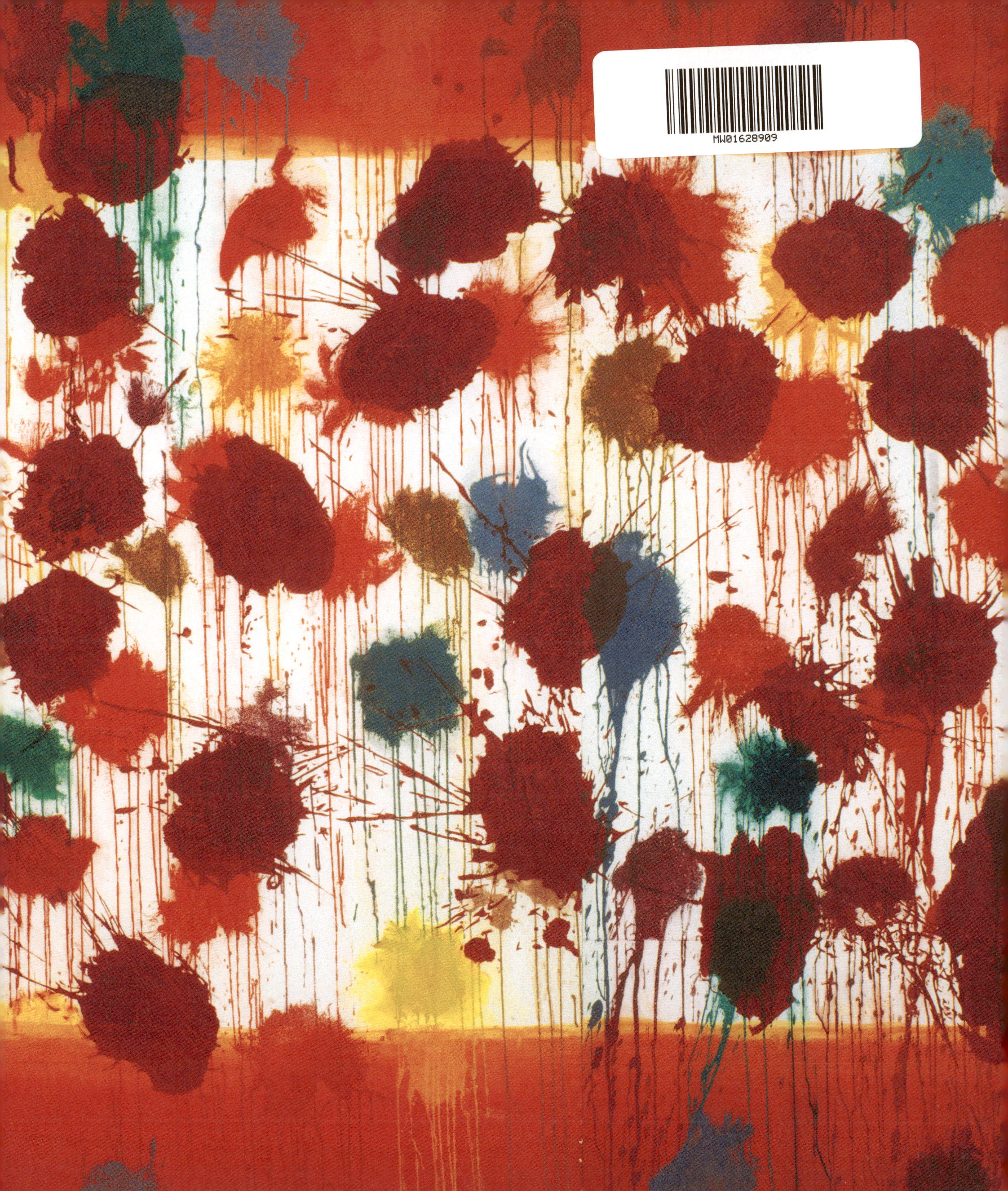

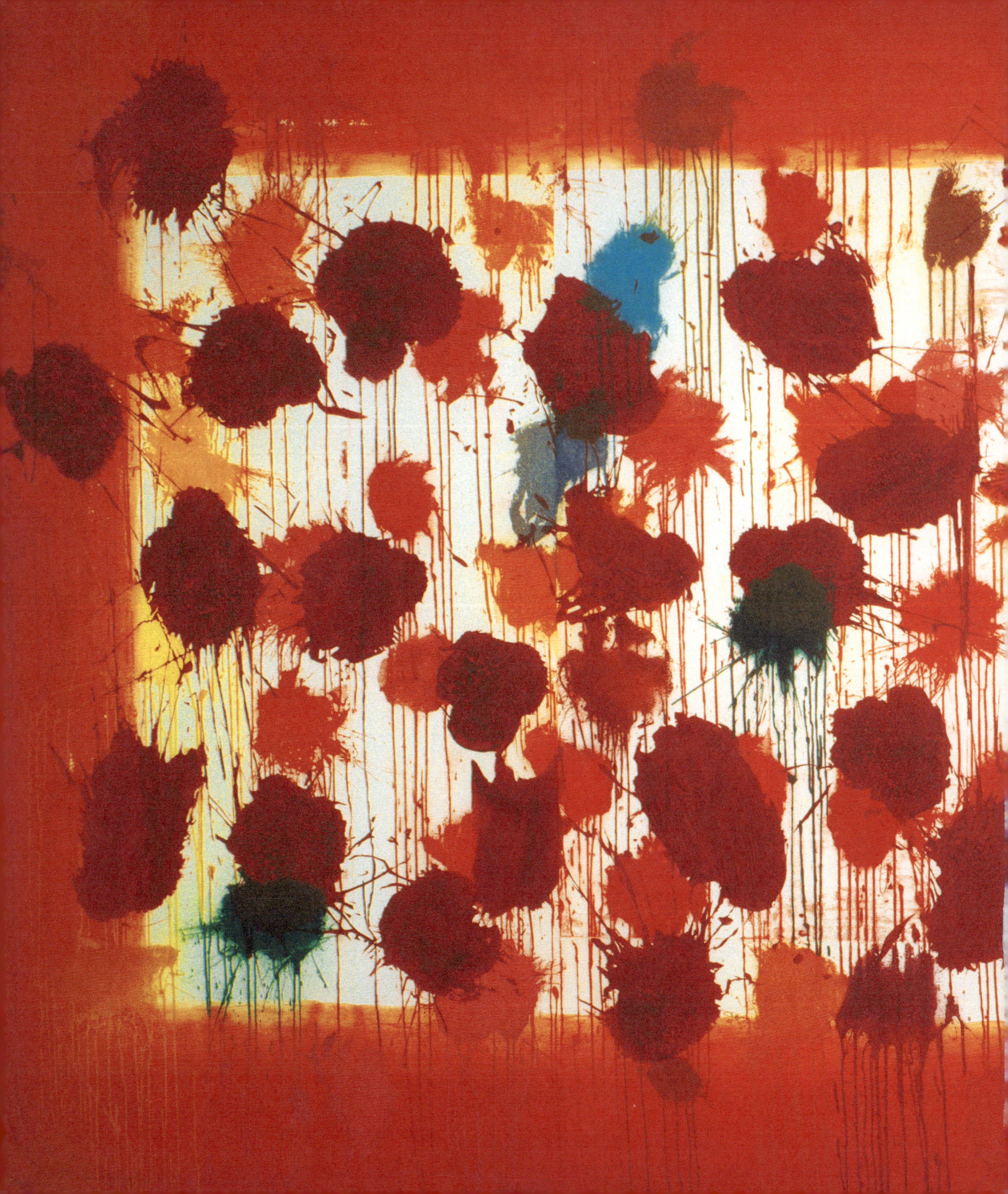

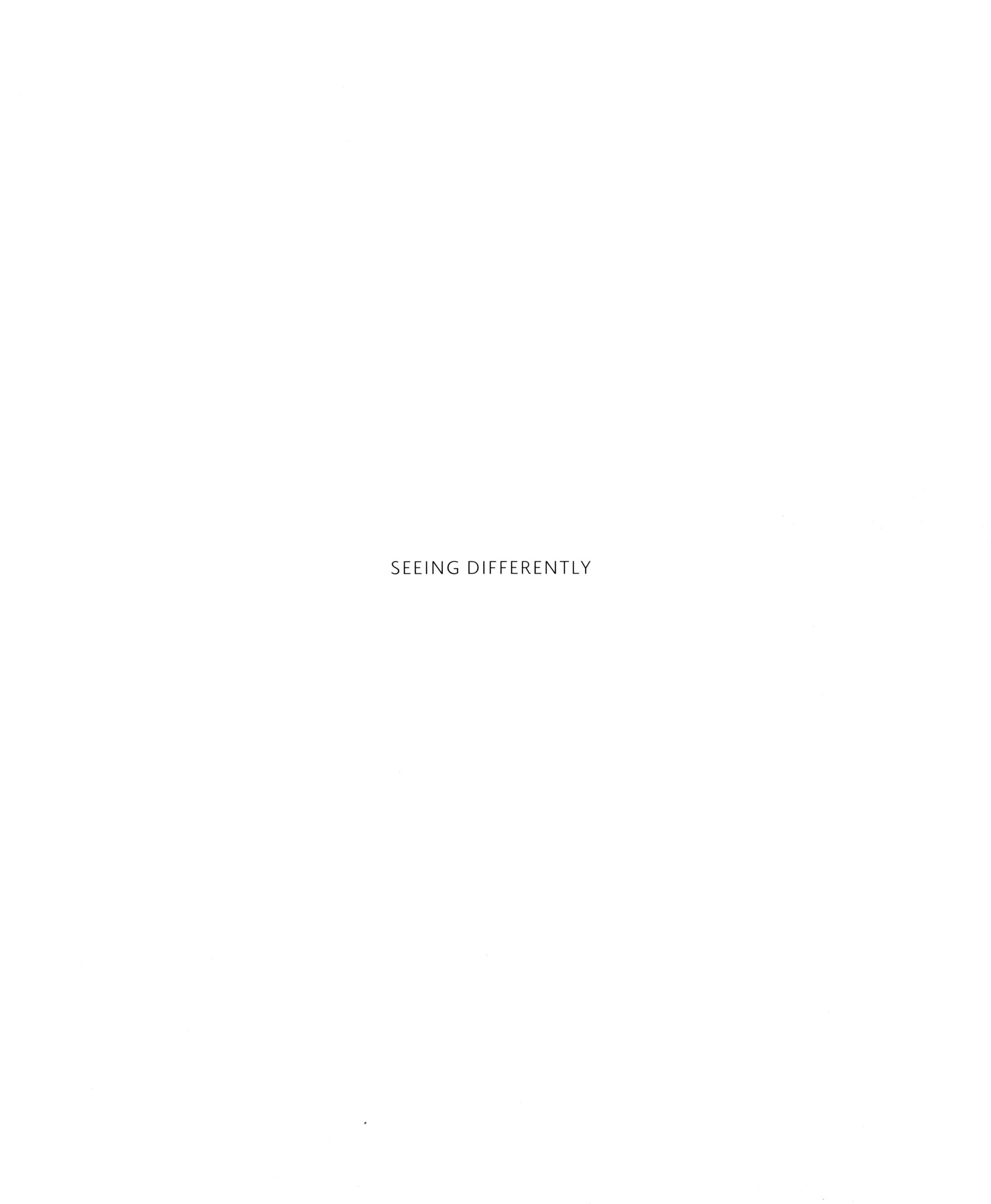

SEEING DIFFERENTLY

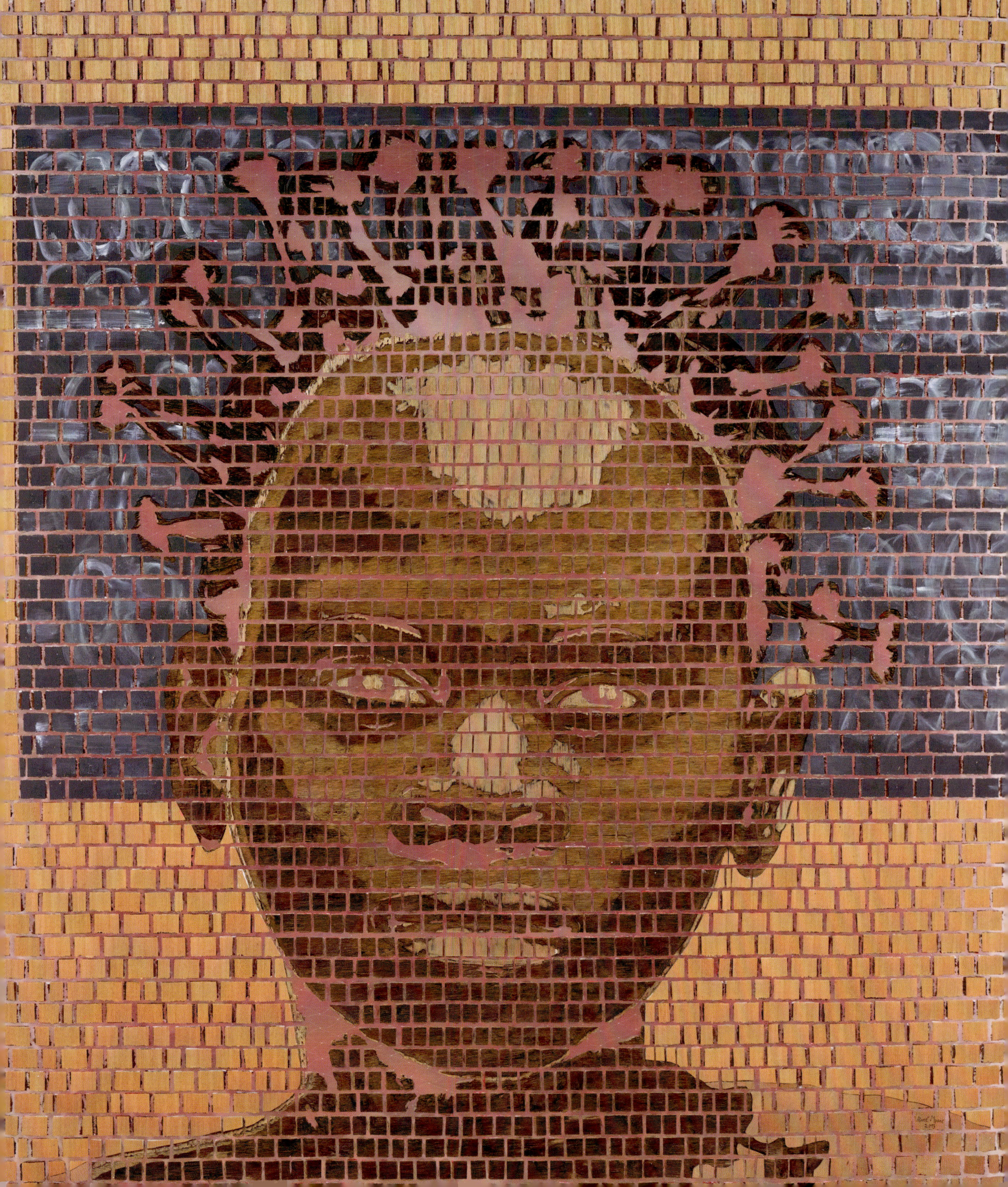

SEEING DIFFERENTLY

THE PHILLIPS COLLECTS FOR A NEW CENTURY

Edited by Elsa Smithgall

Contributions by heather ahtone, Taylor Renee Aldridge, Dominique Baqué, Tina Baum, Enrique Martínez Celaya, Adrienne L. Childs, Makeba Clay, Kate Cowcher, Jessica Stafford Davis, David C. Driskell, John Edmonds, Susan Behrends Frank, Antony Gormley, Wendy A. Grossman, Jeffreen M. Hayes, Liesbeth Heenk, Mary Jane Jacob, Fred L. Joiner, Franz W. Kaiser, Dorothy Kosinski, Lauren Kroiz, Raina Lampkins-Fielder, Jacqueline E. Lawton, Whitfield Lovell, Jennifer Wen Ma, Renée Maurer, Kent Mitchell Minturn, Jed Morse, Charmaine A. Nelson, Alexander Nemerov, Jeremy Ney, Bruce Nixon, Nontobeko Ntombela, Klaus Ottmann, Eliza E. Rathbone, Bridget Riley, Ellington Robinson, Bernardí Roig, Susan Rothenberg, Sean Scully, Alyson Shotz, Elsa Smithgall, Bosco Sodi, Vesela Sretenović, Renée Stout, Lou Stovall, Elizabeth Hutton Turner, and Jenna Wortham

The Phillips Collection, Washington, DC
In association with D Giles Limited

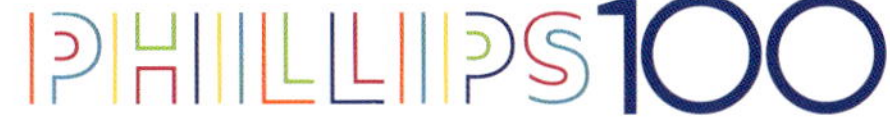

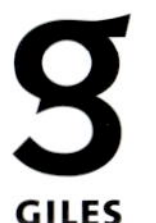

CONTENTS

PLATES WITH SELECTED OBJECT ENTRIES

APPENDIX

FOREWORD

As we prepared to mark the centennial of The Phillips Collection, reality intervened. Instead of preparing to celebrate the birthday of America's first museum of modern art, our galleries were dark and silent, as Washington and the world wrestled with a pandemic. And then a long-in-the-making political and cultural crisis came to a head: tens of thousands gathered near the White House, in the center of Washington and close to our museum, to shout their insistence that Black Lives Matter.

Our anniversary comes at a critical moment in our history, a moment that demands we reflect on our purpose as an institution. We take stock of our past and plan for our future at what feels like a perilous time for so many. What does a museum have to say in the twenty-first century? How do we break out of our own walls and into the wider world?

When Duncan Phillips founded the gallery in 1921, America had just experienced years of technological change, world war, pandemic, and race riots. Humankind numbered fewer than two billion people, many of whom lived in colonies run by faraway European powers. Most people never traveled outside their countries; many never roamed more than a few miles from their hometowns. A visit to an art museum was an experience reserved for the elite.

Today, The Phillips Collection continues a long tradition of displaying side by side artworks of different types, styles, and periods, a practice Phillips pioneered, now adopted by many. We teach, we gather, we host through lectures, films, and music. Digital technology allows us to convey works in forms less solid than actual painting or sculpture, with the Web helping us to fully realize the vision of a museum without walls.

We must be like the Roman god Janus, looking not just to our bold past, but forward to an exciting future. In our second century, the United States will become far more diverse, with most citizens tracing their ancestry not to Europe but to Africa, Asia, and Latin America. Demographics and technology demand that we be nimble, responsive, and smart in order to reach traditional audiences and bring in new ones.

Art and the love of art cannot be sequestered on a quiet side street in Dupont Circle. They must touch new Washington audiences—from immigrant schoolkids to global civil servants to senior citizens. We continue to acquire art from wider and wider circles of new artists. We continue to delight and surprise with the work of creative curators and scholars. We know we must be teachers, provocateurs, companions, and friends, with doors open physically and virtually to a world far wider than Phillips could have imagined in 1921.

Seeing Differently: The Phillips Collects for a New Century brings together creators, curators, and the art that animates and connects them. With this book, you hold in your hands a snapshot of who we are at one hundred years young. It embodies one essential message that has held true since our founding: welcome to The Phillips Collection.

Dani Levinas
Chair, The Phillips Collection Board of Trustees

PREFACE

More than a century ago, the Phillips Memorial Art Gallery (today's Phillips Collection) was born out of an ardent belief in the power of art as a force for public good and social change. Serving community remains at the heart of the Phillips's mission today. This project was shaped in profound ways by the extraordinarily talented group of community advisors who met with Phillips staff over the past year. For their stalwart service and commitment to the Phillips, we gratefully acknowledge: Robin Bell, Zoë Charlton, Vittorio Gallo, Joan Hodges-Wu, Philippa P. B. Hughes, Anika Kwinana, Robin McClain, Mathew McCollough, Tom Minter, James L. Palmer, Christopher Wang, Beverly With, and Dorit Yaron. For her skillful facilitation of the advisory meetings, we thank Swarupa Anila, consultant and vice president of exhibition and gallery development, Royal Ontario Museum.

A book of this magnitude and quality requires the coordinated efforts and hard work of many. We extend warmest thanks to D Giles Limited: Dan Giles, managing director; Allison McCormick, editorial manager; Louise Parfitt, editorial assistant; Louise Ramsay, production director; and Liz Japes, sales and marketing manager. To those who provided invaluable assistance in preparing the manuscript for publication, we also extend our thanks: content editors Johanna Halford-MacLeod and Alexander Karelis, copy editor and proofreader Jenny Wilson, transcribers Deborah Lattimore and Jesse Levit, translators Kevin Gerry Dunn and Jeanine Herman, and indexer Sue Farr. For his fresh and inventive design, we acknowledge Ocky Murray.

Our sincere thanks go to the international group of forty-eight artists, critics, curators, educators, and scholars who contributed to this volume. They have brought a rich, multi-layered understanding to the works discussed and the socio-cultural context of their making. For their illuminating thematic essays exploring less-studied narratives or offering new perspectives on familiar subjects, we gratefully acknowledge: Wendy A. Grossman, Jeffreen M. Hayes, Mary Jane Jacob, Fred L. Joiner, Lauren Kroiz, Kent Mitchell Minturn, Jed Morse, Charmaine A. Nelson, Jeremy Ney, Bruce Nixon, Klaus Ottmann, and Vesela Sretenović.

For their insightful texts on major modern and contemporary works recently added to the collection, we offer warmest thanks to: heather ahtone, Taylor Renee Aldridge, Dominique Baqué, Tina Baum, Adrienne L. Childs, Makeba Clay, Kate Cowcher, Jessica Stafford Davis, Susan Behrends Frank, Wendy A. Grossman, Liesbeth Heenk, Franz W. Kaiser, Raina Lampkins-Fielder, Jacqueline E. Lawton, Renée Maurer, Alexander Nemerov, Nontobeko Ntombela, Klaus Ottmann, Eliza E. Rathbone, Elsa Smithgall, Vesela Sretenović, Elizabeth Hutton Turner, and Jenna Wortham. While none of the writings purports to be a definitive study of a given subject, we hope that the ideas in them will spark further inquiry, dialogue, and reflection.

Nobody appreciated the artist's unique way of seeing the world more than Duncan Phillips. By offering sustained encounters with art in a comfortable setting, he hoped to inspire others to "see beautifully as true artists see." Our book highlights the artist's point of view through texts commissioned from artists in response to works recently acquired by the Phillips—whether their own or by other artists of their choosing. We are grateful to: Bridget Riley, Enrique Martínez Celaya, Antony Gormley, Jennifer Wen Ma, Ellington Robinson, Bernardí Roig, the late Susan Rothenberg, Sean Scully, Bosco Sodi, Renée Stout, and Lou Stovall. The artist's voice also reverberates throughout the book in conversations with John Edmonds, Whitfield Lovell, Alyson Shotz, and the late David C. Driskell. We appreciate their willingness to open themselves and their studios to us. The conversation with Driskell turned out to be one of his last videotaped interviews: we are deeply saddened by the loss of a beloved artist, scholar, educator, and distinguished member of The Phillips Collection's board of trustees.

We thank those who swiftly processed our requests for images: Agence photographique de la RMN: Gladys Pilastrini; Mequitta Ahuja; Art Resource: Jennifer Belt, Diana Edkins, and Gerhard Gruitrooy; Artists Rights Society: Janet Hicks and Lori Zajkowski; Bibliothèque et Archives nationales du Québec: Martin Couture; Calder Foundation: Sandy Rower and Susan Braeuer Dam; Company Gallery: Ken Castaneda; Denver Art Museum: Meghan Shaw; farbanalyze: Selma Ucar; Fine Arts Museum of San Francisco: Susan Grinols; Helen Frankenthaler Foundation: Cecelia Barnett; Lisson Gallery: Charlotte Parmley; Magnum Photos: Michael D. Shulman; Manuel Neri Trust: Anne Kohs and Pam Evans; McCord Museum: Emma Davidson; Michael Rosenfeld Gallery: Dan Munn; neugerriemschneider: Catherina Bonorden; Royal Academy of Arts: Rebecca Lyons; The Scholl Collection: Emanuel Ribas; Southern Illinois University: Nicholas L. Guardiano and Douglas F. Coons; Sperone Westwater: Katherine Borkowski; Sutton Gallery: Brigid Moriarty; and Van Abbemuseum: Margo van de Wiel.

The project marshalled the collective talents, creativity, inventiveness, and energy of the entire Phillips staff. I offer special appreciation for the adept leadership of our senior curator, Elsa Smithgall, who, as project director, worked tirelessly with our community advisors and staff to realize this ambitious project. For their indispensable contributions, I thank: Klaus Ottmann, chief curator and deputy director for academic affairs; Vesela Sretenović, senior curator of modern and contemporary art; Susan Behrends Frank, curator; Renée Maurer, associate curator; Wendy A. Grossman, consulting curator; Kathryn S. Rogge, exhibitions coordinator and manager of academic initiatives; Camille Brown, curatorial assistant; and Rashieda Witter, former curatorial assistant.

Together with the curatorial team, staff across the institution invested their time and expertise to ensure the project's success. I wish to acknowledge: Micha Winkler Thomas, director of strategy and operations; Kristen Paral, manager of museum evaluation and data analysis; Angela Gillespie, director of human resources; Gwen Nathan Young, human resources coordinator; Wendy Ponvert, director of development; Karen Bassiri, director of corporate relations; Chloe Post, major gifts officer; Emily Doll, campaign chief; Bridget Zangueneh, director of institutional giving; Victoria Potucek, grants writer; Elizabeth Temme, director of major gifts; Alexis Englert, manager for major gifts; Victoria Hagar, director of membership; Keith Costas, director of special events; Cherie Nichols, chief financial officer; Ryan Farewell, senior accountant; Fran Marshall, senior accountant; Octaviah Holt, finance associate; Makeba Clay, chief diversity officer; Miriam Magdieli, chief communications officer and director of marketing; Vivian Djen, head of editorial and design services; Hayley Barton, media relations manager; Lia Seremetis, manager of partnerships and marketing; Ann Lipscombe, design and digital communications manager; Anne Taylor Brittingham, director of learning and education strategy; Nehemiah Dixon III, director of community engagement; Miguel Perez, head of public programming; Hilary Katz, manager of teacher initiatives; Erica Harper, head of PreK–12 initiatives; Donna Jonte, manager of art, wellness and family programs; Darci Vanderhoff, chief information officer; Bria Scott-Fleming, IT support specialist; Bob Harris, security operations manager; Bill Koberg, chief of installations; Laura Tighe, collections care manager; Alec MacKaye, installations manager; Elizabeth Steele, head of conservation; Patricia Favero, associate conservator; Sylvia R. Albro, paper conservator; Jeremy Ney, director of music; Abigail C. Winston, concerts manager; Karen Schneider, head librarian; Rachel Jacobson, digital assets librarian; Juli Folk, processing archivist; Trish Waters, registrar for exhibitions; Michele De Shazo, registrar for collection; Laylaa Randera, assistant registrar and preparator; Pete Bernal, shop manager; and Caitlin Hoerr, manager of director's office initiatives and board liaison; as well as Jade Flint, former curatorial intern, and Traka Lopez, former Sherman Fairchild Foundation fellow.

We thank the Sachiko Kuno Foundation, and Dr. Sachiko Kuno herself, for the Foundation's generous support of our centennial music commissions. Our Director of Music, Jeremy Ney, has spearheaded an ambitious suite of new music commissions from a diverse and international group of artists, including composers Benjamin Attahir, Marcos Balter, Lembit Beecher, inti figgis-vizueta, Nathalie Joachim, Gabriel Kahane, Outi Tarkianen, and Paul Wiancko. Each new piece of music will engage with works from our collection, exploring the crosscurrents and dialogues between music and visual art, a subject close to The Phillips Collection's history. The project is a powerful expression of our commitment to interdisciplinary work, and a centerpiece of our renowned concert series which celebrates its 80th season in 2021.

The exhibition and accompanying publication would not have been possible without the generous support of the Henry Luce Foundation. We especially thank its president, Mariko Silver, and its program director for American art, Teresa A. Carbone. For their additional valuable support of this project, we extend warmest thanks to the National Endowment for the Humanities. I would also like to highlight the impact of gifts to our exhibitions endowment with special thanks to the Sherman Fairchild Foundation, Robert and Debra Drumheller, and The Marion F. Goldin Charitable Fund. We are also grateful for generous funding from the Frauke and Willem de Looper Charitable Fund.

The Phillips Collection builds upon the legacy of its visionary founder, Duncan Phillips, and his wife, Marjorie. Additionally, I wish to acknowledge the important stewardship of my predecessors, Jay Gates (Director, 1998–2008), Charles Moffett (Director, 1992–98), Laughlin Phillips (Director, 1972–92), Marjorie Phillips (Director, 1966–72), and Duncan Phillips (Director, 1921–66). We extend our appreciation to the late Gifford and Joann Phillips, Jennifer Phillips, and Liza Phillips, as well as all members of the Phillips family, for their warm and steadfast support.

For their unwavering commitment, I express sincerest thanks to my board of trustees, and to its chairman, Dani Levinas, and former chairs George Vradenburg and the late Vicki Sant. The Phillips family has continued to play an important role on our board. We gratefully acknowledge Alice Phillips Swistel for her wisdom, generosity of spirit, and dedicated service.

Above all, our hearts are full of gratitude to all The Phillips Collection's friends and donors whose generous support has ensured its vitality and made possible the sustained growth of its holdings over its hundred-year history.

As we start our next vibrant chapter, we look forward to expanding the reach and impact of the Phillips by continuing to champion the powerfully diverse artistic expressions of our ever-changing world.

Dorothy Kosinski, PhD
Vradenburg Director and CEO
The Phillips Collection

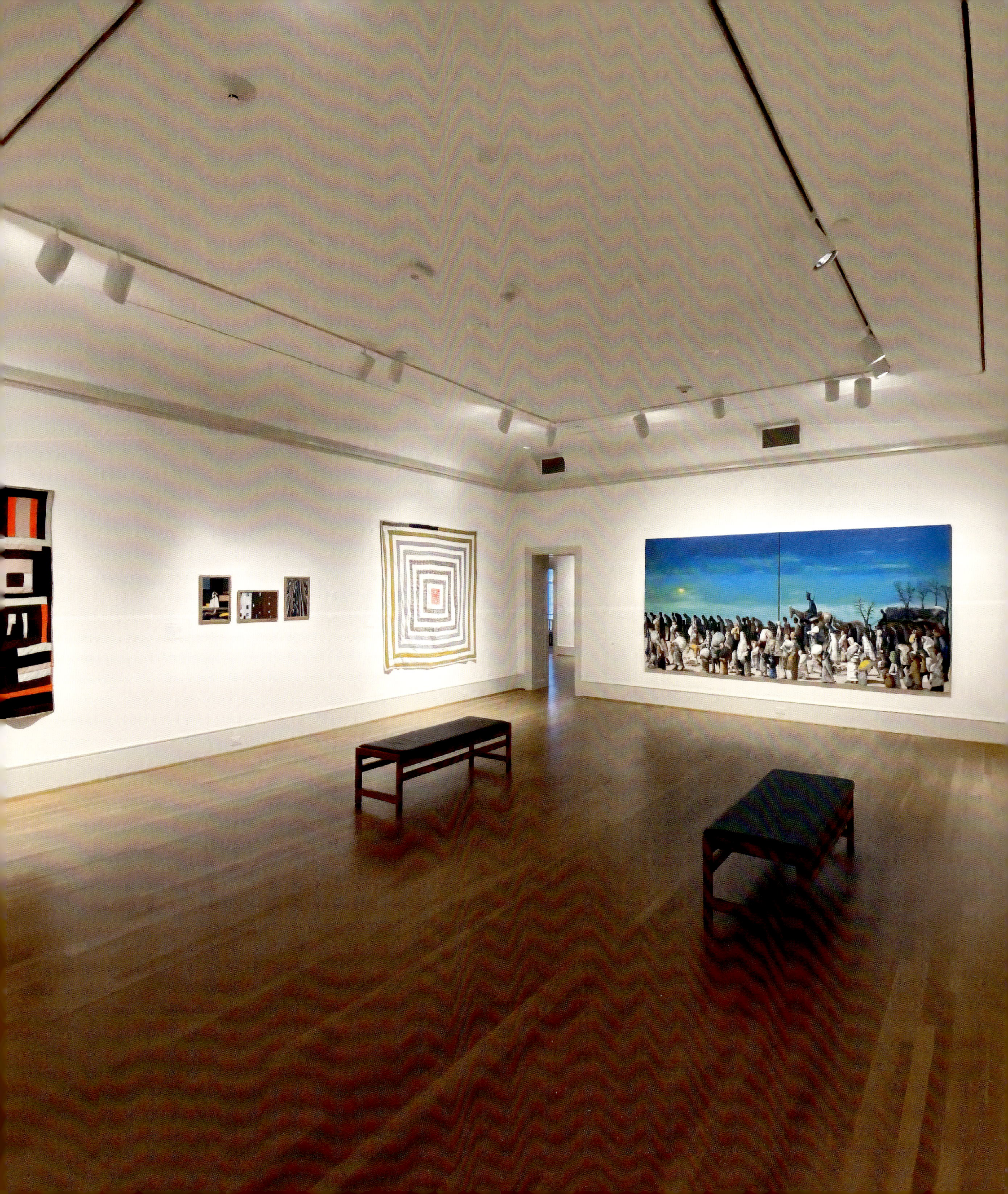

"A VITAL LIVING PLACE"– THE PHILLIPS COLLECTION STILL IN THE MAKING

Dorothy Kosinski

It must be kept a vital living place for enjoyment and must be given ... a sense of frequent rearrangement and of new acquisitions.
—Duncan Phillips, 1965

Duncan Phillips conceived of his museum project as "a memorial ... a beneficent force in the community where I live—a joy-giving, life-enhancing influence, assisting people to see beautifully as true artists see."[1] He had lost his father in 1917; then his older brother, James Laughlin Phillips, succumbed to the Spanish influenza on October 21, 1918. In March 2020, as The Phillips Collection prepares to celebrate the hundredth anniversary of its founding as America's first museum of modern art, the world is gripped by another viral pandemic. The bizarre symmetry between the genesis of the Phillips Memorial Art Gallery and the lead-up to its centennial in 2021 is stunning. With the museum shuttered, the collection unavailable, and exhibitions and programs postponed or cancelled, this eerie parallel beckons us to fully embrace the foundational ideas of the institution.

Duncan Phillips wrote that art saved his life, rescued him from despair.[2] That belief in art as a source of solace, a link to wellness, and an essential positive force in society is a key tenet of our program today. Our Contemplation Audio Tours, our work with veterans and Alzheimer patients, and our intensive work in the schools are all manifestations of an identity that was there from the very outset in 1921. In 2018 we initiated a new chapter in our history, when the Phillips opened a space in the newest building at Town Hall Education Arts Recreation Campus (THEARC), where neighbors include Children's National Hospital, two schools, and also AppleTree Institution, and Boys & Girls Club of Greater Washington. This facility expands and transforms opportunities for exploring art and wellness across disciplines and in one of the most underserved communities in Southeast Washington, DC.

Duncan Phillips enjoyed his creative freedom and, unencumbered by typical museum conventions or boards and committees, he enthusiastically followed his own taste and standards. Uninterested in art historical taxonomy—the *isms*—he reveled in exploring unusual juxtapositions and frequently changing installations in order to reveal the fluid continuum of artistic expression. Change, refreshment, and growth characterized the emerging museum from the outset. He would sometimes sell and sometimes add, occasionally diving

Installation of Main Gallery, The Phillips Collection, March 2020, with (left to right): Mary Lee Bendolph, *"Housetop" variation*, 1998; Jacob Lawrence, panels 57, 31, and 7, *The Migration Series*, 1941–2; Malissia Pettway, *"Housetop,"* ca. 1960; and Benny Andrews, *Trail of Tears*, 2005.

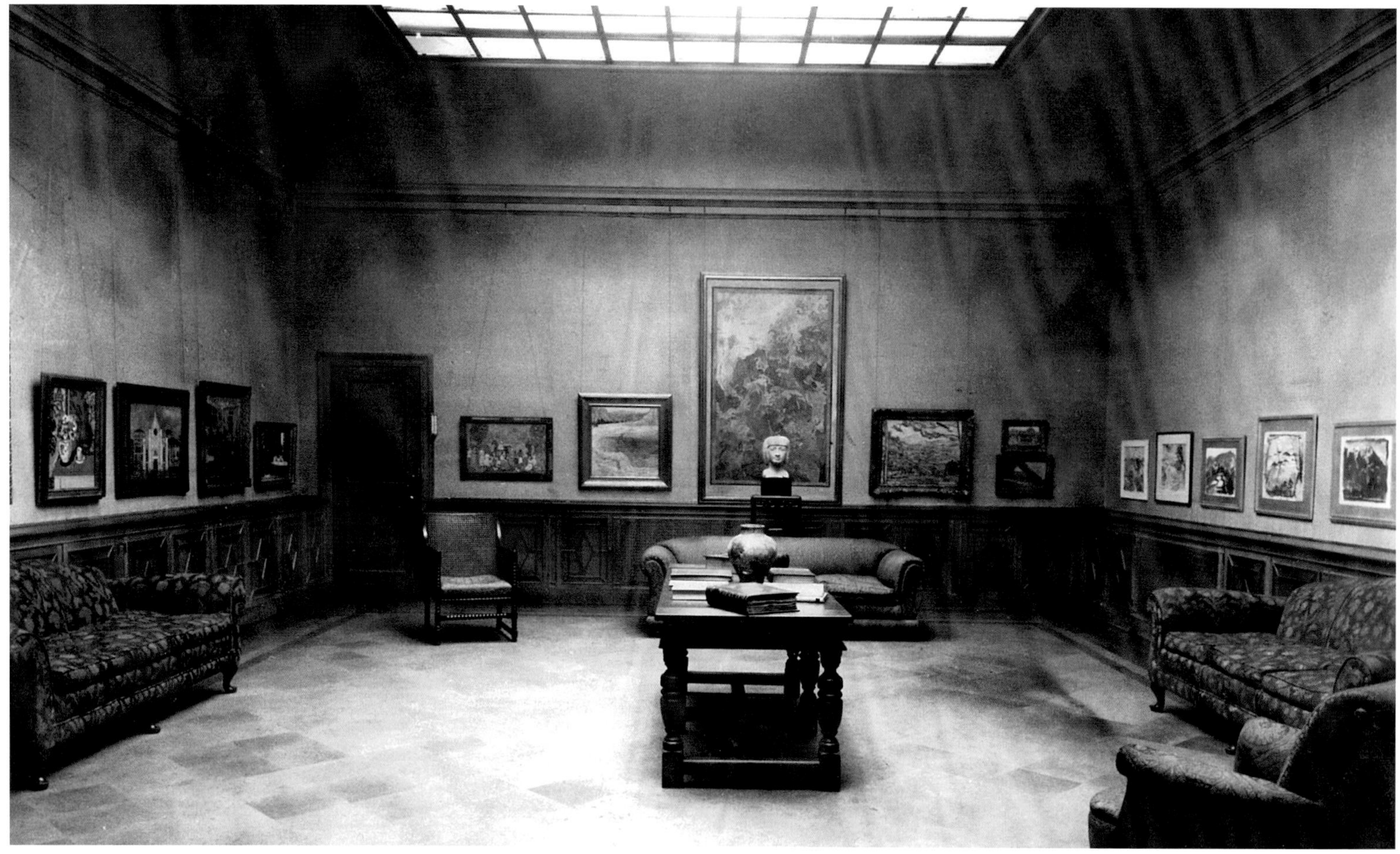

fig. 1
Installation of Main Gallery, The Phillips Collection, 1927, with works by (left to right): Pierre Bonnard, Henri Matisse, Edward Bruce, Édouard Vuillard, Pierre Bonnard, Maurice Prendergast, John Henry Twachtman, Augustus Vincent Tack, Paul Cézanne, and Albert Dubois-Pillet, and an 18th Dynasty Egyptian limestone head.

deep and amassing vast holdings of a favorite artist. He enjoyed encouraging emerging artists with small exhibitions and purchases. This radical dynamism enabled him to thoughtfully study the roots of modern art while at the same time hungrily supporting artists of his own time. It is our hope that *Seeing Differently: The Phillips Collects for a New Century* reveals today's museum's responsiveness to the nimble and curious spirit of its founder, Duncan Phillips, and his wife, painter and co-director, Marjorie Acker.

Phillips defied conventions to create "arrangements for the purpose of contrast and analogy" that rejected arbitrary boundaries of time, geography, race, or gender. His inclusive approach—what he called "unity in diversity"—reflected his conviction that "art is a universal language which defies classification. I teach the universality of art as a unifying spirit and the continuity of human thought and aspiration."[3] Today we continue to abide by that philosophy, as can be seen in recent presentations in the Main Gallery, anchored by two of five recently acquired Gee's Bend quilts (see p. 10). This exciting addition to the collection was achieved through a generous gift-purchase from the Souls Grown Deep Foundation. It is inspiring to experience the introduction of these boldly patterned, large-scale textile compositions into the collection. In one iteration, quilts by Mary Lee Beldolph and Malissia Pettway are juxtaposed with works by Anni Albers, Benny Andrews, McArthur Binion, Jacob Lawrence, Piet Mondrian, and Alma Thomas. Despite the differences between the Dutch artist's aesthetic philosophy and the Gee's Bend quilters' artistic impulses, the radiant patterns in the quilts resonate with the taut dynamic equilibrium of the lines and colors in Mondrian's *Painting No. 9*, 1939–42. The richly patterned drawing by Bauhaus master Anni Albers, *Fox I*, seems to be a linchpin, connecting the different media in the gallery. McArthur Binion's large-scale, oil-stick painting (plate 81) is a dense pattern of labor-intensive striations. Its grid masks a patchwork of repeated elements photocopied from the artist's birth certificate, including place, date, time, and race. The artist's fierce gestural strokes create a disciplined

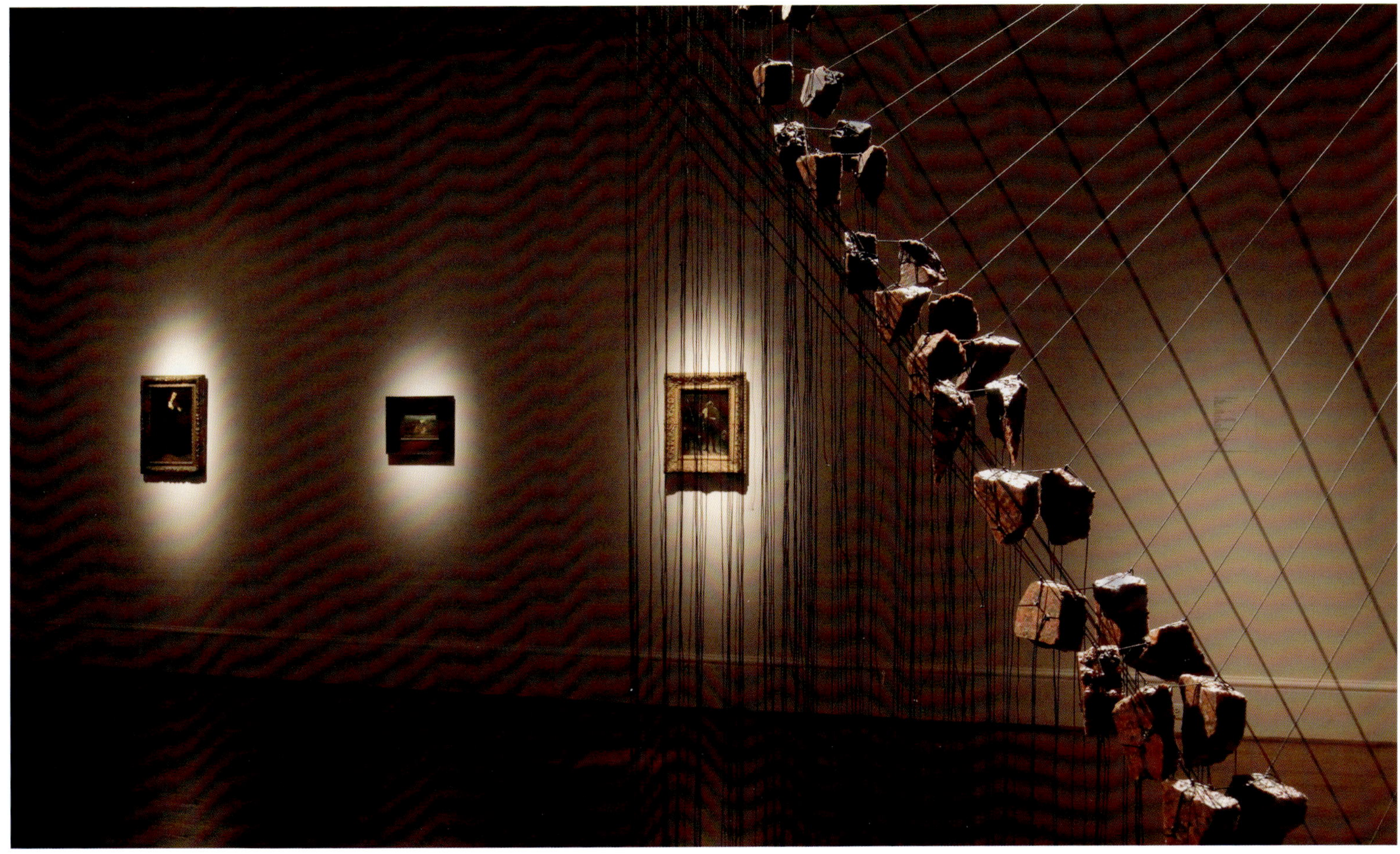

fig. 2
Installation of Barbara Liotta's *Icarus*, 2009, and (left to right): Ferdinand-Victor-Eugène Delacroix, *Paganini*, 1831; Giorgione (?) (attributed), *The Hour Glass*, not dated; and Honoré Daumier, *The Painter at His Easel*, ca. 1870. Intersections: *Icarus* by Barbara Liotta (October 22, 2009–January 21, 2010), The Phillips Collection.

abstract schematic by which he at once obscures, reveals, and controls the most fundamental information of his personal identity. African American quilts have sometimes been acknowledged by artists of Binion's generation as a source of inspiration. This installation prompts one to recall some of Phillips's own innovative installations in the same gallery going back to the twenties: unhesitating juxtapositions of watercolors by the American artist John Marin with oil paintings by the French post-impressionist Pierre Bonnard; an Egyptian head with works by French impressionists, Paul Gauguin, and Augustus Vincent Tack (fig. 1).

Encouraging the living artist was a key motivation for Phillips. He staged an ongoing series of small exhibitions and invariably purchased a work from each project. His dedication to supporting young artists was unwavering. Arthur Dove, John Graham, and Rockwell Kent all received stipends in exchange for Phillips's right to first choice from their yearly production. His dedication sometimes went deep: he amassed eleven works by Milton Avery and forty-eight by Arthur Dove. During the 1950s and 1960s the museum acquired works by Josef Albers, Richard Diebenkorn, Sam Francis, Sam Gilliam, Seymour Lipton, Robert Motherwell, Mark Rothko, Clyfford Still, Mark Tobey, and Bradley Walker Tomlin, all from exhibitions organized by the Phillips. In 2009, the museum picked up this tradition again in earnest, inaugurating Intersections under the direction of Vesela Sretenović, senior curator of modern and contemporary art, and in 2015, the program grew into a partnership with the University of Maryland (see Vesela Sretenović, "Connecting Modern with Contemporary: Intersections at the Phillips" in this volume, p. 108). This series is devoted to individual artists, some local, others international, who undertake an exploration of the collection and the intimate spaces of the galleries—including hallways, and stairwells, even the museum café. Some early projects were executed by Washington artists Barbara Liotta and linn meyers. Liotta's complicated sculptural installation *Icarus*, 2009, soared across the Main Gallery, in company with works she selected from the permanent collection (fig. 2), and was augmented by

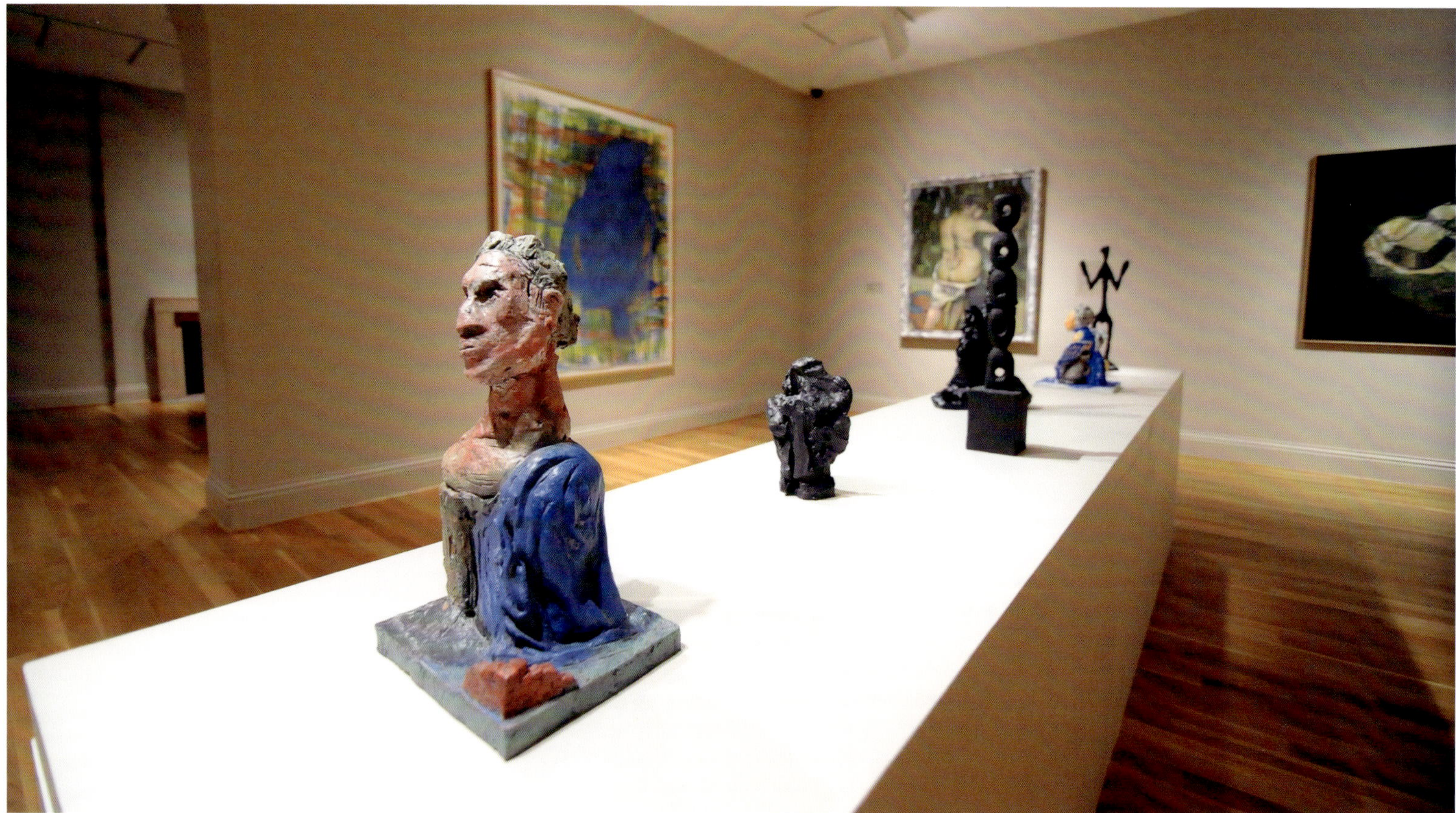

fig. 3
Installation of *Postwar Germanic Expressions: Gifts from Michael Werner*. September 12, 2015–April 17, 2016.

a dance performance, its choreography commissioned from the Washington Ballet. linn meyers's meticulous 2010 wall drawing spanned a doorway and responded to the undulating lines in Vincent van Gogh's 1889 *Road Menders* (see fig. 80). The execution of the drawing took place in public over the course of two weeks, making meyers's process a sort of performance. Indeed, time was intrinsic to the piece, both in terms of its execution and its ephemeral nature: intended from the outset to last for a limited time, it was—to the dismay of many—eventually painted over. Now in its tenth year, Intersections has presented thirty projects, garnering twenty-eight acquisitions for the collection.

Phillips enthusiastically championed certain artists whose work he assembled into in-depth exhibition "units" that are special to the collection. His enthusiasm for John Marin—Alfred Stieglitz, another champion of the artist, poked fun at it—resulted in the amassing of twenty-three works. The collection also includes seventeen paintings by Bonnard. From 1948 to 1982, the museum regularly devoted a gallery to showing selections from the thirteen works by Paul Klee that Duncan Phillips had acquired since 1930. Having bought his first Rothko painting in 1957 and two more in 1960, Phillips established a dedicated space (designed with an awareness of the artist's desires) in 1961, to which the fourth canvas was added in 1964. Phillips's devoted friendship with Tack brought eighty works into the collection. Phillips even contemplated permanently installing the wood-paneled North Library (now the Music Room) with an ensemble of Tack's quasi-abstract, musically inspired compositions.

Recent acquisitions have introduced or built upon existing units of both modern and contemporary art in the collection, including works by Karel Appel, Milton Avery, Jake Berthot, William Christenberry, Rudolf de Crignis, Markus Lüpertz, Alfonso Ossorio, and Renée Stout. The Ossorio Foundation, the Appel Foundation, and the estate of de Crignis were instrumental in making gifts and purchases possible. The works by Lüpertz are part of a transformative gift of forty-six works of art by German and Danish artists from the collection of Michael Werner (fig. 3). The project was initiated through the intervention of Werner's gallerist partner, Gordon VeneKlasen, who was assisting him with placing meaningful groupings of his vast personal collection in

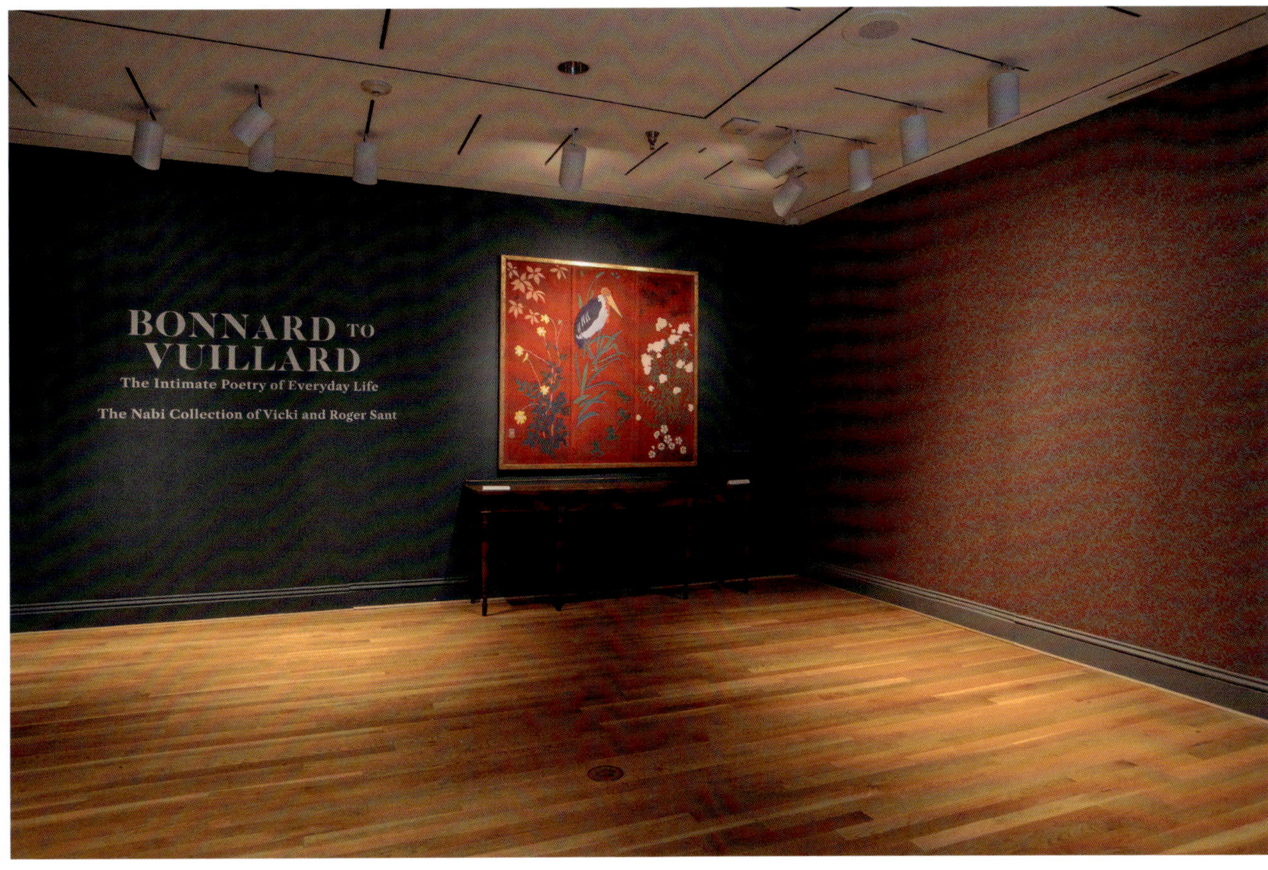

fig. 4
Installation of *Bonnard to Vuillard: The Intimate Poetry of Everyday Life. The Nabi Collection of Vicki and Roger Sant*. October 26, 2019–January 26, 2020.

museums around the world. Werner's generosity has resulted in the Phillips owning groups of works by Georg Baselitz, Jörg Immendorff, Per Kirkeby, Lüpertz, and A.R. Penck, enabling us to present northern European creativity in twentieth-century art in a meaningful way. Beloved artist Bill Christenberry was a revered teacher in Washington, DC, and served on the board of the Phillips for a number of years. Thanks to gifts from him and other donors, we have built a strong Christenberry unit with forty-five sculptures, paintings, works on paper, and photographs. An in-depth collection of over forty works by Nabi artists and an endowment to support its study and presentation (fig. 4), the promised gift of the late Vicki Sant, a former trustee, and her husband, Roger Sant, will in the fullness of time transform the Phillips into a major study center for this particular manifestation of late nineteenth-century European art. Linda Lichtenberg Kaplan, another long-serving Phillips trustee, has promised major gifts of paintings as well as works on paper by artists primarily acknowledged as sculptors. These remarkable groups of acquisitions are the result of thoughtful collecting and loving relationships with the museum, nurtured over decades.

The collection of contemporary art has grown exponentially through the support and generosity of many individuals, notably the late Luther W. Brady, Arthur and Carol Goldberg, the late Gifford and Joann Phillips, Heather Podesta and Tony Podesta, and the family of Anita Reiner. Generous gifts have added an array of acquisitions by international artists as well as artists from this region: Benny Andrews (pl. 25) Angela Bulloch (pl. 105), Maggie Michael, Alyson Shotz (pl. 111), and Arlene Shechet (pl. 122). Video works by Mwangi Hutter (pl. 35) Brian Dailey (pl. 194), John Akomfrah (pl. 20), and Jennifer Wen Ma (pl. 9) are now in the permanent collection. Six ceremonial poles by indigenous Australian artists (pls. 86–91) are a promised gift from Debra and Dennis Scholl, resulting from a major exhibition that took place at the Phillips in 2018 (fig. 5). At the time of the exhibition, one of those artists, Regina Pilawuk Wilson, executed a mural in the Hunter Courtyard at the Phillips. An earlier commission, in 2014, for an exterior mural (fig. 6) was the result of an international collaboration with the Department of State that brought four Senegalese artists to Washington in conjunction with International

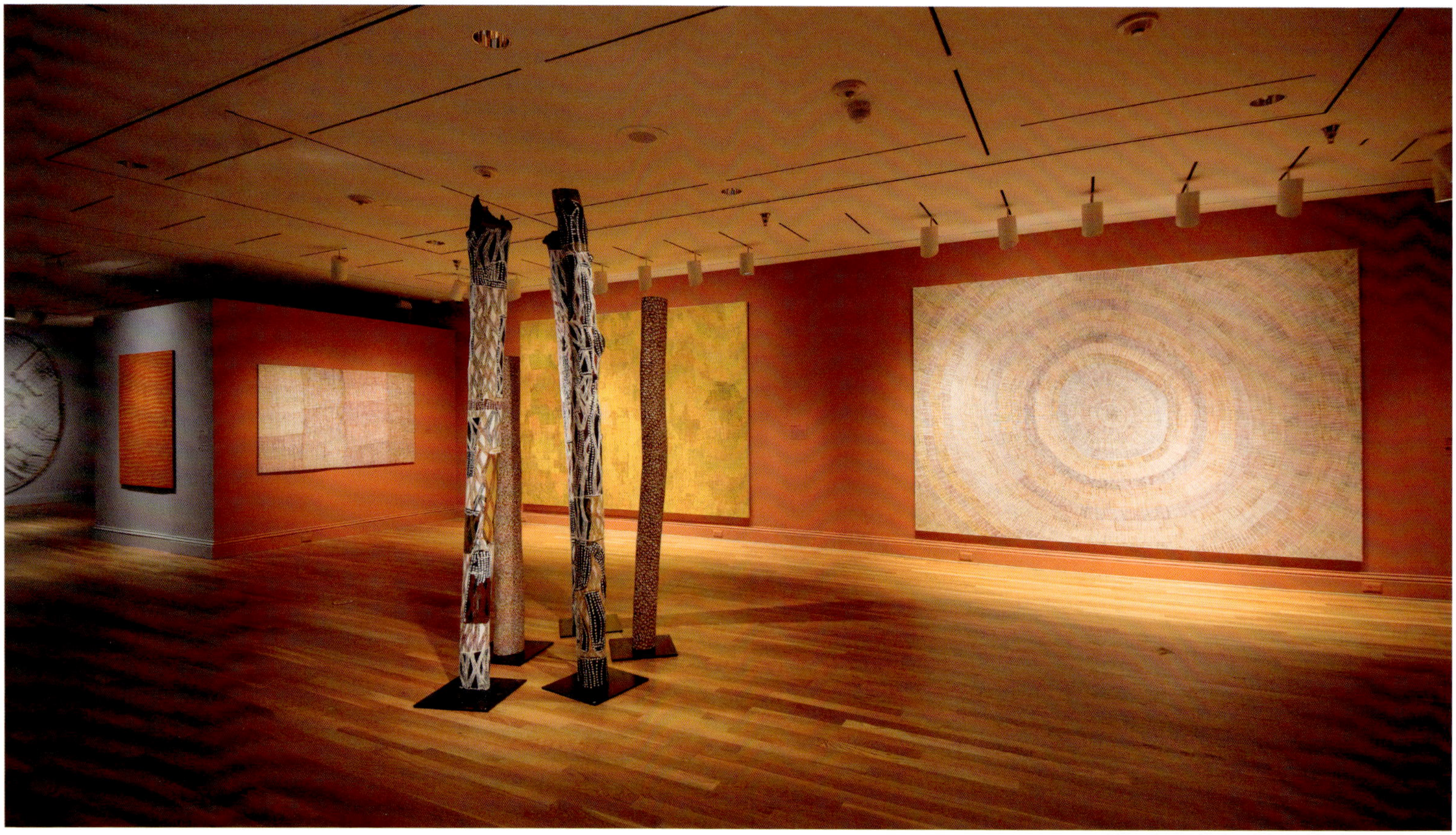

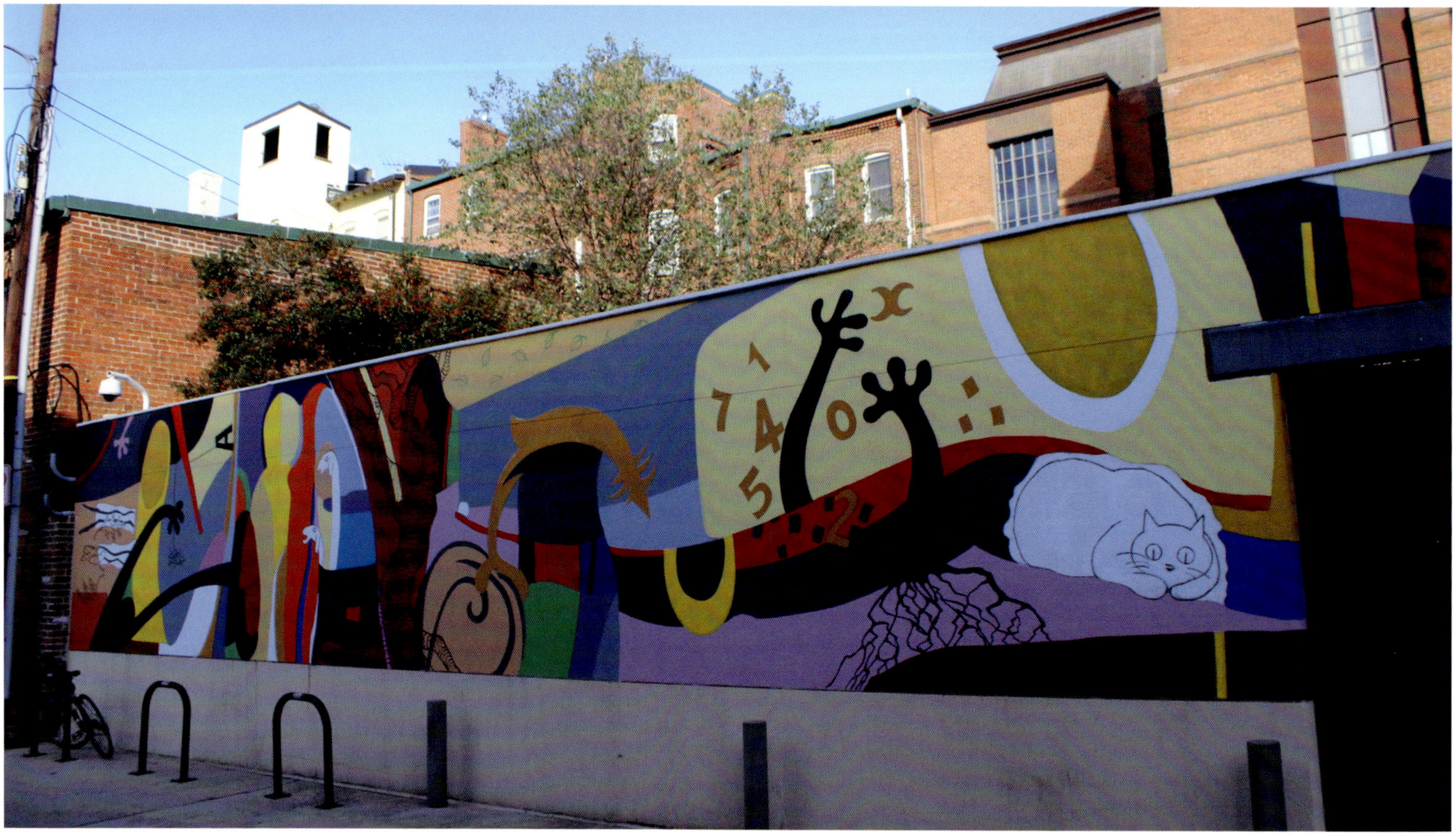

Forum—an annual program organized by the museum in partnership with the University of Maryland to tackle urgent societal and artistic questions.[4] The partnership with the University of Maryland, in its fifth year in 2020, encompasses, in addition to Intersections and the International Forum, two annual series: Conversations with Artists and Leading International Composers. In these, internationally significant practitioners engage in intimate conversations at the Phillips and give one-on-one critiques to students in visual arts and music at the university's College Park campus. The collaboration also supports post-doctoral fellowships in art history, anthropology, and digital culture. Courses in arts integration methodology are co-taught by museum staff and UMD faculty in the School of Education to pre-certificate and certified teachers. Design students conceive and execute in-gallery projects for visitor orientation at the Phillips. The partnership models innovative experiential interdisciplinary STEAM education.

The modern collection has also been enriched by some extraordinary gifts, among them works by Gustave Caillebotte (pls. 47, 48), Alexander Calder (pl. 110), Barbara Hepworth (pl. 180), Bice Lazzari (pl. 174), Roberto Matta (pl. 183), and Man Ray (pl. 185)—thanks to the generosity of Mr. and Mrs. Duane Vieth, the Estate of Mary E. Weinmann, Fenner Milton, the Estate of Barbara Hepworth, Mariagrazia Oliva Lapadula, the Archivio Bice Lazzari, and the Embassy of Italy, and the Rosalind Gersten Jacobs and Melvin Jacobs Collection.

In 2010, the Phillips was the fortunate recipient of two exquisite Howard Hodgkin mural-scale aquatints, *As Time Goes By* (pls. 113, 114), given in memory of Duncan Phillips's son, Laughlin Phillips, who served as director from 1972 to 1992. Upon their acquisition, the two prints—the resplendent red version the gift of the late Luther W. Brady, the equally beautiful blue one that of a group of trustees and other donors—graced opposite walls of our Main Gallery, where they will be seen again during our centennial.

During 2011, the Phillips's ninetieth anniversary year, the museum was grateful to receive Morris Louis's *Seal*, 1959 (pl. 115), from the Marcella Brenner Revocable Trust. *Seal* is a glorious work, measuring almost nine by twelve feet, an unfolding of washes of emerald, sapphire, coal gray, and passages of unpainted canvas. Paradigmatic of the growth and evolution of the permanent collection, the gift had its roots in the artist's own intimate knowledge of the museum and resulted from his widow's appreciation of the important role played in his career by Phillips, as purchaser of one of the first works by the artist to enter a museum collection. Marcella Louis Brenner (d. 2007), planning carefully the distribution of key works in her estate, built on her 2003 gift to the Phillips of four early pen-and-ink drawings and chose *Seal* specifically for the museum. Phillips's purchase of Louis's *Number 182* in 1963 was followed by further acquisitions in the 1990s—a column and a stripe painting given by Washingtonians Philip M. Stern and Judith H. Miller respectively. The result of these thoughtful gifts is an important unit, a meaningful concentration of works by a key artist.

Over the last decade, photography has been the fastest growing segment of the collection, thanks to major gifts from Julia J. Norrell, Kent and Marcia Minichiello, the late Raymond Machesney, Joseph and the late Charlotte Lichtenberg, and the Photography Collectors' Syndicate.[5] In the early years, Duncan Phillips expressed limited interest in photography, although he admired the work of Stieglitz, whose Intimate Gallery in New York was the source of some of Phillips's favorite artists, including Dove, Marin, and Georgia O'Keeffe. Since 2008, the photography holdings have grown to include works by John Edmonds, Ralph Gibson, Laura Gilpin, Man Ray, J. D. 'Okhai Ojeikere, and Ruth Orkin, as well as major groups by Esther Bubley, Bruce Davidson, Walker Evans, Joel Meyerowitz, Jeanine Michna-Bales, August Sander, Aaron Siskind, and Brett Weston, among others.

In the pioneering spirit that inspired the creation of the Rothko Room, the museum unveiled a second such space in 2013, a permanent beeswax chamber by German artist Wolfgang Laib (pl. 203). The acquisition seemed at first a risky or, at the very least, a highly unusual proposition. Within the galleries—domestic rooms dating back to 1897—space is limited at the Phillips. The decision to commit an area in perpetuity to a single work, difficult for any museum, engendered especially intensive discussions at the Phillips. It was inspiring to see how trustees and a broader community of patrons embraced and supported the project financially, partly with an innovative crowd-sourced fundraiser. The chamber is dedicated to the memory of a beloved trustee, Caroline Macomber. The Zenlike simplicity of the room—its creamy golden surfaces glowing in the light of a single bulb, the gentle perfume of the wax—would surely have appealed to her poetic sensibility. I was certain of it, having seen Caroline's

fig. 5 (opposite top)
Installation of *Marking the Infinite: Contemporary Women Artists from Aboriginal Australia.* June 2–September 9, 2018.

fig. 6 (opposite bottom)
Installation of Muhsana Ali, Fodé Camara, Viyé Diba, and Piniang (Ibrahima Niang), *Diocco.* May 2014. The Phillips Collection, Hillyer Court.

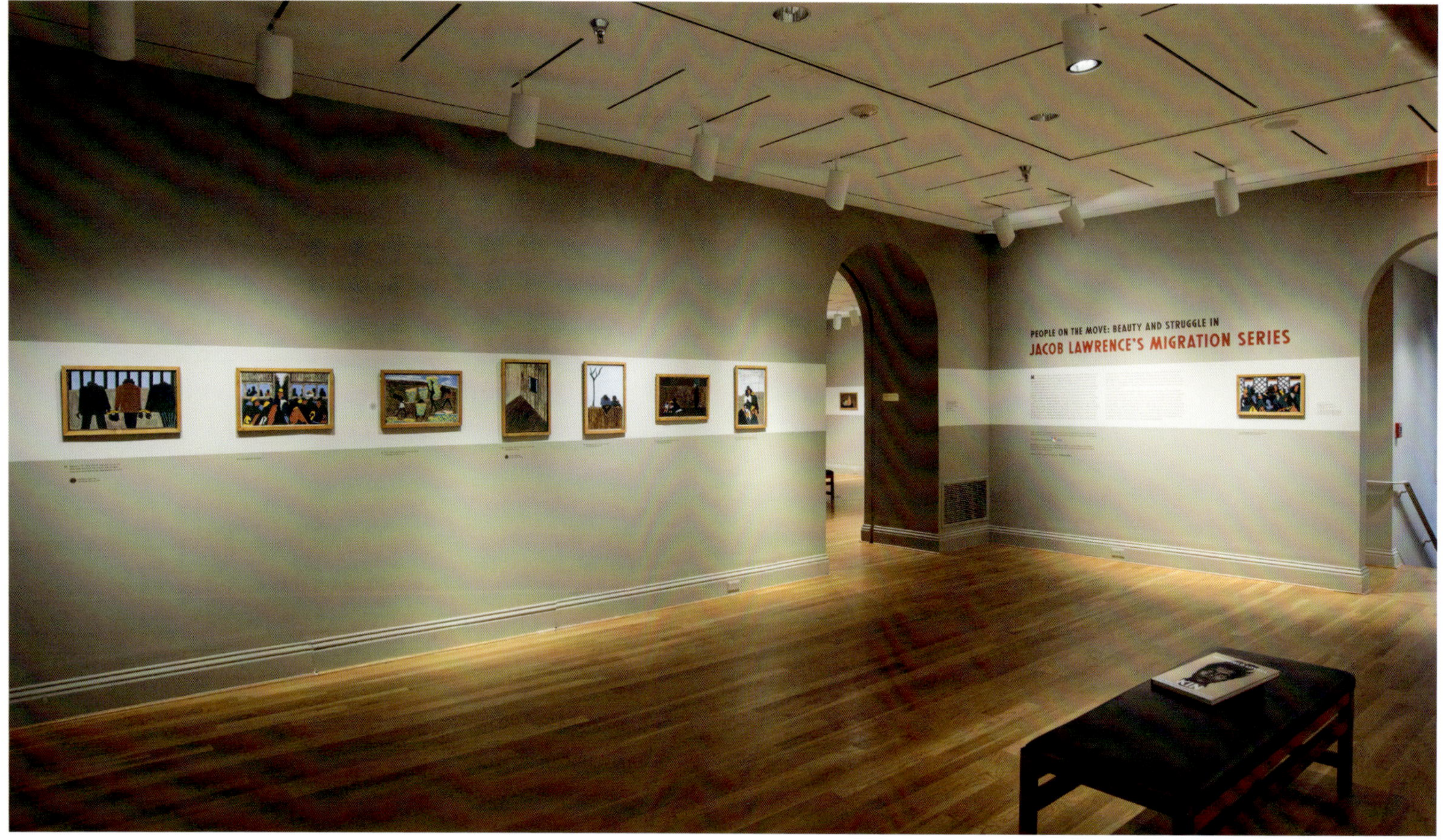

fig. 7
Installation of *People on the Move: Beauty and Struggle in Jacob Lawrence's Migration Series*. October 8, 2016–January 8, 2017.

expansive property on an island off the coast of Maine, where she combined stretches of untamed land and open vistas with garden enclosures. As he began his discussions with Klaus Ottmann, his longtime friend and Phillips chief curator, Laib, whose artistic practice is rooted in elemental materials and the meditative potential of art, carefully chose a small closet-like room for his installation, conceiving it as a response to the Rothko Room that had delighted him so much during his first visit to the museum in 2012. Like the Rothko Room, the wax chamber prompts a slowing of tempo, prolonged contemplation, and sensory awareness. Laib's Wax Room takes its place beside the works by Rothko and Klee that have had their own dedicated spaces.

Duncan Phillips was an early and stalwart proponent of diversity and internationalism in his politics and his collecting. Railing against "adolescent nationalism,"[6] he embraced art from an international standpoint, as a universal expression that crossed boundaries of race and language.[7] He included in his collection works by many naturalized Americans from Hungary, Italy, Japan, Romania, and Russia. During World War II, in 1944, he wrote "all the world contributed to our spiritual and creative resources since all the world is contained in our United States."[8] Similarly Duncan and Marjorie were early proponents of African American artists, collecting works by Sam Gilliam, Lois Mailou Jones, Jacob Lawrence, Horace Pippin, Alma Thomas, and James Lesesne Wells, among others.

Phillips's purchase of Howard University faculty member Wells's *Journey to Egypt* in 1931, the year it was painted, made it the first work by an African American artist to enter a national museum collection in the region. Purchases of works by Richmond Barthé, Allan Crite, Jones, and Pippin followed in the subsequent decade. Thirty panels of Lawrence's *Migration Series* were acquired from Edith Halpert's New York gallery in 1942 (fig. 7). The Phillips Collection offered a rare beacon of encouragement and support to the African American cultural community during decades when Washington, DC, was a harshly segregated city. Presented in a modestly scaled domestic setting, the collection became the model for the first Black-owned gallery in the United States, the Barnett Aden Gallery, founded by Howard

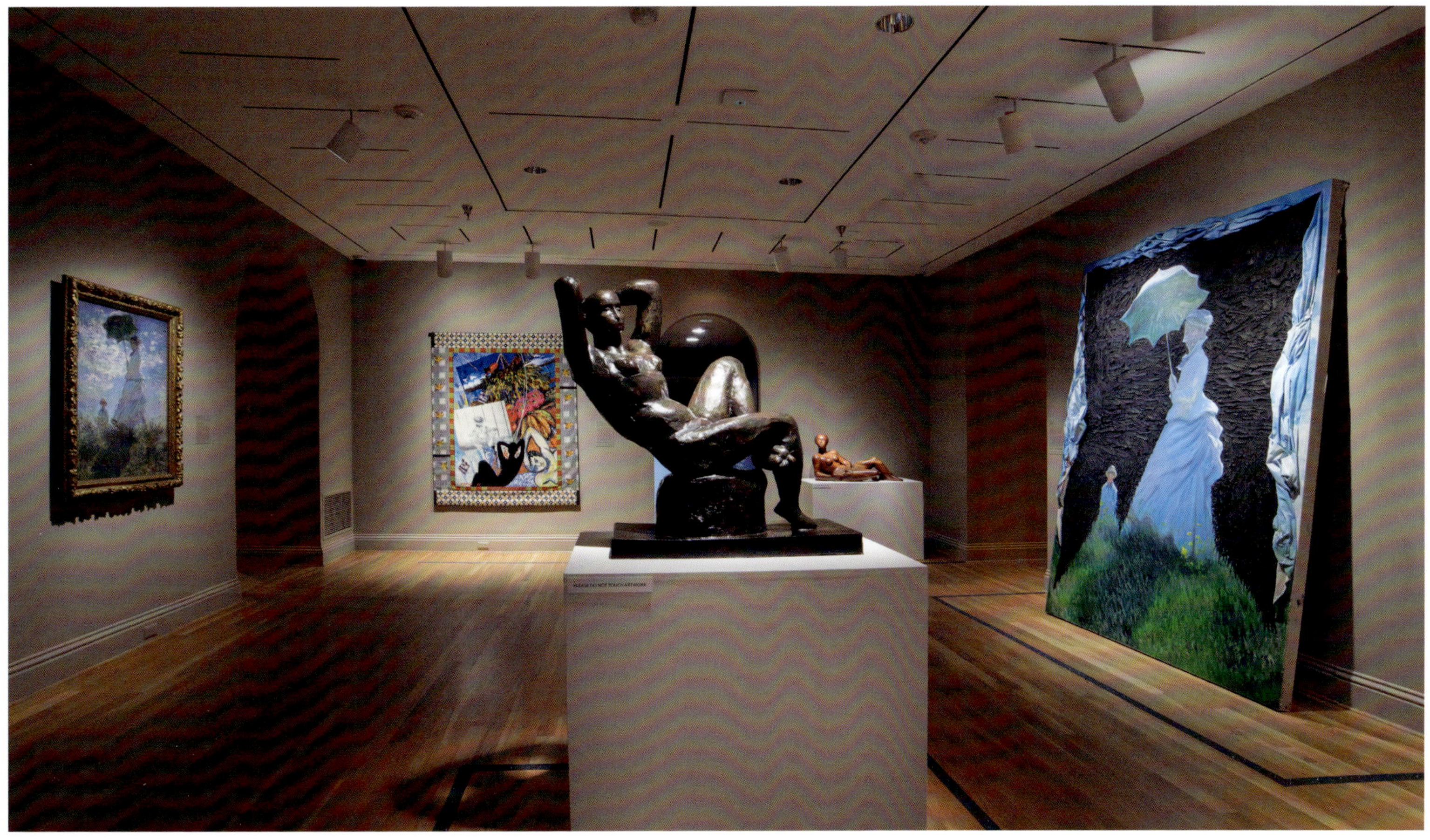

fig. 8
Installation of *Riffs and Relations: African American Artists and the European Modernist Tradition*. February 29, 2020–January 3, 2021.

University professor James V. Herring and Alonzo J. Aden. It was established in their home, where it featured artists regardless of their ethnicity and offered racially diverse exhibitions and programs. Duncan Phillips offered loans of work to the gallery's exhibitions and helped to promote some of the same artists. He also lent work to the Central Public Library, one of the first integrated cultural institutions in Washington, resulting in eight installations.

The late artist and writer David C. Driskell remembered feeling welcome at the Phillips, even courting his wife-to-be, Thelma Deloatch, in the galleries in the early 1950s. "I couldn't go to any other gallery in Washington, any other place, to see my teacher's work, and I think some of it was race consciousness, but for the most part, it was pride that I knew this person, and his work is in the Phillips. It extended that welcome to me."[9] Driskell never forgot the welcoming atmosphere of the collection and the generosity of Duncan Phillips. He embodied that spirit in his later work as a distinguished curator, collector, scholar, educator, and Phillips trustee.

We build on that legacy today. Galvanized by our determination to change the complexion of the permanent collection, in the past five years we have made it a priority to use our limited acquisition funds to broaden the representation of artists from diverse cultures in our collection. Our modest though no less significant strides have yielded acquisitions by John Akomfrah (pl. 20), McArthur Binion (pl. 81), Simone Leigh (pl. 195), Whitfield Lovell (pls. 134, 135), Aimé Mpane (pls. 53, 54), Alejandro Pintado, Zilia Sánchez (pl. 136), and Renée Stout (pl. 192; figs. 37–38), among others. In addition, with support from The Phillips Contemporaries in consultation with Phillips curators, we have acquired our first representative works by such artists as Gwendolyn Knight Lawrence (pl. 10), Nara Park, Ellington Robinson (pl. 133), and Zoë Charlton (pl. 58). Moreover, in 2018, in a concerted step to advance our commitment to diversity, equity, access and inclusion in all facets of our work, we hired a chief diversity officer, Makeba Clay, the first such position created in a US art museum. We have begun to change the course of our exhibitions, programs, and acquisitions

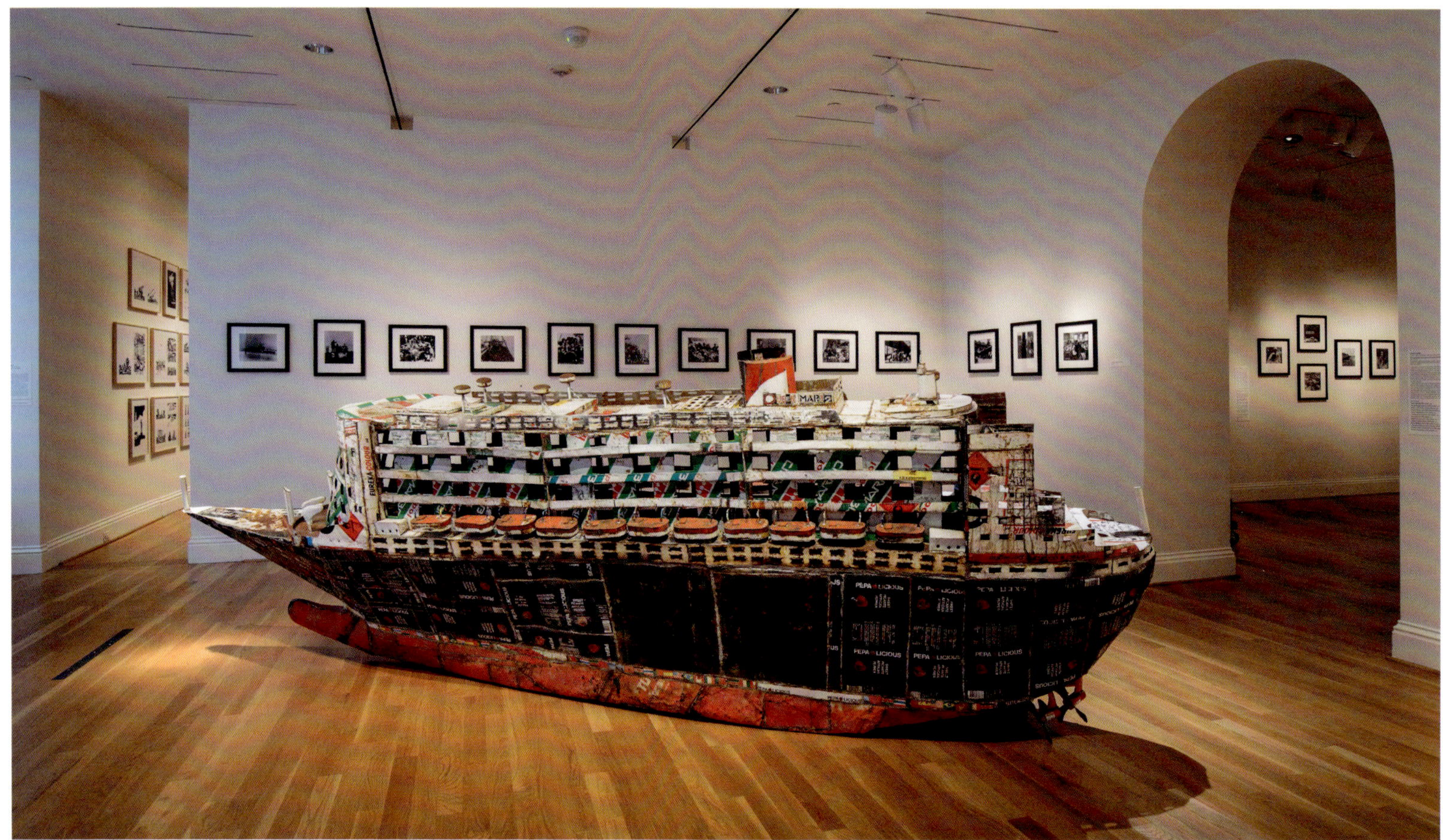

fig. 9
Installation of *The Warmth of Other Suns: Stories of Global Displacement*. June 2–September 22, 2019.

strategy to advance important work in this arena, from probing of urgent topics—such as migration and displacement—to support for veterans, arts education in the schools, engagement in under-resourced communities, and art and well-being.

The Phillips hired its first Black curator, Adrienne L. Childs, to organize *Riffs and Relations: African American Artists and the European Modernist Tradition* (fig. 8), which opened in early 2020. This exhibition illuminated the marginalized history of twentieth- and twenty-first-century African American artists and featured their responses to and interactions with European modernism. Through more than seventy works, the exhibition revealed the poignant ways in which African American artists have drawn on the substance of European art to tell their own stories. Works by Emma Amos, Elizabeth Catlett, Titus Kaphar, Janet Taylor Pickett, and Faith Ringgold were installed with examples by Claude Monet, Henri Matisse, and Pablo Picasso respectively. A year earlier, the Phillips presented *The Warmth of Other Suns: Stories of Global Displacement*, showing seventy-five modern and contemporary artists from the United States and far beyond (fig. 9), whose work posed urgent questions around the experiences and perceptions of migration and the current global refugee crisis. Similarly, in 2018 the museum collaborated with Oscar-winning director Alejandro G. Iñárritu, Legendary Entertainment, and the Emerson Collective on the virtual-reality experience *Carne y Arena* (flesh and sand), based on true accounts from Central American and Mexican refugees. State-of-the-art technology allowed participants to walk in a vast desert landscape and live a refugee's personal journey. In addition, several solo exhibitions have called attention to visionary contemporary voices, including those of Cuban-born artist Zilia Sánchez and American MacArthur grant-recipient Whitfield Lovell. Upcoming projects include solo exhibitions of Lawrence, Thomas, and Driskell.

The link between the foundational tenets of the Phillips Memorial Art Gallery and the core values that drive its strategic direction in the twenty-first century is robust. At its heart is the profoundly shared conviction that art makes a difference, art is relevant to the quality of people's lives, and art affects society. On December

15, 1940, just one year before the attack on Pearl Harbor and the US entry into World War II, Duncan Phillips participated in a symposium at the Phillips about "The Place of the Arts in the World Today." He wrote: "But art is the antithesis of war. Art is the greatest natural language between the different tribes and races. It is the symbol of creative and social forces which unite men, the rallying point of opposition to all those destructive anti-social forces which divide them. Art offers the only universal currency of thought-exchange and fellowship of the likeminded."[10] We share Duncan Phillips's passionate belief in the power of art to reveal our shared humanity, build empathic citizens, and provide spiritual healing and renewal. His idealistic vision speaks just as well to the divisiveness, factionalism, and strife that wrack our tumultuous world in 2020, as to the war, racism, and murder that enveloped his world in the 1930s and 1940s. The country has not only been wrestling with a worldwide health and economic crisis from the coronavirus pandemic but also confronting its centuries-long history of systemic racism in the face of deadly police brutality against Black people and other people of color.

Artists such as Jefferson Pinder have been responding to our nation's brutal history of deadly violence against Black people. In 2015, the Phillips collaborated with the David C. Driskell Center at UMD to present Pinder's *Dark Matter(s)* at Dupont Circle and the Driskell Center. Working with the international b-boy crew Lionz of Zion, Pinder directed a moving performance that wrestled with the nature of violence and control in the aftermath of the deaths of Michael Brown, Freddie Gray, and Eric Garner. Soon after, the Phillips showcased *Question Bridge: Black Males*, a video installation featuring more than 1,600 questions and responses documented by artists Chris Johnson, Hank Willis Thomas, Kamal Sinclair, and Bayeté Ross Smith. The project provided a powerful vehicle for healing and open dialogue that gave voice to the diversity of human expression within America's Black male population.

As a global crisis looms before us, we redouble our commitment to leveraging our position as an arts institution in the nation's capital to better lives; to use our privilege to challenge the system of white supremacy; and to continue to amplify marginalized voices. We are committed to continuing our founding mission to use the intersection of arts and education to build empathy, increase equity, and, most importantly, stand shoulder-to-shoulder with our colleagues and community to do the critical and hard work to combat discrimination. As we mark our centennial and begin a new chapter, we are full of hope for a better, more inclusive and diverse Phillips in the next century and beyond. Duncan Phillips's resounding words ring true to this day: we are a "Collection Still in the Making."

The epigraph is from Duncan Phillips, "Statement of My Wish for the Future of The Phillips Collection," January 26, 1965, n.p. The Phillips Collection Archives, Washington, DC.

1 Duncan Phillips, *A Collection in the Making* (New York: E. Weyhe; Washington, DC: Phillips Memorial Gallery, 1926), 4. Originally founded as "The Phillips Memorial Art Gallery," the museum was renamed Phillips Memorial Gallery in ca. 1923, then The Phillips Gallery in October 1948, then The Phillips Collection in July 1961.

2 Phillips, *A Collection in the Making*, 3.

3 Duncan Phillips, *The Arts in War Time* (Washington, DC: National Gallery of Art, 1942), n.p. The Phillips Collection Archives, Washington, DC. Duncan Phillips, "A Collection Still in the Making," *Formes*, no. 9, November 1930: 9.

4 The Senegalese artists Muhsana Ali, Fodé Camara, Viyé Diba, and Piniang (Ibrahima Niang) were part of a larger group of painters who had created a mural at the US Embassy in Dakar in May 2014. They traveled to DC as part of a cultural exchange organized by the State Department's Art in Embassies program to paint an original mural at The Phillips Collection. This mural was generously supported by Toni A. Ritzenberg, CulturalDC, Millennium Arts Salon, International Arts & Artists, and the Cameroon American Council.

5 The Photography Collectors Syndicate has included the following individuals who have made significant donations to The Phillips Collection: Michael and Joyce Axelrod, Kate Axelrod and Peter Ocko, Earl and Sue Cohen, Adam and Susan Finn, Jordan and Devinah Finn, Lisa Finn, Cam and Wanda Garner, Clay J. Ide, Michelle and Stan Kurtz, Saul Levi, Mel and Gail Mackler, Leo and Nina Pircher, Kenneth Pollin, Robert and Kathi Steinke, Jeff and Jill Stern, and Gabriel Wisdom.

6 Duncan Phillips, foreword to *The American Paintings of The Phillips Collection* (Washington, DC: Phillips Memorial Gallery, 1944).

7 Phillips, foreword to *American Paintings*.

8 Phillips, foreword to *American Paintings*.

9 David C. Driskell, oral history interview with Donita Moorhus, December 23, 2008, transcript, 9–10, The Phillips Collection Archives, Washington, DC.

10 Duncan Phillips, "The Place of the Arts in the World Today," *A Bulletin of the Phillips Memorial Gallery*, January 1941, n.p.

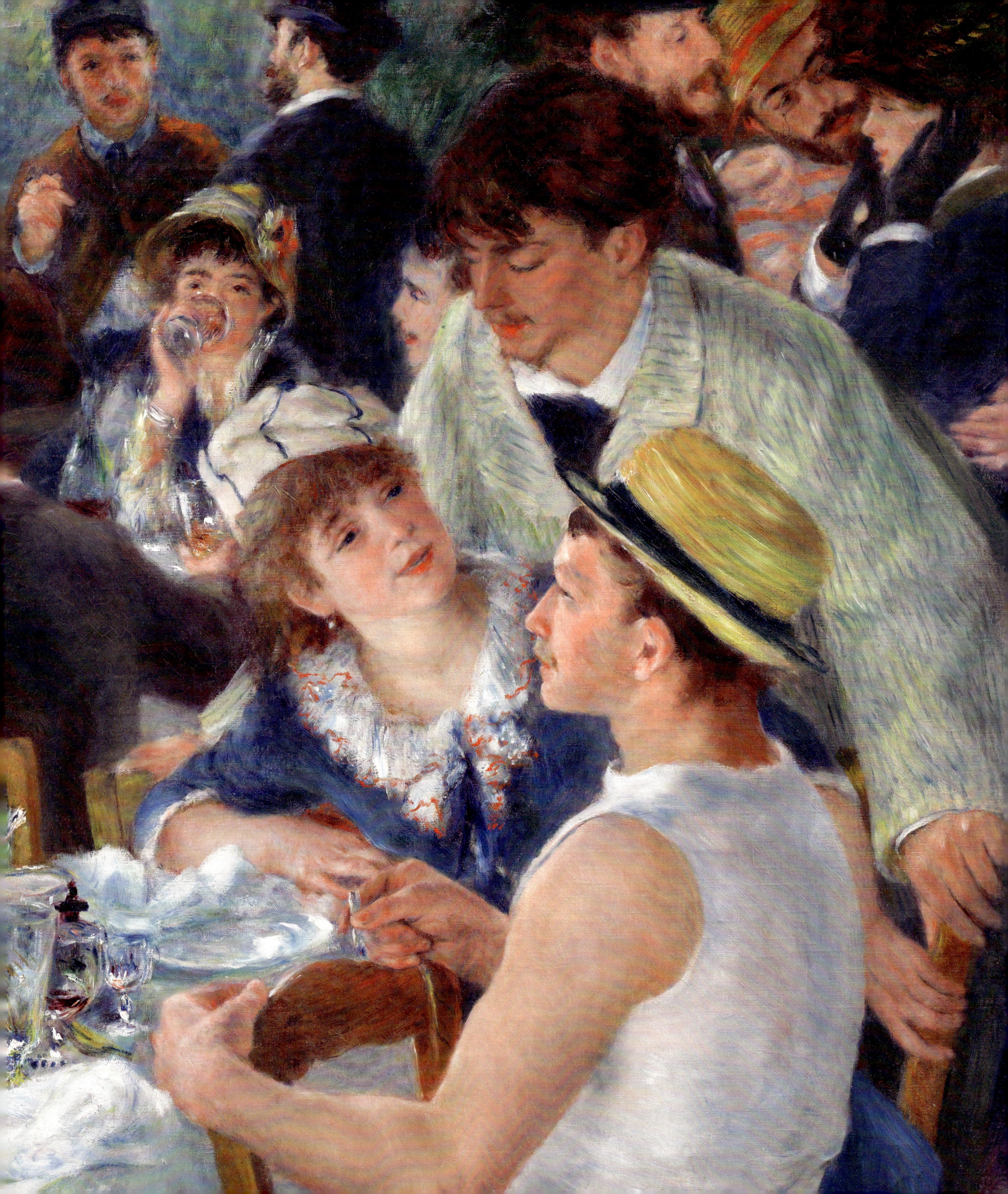

REFLECTIONS ON PIERRE-AUGUSTE RENOIR

Bridget Riley

(opposite)
Pierre-Auguste Renoir, *Luncheon of the Boating Party*, detail, 1880–81
The Phillips Collection, Washington, DC, Acquired 1923.

In 1985, the Hayward Gallery in London mounted a great Renoir exhibition. It astonished the younger painters in England, who flocked to see it: the painter's delight in his medium, the actual application of paint, its color, its vibrancy, and the intensity of touch. Not since the Renaissance had such glazing been seen.

I was drawn to *Madame Clémentine Valensi Stora (L'Algérienne)* (fig. 10). Its harmonies of red and yellow ochres lead from the arm of the chair through the sash, shawl and headdress, framing the pale, fresh oval of Madame Stora's face. Her dark eyes—with highlights—lock with the viewer's, whose eye, in turn, seeks and finds a mysterious color correspondence in the darkness of the hanging behind her. The loose, bright brushwork of her transparent, gauzy sleeves, and the simple treatment of her arms and hands as they lie in her lap offer a strong contrast to the mid-tone blue, which passes up through the reds and ochres, leading to the shine in her eyes.[1] This beauty attained an extraordinary sensuality, which many of us who visited the exhibition found almost overwhelming. Renoir, however, had a firm grip on his talents, held in check by a strong sense of the great tradition of Western painting.

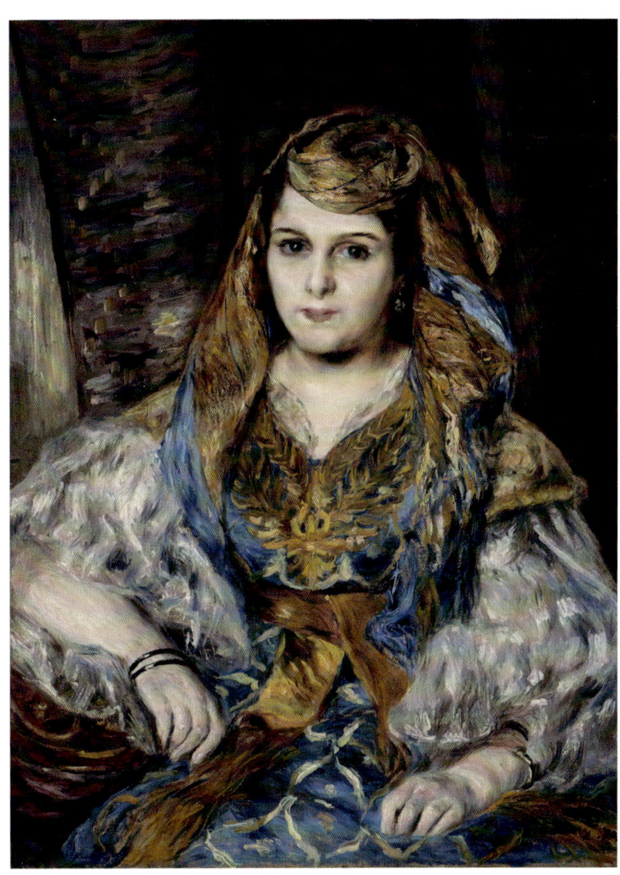

fig. 10 (right)
Pierre-Auguste Renoir *Madame Clémentine Valensi Stora (L'Algérienne)*, 1870
Oil on canvas, 33 1/4 × 23 1/2 in.
Fine Arts Museum of San Francisco, Gift of Mr. and Mrs. Prentis Cobb Hale in honor of Thomas Carr Howe, Jr., 1966.47.

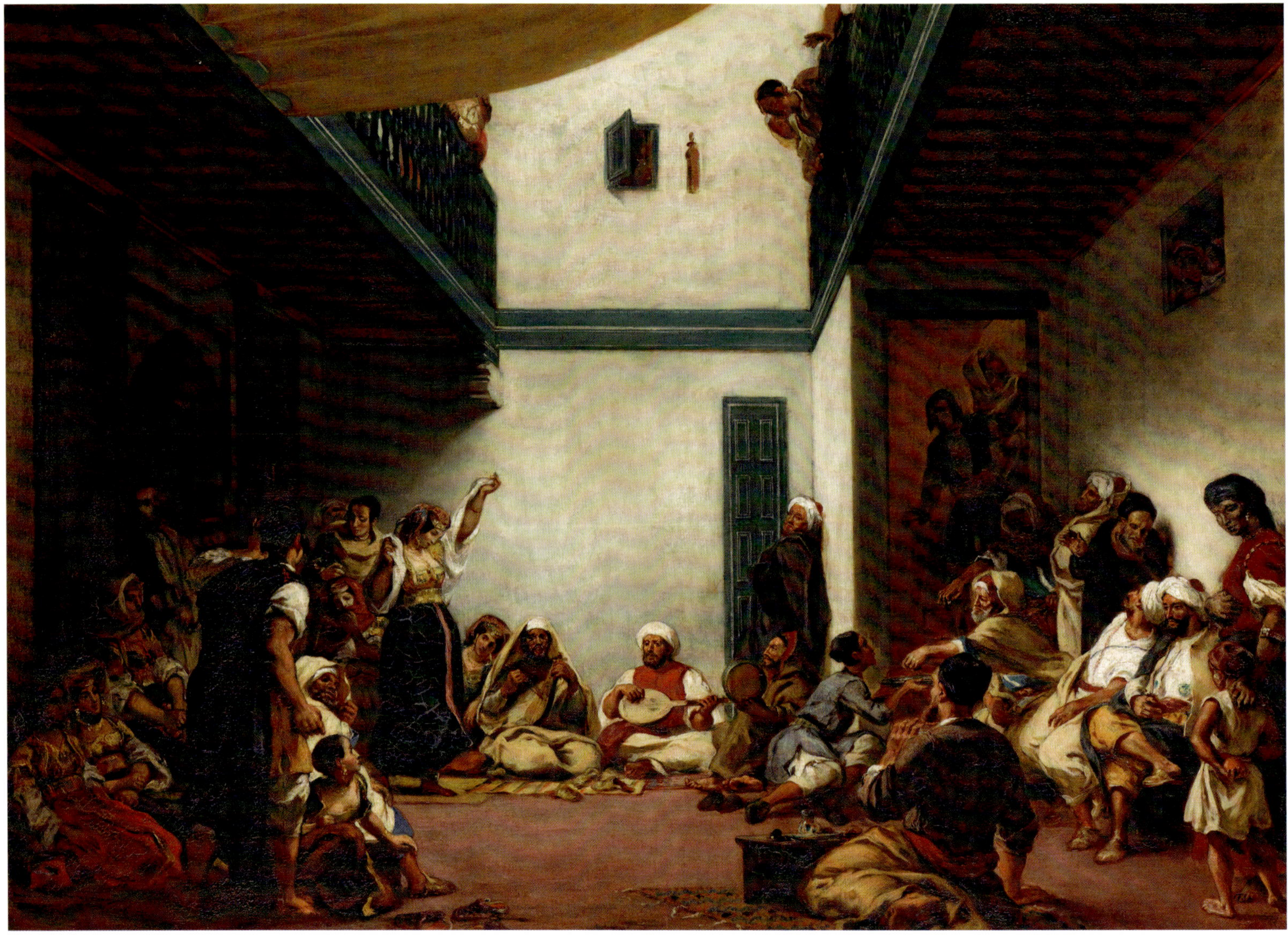

fig. 11
Ferdinand-Victor-Eugène Delacroix
***Jewish Wedding in Morocco*, 1841**
Oil on canvas,
41 1/4 × 55 in.
Musée du Louvre, Paris, France.

Renoir's gifts were prodigious. In his essay in the catalogue that accompanied the exhibition, Lawrence Gowing compared them to those of Rubens in their scale, range, and resourcefulness.[2] He developed his natural gifts through attentive and careful study in the Parisian museums, declaring Eugène Delacroix's *The Women of Algiers in Their Apartment* (1834; Louvre, Paris) to be "the most beautiful painting in the world." Renoir's famous copy of Delacroix's *Jewish Wedding in Morocco* (1875; Worcester Art Museum, Worcester, Massachusetts)[3] (fig. 11) earned him the nickname of "Delacroix blonde," a direct reference to the importance the master attached to "the mid-tone" in the use of color.

Hanging on a wall by itself and presiding over the whole exhibition was *Luncheon of the Boating Party* (fig. 12). It is, one feels, a Sunday outing. Enveloped in the soft, indirect reflected light of the awning, it is a perfect example of *peinture blonde*, as it was known in studio parlance, indicating the predominance of "the mid-tone" in impressionist practice.

The whole scene of *Luncheon of the Boating Party* is shot through with sight lines and glances. It is an interlocking structure of people observing, trying and hoping to catch one another's eyes: watching, speculating, considering their chances, connecting and not connecting. At the lower right, a young man gazes intently at a young woman on the far left playing with her dog, wishing he were the little dog. This avoidance of exchange holds a frontal plane across the painting with a poignancy that recalls the powerful glances between Bacchus and Ariadne (1522–23; National Gallery, London) and Diana and Actaeon (1556–59; National Galleries

fig. 12
Pierre-Auguste Renoir
***Luncheon of the Boating Party*, 1880–81**
Oil on canvas,
51 1/4 × 69 1/8 in.
The Phillips Collection,
Washington, DC,
Acquired 1923.

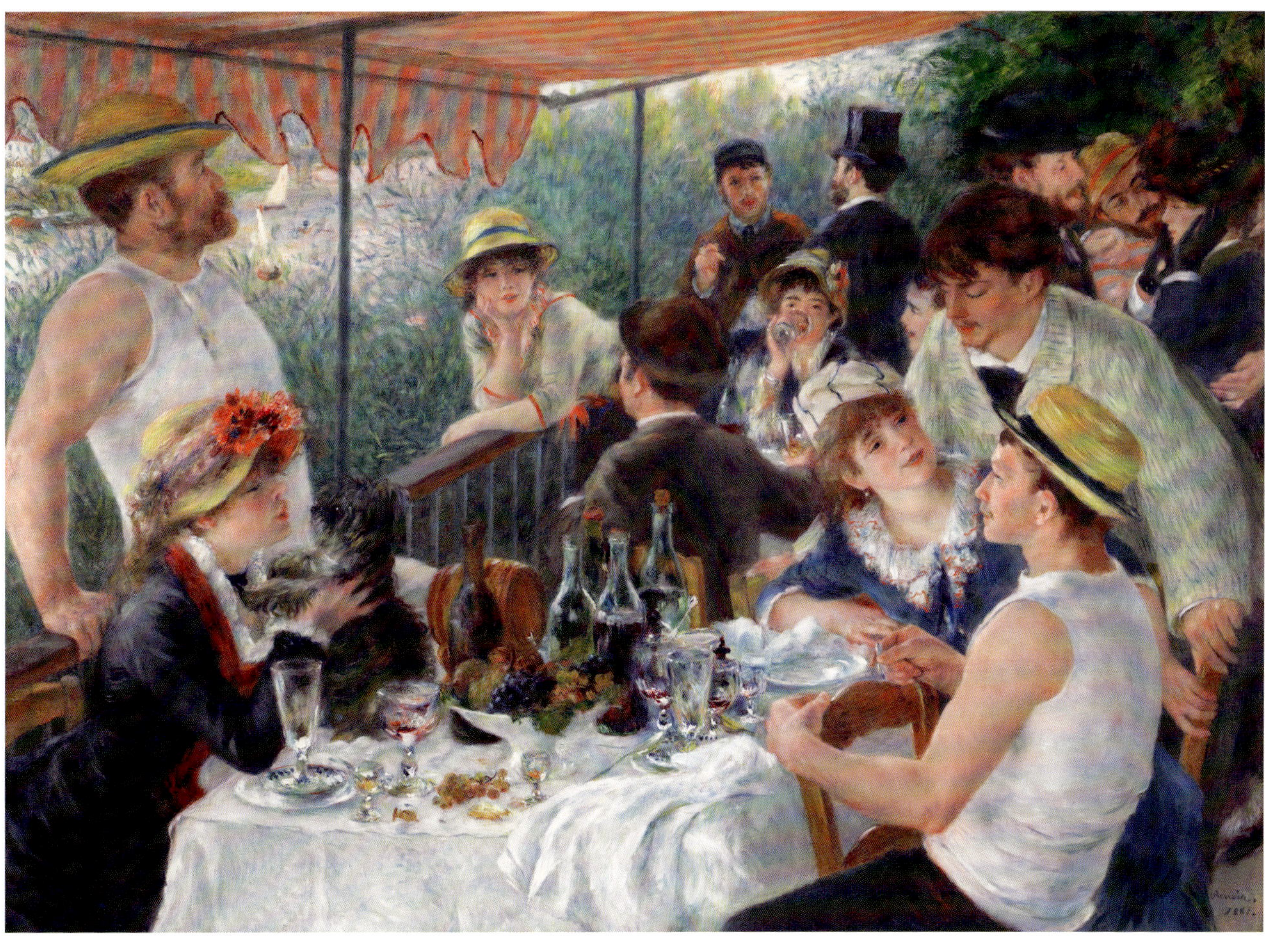

of Scotland and National Gallery, London), with which Titian orchestrates these great Renaissance paintings.

Renoir was passionately interested in all matters of color. I was enthralled by his use of red, one of the most difficult colors for a painter, by virtue of its strength. He takes red through every possible modulation and every shade of light and dark, using it as contrast or harmony. The red movement in *Luncheon of the Boating Party* supports the network of sight lines and glances. Tiny touches picking up lips, scarves, artificial flowers, ribbons and trimmings, carry red into the depths of the picture plane, returning it by the way of subdued stripes in the awning above, to the foreground of the viewer's gaze.

1 The portrait of Madame Stora was exhibited at the 1870 Salon, where some contemporary critics noted it as a testimony of Renoir's growing admiration of Delacroix. By 1906 it was in the possession of Claude Monet, who kept it until he died. See Anne Distel, catalogue entry 17, in John House and Anne Distel, *Renoir: Hayward Gallery, London* (London: Arts Council of Great Britain, 1985), 195.

2 Lawrence Gowing, "Renoir's Sentiment and Sense," in House and Distel, *Renoir*, 30–31.

3 In the 2016 National Gallery, London exhibition *Delacroix and the Rise of Modern Art*, Renoir's portrait of Madame Stora was hung next to his 1875 copy of Delacroix's *Jewish Wedding in Morocco*. This was also included in the Hayward Gallery Renoir exhibition in 1985.

"IT IS THE COLOR OF COURSE"

Klaus Ottmann

Red first shouted at me from a bed of pelargoniums.... I was four. This red had no boundary, was not contained. These red flowers stretched to the horizon.
—Derek Jarman

Duncan Phillips's collection of paintings, the bulk of it assembled between 1918 and his death in 1966, is suffused with color, arguably more so than most other collections. As Paul Richard has written, "for those who can hear color chords, the Phillips is a symphony."[1] Speaking of Jean Siméon Chardin's *Le jeune homme au violon* (*Young Man with Violin*) (1734–35), which he saw at the Louvre in Paris, Phillips, who described his interest in painting as "less psychological than esthetic," commented on the palette: "Against a coat of exquisite grayish green velvet a rich-toned flame-tinted violin sounds a delicate colour chord."[2]

Phillips's choices, ranging from Europeans like Vincent van Gogh, Pierre Bonnard, and Henri Matisse to Americans including John Henry Twachtman, Thomas Eakins, Albert Pinkham Ryder, Augustus Vincent Tack, Arthur Dove, Jacob Lawrence, Milton Avery, Mark Rothko, and Sam Gilliam, attest to his penchant for both bold color and subtle hues. His collection was shaped in no small measure by a deep belief in the "joy-giving and life-enhancing" potence of color—one he first experienced aged four, when his parents took him to the circus in Paris. Frightened by the performance of a clown, he would only be comforted by a bouquet of red, blue, and yellow flowers in his parents' hotel room. In her recollections of Phillips, his wife wrote: "He later remembered that he could not let the bouquet out of his sight and always thought that was his first real aesthetic experience of color."[3] This episode in Marjorie Phillips's recollections brings to mind one of the more spiritual and colorful paintings in The Phillips Collection, Odilon Redon's *Mystery* (fig. 13), an image of a pensive human figure contemplating a brightly colored bouquet. The dreamlike quality of the composition suggests multiple layers of meaning.

Many years later, in 1917, when his father died suddenly, and the following year, when his brother succumbed to the Spanish flu, Phillips again turned to color for comfort, this time finding it in the paintings he had been acquiring:

> There came a time when sorrow all but overwhelmed me. Then I turned to my love of painting for the will to live....So in 1918

fig. 13
Odilon Redon
***Mystery*, ca. 1910**
Oil on canvas,
28 3/4 × 21 3/8 in.
The Phillips Collection,
Washington, DC,
Acquired 1925.

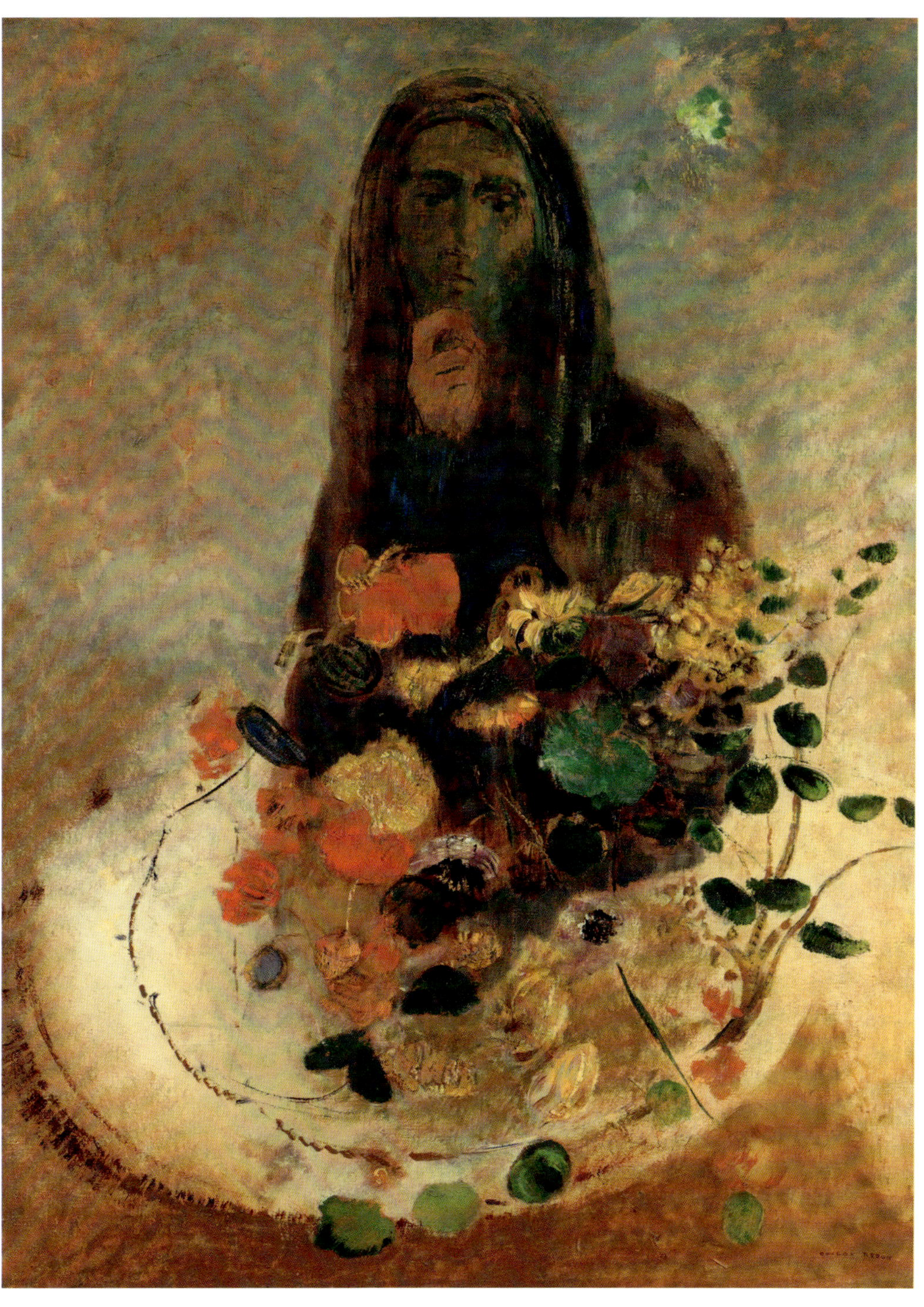

I incorporated the Phillips Memorial Gallery, first to occupy my mind with a large, constructive social purpose and then to create a Memorial worthy of the virile spirits of my lost leaders—my father… and my Brother.… I saw a chance to create a beneficent force in the community where I live—a joy-giving, life-enhancing influence, assisting people to see beautifully as true artists see.[4]

None, however, have embraced color more unabashedly, of course, than those who create with it—painters, and, increasingly since the 1960s, filmmakers. Bonnard's profusion of colors and textures come to mind, as do Rothko's glowing rectangles of color, inspired by the philosophies of Søren Kierkegaard and Friedrich Nietzsche and his study of the Jewish Kabbalah. So do Yves Klein's immaterial blue monochromes, or the innovative use of color in films: Michelangelo Antonioni's *Il deserto rosso* or Jean-Luc Godard's *Pierrot le fou*. In the latter, the American filmmaker Sam Fuller, when asked to define cinema, says: "Film is like a battleground: love, hate, action, violence, death—in one word, emotions." Rothko, whose paintings influenced Antonioni's films,[5] regarded his floating color rectangles as "actors" in an emotional drama and was "interested only in expressing basic human emotions—tragedy, ecstasy, doom, and so on,"[6] which is echoed in his stated desire to "communicate ... basic emotion."[7]

PAINTERS USE RED LIKE SPICE!
—Derek Jarman

All works of art are endowed with a certain self-revelatory quality that does not depend on outside references. For the Dutch CoBrA artist Karel Appel, everything begins with the color red (see fig. 14): "The hardest part is to start a painting; after that, it's easy. You have to choose the colour. It's very important to start with red."[8] For Appel, red is the point zero of painting, as it was for Eugène Delacroix, Bonnard, Matisse, and Rothko. As the French philosopher Jean-François Lyotard observes, "colour enters matter as what vibrates before the yes and the no, which is there before form and concept."[9] The American mathematician, philosopher, and logician Charles Sanders Peirce regarded the color red as a key example of "Firstness," which to him is "possibility."[10] Any work of art possesses Firstness—for example, a red painting. It has the potential of presence. It begins in the artist's studio with the mere possibility of the color red. But it only "exists" when we perceive it.

Rothko, largely self-taught, having painted for more than half of his life in a figurative style, became an abstract painter almost against his will. Having painted figures, still lifes, and street scenes in the 1920s and 1930s, and having achieved a greater sense of freedom from representational constraints in his semi-abstract paintings inspired by Greek mythology, he moved into pure abstraction in 1946, arriving at his color-immersive signature style in 1949, after seeing Matisse's painting *The Red Studio* (1911) at the Museum of Modern Art in New York. Rothko visited the museum every day for months to study it. He likened its enveloping sense of color to music and once told his wife, Mell, that they owed both his artistic achievements and their material possessions to Matisse's *Red Studio*: "You remember when I used to pass my days at the Museum of Modern

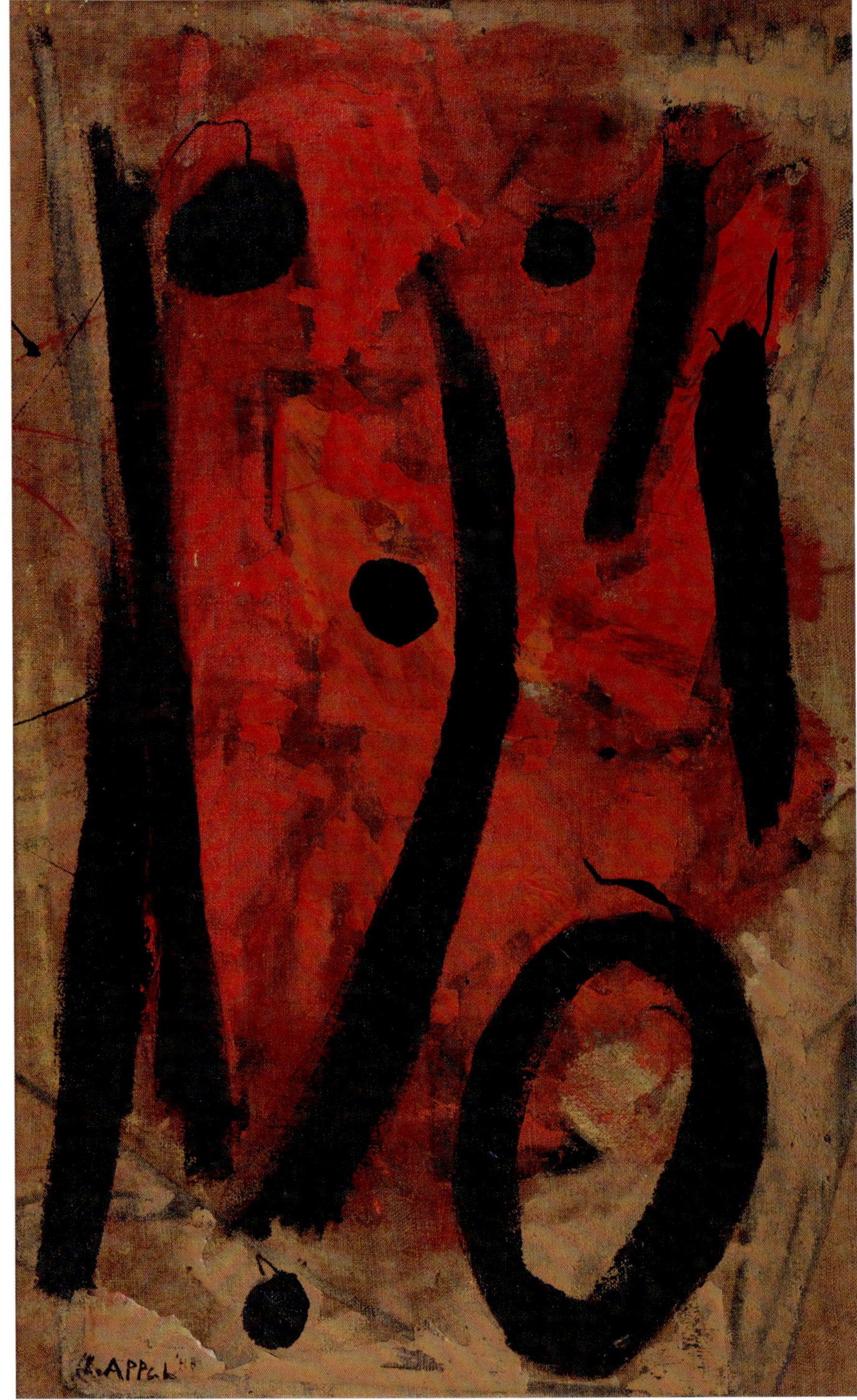

Art looking at Matisse's *Red Studio*? ... You thought I was wasting my time. But this house you owe to Matisse's *Red Studio*. And from those months and that looking every day all of my painting was born."[11]

Rothko took the notion of color as form, carrying emotive and existential content, from his study of

fig. 14 (opposite)
Karel Appel
***Tekens in Rood (Signs in Red)*, 1948**
Oil, lacquer, and newspaper on burlap mounted on canvas, 51 5/8 × 31 1/2 in.
The Phillips Collection, Washington, DC,
Gift of the Karel Appel Foundation, 2016.

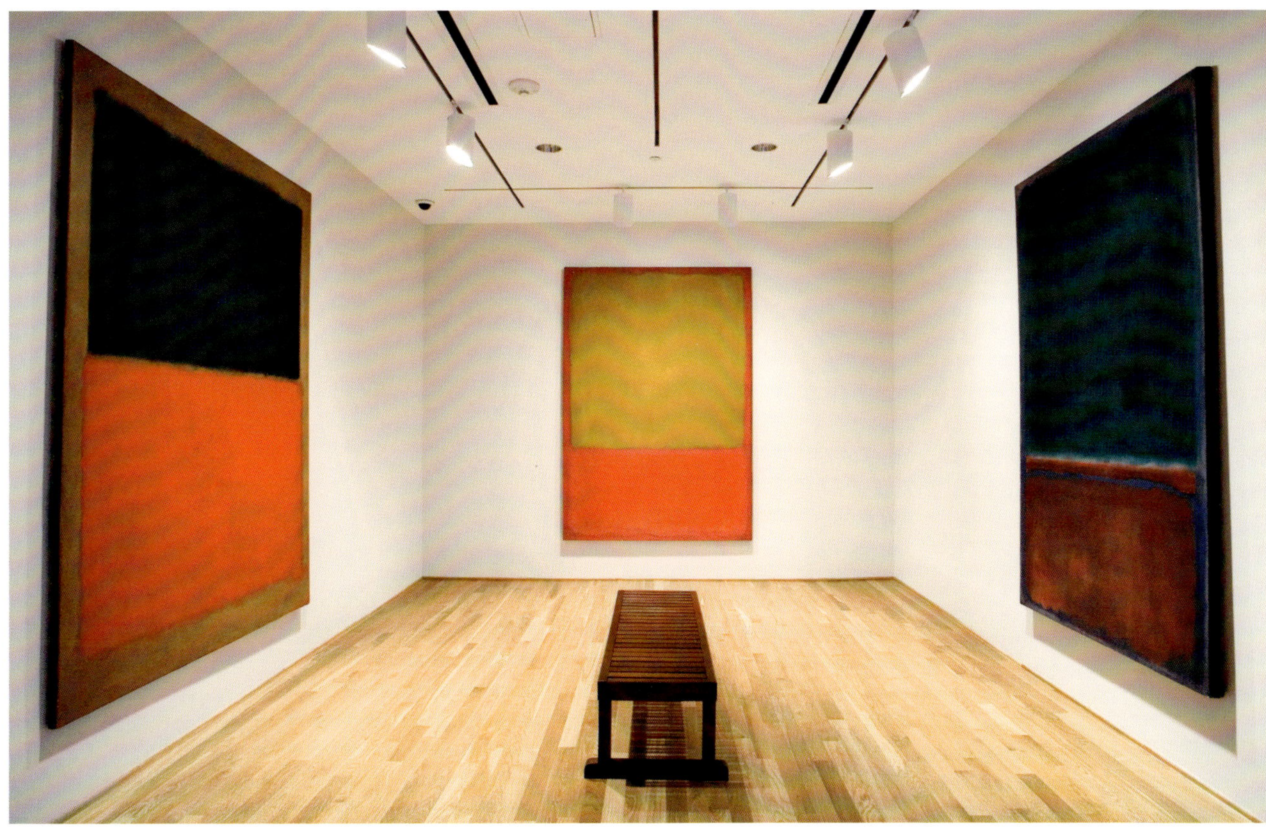

fig. 15 (right)
The Rothko Room at The Phillips Collection, 2006. Left to right: *Green and Tangerine on Red*, 1956; *Ochre and Red on Red*, 1954; *Green and Maroon*, 1953.

Matisse's painting. Combining this with his passion for and knowledge of theater and film, he extended color into space, constantly negotiating between the depth and the surface of his paintings, by expanding the color outward while, at the same time, contracting it inward.

Rothko told Katharine Kuh, a curator at the Art Institute of Chicago: "Since my pictures are large, colorful and unframed, and since museum walls are usually immense and formidable, there is the danger that the pictures relate themselves as decorative areas to the walls. This would be a distortion of their meaning, since the pictures are the opposite of what is decorative. . . . By saturating the room with the feeling of the work, the walls are defeated."[12]

No space I know has been more saturated by the emotive potence of color than The Phillips Collection's Rothko Room (fig. 15). Duncan Phillips may have been introduced to Rothko's work in 1950 by the artist Theodoros Stamos: "I told him that I think it's important that he get at least one [Rothko], and I told him why. I told him that he is so strongly related to Bonnard that if he looked at some black and white Bonnards he would see it clearer, and then focus on the color. We discussed that for a long time."[13]

From an exhibition in 1957 at The Phillips Collection of six paintings by Rothko, Phillips acquired *Green and Maroon* (1953). In 1960, he held a one-person show of Rothko's works, acquiring from it *Green and Tangerine on Red* (1956) and *Orange and Red on Red* (1957). When Phillips added an adjoining building to accommodate his growing collection in 1960, he created a small gallery for his "unit" of Rothko paintings, making the Phillips the first American museum to dedicate a space to the artist's work. From the outset, the room was intended as a meditative respite, and was even referred to by Phillips as a type of "chapel." Since then, the Phillips has grown its Rothko holdings through several gifts (see fig. 16) although the original configuration of the Rothko Room has remained virtually unchanged.

Grey is the sad world
Into which the colours fall
Like inspiration
Sparkle and are overwhelmed...
—Derek Jarman

A number of works acquired by Duncan Phillips are surprisingly muted and subtle in color. Their colorific effect only becomes activated when they are placed in conversation with other works. A powerful work by Francis Bacon, *Study of a Figure in a Landscape* (1952), is a case in point. When installed next to Van Gogh's small *House at Auvers* (1890) with its immense fields of dense green, the focus of Bacon's large study depicting a dark, gray, human figure crouching in long grass seems to shift from the figure to the sparse blades of green within his field of long yellow grass.

A golden colour appears when what is yellow and sunny gleams.
—Derek Jarman

Yellow is related to gold. When experiencing Wolfgang Laib's *Wax Room* (see fig. 25; pl. 203), with its walls covered in yellowish-amber wax (which, according to the artist, refers to both the life-sustaining power of honey and the gold leaf used in fourteenth-century Sienese painting), its auric effect becomes apparent only when the wax is activated by the soft gleam of the lightbulb hanging from the ceiling of the room.

Artists like Rothko, Laib, and the Danish artist Poul Gernes—one of whose works the Phillips recently acquired (pl. 75)—practice painting as an ideological formalism of color and space. On one of his notecards, Rothko wrote: "Addition to experienced color and space.... Once color is out of the paint can, it is in the world of human action in relation to the time and the event of the day and the eyes for whom the time and events occur." For Rothko, as for Laib and Gernes, color and space pertain to the experience of the human condition and thus have both aesthetic and ethical qualities.

Blue gives other colours their vibration, Cézanne. TRUE BLUE.
—Derek Jarman

When Duncan Phillips called his collection an "intimate museum combined with an experiment station,"[14] he was not speaking simply in spatial terms, but also about a psychological experience, about emotions tied to color, as epitomized by Bonnard and Rothko, which he later described, in reference to Bonnard, as substituting "for the merely visual sensation a new kind of impressionism of the *total sensation*, including the *conception of the mind*."[15] Phillips, who ultimately regarded Rothko as one of the greatest contemporary American artists, detected in his paintings "an enveloping magic which conveys to receptive observers a sense of being in the midst of greatness." He continued, "It is the color of course. These canvases which have been called empty by the resistant skeptics and which certainly depict nothing at

fig. 16
Mark Rothko
***Untitled*, 1968**
Acrylic on paper mounted on hardboard,
23 13/16 × 18 11/16 in.
The Phillips Collection, Washington, DC,
Gift of the Mark Rothko Foundation, Inc., 1985.

all are nevertheless a vibrant life-enhancing experience to those who make themselves ready for them."[16]

The affinity for color remains an essential characteristic of The Phillips Collection. Many of the acquisitions of the past twenty years attest to this: works by Appel, Stephen Dean, Rudolf de Crignis, Helen Frankenthaler, Gee's Bend quiltmakers (Mary Lee Bendolph, Aolar Mosley, Arlonzia Pettway, Lucy T. Pettway, and Malissia Pettway), Gernes, Gilliam, Per Kirkeby, Laib, Morris Louis, Markus Lüpertz, Joseph Marioni, Aimé Mpane, Susan Rothenberg, Kate Shepherd, John Walker, and Franz Erhard Walther—to name but a few.

Wittgenstein once remarked that "man has the drive to run against the boundary of language.... This running against the boundary of language ... points to something."[17] Color is such a boundary, one that points to something mystical, undefinable, non representable: "There is indeed the inexpressible. This shows itself; it is the mystical."[18] It is in Redon's bouquet of flowers, in the grasses of Van Gogh and Bacon, and in the red, blue, and green color fields of Mark Rothko that, in Wittgenstein's famous dictum, ethics and aesthetics become one, and the ethical responsibility of color is practiced at its fullest.

The epigraphs in this essay are from Derek Jarman, *Chroma: A Book of Colour—June '93* (London: Vintage, 1994), 31, 33, 56, 92, 105.

1 Paul Richard, "The Shadow of Duncan Phillips," *Washington Post*, June 15, 1986, https://www.washingtonpost.com/archive/lifestyle/style/1986/06/15/the-shadow-of-duncan-phillips/1917cddc-a303-4780-8bfa-dd1066f3e9c5/. Accessed April 2020.

2 From Duncan Phillips's travel journal, Paris, 22 August 1911, cited in Marjorie Phillips, *Duncan Phillips and His Collection* (New York and London: W. W. Norton, 1982), 41.

3 Phillips, *Duncan Phillips and His Collection*, 32.

4 Duncan Phillips, *A Collection in the Making: A Survey of the Problems Involved in Collecting Pictures Together with Brief Estimates of the Painters in the Phillips Memorial Gallery* (New York: E. Weyhe; Washington, DC: Phillips Memorial Gallery, 1926), 3–4.

5 Antonioni referred to himself as "a filmmaker who paints" (A. Tassone, "Entretien avec Michelangelo Antonioni," *Positif* 292 [June 1985]: 38–45). Antonioni's first exhibition of his own paintings took place at the Galleria Nazionale d'Arte Moderna in Rome in 1983. He is said to have told Rothko: "Your paintings are like my films—they're about nothing, with precision." Quoted in R. Gilman, *Common and Uncommon Masks: Writings on Theatre, 1962–1975* (New York: Vintage Books, 1972), 34.

6 Quoted in Annie Cohen-Solal, *Mark Rothko: Toward the Light in the Chapel* (New Haven, CT, and London: Yale University Press, 2015), 148–49.

7 Cohen-Solal, *Mark Rothko*, 149.

8 Karel Appel in conversation with Hans Ulrich Obrist, April 2005, in *Bonnard, the Work of Art: Suspending Time*, ed. Suzanne Pagé (Aldershot, UK: Lund Humphries, 2006), 271.

9 Jean-François Lyotard, *Karel Appel: A Gesture of Colour/Karel Appel, Un geste de couleur*, trans. Vlad Ionescu and Peter W. Milne (Leuven: Leuven University Press, 2009), 159.

10 See Charles Sanders Peirce, *The Essential Peirce: Selected Philosophical Writings, Volume II (1893–1913)* (Bloomington: Indiana University Press, 1998), 268.

11 As recounted by Italian writer Gabriella Drudi in a letter to the art critic Dore Ashton. Dore Ashton, *About Rothko* (New York: Oxford University Press, 1983), 187.

12 Quoted in Katharine Kuh, *My Love Affair with Modern: Behind the Scenes with a Legendary Curator* (New York: Arcade, 2006), 147–48.

13 Theodoros Stamos to Grayson Harris, September 9, 1991, The Phillips Collection Archives, Washington, DC.

14 Phillips, *A Collection in the Making*, preface, n.p.

15 Phillips, *A Collection in the Making*, 52.

16 Cited by Marjorie Phillips in *Duncan Phillips and His Collection*, 288.

17 Quoted in B. F. McGuinness, ed., *Ludwig Wittgenstein und der Wiener Kreis: Gespräche, aufgezeichnet von Friedrich Waismann* (Frankfurt am Main: Suhrkamp Verlag, 1984), 68–69 (my translation).

18 Ludwig Wittgenstein, *Tractatus Logico-Philosophicus*, trans. C. K. Ogden (London: Routledge & Kegan Paul, 1981), 6.522.

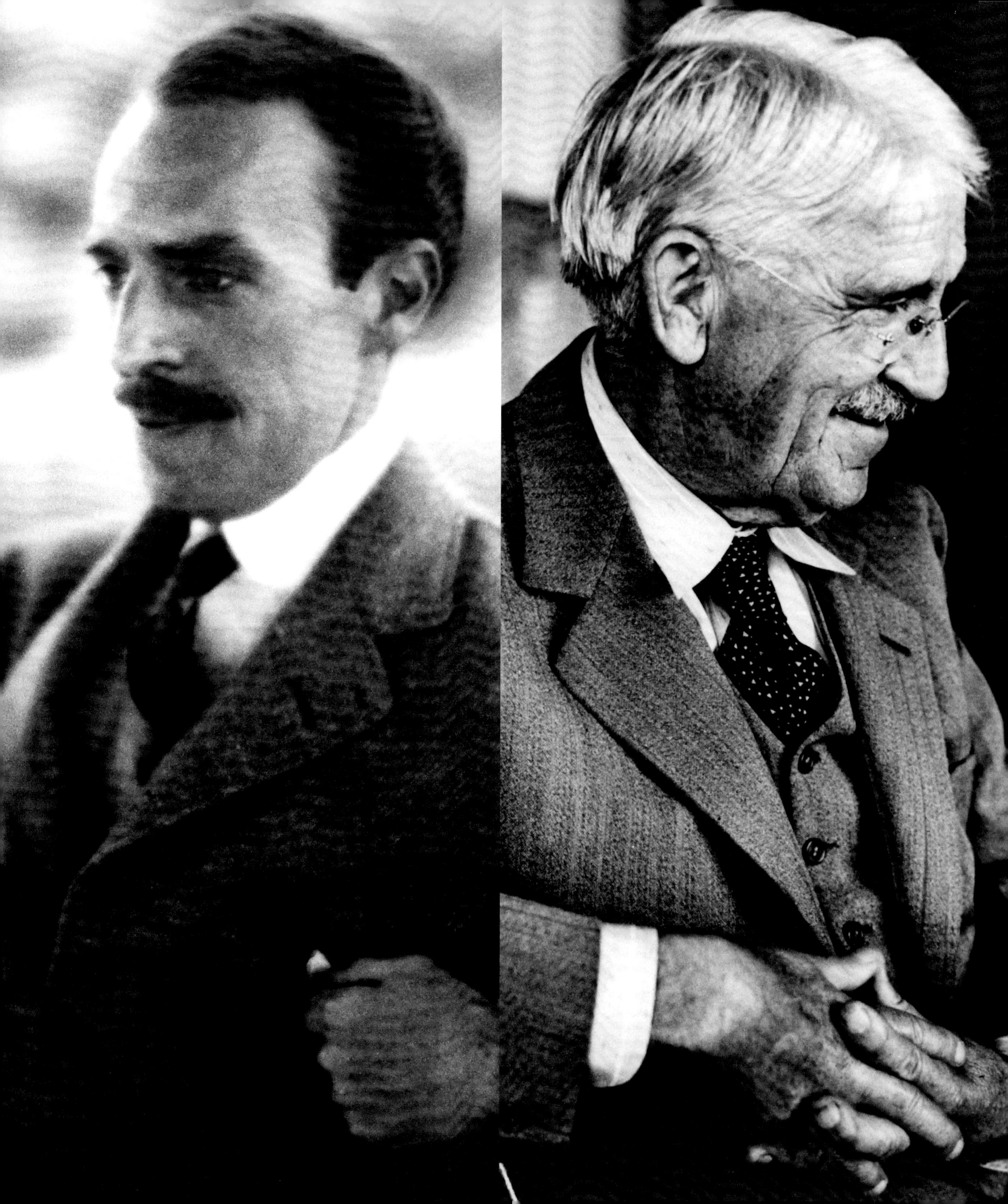

NOT THE EYE BUT THE BEHOLDER: THE SHARED VISION OF DUNCAN PHILLIPS AND JOHN DEWEY

Mary Jane Jacob

(opposite left)
Portrait of Duncan Phillips, ca. 1922.

(opposite right)
Photo of John Dewey Smiling in Profile, 1950
Special Collections Research Center, Morris Library, Southern Illinois University, Carbondale.

To Duncan Phillips, art was personal. It started with buying paintings but grew, through cycles of sympathetic identification with the artist and viewer, to have wide public impact as he became a protagonist in the story of the founding of American modern art museums in the early twentieth century. The sorrow stemming from the passing of his father and, soon after, his only sibling was motivation to build a memorial in the form of a museum that became The Phillips Collection (fig. 17). The joy he found in marrying an artist, Marjorie Acker Phillips, sustained and enriched that vision. It was an endeavor through which Phillips found what philosopher John Dewey called his vocation, not just a livelihood but his life's work.

As a well-to-do, well-educated young man, it is fair to say that Duncan Phillips was in search of a life. While this is true for all who seek meaning, he was enabled along this path. At a young age, his father had retired and relocated the family from Pittsburgh to the District of Columbia. There Duncan was not only afforded a fine education but also the ability to develop his own interests outside a business career. By age thirty, he and his brother had a yearly stipend of $10,000 to purchase art (some $250,000 today). The freedom money buys does not ensure success: it takes care and conscious intent to create a way of working and living that are in harmony. In this task Phillips used his gifts not just to pursue art as a fancy or even a profession, but as a vehicle for self-realization. He knew that looking at art was not just an intellectual exercise or diversion but that when we bring to the viewing our whole being, it is possible to have transformative aesthetic experiences.

When in 1914 he wrote his first book, *The Enchantment of Art*, he acknowledged the formative role of an experience "when the enjoyment of artistic beauty made it wonderfully well worth while." Then he set out: "the purpose of this book is the purpose of art itself; to stimulate the appreciation of life and to intensify the joy of living," while at the same time sensing that "the Enchantment of Art is a subject as big as life and as enduring."[1] By 1926, with *A Collection in the Making*, he said his museum project was to be "a joy-giving, life-enhancing influence" in his community, "assisting people to see beautifully as true artists see."[2] His passion had become his mission.

Phillips's understanding of art—that it enriches life—is central to John Dewey's 1934 thesis on aesthetics, *Art as Experience* (fig. 18). In that now-classic book, Dewey

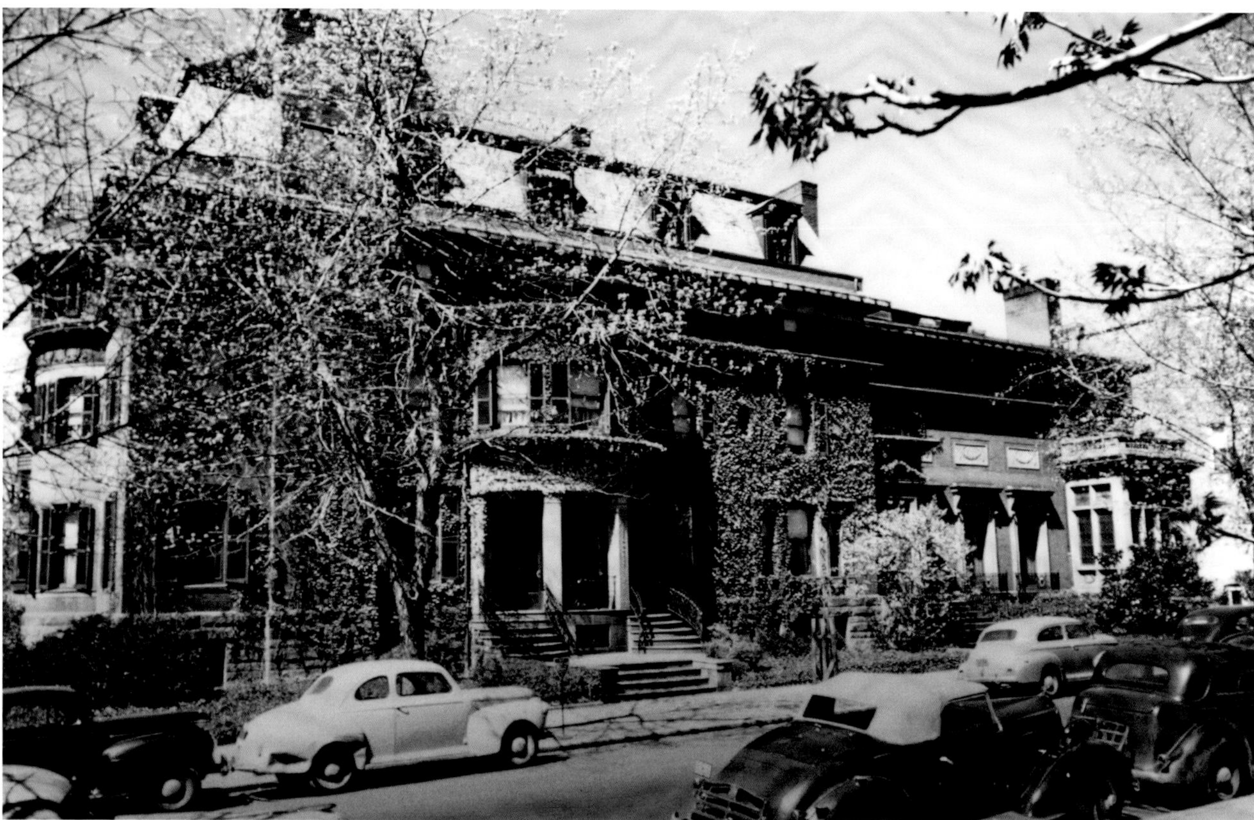

fig. 17
The front of The Phillips Collection, then the Phillips Memorial Art Gallery, ca. 1930s.

laid out just how aesthetic experience helps us live life more consciously. It is "heightened vitality" that "keeps alive the power to experience the common world in its fullness," at once essential to individual life and for a healthy and humane society.[3]

Phillips was an exceptionally attentive reader of Dewey, and this book came at the right time. Phillips's own aesthetic experiences had taken shape through his collecting, his writings, and the founding of his museum. His studied analysis of Dewey is revealed in his personal copy, annotated and further animated by conversations with himself and with the author in the margins.[4] The next year, in a major three-part essay devoted to "Personality in Art," Phillips applied Dewey as he expounded on his views on art and society.[5]

Aesthetic Experience

What makes an aesthetic experience unlike other experiences, as John Dewey tells it, is that as it runs its course and we make meaning, it becomes part of our being. So more than cultivating good taste, when we encounter a work that truly touches us, we take it in not just with our eyes but with our whole selves. We come to realize what is vital to us, literally having the sensation of vitality. This is a growing process fundamental to living, Dewey posited, and it enables us to cope with inevitable change, all the more evident in modern times. This biological truism also takes on a social dimension as we grow in consciousness and become cognizant of the consequences of our actions on the world around us.

The belief that art is a part of the "processes of living" struck a chord for Phillips.[6] This was the experience he first called "enchantment" in 1914. Ten years before Dewey, in 1924, he had written: "The greatest thing art can suggest is the rhythm of life itself."[7] In 1929, he spoke of it as providing a "sense of well-being and enriched capacity for living," and employed this concept to define art as "the one method of communication which is also a symbol of life itself, of life with its rhythms and its complexity of independent relations."[8] In 1931, as he took on the subject in an essay dedicated to aesthetic experience, he elaborated: "art must first be respected as a living, growing, changing child of man, having its own organic life, based on the same principles of rhythm and interdependence as those by which we live and with its own emotions in line, form, color, light, space, proportion, contrast, repetition, subordination, accent, continuity, harmony, unity and in one word *relations*."[9]

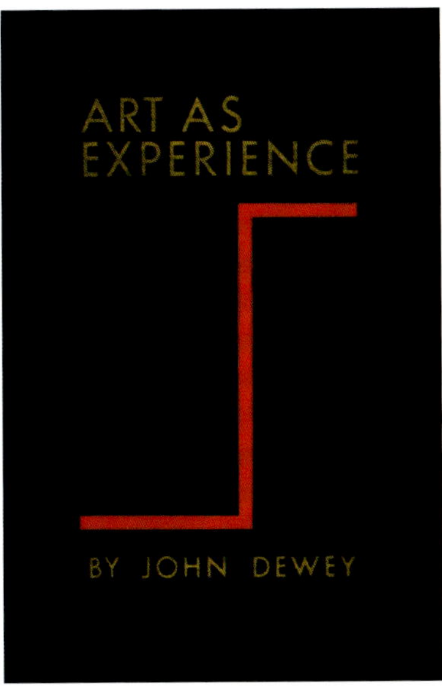

fig. 18
Cover of John Dewey's *Art as Experience* (1934).

In this essay he defended the pleasure derived from viewing art because one grows as life is enriched, in contrast to Leo Stein whose emphasis on "pure aesthetics" took the life out of a work of art, rendering it "just another bit of knowledge."[10]

With clear conviction, Phillips sets out his terms for aesthetic experience: "Beauty is in us, not in objects."[11] When Dewey's book appeared three years later, what a kinship he must have felt as he read the opening lines: "the actual work of art is what the product does with and in experience."[12] Later in the volume, Phillips marks "Fine passage!" as he paraphrases Dewey in the margin: "The uniquely distinguishing feature of esthetic experience is the fact that no real distinctions between self & objects exists in it" (fig. 19).[13] So Phillips knew to be true, as Dewey wrote, that a work of art is art "only when it lives in some individualized experience," and is "recreated every time it is esthetically experienced."[14]

Importantly, Dewey made explicit that aesthetic experience is not the sole province of works of art. Thus, he identified the primary form that exists in nature or some other aspect of living, and the subset that is the rarefied form of works of art. The philosopher was incensed at the lack of recognition of this fact and by philosophies that set art apart in a realm of its own. He also pointed to how this is expressed in museums that wrongheadedly define a hierarchy of types of works and cultures. Therefore, he claimed as motivation for writing this book: "The task is to restore continuity between the refined and intensified forms of experience that are works of art and the everyday events, doings, and sufferings that are universally recognized to constitute experience."[15]

fig. 19
Duncan Phillips's annotation on p. 248 of John Dewey's *Art as Experience* (1934).

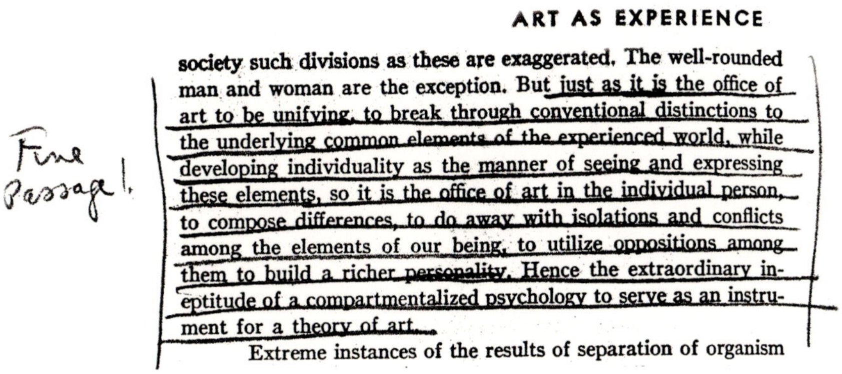

ART AS EXPERIENCE

society such divisions as these are exaggerated. The well-rounded man and woman are the exception. But just as it is the office of art to be unifying, to break through conventional distinctions to the underlying common elements of the experienced world, while developing individuality as the manner of seeing and expressing these elements, so it is the office of art in the individual person, to compose differences, to do away with isolations and conflicts among the elements of our being, to utilize oppositions among them to build a richer personality. Hence the extraordinary ineptitude of a compartmentalized psychology to serve as an instrument for a theory of art.

Extreme instances of the results of separation of organism

Fine Passage!

Phillips seized on this point with a call for common sense. Writing the next year in "Personality in Art," he asks us to recognize that in the course of living we all have had Dewey's "isolated experiences which were like works of art in their unity, their irrelevant sequences, and their contributory relations." As he marshaled the philosopher's two-tier structure to discredit the theories of Roger Fry and Clive Bell that isolated art from life and divided ordinary experiences from experience of works of art, he took heart, stating: "Such experiences are evidence enough for Dewey that the aesthetic is not self-sufficient and extraordinary after all."[16]

The Experience of the Artist

For Phillips, art begins with artists, their life experiences playing a central role in their work. "Nothing," he proclaimed, "has ever taken the place of expressive personality in art. The greatest humanitarians of painting, Giotto, Michelangelo, Rembrandt, and Daumier, to name but a few, were great not because of their subjects but because of themselves."[17] Writing in 1935, he concluded in Dewey-like fashion: "Since the aesthetic experience is a consummated adjustment of the self to its surroundings, a fulfillment of the wish to interact with environment as a force, then the substance of an individual's art is bound to depend both upon his own character and the character of the period; upon his past and his present and upon what kind of experiences have most insistently stirred and moulded him."[18]

According to Dewey, art-making proceeds according to the "individual person with all his characteristics of temperament, special manner of vision, and unique experience."[19] Yet the resulting work is more, as "imaginative quality dominates, because meanings and values that are wider and deeper than the particular here and now in which they are anchored are realized by way of *expressions*."[20] Phillips paraphrases this thought: "art is the fusion in one experience of the pressure on self of conditions and the spontaneity + novelty of personal vision."[21] "What most of us lack in order to be artists," Dewey clarifies, "is not the inceptive emotion, nor yet merely technical skill in execution. It is the capacity to work a vague idea and emotion over into terms of some definite medium"—to which Phillips notes in the margin: "True."[22]

Dewey also affirmed Phillips's understanding that the artist's processes are not rigid, *cannot* conform to rules, but rather evolve through an act of discovery like experiments in the scientist's laboratory. Dewey speaks of the "unexpected turn" that arises when "something which the artist himself does not definitely foresee" leads to an innovation. It is "fulfillment of an experience for its own sake."[23] In the modern era, the quest for the new was paramount. Phillips writes, as he reflects on Dewey in 1935: "The artist was born to be an experimenter, and in an experimental age he is in his element, thoroughly invigorated by a congenial and stimulating atmosphere."[24]

Identifying with artistic expression—as a collector, museum director and, most of all, sympathetic viewer—Phillips time and again defended the individual artist's uniqueness. He called this "personality," stating: "The union in art of substance and form not only implies personality but is inconceivable without it. Art is a language of personality and if personality is suppressed then follows that art is suppressed also."[25] While he believed artists benefit from a rootedness that contributes to their personality, Phillips also felt artists must "portray the special character of their own environments in such a way as to win the interest, understanding, and sympathy of their fellow human beings anywhere in the world. But to do this they must express their own individual reactions. They must have something to say, something which relates to their subjects but which grows out of themselves."[26] He would have agreed with Dewey that self-expression must not be self-contained, closed, and private.[27] Art must communicate. So Phillips repeated Dewey's words in the margin: "the more a work of art embodies what belongs to experiences common to many individuals, the more expressive it is."[28]

If the "making of art is a process of boiling down a great deal of life into the essence of art, a process of condensation," Phillips reasoned, then the "appreciation of art is a process of living oneself out into its multitudinous separate manifestations—a process of expansion."[29] This requires, Dewey pointed out, openness on the part of the viewer, not only being receptive but surrendering, a transmission of energy to the point of saturation—"immersion so complete that the qualities of the object and the emotions it arouses have no separate existence." During this process, the visual is only one of a myriad of stimuli that all play a part; the eye "never *functions* in isolation." Thus, "a beholder must *create* his own experience."[30]

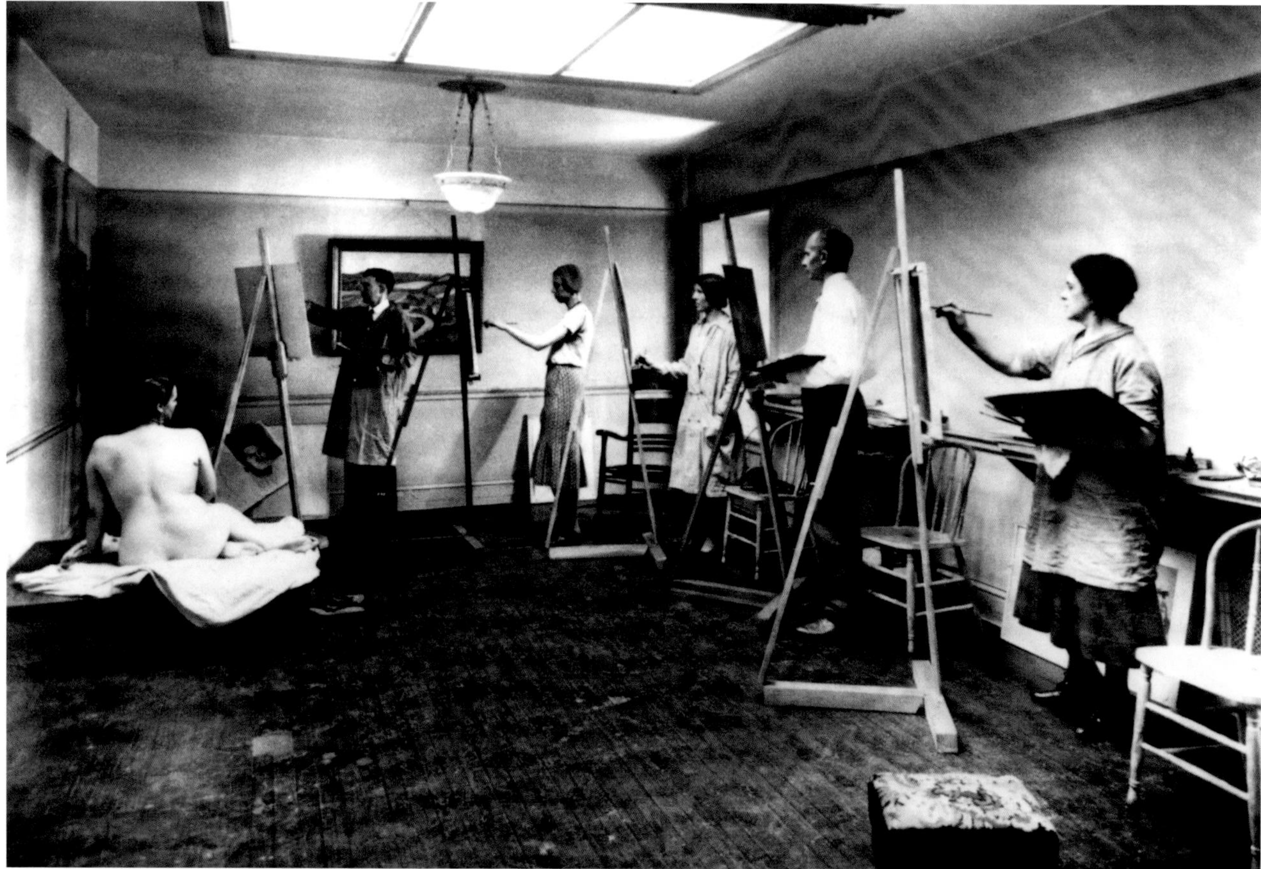

fig. 20
Phillips Gallery Art School with nude model, ca. 1931–33.

fig. 21 (left)
House galleries at the Phillips (formerly the east and west parlors), 1931.

fig. 22 (right)
Dining Room, with Pierre Bonnard's *The Palm*, 1931.

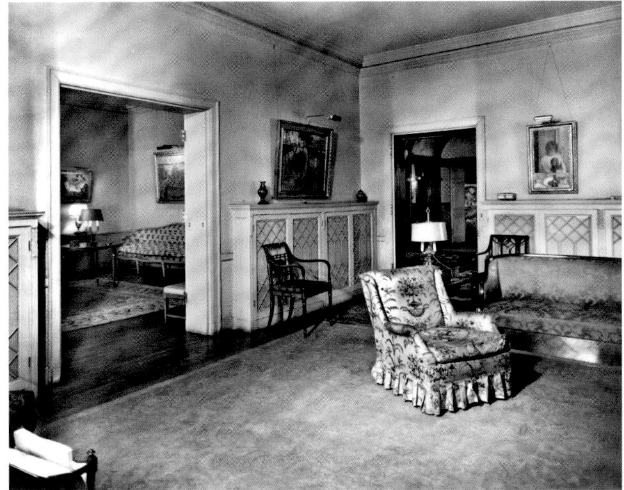

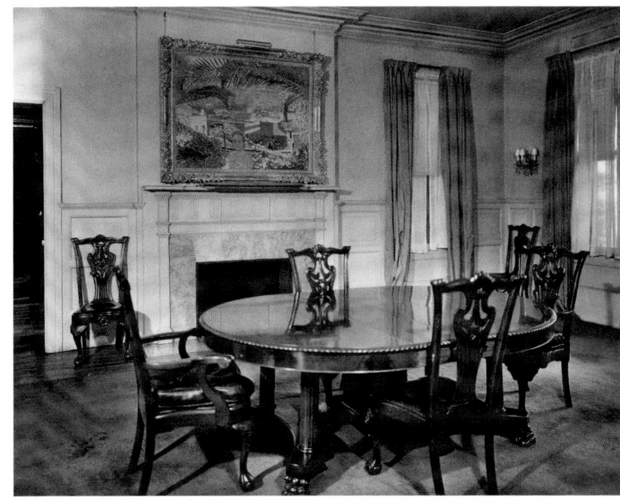

Dewey's understanding that the viewer completes the work of art would over time affect new directions in art as well as institutional practices. Phillips understood this. Already in 1931 he had written: "That beauty is subjective, that each of us makes his own beauty out of his inner consciousness is one of the two points which I consider essential to an understanding of the aesthetic experience. The other is that art, at least in so far as it is a science of the means of expression, is objective, that it can be learned like any other game, that it is impersonal, more or less disinterested, transcendent of self, in the exacting and exclusive task of creation."[31] So he annotated in 1934: "A triad the speaker the thing said the one spoken to the external object is the connecting link between artist and audience."[32] While both men promoted art as a universal language, they agreed it had to be acquired. Phillips put this into action from the outset in 1921, believing, "[w]e can all learn to see in that way—just as we hear in that way when we listen to great orchestral music."[33] Modern art posed even greater challenges for unfamiliar audiences; by the museum's second decade Phillips had hired former Yale classmate, C. Law Watkins, to launch public programs and the museum's art school (fig. 20). In the emerging field of art appreciation, Watkins developed a pedagogical approach that blended art history and theory with lessons in the formal qualities of a work in order to enable viewers' looking.[34]

Prototyping a New Museology

Phillips's understanding of Dewey's central thesis that all life is experience is evident in the opening to his three-part treatise on "Personality in Art": "To understand the aesthetic [Dewey] believes 'one must begin in the raw.'"[35] When three years later Dewey came to lecture at the Phillips,[36] he expounded on his wider view of art:

> If we approach the matter from our end we get a more flexible approach and one that is more inclusive, one that is more tolerant. It recognizes that we may have this experience in the presence of all kinds of things—the graciousness of a person in approach and intercourse in relation to other people—that great deeds of people not merely of those who are recognized as heroes, but humble people, may then have the grace or nobility because of the way that they strike us. If we approach from this side it seems to me that it tends to enlarge us. If we become more on the lookout for the moments of this kind of experience we do not think of them as experiences we have to have by going to certain places, but that we may have at any time of day in connection with any, not everyone, but with contacts with objects, scenes, persons that are not in any way labeled to be works of fine art....
>
> [W]e must not be overawed by the idea of works of art.... [M]useums, often calling themselves museums or galleries of fine art, often have in them utensils like rugs, carpets, vases, weapons, etc., that at the time of their origin were things of daily use ... but they have the power of exciting an experience which, so far as it goes, has the quality which the great works of art have.[37]

Surely Dewey would have appreciated the domesticity of Phillips's museum. For Phillips the continuity of life and art was actual. Therein lay the purpose of his enterprise: to demonstrate a way of being at home with art, making it part of one's life, and to ignite the potential within visitors to find aesthetic experiences in their daily lives (figs. 21, 22). Welcoming persons unknown to him with the generosity of a personal invitation and making them comfortable was a strategy to open them up to the art experience. This sense of familiarity is evoked by Marjorie Phillips when, in reference to *A Collection in the Making,* she says her husband's words were "written almost as if he had spoken them to a friend in the gallery."[38]

Making a museum for Duncan Phillips was an act of faith in the restorative pleasure of art. Thus, he made his pioneering efforts on behalf of modern European and American art even more radical by opening the doors of his home in 1921. While earlier the home of Leo and Gertrude Stein had served as a gathering place, their salon was not for the public, and Katherine Dreier's Société Anonyme, which preceded the Phillips by one year, and other modern museums that followed (most famously the Museum of Modern Art in New York in 1929), were founded in dedicated locations. It was only Albert Barnes in 1922 who, like Phillips, created a gallery in a space that also served for personal use.

In his museum, Phillips shunned the museum convention of an installation based on chronology or national school, choosing instead to assemble exhibition "units" that would allow full immersion in an individual's artistic personality. He set up conversations between artists to test their ideas in dialogue with each other (fig. 23).[39] While his focus was the art of his time, he showed some works of earlier centuries to further illuminate the interests and motivations that artists have shared over time. As his collection developed, Phillips continued to assemble and present exhibition units for artists, including among others Arthur Dove, John Marin, Pierre Bonnard, Paul Cézanne, and Paul Klee, in changing temporary installations. However, toward the end of his life this took an unanticipated turn that would prove influential for the course of contemporary art.

On the first floor, Marjorie Phillips writes, "off to the side is a small but poetic and distinguished Mark Rothko room." There, in 1960, her husband had installed three canvases by this artist (fig. 24). This room, the first devoted permanently to a single artist, was unlike any other in the museum: a gravitational force more than a unit, so exceptional was these paintings' command of the space. Their emotive power when shown in proximity in a dedicated space had the ability to transport the viewer beyond its confines. Phillips felt this, and we are told he "derived untold pleasure from this room, which became for him and for so many other people a little chapel for meditation."[40]

The Rothko Room had an astounding effect on the artist, prompting him to consider his paintings environmentally. Their spatial and emotional potential was consummated a decade later with the Rothko Chapel in Houston, where private prayer in the presence of art became overt. Over time, artists would participate in the installation of their work and, with the birth of installation art as a genre, by the 1970s they would take on exclusive control. Contemporary practices would expand to encompass space and time, as art came off

fig. 23 (below)
Main Gallery at The Phillips Collection featuring work by Bradley Walker Tomlin, Henri Matisse, and Nicolas de Staël, 1963.

fig. 24 (bottom)
The Rothko Room in The Phillips Collection's original 1960 annex with Jackson Pollock's *Collage and Oil* (ca. 1951), ca. 1960–63.

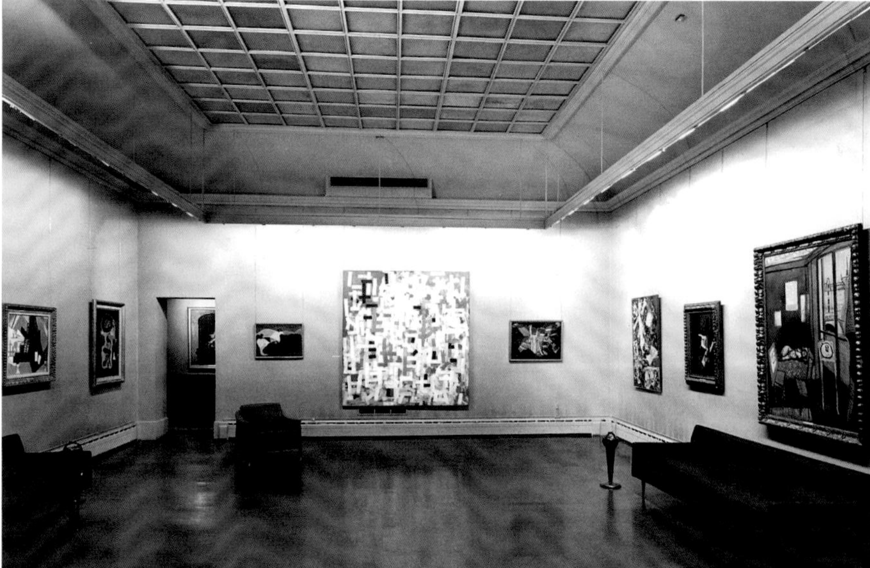

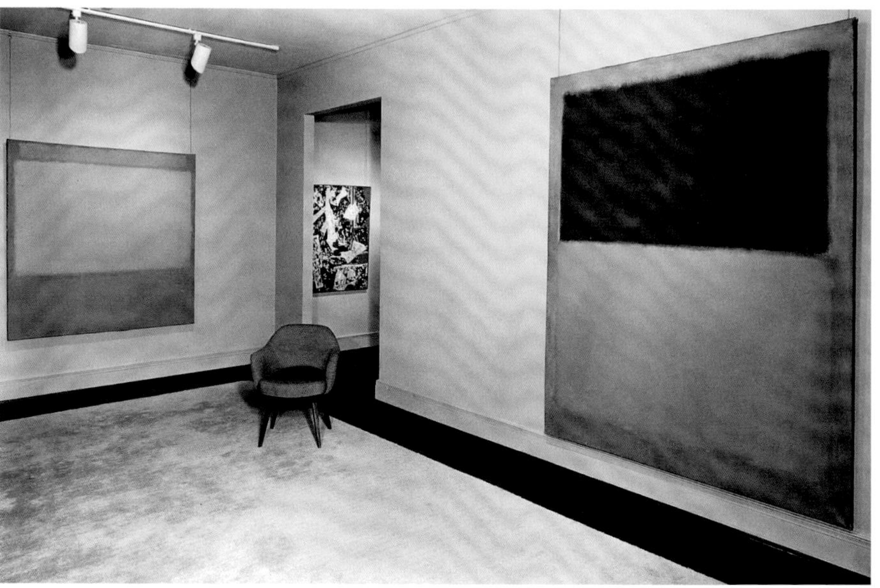

the canvas and out of the studio. Collectors, museums, and public agencies would revive the tradition of commissioning. All this was part of the legacy of this small poetic room where discrete art objects could be imagined as a single work of art.

In 2013, the Phillips commissioned a second artist's room (fig. 25). The choice of artist, Wolfgang Laib, was inspired. Working in harmony with the rhythms of nature, he seeks to bring life-giving energy to art. In Laib's *Wax Room: Wohin bist Du gegangen - wohin gehst Du?* (*Where have you gone - where are you going?*),[41] he achieves with beeswax the otherworldliness that Rothko conveys through color. Stepping into the wax room requires openness to a sensory, emotional, and spiritual experience through which one may enter another dimension of time and space.

We might imagine Phillips would have been profoundly moved by Laib's project. Like Rothko's, it offers the kind of aesthetic experience that Dewey once described as taking "up into itself meanings covering stretches of existence wrought into consistency."[42] Phillips had evoked much the same when he wrote, "art-appreciation or, if you prefer, aesthetic contemplation is that other eternal play instinct for vicariously experiencing ... identifications of man with nature, of idea with plastic form."[43] And they both might have appreciated Laib's intention that art has the power to heal, not just the individual but humankind. "You can see it from the past," this artist remarked, "ultimately art and culture, not wars and confrontations, have stimulated change in people.... I am still of the opinion that—and this may sound insanely naïve—art changes the world."[44]

The Place of Art in the World Today

"Art has a mission for such a time as ours," wrote Phillips in 1929, continuing: "For art also deals with humanity and is of personal expression the very essence."[45] Then he set out two goals: on the one hand, to raise the level of public appreciation of art, and on the other, for artists to rise to "a higher destiny than to provide entertainment for a few of their protectors from public ignorance and indifference."[46]

Dewey believed a higher purpose for art was democracy, taking this up not only in *Art as Experience*, but also in *Education as Experience, Democracy and Education*, and elsewhere, noting art's ability to foster empathy. This quality of human experience is necessary to understanding just what equality means: an ideal basis for a democratic society, but one which demands balancing the rights of the individual with the common good. So when Dewey said, "Works of art are means by which we enter, through imagination and the emotions they evoke, into other forms of relationship and participation than our own,"[47] Phillips responded that there is "great hope for human progress in a receptivity of mind, a sympathetic search for participation in alien experience."[48]

Additionally, in artists' agency Dewey found a model for living in a democracy. Fully committed to their work, artists live their art. As they seek expression, they both realize themselves and seek to communicate to a wider community. So when reading Dewey, Phillips had transposed the philosopher's words to emphasize the social power of art, writing in his copy: "Civilization is uncivil because human beings are divided into non-communicating sects, races, nations, classes and cliques. Works of art are the most intimate and energetic means of aiding individuals to share in the arts of living."[49] Already in 1929, Phillips had stated: "Art is the greatest unifying and it is also the greatest clarifying force of the universe, and it is not for more than a moment to be regarded as merely a racial or national expression or the exclusive interest and business of a technically trained few."[50] This he put into action as he fought against the narrow-mindedness of nationalism. By 1935, taking exception to the fanatical position of critic Thomas Craven who advocated a strict Americanism in art, and campaigning against legislation that would restrict importation of foreign art, Phillips wrote: "The participation of the intelligent artist in alien cultures cannot fail to broaden and deepen him, and as it passes through the alembic of his mind and merges with himself it helps make the whole world kin."[51]

At the same time, one year after *Art as Experience* was published, it was Dewey who inspired the philosophical footing for the creation of the Federal Art Project within the Works Progress Administration. Phillips played his part, serving as chair of the committee for the Washington, DC area for the Public Works of Art Project, and overseeing the commissioning of artists. During this period, he also pursued a "passionate concern to find avenues to peace" both before and after World War II, as Marjorie Phillips tells it,[52] and here we can recall Dewey fighting to outlaw war when the Great War was to be the last. In all these activities, both collector and philosopher saw art as a way forward for society.

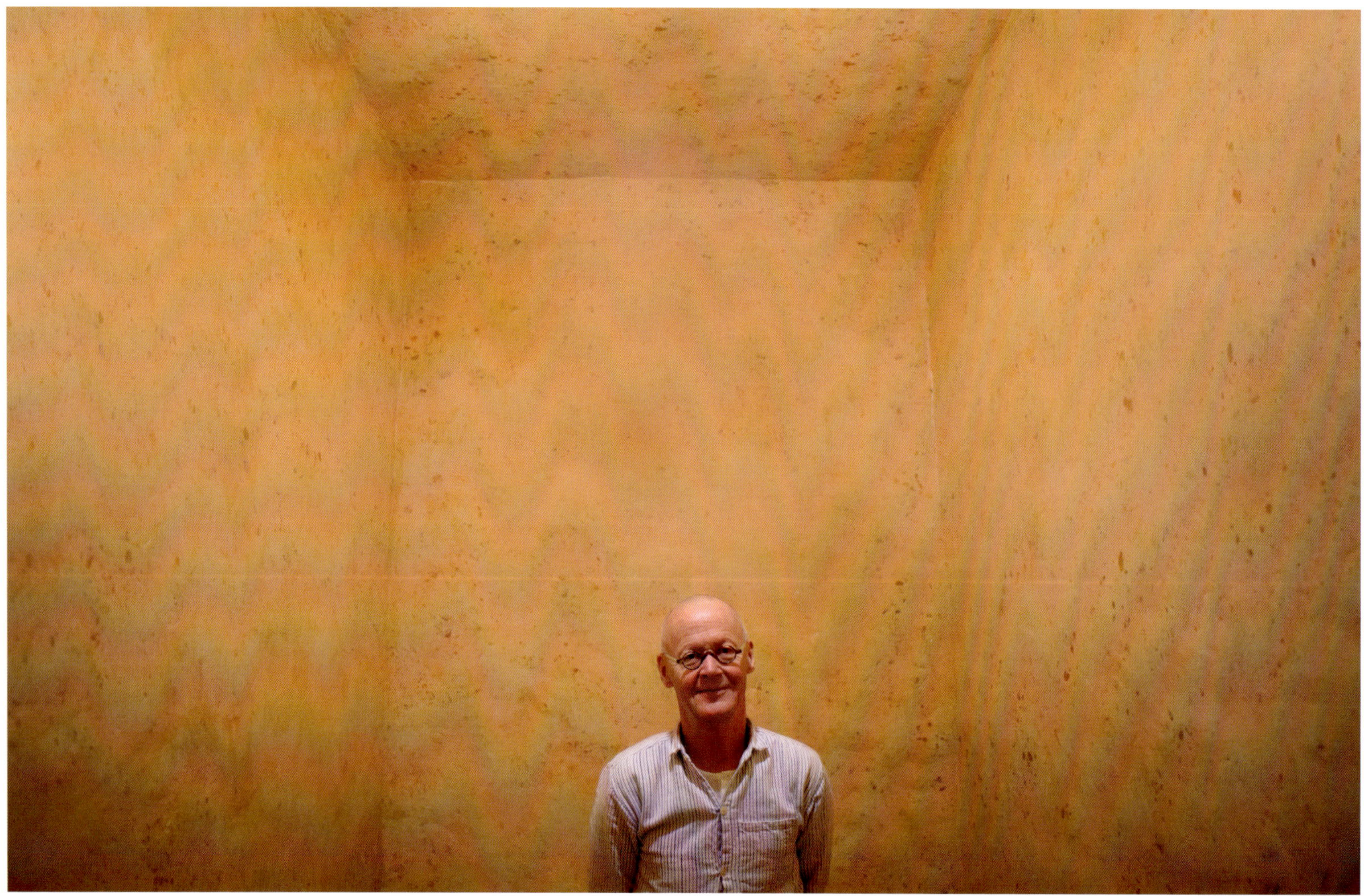

fig. 25
Wolfgang Laib in his *Wax Room (Where have you gone - where are you going?)*, 2013
The Phillips Collection, Washington, DC.

Duncan Phillips never wavered in his belief in art and artists. In December 1940, when the cultural landscape was being threatened by World War II, he defended the value of art:

> If it is escape to turn from death to life, from weariness to refreshment of soul, from destruction to creation, from despair about humanity to appreciation of the various subtle refinements in human sensibility, qualities of the human mind which survive the centuries and mock the conquerors, then escape, as long as it is possible, to sane living and thinking is what a threatened civilization needs to justify its fight and to give it added purpose. Not in spite of but because of the fact that we hate Hitler we should see to it that our orchestras continue to play Beethoven.[53]

"Art is a social communication and a national asset but never more so than when it is a miracle of personal expression," for Phillips. Ultimately, "art must be the last stand, as it will be the eternal stronghold of the individual."[54]

Phillips remained true to his vision of the value of art over a lifetime—making a life through his appreciation of works of art, defending the artist's individual spirit in courageous pursuit of expression. Finally, it lives in an institution where he could share what he had come to know through experience—that art is not for art's sake but "for the sake of life."[55]

1 Duncan Phillips, "Preface to the First Edition," in *The Enchantment of Art, as Part of the Enchantment of Experience Fifteen Years Later* (Washington, DC: Phillips Publications, ca. 1927), n.p. In 1991, with her book *The Reenchantment of Art*, Suzi Gablik opens with her mission to "restore to our culture its sense of aliveness" and in like manner she also calls her volume a deeply personal account outside the normative categories of art books, but directed toward "the whole being." In doing so, she situates art's role within larger questions of social and environmental responsibility, calling for a paradigm shift away from autonomous individualism, touted by modernism, and which has come to operate so comfortably within capitalism. See Gablik, *Reenchantment of Art* (New York: Thames & Hudson, 1991), 1–4.

2 Duncan Phillips, *A Collection in the Making* (New York: E. Weyhe; Washington, DC: Phillips Memorial Gallery, 1926), 4.

3 John Dewey, *Art as Experience* (New York: Penguin, [1934] 2005), 18, 138, 333.

4 Duncan Phillips, handwritten comments in photocopy of John Dewey, *Art as Experience* (New York: Capricorn Books, 1934), The Phillips Collection Archives, Washington, DC. Prior to dismantling Duncan Phillips's library, photocopies were made of several of his important annotated books, including Dewey.

5 Duncan Phillips, "Personality in Art: Reflections on Its Suppression and the Present Need for Its Fulfillment," *American Magazine of Art* 28, no. 2 (February 1935): 78–84. Duncan Phillips, "Personality in Art, II: Reflections on Its Suppression and the Present Need for Its Fulfillment," *American Magazine of Art* 28, no. 3 (March 1935): 148–55. Duncan Phillips, "Personality in Art, III: Reflections on Its Suppression and the Present Need for Its Fulfillment," *American Magazine of Art* 28, no. 4 (April 1935): 214–22.

6 Dewey, *Art as Experience*, 25.

7 David Scott says this quote, and the one following, in Duncan Phillips, essay for *Exhibition of Recent Decorative Paintings by Augustus Vincent Tack*, exh. cat., 1924, n.p.

8 Duncan Phillips, "Art and Understanding," in *Art and Understanding* 1 (November 1929): 7, 8.

9 Duncan Phillips, "The Aesthetic Experience," in *The Artist Sees Differently: Essays Based Upon the Philosophy of a Collection in the Making* (New York: E. Weyhe; Washington, DC: Phillips Memorial Gallery, 1931), 38.

10 Phillips, "The Aesthetic Experience," 32–33. See also Leo Stein, *The A-B-C of Aesthetics* (New York: Boni & Liveright, 1927).

11 Phillips, "The Aesthetic Experience," 29.

12 Dewey, *Art as Experience*, 1.

13 Phillips, comment in Dewey, *Art as Experience*, 248.

14 Dewey, *Art as Experience*, 113.

15 Dewey, *Art as Experience*, 1–2.

16 Phillips, "Personality in Art, II," 148.

17 Phillips, "Personality in Art, II,"154.

18 Phillips, "Personality in Art, II,"152.

19 Dewey, *Art as Experience*, 299.

20 Dewey, *Art as Experience*, 273.

21 Phillips, comment in Dewey, *Art as Experience*, 281.

22 Phillips, comment in Dewey, *Art as Experience*, 75.

23 Dewey, *Art as Experience*, 144.

24 Phillips, "Personality in Art, III," 216.

25 Phillips, "Personality in Art," 84.

26 Phillips, "Personality in Art," 83–84.

27 "Art would not amplify experience if it withdrew the self into the self nor would the experience that results from such retirement be expressive." Dewey, *Art as Experience*, 107.

28 Phillips, comment in Dewey, *Art as Experience*, 285.

29 Phillips, "The Aesthetic Experience," 29.

30 Dewey, *Art as Experience*, 288, 104, 56.

31 Phillips, "The Aesthetic Experience," 28.

32 Phillips, comment in Dewey, *Art as Experience*, 106. Extra spaces and underline are Phillips's.

33 Phillips, *A Collection in the Making*, 5.

34 Watkins's teaching exhibitions "Emotional Design in Painting" and "The Functions of Color in Painting" in 1940 and 1941 were exercises in deconstructing formal design elements. Concurrently chair of the art department at American University, there he added art courses that could offer credit for those pursuing any degree, thereby fulfilling Phillips's youthful dream of making the rewards of art available to those other fields, which was prompted when Yale eliminated its sole art history class. See Duncan C. Phillips, Jr., "The Need of Art at Yale," *The Yale Literary Magazine* 72, no. 9 (June 1907): 355–61. By 1943, Watkins also created a four-year course for artists at American University, the first of its kind. He declared at that time: "The artist who has not been drafted to serve in the war will make the highest eventual contribution to society by continuing to learn and practice the eternal constructive realities of the arts." C. Law Watkins, "Art and Reality," *College Art Journal* 2, no. 4, part 1 (May 1943): 118–19, https://doi.org/10.2307/773342. Accessed April 2020.

35 Phillips, "Personality in Art," 78.

36 John Dewey delivered a lecture to the Washington Dance Association at the Phillips Memorial Gallery on November 13, 1938. Transcript in Fletcher Free Library, Burlington, Vermont. See also John Dewey, "The Philosophy of the Arts," *The Collected Works of John Dewey, 1882–1953*. (2nd Release). Electronic Edition. *The Later Works of John Dewey, 1925–1953. Volume 13: 1938–1939, Essays, Experience and Education, Freedom and Culture, and Theory of Valuation*, 359.

37 Dewey, "The Philosophy of the Arts," 359.

38 Marjorie Phillips, *Duncan Phillips and His Collection* (New York and London: W. W. Norton; Washington, DC: Phillips Collection, [1970] 1982), 113.

39 Marjorie Phillips, *Duncan Phillips and His Collection*, 165. This term recalls Frank Lloyd Wright's use of the term "experimental station" in a speech given at Hull-House in Chicago to refer to devoting a space and means by which the artist could study and test the capabilities of the machine for making in the modern age. See Frank Lloyd Wright, "The Art and Craft of the Machine," *Brush and Pencil* 8, no. 2 (1901): 12, https://doi.org/10.2307/25505640. Accessed April 2020.

40 Phillips, *Duncan Phillips and His Collection*, 288.

41 This is Laib's fourth permanently installed wax room, followed by *From the Known to the Unknown—to Where is Your Oracle Leading You?* (2011–14) made for Anselm Kiefer on his property in Barjac, France. The first wax room, *La Chambre des certitudes* (The Room of Certitudes; 2000), a space completely covered in beeswax, is built into a mountainside in the French Pyrenees and reached only by foot; the second wax room, *pensatoio* (2009), is at the Chasa dal Guvernatur in Sent, Switzerland; and the third wax room, *Without Place, Without Time, Without Body* (2004), is located on Laib's property in a hillside near his studio in southern Germany.

42 John Dewey, *Experience and Nature* (New York: Dover Publications, [1925] 1958), 371.

43 Phillips, "The Aesthetic Experience," 29.

44 Peter Lodemeyer, "Time—Space—Existence: A Conversation with Wolfgang Laib," in *Sculpture* 27, no. 2 (March 2008): 28.

45 Phillips, "Art and Understanding," 15.

46 Phillips, "Art and Understanding," 12–13.

47 Dewey, "The Philosophy of the Arts," 347.

48 Phillips, "Personality in Art," 83–84.

49 Phillips, comment in Dewey, *Art as Experience*, 336.

50 Phillips, "Art and Understanding," 16.

51 Phillips, "Personality in Art, III," 217.

52 Phillips, *Duncan Phillips and His Collection*, 208. See "The War Years," 207–34.

53 Duncan Phillips, "The Place of the Arts in the World Today," in *A Bulletin of the Phillips Memorial Gallery* (Washington, DC: Phillips Memorial Gallery, 1941), n.p. This is a published version of Phillips's address at a symposium under the auspices of the Washington Dance Association at the Phillips Memorial Gallery, December 15, 1940. Later adapted versions of the speech appeared in Duncan Phillips, "The Place of Arts in a War-Torn World," *St. Louis Post-Dispatch*, January 27, 1941; and Duncan Phillips, "The Arts in War Time," Address before the American Association of Museums, Williamsburg, Virginia, May 19, 1942. National Gallery of Art pamphlet, 1942.

54 Phillips, "The Place of the Arts in the World Today," n.p.

55 Phillips wrote: "For the artist life is for the sake of art. For the appreciator art is for the sake of life." Phillips, "The Aesthetic Experience," 29.

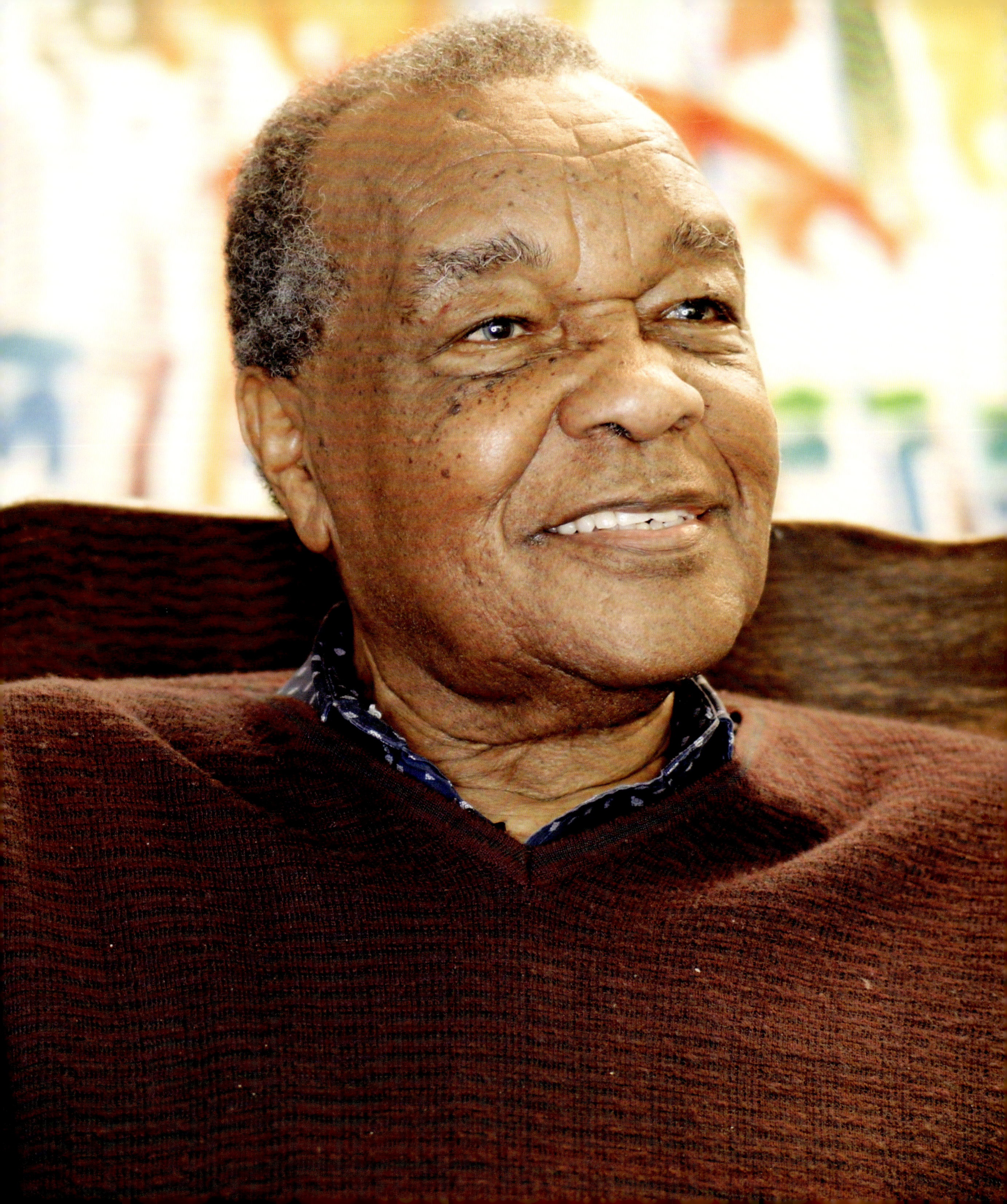

Elsa Smithgall: You have a special perspective on the Phillips and the role it's played for you personally as an artist, and in the larger cultural community in Washington [DC], since the 1950s. It's something you have reflected on previously in your 2008 Phillips Collection oral history, upon which this conversation builds.[1] A natural place to start is the moment when you made the decision as a very young person to take the train from Appalachia to Washington, heading to what you hoped would be an education at Howard University, and what turned out to be the discovery of your calling as an artist.

David Driskell: When I came to Howard University in 1949—and I should make the distinction of saying I did not enroll in art in 1949—I actually just went on the campus and pretended I was enrolled, because school had been in session three weeks when I arrived, and even though they told me that, I still went to class, wrote home and told my parents, "I'm in college." Well, I was there in spirit, and physically I was there.

I just kind of went in and sat in on the history classes because I had plans of majoring in history. It was not until a year later—when I was properly enrolled, in January of 1950, taking history courses and humanities and the general introduction that freshmen would be taking—[that] in the back of my mind was this notion, "Well, you're going to be an art minor. You're going to do a minor in art, not a major."

WASHINGTON WAS STILL A SEGREGATED CITY AND THERE WEREN'T THAT MANY PLACES THAT A BLACK PERSON COULD GO IN THE CULTURAL WORLD AND REALLY FEEL ACCEPTED.

So it was a year later, in 1951, that I finally decided to take an art course, and I took a drawing course with James Wells. [Then] I looked up one day and standing behind me was this gentleman, very well dressed and well spoken. He said, "What is your name? I don't think I know you." And I told him my name. He said, "Are you an art major?" And I said, "No." I said, "I'm a history major." He looked down at my work and he said, "Well, you don't belong over there. You belong here." That was my introduction to James A. Porter [later Art Department chairman]. Next semester, I changed my major and started taking art courses.

I had been to the Phillips prior to that, on the advice of a friend who was not an art major but who had great interest in art. Bill Taylor was a sculptor. I'd made his acquaintance through Earl Hooks, my classmate. Bill would go to the various museums on Sunday, and after I met him, he said, "Well, you've got an interest in art. You've got to go to the museums." Bill was a few years older than I. He had not had formal college training. He had studied with Alma Thomas at Shaw Junior High [in Washington, DC] and had pretty much been on his own. And that's how I first learned about the Phillips. He told me it was a nice place to take my girlfriend [Thelma Deloatch] on Sunday afternoon [Driskell and Deloatch married on January 9, 1952]. So I started pretty much doing that, going to the Phillips on Sunday afternoon.

Washington at that time was still a segregated city and there weren't that many

David Driskell at his Hyattsville, MD studio, February 2020.

IN CONVERSATION WITH

DAVID C. DRISKELL

In loving memory.
Adapted from an interview with Elsa Smithgall that took place in the artist's Hyattsville studio, February 12, 2020.

places that a Black person could go in the cultural world and really feel accepted, and I give credit to both Alma Thomas and to Bill Taylor for saying, "Go to the Phillips," before my teachers told me to do that. "Go to the Phillips and look at all the masters. They're there. The modern masters are there." And that's what I did.

ES: One of the artists you encountered there was, in fact, James Wells. What was it like seeing his work at the Phillips?

DD: Well, it was a great experience being able to say, "That's my teacher," or "I studied with him." And even if I went there with the intention of looking at the other artists, I'd always go to see Wells (fig. 26), because there was not only just the physical connection, but it seemed like something very, very special. And I don't know that I processed it so much in terms of race then, because African American artists weren't really expected to be seen in those places, and without being unkind about it, I had learned early on that there was a difference between going to the Phillips and going to the Corcoran [Gallery of Art]. I simply did not feel the welcome at the Corcoran that I felt at the Phillips.

I'D HEAR CONCERTS SUNDAY AFTERNOON IN THE MUSIC ROOM, AND THERE WAS A SENSE OF BELONGING, WHICH WAS MOST WELCOMING.

Also, once I was enrolled, Lois [Mailou] Jones told us the true story of how she was excluded from exhibition at the Corcoran. She was very much interested in Cézanne and French landscape, still-life painting, and, of course, the city scenes very much like Maurice Utrillo, and I had seen his work at the Phillips, and I felt a kinship between what Lois was doing and what I had seen in his work. So there was this relationship which was developing all of the time of my experiencing art on one level, and then I'd go back to the Phillips and see it on another level.

I went to the National Gallery [of Art]. I felt like nobody was going to come up and say, "What are you doing here?" [laughs] And I would go there to eat at the cafeteria. In those days, 1949, 1950, maybe as late as 1951–52, African Americans were very limited as to where they could go publicly, with the exception of the U Street Corridor, where there were Black-owned businesses, cafeterias, etc. But one could eat at the National Gallery,

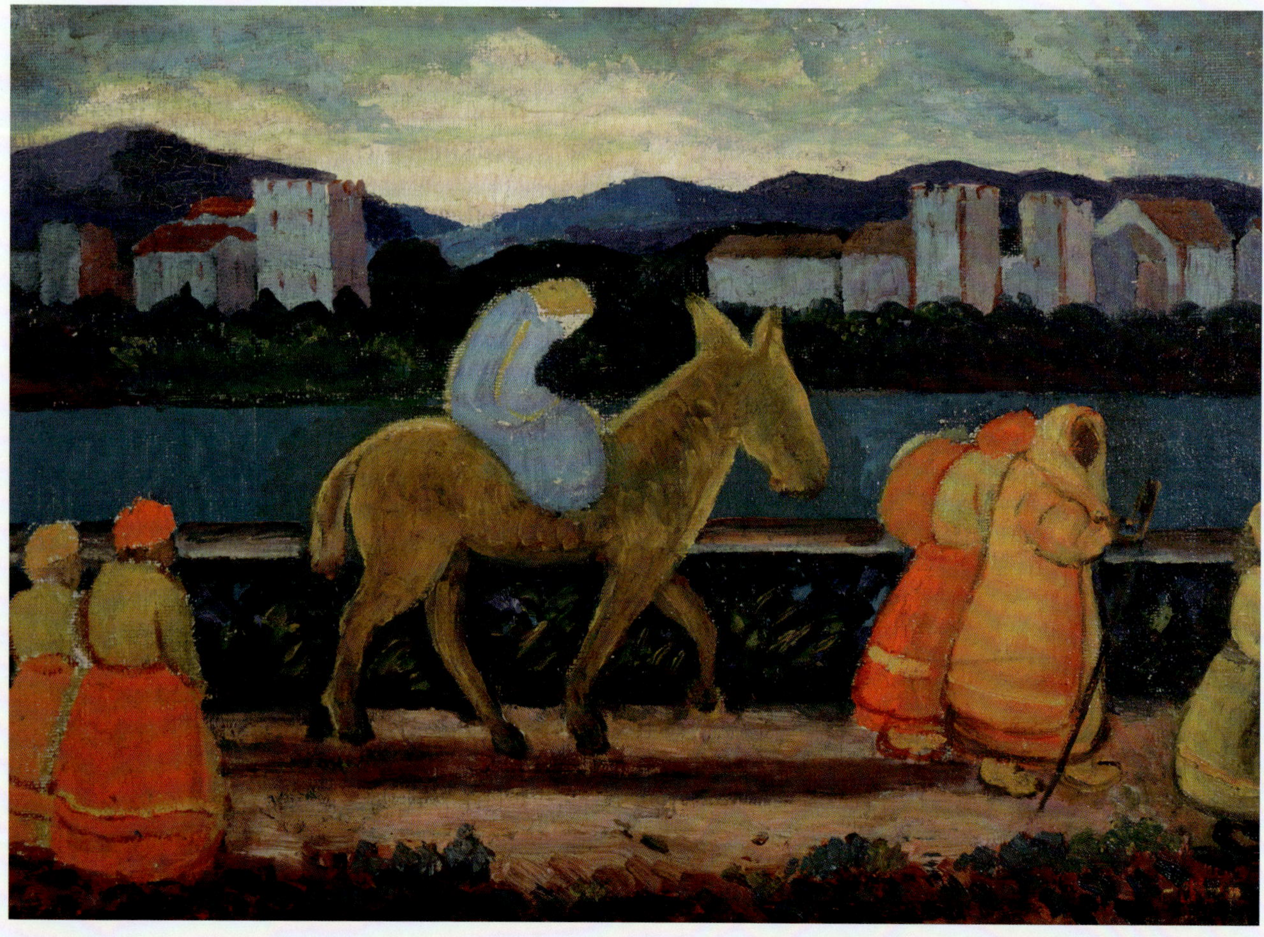

fig. 26
James Lesesne Wells
***Journey to the Holy Land*, undated**
Oil on canvas board, 14 1/2 × 19 3/4 in.
The Phillips Collection, Washington, DC, Acquired 1935.

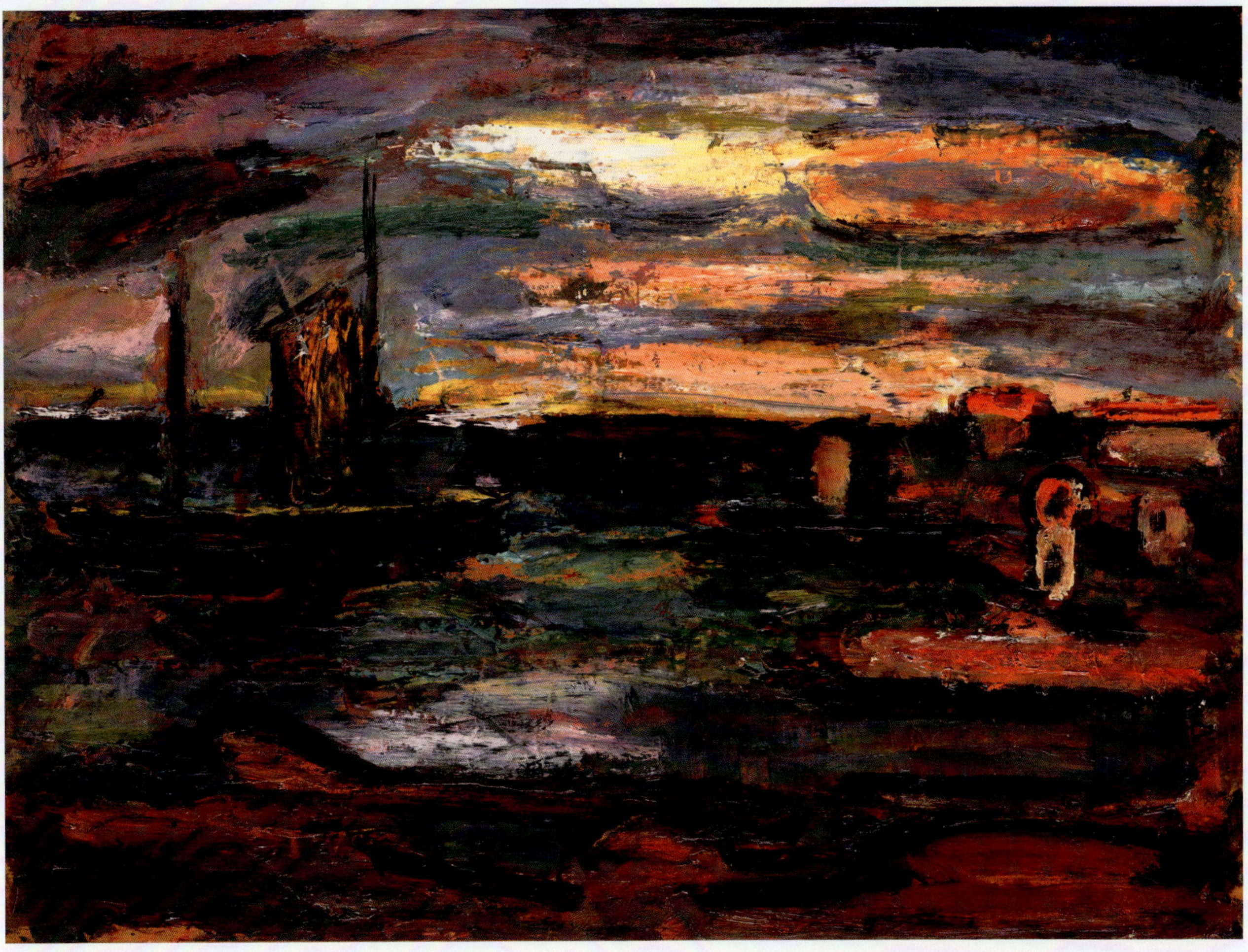

fig. 27
Georges Rouault
Afterglow, Galilee,
before 1931
Oil on paper mounted on canvas,
19 3/4 × 25 5/8 in.
The Phillips Collection, Washington, DC,
Acquired 1939.

at the Savarin Restaurant in Union Station, and at the Methodist Building across the street from the Capitol and the House of Representatives. You couldn't even eat at a Peoples Drug store counter.

So my real treat for Sunday afternoons would be: I could go to the Phillips, or to the National Gallery, or take the streetcar all the way out to Cabin John [Maryland]. You'd pay an extra ten cents to go out to Cabin John, but you couldn't get off and go into the amusement park. It was all white. So I would take the car for my Sunday evening rides out there to see the landscape, see nature.

But getting back to the Phillips, that was the stable place. I could go there and I'd hear concerts Sunday afternoon, in the Music Room, and there was a sense of belonging, which was most welcoming, and that wasn't ordinary in Washington at that time in the cultural community.

ES: There were other galleries, private and somewhat non-traditional spaces: Barnett Aden, Jefferson Place Gallery, Howard University Gallery, the Watkins Gallery at American University...

DD: And the Wyatt Gallery and later the Franz Bader [Gallery].

ES: How did the Phillips fit within that local gallery scene?

DD: As early as 1952, I started driving a taxi in Washington, and as part-time work I worked at the Barnett Aden Gallery with Professor [James V.] Herring [co-founder of the gallery, and also Howard University Art Department chairman until 1953]. I was there in the evenings, for the most part, and it gave me a chance to study and also to meet people who came to the gallery. They would often have openings, which were major for the time, because they had very important artists coming in, and I can recall having met some of the local poets. They would have salons of sorts: Georgia Douglas Johnson, the very last of the Harlem Renaissance poets that came to Washington; May Miller—May Miller

MY REAL TREAT FOR SUNDAY AFTERNOONS WOULD BE: I COULD GO TO THE PHILLIPS, OR TO THE NATIONAL GALLERY, OR TAKE THE STREETCAR ALL THE WAY OUT TO CABIN JOHN.

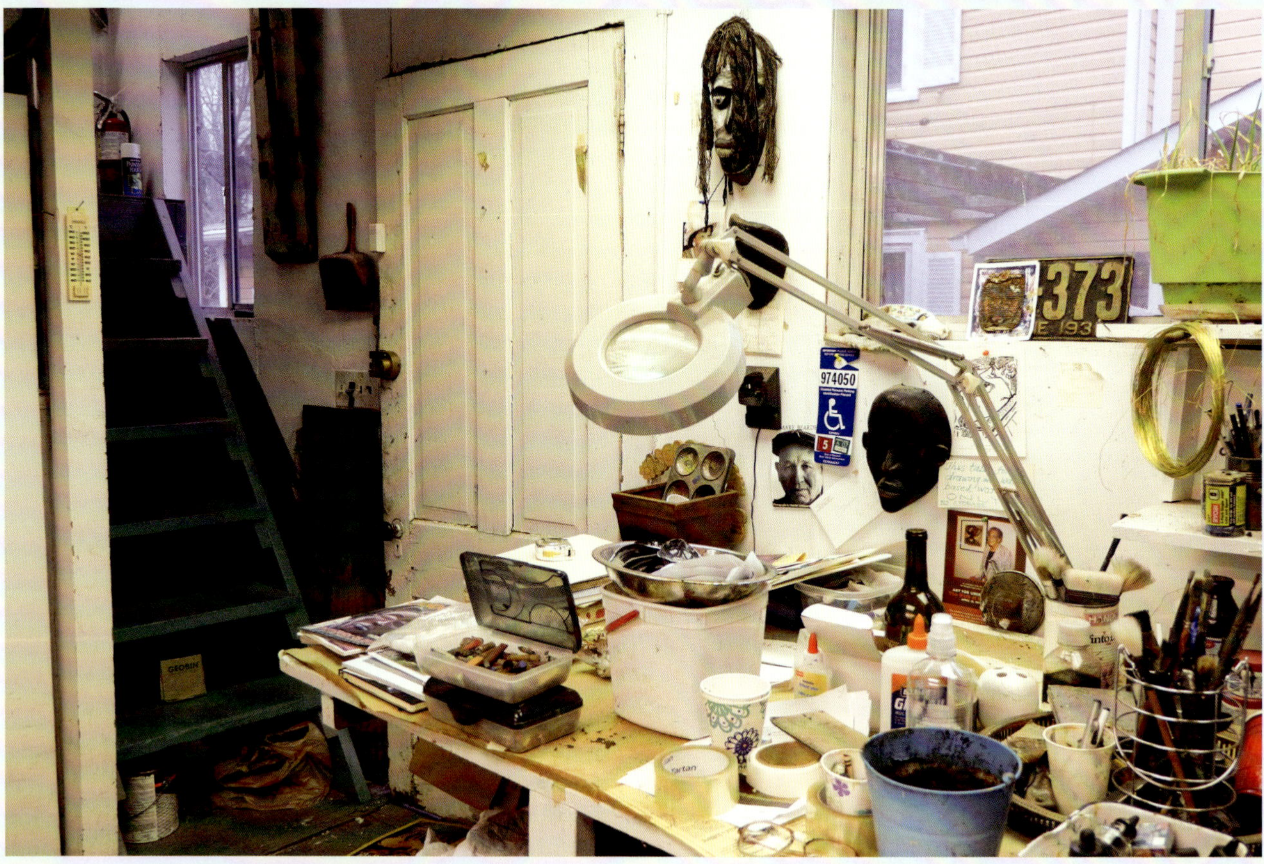

fig. 28
David Driskell's Hyattsville, MD studio, February 2020.

Sullivan—the daughter of the dean at Howard University's College of Liberal Arts. She was a poet. And I remember Langston Hughes came into town.

Most of the time, I would be in the back, taking care of the dishes or something like that, but I wasn't confined to that area, and Professor Herring made it very clear that I was welcome to come in and mix with the artists. That was where I first met Romare Bearden, Theodoros Stamos, I. Rice Pereira, and several other artists. It was not just Black artists who were there. Yes, it was to showcase mainly African American art, but American artists, in general, would come.

That's where I first met Mr. Duncan Phillips, and I want to say it was around 1952. He came to visit, and I want to say it was a group show in which I. Rice Pereira, Theodoros Stamos, and a few others were included. Mr. Herring said occasionally [Phillips] would follow up with purchases of artists that he had seen there.

I don't recall having ever met Mrs. Phillips. I remember going to the gallery—we called it the Phillips Memorial Gallery at that time—and seeing her work, and in my mind it was a picture of a baseball park, of Griffith Stadium.

And there was a woman painter at American University who did still life, and I want to say I saw her work there: [Sarah] Baker.

I remember being interested in Baker's still lifes because they tended a little more toward modernism. But the baseball stadium stands out in my mind, and it was interesting to me when somebody finally told me that the painter was the wife of Mr. Phillips. You know, you'd see a Cézanne here and a Marjorie Phillips there. [laughs] You'd go up the steps and there was a Rouault, perhaps a[n Albert Pinkham] Ryder. So it was a very interesting mix, a very interesting atmosphere.

Now, at Howard, there were often group shows, and that's how I came to know the work of people like Archibald Motley. Howard owned a number of those works—Charles White, Jacob Lawrence, etc. Lois [Mailou Jones] was my teacher as well. I studied watercolor painting [with her], because she didn't teach oil painting, she taught watercolor painting and design. But I still say mainly what I learned about color and color relationships, I learned from Lois because she was such a great colorist.

ES: It's interesting that Duncan Phillips lent works to Barnett Aden's exhibitions. It sounds as though you may have met him right at the time he had lent I. Rice Pereira's *Transversion* to their ninth anniversary exhibition, in the fall of 1952. He had bought it from them, then they did a show and asked if he would lend it.

DD: I would suspect that was about the time and the occasion.

ES: How was the Barnett Aden Gallery patterned after the Phillips, and in what ways did it differ?

DD: Well, 127 Randolph Place Northwest was not a major house. It was modest in certain ways. As one walked in, to the left was the living room. Down the hallway, past the living room, was an open area which was more like a reception area, and that's where the desk was that people signed in at when they came in. Then beyond that was the dining room, which was wall space for the most part, but they had built some shelves there.

By the time I started working there, it was literally a shop called Quan Yin in that section of the dining room—there were very few paintings hung in that area—until they moved over near Seventh and T Northwest, where there was an actual building that they called the Quan Yin that was devoted to art objects that people didn't normally buy or couldn't get in Washington.

[But] Professor Herring and Mr. Aden had many acquaintances in New York with the gallery people: Edith Halpert, Anita Kraushaar, [Jeff Berman's] ACA Gallery, and the Wildenstein Gallery, where I first learned about Norman Lewis's work. Of course, they didn't have the space, the money, but they were trying to pattern their whole gallery scene after the Phillips in the sense of the comfort, the welcoming, the level of excellence. When I first experienced this at the Phillips, I thought, "People live like this? I want to live like this." [laughs] So I started trying to collect art. The very first piece was a print by Professor Wells. A little later, I acquired a [Rouault] print [purchased from itinerant Baltimore dealer Ferdinand Roten].

And they were authentic works that were not terribly expensive. I have a little Renoir hanging in the hall, also from Roten, that I acquired early on. I have a small page from a *Book of Hours*. As I was being taught art, I was buying in different categories. I remember a Persian tile that I bought that inspired some of my own work later, with a falconer [on horseback].

Anyway, those objects would stay in my mind for a period of time and I would think, "That's a section of art that I could deal with"—ceramics, the decorative arts, and what have you. Meantime, I'm taking courses at Howard University, which emphasizes all of those art forms. One thought more about the practice of art at American University and perhaps at Catholic University, but Howard had an extensive curriculum in art history, including studies on the master's level, and they were not all African American professors. It was about half and half as far as the racial makeup.

ES: I think Morris Louis was on the faculty.

IF I WAS GOING TO GO INTO EXPRESSIONISM, I WANTED IT TO HAVE THAT KIND OF HEAVY-HANDED FEEL ABOUT IT.

DD: Morris Louis came on the faculty in 1953, the year that I came back from Skowhegan [School of Painting and Sculpture], and he was the most abstract of all of the painters [at Howard]. I'd been studying with Jack Levine. I [was] going to be a social commentary artist, and Professor Porter said to me, "We have a new instructor. I want you to take a course with him. His name is Morris Louis." I said, "Oh, no. He's an abstract painter. I can't study with him." And Professor Porter said, "You will study with him." [laughs]

ES: In the end, did you feel that it was worthwhile?

DD: Oh, yes. It just opened up my whole way of seeing form, of painting. Carl Alexander was in that class, and I think he and I may be the only ones left who studied with Morris Louis at Howard. Carl took him *very* seriously; I didn't. I learned a great deal from him, but I knew I wasn't going to go totally abstract. Morris, I would say, was not highly regarded in the Washington community at that time. He was making his way, as was Ken Noland. There were others who were perhaps more widely known, and [working in] different styles, like Samuel Bookatz.

ES: When you visited the Phillips with your teachers, did you feel that what you saw was being connected to what you were learning from Wells or Jones?

DD: Yes, definitely. In particular, Miss Jones would say, "Well, this is a good example of what I was trying to tell you about."

ES: You've talked a little bit about Cézanne or Matisse or Rouault, in terms of an influence on your early formative period...

DD: And Braque.

ES: What spoke to you in Rouault's work?

DD: The boldness of his form, the stroke—it seemed to me that his painting was always an extended form of drawing—and the dark, heavy line that articulated certain things that one couldn't describe with paint alone. And there was a kind of expressionist feel that I thought was there; that if I was going to go into expressionism, I wanted it to have that kind of heavy-handed feel about it, not so much the quiet flow of a Morris Louis, maybe fluid, but not *that* fluid.

I'd been introduced to most of those [Rouault] paintings at the Phillips (see fig. 27) and at the National Gallery....

ES: What about the spirituality in Rouault?

DD: To separate the real meaning of spirituality over and against religiosity in the sense of a religious subject—there was something very, very profound, I feel, about the dynamics of how he was able to communicate spiritually and make me feel that I was part of that experience. I didn't necessarily feel that with Raphael and some other painters.

ES: I thought we'd look at another important decade, against the backdrop of the civil rights movement. You leave your teaching post at Talladega College in Alabama, in 1962, to ...

DD: ... take the professorship at Howard ...

ES: ... and the role of directing the Barnett

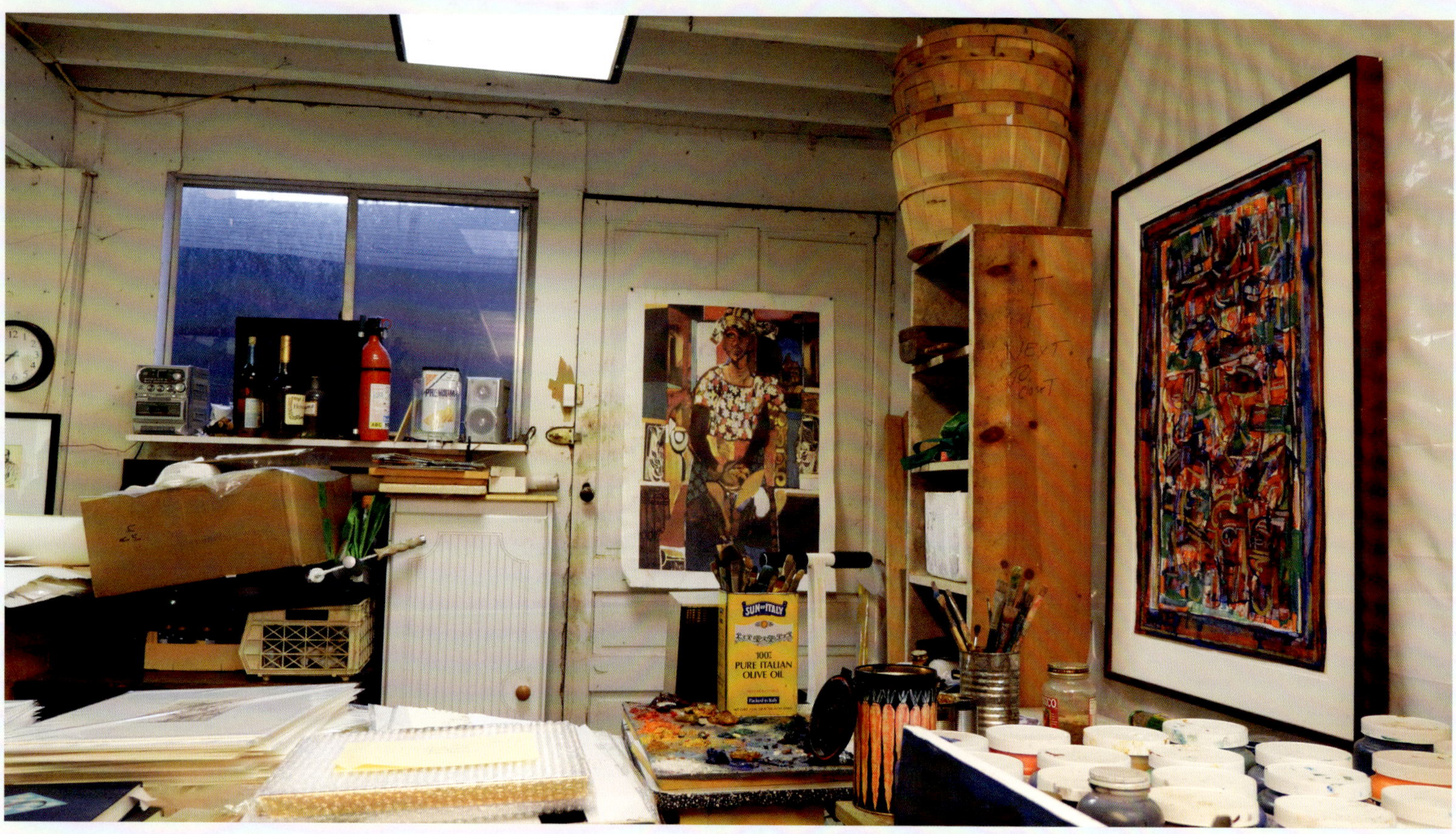

Aden Gallery after [Alonzo J.] Aden's death. It's interesting to think about the Phillips expansion in 1960, with the new Rothko Room. Do you have memories of that?
DD: We called it the Rothko Chapel. [laughs] I really felt a kind of a spiritual relationship to Rothko's work, even though I didn't paint in that style. When I went there, I really felt as though I was almost on sacred ground, just absorbing the essence of what it was that color was able to do, and the way it did it geometrically as well as in his formal analysis of a limited palette that could say so much. I didn't try and adapt it for myself, but as I look back, I learned a great deal from it. I learned how to flatten out form, how to introduce elements of geometricity in my work, and it was a totally different kind of experience for me. I would take my students there. Mary [Lovelace] O'Neal was one of the students that I would take over with me to the Phillips in the sixties. She said to me just last Thursday, "Mr. Driskell, remember how I would call you late at night and say, 'How did Rothko make that red?'" Lou Stovall was in that class. Sylvia Snowden....

I REALLY FELT A KIND OF A SPIRITUAL RELATIONSHIP TO ROTHKO'S WORK, EVEN THOUGH I DIDN'T PAINT IN THAT STYLE.

Then I taught a course which was not a painting course, but it bordered on philosophy and aesthetics, in 1962–63; it was really about protest art and what would have been characterized at that time as Black art, but we weren't using that title. So even at Howard, a Black university, we didn't put it in the curriculum like that. So I had the course really pretty much in disguise. We called it "Modern Art and Aesthetics." And in that class was Stokely Carmichael, who was Mary O'Neal's boyfriend; Jessye Norman, who became the famous opera singer; a famous collector now, Walter Evans; Harold Wheeler, who became a very important modernist composer.
ES: Speaking of "Modern Art and Aesthetics" made me think about your aesthetic philosophy. You have a deeply spiritual and intellectual world view. And there are a number of writers and thinkers that have been important to you.
DD: Yes, I was developing this interest in philosophy. In some cases, they were connected to religion in certain ways: [Bernard] Faucon, [Jacques] Maritain, [Paul] Tillich, and others. I was reading way beyond art to try and match it up with the philosophy of the times. It wasn't my original thinking to do that, so much as the thinking of my graduate advisor at Catholic University, a woman by the name of Nell Sonneman, who was a textile artist and had

figs. 29 & 30
David Driskell's Hyattsville, MD studio, February 2020.

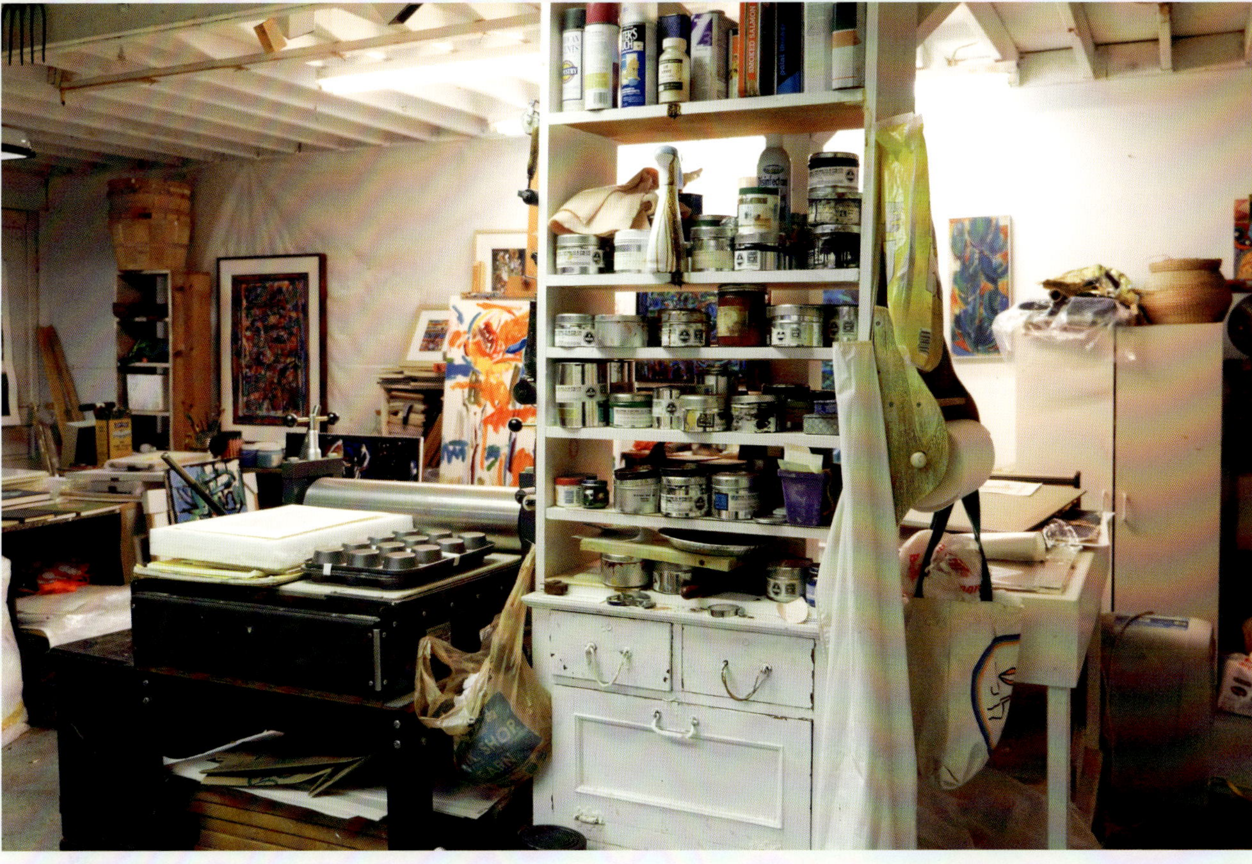

this sense of how to make—I would say, in fundamentalist [religious terms]—the connection between heaven and earth, in the sense of the beauty, the dream of what the perfect form must be like, in the sense of Plato or Aristotle.... She would say, "You can only do so much, but what you do must be so well done that the angels in heaven will rejoice when they see it." You know, I'm from a fundamentalist Baptist background, with a father who preached fire and brimstone, heaven, hell, [laughs] so all of this was making a lot of sense to me on an intellectual level.

My father, when I was in the fifth grade, gave me this book called *Basic Teachings of the Great Philosophers*. I think the author was S. E. Frost. Plato, Aristotle, Socrates, you name it, Kant, all the way up to modern philosophy. And yet he never preached about anything like that, and I, even now, keep thinking, why did he give me that book and insist I read it?

When I arrived at this little four-room high school in Forest City, North Carolina, in 1945, I knew who Aristotle was, I knew who Plato was. Nobody else seemed to know. And it was this dormant period until I arrived [at] college and had courses in the humanities with people like Nathan Scott, Alain Locke, and Frank Snowden, and then it all came back. It gelled.

I think it has influenced my own art in certain ways. Tillich, for example, said there's more spirituality in the sense of a human encounter in Cézanne's *Apples* than one finds in *The Madonna* by Raphael. [laughs] Now, that's a big statement. But I also was taken with his notion about the courage to be: you can't let race, gender, any of those things get in the way of what you know your calling is, and that was buttressed by, later on, my reading works of Rollo May, *The Courage to Create*, all the way down to the little book that Joshua Taylor wrote, called *Learning to Look*, which I would require all my students to read.

So I was trying to mix all of these things in. I said to Adrienne Childs the other day, when she was asking me some questions about [my painting] *Red Still Life*, "Well, you can never paint enough still life." I never get tired of painting a still life. It's part of nature. It's a challenge. It has the tenets of beauty and all those things that you tempt yourself to do and hopefully come out victorious with. That's why I could stand and look at a Cézanne, a Renoir, a Matisse, all day and never get tired.

ES: You brought up nature, another theme that runs through your work. It would be interesting to hear your perspective, as the son of sharecroppers, on the importance of the land, and your upbringing....

DD: Yes, I think having grown up in what we call the "country," out of doors, not experiencing the real feel of city life or anything like that until I was an adult,

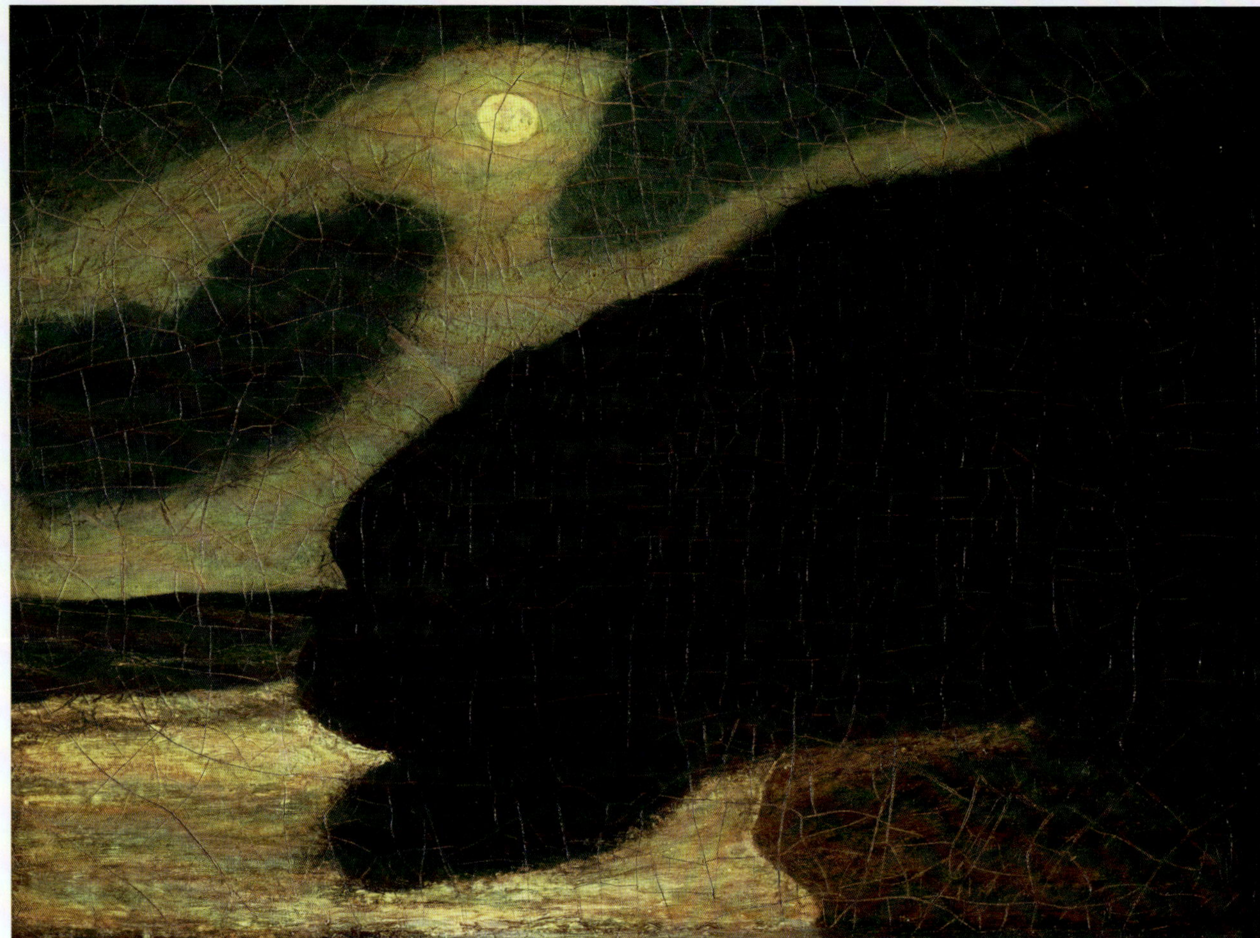

fig. 31
Albert Pinkham Ryder
***Moonlit Cove*, early to mid-1880s**
Oil on canvas,
14 1/8 × 17 1/8 in.
The Phillips Collection,
Washington, DC,
Acquired 1924.

it was just something about having this relationship with things that grow, things that we rely upon in so many ways, the plants that we consume for food, the plants that we use in building our houses, the farming ethic in general.

YOU CAN NEVER PAINT ENOUGH STILL LIFE. I NEVER GET TIRED OF PAINTING A STILL LIFE.

And though my parents were not educated with college degrees, they had great respect for nature. I would follow my mother around in the woods as a kid, because we had no doctors in the community, and she would select certain things to make teas for us if we had a cold or other illness. So there was that curiosity, that interest. My father grew the usual vegetables in the garden. We had a cotton field, we had a corn field, things like that, we had fruit trees. I would watch [my mother]—this was in the thirties and forties—as she canned, preserved, dried, so that we were all but self-sufficient. Now, I don't have to do that, but a little rubbed off on me: a part of my gardening is to grow as many—in Maine, of course—fresh vegetables as I can. I have fruit trees: peaches and pears and apples and plums. My wife, Thelma, came up pretty much in the same tradition, so she will preserve some, she will make jam from some. I will do the regular canning. So it [became] part of my lifestyle because it was so important back then.

It still plays a very important role in my own work. I watched my mother go out and dig clays, yellow clays or ochres, the red clays, other clays to dye the cloth that she would put in her quilts; or the berries she would pick, like the pokeberry, that she would make colors from. In some of these drawings from my sketchbooks, the inks are made from the black walnut hull and the pokeberry.

In so many of my nature studies, especially the ones at night, I will have a moon. You don't stop seeing because night comes, and you don't avoid the brightness of the day. They're all part and parcel of that wonderful experience of living, and being able to interpret it.

There's an interesting and, I would say, rightful place, where one blends nature in with self, and for me, it's been all but a saving grace of sorts.

ES: Coming back to Ryder, how do you feel about his work vis-à-vis nature?

DD: It's interesting that Ryder was one of the artists that I was taken with when I first came to the Phillips: the night scene (fig. 31), of course, the *Dead Bird*, related to nature, and so forth. I'm sure he was probably looked upon by some as being out of step with time. But here we are and his work is still with us, and there's a mystery, I think, about how he saw the world. Who would think to paint a dead bird? The empathy that he had with the loss of life of this little creature.

I think the gift of the artist, as with Ryder and so many others who moved beyond the ordinary, was to see beyond the contours of time and space and create their own definition of form. And I think that's what singles out the best amongst us. When you step outside the ordinary and refuse to get back in line, then you're making a difference. Kandinsky did it; so many artists that we could name, you know, were able to take that leap of faith. And I think it requires that.

ES: Hokusai apparently believed that he would reach the peak of his abilities at the age of 110. As you approach your ninetieth birthday, how do you see your work in the bigger context of your life's journey?

DD: Well, first of all, I feel very blessed, very fortunate, to have had the experiences that I have had in life through art, not from the point of view of being acclaimed or having the reward of riches ... so much as the notion that what I have done is being looked upon and passed on to others as a pattern worthy of repeat[ing], and part of it is my belief that everybody has a calling, everybody has a field that they are supposed to be dedicated to, and that if one can define that field beyond self and be inclusive of others, then that's one of the most important things that could be done; if you can pass it on, if you can say, "Here is my gift to you."

If I have imprinted anything at all that can be passed on to those who are willing carriers, then I will feel as though I have done something important and worthy of my having been here.

I FEEL VERY BLESSED, VERY FORTUNATE, TO HAVE HAD THE EXPERIENCES THAT I HAVE HAD IN LIFE THROUGH ART.

The more we see ourselves in that relationship of adjacent and adjoining and relating to others, the larger we become, and I think art is one of those areas of endeavor that allows us to do that, to be separate and apart, yet so well connected that somebody else will want to hold on and hang on.

I often say: try and visualize the world without the concept of making. What would it be like if we didn't make things? I can't imagine. And yet here we are, some of us entrusted with that responsibility, and that's why I think it's sacred. I would say to my students, "Art is a priestly calling. If you're not going to be dedicated to it, go and search for something else, because you're supposed to be adding to the information of the world."

ES: You're still making art (figs. 28–30). What's driving this latest burst of artistic work?

DD: I'm probably trying to build on what I've already done, but at the same time, make it stronger, make it have more meaning, not necessarily [so much] from the point of view of visual definition as from a spiritual point of view.

ES: One last question to bring us back to the Phillips. What is your wish for the Phillips in the twenty-first century and beyond?

DD: Well, I know visual service will continue to be an important element of its mission, but I also think it's larger than that. The Phillips has the challenge of not being ordinary, [of looking] beyond time and place to a new vision. I don't know what that is, [how] I would even define it, but it would be inclusive of all of the things that you have done, while at the same time looking to the future.

So how can this great modern museum, one of the first modern museums, transcend time and place and continue to be a leader not just in the nation's capital, but for the nation and for the world? I think that's the vision that Mr. Phillips had from day one: that this wouldn't be just an ordinary museum, an ordinary gallery, [but] a universal place, a place where ideas are born, implemented, explored, and continued in the sense of human conquest, human endeavor, particularly in the area of the humanities, where we are concentrating on our inner soul, seeing beyond what we thought we could see, doing beyond what we thought we could do, and continu[ing] to be the leader in that sense.

1 David C. Driskell, oral history interview with Donita Moorhus, December 23, 2008, The Phillips Collection Archives, Washington, DC.

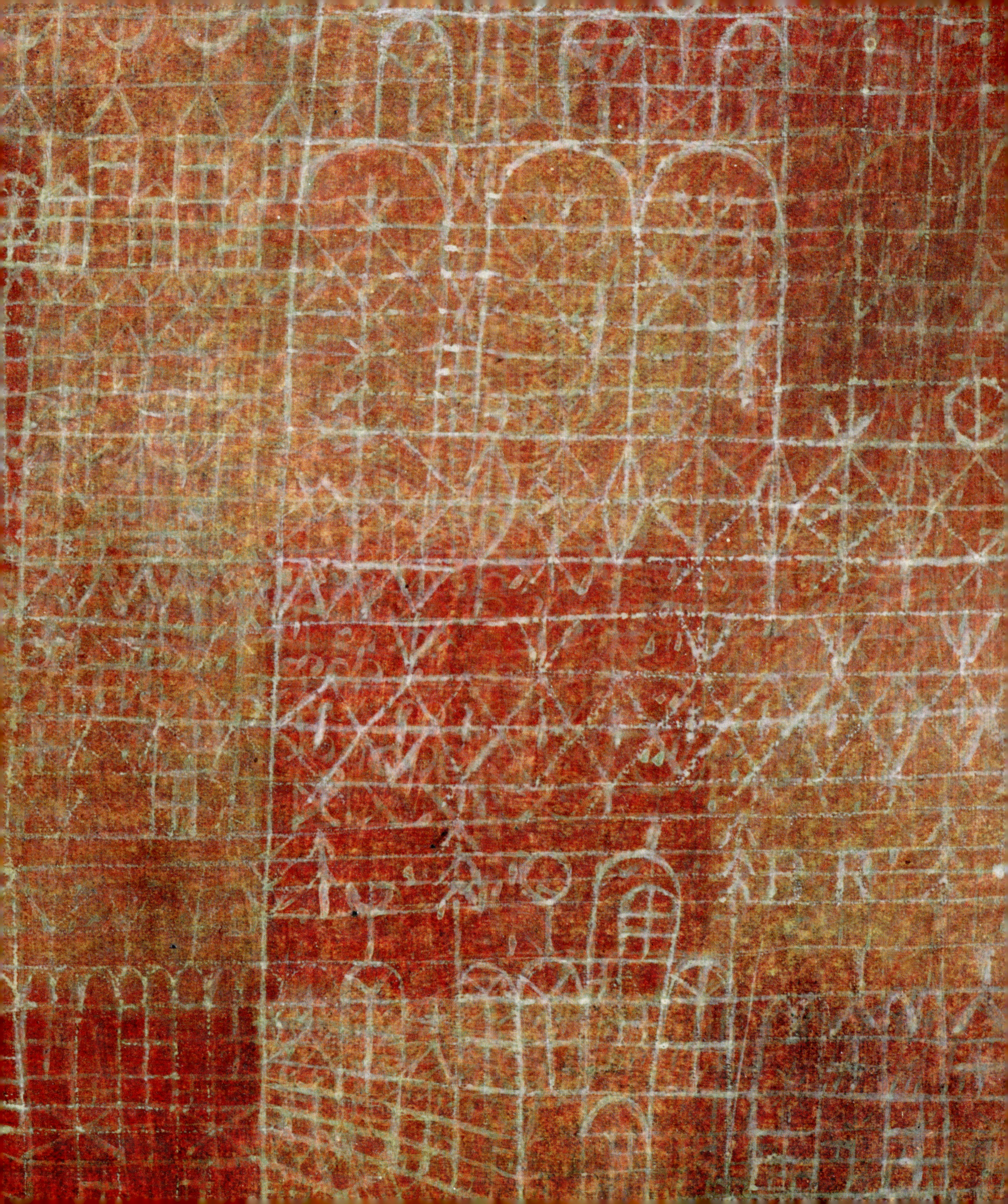

UNRAVELING THE ABSOLUTE: PAINTING MUSIC AT THE PHILLIPS COLLECTION

Jeremy Ney

Art does not reproduce the visible; art makes visible.
—Paul Klee

Before painting, there was jazz.
—Sam Gilliam

When Duncan Phillips purchased Eugène Delacroix's painting of the nineteenth-century virtuoso Niccolò Paganini in 1922 (fig. 32), he recognized the great power possessed by this small image. Phillips, for whom beauty and the desire to "see beautifully as true artists see" were guiding principles,[1] wrote about the painting often, viewing it as atypical of Delacroix's art, showing novel experiments with color, line, light, and shade, techniques that were to serve as "plastic expression of passionate emotions."[2]

What beauty did Phillips see in Delacroix's portrait of Paganini? The answer lies as much in the painting's surface effects as it does in the currents of nineteenth-century aesthetic thought that helped shape Phillips's early intellectual foundations. This "tiny-soul portrait" of Paganini, as Phillips described it,[3] is representational in the sense that we see the virtuoso in the act of music-making. However, the painting's allure is not necessarily in the accuracy of physical depiction but in what Phillips described as its "psychological insight"[4]—Delacroix's rendering of an internal state of mind. Paganini is seen absorbed in the moment of performance. His eyes closed, body contorted, he appears to be overpowered by the metaphysical and transcendent power of music. By enacting the immanence of music—an invisible art—his physical presence is threatened by an enveloping darkness that floods the canvas. Thus, the realism within the image is transfigured by a sensory, visual evocation of mood or "passionate emotion" as Phillips described it.[5] Within the play of corporeal absence and musical presence in the painting, Paganini becomes a symbol, a visual manifestation of "the music itself." As the art historian Anne-Birgitte Fonsmark has commented, "it is not only Paganini that is portrayed here, but the very essence of music."[6]

This painterly claim to the "essence of music" unfurls a series of necessarily rhetorical questions. What, first of all, is music? Is it—as Arthur Schopenhauer claimed—a solely sounding art,[7] something separated from other realms of life and art; wordless, non-referential, abstract? In the

(opposite)
Paul Klee, *Cathedral*, detail, 1924
The Phillips Collection, Washington, DC, Acquired 1942.

nineteenth and early twentieth centuries, this concept of instrumental music's autonomy was attractive to artists in other media who wished to transcend formal boundaries, leading theorists like Walter Pater to claim in 1873 that, "all art constantly aspires to the condition of music."[8] The evidence of Pater's principle was clear enough in his own time: from the utopian idea of synesthesia espoused in the poetry of Charles Baudelaire and Stéphane Mallarmé, and manifested in the Wagnerian poetics of the *Gesamtkunstwerk*, to the "musicality of painting" initiated by Delacroix and adopted by Paul Gauguin and his Nabi disciples, such as Pierre Bonnard, the nineteenth century was a period of frenzied inter-artistic exchange.[9] The notion of correspondence and convergence between art forms became a kind of aesthetic orthodoxy, and the status accorded to music for its autonomous, absolute nature continued into the twentieth century, influencing both the theory and practice of visual art.[10] Music offered visual art a radical break from representation, and the musical analogy became a potent talisman for the emergence of visual abstraction. Indeed, many works in The Phillips Collection bear witness to this aesthetic affinity between visual art and music, from Delacroix to Wassily Kandinsky, Paul Klee, and Arthur Dove, among many others.

Yet, to provide a more nuanced view of music's influence on works of art owned by the Phillips also means challenging some assumptions about what constitutes "music" within the study of the visual arts. In recent music scholarship, new interdisciplinary models of exploring sound and music have broadened approaches to musical meaning, exploring concepts that seek to capture the totality of music in its various social and material dimensions.[11] Such necessary scholarly work has also exposed the contingency of the term "music" as a universal category, urging us to recognize but also look beyond the totalizing nature of the parallel canons of European Western art and Western classical music. No study of a collection as rich and variegated as the Phillips's could, for instance, exclude the influence of blues, jazz, and other African American musical idioms. In this context, rather than attempting a complete survey of manifestations of musical ideas in works of art at The Phillips Collection, this contribution is necessarily selective, exploring ways in which art and music can be entwined, with an emphasis on the work of four artists: Kandinsky, Klee, Sam Gilliam, and Renée Stout.

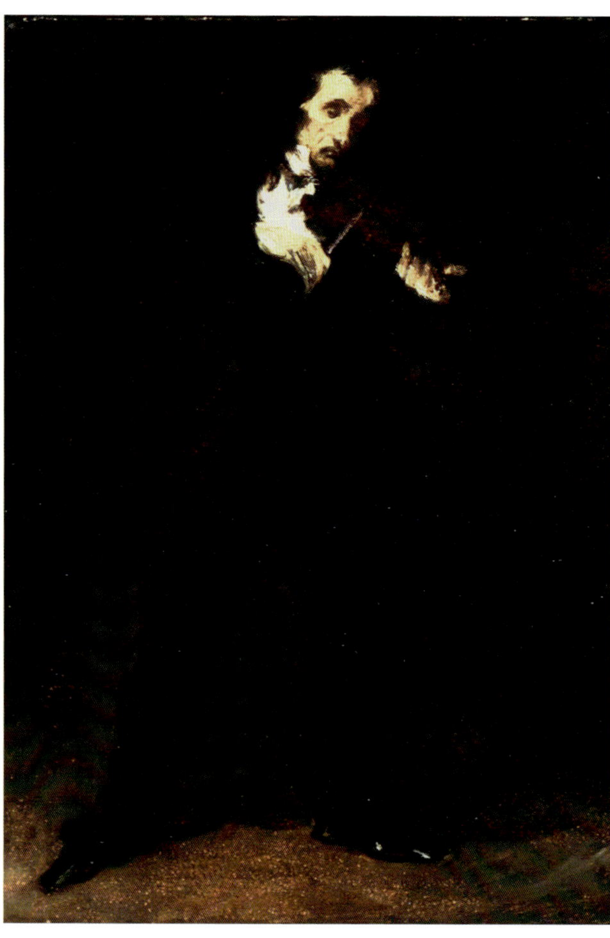

fig. 32
Ferdinand-Victor-Eugène Delacroix
***Paganini*, 1831**
Oil on cardboard, 17 5/8 × 11 7/8 in.
The Phillips Collection, Washington, DC, Acquired 1922.

Paradoxes, Provocations, and Polyphony

Following a performance of his music at The Phillips Collection in December 2012, the noted German composer Matthias Pintscher said: "It goes without saying that visual impressions cannot be composed, or 'set to music'—there is no genuine, interdisciplinary way to translate between forms that are heard and those that are seen."[12] His observation gestures toward a distinction that is often seen as self-evident: that music is a temporal, time-based art, whereas painting is fixed and spatial. The perceptual process in each art form is fundamentally different, governed by the fact that listening and seeing are not interchangeable modalities. Correspondence between music and visual art must therefore wrestle with this distinction between temporal and spatial forms.

Synesthesia offered one way in which artists reconciled these two poles of aesthetic experience. Synesthesia is a neurological condition shared by many prominent artists, in which stimulation in one sense immediately triggers perception in another (for example, a specific

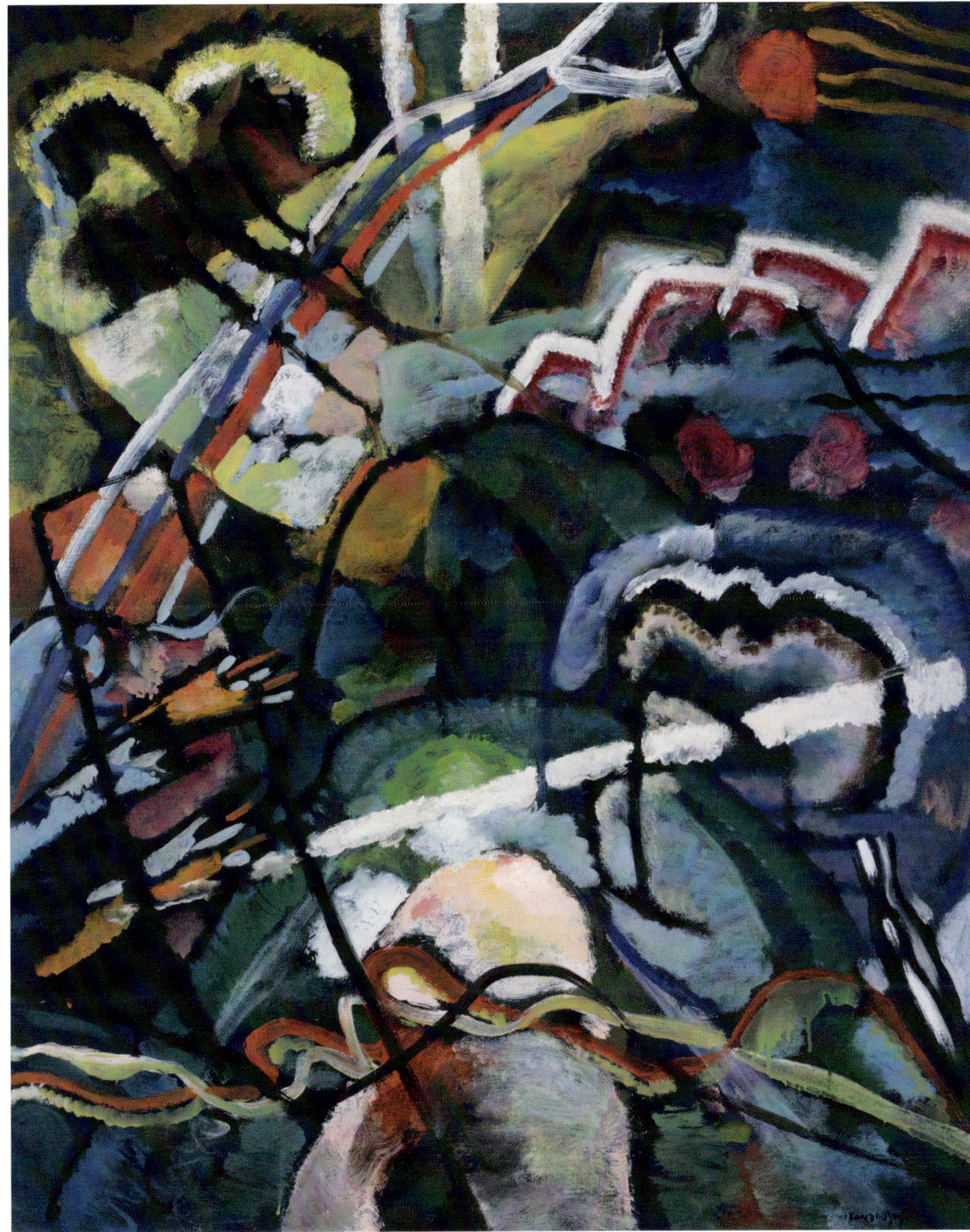

fig. 33
Wassily Kandinsky
***Sketch I for Painting with White Border (Moscow)*, 1913**
Oil on canvas,
39 3/8 × 30 7/8 in.
The Phillips Collection,
Washington, DC,
Gift from the estate of
Katherine S. Dreier, 1953.

sound triggering a vivid color).[13] It can also be understood as the manifestation of a cultural sensibility, a way of relating art to music through metaphor and allegory. Both forms captured the imagination of the international artistic avant-garde in the nineteenth and early twentieth centuries, with artistic discussion of synesthesia reaching its peak in the writings and art of the Russian artist Wassily Kandinsky. Kandinsky was interested in the emotive potential of color as a pure form, and he found inspiration in instrumental music's abstract, non-referential qualities. The supposed immediacy of music's sensory effect appealed to Kandinsky because it had been understood since Schopenhauer that musical-emotional response was non-subjective. As the theorist Rei Terada has illustrated, instrumental music (music without words or narrative function) as a form is "all too transparent, a language so fine that no content can penetrate it."[14] Such emotional transparency provides the ultimate vector for the visual artist; by using the example of music, one could stir and arouse emotion visually without representing any specific objective emotional reality. Such an effect of "purity" also became a potent tool for American visual artists like Dove, who claimed that "anybody should be able to feel a certain state and express it in terms of paint or music.... [Art] is nearer to music."[15]

The 1913 painting *Sketch I for Painting with White Border (Moscow)* (fig. 33) illustrates Kandinsky's philosophical and practical linking of art and music. The painting coincides with a radical moment in his thinking, two years after the publication of his aesthetic treatise, *Concerning the Spiritual in Art*, in which he proposes a theory of non-representational painting that synthesizes sounds (*Klänge*) with colors and forms, intentionally erasing the barriers separating artistic media.[16] In this preparatory study, Kandinsky is working out how to create a non-figurative visual art that is still structurally coherent. The motifs of the troika and a horse with rider are just discernible at the upper left and middle right of the composition, hovering on the edge of representation and abstraction. Kandinsky deliberately dissolves each motif, looking to "rid them of their association with the material world and release their spiritual inner sounds."[17] In seeking to transcend imitation and attain a higher spiritual and aesthetic domain, Kandinsky incorporates principles drawn from music: its condition as an absolute artform that is separated from imitation of the physical world, and the rational properties of musical composition demonstrated in the proportional relationships of keys, scales, harmony, and rhythm. Kandinsky claims these ideas for painting, finding new means to express visually what his friend the composer Arnold Schoenberg described as the "true essence" of art: an inner spirituality derived from the resources of the artwork as a self-sufficient system.[18]

Influenced by Kandinsky's theories and movement toward abstraction, the points of contact between music and art began to deepen significantly in the twentieth century. Visual artists on both sides of the Atlantic

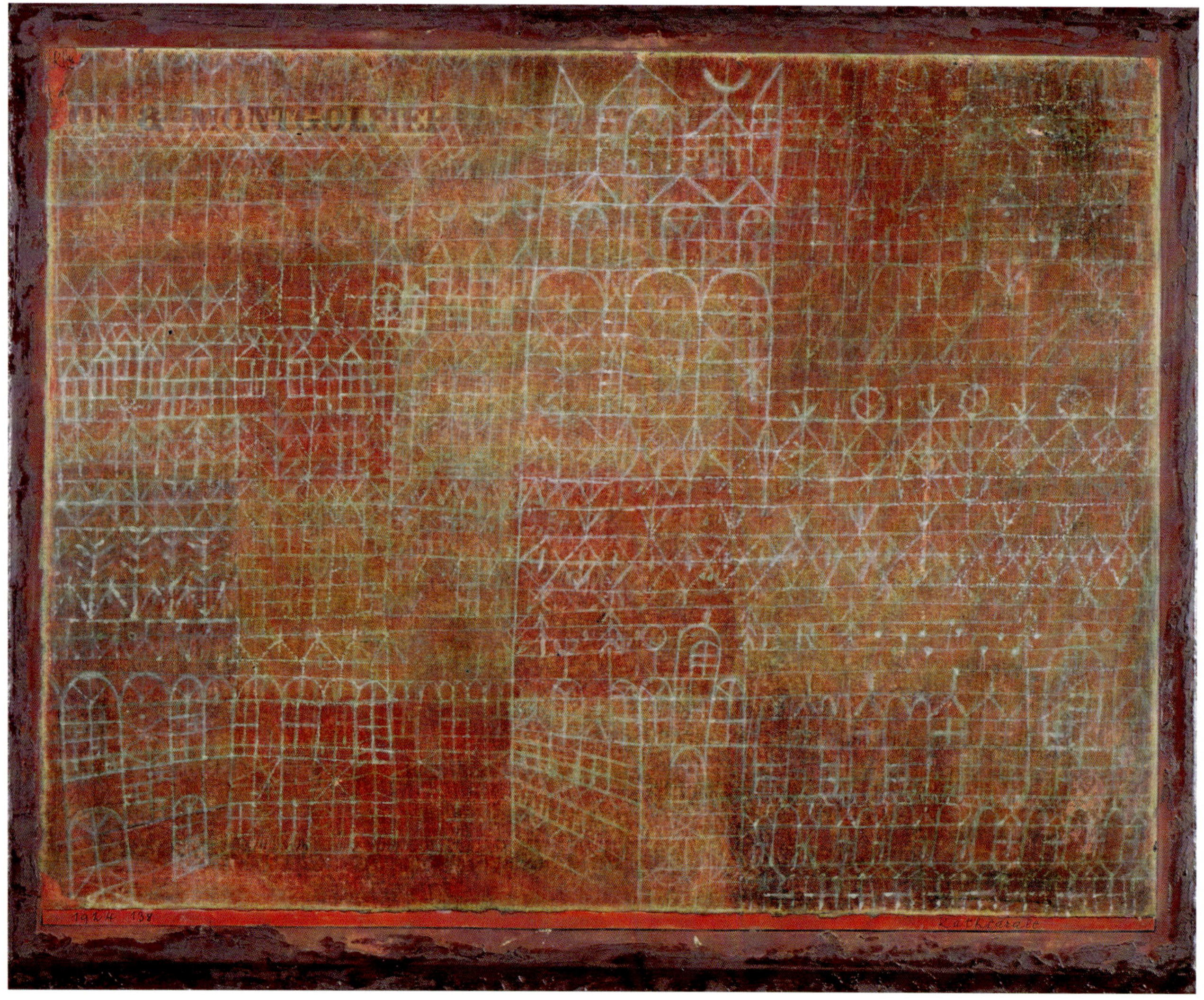

fig. 34
Paul Klee
***Cathedral*, 1924**
Watercolor and oil on paper mounted on cardboard mounted on wood panel, 11 3/4 × 13 7/8 in.
The Phillips Collection, Washington, DC, Acquired 1942.

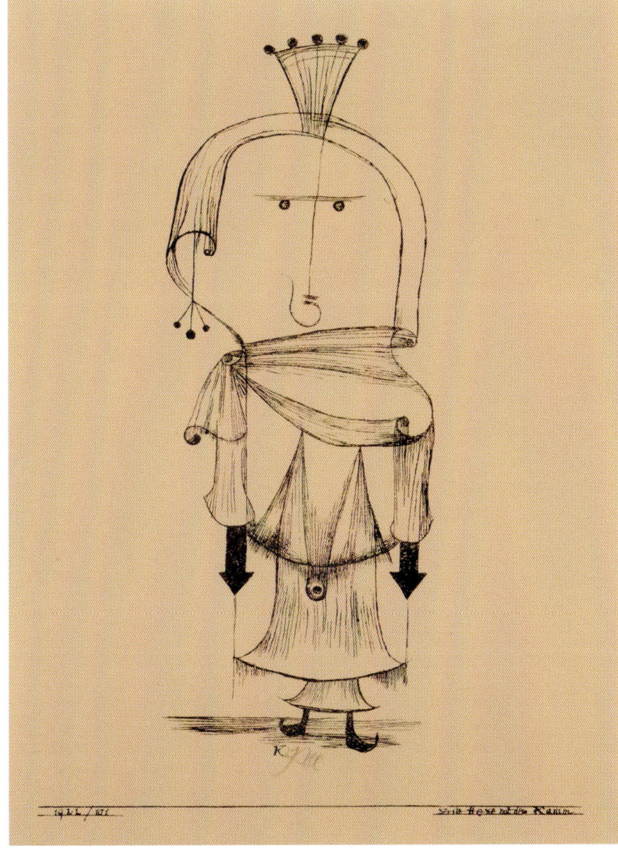

fig. 35
Paul Klee
***The Witch with the Comb*, 1922**
Lithograph with graphite pencil inscription, 19 1/4 x 13 in.
The Phillips Collection, Washington, DC,
Gift of B. J. and Carol Cutler, 2006.

began to translate musical concepts such as the forms and structures of polyphonic music to a visual idiom. Polyphonic music (music with multiple overlapping voices called "subjects" that combine in patterns to create rich textures) is associated with the fugues of J.S. Bach. In the era of cubism and the later years of the Bauhaus, his music was hailed as the pinnacle of pure form, praised for its purity, logic, rigor, and economy of means.[19] Polyphonic music of the Renaissance and the early-classical era came to be seen in visual terms as "architectural,"[20] providing new technical and structural avenues for visual artists to exploit. The constructivist impulse permeated the teaching and practice of Bauhaus artists, notably the Swiss-born artist Paul Klee.

A classically trained violinist, Klee was deeply inspired by polyphonic music, particularly that of Bach. As early as 1918, Klee was exploring its relationship to art. He noted in his diary: "polyphonic painting is superior to music, to the extent that the temporal element is here replaced by the spatial element. The notion of simultaneity appears here in an even richer form."[21] The grid-like structure of his painting *Cathedral* (fig. 34) — alternating blocks of color overlaid with delicate white calligraphic forms—compels the eye to scan its surface, picking out points of emphasis. The barely perceptible irregularity in the shapes of the color blocks creates the impression of a subtle, undulating rhythm. The lines weave in and out of the foreground, playing with depth and plane in dynamic motion as a simultaneous yet distinct "polyphonic" subject.

Klee identified drawing and line in active terms—taking "a line on a walk," "moving freely without goal"[22]—thus drawing our attention to the materiality of the line in motion and the physical action of the artist's body in the moment of creation. The lithograph *The Witch with the Comb* (fig. 35) is a study in this process of formation and movement. Beginning with the playful curved line of the mouth, we follow the line through a composition that establishes a series of dynamic and opposing rhythmic forces: the tension between the upward-pointing comb and the downward-pointing earring; and the sinuous, flowing and spiraling lines of fabric set against the counter-rhythm of the pendulum motion of an eye shape in the middle of the composition. These subtle visual effects are blunted by the force of two downward arrows, Klee's favored symbol for playful misdirection.[23] In the focus on formation rather than form, drawing becomes the act of making visible, a simultaneous process of arrival and dissolution. In this context, the musical analogy ceases to be in the coloristic effect of vague musical emotion, or a sense of purity borrowed from music's nature as an "absolute" art; rather, Klee's line is akin to the physical quality of sound production, of body and instrument sounding from silence, shaping the gesture of sound in its material present.[24] Since Klee was a talented violinist and life-long lover of music, it is not farfetched to interpret this affective affinity for the parallel acts of coming to image and coming to sound.

Klee's assimilation of music into his practice had valuable lessons for future generations of artists inside and outside the realm of the visual, and his translation of the element of time and rhythm went beyond musical analogy toward more universal concepts. His "line on a walk" anticipates a new postmodern direction, with artists like John Cage introducing new doctrines of abstraction that would test the durability of Walter Pater's assertion that "all art constantly aspires to the condition of music": in the heady interdisciplinary experimentation of the mid-century international avant-garde, art would begin to aspire to a new condition of performance.[25]

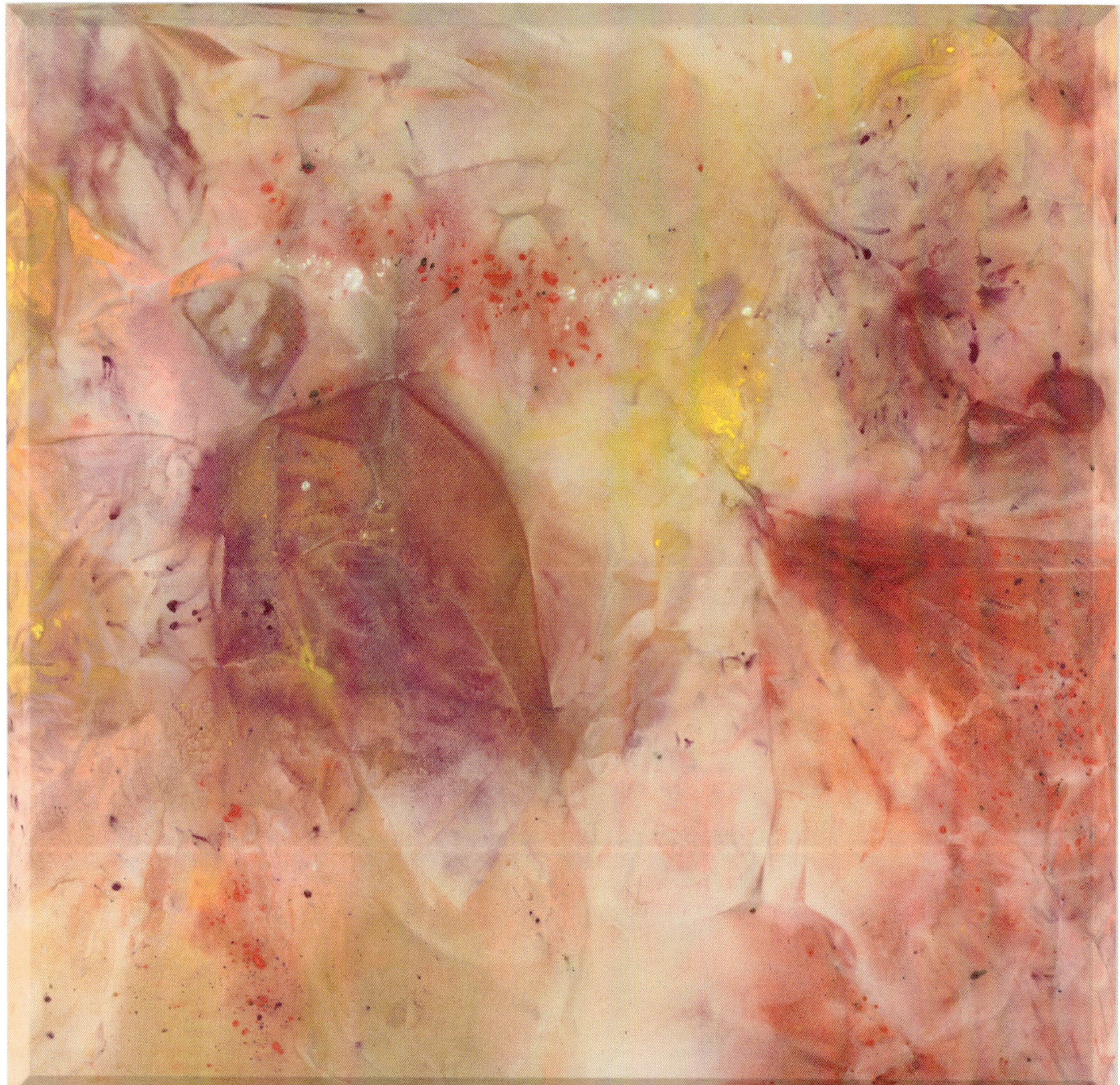

fig. 36
Sam Gilliam
***April*, 1971**
Acrylic on canvas, 60 × 60 × 2 1/2 in.
The Phillips Collection, Washington, DC, Bequest of Mercedes H. Eichholz, 2013.

Jazz, Blues, and the African Diaspora

In the study of correlations between art and music, critical omission of the influence of blues and jazz has been described as the result of a "racial blind spot," with the European canon dominating scholarship on the topic.[26] However, in American culture of the twentieth and twenty-first centuries, the influence of African American musical vernacular is indelible. The fraught history underpinning African American music—both its origins in slavery and its critical erasure resulting from twentieth-century prejudices related to "high" and "low" art forms—calls into question the Eurocentric view of music's condition as an absolute art and undermines the idea that music could be politically neutral or transcend issues of race, gender, or class. Since blues, jazz, and improvisatory forms of African American music are rooted in lived experience, how might we identify the traces of these musical forms in different artists' work?

Sam Gilliam has spoken frequently about the influence of jazz on his art. When he moved to Washington, DC, in the early 1960s, he promoted concerts, bringing the Modern Jazz Quartet and Marian Anderson to the city during the era of civil rights.[27] Painting in his DC studio, Gilliam listened to the vanguards of bebop: Ornette Coleman, John Coltrane, Dizzy Gillespie, and Thelonious Monk, radical improvisers who pioneered a liberated Black musical aesthetic rooted in African and African American cultural history.[28] Gilliam has talked about his associations with John Coltrane's music and the aural impression of his "sheets of sound"—a conscious visual metaphor for Coltrane's innovations in jazz harmony and rhythm.[29] "Coltrane worked at the whole sheet," Gilliam has remarked; "he didn't bother to stop at bars and notes and clefs and various things, he just played the whole sheet at once."[30] This statement describes the musician in visual terms that appear to show his ability to transcend the sequential function of music. Gilliam has also identified with the performance of jazz musicianship, saying, "jazz leads to the acrobatics of art,"[31] revealing his affinity with the bodily, affective presence of a musician like Coltrane in the "acrobatic" moment of improvisation.

Gilliam remained wholly committed to abstraction in the 1960s and 1970s, at a time when the Black Arts Movement (BAM) sought to frame Black art through a "socially responsible aesthetic" that was rooted in figuration and realism.[32] Gilliam's abstraction allowed him to move more fluidly through questions of race and self-identity, and he chose to relate to them freely as one element among many, rather than as a matter of fate. His engagement with jazz was similar; it is not always explicit in his work, but it is central to the mosaic of his artistic identity. His statement that, "before painting, there was jazz" is revealing in this context.[33] As the French philosopher Gilles Deleuze has observed, the blank canvas is already filled with the ideas that the artist brings to the painting.[34] He calls this "the painting before the painting."[35] Gilliam's decisive "before painting, there was jazz" compels us to interpret the aural trace of jazz influence in his work.

The Phillips's beveled-edge painting, *April* (fig. 36), reveals Gilliam's intensely performance-like process, which—like jazz—requires a balance between structure and improvisation. At this time, he applied paint freely to canvases placed on the floor, folding the material while the paint was wet, a procedure that introduced improvisatory elements to the final composition.[36] The title, *April*, signals a conceptual link to earlier paintings, *April 4* (1969) and *Red April* (1970), both of which refer to the assassination of Dr. Martin Luther King (April 4, 1968), rooting the multiple *April* paintings in a shared, humanistic social consciousness.[37] In 1971, Gilliam also produced *Lady Day*, an explicit homage to the jazz singer Billie Holiday, which shares the same coloristic, sensuous lyricism as *April*. While the titles of the canvases flag their social, political and cultural concerns, these are also rendered ambiguous through the process of abstraction. Within Gilliam's process of defamiliarization through abstraction, he found a model in the experimental attitude of the practitioners of bebop, who recombined and transformed the elements of jazz through a process of hybridization and synthesis that created a new art form focused on individual freedom and agency. The radicalism of artists like John Coltrane formed the perfect analogue for Gilliam, who sought a similar individualistic style unconstrained by disciplinary boundaries.

The painter and sculptor Renée Stout has also deployed explicit and oblique references to music in ways that subtly reveal the conceptual depths of her work. Stout takes inspiration from the blues tradition of the Mississippi Delta, and her visual explorations of the blues are linked to her parallel interest in African history and the diasporic traditions that have shaped the musical, social, and spiritual origins of the blues as the "first completely personalized form of African-American music."[38] Stout's work frequently recalls elements of African culture and places them in dialogue with the African American experience, generating objects that are suffused with what the theorist Paul Gilroy has called "diasporic intimacy."[39]

The mixed media sculpture *Elegba (Spirit of the Crossroads)* (fig. 37) invokes the complex Yoruba trickster deity. Elegba (or Eshu or Èsú in other African cultures) is god of the crossroads, a spiritual location where an individual must confront difficult life decisions. The crossroads metaphor simultaneously signals a site of danger or opportunity, and Elegba is believed to hold the spiritual potential to effect change. In West African Yoruba culture, where music, dance, religion, and spirituality are united in an indivisible network of social practices, Elegba can be called upon by humans through ritual and divination, to influence events in this world. In her exploration of the powerfully affective spirit of the crossroads, Stout recalls the legend of musician Robert Johnson, who in blues folklore sold his soul to the devil at the crossroads in exchange for becoming a virtuoso blues guitarist.

In Stout's 2017 painting, *Mannish Boy Arrives (for Muddy Waters)* (fig. 38), the shape of the Elegba sculpture seems to manifest itself with a bright orange light that appears to signal a path forward, perhaps indicating a

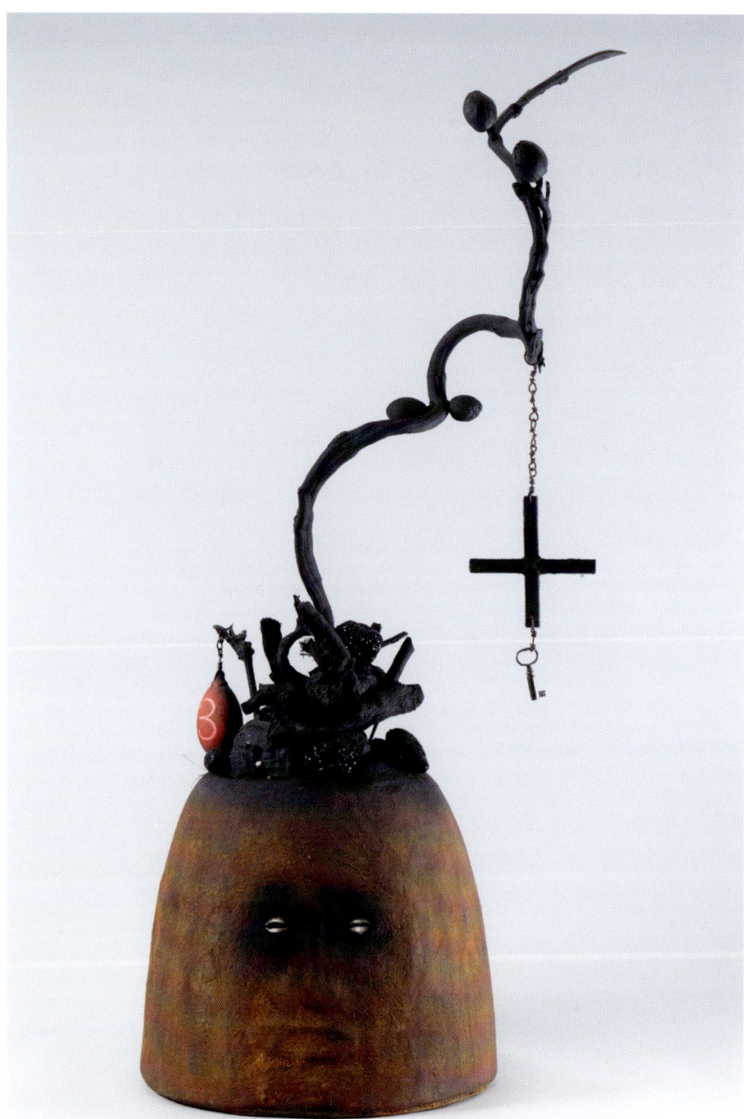

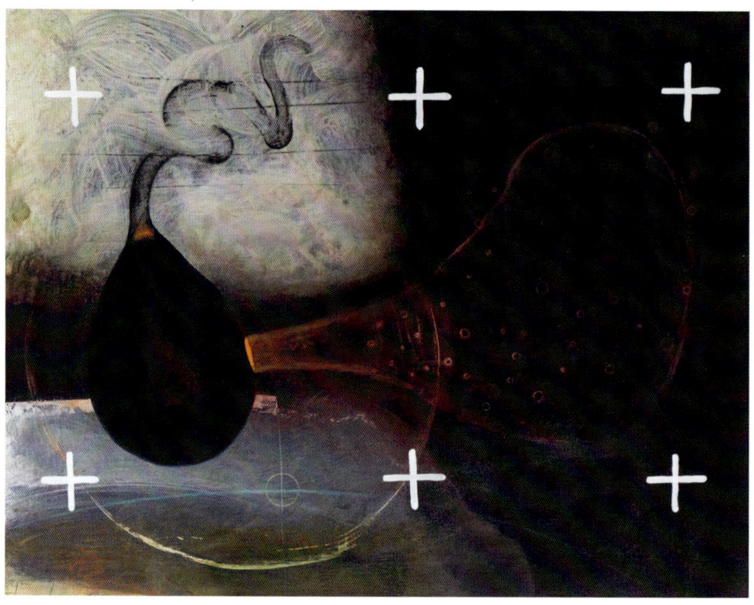

fig. 37
Renée Stout
***Elegba (Spirit of the Crossroads)*, 2015–19**
Mixed media,
39 × 17 × 13 in.
The Phillips Collection,
Washington, DC,
Gift of the artist and
Hemphill Gallery, 2019.

fig. 38
Renée Stout
***Mannish Boy Arrives (for Muddy Waters)*, 2017**
Acrylic and latex on wood panel,
16 x 20 in.
The Phillips Collection,
Washington, DC,
Director's Discretionary Fund,
2018.

choice to make at the crossroads. In the song *Mannish Boy*, bluesman Muddy Waters sings "I'm a hoochie-coochie man," invoking a veiled double meaning: the sexually provocative nineteenth-century dance and the hoodoo spiritual traditions that connected enslaved Africans of the Mississippi Delta (his birthplace) to their ancestral homeland. The "diasporic intimacy" of these traditions, as the scholar George Lipsitz has observed, allowed "displaced Africans in the American South to keep alive memories of the continent they came from through a wide range of covert practices."[40] Stout's deployment of the Elegba icon in *Mannish Boy Arrives (for Muddy Waters)* is similarly covert and coded, and the image of the crossroads serves a blues-tinged metaphysics, an imagined transitional and transcultural site where African ancestry and African American experience meet. Renée Stout's sculptures and paintings thus perform the cultural memory of the blues, conjuring a space in which the silent past resonates in the visual present.

Coda: Sites for Sight and Sound

Thinking with and through music—via its structures and forms or its vast cultural footprint—can yield new interpretations of works of visual art. In the context of the twenty-first century, in which artists continue to dissolve formal boundaries and the concept of genre, the critical lens on music and the visual arts has widened to encompass new objects and territories. In this expanded disciplinary framework, the possible points of contact between music and the visual arts become more energetic, dynamic, and interpretive. It becomes clear that in order to advance the spirit of intention laid down by Duncan Phillips, "to see as true artists see," we are compelled to open ourselves to a diversity of artistic perspectives. In its milestone centennial year, The Phillips Collection has responded to this imperative with several new commissioned musical works that explore the enlivening dialogues between visual art and music. The spirit of such a cross-disciplinary endeavor sparks a final question: can music transform what we see, and could a work of art help us hear in new ways? To confront such an intersensory provocation, we would do well to heed the words of jazz saxophonist Charlie Parker, who encouraged his audiences to "hear with your eyes and see with your ears."[41]

The epigraphs in this essay are from Paul Klee, "Creative Credo," 1920, and Sam Gilliam, quoted in Jim Lewis, "Red Orange Yellow Green and Blue Period," *W* magazine, November 28, 2014.

1 Duncan Phillips, *A Collection in the Making* (New York: E. Weyhe; Washington, DC: Phillips Memorial Gallery, 1926), 4.

2 Phillips, *A Collection in the Making*, 20.

3 Phillips, *A Collection in the Making*, 20.

4 Phillips, *A Collection in the Making*, 20.

5 Phillips, *A Collection in the Making*, 20.

6 Anne-Birgitte Fonsmark, *Delacroix: The Music of Painting* (Copenhagen: Ordrupgaard, 2000), 15.

7 See Lydia Goehr, "All Art Constantly Aspires to the Condition of Music Except the Art of Music: Reviewing the Contest of the Sister Arts," in *The Insistence of Art: Aesthetic Philosophy after Early Modernity*, ed. Paul A. Kottmann (New York: Fordham University, 2017), 140–69.

8 Walter Horatio Pater, "The School of Giorgione," in *Studies in the History of the Renaissance* (New York: Oxford University Press, 2010), 124.

9 Fonsmark, *Delacroix: The Music of Painting*, 42.

10 See Simon Shaw-Miller, *Eye hEar: The Visual in Music* (Farnham, UK: Ashgate, 2013), 3.

11 Georgina Born's 2007 article, "For a Relational Musicology: Music and Interdisciplinarity, Beyond the Practice Turn," illustrates key debates and antagonisms that have tested musicological discourse since the 1980s and 1990s. See *Journal of the Royal Musical Association* 135, no. 2 (2010): 205–43.

12 Matthias Pintscher appeared as part of the Leading International Composers series at The Phillips Collection in 2012.

13 The topic of synesthesia was researched extensively in the nineteenth century, with scientific studies conducted by German physician Georg Sachs, and anthropological studies by English theorist Francis Galton, among others.

14 Rei Terada, *Feeling in Theory: Emotion after the "Death of the Subject"* (Cambridge, MA: Harvard University Press, 2001), 94.

15 Quoted in Judith Zilczer, "Music for the Eyes: Abstract Painting and Light Art," in *Visual Music: Synaesthesia in Art and Music Since 1900* (New York: Thames & Hudson, 2005), 62.

16 See Daniel Albright, *Putting Modernism Together: Literature, Music and Painting, 1872–1927* (Baltimore: Johns Hopkins University Press, 2015), 128.

17 See Elsa Smithgall, "Undreamt Possibilities: Kandinsky's *Painting with White Border*," in *Kandinsky and the Harmony of Silence: Painting with White Border*, ed. Elsa Smithgall (Washington, DC: Phillips Collection; New Haven, CT, and London: Yale University Press), 23.

18 Quoted in Mark Evan Bonds, *Absolute Music: The History of an Idea* (Oxford: Oxford University Press, 2014), 281.

19 See Philippe Junod, *Counterpoints: Dialogues Between Music and The Visual Arts* (London: Reaktion Books, 2017), 104.

20 Henri Nouveau, quoted in Junod, *Counterpoints*, 238.

21 Quoted in *The Diaries of Paul Klee, 1898–1918* (Berkeley, Los Angeles, London: University of California Press, 1964), 374.

22 Paul Klee, *Pedagogical Sketchbook* (London: Faber & Faber, 1953), 6.

23 Philip Larson has identified Klee's various uses of arrows to signify male sexuality, aggression, or misdirection. See Larson, "Paul Klee's Music," *On Paper* 2, no. 6 (July–August 1998): 21.

24 There is a significant body of musicological literature that discusses the materiality of sound. A good starting point in this context is Carolyn Abbate's 2004 article, "Music—Drastic or Gnostic?," *Critical Inquiry* 30, no. 3 (2004): 505–36.

25 See Peter Vergo, *The Music of Painting: Music, Modernism and the Visual Arts from the Romantics to John Cage* (New York: Phaidon, 2010), 11.

26 See Graham Lock, "Introduction: The Hearing Eye," in *The Hearing Eye: Jazz & Blues Influences in African American Visual Art*, ed. Graham Lock and David Murray (Oxford: Oxford University Press, 2009), 1.

27 Sam Gilliam in conversation with Jonathan P. Binstock, February 2017. Printed in *Music of Color: Sam Gilliam 1967–1973* (Cologne: Walther König, 2018), 16.

28 Binstock, *Music of Color*, 114.

29 Wadsworth Jarrell in conversation with Graham Lock, in Lock and Murray (eds.), *The Hearing Eye*, 155.

30 Quoted in Binstock, *Music of Color*, 123.

31 Sam Gilliam, "Sam Gilliam Talks about the Influence of Jazz Music" (April 23, 2011), https://www.youtube.com/watch?v=T8chkNLRdLo. Accessed April 2020.

32 Binstock, *Music of Color*, 114.

33 Quoted in Binstock, *Music of Color*, 123.

34 Gilles Deleuze, *Francis Bacon: The Logic of Sensation*, trans. Daniel W. Smith (Minneapolis: University of Minnesota Press, 2003), 71.

35 Deleuze, *Francis Bacon*, 73.

36 Binstock, *Music of Color*, 137.

37 Binstock, *Music of Color*, 129.

38 See Lawrence W. Levine, *Black Culture and Black Consciousness: Afro-American Folk Thought from Slavery to Freedom* (Oxford: Oxford University Press, 1977), 221.

39 Paul Gilroy, *Ain't No Black in The Union Jack* (Chicago: University of Chicago Press, 1987), 156.

40 George Lipsitz, "Diasporic Intimacy in the Art of Renée Stout," in Marla C. Berns, *Dear Robert, I'll See You at the Crossroads: A Project by Renée Stout* (Seattle and London: University of Washington Press, 1995), 10.

41 Quoted by Art Blakey in Arthur Taylor, *Notes and Tones: Musician-to-Musician Interviews* (London: Quartet Books, 1983), 248.

"LEARNING TO LOOK & SEE"

Fred L. Joiner

Several years ago, the late David Driskell gave a talk in DC at a venue that now escapes my memory, but he left me with a lesson I will never forget.

He cited a book called *Learning to Look: A Handbook for the Visual Arts* by Joshua C. Taylor as having been an influential text in helping him to develop his vision of what made good art and helping him to determine if something was well made.

He talked about his many road trips to Maine and the junk shops along the way and the treasures he found in unexpected places because he learned how to look. Continuing to sharpen his eye caused him to reexamine everything around him.

I wish that I had gotten Driskell's lesson in looking when I first arrived in Washington in 1993; it was one I would fully realize much later after hearing his talk. Still, I did understand that it was a much more manageable city compared to New York, and it was overflowing with a rich history of African Americans. From the old M Street High School,[1] to the salons of Georgia Douglas Johnson and Alma Thomas, to the classrooms of Alain Locke and Sterling A. Brown, and the theatre district (in particular, the Greater U Street neighborhood and the Howard Theatre), the city was brimming with this history and it was palpable.

Pilgrimage: From Riches to Riches

My wife and I decided to leave the sable richness of Washington in October of 2013 to embark on a three-year stay in Bamako, Mali. She accepted a job in Bamako doing public health work, and I enrolled in graduate school for an MFA in Creative Writing. I was elated. This was the trip that I had been trying to figure out how to make most of my adult life.

While I would be living in Mali for an extended period, this trip was a pilgrimage of sorts for me because I had long felt a connection with West Africa due to my parental and ancestral roots in Coastal South Carolina and Georgia. It was reinforced by the study and research I had done in DC.

Although nothing could totally prepare me for what I would experience, I felt ready to engage with this new adventure in hopes that it would inform my writing, expand my worldview, and shift my thinking about artfulness, as well as art-making and how it functions in other contexts, both cultural and geographic.

In spite of the bleak picture I was given of West Africa, I was fortunate to have had a counterweight to that picture in my family and community. Besides, after twenty years in DC and the education that it afforded, I knew I would find more than bleakness in a place so rich with culture.

Time, Timing, Grace, & Everyday Magic, or Finding Art & Poetry in Everyday Things

In my study and my thirst for knowledge about West Africa, I had seen many images and videos of people carrying things on their heads while going about their everyday lives, but being on the ground, immersed in the context from which those images came, was an invaluable education.

What struck me most was the grace and elegance with which people seemed to move—especially the women. It was not only their grace in movement, but also the contrast between how easily they moved from place to place and how busily they went about

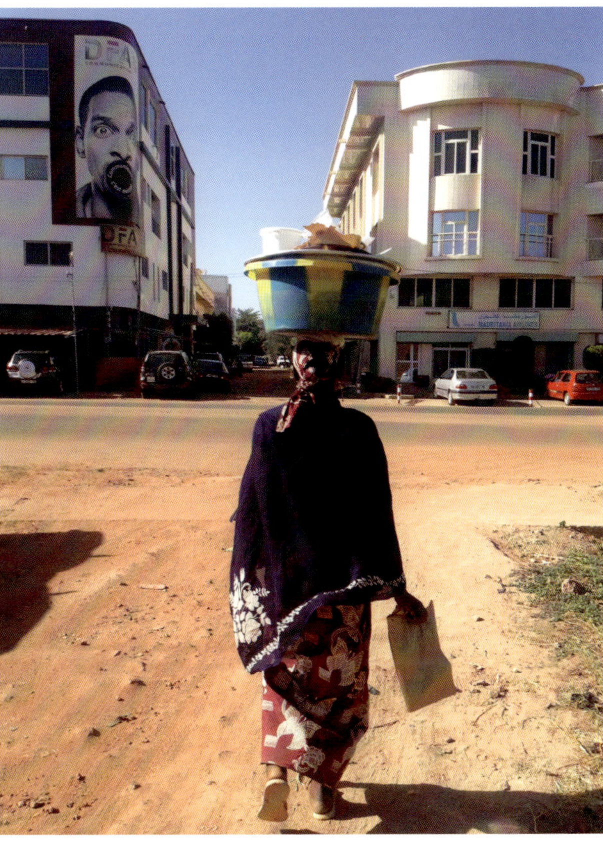

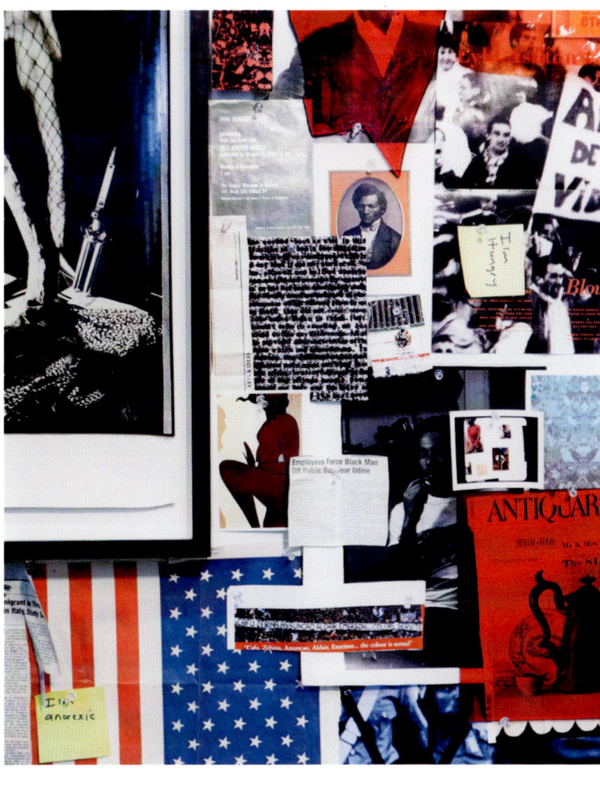

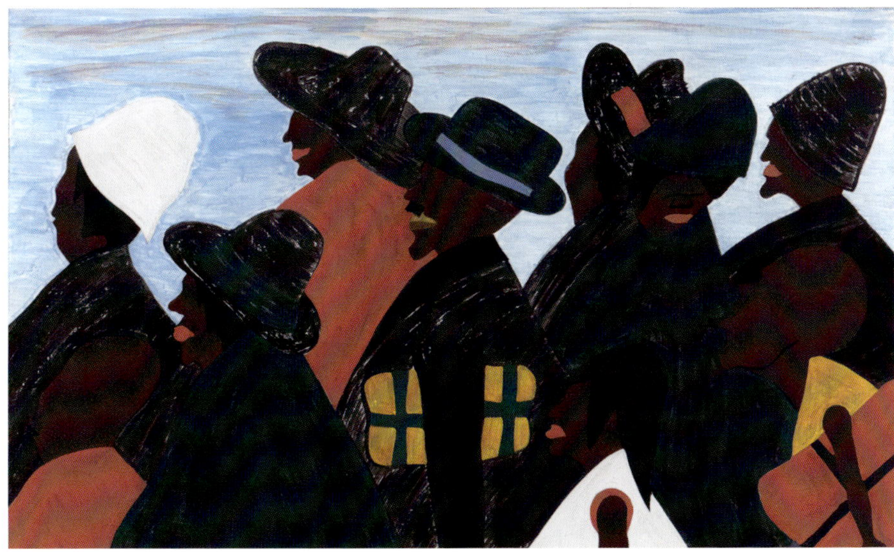

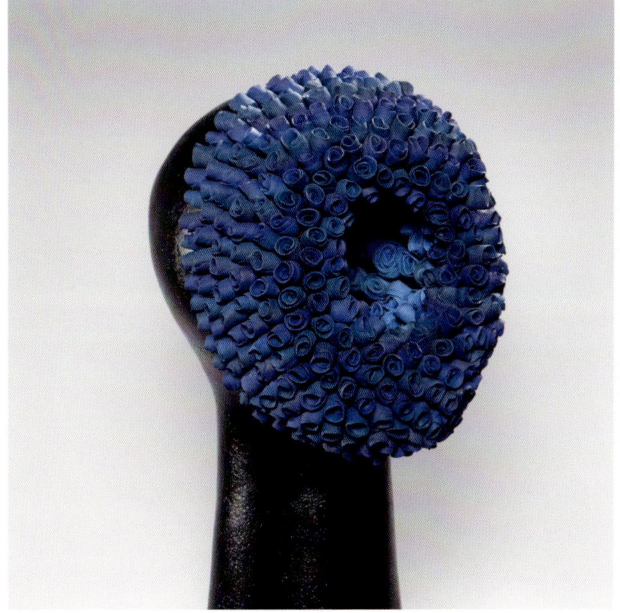

(clockwise from top left)

fig. 39
***Royalty*, 2013**
Image courtesy of the author.

fig. 40
Lyle Ashton Harris
***Blow Up II (Armory)*, detail (from "America Now + Here: Photography Portfolio 2009"), 2005**
Chromogenic print,
24 × 20 in.
The Phillips Collection,
Washington, DC,
Gift of Carolyn Alper, 2010.

fig. 41
Simone Leigh
***No Face (Crown Heights)*, detail, 2018**
Terracotta, graphite ink, salt-fired porcelain and epoxy,
20 × 8 × 8 in.
The Phillips Collection,
Washington, DC,
Director's Discretionary Fund, 2019.

fig. 42
Jacob Lawrence
***The Migration Series*, Panel no. 35: They left the South in great numbers. They arrived in the North in great numbers, between 1940 and 1941**
Casein tempera on hardboard,
12 × 18 in.
The Phillips Collection,
Washington, DC,
Acquired 1942.

their work; work essential to the proper functioning of the country, transporting food to the market for sale, transporting finely tailored bazin and wax-print, most times while also carrying at least one child, with another one or two in tow. As much as I think the women made a dance of their work, I also think it may have to do with time and timing, the unrushed attention, steps, and deliberation it takes to carry life on your hips and sustenance on your shoulders, to move through the Sahel's heat at a pace that cools you, to move through the streets of a city freighted with the weight of life in a country where so little is under your control.

During my first month in Mali, I often walked out of our apartment with my phone and film cameras, to take a walk, to take pictures (fig. 39), and to learn my way around the neighborhood. I told myself that no matter how long I stayed in West Africa, I never wanted to allow myself to not see and marvel at the everyday magic of the women in Mali.

the everyday magic
of thriving in a world
that totalizes you, reduces
all your complexity
to fetish,
to an oddity
of obedience

& dust under the foot
of everything, the paradox
of being unthought,
thought of as nothing

& yet being the soil
& sustenance that nurtures
everything.

As I walked down the orange dirt road, I saw my friend's sister, a strong but slight woman with shoulders barely wider than her narrow hips, carrying three enormous metal pots on her head. She was gliding. She was taking the pots to the small shanty restaurant their family owned about five miles away. These pots were very heavy, probably weighing about forty pounds altogether, but she refused my help and went along her way. Before she was out of earshot I asked her if I could take a photo of her. She agreed and the seed of a poem sat with me for many months before I could put pen to paper.

Anatomy of Malian Woman

Head
a cornucopia crown
atop
a neck
an archetypal posture
atop shoulders that shoulder
a day's work

Back
the spine of a notion
the face on a bill
that folds into
the pocket of a man
that lays her on
that ladder of bone. Legs open.
the birth of a nation

Hips
always at work
carrying
always in motion
children clinging like dust

Feet
dressed in royalty's
dust, Harmattan's winds
dance after her steps.

In the Womb

Providentially, around that same time, I was revisiting Pablo Neruda's collection of poems, *Odes to Common Things*, which not only reminded me of the poetry of everyday things and where else poetry can be found, but also where *art* can be found. The more time I spent in Mali (and in the region), the more I saw myself in the people, and the more connections I started to make between my US low-country-born elders and ancestors from Coastal South Carolina and Georgia, and my Family Across the Sea.[2] More and more I began to see the artfulness of their living that comes from the beauty they create in thriving, in refusing to be ruled by erasure, to literally be the Bamana or Bambara.

It was in the midst of this womb of ideas that I was introduced to Simone Leigh's work.

I cannot see
Simone Leigh's work
& not think
of the women who made
me   the ancient, sable
pillars of my spine,
& not see
the world
that seeks to unmake
them, to unsee them,
then when seen
only see them as spectacle
or receptacle.

Embarrassingly, I was introduced to Simone Leigh's work only after briefly meeting her in Senegal. My wife and I were on a short vacation in Dakar, before heading back to the United States to birth our oldest daughter, Naomi. It was our good fortune that not only was Senegal's longstanding biennial, Dak'Art, convening but the Global Black Consciousness Conference was also taking place. After meeting Leigh in the afternoon, I made a point to find her work at Dak'Art and to do some more research on her. When I found her work at the conference, it immediately caught my attention because its title came from a Gwendolyn Brooks poem, "my dreams, my works, must wait till after hell".... I was quite surprised, because I had been told she was a sculptor, and this piece was a video installation.

Since then I have tried to follow Leigh's work, and I was pleasantly surprised again to see that *No Face (Crown Heights)* (fig. 41) has found a home at the Phillips.

They look at us
& think us empty
but we are full of all
of us, all our wombs
& hands have made these things.
Call us, I Am.
No Face (Crown Heights)

It is overdue as an investment in living Black artists, and Black women artists in particular. It is important as a cultural artifact that is crafted in the present, but moves both forward and backward in time, making use of contemporary techniques and traditions across the Black Atlantic, the Low Country Southern US, and well into the ancient, creative heart of Africa.

It meant the world to me to walk into the Phillips as a nineteen-year-old and see the work of Alma Thomas, Horace Pippin, Sam Gilliam (pl. 116; fig. 36), and of course Jacob Lawrence (fig. 42). I can only imagine what it will mean to today's youth of color to see the work of Renée Stout (pl. 192; figs 37–38), Mary Lee Bendolph (pl. 78), Lucy T. Pettway (pl. 76), Malissia Pettway (pl. 77), Whitfield Lovell (pls. 134–135), Wilmer Wilson IV, Lyle Ashton Harris (fig. 40), and others whose works give the viewer an ever fuller vision of African American and diasporic African life.

Seeing this and other recent investments in Leigh's work gives me hope that more portals of collaboration will open and more communities will be built around this work and work like it which challenges hegemonic collecting initiatives that have kept so many Black artists out of critical conversations in the art world. I think the presence of work like Leigh's will inspire future generations of artists, who may not see how their obsessions, work, and practice fit into a larger discussion about contemporary art, or who may not yet understand the value of their work, which may center on subjects that have historically been unseen, erased, or made invisible.

The fact that Leigh's work is in a collection like the Phillips is an acknowledgment of the artfulness and genius of Black women's ability to make living look like magic and art. To see this is to recognize their ability to make art out of survival, or even to make art out of the things that, like Lucille Clifton said, "everyday have tried to kill them and have failed,"[3] or, like Neruda said, to make poetry and odes to the genius and beauty of common things, everyday things. This work holds up a mirror to our own richness, moving in our time, urging us to self-define and to take up as much space as we require.

1 The M Street High School, now the Perry School, was once one of the country's most important preparatory schools for African Americans.

2 *Family Across the Sea* is a documentary that shows the connections between Coastal South Carolinians and communities in West Africa.

3 In her poem "won't you celebrate with me," Lucille Clifton wrote: "... everyday / something has tried to kill me / and has failed." See https://www.poetryfoundation.org/poems/50974/wont-you-celebrate-with-me. Accessed April 2020.

EXCELSIOR AND THE CONTEMPORARY

Kent Mitchell Minturn

Acquired by The Phillips Collection in 2008, Alfonso Ossorio's mesmerizing assemblage *Excelsior* (fig. 43) consists of a wide array of miscellaneous objects and materials—seashells, bones, prosthetic glass eyes, marbles, coins, brass, sand, rope, and two halftone reproductions (of a young saint or martyr at the top, and an older man, possibly a pensive St. Paul, at the bottom)—secured to a wooden board. Also attached are a thin branch and piece of driftwood that divide the vertically aligned composition into roughly symmetrical halves. The work represents one of the first instances in which Ossorio abandons oil paint as his primary binding agent for a plastic polyvinyl resin and glue paste.

Born in Manila to a Spanish father and Chinese-Philippine mother, Ossorio was raised in a strict yet multicultural Roman Catholic environment. His childhood, he later said, was not particularly happy.[1] He was educated at Harvard University where, in 1938, he wrote a senior thesis on "Spiritual Influences on the Visual Image of Christ." During World War II, he served as a medical illustrator for the United States Army. From early 1950 until the fall of that year, Ossorio returned to the Philippines—to Victorias, in the island province of Negros Occidental—to paint a mural depicting Christ on Judgment Day, in the Chapel of St. Joseph the Worker, a church erected for the employees of his family's sugar refinery.[2]

The mural project was constraining, requiring Ossorio to stay within the confines of traditional Christian iconography.[3] As a release, he began a series of approximately four hundred drawings, gouaches, and watercolors. Fast, spontaneous, and free, they readily oscillate between figuration and abstraction (see fig. 44). Here, Ossorio took liberties and tried something new, a wax-resist technique that he admitted he had borrowed from Romanian surrealist Victor Brauner, whose work had appeared in a recent issue of *Cahiers d'art*.[4] The Victorias drawings, as they came to be known—technically, they are paintings—were the subject of a book written by fellow artist and friend Jean Dubuffet. In it, he rightly refers to them as Ossorio's "over-flow," decorations for his "own personal and private Church."[5]

In their freedom and experimentation, these works anticipate Ossorio's *Congregations* series, of which *Excelsior* is a major early example. The remarkable photos taken of Ossorio's studio during the 1960s show a variegated collection of objects grouped on

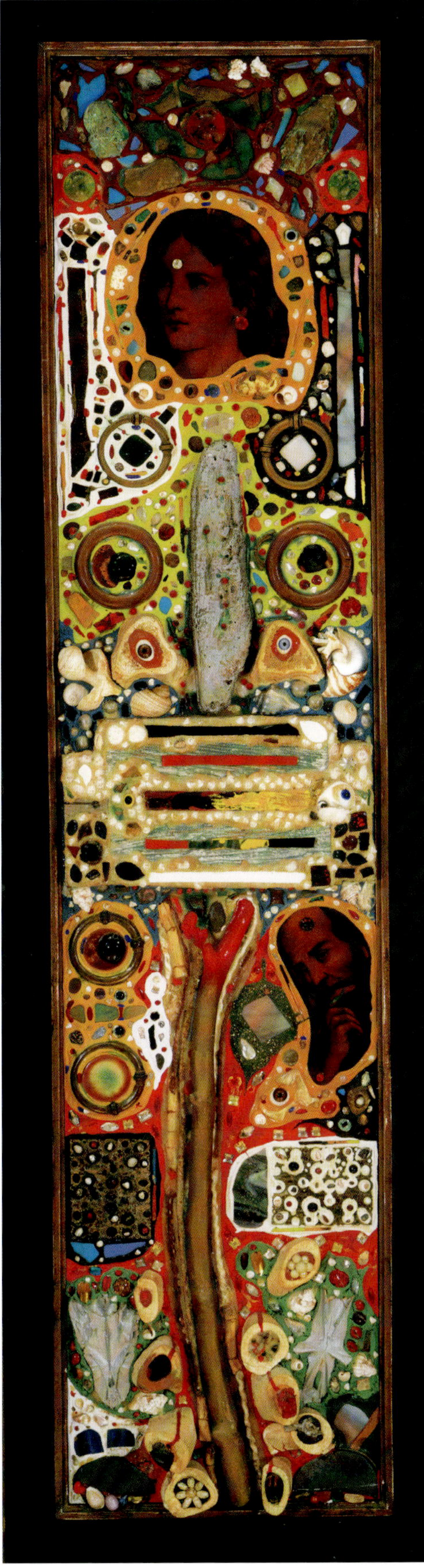

fig. 43
Alfonso Ossorio
***Excelsior*, 1960**
Mixed media assemblage, 56 × 12 in.
The Phillips Collection, Washington, DC,
The Dreier Fund for Acquisitions, 2008.

the floor and hung on the walls, organized by some impenetrable and idiosyncratic classificatory system, and give insight into his working methods. Scholar Ellen G. Landau has related Ossorio's creative process to the structuralist activity of bricolage (from the French for the improvisational puttering of the handyman or do-it-yourselfer) as described by anthropologist Claude Lévi-Strauss in *La Pensée sauvage* (1962). According to Lévi-Strauss, the rules of the bricoleur's "game are always to make do with 'whatever is at hand,' that is to say with a set of tools and materials which is always finite and is also heterogeneous." Further, he argues, the bricoleur "has to turn back to an already existent set made up of tools and materials, to consider or reconsider what it contains and, finally and above all, to engage in a sort of dialogue with it and, before choosing between them, to index the possible answers which the whole set can offer his problem."[6] The analogy is tempting. Indeed, Ossorio's artistic ritual involved tinkering and *ad hoc* maneuverings. In an interview with the Archives of American Art, he explained:

> I do a sketch of a background. The ground is done first. Then I place the objects on the panel that they'll finally end up on. Once that is more or less settled they're all removed, put on another table, and I put the pastes and the adherents on and work that way. Which means that always there is a certain amount of adjustment to make simply because of displacement of volume and that sort of thing. Frequently there are changes as I work on the final panel.[7]

But in many ways the structuralist paradigm is too reductive, tending to diminish Ossorio's agency and authorship, and failing to take into consideration his biography and religious beliefs. Whereas it is true that Ossorio repeatedly uses a certain set of materials in his *Congregations*—especially osso buco bones, eyes, mirrors, fake jewelry, and seashells—his set is neither finite nor unchanging. Many of the *Congregations* contain one-off elements, like the two-dimensional illustrations from an art tome in *Excelsior*. His strategy is perhaps better understood as "Repeat and Change," to borrow a title from another *Congregation* completed the same year. It is not only the objects and materials that evolve over time, but the format of the works as well: the *Congregations* eventually expand beyond their frames, becoming freestanding sculptures. Further, what Ossorio includes is not haphazard; his materials

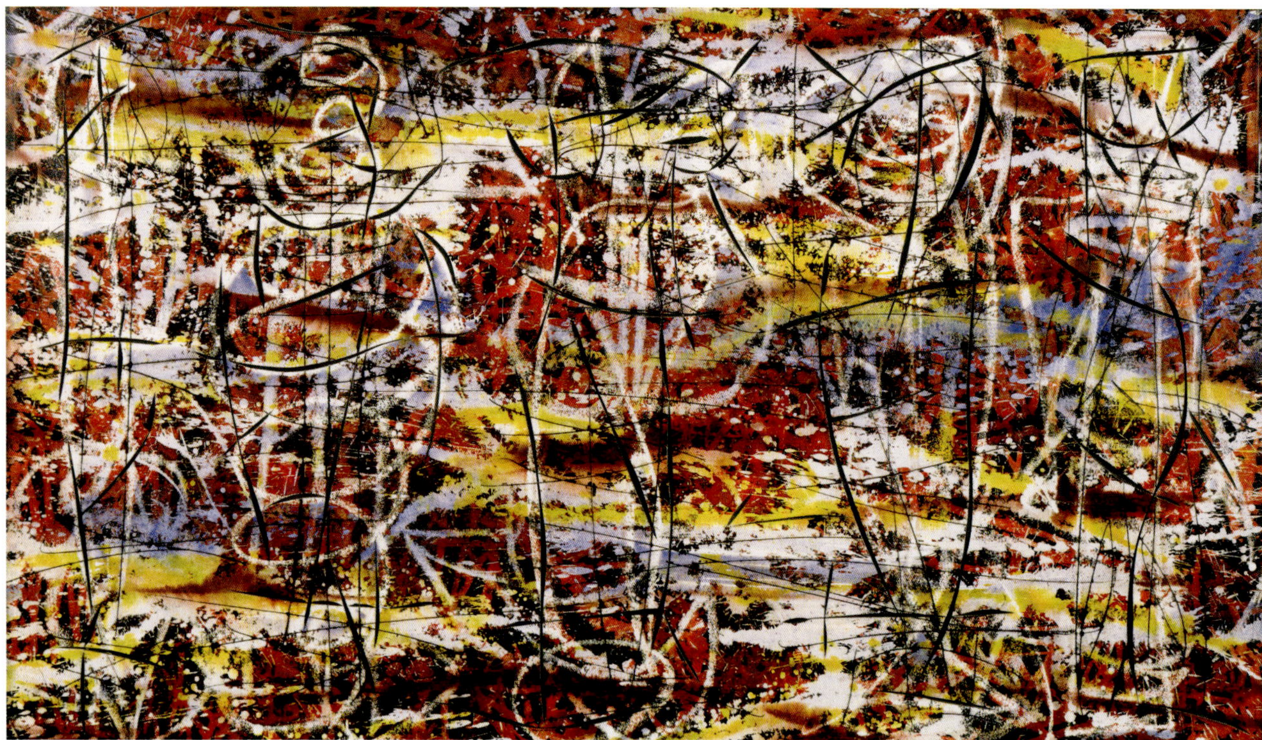

fig. 44
Alfonso Ossorio
***Five Brothers*, 1950**
Watercolor, wax resist, and pen and brush black ink on illustration board, 18 3/8 × 30 1/4 in.
The Phillips Collection, Washington, DC, Acquired 1951.

are not just things he had "at hand." Those who knew him and visited his studio are quick to recount how many of these materials were carefully chosen and had to be mail-ordered. Also, Ossorio was not simply "turning back" and looking at some pre-existing model or set of possibilities for inspiration. This was essentially the argument of curator William Seitz, who included Ossorio's *Excelsior* in the Museum of Modern Art's groundbreaking show, *Assemblage* (1961). Seitz's vague definition of assemblage—"setting one thing beside another without a connective"—and his attempts to relate Ossorio's piece to the prewar collages, montages, readymades, and objets trouvés found in works by Jean Arp, Georges Braque, Marcel Duchamp, Pablo Picasso, and Kurt Schwitters do not tally with the artist's actual practice.

A constant in the *Congregations* is Ossorio's unprecedented inclusion of glass eyes. About these, he said:

> I've employed a great quantity in a great many pictures. They do remain concentric circles. They are a visual element in that sense. But they have the added overtones of being animal eyes, human eyes; they have all that sudden sense of dedication or power. They have multiple meanings.[8]

His early *Congregation, Cyclops and Argus II* refers directly to the mythological figure with eyes covering his body, the origin of the phrase "to be followed by the eyes of Argus," that is, to be the subject of intense scrutiny. We can imagine that by 1960 Ossorio had grown weary of how others saw him; he was often overlooked, perceived—or written off—as a wealthy collector, a Hamptons socialite, a gallery director (Signa Gallery, East Hampton), or a derivative follower of Jean Dubuffet and Jackson Pollock. He was also openly gay. Ossorio's *Congregations* turn this gaze back on the observer and remind us that these eyes, which are always open and staring, cannot truly see.

The *Congregations* are shockingly original and forward-looking, blending high and low, avant-garde and kitsch, handmade and mass-produced, private and public. They pave the way for the advanced practices of a host of younger artists in the last three decades of the twentieth century, including John Chamberlain, Bruce Conner, Ed Kienholz, Julian Schnabel, and Richard Tuttle. Mike Kelley's late 1990s *Memory Ware Series* (see fig. 45), with its emphasis on heterogeneity, nostalgia, and a mixing of the public and the private, seems particularly indebted to Ossorio.

Further, *Excelsior* is singularly important because it reintroduces overtly religious subject matter, in a non-

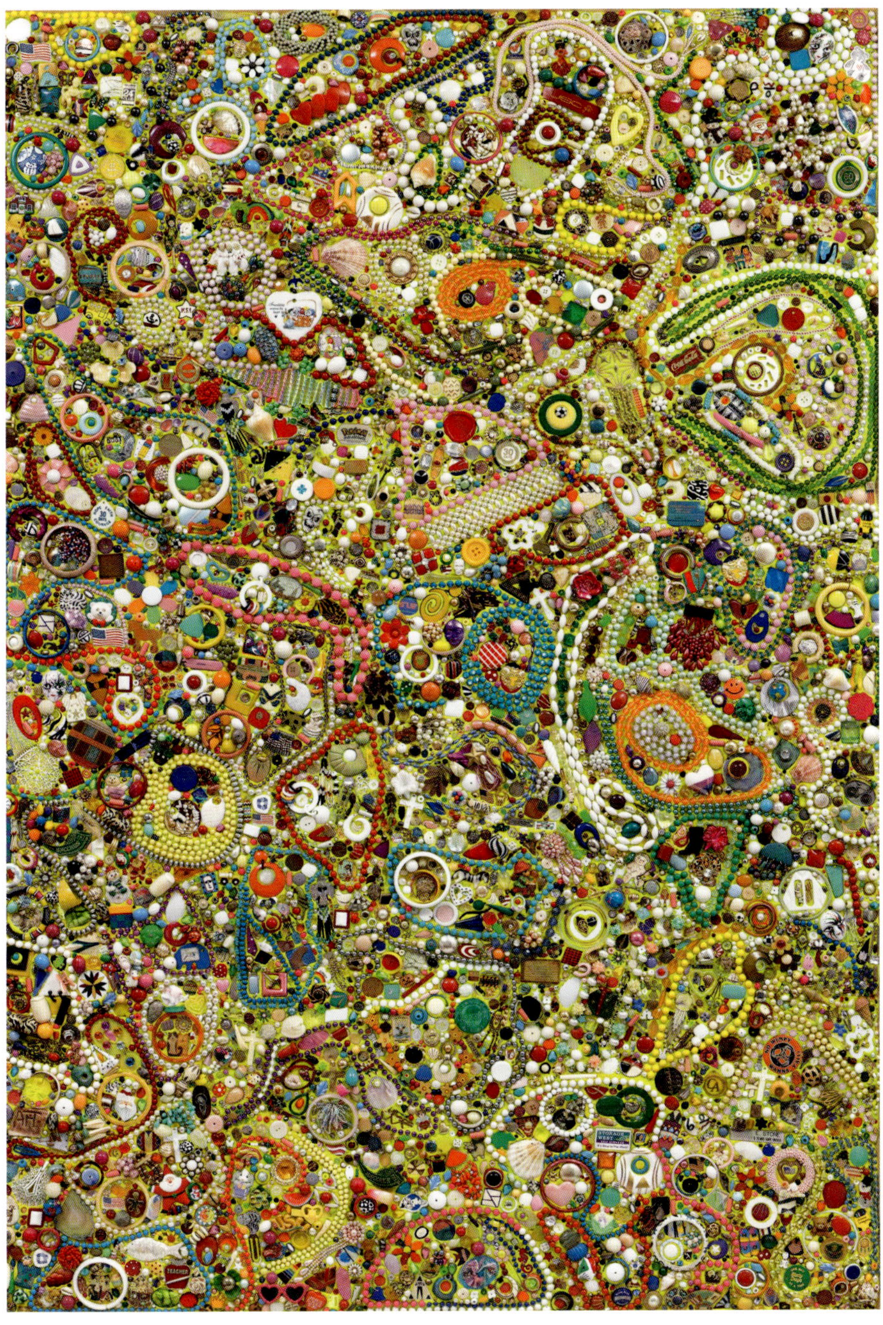

fig. 45
Mike Kelley
***Memory Ware Flat #41*, 2003**
Mixed media on wood panel, 76 1/4 × 52 1/8 × 4 in. Collection Metro Pictures, New York.

abstract manner, into advanced postwar American art.[9] It bravely and unabashedly hypostatizes ideas central to Ossorio's own unorthodox belief system:

> Religion is tying together, as far as one can, certain ultimate verities in terms of what makes up a human being, what makes up the forces in our existence.... The human being is the link between God and the material world. Which is the whole idea of the sacrifice of the mass. It's all one kettle of fish. It is simply that it is all one unity. Even a little waste piece of plastic or a bone is just as much alive as the abstract concept of God, which is meaningless unless it is incarnated.[10]

Etymologically, the exclamation "excelsior" means to move above and beyond. Ossorio's assemblage ultimately asks the contemporary viewer to bear witness to his move beyond Catholicism to a humbler artistic catholicism.

1 See Francis V. O'Connor, "Alfonso Ossorio's Expressionist Paintings on Paper," in *The Child Returns 1950—Philippines Expressionist Paintings on Paper, November 5, 1998–January 9, 1999* (New York: Michael Rosenfeld Gallery, 1998), 4–16.
2 Adé de Béthune, "Philippine Adventure," in *Liturgical Arts* 19 (August 1951): 112–13.
3 Eric Torres, *The Chapel of St. Joseph the Worker* (Negros Occidental: Victorias Milling Company, 1967).
4 Ossorio, quoted in "Interview: Alfonso Ossorio Talks with Paul Cummings," *Drawing* 7, no. 5 (January–February 1986): 107. Victor Brauner, "Dessin à la bougie," *Cahiers d'art*, 20–21 (1945–46): 314.
5 Jean Dubuffet, *Peintures initiatiques d'Alfonso Ossorio* (Paris: La Pierre Volante, 1951), 18.
6 Ellen G. Landau, "Alfonso Ossorio: Behind the Congregations," in *Alfonso Ossorio: Congregations* (Southampton, NY: The Parrish Art Museum, 1997), 23–29, 27. For the Lévi-Strauss passage, see the English translation, *The Savage Mind* (Chicago: University of Chicago Press, 1966), 17.
7 Alfonso Ossorio, oral history interview with Forrest Selvig, November 19, 1968, Archives of American Art, Washington, DC, https://www.aaa.si.edu/collections/interviews/oral-history-interview-alfonso-ossorio-5517. Accessed April 2020.
8 Alfonso Ossorio, oral history interview with Forrest Selvig.
9 Cf. Thomas Crow, *No Idols: The Missing Theology of Art* (Sydney: Power Publications, 2017), especially the final chapter, "Conclusion and a Return to Catholicism."
10 Alfonso Ossorio, oral history interview with Forrest Selvig.

IN THE ROUND: FROM DRAWING TO SCULPTURE

Jed Morse

At first glance, drawing and sculpture could not be more divergent forms of expression. Drawing appears cerebral, delicate—the rendering of a believable three-dimensional image on the flat plane of the paper. Sculpture embodies the physical, manipulating masses of material—clay, wood, stone, metal—with the strength of the artist's own hands or the forces of industrial manufacturing. With the incorporation of mold makers, foundries, and fabricators, sculpture can be a communal act. Drawing, on the other hand, is often a solitary pursuit, akin to writing, with the creator facing the blank sheet of paper with all of the potential and anxiety it represents. But the two art forms have been intimately linked for centuries. In the eighteenth and nineteenth centuries, academies trained artists to draw by having them recreate on paper what they saw in plaster casts of ancient Greek and Roman sculptures. Those who were to specialize in sculpture, in turn, learned to think through drawing, planning their sculptural compositions on paper first before dedicating the time and resources required for sculpting. In the twentieth century, artists began to reconsider and, sometimes, cast aside such rigid artistic traditions of pedagogy and practice, making relationships between drawing and sculpture less prescribed, more fluid, immediate, and indeterminate.

Although Seymour Lipton had no formal artistic training, his practice largely followed the traditional model established by art academies of centuries past: setting ideas down quickly in black crayon on typing paper, then developing the forms in small maquettes before realizing them at full size. Lipton's rational practice, however, relied on the automatism and psychological freedom advocated by the surrealists and

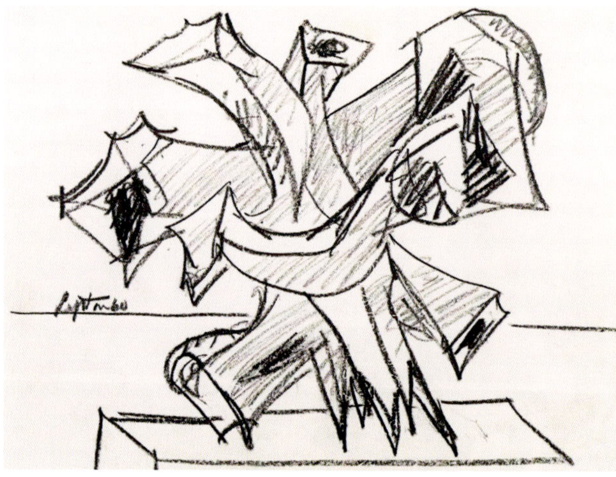

fig. 46
Seymour Lipton
***Untitled*, 1960**
Black crayon on paper,
8 1/2 × 11 in.
The Phillips Collection,
Washington, DC,
Gift of Alan Lipton, 2009.

fig. 47 (left)
Manuel Neri
***Amante Series No. 14*, 2009**
Watercolor and charcoal on paper,
16 1/8 × 11 3/4 in.
The Phillips Collection, Washington, DC,
Gift of the Manuel Neri Trust, 2018.

fig. 48 (top right)
Manuel Neri
***Amante Series No. 1*, 2009**
Watercolor and charcoal on paper,
16 1/8 × 11 3/4 in.
The Phillips Collection, Washington, DC,
Gift of the Manuel Neri Trust, 2018.

fig. 49 (bottom right)
Manuel Neri
***Amante Series No. 5*, 2009**
Watercolor and charcoal on paper,
16 1/8 × 11 3/4 in.
The Phillips Collection, Washington, DC,
Gift of the Manuel Neri Trust, 2018.

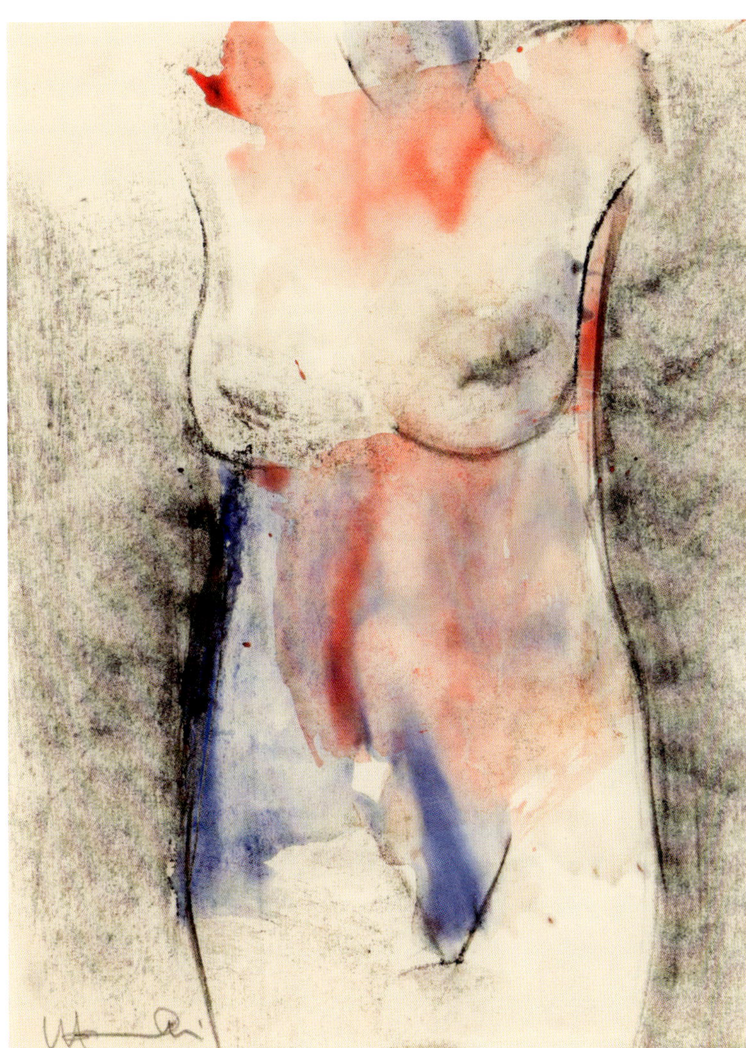

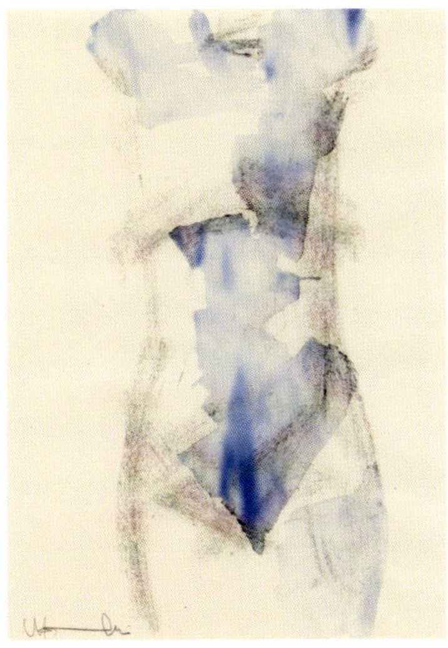

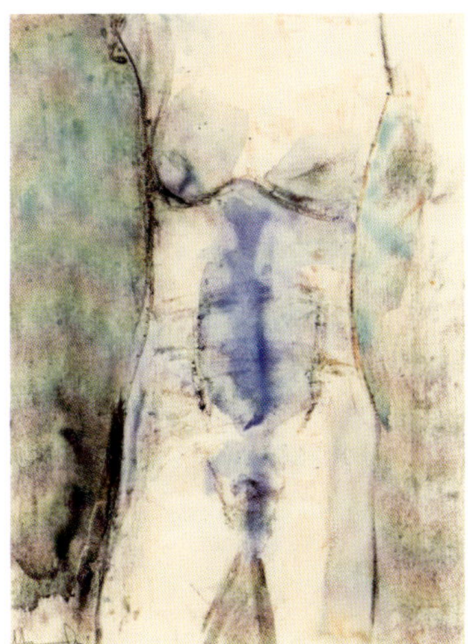

abstract expressionists, movements in which the artist participated. Lipton explained in 1949:

> On an instinctive level, I explore new worlds of three-dimensional form, making drawings and small plasticene models preparatory to finished work. This is a withdrawal into a subjective, imaginative and almost automatic world of formal invention and discovery. It is a reaching for formal equivalents to the substance of experience. It is also a realm of free play of forms for the sake of form. It is not an anarchic world, however, because it is guided somewhat unconsciously by the compass of previous experience.[1]

Lipton's sketched sculptural dreams often took surprisingly vivid physical forms. His drawings invariably ground the imagined object in space, rising from a ground-level plane, pedestal, or architectural support, lending the drawings a sense of ambient space and the depicted forms a sense of scale. Sculptural forms often developed over time through multiple iterations on paper, ranging from quick sketches to careful renderings. *Untitled*, 1960 (fig. 46), is one of several related drawings of a sculptural idea that would eventually take monumental form in *Archangel*, a commission for Philharmonic Hall at Lincoln Center in 1963.

Many sculptors have used both sculpture and drawings as a way to explore a motif repeatedly. Manuel Neri, an important figure of the Bay Area Figurative movement, began drawing and sculpting the female figure in the late 1950s as a symbol of humanity in general. At once awkward, sensual, and violent in tone, Neri's works highlight the profundity of human experience, often incorporating elements that blur distinctions between physical and psychological space, as well as classicism and modernity. *Torso Bronze Maquette I*, 1993, in The Phillips Collection, exhibits a rough, abraded surface suggesting psychological tensions; whereas *Torso Maquette II*, 1993, also in the Phillips, appears honed and smooth through much of the figure, but coarse where the limbs would be, recalling an ancient fragment. Neri drew studies before, during, and after the production of his sculptures, continually mining the expressive potential of the subjects' balance, proportion, and pose, as well as his handling of the materials. The *Amante Series* of 2009 returns again to the motif of the torso, shifting its potential meanings through subtle adjustments in orientation and application of pigments, with *No. 14* well-defined and sensuous, *No. 5* wan and emaciated, and *No. 1* fleeting and ephemeral (figs. 47–49).

Much of the interwoven relationship between drawing and sculpture in the twentieth century can be attributed to the separation of drawing from depiction and the use of line in service of invention or expression alone. New materials available to sculptors, such as wire and nylon monofilament, encouraged the affiliation between the two practices. Spanish sculptor Julio González, who forged and welded his own iron compositions as well as Pablo Picasso's initial welded sculptures in the late 1920s and early 1930s, famously likened the process to "drawing in space." Artists have been exploring the expressive possibilities of a line elaborated in space since the early part of the twentieth century, from Alexander Calder's whimsical *Hollow Egg*, 1939 (pl. 110), to Alyson Shotz's analytical *Allusion of Gravity*, 2005 (pl. 111).

David Smith, who first encountered González's and Picasso's welded sculptures in 1930 in the pages of the French avant-garde periodical *Cahiers d'art*, became the primary purveyor and investigator of this new relationship between sculpture and drawing. Smith made works on paper and canvas throughout his career, alongside his sculptures. At times his sketches and drawings took the form of studies for his sculptures, but his work on paper also took on a life of its own. Drawing and sculpting were parallel practices of artistic and self-exploration that were mutually reinforcing but often had no apparent connection to each other. Drawings in brush and egg ink, such as *Untitled*, 1959 (fig. 50), are emblematic of Smith's parallel investigations on paper and embody the statement in his 1957 sketchbook: "my drawing is meant to reveal me as one man, it comes from my life, my problems ... nothing put down with force and conviction is meaningless."[2] His sculptures, such as *Bouquet of Concaves*, 1959 (pl. 74), often exhibit the physical tension between tight, planar composition (more akin to drawing) and three-dimensional elaboration in space. Part of this is due to the nature of Smith's practice of building welded steel sculpture: he often laid out bits of steel on the floor of his studio to work out his compositions, seeing them initially as relatively flat arrays of shapes, welding them together, then standing them up and expanding the sculpture in depth. In turn, seeing the outline of the composition burned onto the floor by his torch led Smith to similar explorations of abstract compositions on paper and canvas known as the *Sprays*.

Sculptors often bring their form-making concerns to their image making, attending to the tactility

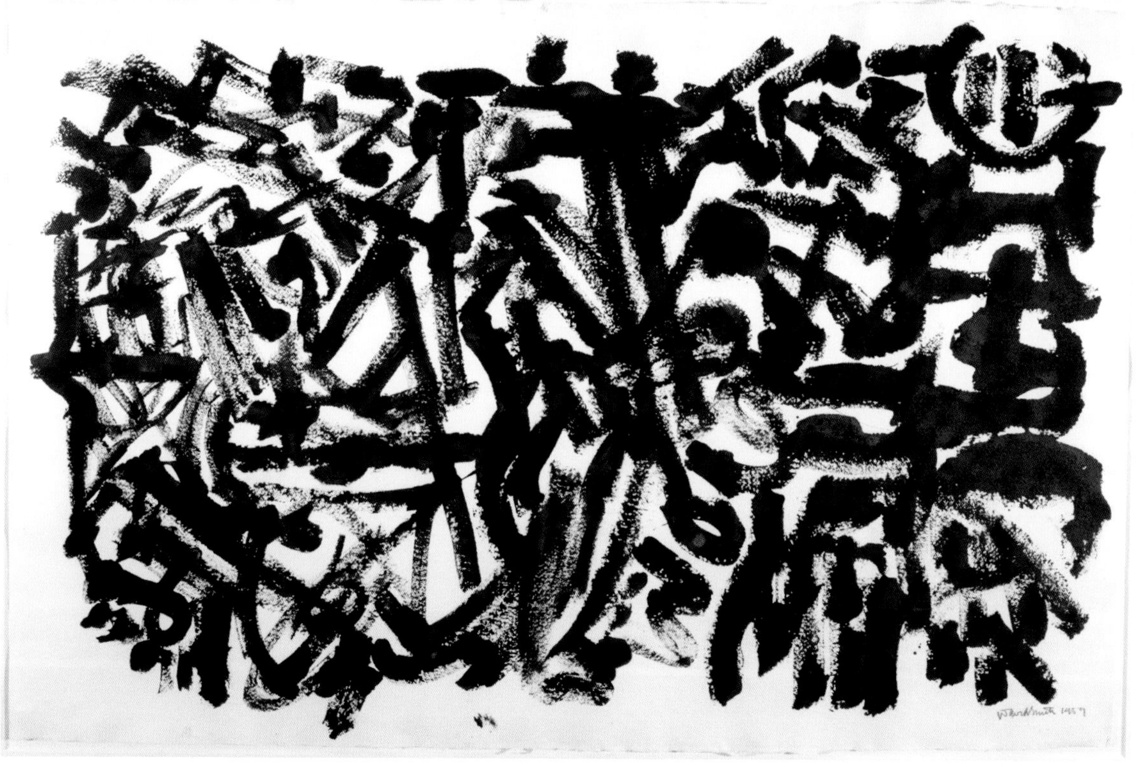

fig. 50
David Smith
***Untitled*, 1959**
Black egg ink on handmade paper, 27 × 39 1/2 in.
The Phillips Collection, Washington, DC, Gift of Linda Lichtenberg Kaplan, 2004.

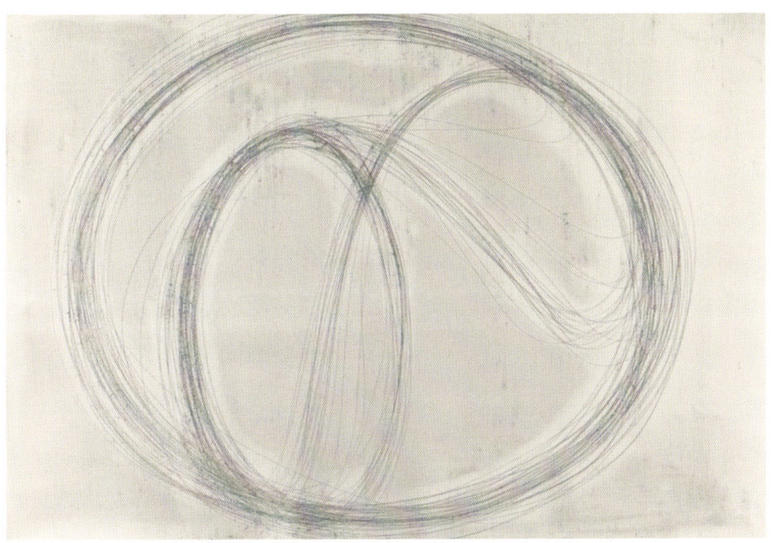

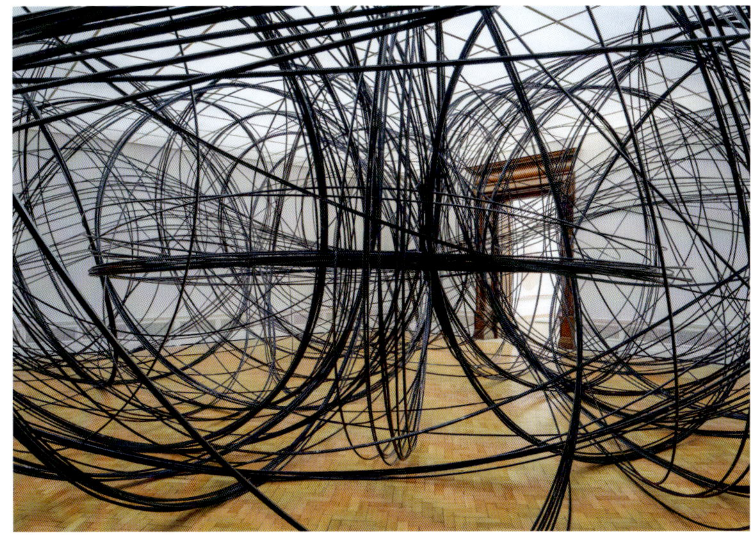

fig. 51 (left)
Antony Gormley
***Clearing 104*, 2009**
Carbon and casein on paper, 30 1/4 × 43 3/4 in.
The Phillips Collection, Washington, DC,
Gift of the artist, 2012.

fig. 52 (right)
Antony Gormley
***Clearing VII*, 2019**
Approximately 8 km (5 miles) of 1/2 in. square-section 16 standard wire gauge aluminum tube, dimensions variable. Installation, *Antony Gormley*, Royal Academy of Arts, London, September 21–December 3, 2019.

and physicality of their work on paper as they would their sculpture. Joel Shapiro has explored the myriad formal and expressive possibilities of highly distilled arrangements of geometric forms in bronze and pigmented wood. Alongside this sculpture practice he has made hundreds of works on paper. Many of these, such as *Untitled* (1997; The Phillips Collection), investigate similar concerns to the sculptures, but expand on them through Shapiro's attention to the material particularities of the medium. Charcoal and pastel forms resemble his pigmented wood structures, but the artist spreads and smears the pigment on the paper, exploring an atmospheric quality specific to the space of the page. Similarly, Richard Serra has pushed his drawings and prints to express qualities he elicits from his monumental steel sculptures. Etchings such as *Venice Notebook Series #19* (2003; The Phillips Collection), which derive from aerial drawings he made of his work in the 2001 Venice Biennale, push the limits of the medium to deliver a printed image that conveys the weight, obduracy, movement, and tactility of his sculpture.

New generations of artists continue to expand upon the nature of both sculpture and drawing. The work of Antony Gormley explores existential questions of time and space through a fixation on the experience of the human body. The drawing *Clearing 104* (fig. 51) relates to a series of musings on the rationalization and delimiting of space that culminated in an ongoing series of room-filling installations of kilometers of curled aluminum tube which started in 2004. Gormley wrote of this project that he "was trying to destroy the fixed co-ordinates of a room and make a space/time continuum (a line without end) that was both a thing and a drawing."[3] His drawing represents the concept contained in the installation in a single, fluid, continuous gesture occupying the space of the page, much as the aluminum tube is a single, fluid, continuous gesture in the space of the room (fig. 52).

With each expansion of means come significant conceptual shifts. As the world changes, artists reconceive how and why to make art. For some artists, digital sketches and renderings have become significant ways of exploring ideas in progress, just as computer-aided modeling and carving have become the preferred means of production for others. The relationship between media in service of expression will, undoubtedly, continue to evolve in ways as yet unimagined.

1 Seymour Lipton, "Experience and Sculptural Form," *College Art Journal* 9, no. 1 (Autumn 1949): 53.
2 David Smith, handwritten notes, 1957, Sketchbook 51: 285. Reprinted in Susan J. Cooke, ed., *David Smith: Collected Writings, Lectures, and Interviews* (Oakland: University of California Press, 2018), 289.
3 Antony Gormley, http://www.antonygormley.com/projects/item-view/id/240#p0. Accessed April 2020.

SAN FRANCISCO MODERN: FRANK LOBDELL AND MANUEL NERI

Bruce Nixon

In the decades following World War II, artists on the West Coast labored in the shadow of a peculiar paradox. On the one hand, they were largely overlooked by the cultural establishment back East, a situation that allowed them to develop in ways quite free from the pressures of the marketplace, critical taste, or the needs of the major museums. As a result, the region would, over a period of fifteen or twenty years, produce a striking number of artists characterized by their individuality, intelligence, and originality, and by little, if any, adherence, to prevailing fashions in New York; artists who will never fit neatly into any overarching narrative of American visual life in the latter twentieth century. On the other hand, artistic careers tended to be constrictive, often poorly understood, supported chiefly by teaching posts, confined within the obstinate, unjust borders of regionalism. Some broke through the cultural ceiling—Richard Diebenkorn, Wayne Thiebaud, Mark di Suvero, perhaps Bruce Conner and Ed Ruscha—but for everyone else, the climb toward national attention and critical acceptance would be more arduous, a slow campaign to overcome the kinds of prejudices and arbitrations that might naturally be anticipated from a powerful, centralized cultural hierarchy.

The new century has brought a gradual shift, precipitated in part by a general opening of interest within the art world and in part by activities on the West Coast itself, as critics and historians in San Francisco and Los Angeles began documenting and assessing their own legacy with the care it so clearly deserves. Museum practice followed, and exhibition and collection programs in institutions around the country now incorporate the postwar West Coast on a more frequent basis. With this in mind, we turn to recent gifts to The Phillips Collection, a selection of drawings and prints by Frank Lobdell, and one of drawings and sculptures by Manuel Neri—two artists who utterly personify the mixed blessings of an art life on the West Coast between 1945 and the late 1960s, the point at which, historically, artists there became more routinely involved in national trends. The gifts enhance and expand the representation of West Coast modernists in the collection beyond Diebenkorn.

Lobdell arrived in San Francisco in 1946 with the intention of resuming art studies that had been interrupted by the war. He quickly found himself in the midst of a bustling group of painters, most of whom were, like himself, recent veterans, determined

fig. 53
Frank Lobdell
***1742 II*, 1966**
Color lithograph,
overall: 32 × 20 in.
The Phillips Collection,
Washington, DC,
Gift of Ann Kohs in honor of
Eliza Rathbone, 2015.

to apply the new, exhilarating means of gestural painting to their experiences of modern warfare. Lobdell had been in a battalion that tracked the retreat of the German army across France, and he had witnessed acts of atrocity that would leave an indelible imprint. While they were never a descriptive subject for him, they inform a tragic vision of human destiny that has invested his output with tremendous energy and moral force.

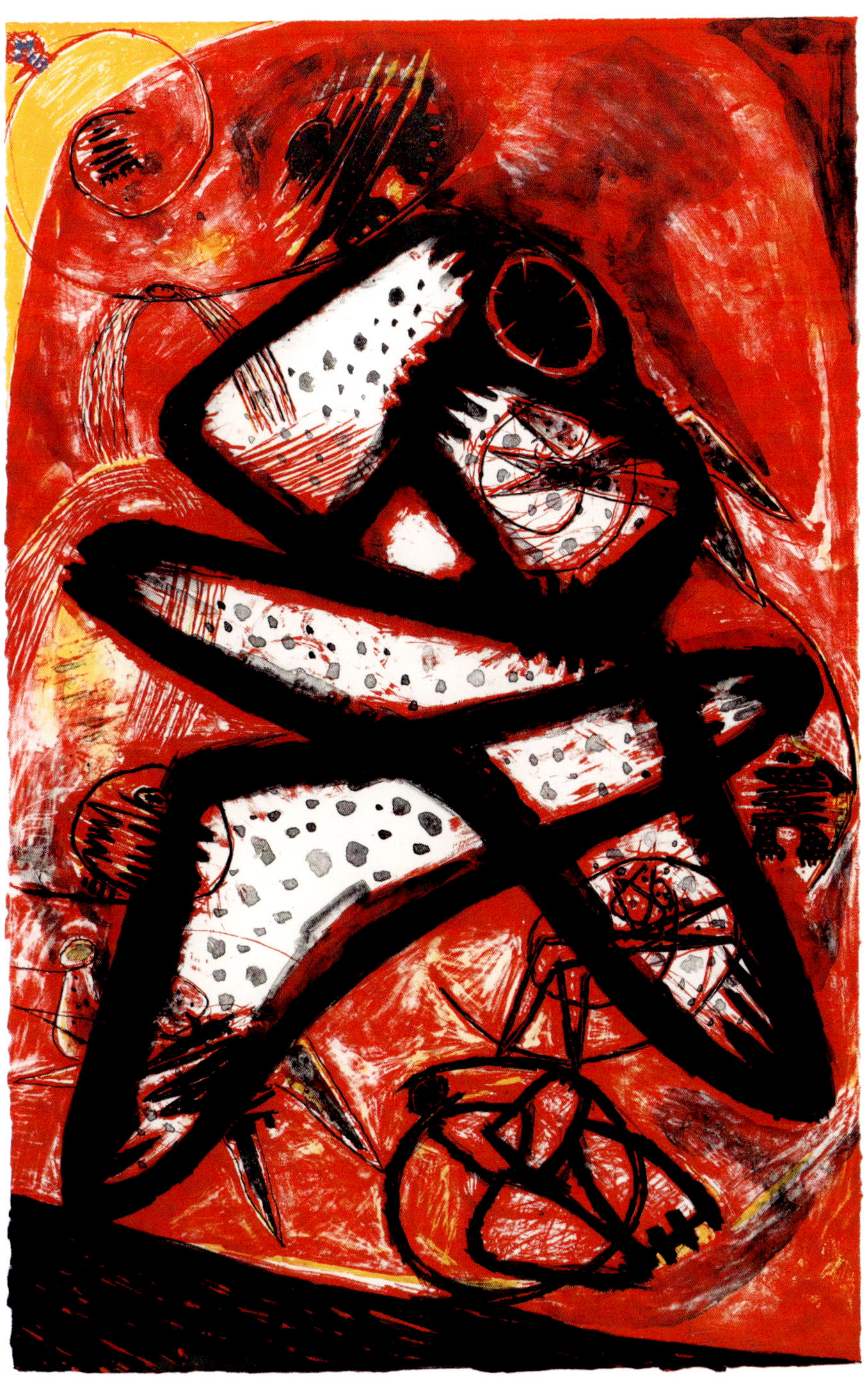

At the center of the Phillips's Lobdell holdings is an edition of thirty-two prints (see fig. 53) done in 1966 at the Tamarind Lithography Workshop in Los Angeles. Before he left for the residency there, Lobdell hung a huge canvas on the wall of his Palo Alto studio, a canvas that would become the magisterial *Summer 1967 (In Memory of James Budd Dixon)* now in the Fine Arts Museums of San Francisco (fig. 54). Lobdell used the weeks at Tamarind to give detailed study to fresh developments in his imagery, and the unblinking intensity, concentration, and visual intelligence of the series fully embody his working process. We can see him probing precedents to which he felt affinities—Pablo Picasso's *Guernica* (Museo Reina Sofía, Madrid), and Francisco de Goya's *Caprichos*—and then exploding them, transforming them, recreating them in the service of his own language of nightmare. The edition is crucial. Its insights would spill across *Summer 1967*, a painting that captures the transition from Lobdell's more purely abstract expressionism of the 1950s and early 1960s—the fraught spaces and smoldering interior illumination, the surfaces like alligator skin that close around isolated figural forms—and, beginning in the early 1970s, his pursuit of the vivid, articulate pictographic language that continued for the remainder of his career. The Tamarind lithographs find the core of this imagery already on confident display, assisted by Lobdell's bold colorism, another quality that would assume a lyrical beauty in the years to come.

Lobdell's work is also represented by a series of figurative drawings in ink (see pl. 140), and while they are not typical of Lobdell's goals for his paintings, they reflect his relationship with his own artistic life. They were made in weekly sessions at the San Francisco Art Institute with the model, a longstanding practice with a group that included Diebenkorn, Nathan Oliveira, and Elmer Bischoff, among others. While Lobdell's work would always be loosely figural, it was not, strictly speaking, figurative. But he had a sense of unity with the Western art tradition, and working from the figure was intrinsic to that tradition; here he brings himself into direct contact with it. The Phillips Collection includes drawings of Diebenkorn's from these same sessions, and we can see how different the two were. Still, Lobdell was a compulsive draftsman who used works on paper as a mode of research directed toward his canvases, and the figure drawings are no exception; they reflect his uncompromising eye in combination with his gifts for visual pattern and implacable structure.

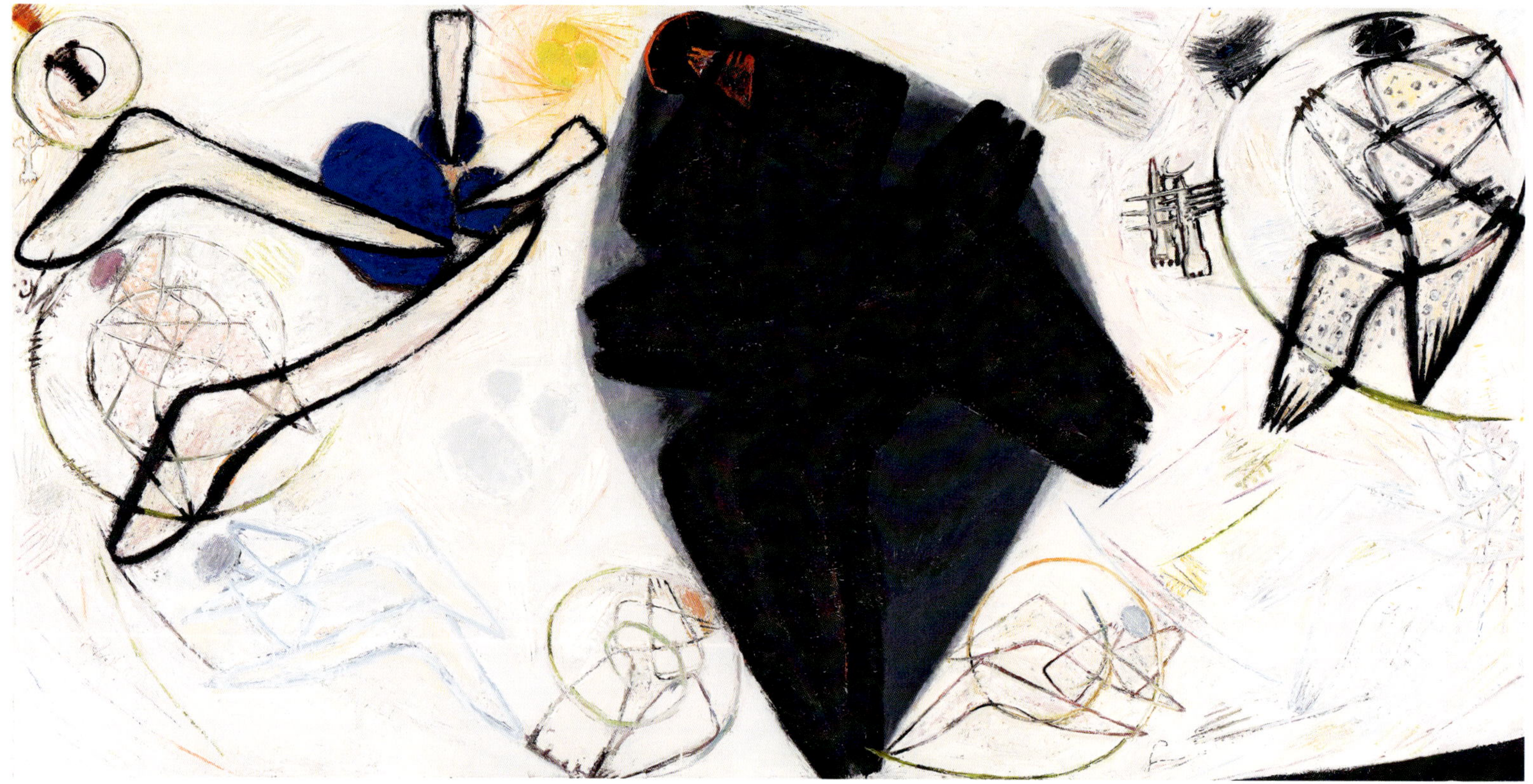

fig. 54
Frank Lobdell
***Summer 1967 (In Memory of James Budd Dixon)*, 1967**
Oil on canvas,
90 1/2 × 173 1/2 in.
Fine Arts Museums of San Francisco, Gift of Judson, Heather, and Charlotte Lobdell, 2002.150.

The abstract expressionist group in San Francisco is an underappreciated episode in postwar American painting, but in truth, it was short-lived and began breaking up by the mid-1950s. For the time being, the Bay Area lacked the necessary infrastructure of galleries, patronage, critical encouragement, and museum support, and yet, even as those painters went their way, another group soon replaced them. These artists were younger, typically born around 1930, and were associated with the Beat insurgence in San Francisco. This is the scene from which Manuel Neri emerged before the end of the 1950s. Although the Beats are still more widely familiar as a literary movement, the artists in San Francisco demonstrate remarkable range—Neri worked alongside Wally Hedrick, Bruce Conner, Joan Brown, Jay DeFeo, and others less known. He would benefit from the environment of tolerance, incessant activity, and experimentation—the freedom to pursue the sculptural figure at a time when the art mainstream looked upon it with undisguised disdain—and by the early 1960s Neri had plunged into a study of the form that is unique in twentieth-century American art.

Neri is now associated with the full-sized standing figure in plaster and bronze—the low cost of plaster, its speed of handling, and its lack of preciousness were all essential to his early methodology. He might be a kind of anti-Giacometti, interested not in the uncertainties and contingencies of human perception but in the capacity of the figure to communicate ideas and psychological states across space. Neri never placed much trust in words—figural gesture offered a truer rendering of internal reality. At the same time, few artists have ever been as sensitive to the fullness of their formal traditions, and if Neri's figures stand comfortably alongside the postwar European humanism of an Alberto Giacometti or a Marino Marini, he also absorbed the forms of antiquity and the Renaissance at firsthand. His interests are synthetic, pressing toward an unequivocal individuality of visual language, and toward sculptural surfaces of unusual texture, surfaces that draw the haptic eye and lead it across the entirety of the form.

Such motives are obvious even in the small partial or fragmented figures from the late 1970s, such as the idiosyncratic partial figure, *Posturing Series No. 2* (fig. 55), but they are never absent from any of Neri's work, and appear in the drawings as well. Neri was another indefatigable draftsman who worked almost daily from the model, and he produced thousands of sheets during his career. The drawings serve a number of functions, including considerations of pose and the deployment of

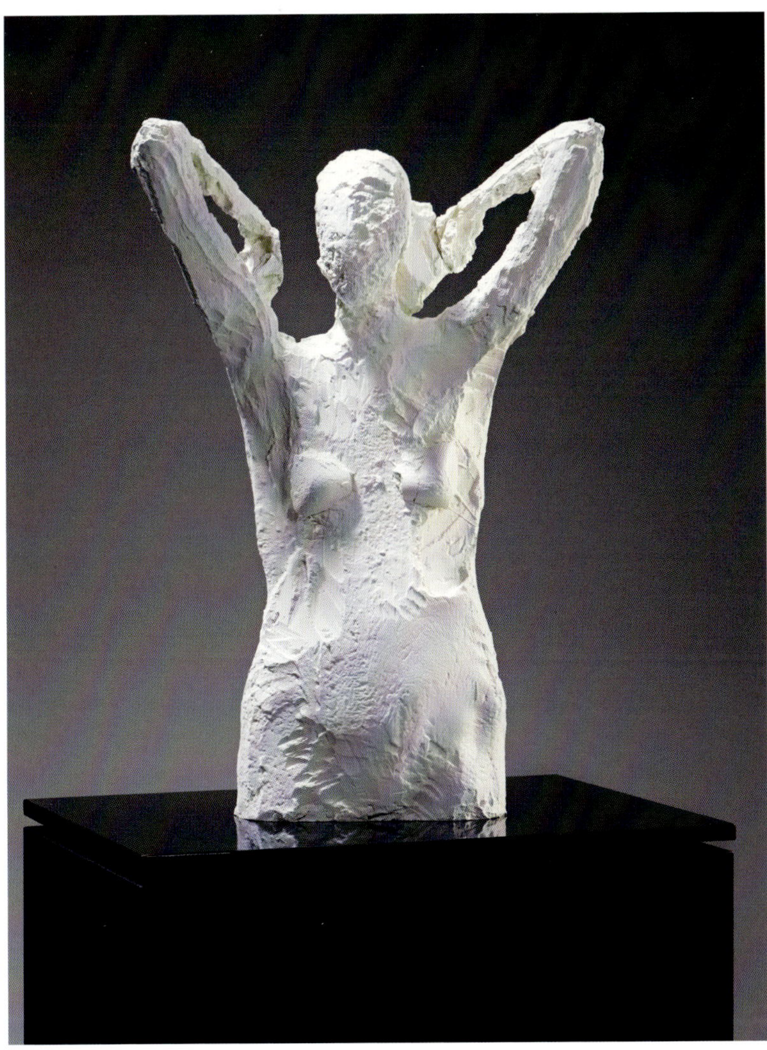

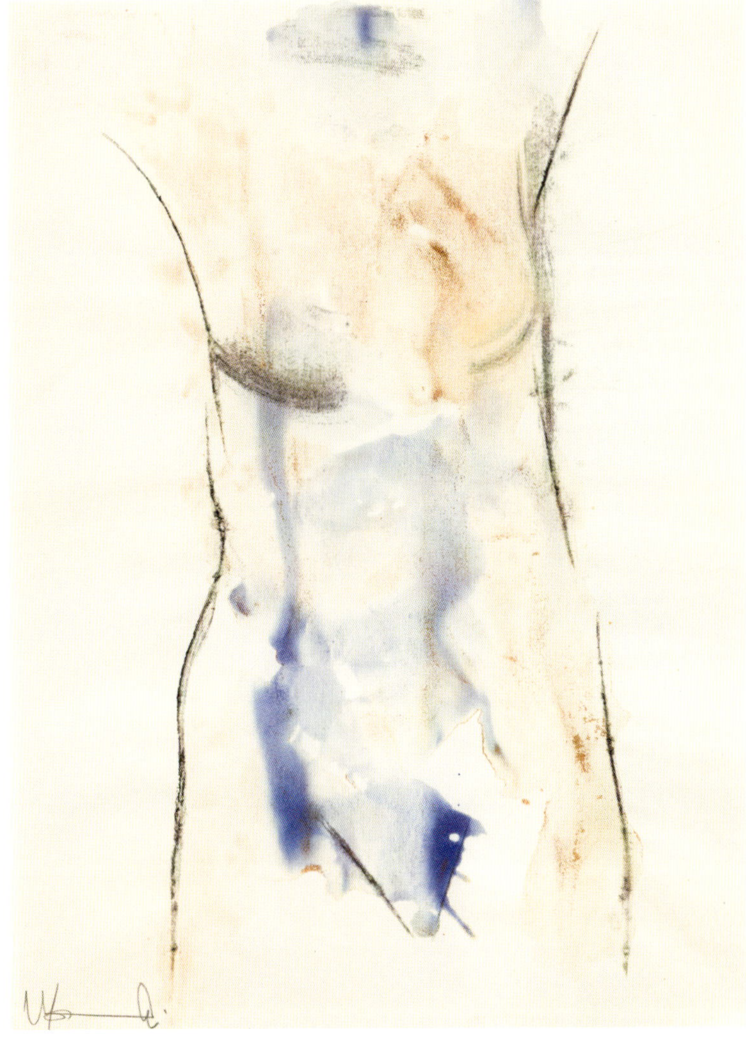

fig. 55 (left)
Manuel Neri
***Posturing Series No. 2*, 1978**
Mold 2007, cast 2006
Bronze with patina, sealant, and oil-based pigments with yellow glaze,
31 x 21 1/2 x 12 in.
The Phillips Collection, Washington, DC, Gift of the Manuel Neri Trust, 2018.

fig. 56 (right)
Manuel Neri
***Amante Series No. 10*, 2009**
Watercolor and charcoal on paper,
16 1/8 × 11 3/4 in.
The Phillips Collection, Washington, DC,
Gift of the Manuel Neri Trust, 2018.

color, which was eventually transmitted to the bronze editions. Neri treated the bronze figures like canvases, lavishing their surfaces with poetic, richly gestural color. The *Amante Series* (see figs. 47–49; 56) moves in these directions, but all of the works are representative of Neri's mature career, reflecting his achievement as one of the most important American figurative sculptors of the late twentieth century.

Few, if any, of the artists of the postwar West Coast were antagonistic toward New York, or deeply troubled by mainstream indifference. They were not the anti-New York; they were, rather, the not-New York, and those who had the capacity to develop on this open terrain would thrive. Lobdell and Neri demonstrate the point. Although Lobdell may well be the most under-recognized major American painter of the era, among his colleagues, others are ripe for recovery: Hassel Smith, Jack Jefferson, Edward Corbett, James Budd Dixon. Jay DeFeo, who died in 1989, is now recognized as a major figure of the period, but the Beat scene in the Bay Area produced additional artists of note; examples would include Wally Hedrick or Alvin Light. As the acts of recuperation continue in the years to come, an institutional documentation of postwar West Coast art activity can only expand our understanding of the richness and deep textures of American art during the period, reminding us always that the entire story will never be contained in a single narrative.

PHYSIOGNOMY AND A FISHERMAN: AUGUST SANDER AND FORREST BESS

Lauren Kroiz

A beech tree's smooth trunk suddenly bulges, growing instantly gnarled at half its height (fig. 57). Above, a dense network of branches fills the upper two thirds of August Sander's arboreal photograph. Dry grass and bare earth give way to a light gray blur in the middle ground, creating a blank setting that frames the tree like the page of a botanical illustration. Focused on the trunk and the complex disorderly branches, so dense they block much of the light, Sander's photograph is not picturesque. It does not represent the tree's shape, barely including leaves and giving no hint of its canopy. Instead, Sander treats this beech as a specimen for the observation of isolated detail. Most famous for his portraits of German people, he located his photographs of nature along with them as part of a larger physiognomic project. In his writings and images, he argued that physiognomy represented the possibility for innate and immediate insight through vision. Beyond the appearance of an individual, Sander proposed, "Everything that happens has a face, and the total expression of this is called physiognomy."[1] The pseudo-science of discovering character in faces led him to discern the forces at play in both the human and non-human world.

Sander's approach to the landscape was in sympathy with many twentieth-century American modernists whose work has recently been acquired by The Phillips Collection, notably the painter and fisherman Forrest Bess. In small abstract paintings, Bess drew on personal visions he called "a form of cultivated seeing into the darkness," probing the forms of nature for deeper truths.[2] Although photographs of nature like Sander's may appear neutral or objective in contrast to Bess's paintings, Ólafur Eliasson's 2013 *Kaleidoscopic telescope* reminds us that observing our universe and perceiving ourselves cannot be separated (fig. 58). When we gaze through Eliasson's doubled device, our own observing eye appears at the scope's other end, multiplied by the mirrors into an orb, a kind of planet or universe. Eliasson explains his attempt to uncover "relationships between having an experience *and* simultaneously evaluating and being aware that you are having this experience."[3]

This essay draws on recent acquisitions by Sander and Forrest Bess in the Phillips to explore the ways their landscapes might teach us to perceive as observers and participants, alive to the interplay of forces within our world and ourselves.

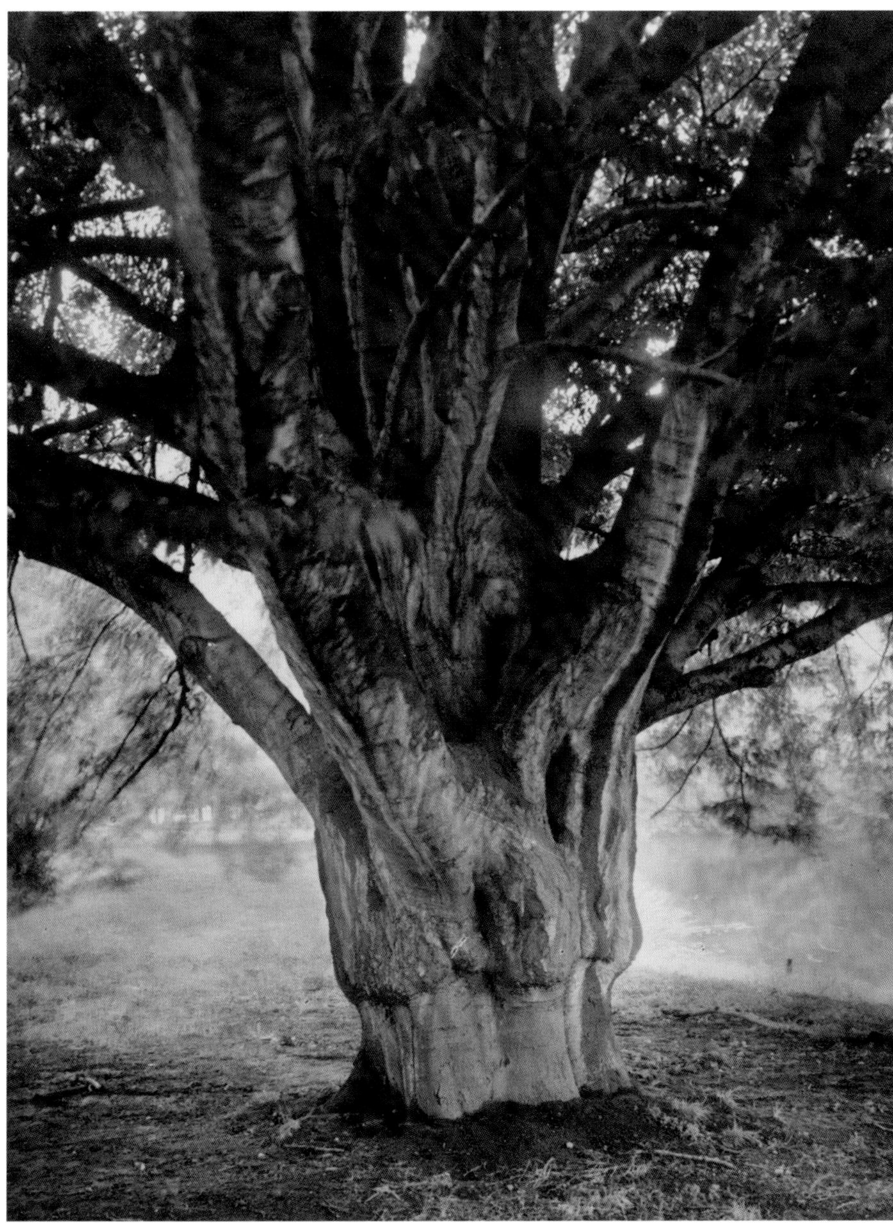

fig. 57
August Sander
***Beech Tree*, ca. 1936**
Gelatin silver print,
9 1/4 × 6 7/8 in.
The Phillips Collection,
Washington, DC,
Gift of Kent and Marcia
Minichiello, 2006.

In landscape we recognize the human spirit of the time, which we are able to capture with the help of the camera.... Landscape, its boundaries defined by a common language, conveys the physiognomy of a nation's chronological state.
—August Sander, 1931[4]

August Sander was born in 1876 in the iron-rich, heavily wooded town of Herdorf to an herbalist mother and a miner father. Sander himself worked in the ore mine as a youth.[5] His introduction to photography came there when a technician visited to document views of the valley. Herdorf operated as a particular place in which nature and industry were closely related.[6] However, Sander's understanding of the landscape also broadly resembled that of many Germans of his era, shaped by journalist and folklorist Wilhelm Heinrich Riehl, whose massive three-volume work *The Natural History of the German People* was published between 1851 and 1855. Against the background of an industrializing Europe, Riehl argued that the forest represented the heart of German culture. Linking nation and nature, he and his followers had early popular successes preserving German forests, including several sites that Sander would later photograph.[7]

Forests had symbolic appeal for the Romantics and the political Left. The Third Reich found in Riehl's work inspiration for its *Blut und Boden* (Blood and Soil) politics.[8] Sander's physiognomic work often relied on archetypes that at first glance seem amenable to the National Socialist project. However, in 1936, his book *Face of Our Time* was confiscated by the Nazi government and destroyed.[9] That year Sander authored an article entitled "Der deutsche Wald" (The German Forest) and illustrated it with *Beech Tree*. He explained:

> Taking a quick stroll through the German forest today, we can neither ignore its origins nor its changes over the course of time. It is man, time and again, giving landscape its form.[10]

The discontinuity in the bark of the beech tree in Sander's photograph resulted from coppicing, an ancient forest management method that relies on the ability of some tree species to regrow new shoots from a stump and on the longevity of coppiced trees, which remain juveniles and survive for centuries.[11] New branches generated from the base curve outward and then upward, accounting for the tangled web in *Beech Tree*. In actively managed woodland with a system of rotating parcels, instead of clear-cutting for timber, limbs would be harvested and regrown. Preventing the upper canopy from over-shading the forest floor and understory, coppicing promoted biodiversity. During the Middle Ages, in what would become Germany, coppicing maintained a low forest, easily harvested by hand. The practice began to decline in the eighteenth century, as firewood and charcoal gave way to coal. By 1936, it would have been historic. Thus Sander's photograph of a specific beech tree points to both a property of the plant and a history of its human use.

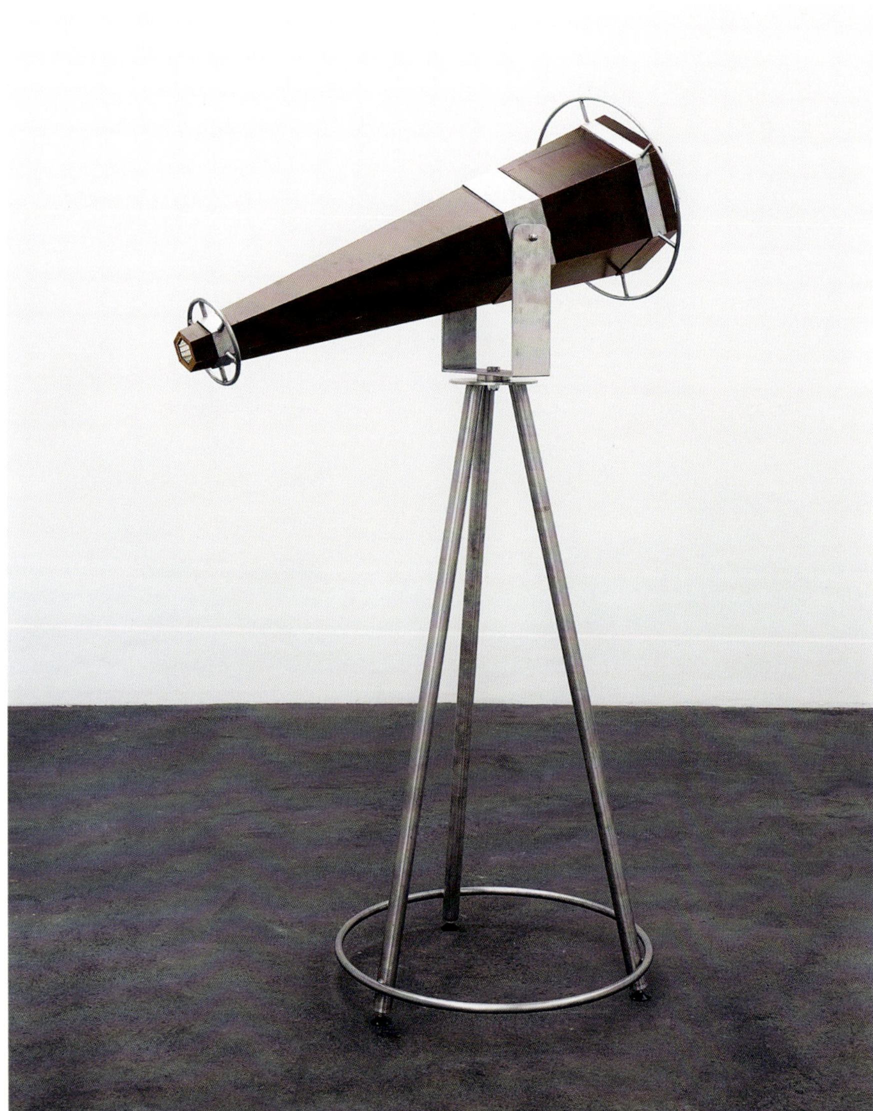

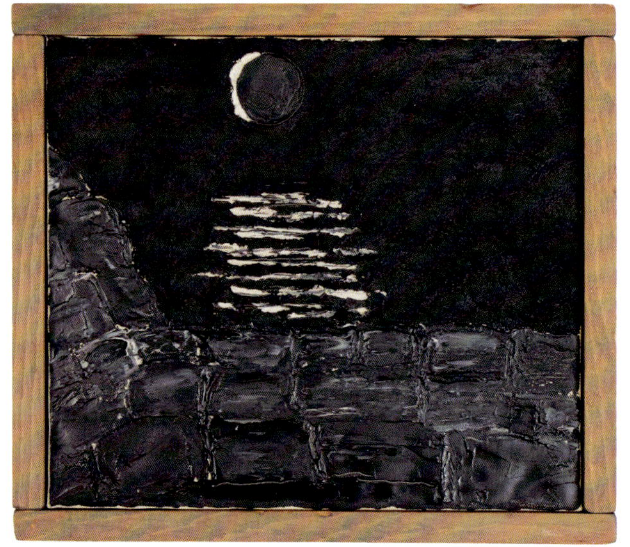

fig. 58 (left)
Ólafur Eliasson
***Kaleidoscopic telescope*, 2013**
Stainless steel, wood, and mirror, 76 3/4 × 47 1/4 × 28 3/8 in.
The Phillips Collection, Washington, DC, Gift of the Heather and Tony Podesta Collection, 2019.

fig. 59 (right)
Forrest Bess
***Untitled (Black Seascape with Moon)*, 1951**
Oil on canvas, 9 × 10 3/4 in.
The Phillips Collection, Washington, DC, Promised Gift of Miriam Schapiro Grosof.

Sander's photographs often demonstrate human presence in the landscape more overtly. In *Birches in the Woods* (pl. 52), an earthen path cuts diagonally across the foreground. In *Deerpark, Cologne* (pl. 50), a low metal rail cuts at a slight diagonal across the bottom of the composition. The latter captures the *Stadtwald* (city forest) in the city where Sander lived. The park included a herd of tame fallow deer, named for their pale brown color and kept as ornamental species since the Roman period. As collectors Kent and Marcia Minichiello point out, in Sander's photographs of nature, human presence is everywhere, but people are not.[12]

I have no choice but to follow the vision.... As a fisherman, there are times when all conditions—weather, water, wind, are unfavorable, yet, there is the feeling that fish can be caught, and by following this feeling—it becomes so. I think that the search for Truth transcends all.
—Forrest Bess, 1951

So Forrest Bess explained his work to his local community in the southeastern Texas newspaper the *Bay City Tribune* just months after exhibiting his small biomorphic abstractions at the influential Betty Parsons Gallery in New York.[13] Bess collapsed his role as painter and fisherman, claiming both as aspects of the same search for truth. Bess understood nature as itself abstract, relying on his own experience and the work of artists he admired, particularly Vincent van Gogh.

Cultivating a vision that might contradict the surface appearance of nature, Bess offers one alternative to Sander's physiognomy. Observing the elements might suggest one path (no fishing), but a vision or feeling could both demand and create a different course for its follower (fish caught).

Bess's attention to fish and the sea in his metaphor can be explained biographically. The artist spent his life near the small town of Bay City, Texas, on the Gulf of Mexico. During World War II, Bess enlisted in the Army and was brutally beaten after revealing his homosexuality. He suffered a nervous breakdown. He had painted as a young man and his doctor advised him to paint the visions he had experienced since childhood as a form of therapy. Returning to his family's fish-bait camp on the flat water of the East Matagorda Bay, Bess painted *Untitled (Black Seascape with Moon)* in 1951 and made its simple wooden frame (fig. 59).

In the small black and white oil painting, a sliver of waning crescent moon heads toward the darkness of a new moon.[14] Bess differentiated the parts of the seascape not with color, but with texture. A heavy impasto pattern of rounded rectangles, like boulders or crocodile skin, forms the horizon line along the lower third of the painting. Off-white, lightly yellowed lines beneath the moon suggest its reflection on the water. The restricted moonlit palette recalls Bess's apparently contradictory phrase—a "seeing into the darkness."[15]

In his visions, painting, and writings, Bess called for the uniting of opposites, civilization and nature, as well as male and female. Attempting to annihilate the latter opposition and achieve immortality, the artist also experimented with hermaphroditism, performing self-surgery to transform his body. In the mid-1950s, Bess used dense alchemical symbols to explain how the wound he had opened in his perineum functioned as the "entrance to the world within myself."[16] Neither Bess's body nor his esoteric theories explain *Untitled (Black Seascape with Moon)*, but his worlds exist in relation to each other. Bess's landscape of buckling surfaces in sculpted viscous black suggests the mutability of the physical world and the feeling of its animation.

Looking at these similarly small-scaled black and white acquisitions together, can we learn to see both physiognomy and into the darkness?

1 August Sander, "Photography as a Universal Language" [1931 lecture for Cologne Westdeutscher Rundfunk], in August Sander and Gabriele Conrath-Scholl, *August Sander: Seeing, Observing, Thinking*, trans. Daniel Mufson (Munich: Schirmer/Mosel; Cologne: Photographische Sammlung/SK Stiftung Kultur; Paris: Fondation Henri Cartier-Bresson, 2009), 28.

2 Forrest Bess to Meyer Schapiro, ca. 1950, Schapiro Papers, Archive of American Art, Smithsonian Institution, reel 3458, frame 26, quoted in Clare Elliott, *Forrest Bess: Seeing Things Invisible* (Houston: Menil Collection, 2013), 13.

3 Chris Gilbert, interview with Ólafur Eliasson, *Bomb Magazine*, July 1, 2004, https://bombmagazine.org/articles/olafur-eliasson/. Accessed April 2020.

4 August Sander, *Wesen und Werden der Photographie* (Nature and Evolution of Photography) [1931 lecture for Rundfunkvortrag], quoted in Susanne Lange and Gabriele Conrath-Scholl, "August Sander: The Physiognomy of Landscape," in The Phillips Collection, *August Sander: Photographs of the German Landscape* (Washington, DC: Phillips Collection, 2004), 61.

5 Stephen Bennett Phillips, "Introduction," in The Phillips Collection, *August Sander: Photographs of the German Landscape*, 17.

6 Gabriele Conrath-Scholl provides insightful reading of Sander's early life in "Perspective—Notes on the Work of August Sander," *August Sander: Seeing, Observing, Thinking*, 11.

7 Phillips, "Introduction," 18. Sander focused his explorations of the forest on the evolution of the Rhineland-Palatinate landscape.

8 Phillips, "Introduction," 23.

9 See Kent and Marcia Minichiello, "A Collector's Perspective on August Sander's Landscape Photographs," in The Phillips Collection, *August Sander: Photographs of the German Landscape*, 30.

10 Sander, "Der deutsche Wald," in *Klöckner-Post* (1936), quoted in "Botanical Studies," cited in The Phillips Collection, *August Sander: Photographs of the German Landscape*, 76.

11 Thank you to my colleagues Margaretta Lovell and Joe R. McBride for this identification.

12 Kent and Marcia Minichiello, "A Collector's Perspective on August Sander's Landscape Photographs," 41.

13 Forrest Bess, "Finally, A Bit of Prophecy," *Bay City Tribune*, May 9, 1951, reprinted in Chuck Smith and Robert Thurman, *Forrest Bess: Key to the Riddle* (New York: powerHouse Books, 2013).

14 In the systematic set of symbols Bess developed in the early 1960s, the crescent moon represented a young woman. Elliott, *Forrest Bess: Seeing Things Invisible*, 101.

15 Forrest Bess to Meyer Schapiro, ca. 1950, Schapiro Papers, Archive of American Art, Smithsonian Institution, reel 3458, frame 26, quoted in Elliott, *Forrest Bess: Seeing Things Invisible*, 13.

16 Bess to Schapiro, January 10, 1955, quoted in Robert Gober, "The Man that Got Away," in Elliott, *Forrest Bess: Seeing Things Invisible*, 91.

LIFTING INTO THE FOREGROUND: A MEDITATION ON JOSEPH HOLSTON'S *CHARITY*

Jeffreen M. Hayes

The complexity of human existence is connected to the beauty of art, which begins with the artist's process, then moves with their hand, and ends with the experience of the object. When we encounter art, if we are open to the artist's vulnerability, we see and feel how artists contribute to the shaping of the self.

When I interned at Orlando Museum of Art, I experienced my first moment of seeing myself reflected in art. As an undergraduate, I had studied the history of medieval and baroque art and explored career options in art museums. My professor, Philip Bishop, encouraged me to intern at the local museum—Orlando Museum of Art—for credit. The only department accepting interns was Education, and it was an opportune time because the museum was preparing to host Kerry James Marshall's *A Narrative of Everyday* (1998).

The exhibition consisted of two large paintings from the mid-1980s, *The Garden Project* series (see fig. 60), an untitled fifty-foot woodcut, and a video. Each of these works centered figurative representations of Blackness and the Black experience that sways between what is, what is imagined, and what could be. Black bodies at leisure—in joyful scenarios, expressing intimacy, all in and against a world that intentionally attempts to snuff out simple pleasures of humanity in Black people—are the stars of Marshall's body of art.

I remember it so distinctly because it was the first time I saw me. I saw me in the composite of black skin, the broad noses, full lips, and the eyes. The eyes.

In representations of Black bodies in American visual and material culture, the stereotypical images exaggerate the physical features and skin tone that mark Black people as different, as Others. Skin as dark as night, bulging eyes whose whites stand out, lips oversized as if swollen from an allergic reaction. These are representations created by white people for white consumption, exemplified by their beliefs in Otherness and their inhumanity toward Black people. Images and objects of this nature continue to have a lasting impact on visual culture.

That is why art is a necessary avenue to seeing oneself. It is why museums need to exhibit works of art that speak to the human condition. In that act of justice, institutions will be inclusive of the lived experiences of all. There is power in the museum stating, through its exhibition practices, that we see you and you are part of all of us. It is where and how community comes to bear. We know this through the eyes of the visitor, when they

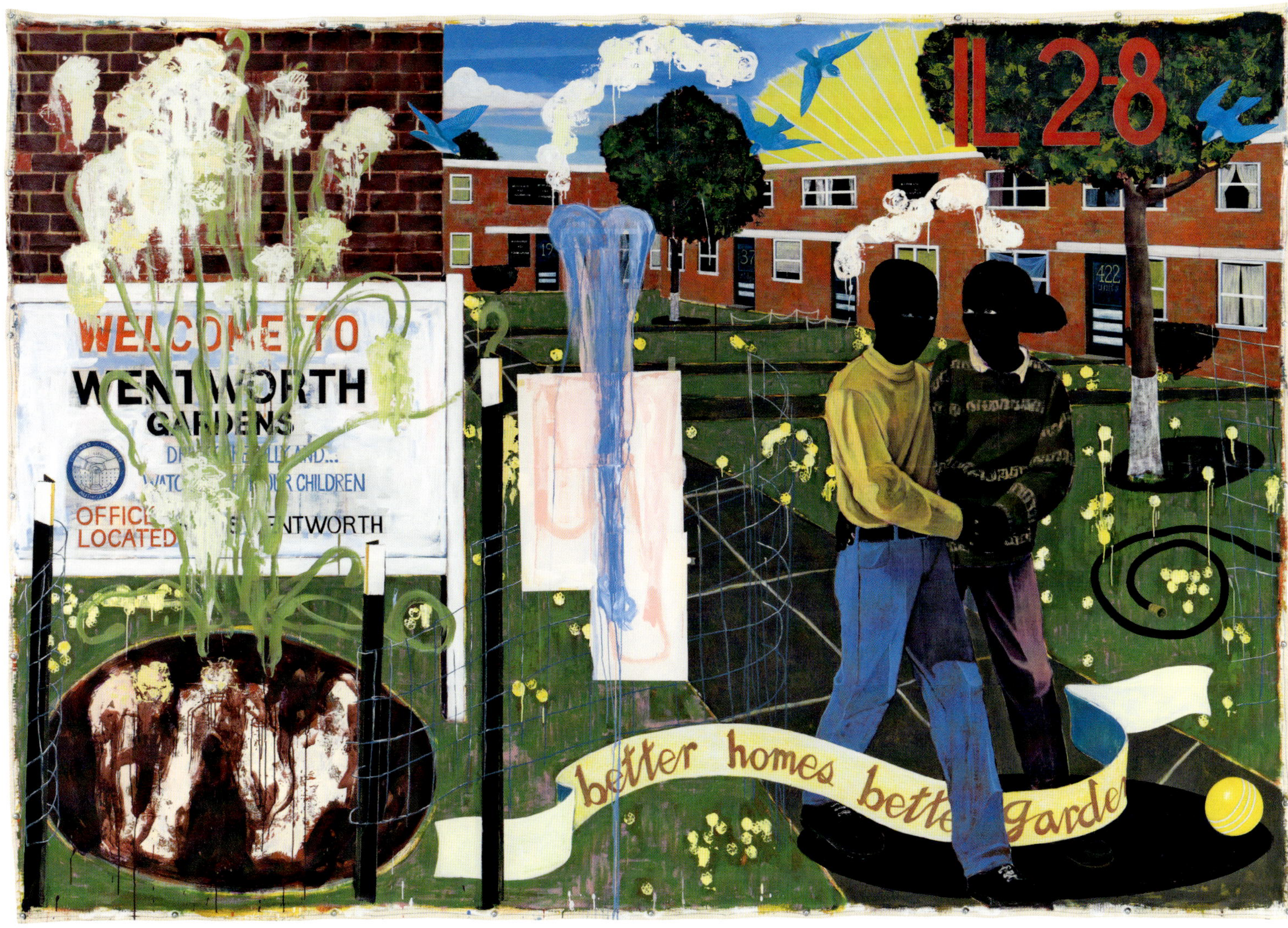

fig. 60
Kerry James Marshall
***Better Homes, Better Gardens*, 1994**
Acrylic and collage on unstretched canvas, 100 × 142 in.
The Denver Art Museum, Funds from Polly and Mark Addison, the Alliance for Contemporary Art, Caroline Morgan, and Colorado Contemporary Collectors: Suzanne Farver, Linda and Ken Heller, Jan and Frederick Mayer, Beverly and Bernard Rosen, Annalee and Wagner Schorr, and anonymous donors.

connect with a powerful work of art. The art of Joseph Holston offers the ability to connect the soul of the figure to the soul of the viewer.

Holston's *Charity* (fig. 61) is one work of art that draws the viewer in, not only through the eyes of the figure sitting looking at you, but also by the medium and scale. The work, an etching, is a portrait of an elderly Black woman, sitting in a wooden chair, inspired by a photograph of an unknown woman that Holston came across in a book or magazine.[1] Early in his career as a painter-printmaker, the artist created subjects that were depicted in both paintings and prints. *Charity* is one such work that represents his process, and it has a compelling story to go along with it.

Having encountered the image of the woman in a publication, Holston was inspired to make a painted version in oil. When his mother saw the painting, she said, "That's Charity." Holston's mother was referring to a woman she knew in her hometown, Harriman, Tennessee. Researching the matter, the artist learned that in the 1920s and 1930s, a Charity Copeland, who shared his mother's maiden name, lived in Harriman.[2] Although the woman was not named in the publication, her image immediately sparked Holston's mother's memory. Holston titled the painting *Charity*, which is a beautiful way to honor the circular notion that, even as strangers, we are connected, and art is the portal that connects us.

In this vein, Charity acts as a portal, particularly in the way that Holston positioned her in the etching. Her face is on the horizontal-vertical axis, while her body is angled on the diagonal. Her right arm rests on the

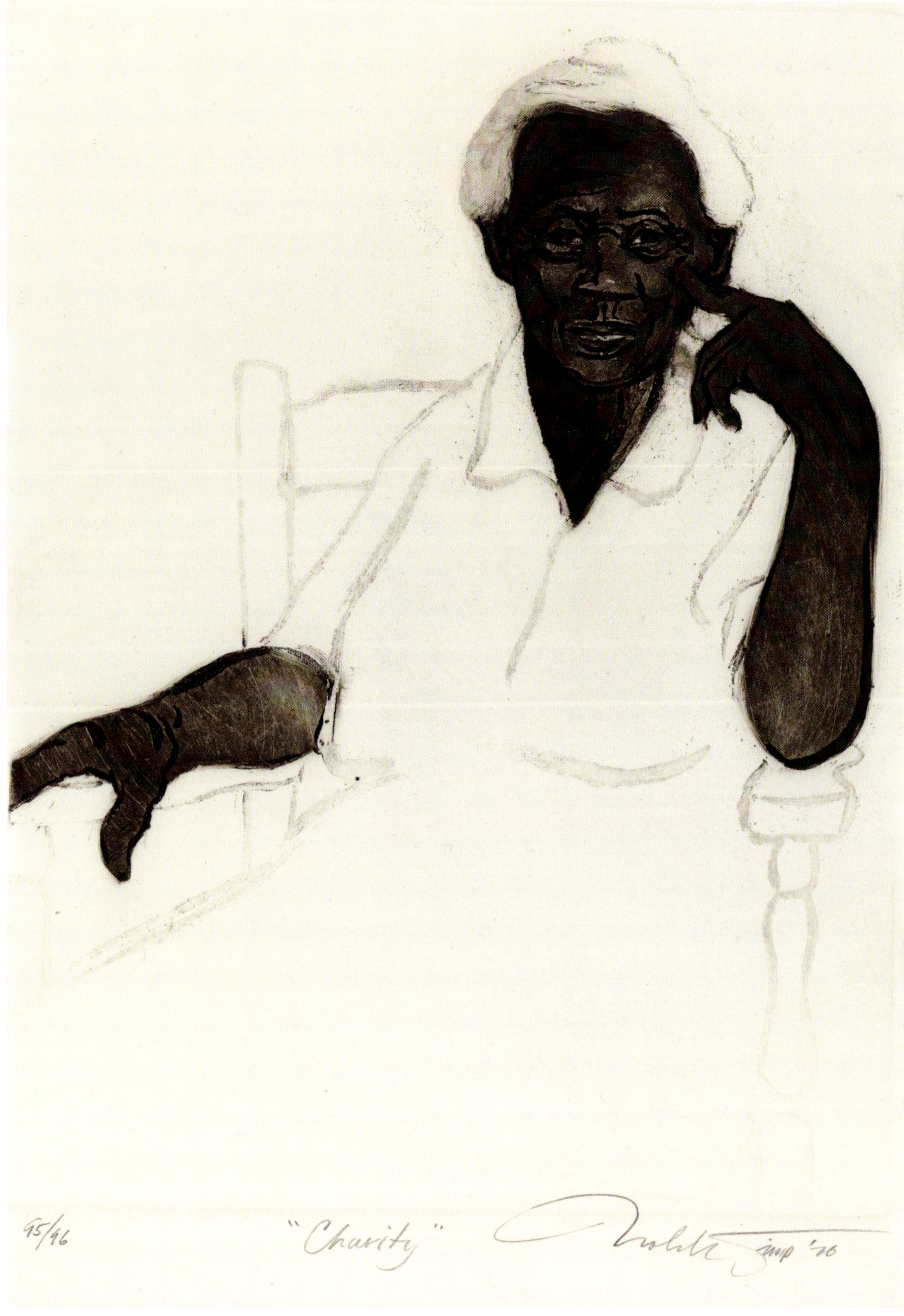

fig. 61
Joseph Holston
***Charity*, 1976**
Aquatint with sugar-lift on paper,
overall: 11 3/4 × 8 5/8 in.
The Phillips Collection, Washington, DC,
Gift of Joseph and Sharon Holston, 2014.

arm of the chair, with her hand gripping the end of it, and her left arm is raised with her index finger touching her face. The placement of her body, when delineated in the simple lines of an *X*, recalls the African Kongo cosmogram representing the "four moments of the sun" (dawn, noon, sunset, second dawn) that connect the physical world with the spiritual world. Symbols of the cosmogram traveled from Africa to the Americas with the transatlantic slave trade and were passed down in African American communities. While referring to the Kongo cosmogram may not have been the artist's intention, being open to the traces of the African diaspora demonstrates how portals can exist.[3] This is particularly poignant when you consider Charity's body and age, as Holston depicts her.

The artist highlights Charity's skin tone, age, and facial features. Of these characteristics, her eyes indicate Charity's identity and what she wants the viewer to know about her. There is a depth to the experience visible in her eyes as her brows furrow. Holston highlights them with a lighter shade of sepia above the brows, directing the viewer to look as deeply into her eyes as Charity looks at us. The clarity in her eyes and gaze tells us that she has lived many lives.

As our eyes move down from hers to the rest of her face, the life lines, carefully etched, give us a sense of Charity's strength. Holston's attention to the details in the face add a three-dimensional weight and sculptural quality to the etching, suggesting Charity's nature. Her firmness is reflected in her relaxed body, which is placed off-center. She has survived a life of hardship as a Black woman and has a story to tell, a story that we can imagine and be open to hearing because the museum makes space for it to be told.

Holston, a skilled printmaker, used the sugar-lift aquatint etching technique. In this, a water-soluble substance, like ink mixed with sugar, is applied to the metal plate by drawing the image directly onto it. A pen or paintbrush is used for the application. Once the substance is dry, the plate is covered with a varnish, then dipped into a water bath. During this process, the water lifts the sugar mixture from the plate. After a further acid bath, what is left is the incised or etched image drawn with the mixture.[4]

The technique parallels the way Holston approaches Charity's identity. He not only brings her to life but also lifts her from the background, from the margins, and places her squarely at the center, a pillar in the Black community. Black women are the foundation and the backbone of the Black community, and Black women elders hold a special place because of their experience and their wisdom. In the eyes of Charity, I see the eyes of Black women in my family and my circle. Her dignity and strength are unparalleled, and Holston captures this brilliantly in the simplicity of this print.

Dignity is a state of humanity that helps to ground our sense of self. When we do not experience it, art can serve as a reminder and bring us back to who we are and who we aspire to be. Art affirms our being. Joseph Holston exquisitely offers up the affirmation, uplifting Blackness and demonstrating that creating space for it to exist within the history of art and in museums does not mean that there must be a compromise on the subject or content. No, Holston shows us that there is room to hold space for Blackness and, with that gesture, there is an invitation to see oneself.

1 Email exchange with Sharon Smith Holston and Joseph Holston, April 14, 2020.

2 Email exchange with Sharon Smith Holston and Joseph Holston.

3 See Robert Farris Thompson's *Flash of the Spirit: African and Afro-American Art & Philosophy* (New York: Vintage Books, 1984) and Park Ethnography Program: African American Heritage & Ethnography, https://www.nps.gov/ethnography/aah/aaheritage/lowCountry_furthRdg4.htm. Accessed April 2020.

4 For more details on the process, see "Sugar-lift aquatint by Pablo Picasso" at El Blog del Museu Picasso de Barcelona, http://www.blogmuseupicassobcn.org/2015/07/sugar-lift-aquatint-by-pablo-picasso-the-delicacy-of-the-etching-of-pictorial-effects/?lang=en. Accessed April 2020.

BRUCE DAVIDSON'S BLACK FEMALE SITTERS

Charmaine A. Nelson

On what was almost assuredly a cold winter's night, on March 5, 1787, an eighteen-year-old enslaved Black woman, disparagingly described as "a NEGRO WENCH named BETT," escaped from her owners, the West Indian merchants James Johnston and John Purss.[1] That we know of Bett at all is mainly due to the printing of a fugitive slave advertisement in the *Quebec Gazette* the following day (fig. 62), an advertisement detailing her escape down to the hour—"between seven and eight o'clock." Incredibly, Bett's escape was one of only five documented winter escapes of an enslaved person in the British-controlled province of Quebec. But more incredible still, the notice described Bett as "big with child, and within a few days of her time."

The sexuality and maternity of enslaved women have been important topics of inquiry for scholars of transatlantic slavery. The matrilineal order of this race-based slavery exposed enslaved Black women and girls to sexual violence, turning their fertility into a prized economic commodity by ensuring that any child born to an enslaved mother became the property of her owner. For slave owners across the Americas, ownership of enslaved women included sexual access to their bodies and the possible issue of such access. It should be obvious, therefore, that the child that Bett carried in her womb may have been the mixed-race product of the sexual coercion or rape she had suffered at the hands of Johnston or Purss.

Slavery's four-hundred-year history deeply impacted the visual representation of enslaved and free Black women. While some of the earliest representations of the enslaved were textual descriptions in auction, fugitive, and sale advertisements, both enslaved and free Blacks were also documented across various media, including drawings, prints, paintings, and sculptures. But certain patterns, largely informed by racial stereotypes, became prevalent in Western art. Black women were persistently represented as sexually available and aggressive, and simultaneously invisible as parents of their own children.

The hypersexualization of Black females in Western art was obviously justified by the desire of slave owners to exploit them as breeders of new human property. A case in point is *Portrait of a Haitian Woman*, produced by the French-Canadian artist François Malépart de Beaucourt (fig. 63). The most remarkable elements of the painting, originally known as *Portrait of a Negro Slave*, are the exposure of the Black woman's breast and

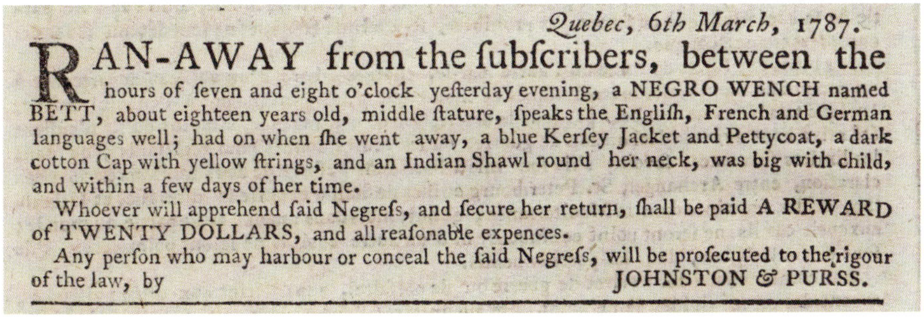

Quebec, 6th March, 1787.

RAN-AWAY from the ſubſcribers, between the hours of ſeven and eight o'clock yeſterday evening, a **NEGRO WENCH** named **BETT**, about eighteen years old, middle ſtature, ſpeaks the Engliſh, French and German languages well; had on when ſhe went away, a blue Kerſey Jacket and Pettycoat, a dark cotton Cap with yellow ſtrings, and an Indian Shawl round her neck, was big with child, and within a few days of her time.

Whoever will apprehend ſaid Negreſs, and ſecure her return, ſhall be paid **A REWARD** of **TWENTY DOLLARS**, and all reaſonable expences.

Any perſon who may harbour or conceal the ſaid Negreſs, will be proſecuted to the rigour of the law, by **JOHNSTON & PURSS.**

fig. 62
James Johnston and John Purss, "RAN-AWAY from the subscribers," *Quebec Gazette*, published March 6, 1787, vol. 1125, p. 2, Bibliothèque et Archives nationales du Québec (BAnQ), Montreal, Canada.

its deliberate juxtaposition with the prominent tray of tropical fruit.[2] The message is clear. Smiling out at the viewer, the pretty, well-groomed, dark-skinned servant offers us her body as she stages the array of fruit, also for our delectation. However, the sitter's enslaved status and her exposed breast alert us to the power imbalance that characterized the production of the portrait. Originally from St. Domingue (later Haiti), the sitter, Marie-Thérèse-Zémire, was most likely purchased in the French Caribbean colony during the Haitian Revolution and forced to migrate back to Montreal in 1792 with the white artist and his wife. Owned by the Beaucourts, Marie would have had no choice but to sit for her portrait in the way François demanded. Therefore, the exposure of her breast, coupled with her smiling face, invites an invasive sexualized gaze that does not accord with the coercive experience of sitting for François that Marie no doubt suffered. Clearly, then, portraiture allowed the artist or the patron—in this case, François—to mask his power over Marie and to re-present her coerced engagement as a congenial and self-directed sexual offering.

To the extent that Marie's breast symbolizes both her sexual and maternal labor, François's contrived narrative of her happy self-exposure also points to the aftermath of the sexual violence that Black women routinely suffered: the children, often mixed-race, that they bore. While the development of photography led to a plethora of images of proud white mothers and their offspring, it also led to a similar explosion of images of Black women and white children. This latter group of images is not surprising if we understand that the customary labor of many enslaved Black domestics was the care of the white slave owners' children, the boys and girls who would one day grow up and own their Black surrogate mothers. Even after the demise of slavery, portraits of Black women posed with white children, like *Baby Paikert and nurse, Montreal, QC, 1901* (fig. 64), much like Marie's portrait, illuminate the coercive dimensions of portraiture that applied when the sitter was not the patron of her own likeness. Such photographs announce the symbolic value of the domestic servant, whose Black body proclaimed the wealth and privilege of the absent white parents and the preciousness of the white child, customarily posed on her lap. But they also call us to consider the chronically absent and strategically neglected Black child, that of the enslaved mother, who was forced to divert her attention and biological resources (quite literally, her breast milk) away from her own enslaved children and instead to free white ones.

Three photographs of Black women in The Phillips Collection, all by the white American photographer Bruce Davidson, directly reflect (but arguably do not replicate) these legacies of the sexualization and maternity of enslaved women. Born in Oak Park, Illinois, in 1933, Davidson joined the prestigious Magnum Photos collective in 1958, garnering praise for his documentation of the civil rights movement.[3] Following in the footsteps of Black American photographers, like James Van Der Zee, Gordon Parks, and Roy DeCarava—artists who became renowned for their sympathetic and insightful representations of Black individuals and communities—Davidson was doubtless changed by his documentation of the systemic state-sponsored violence and peaceful

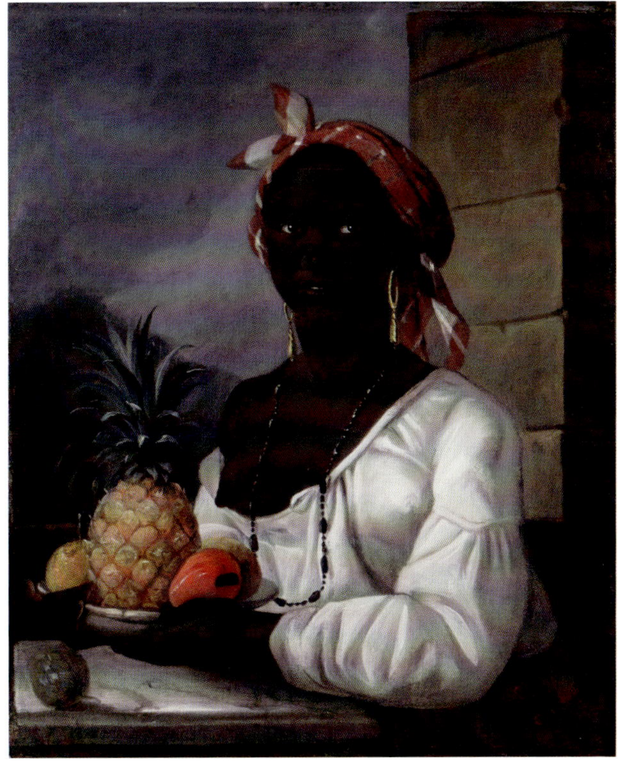

fig. 63
François Malépart de Beaucourt
***Portrait of a Haitian Woman* (formerly *Portrait of a Negro Slave* until 2011), 1786**
Oil on canvas laid on canvas, 27 1/8 × 21 7/8 in.
McCord Museum, Montreal, Gift of Mr. David Ross McCord M12067.

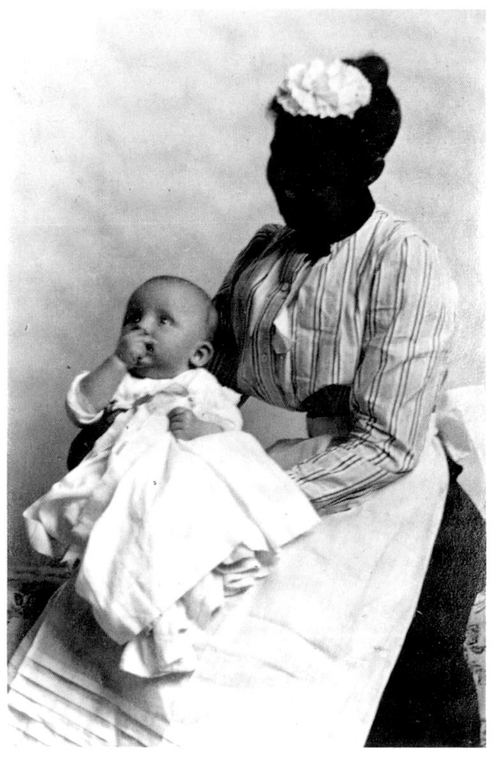

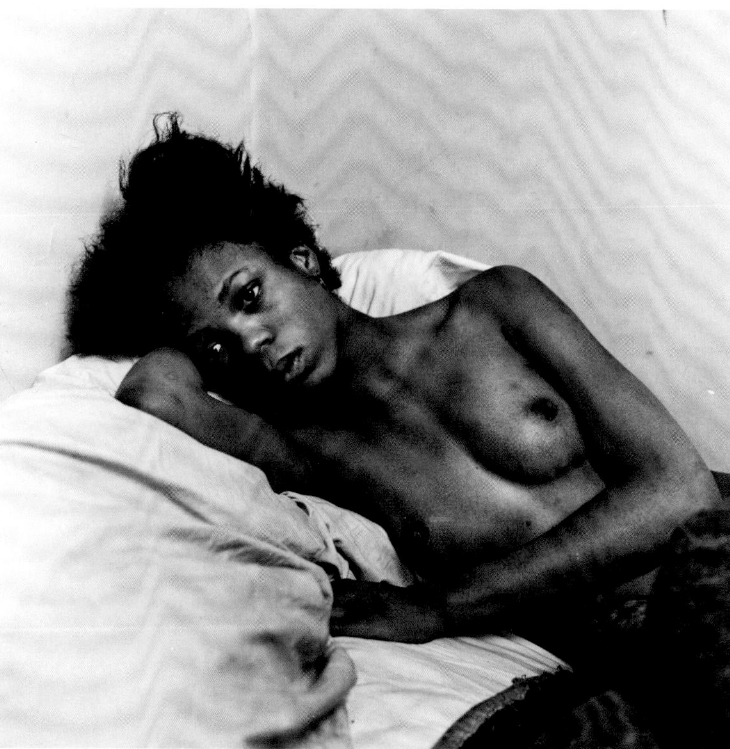

fig. 64 (left)
William Notman & Son
Baby Paikert and nurse, Montreal, QC, 1901
Silver salts on paper mounted on paper, 3 3/8 × 2 1/8 in.
McCord Museum, Montreal, Purchase from Associated Screen News Ltd. II-138937.1.

fig. 65 (right)
Bruce Davidson
Nude Woman on Bed (East 100th Street series), 1966–68
Gelatin silver print, 11 × 14 in.
The Phillips Collection, Washington, DC, Gift of Leo and Nina Pircher, 2013.

human rights protests of 1960s America. This, coupled with his Yale University philosophy background, produced a decidedly compassionate gaze, one through which the viewer (like the one behind the camera) appears to acquiesce to the portrait subject.

The unclothed Black woman in Davidson's *Nude Woman on Bed* (fig. 65) defies the Western legacy of the hypersexualized Black female subject. Instead, seemingly alone and on a dishevelled bed with hair not yet groomed, the young woman lies on her side, a far-off expression on her face that indicates introspection rather than invitation. Unlike François, in his much earlier painting of Marie, Davidson positions viewers as voyeurs who explore the unnamed woman's solitary state, seemingly without invitation. If she waits for someone, it is certainly not the viewer, since she does not acknowledge us or meet our gaze. If the youthful beauty of her exposed breasts provokes excitement within us, the source of such sentiment is clearly our own.

Davidson's more compassionate exploration of Black females also extended to the elusive pregnant woman. Davidson's *Pregnant Woman in Pink Dress Against Yellow Rail* (fig. 66) and *Standing Pregnant Nude* take expectant Black mothers as his focus. Unlike the sitter in *Nude Woman on Bed*, both of the pregnant women in these images stare out at the viewer, one fully clothed in a public space and the other unclothed in a private one. Standing on the dimly lit subway stairs, the woman in *Pregnant Woman in Pink Dress Against Yellow Rail* turns to meet the photographer's gaze as if asked to stop and pose in the middle of her descent. The light material of her pink dress allows us to see her protruding stomach, the evidence of her growing child. Her expression appears to be content, calm, peaceful—not an outright smile, but clearly one of a person comfortable with herself and her surroundings.

The expression of the model in *Standing Pregnant Nude* strikes a different tone. Davidson crops her at the knees, allowing us to view her frontal nudity, which includes her engorged breasts and protruding stomach. Her left hand balances on a TV dinner tray set out in front of a television set in a living room illuminated by partial sunlight that streams through drawn curtains. Unlike the model in *Nude Woman on Bed* she gazes at us directly, and unlike the model in *Pregnant Woman in Pink Dress Against Yellow Rail*, her gaze is not compliant. Instead, the cock of her head and her hip, both to the left, signals confidence, even defiance. Cognizant of the beauty of her unclothed body, she is proud of herself, and her self-exposure is not an offering. Composure and self-possession characterize her regard.

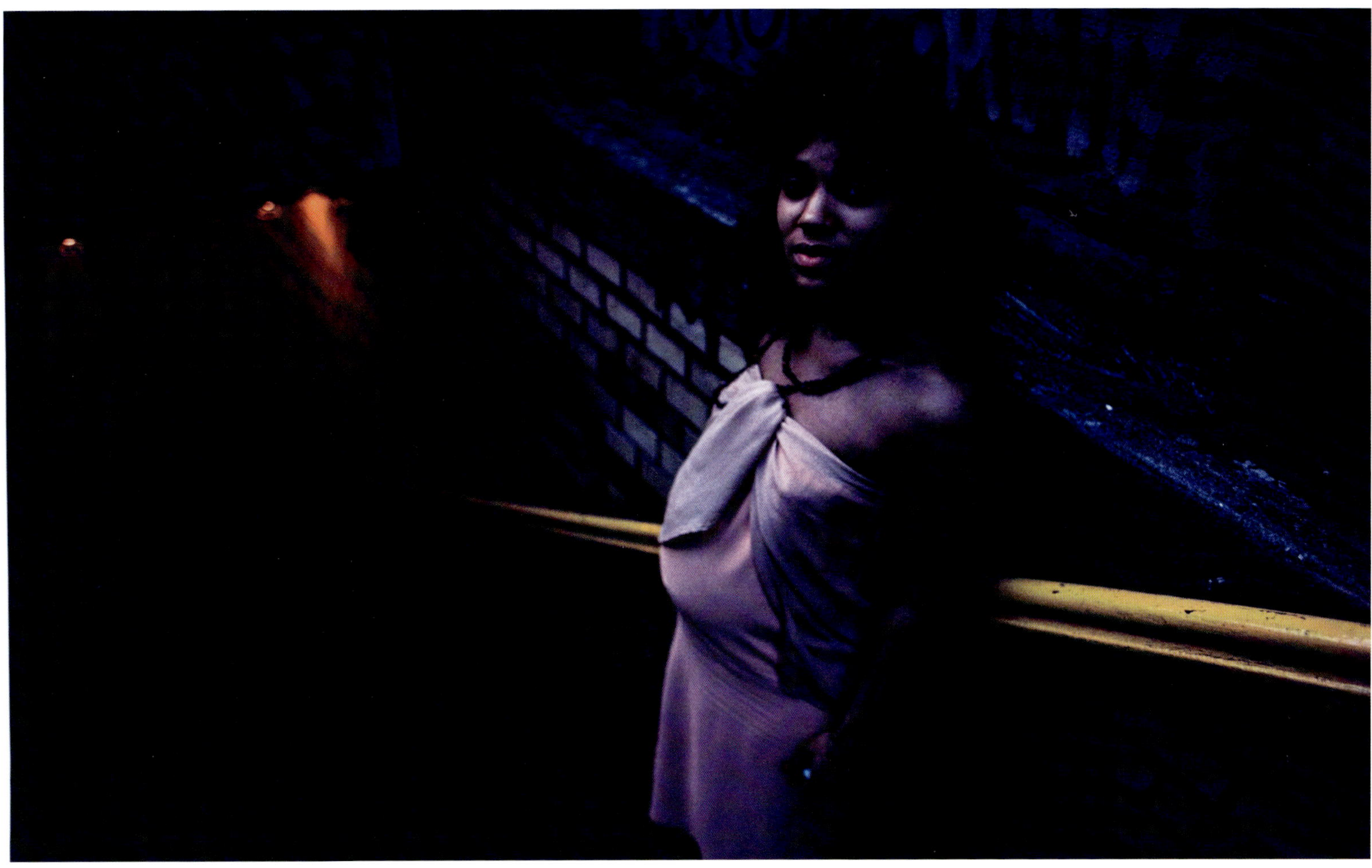

fig. 66
Bruce Davidson
***Subway, New York (Pregnant Woman in Pink Dress Against Yellow Rail)*, 1980s**
Dye transfer print,
20 × 24 in.
The Phillips Collection, Washington, DC,
Gift from the Collection of Michael and Joyce Axelrod, Mill Valley, California, 2013.

While all three of Davidson's photographs blend the genres of portraiture and figure study, *Nude Woman on Bed* and *Standing Pregnant Nude* also incorporate the Western tradition of the nude. Whereas the plights of Bett and Marie were exposed and memorialized in their textual (fugitive slave advertisement) and visual (oil portrait) representations by the white men who owned them, such exploitative modes of representation sadly did not perish with the abolition of slavery. Furthermore, Marie's hypersexualization and Bett's maternal trauma were both indelibly connected to the systemic and institutionalized exploitation of enslaved women as breeders of new property. This debased legacy led to a deficit of images of Black women as beautiful, composed, careful, self-possessed, introspective, intelligent, and in control of their own bodies and pleasure for their own ends. Davidson's singular portraits defy many of the standard stereotypes of Black female subjects that emerged from slavery and have persisted long after its demise. Not only are his female sitters poised, introspective or outright defiant, they refuse the viewer the customary pleasure of a sexualized offering, even of their unclothed bodies. They have allowed themselves to be captured and memorialized, but unlike Bett's unauthorized textual portrait and Marie's painted one, these images seem not to be fully for us, but compassionately, and finally, for them.

1 James Johnston and John Purss, "RAN-AWAY from the subscribers," *Quebec Gazette*, March 8, 1787, transcribed in Frank Mackey, *Done with Slavery: The Black Fact in Montreal, 1760–1840* (Montreal: McGill-Queen's University Press, 2010), 329.

2 For more on the specific use, symbolism, and meanings of the fruit still life, see Charmaine A. Nelson, "The Fruits of Resistance: Reading *Portrait of a Negro Slave* on the Sly," in Nelson, *Representing the Black Female Subject in Western Art* (New York: Routledge, 2010), 76–87.

3 *Bruce Davidson* (New York: Museum of Modern Art, 1966), exhibition brochure. For a profile of Davidson, see the Magnum Photos website, https://pro.magnumphotos.com. Accessed April 2020.

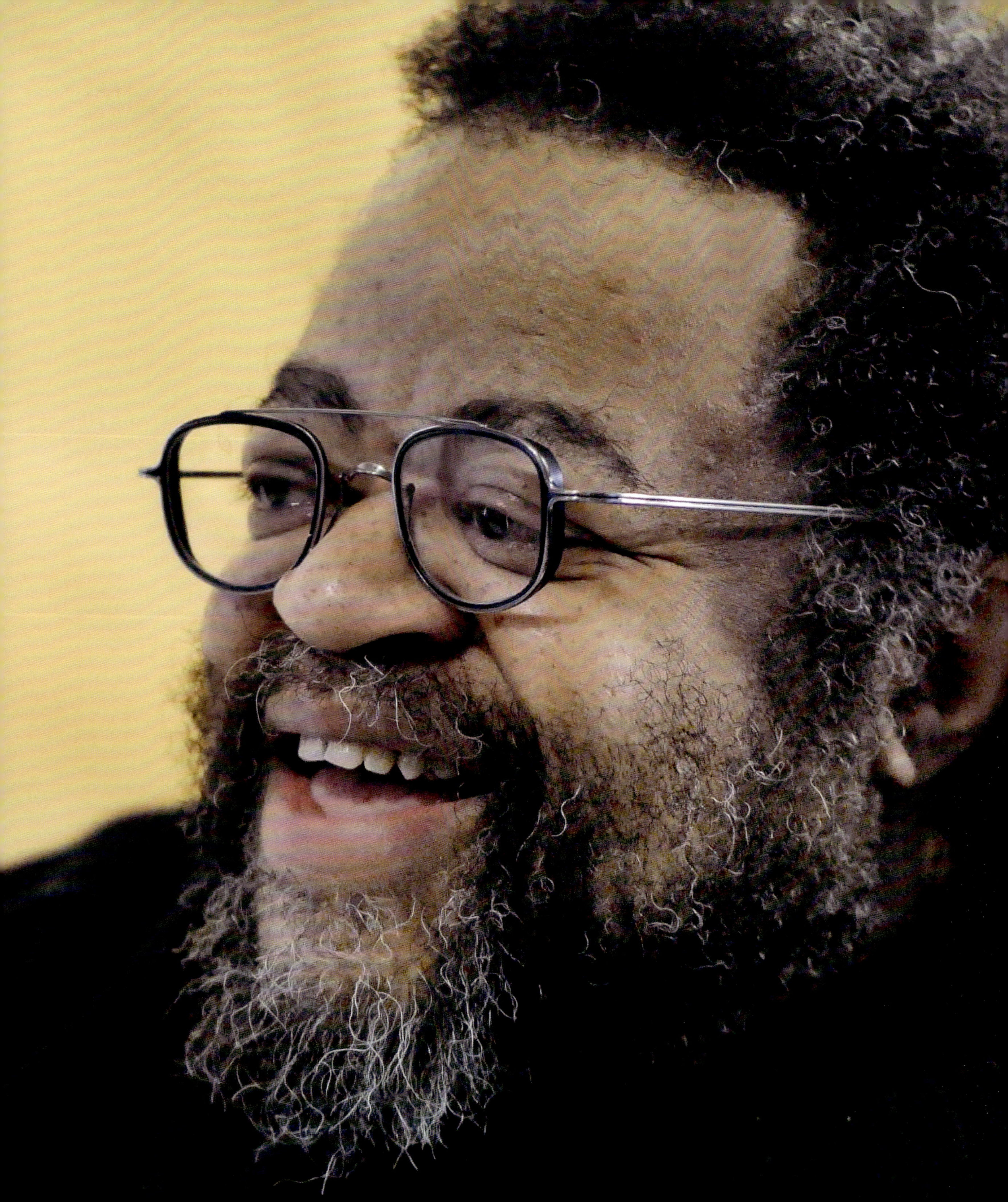

Elsa Smithgall: You showed artistic promise from a young age. How were you encouraged and nurtured by parents and teachers?

Whitfield Lovell: When I was a little toddler, I got a hold of some crayons and I drew all over the walls, all over the door, and all across the living room, and my parents decided not to chastise me or even to acknowledge that I had done something wrong, because they thought that might stunt my creativity. "And who knows? He might grow up to be an artist." Right? So I thank them for that.

Very early on, I was into music. I sang and I studied piano. I wrote songs and made up tunes for them. But I always loved to draw. At the age of thirteen, in junior high school, I had a really wonderful art teacher, Margaret Nussbaum, who spent her lunch hours looking at my drawings, so that gave me the encouragement to go home and draw. I made drawings every night. I didn't even do my homework. And I'd bring them in the next day and she'd look at them and give me critiques. Margaret Nussbaum, Linda Jacobs, and Elena Maeztu: they were the three art teachers in the school, and they all helped critique my drawings.

I was accepted at the Fiorello H. LaGuardia High School of Music and Art. It was a fabulous three years. I also began writing poetry and short stories while I was there. If you could write a poem that showed sensitivity or make a drawing that showed emotion, feeling, that was valued.

I went on to study at a specialized art college [Maryland Institute College of Art]. Not long after that, I decided not to focus on portraiture as my artistic expression, because it seemed like the role of the portrait artist was to make a depiction on commission that would immortalize and ultimately flatter the person in a way that might weaken the artwork. I actually started doing a lot of figures with no heads just to get away from portraiture. There were logical progressions that led me to where I am now. At some point, I got back into making images of people. I don't think of them as portraits, but rather as artworks using heads and faces. I work generally from photographs.

ES: How did photographs become an important part of your work?

WL: I see my past, my childhood, in black and white. My father [Allister Lovell] made his living working for the post office but

MY FATHER MADE HIS LIVING WORKING FOR THE POST OFFICE BUT HE WAS ARTISTICALLY TALENTED.

he was artistically talented. He became a self-taught photographer. I helped him in his darkroom from the time I was about five, and I watched the images come to life in the photo solution. We often looked at family pictures. My father took so many photos that we had shoeboxes full of them. My grandmother had her pictures of her relatives, her parents, and her cousins in albums, but we had boxes of pictures. It was a wonderful pastime to look at the pictures and talk about the people. I learned about people I had never met, whom I was related to, and I learned things about people I knew by seeing them at younger ages and in different situations. I have all my grandmother's photo albums. There's something about the lives of the people in them that deserves to be told, these human beings who were practically invisible, certainly in a museum setting, and *that* is amazing to me.

Whitfield Lovell in his Manhattan studio, March 2020.

IN CONVERSATION WITH

WHITFIELD LOVELL

Adapted from an interview with Elsa Smithgall that took place in the artist's Manhattan studio, March 10, 2020.

I worked with my father's photographs for a good ten years. Then I began drawing from photographs of African Americans that I found in flea markets and online. I feel that the people whose images I'm using are stand-ins for ancestors, the people that I'll never meet. Mortality drives me and keeps me fascinated with these images. I love the fact that when this person's photo was being taken, there was no thought that some artist would draw from it and that it would end up in a museum—maybe the museum whose floors they scrubbed at one time, and now they're on the wall? For me, that's very special, and I just never, never get tired of it.

ES: How does your work engage with history?

WL: History is very much alive. Most people think of time in a linear sense—the end of this era, the beginning of another—but for me, the souls, the spirits who walked the Earth before we did, are somehow still with us. They shaped what we're doing now and we're affected by all of the things they did.

ES: Objects are integral to your work. What meaning do they hold for you?

WL: Objects have meaning because they were used in daily rituals. Somehow that object—a pot or a pan or a hat that someone wore—is imbued with a lot of spiritual power because it's been used. I see beauty in these objects, and I think that the right image juxtaposed with the right object sets it off. It's like you're taking two things, and you put them together and you get a third thing. I love that moment when it clicks.

ES: There's something so poetic in your imagery.

FOR ME, THE SOULS, THE SPIRITS WHO WALKED THE EARTH BEFORE WE DID, ARE SOMEHOW STILL WITH US.

WL: What I love about poetry is that a poet can say so much without coming out and saying it. I see my tableaux and *Kin* series and all my artwork as being strong metaphorically; they say things that can't always be put into words. I try not to be literal.

ES: In addition to poetry, music plays an important role in your practice.

WL: When I was a child, my parents had quite a jazz collection, so I listened to a lot of singers like Sarah Vaughan, Ella Fitzgerald, Barbra Streisand, and Nat King Cole. The vocals were just so mesmerizing that I asked my mother to get me voice lessons.

My mom had an album or two by Nina Simone, which my sister and I used to listen to. By the time I was a teenager, I was a really huge fan of her music. I've heard—and probably own—every recording she ever made. Her music helped me quite a bit getting through art college. The competition in art school is so intense, and the feedback you get is so unreliable. I dealt with a lot of racism, because this was the late seventies and there were very

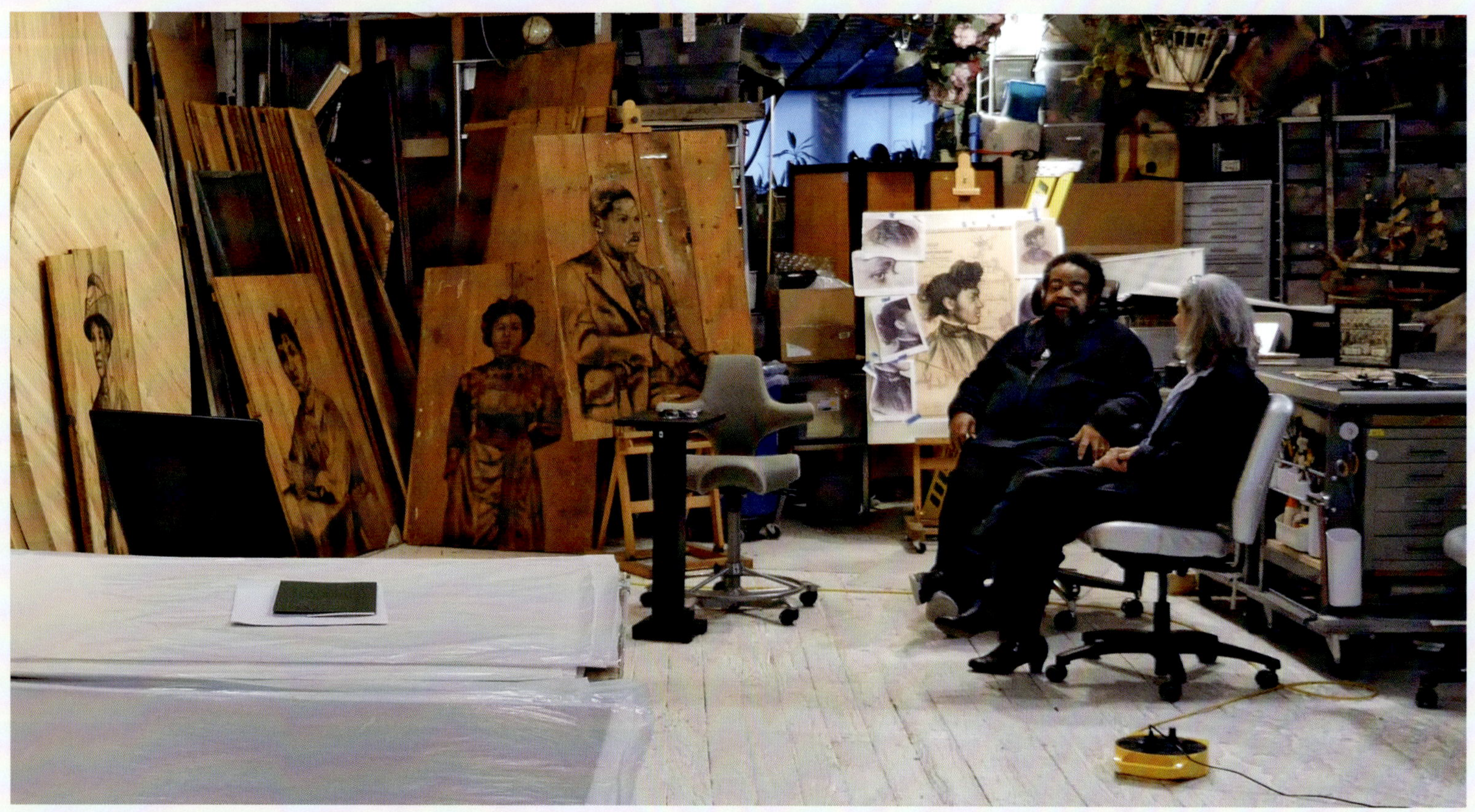

fig. 67 (opposite)
Whitfield Lovell and Elsa Smithgall in the artist's Manhattan studio, March 2020.

fig. 68 (right)
Whitfield Lovell's Manhattan studio, March 2020.

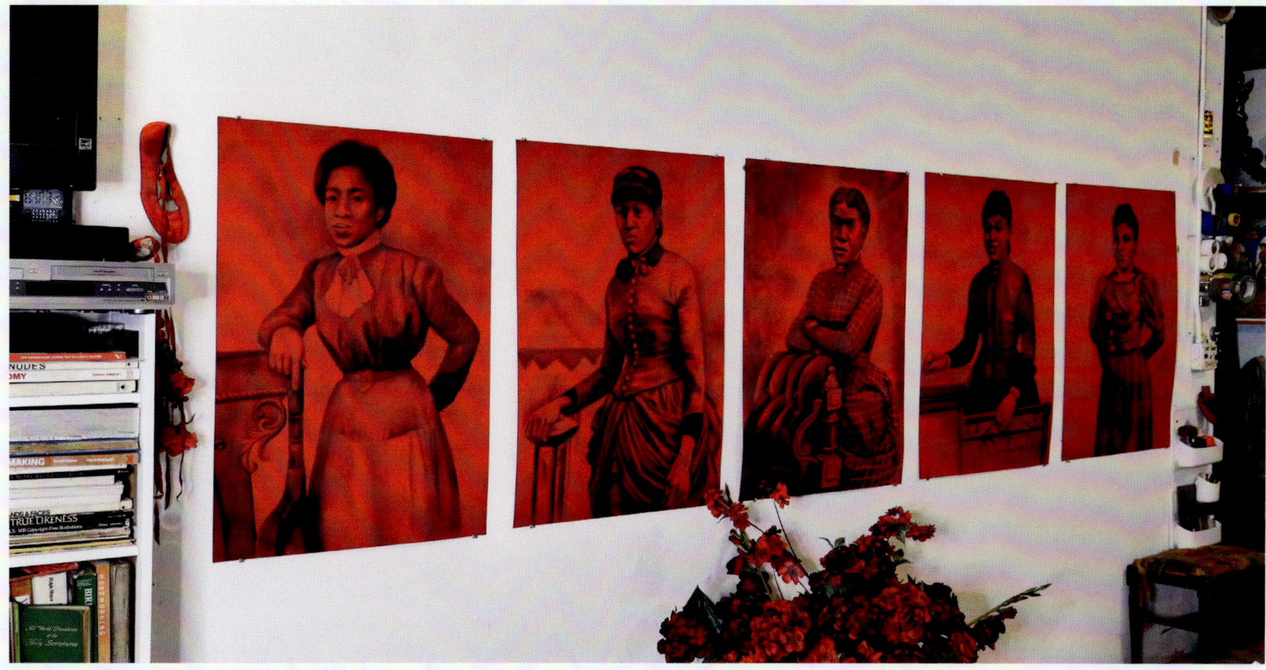

few kids of color attending art schools. Listening to Nina's music helped me find the strength to find my own voice artistically. She could take the lightest sort of nursery rhyme and sing it as if it were an emotional masterpiece. I realized that I had to have that special something in every artwork that I did. It wasn't enough to be able to draw. There had to be some special quality in each piece that transcended skill and moved people. I have to credit Nina for helping me realize that.

ES: Who have been your mentors or role models?

WL: When I say mentors, I don't mean that I've tried to emulate them artistically, because I certainly never have, but that I learned how to be a better person and a stronger artist by observing them. When I was in high school, I was told to meet this woman named Lowery Stokes Sims who worked in education at the Metropolitan Museum of Art. And she said, "There's this guy here who's really great. His name is Randy Williams. You really ought to take his class." He became my mentor from the time I was fifteen until I was about twenty-four. Every time I experienced discouragement, racism, rejection, even outside the art school environment, he would say, "You'll be okay. Don't let that bother you." And that meant a lot. I consider Carrie Mae Weems, whom I met through Lorna Simpson, one of my mentors. She's not only a great artist, but she's a wonderful spirit.

Aesthetically, among photographers, I love James Van Der Zee, Roy DeCarava, and Lee Friedlander. In 1990, I took a trip to Mexico. I was blown away by Frida [Kahlo] and Diego [Rivera] and how they used symbolism. They gave me license to work autobiographically. Betye Saar was another role model for me, and working with her at Skowhegan [School of Painting and Sculpture] was really important; also meeting Elizabeth Catlett, who was a visiting artist there. Howardena Pindell is another role model, like a hero for me.

ES: You have been an important mentor to others. What advice do you have for young artists today?

WL: I taught at Skowhegan one full summer and two half-summers, and I call my Skowhegan students my children, although they're pushing forty now. I think the important thing is to not rush for the commercial trappings. The art world has become very much about getting a gallery. When I came along, Black people didn't have galleries. We made art because we had to. I have known many people who made art their entire lives and never had gallery or museum shows, or they had them for a brief time and it didn't last, and yet they had to make art, so they found a way.

Some of the people who came ahead of me were David Hammons, Camille Billops, Emma Amos, Jack Whitten. Al Loving was incredibly encouraging. He had a little success and attention, but not nearly as much as his life's work warranted, but he made art with a passion. I knew that making money from the art wasn't the important thing. The important thing was making the work good, making it meaningful enough that one hundred years from now people would want to look at it, and find it worthwhile.

LISTENING TO NINA'S MUSIC HELPED ME FIND THE STRENGTH TO FIND MY OWN VOICE ARTISTICALLY.

Finding your own artistic voice has a lot to do with understanding who your people were, where they came from and how they got here, and the kind of attitudes that you picked up from them. You might deal with it in a representational way or you might deal with it in abstraction, but it's part of who you are, and you have to understand who you are.

ES: There's a humanistic quality to your art that invites empathy.

WL: I hope that my work inspires empathy cross-culturally and is not thought of as Black art for Black people. If my work can help teach people something, or help people see things in a different way or have more compassion for the ancestors, then I have done a lot more than I ever expected to, and I'm happy about that.

I HOPE THAT MY WORK INSPIRES EMPATHY CROSS-CULTURALLY AND IS NOT THOUGHT OF AS BLACK ART FOR BLACK PEOPLE.

ES: What are you making at the moment?

WL: When I was at the American Academy in Rome last year, I started a series called *Winterreise*. It's silver Conté on black paper. I walked into the art supply store there and found the silver Conté and this black paper, and I always wanted to work with that.

In Rome, I felt I should be listening to Puccini and Verdi, but I found myself listening to Schubert. That was the mood I was in. I had recently had a few deaths in my family, and so his *Winterreise*, which means "winter's journey," was actually very close to my experience, because it's a song cycle with twenty-four songs, and it's about a man literally taking a journey through a snowstorm to run away from grief and loss of love. And so this was like completely where my head was, and it was winter and it was Rome, and so I did one drawing for each song. They are going to get objects and be encased, the way the *Kin* series is, with objects that loosely relate to the song cycle. There were things that Schubert mentioned in the song cycle, like black coals and leaves and branches, things like that. So I'm working on the objects now. But I actually did twenty-seven drawings, more than I needed to do (figs. 67, 68).

ES: Let's talk about the three *Kin* in The Phillips Collection, which were featured in our exhibition of your work (figs. 69, 70).

WL: The young man with that furry hat in *Kin XXXV (Glory in the Flower)* (pl. 134) made me think of my childhood; he had a Harlem or Bronx look about him. And the radio made me think of the kind of music that we heard at that time. The "glory in the flower," to me, sets it off because it brings a tenderness to the way we view this young man. There's something beautiful about that kind of youth, and at the same time, Black males are the most

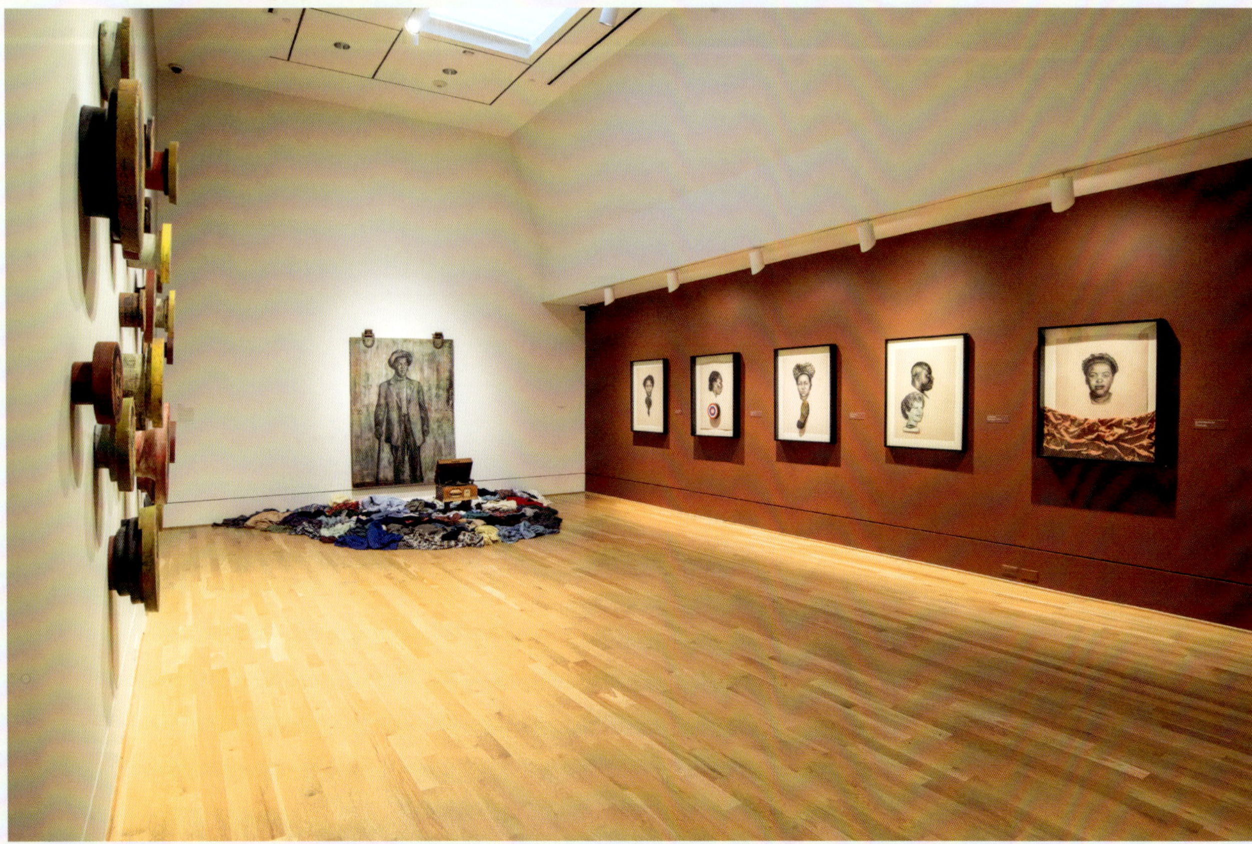

fig. 69 (left)
Installation of *Whitfield Lovell: The Kin Series and Related Works*, October 8, 2016–January 8, 2017, The Phillips Collection.

fig. 70 (opposite)
Installation of *Whitfield Lovell: The Kin Series and Related Works*, October 8, 2016–January 8, 2017, The Phillips Collection.

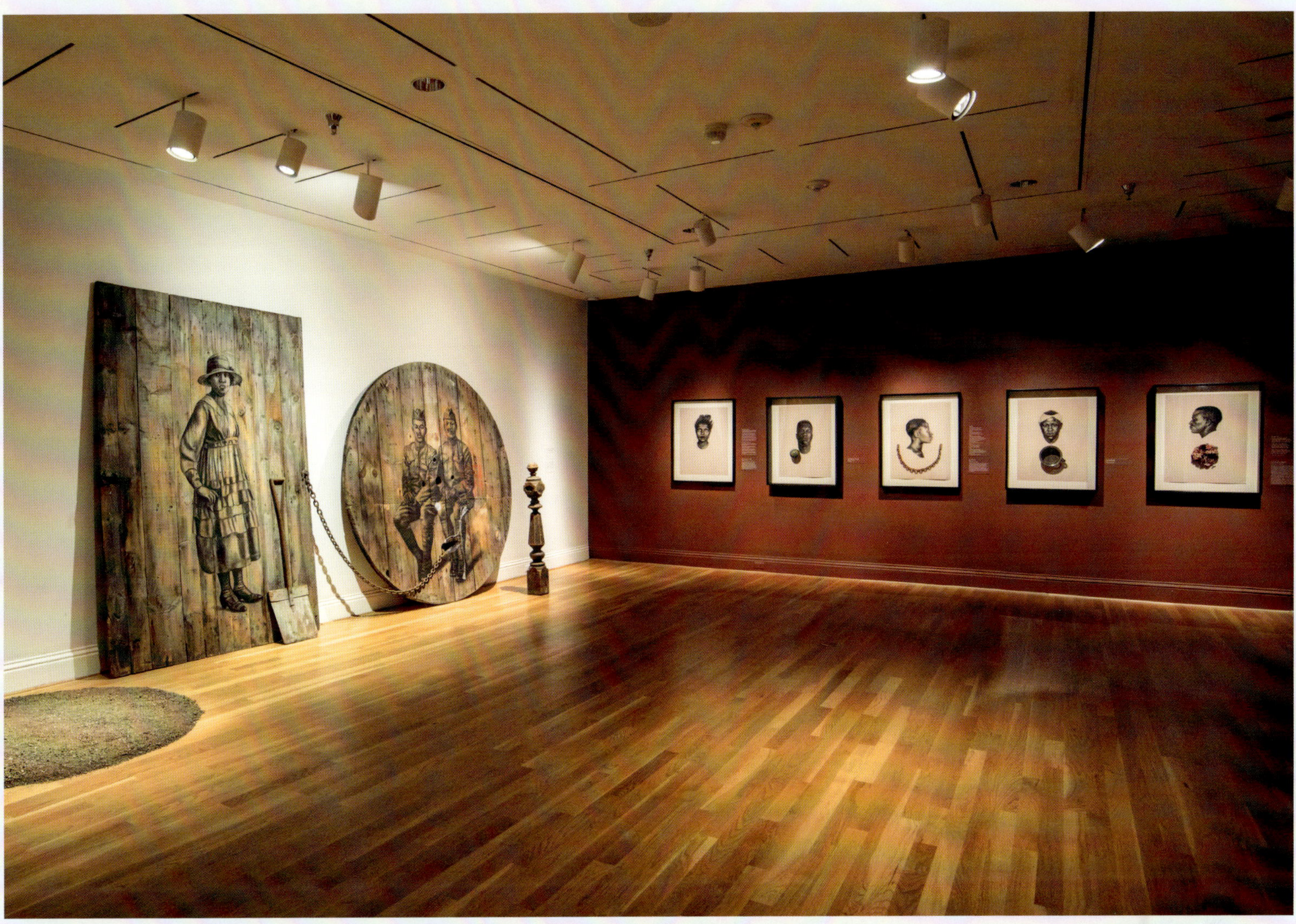

"endangered species" in the country, so I wanted to allude to that.

In *Kin XLI (Fauna)*, I loved the way that the man and the bird were both looking sideways in similar fashion. When you think about it, birds—and blackbirds, in particular—are often thought of as representing spirits. Nina Simone had a song: "Why you want to fly, blackbird? You ain't ever gonna fly." So that's what I was thinking about when I did that piece.

Kin XLV (Das Lied von der Erde) (pl. 135)—"The Song of the Earth" is one of my favorite pieces. The tear and the ruffling of her hair express so much of the pathos and the sadness of life, and I'm not just talking about Black people. I'm talking about the human experience. We're all born, we age, we suffer, we feel, and then we pass away, and everyone has that experience. Queens and princesses, servants, everyone shares that human experience.

ES: How would you like your work to be displayed in a museum such as the Phillips?

WL: I would like my work not to be segregated—Black art here, modernists there. It's the spirit in the artwork that's important. It's not like we're learning something by seeing what this group does and seeing what that group does. You learn more in a diverse culture by seeing the best of everything.

ES: Circling back to the occasion for this interview, the Phillips's centennial, what is your wish for the museum in the next century?

WL: I would like to see the Phillips continue to seek out diversity, and for museums in general to be as diverse and inclusive as the world. There's interesting work being done by African American artists as well as others. There's a generation or two or three before me that we need to catch up on. That work is still out there, and it should be brought in and appreciated and honored.

RETHINKING PHOTOGRAPHY AT THE PHILLIPS COLLECTION: LOOKING BACK/LOOKING FORWARD

Wendy A. Grossman

[Alfred Stieglitz] challenged the misconception that a photograph must remain mechanical and he affirmed that by a camera's mechanism an artist can produce miracles of sensitized individual perception and interpretation.
—Duncan Phillips, 1947

The avant-garde photographic activity flourishing in the interwar period was not what opened Duncan Phillips's eyes to the artistry of the medium; rather, it was Alfred Stieglitz. Phillips wrote in 1926, "As yet the photograph has been perfected by only one or two men, notably Alfred Stieglitz."[1] He first translated this assessment into action a decade later by publishing an article extolling the creative potential of the camera and proposing an exhibition of Stieglitz's photographs.[2] It was not until 1945, however, that photographs would be accessioned into the museum's collection. The story of The Phillips Collection's now significant photography holdings can be traced from the founder's tentative endorsement and his gradual seduction by the medium to its robust and multifaceted presence of over fifteen hundred works in the institution today.

The past two decades have seen a striking increase in The Phillips Collection's photographic acquisitions, growing over twentyfold since the start of the new century.[3] How this expansion came about is a testament to the central place photography occupies in the contemporary art world as well as a little-explored facet of the museum's history. Considered here are the forces that have shaped the museum's approaches to collecting and exhibiting photography, as well as the way in which these new works have come to join conversations about modernism at the institution's core and Phillips's ideas about artistic dialogues.

Duncan Phillips's taste in photography was forged by his relationship with Stieglitz, built over decades of working together to promote American artists in whose work they shared an interest. He was impressed by Stieglitz's modernist sensibilities, his advocacy for recognition of photography as a modern art form, and, in particular, the evocative imagery of his metaphorical *Equivalents* series (see fig. 71). Phillips's endeavors to exhibit and acquire prints from that series, begun in 1937, came to fruition with Georgia O'Keeffe's bequest of nineteen of these images following the photographer's death. In her August 11, 1949 letter about the gift, O'Keeffe wrote: "Stieglitz so often spoke of intending to send [the photographs] himself. I think they will feel

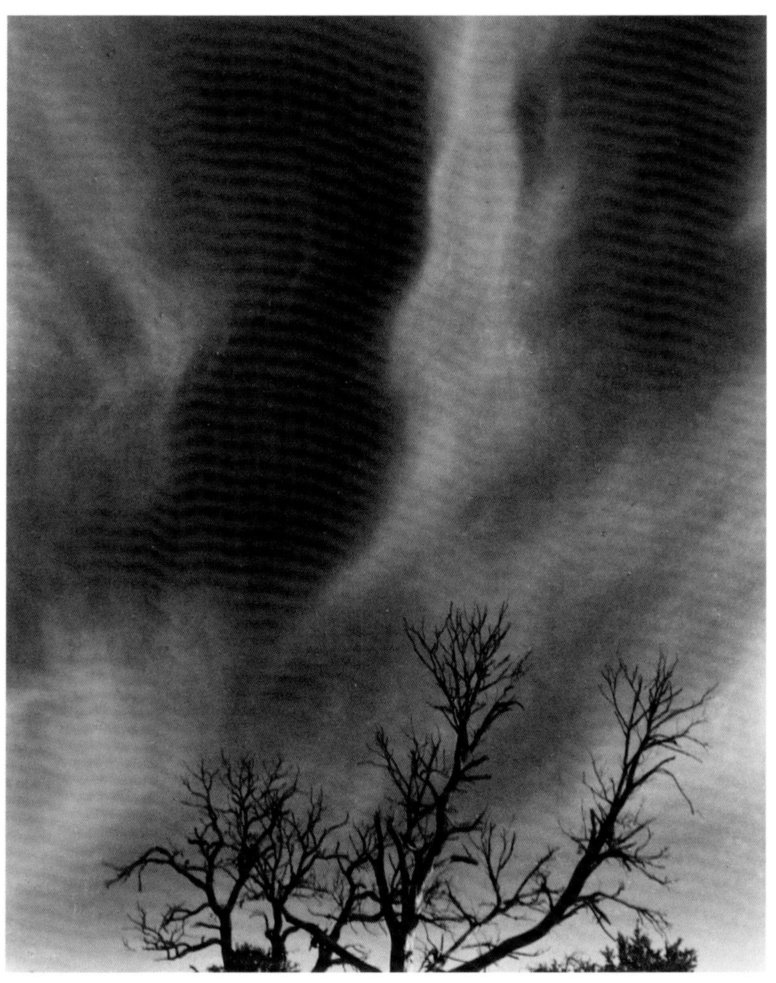

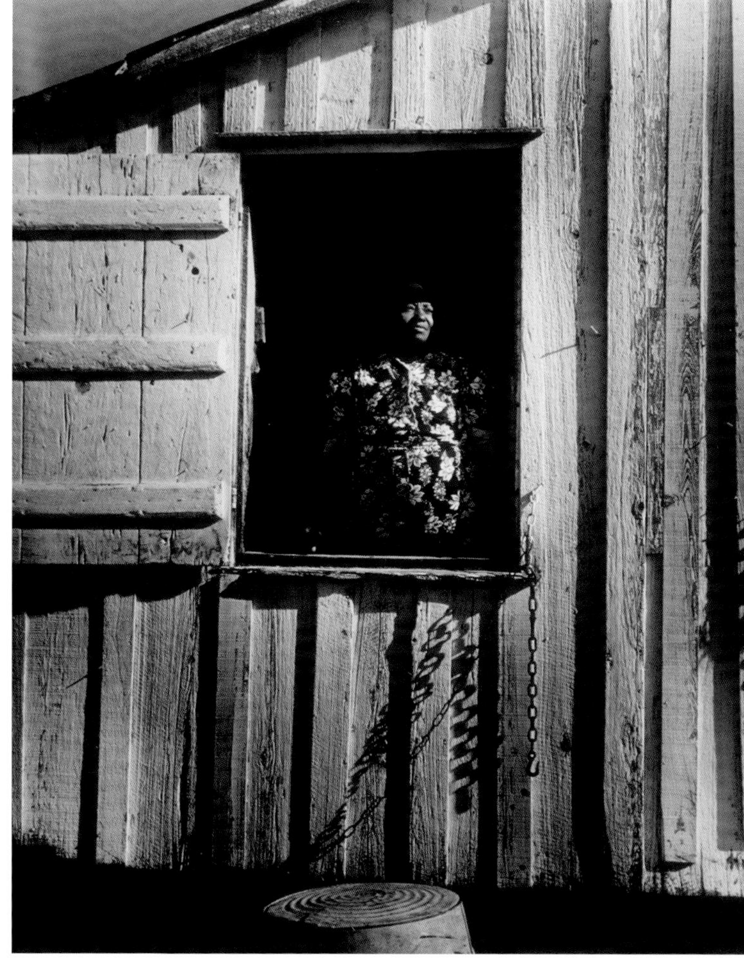

fig. 71 (left)
Alfred Stieglitz
***Equivalent*, 1925**
Gelatin silver print,
4 3/4 × 3 5/8 in.
The Phillips Collection,
Washington, DC,
The Alfred Stieglitz
Collection, gift of Georgia
O'Keeffe, 1949.

fig. 72 (right)
Clarence John Laughlin
***Black and White No. 2*, 1940**
Gelatin silver print,
14 × 11 in.
The Phillips Collection,
Washington, DC,
Acquired from the artist,
1948.

very much at home with you."[4] With this bequest, The Phillips Collection joined a select group of museums in the United States whose photographic collections were similarly nurtured.[5]

The value Phillips placed on maintaining connections with living artists he admired is further reflected in his activities with photographers. Prior to the Stieglitz bequest, he had begun in the mid-1940s to collect photographs by Clarence John Laughlin, a Louisiana photographer with whom he maintained a long personal relationship. He gave Laughlin one of his first solo museum shows in 1943, and acquired twenty-seven of his works between 1945 and 1956. Photographs like *Black and White No. 2* (fig. 72)—with its dramatic interplay between formal and conceptual concerns and pointed commentary on race—clearly resonated for the collector, who was one of the photographer's earliest supporters.[6]

Some of the last photographic works Phillips acquired and exhibited were also by an individual he knew and admired as a visitor to the museum, Henri Cartier-Bresson.[7] Five photographs covering three decades of this renowned French photographer's career were exhibited and entered into the collection in 1964, two years before Phillips's death. It is not difficult to see how work such as the photographer's dynamic portrait of Swiss sculptor Alberto Giacometti (fig. 73) melded with Phillips's other collecting interests, including the monumental bronze head by Giacometti he had acquired two years before.

It wasn't until the 1990s, however, that the museum made a conscious institutional decision to build its photography collection, using its limited acquisitions budget to acquire classic modern photographs in the tradition of Stieglitz and his circle. A substantive core of gifts acquired in the mid-1990s and 2000s with support from the Phillips Contemporaries and other friends of the museum include iconic works of high modernism by Berenice Abbott (pl. 1), Ansel Adams (pl. 171), Cartier-Bresson (pl. 169), Imogen Cunningham (pl. 60), André Kertész, Aaron Siskind (pls. 112, 167, 200–202), Paul Strand, and Edward Weston (pl. 61). The emphasis in these works on the medium's formal qualities and experimentation with perspective, light, and cropping epitomize the modernist photographic aesthetic. Phillips's philosophy toward collecting "units" of artists' work that encapsulate their entire careers is carried on in the way the museum's photographic collection has been built, with Siskind being one of the first to be accorded this treatment.[8] Subsequently, the collection has become a major repository of works by Esther Bubley, William Christenberry, Alvin Langdon Coburn, Bruce Davidson, Walker Evans, August Sander, and Brett Weston, among others.

A series of special exhibitions have raised the profile of photography at The Phillips Collection, a development that has also served to galvanize related donations. This scenario is reflected in the acquisitions of numerous German landscapes by Sander (see pls. 50–52), over 150 abstract photographs by Brett Weston spanning seven decades of his career (see pls. 16, 166), Evans's images of African sculptures from the photographic portfolio accompanying the seminal 1935 exhibition *African Negro Art* at New York's Museum of Modern Art (see pl. 124), and Man Ray's photograph of a mathematical model that inspired one of the canvases in his *Shakespearean Equations* series (see fig. 97; pl. 185).[9] The latter image is noteworthy as an outlier of sorts in the collection, representing as it does the radical interwar photographic activities of this dada/surrealist artist.[10]

The museum's collecting strategy received a critical boost in 2012 from the Photography Collectors Syndicate, a philanthropic organization of photography aficionados.[11] Gifts from members of the syndicate that have driven the exponential growth of the collection with in-depth work from individual photographers include over 170 works by Ralph Gibson (see pls. 2, 165) and over 160 by Joel Meyerowitz (see pls. 12, 13), whose early advocacy of the use of color film as a serious art form in the 1960s made him a pioneer in the history of American photography.[12] Similarly acquired photographs have filled the previous gap in the unit of Siskind's work with images from his Harlem series, a portfolio of photographs representing his early career as a member of the Photo League (see pl. 168).

While current museum collecting activities in photography are no longer guided by the taste of an individual collector, they are habitually informed by Phillips's interest in fostering creative conversations through contrast and analogy. Indeed, this paradigm has served as a key organizing principle in installations of the collection, as well as in numerous exhibitions mounted in the museum both during the founder's lifetime and in the ensuing decades.[13] The museum's expansive 2012 exhibition *Snapshot: Painters and Photography, Bonnard to Vuillard* is a quintessential expression of this conversation model. The synergistic relationship between the museum's new photographs and work in other mediums in its permanent collection

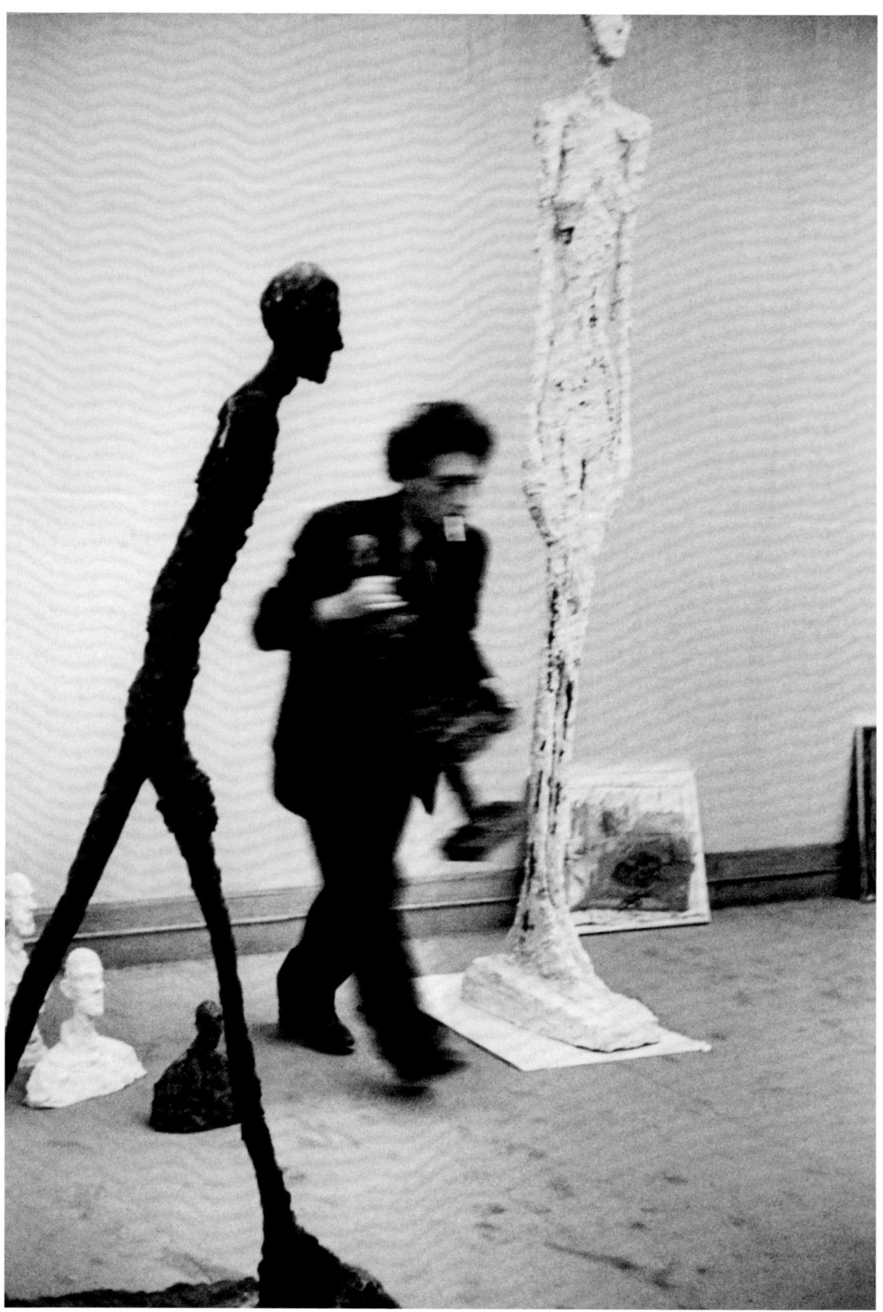

fig. 73
Henri Cartier-Bresson
***Giacometti*, undated**
Gelatin silver print,
13 3/4 × 9 1/4 in.
The Phillips Collection,
Washington, DC,
Acquired 1964.

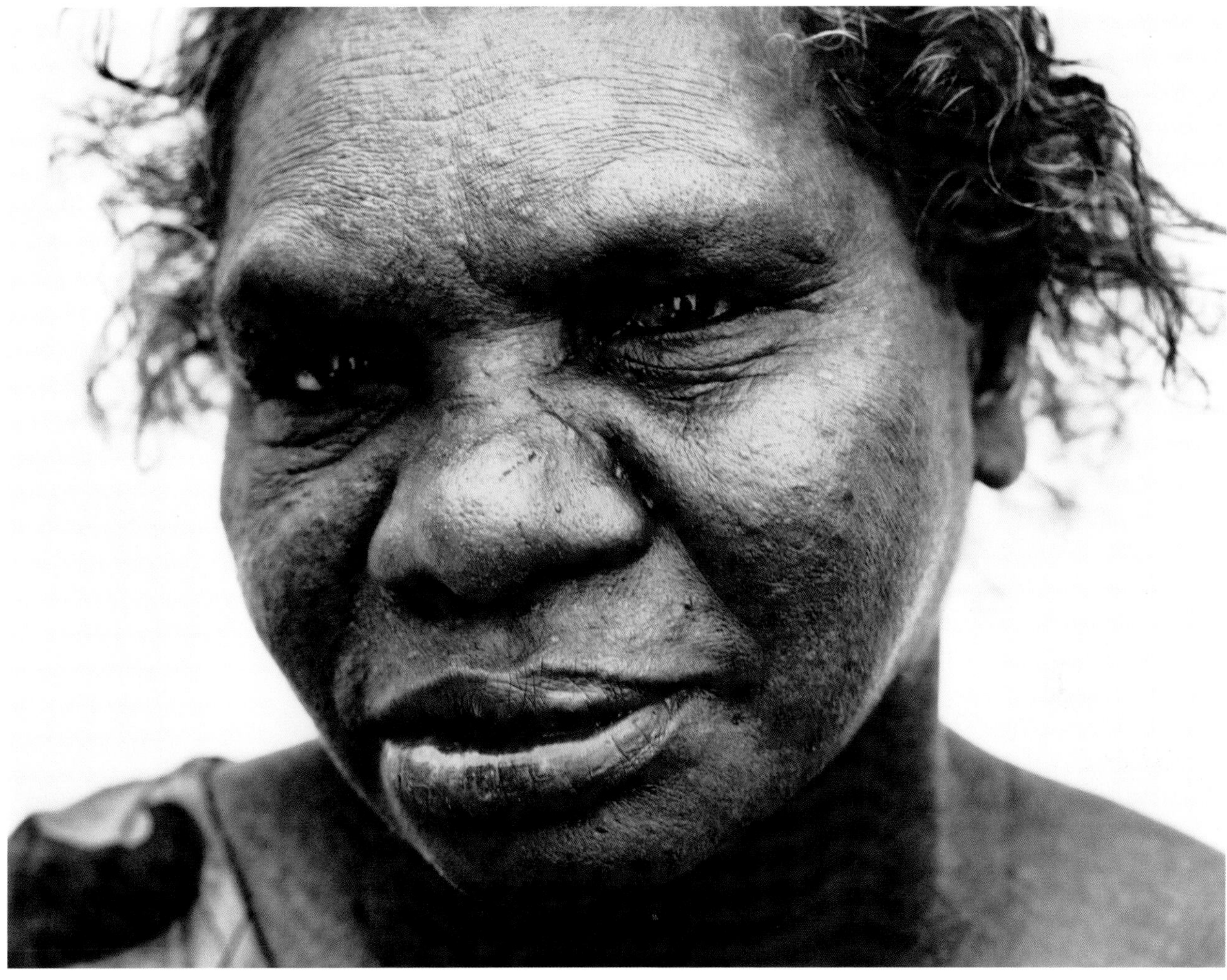

fig. 74
Ricky Maynard
Wik Elder, Gladys,
ca. 1938–39
Pigment print on paper,
12 × 16 in.
The Phillips Collection,
Washington, DC,
Acquired 2017.

is further underscored in the Phillips anniversary tribute, illustrated in the manner in which so many of the recent photographic acquisitions fit seamlessly within its thematic constructs.

The museum's contemporary art program, Intersections, has similarly encouraged conversational engagement with the permanent collection, thereby contributing to the increasing representation of living artists in the museum's photography collection. Emblematic of the acquisitions facilitated by this program is Allan deSouza's *The World Series* (see fig. 81), a group of thirty color photographs created in response to panels of Jacob Lawrence's *The Migration Series* in The Phillips Collection. This meditation on the rites of passage in a contemporary migration of the artist's imagination exposes the human condition of people in transition in today's world.[14]

The significant growth in the photographic holdings provided the stimulus in 2015 for *American Moments*, the Phillips's first major exhibition to celebrate gifts of photographs. Drawn exclusively from the burgeoning permanent collection, the exhibition featured 133 works by thirty-three photographers, whose images reflect a broad swath of mid-twentieth-century America. Revisiting selected images from this endeavor six years later in this centenary celebration offers the opportunity to examine them within new contexts and appreciate how the photographers' creative visions resonate with the museum's collection as a whole. Illuminated in this new framework is the distinctive fashion in which American photographers such as Esther Bubley (pls. 151, 152), Bruce Davidson (pls. 7, 8, 153), and Alfred Eisenstaedt (pl. 155) embraced the medium for its social, political, and aesthetic potential. Striking portraits by W. Eugene Smith (pl. 129) and Laura Gilpin (pl. 93), and Depression-era sociopolitical exposés by Walker Evans (pls. 144, 154), further illustrate how photographers

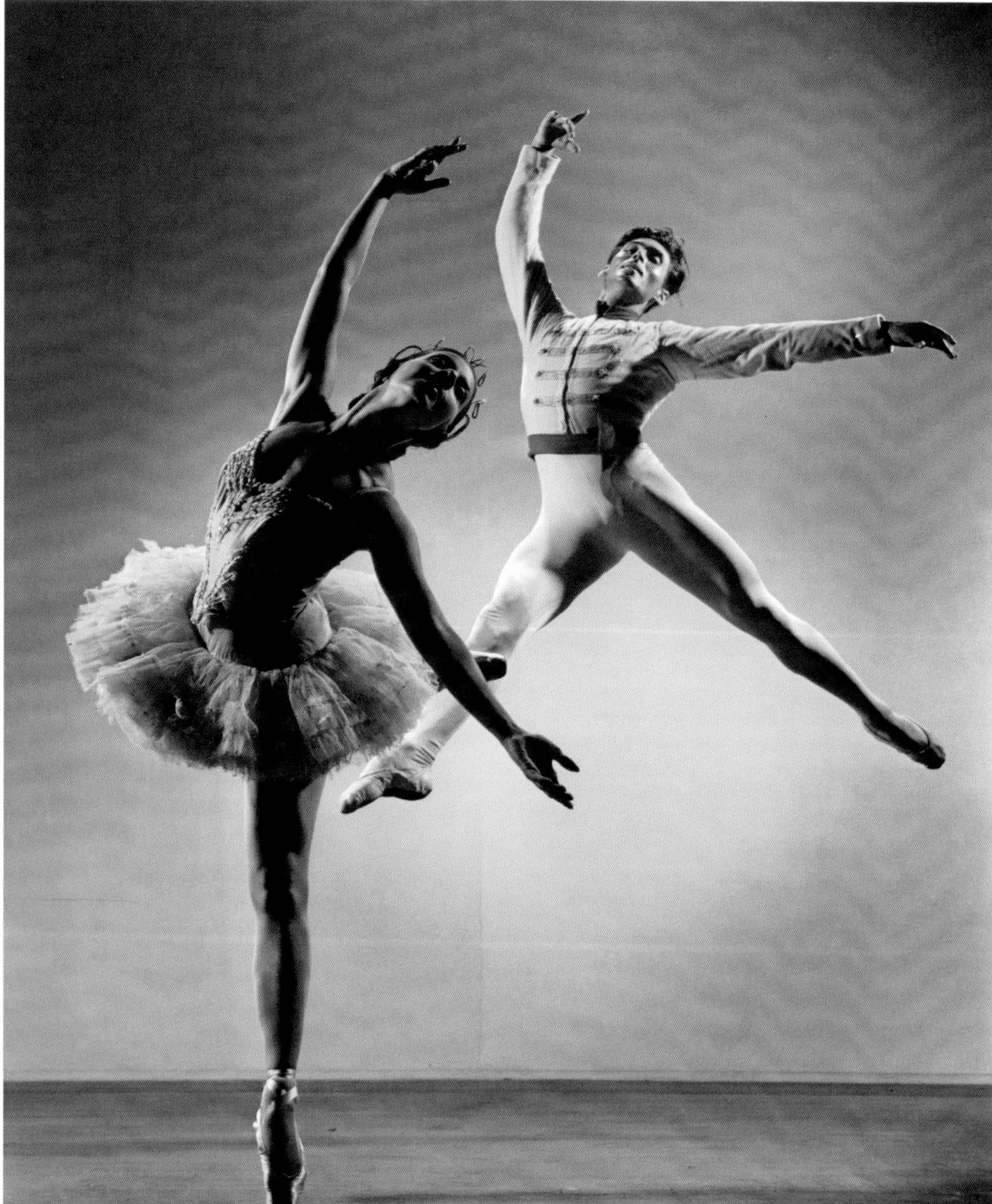

fig. 75
Gjon Mili
***Alicia Alonso and Igor Youskevitch Performing*, 1947**
Gelatin silver print,
14 × 11 in.
The Phillips Collection,
Washington, DC,
Gift of Cam and Wanda Garner,
2013.

employed the medium as an incisive representational or documentary means of expression.

The socially conscious tradition of these New Deal-era photographers finds poignant counterpoints in contemporary works that have subsequently entered the collection, such as John Edmonds's haunting image from his *Hoods* series (pl. 30). Photographs in this series, in his words, "act as radical affirmation that this—the push for visibility, for safety, for justice, for empathy—is not only up to me, but also up to you."[15]

The broad range of formal and conceptual concerns manifest in works in the museum's collection today encompasses the multiplicity of ways in which photography has operated at the heart of both modernist and post-modern discourses. Bracketing the historical and aesthetic span of the collection on one end is Alvin Langdon Coburn's 1911 *The Great Temple, Grand Canyon* (pl. 6), an exemplar of pictorialism and the international movement's efforts at the turn of the century to claim a place for photography in the realm of fine art. On the other end are works by contemporary artists such as Anselm Kiefer (pls. 26; 179) and Annette Messager (pl. 128), whose multimedia artworks incorporate the photographic medium in ways that defy simple categorization. While the Phillips's photography collection remains predominantly twentieth-century

American, the institution's initiatives on diversity and efforts to present a more global perspective notably inflect its new acquisition practices. Recent additions of photographs by Tasmanian Ricky Maynard (fig. 74), Albanian Gjon Mili (fig. 75), Nigerian J. D. 'Okhai Ojeikere (pls. 31–34), Korean Nikki S. Lee, and other international artists are incorporating previously unheard voices into the museum's creative dialogues. Works by Lee from several of her performance projects, along with photographs such as those by British artist Sam Taylor-Johnson (pl. 142), Jeanine Michna-Bales (pls. 21–24) and others, also reflect the greater visibility of female artists in the museum's rapidly growing contemporary collection.

In terms of subject matter, style, technique, intentionality, and scale, the new acquisitions offer an instructive study in contrast and an opportunity to gain greater appreciation for the range of artistic activity that falls under the rubric of photography. Indeed, such examples in the museum's collection present a history of twentieth- and twenty-first-century photography in microcosm, tracing the story from analog to digital practices and from the ubiquity of the black-and-white gelatin silver print as a modernist vehicle to the diversity of formats and techniques used in contemporary practices. Revealed in this trajectory is how conventional approaches to the medium, and even the very definition of photography, have undergone radical change from Duncan Phillips's initial acquisitions to this moment of the museum's centennial. No longer a stepchild, photography has gained its place in The Phillips Collection as in other major museums, as a fully recognized, vital, and still evolving art form.

The epigraph is from *Stieglitz Memorial Portfolio, 1864-1946* (New York: Twice a Year Press), 1947.

1 Duncan Phillips, *A Collection in the Making* (New York: E. Weyhe; Washington, DC: Phillips Memorial Gallery, 1926), 7. The fact that Phillips attributed the perfection of photography to just one or two *men*—despite the pioneering role of a number of female practitioners in the history of photography—should not pass unnoted. The esteem in which Phillips held Stieglitz, and his belief in his importance, is further reflected in his role in advising Georgia O'Keeffe to donate Stieglitz's work to the newly founded National Gallery of Art. See Sarah Greenough, *Alfred Stieglitz: The Key Set* (New York: Harry N. Abrams, 2002), XI, L, n. 5.

2 Duncan Phillips, "Personality in Art, II: Reflections on Its Suppression and the Present Need for Its Fulfillment," *American Magazine of Art* 28, no. 3 (March 28, 1935). On Phillips's efforts to secure the loan of Stieglitz's photographs for an exhibition, see Elizabeth Turner, *In the American Grain: Arthur Dove, Marsden Hartley, John Marin, Georgia O'Keeffe, and Alfred Stieglitz* (Washington, DC: Counterpoint, 1995), 153.

3 Since the turn of the twenty-first century, over fifteen hundred photographs have been added to the sixty-six prints accounted for prior to that time.

4 Correspondence from Georgia O'Keeffe to Duncan and Marjorie Phillips in the museum's archives.

5 For a full list of museums that received photographs as gifts from Stieglitz during his lifetime, or received or acquired them from the Alfred Stieglitz Estate, see Greenough, "Notes to the Reader/Stieglitz Collections," in *Stieglitz: The Key Set*, pp. LIX–LXI. The place of photography in institutional collecting practices touched upon here is a relatively recent field of inquiry. See Elizabeth Edwards and Christopher Morton, eds., *Photographs, Museums, Collections: Between Art and Information* (London: Bloomsbury, 2015).

6 Correspondence between Phillips and Laughlin in the museum archives chronicles their relationship. See also A. J. Meek, *Clarence John Laughlin: Prophet without Honor* (Jackson, MS: University Press of Mississippi, 2007), 78, 80, 84, 86, 88, 117, 119, 208 n. 18.

7 See "Exhibitions at the Phillips Collection," in Erika D. Passantino and David W. Scott, eds., *The Eye of Duncan Phillips: A Collection in the Making* (New Haven, CT: Yale University Press; Washington, DC: Phillips Collection, 1999), 659–74.

8 In the early 2000s, then-curator Stephen Phillips identified Siskind as a major figure in twentieth-century photography whom The Phillips Collection should consider a "unit" artist to be focused upon for acquisitions.On Duncan Phillips's philosophy about collecting "units," see Passantino and Scott, *The Eye of Duncan Phillips*.

9 Exhibitions that occasioned these gifts are: *August Sander: Photographs of the German Landscape* (2004); *Brett Weston: Out of the Shadow* (2008); *Man Ray, African Art, and the Modernist Lens* (2009); and *Man Ray–Human Equations: A Journey from Mathematics to Shakespeare* (2015).

10 Prior to this acquisition, Man Ray was represented in the collection solely by his 1914 canvas, *The Black Tray*, which Phillips purchased in 1927.

11 The Photography Collectors Syndicate was founded in 2001 by Howard Greenberg and Michael Axelrod. See "Dedicated Donors: Jill and Jeffrey Stern and the Photography Buyers Syndicate," *Magazine of the National Museum of Women in the Arts*, Fall 2019: 7.

12 See Joel Meyerowitz and Colin Westerbeck, *Joel Meyerowitz. Where I Find Myself: A Lifetime Retrospective* (London: Laurence King, 2018).

13 Examples include: *Two Photographs by Edward Steichen of Rodin's Balzac* (1956); *Sculpture Seen Anew: The Bronze Age to Brancusi: Photographs by C. J. Laughlin* (1960 and 1965); *Two Lives: Georgia O'Keeffe and Alfred Stieglitz, A Conversation in Paintings and Photographs* (1992); *Brancusi: Photographs and Sculpture* (1994); *In the American Grain: Arthur Dove, Marsden Hartley, John Marin, Georgia O'Keeffe, and Alfred Stieglitz* (1995); and *Americans in Paris: Man Ray, Gerald Murphy, Stuart Davis, Alexander Calder* (1996).

14 Vesela Sretenović, *Intersections@5: Contemporary Art Projects at the Phillips* (Washington, DC: Phillips Collection, 2015), 38–39.

15 John Edmonds, "John Edmonds: on the hoodie," *Financial Times*, January 5, 2018: https://www.ft.com/content/e7172732-f014-11e7-ac08-07c3086a2625. Accessed April 2020.

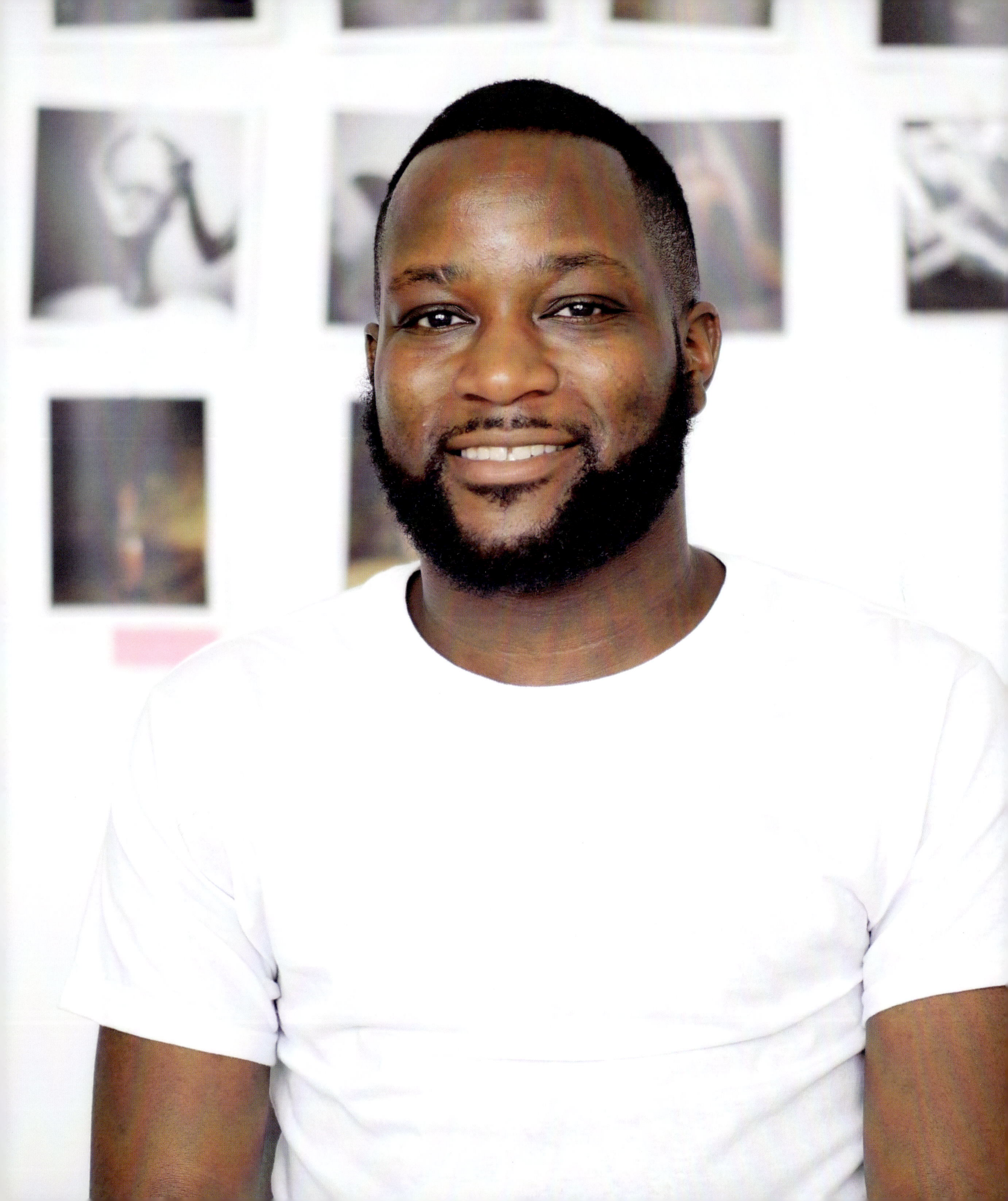

Elsa Smithgall: You have strong DC roots. What was it like spending your formative years in the area?

John Edmonds: Growing up in DC was really enriching because you have museums like the Smithsonian Institution and the Phillips with all these incredible canonical works of art that you may or may not have studied in grade school or learned of in an art history class in college. When I was a student at the Corcoran College of Art and Design, it was a different time. Obama was in office. The Corcoran hosted a show called *30 Americans* in 2011, a tour de force highlighting thirty African American contemporary artists who have had tremendous influence on art today. That show changed my life in so many ways. I saw Black art that spoke directly to the complexity of the times, and it wasn't just the work of these incredible artists, who were making art about their world and how they're seen or their aspirations: many of them came to DC to give lectures. I was fortunate enough to have studio visits with many of them, such as Kara Walker, and Hank Willis Thomas. Hank has become an important mentor to me. It was all a really exciting time, and it was at that point that I committed to being an artist.

ES: Were there any challenges that you experienced as an emerging artist in DC?

JE: There are definitely obstacles related to being in a city where there is a contemporary art scene without a high level of visibility: figuring out how to penetrate and become an active member of that community. But there's a unique intellectual rigor in DC; interesting and complex ways that art and politics converge.

While I was in DC, there was this divide between contemporary art practices in sound and performance and this really kind of historical and, in many ways, bureaucratic idea of understanding art and art-making. How to find a way to bring together the two worlds that I am part of? Growing up in DC really helped me develop my worldview.

ES: How did your interest in photographic portraiture develop?

JE: I was commuting by train between DC and Prince George's County [Maryland], where my family lives, and I began paying close attention to people around me. I started approaching young African American men, asking if I could make their portraits. Photography became a way for me to gain access and to have intimate and private kinds of engagements with strangers.

ES: During your visits to The Phillips Collection, were there particular works that you admired?

JE: I remember many encounters having a tremendous impact on me. A few years ago, a Sam Gilliam that I had never seen before [*Red Petals*, 1967] really stood out to me—it wasn't like the Gilliams that I'm familiar with, the large kind of draperies. I really respect and admire the Phillips for highlighting work that artists may not be as recognized for; it's something museums should do. And the Rothko Room—you can feel that sense of spirituality, that feeling of being overcome by something greater than yourself.

ES: Issues of self, representation, community, and the spiritual coalesce in your work, from the *Immaculate* series through the *Hoods*, *Du-Rags*, and *A Sidelong Glance*. Does a spiritual view of humanity inform your interest in expressing the beauty and intimacy of self?

JE: Absolutely. In all these bodies of work, what you see is photography used as a tool for connecting with others and for more humanistic introspection. What really

John Edmonds in his Brooklyn studio, March 2020.

IN CONVERSATION WITH

JOHN EDMONDS

Adapted from an interview with Elsa Smithgall that took place in the artist's Brooklyn studio, March 11, 2020.

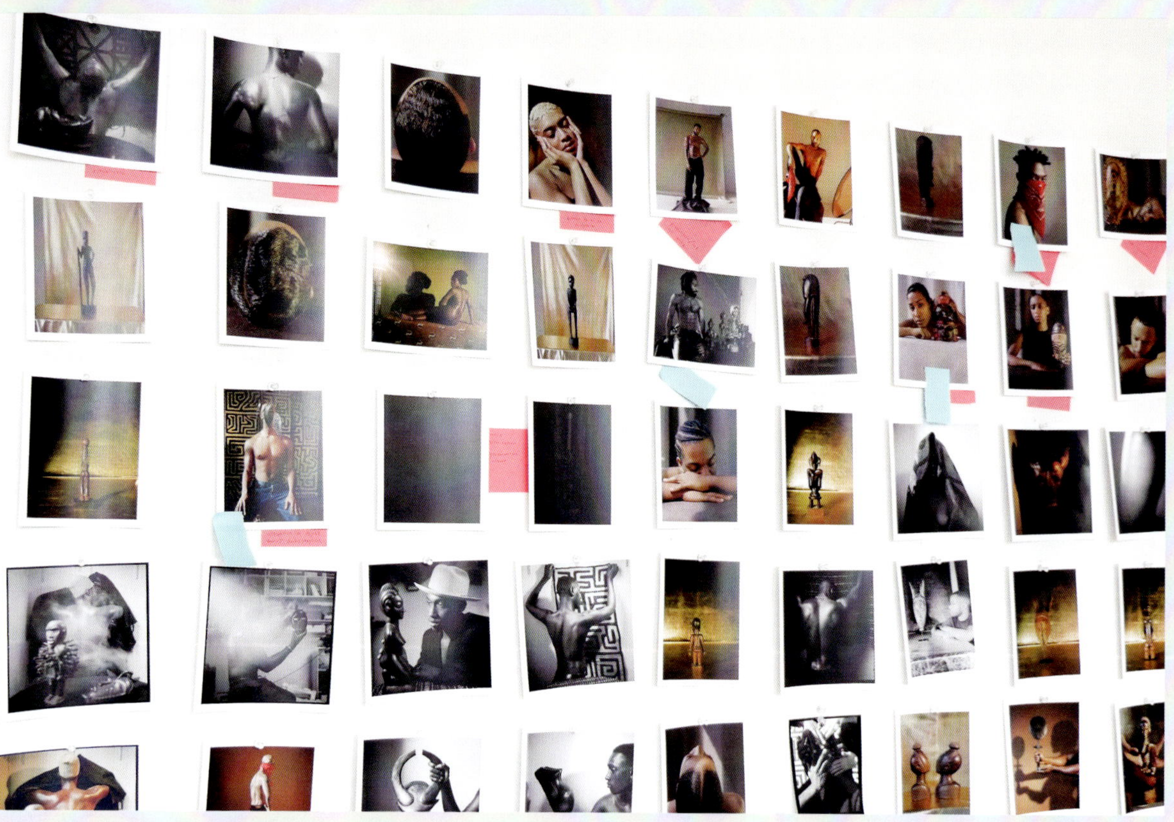

figs. 76 & 77
John Edmonds's Brooklyn studio, March 2020.

drives all of the work is a desire to revere others and myself through the medium. I have been to Ghana and Jamaica and places where there is a sense of disruption from colonialism. The larger question for me is my place in this picture—in this larger story of diaspora and displacement and the desire for connection.

ES: Speaking of Ghana, how did African art objects find their way into your *A Sidelong Glance* body of work?

JE: I remember that the first time I saw something that resembled an African art object was in my own home, when I was a young child. We had all these pseudo-African masks. I took them as completely authentic because they were part of my everyday experience. In 2017, at a friend's house—this is where *A Sidelong Glance* begins—in his living room, I saw one of these objects that reminded me of the ones that I grew up with. I was struck by how many of these African art objects were created with this connection to human likeness. That moment of rediscovering these objects that I had an innate connection to, in a space with people who are like extended family to me, prompted this desire to incorporate them into my practice.

ES: The *A Sidelong Glance* works speak to an earlier history of photographs of African art by artists like Rotimi Fani-Kayode, Carl Van Vechten, Man Ray, Alfred Stieglitz, Walker Evans, and others. How do you think about reimagining the narrative of these earlier images?

I HAVE BEEN TO GHANA AND JAMAICA AND PLACES WHERE THERE IS A SENSE OF DISRUPTION FROM COLONIALISM.

JE: The words "imagine" and "reimagine" are deeply connected to the root word "image." So much of my work is about reimagining. As far as these canonical works by artists like Walker Evans and Rotimi Fani-Kayode are concerned, I was always interested in the different ways that these artists engage with the African art objects and in how much those differences had to do with their worldviews. You have someone like Rotimi Fani-Kayode, who is Black British, and from an esteemed Yoruba family. He is negotiating these different aspects of his personhood, who he is in the world, through the photographic medium. Then you have other artists from completely outside the culture, who incorporate African art objects into their work—Man Ray, for example. I'm interested in what happens when the same objects are in different hands. What happens when they're in the hands of someone with a connection to Africa—whether it's ancestral or a general longing for a view of this place, its beauty, its truth? Because when you look at Man Ray or Walker Evans insistently using these objects, there's a lack of context and a kind of sucking of life out of the actual object. My own position as an artist is not a contentious one: it's one of wondering how I open a subject up even more, for people to be able to receive these objects with the reverence that they're actually due. My ambition is to kind of reify them.

At the end of 2017, I started making the *A Sidelong Glance* photographs right on the heels of the *Du-Rags* pictures. At the time, I wasn't sure exactly where the work was headed, but I knew that I wanted to wave the hair of the models and that I wanted this sense of warm, golden light that was very much a part of the earlier kind of photographs that I had made. The people in *A Sidelong Glance*, like many of the models in my other works, are everyday people that I see in New York—friends and acquaintances and people who have had an impact on me; a specific creative community that occupies Brooklyn and the Lower East Side. Those pictures became the beginning of documenting this group of people in the same way that Carl Van Vechten, in the twenties and thirties, was documenting all the writers and thinkers and philosophers and tastemakers of his time. I was interested in how photography has this kind of intrinsically documentary or indexical nature. It felt as though I was seeing that kind of community come into themselves as people, as thinkers. So there's the canonical nod, but at the same time, they are pictures of friends and acquaintances and people that I have seen who have had an impact on me. There is a relationship that unfolds through photographic practice.

ES: Who are your artist heroes?

JE: In an art context, I look less at photography than at sculpture and painting, two mediums I've always liked as ways of thinking about light. I'm very much interested in light as a metaphor for revelation or enlightenment or discovery. Most of the artists that I find really inspiring and compelling are my peers and friends; also the makers of these African sculptures. That's why I went to Ghana—to see that kind of rigorous process. When I think of modernism, I don't think of Picasso or Modigliani; I think of African art. I think about these forms that have influenced almost every aspect of visual culture. I want to re-center that, because these objects have been overlooked. So, the people who make these African art objects, they have been one of my hugest inspirations.

ES: What do you find most compelling about the medium of photography?

JE: The thing that really excites me and really draws me to photography is that

IN AN ART CONTEXT, I LOOK LESS AT PHOTOGRAPHY THAN AT SCULPTURE AND PAINTING, TWO MEDIUMS I'VE ALWAYS LIKED AS WAYS OF THINKING ABOUT LIGHT.

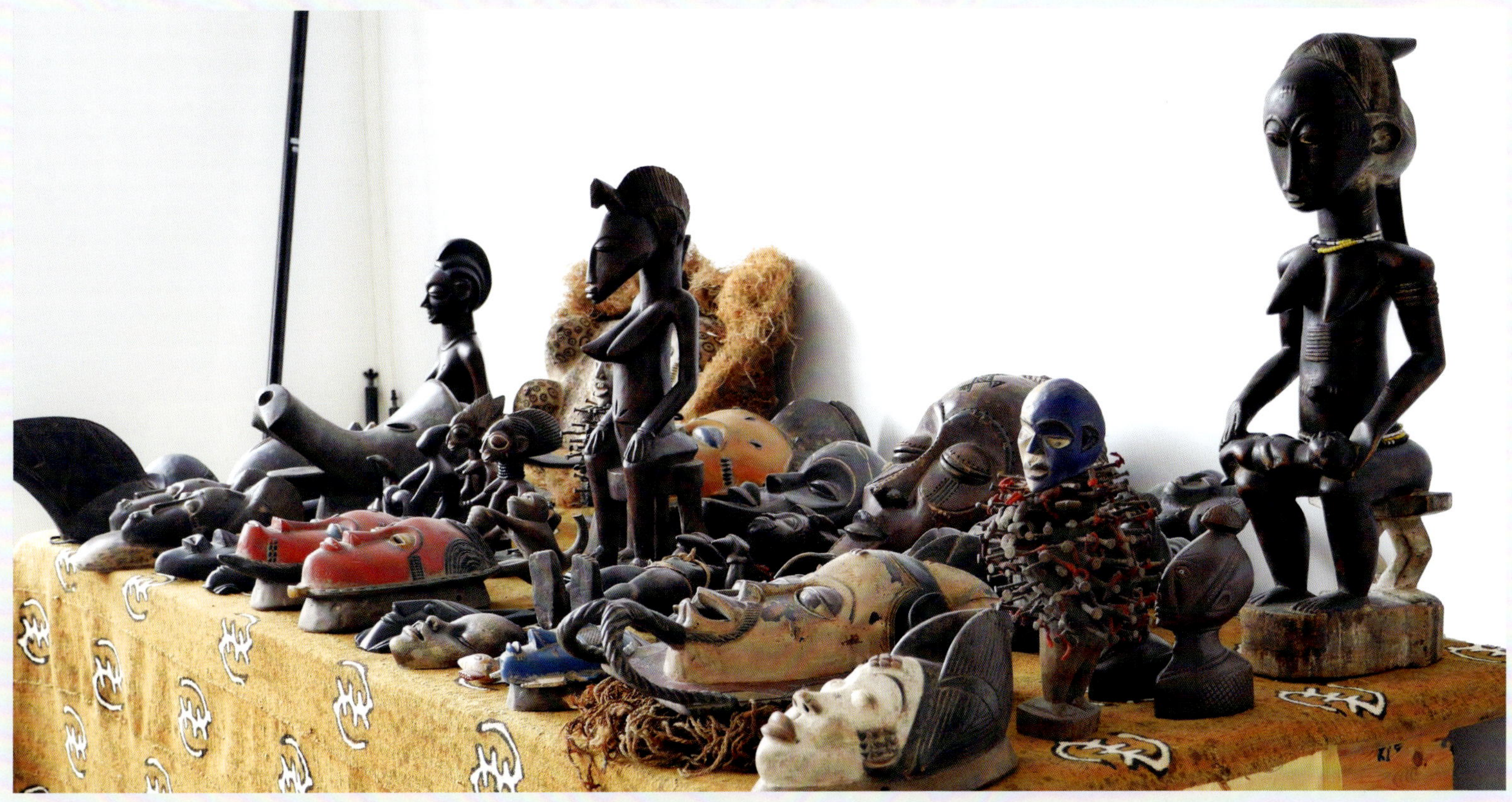

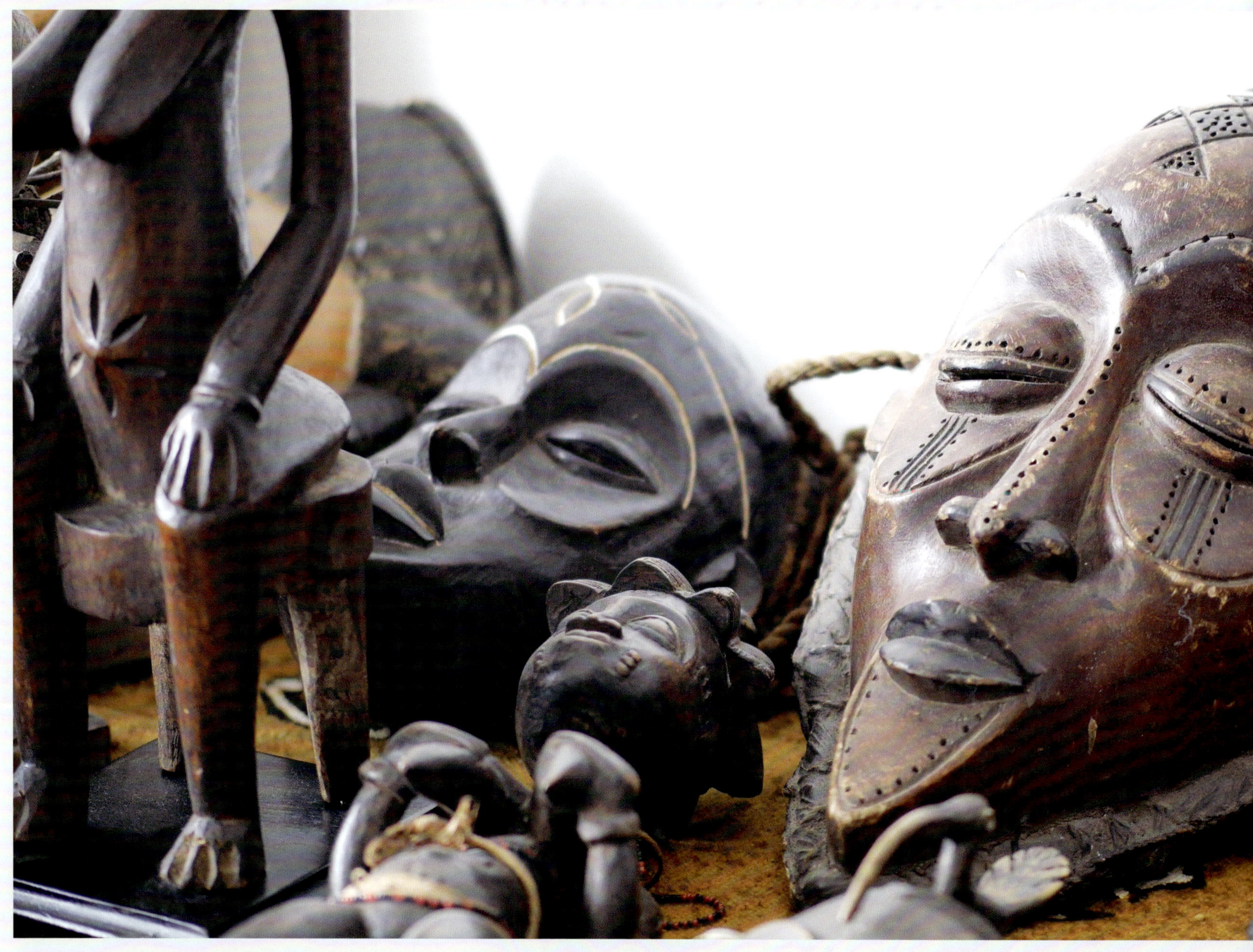

it is so ubiquitous. Photography is part of our world, and it's how we are able to understand the world around us. It's also exciting for the way it can intersect with different media—sculpture, painting; the relationship it has had to other media.

I like the open-endedness of photography, all the different ways of working—with a 4 × 5 camera, or a digital camera, or cameraless, or in a darkroom. There are so many different ways that photography can be used, and I think that what's really exciting about it is how it always asks, no matter whose hands it is in: how are you going to use me? It's an incredible medium, and it's one that just keeps on giving.

ES: In your monograph, *Higher*, Shane Lavalette quotes you as saying: "I hope my work can reflect the reality of this country right now." That idea resonates in your work, including your *Hood* series, which calls to mind the death of Trayvon Martin and its context of systemic racism. To what extent are you thinking about photography as an instrument for political and social change?

JE: Photography can speak to issues and concerns in the world. The question I ask in all my work is what the essential tools are for viewers to see themselves as a part of how the image is read, received, and consumed. I try to make work from a place of introspection. As an artist, I am not reactive but I am responsive, and I am responsible to the concerns that I have not only as an artist, but as a citizen. No matter how set up

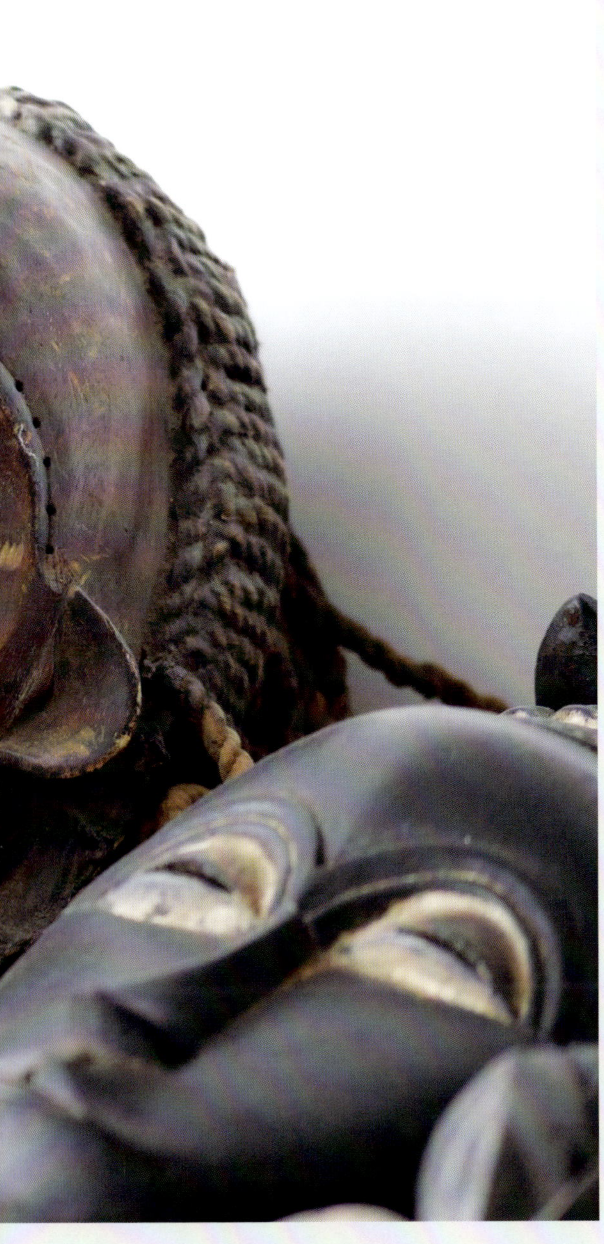

fig. 78
John Edmonds's Brooklyn studio, March 2020.

or constructed the image, it has to speak to reality and remind us directly of experiences of our time.

I began the *Hoods* pictures while I was living in New Haven. It was a project about a simple item of clothing worn by many people of all races, ages, and genders (see pl. 30). I was interested in how people would respond to this racially coded item in images where the identity of the wearer was completely obscured or opaque. Claudia Rankine uses the term "racial imaginary"—the lens of whiteness, something that is very much part of the American psychological landscape. In a kind of passive-aggressive way, those *Hoods* pictures address this large elephant in the room. I'm working in a public space in this very sore-thumb kind of way, with a camera on a tripod, when I'm making those pictures. I have all these hooded jackets with me, and I'm casting people as they walk by, costuming them with clothes from my own wardrobe. I often talk about those pictures in terms of "self-portraiture"—in quotation marks, because I'm not necessarily the subject. The self-portrait can be located in the viewer locating him- or herself within the dynamic of looking.

It's a figure in a hood, but the issue is how as a society we racialize and create fictions around those we do not know. I tell my students photography is not merely about how interesting the composition is or how great the light is, because those are all things that a competent person can, with practice, control. What is important is for a picture to make you slow down and ask yourself: what am I seeing?

ES: Tell us a bit about your studio practice (figs. 76–78) and what drives your creative thought process?

JE: You have to work with things not going exactly your way, and say, "Okay, what else can transpire, given the circumstances that we are working with?" It ends up being a really beautiful kind of call and response, or freestyle. It wasn't until now that I actually thought about that as an analogy for the work, but that's what it is. How do I pull all these different things together to make a picture that says something more than my immediate engagement with the model? I want to speak to larger concerns around humanity, not simply representation, but humanity and creating records of existence.

NO MATTER HOW SET UP OR CONSTRUCTED THE IMAGE, IT HAS TO SPEAK TO REALITY AND REMIND US DIRECTLY OF EXPERIENCES OF OUR TIME.

ES: In this digital age, what attracts you to historical, analog techniques in photography?

JE: This is a solarized photograph on the wall, and it's a very dark image. I made many of them to be that way. I'm interested in early photographic practices and what they allow on a craft level, because that is something that's not really being considered right now. I'm excited when I see work that *does* take the past into consideration, because I feel so fortunate to have followed right on the heels of photographers who were able to learn analog photography in such a close and intimate way.

ES: What is your wish for the future of the Phillips in the next century?

JE: Selfishly, it's to see more shows of younger artists; more artists addressing contemporary concerns.

CONNECTING MODERN WITH CONTEMPORARY: INTERSECTIONS AT THE PHILLIPS

Vesela Sretenović

Contemporary art has been at the core of The Phillips Collection from its inception. Although the museum may be best known for its exquisite collection of modern painting, most of it dating from the late nineteenth century to the mid-twentieth, by Americans and Europeans—from Arthur Dove, Jacob Lawrence, Georgia O'Keeffe, and Mark Rothko to Pierre Bonnard, Paul Klee, Henri Matisse, Pierre-Auguste Renoir, and Nicolas de Staël—its founder, Duncan Phillips, stated his focus early on: "Our emphasis is on the art of our time with a few great masters of the earlier centuries as inspiration and source material."[1] Championing living artists, Phillips exhibited their work, wrote about it, and acquired it for his museum. As he said, "I am attracted to qualities of contemporary art precisely because they thrill me with refreshing differences from any qualities I have cherished before, and I admire the aesthetic interpretations of the age we live in—even the symbols for the anarchy, the turmoil and the inner tensions."[2]

Since Phillips's death in 1966, the museum has continued to build on this legacy of exhibiting and acquiring contemporary art. Presentations in just the past two decades include solo exhibitions of George Condo, Moira Dryer, Antony Gormley, Ellsworth Kelly, Per Kirkeby, Robert Ryman, Zilia Sánchez, Sean Scully, and Frank Stella, among others. Notable twenty-first-century site-specific commissions include a wax room by Wolfgang Laib (see fig. 25; pl. 203) and two outdoor sculptures by Ellsworth Kelly (pl. 98) and Angela Bulloch (pl. 105).[3]

The Phillips's centennial is a good moment to reflect on the institution's evolution and to consider how trends in contemporary art have shaped its exhibitions, programs, and collection as a whole. Moreover, it offers an opportunity to celebrate the tenth-plus anniversary of its first series of contemporary art projects—Intersections.[4]

In the aftermath of the 2008 market crash and the great recession, with its toll on the world economy, including the arts (their production, presentation, and funding), the question was how to engage with art in a new century shaken by a deep financial crisis and driven by fast-paced lifestyles, social media, and globalization, especially at an institution like the Phillips that has remained loyal to modernist canons. Inaugurated in 2009, Intersections came from a search for exhibition models and themes that would bridge the art of past and present. Remembering Duncan Phillips's words "that

fig. 79 (opposite top)
Installation of Sandra Cinto's *One Day, After the Rain*, 2012, inspired by Arthur Dove landscapes in The Phillips Collection. Intersections: *One Day, After the Rain* by Sandra Cinto (May 19, 2012–August 18, 2013), The Phillips Collection.

fig. 80 (opposite bottom)
Installation of linn meyers's *at the time being* and Vincent van Gogh's *The Road Menders*, 2010. Intersections: *at the time being* by linn meyers (February 11–August 22, 2010), The Phillips Collection.

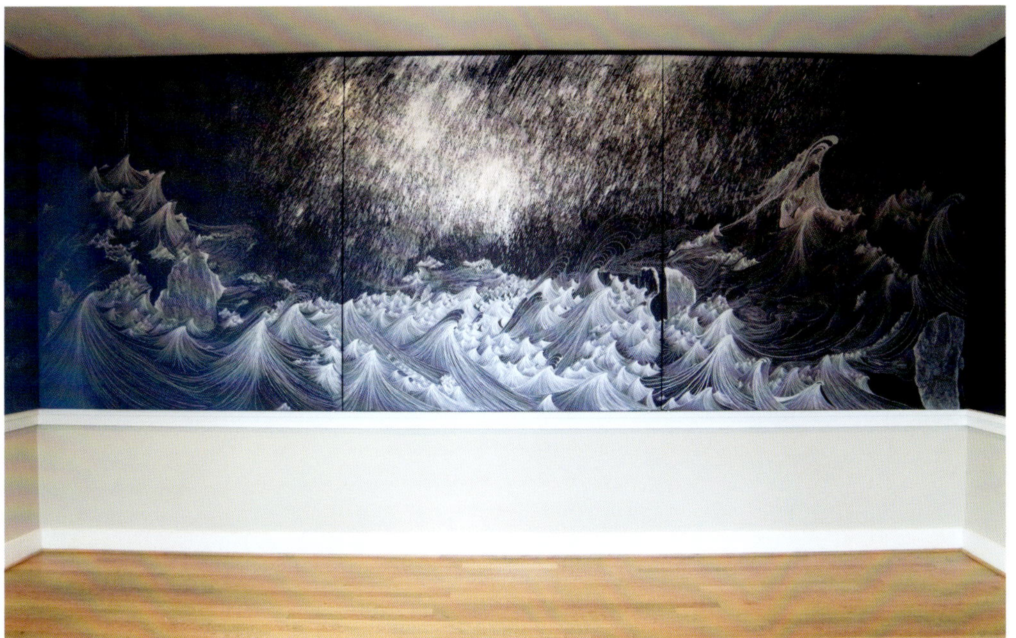

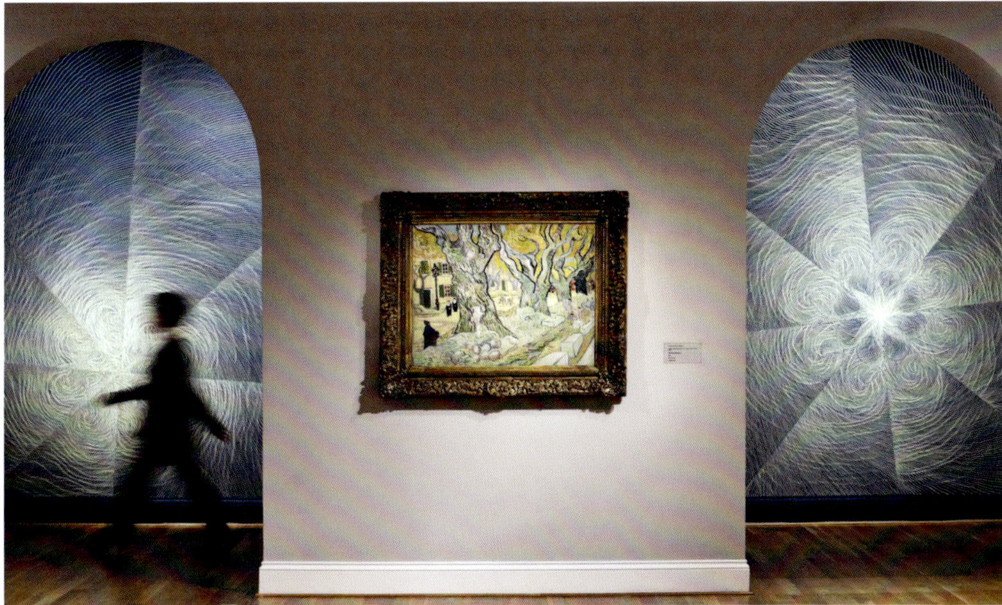

we should be as sympathetic to change and progress in art as in science,"[5] and that the Phillips—at the time called the Phillips Memorial Gallery—is "not a fixed, unchangeable institution," but rather a museum that "acts promptly,"[6] Intersections was envisioned as an ongoing series of contemporary art projects reflective of current artistic and social issues and honoring the founder's engagement with living artists and contemporary art.

The main premise of the series is to invite living artists to create new projects—or, on occasion, install existing work—in response to the Phillips's permanent collection and the distinctive architecture of its 1897 Georgian Revival mansion, creating unexpected dialogues between the art of the past and the present; that is, between modern and contemporary works.[7] This accords with Duncan Phillips's way of displaying art to highlight visual conversations among artists and artworks, regardless of nationality and chronology. As he put it, "My arrangements are for the purpose of contrast and analogy. I bring together congenial spirits among the artists from different parts of the world and from different periods of time and I trace their common descent from old masters who anticipated modern ideas."[8] Moreover, the Intersections series echoes Phillips's view of his museum as a laboratory—or an "experiment station,"[9] as he described it—where works of art were constantly recontextualized and reexamined in changing installations.

The connections implied by the name of the series—between the museum's holdings and newly commissioned works, traditional themes and current approaches, and historical architecture and site-related artistic installations—are not always obvious or, indeed, only visual; they may be dialogues with institutional history, aesthetic concepts, or architectural setting. The goal of Intersections is not only to reveal links and contrasts between artworks and architecture, but also to create intriguing relationships, teasing the way we look at and think about art. Intersections projects are conceived as an unfolding sequence of temporary, unconventional interventions that, like nomads, always occupy different places in the museum. Furthermore, the series shows art of the past in a new light, focusing on the continuity of modern and contemporary art.

Another underlying aim of Intersections is to go beyond traditional exhibition formats—whether chronological or thematic—and the modernist neutrality of "white cube" spaces.[10] Instead, the goal is to pursue innovative practices and to activate non-traditional museum spaces—café, stairwells, corridors, bridges, courtyard and other outdoor spaces—with art produced specifically for them. Another aim is acquisition of a work by each participating artist, not necessarily a work that was part of the initial project, but one that is in some way representative or emblematic of it. In the long run, these acquisitions will be records of the Phillips's exhibition history as well as expressions of the idea of contemporaneity of the early twenty-first century.

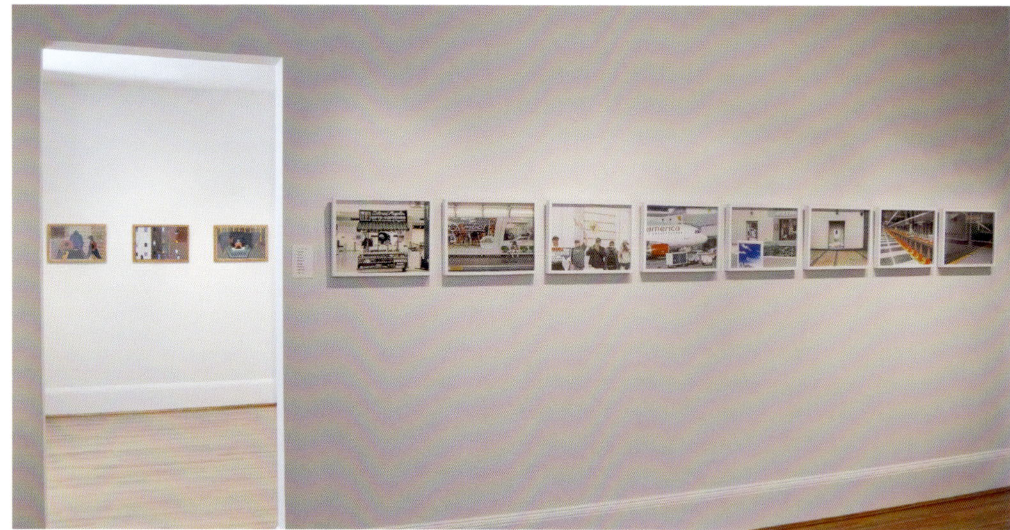

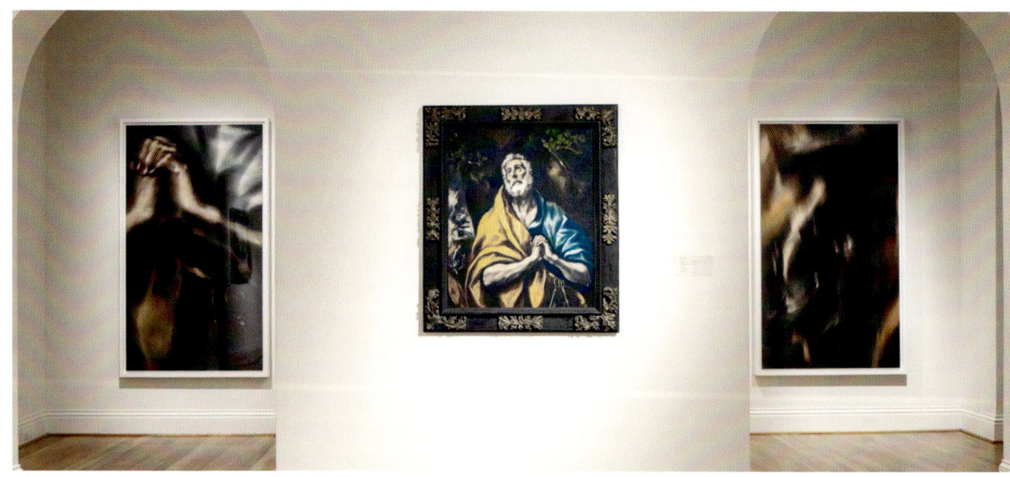

fig. 81 (top)
Installation of Allan deSouza's *The World Series* (2012), inspired by Jacob Lawrence's 1941 *Migration Series*. Intersections: *The World Series* by Allan deSouza (June 23–October 30, 2011), The Phillips Collection.

fig. 82 (bottom)
Installation of Bernhard Hildebrandt's *Keys*, 2013, and *MM*, 2013, with El Greco's *The Repentant St. Peter*, 1600–14. Intersections: *A Conjugation of Verb* by Bernhard Hildebrandt (June 27–September 22, 2013), The Phillips Collection.

Since 2009, there have been thirty Intersections projects, presenting emerging and well-established artists of different racial and ethnic backgrounds, most of them women, from the United States and abroad. The projects have been aesthetically and conceptually varied, employing a multitude of approaches and media, including: painting and drawing (Sandra Cinto [fig. 79], Tayo Heuser, Jean Meisel, linn meyers [fig. 80], and Kate Shepherd); photography and video (Allan deSouza [fig. 81], Bernhard Hildebrandt [fig. 82], Jennifer Wen Ma, Vesna Pavlović, and Nicholas and Sheila Pye); sculpture (A. Balasubramaniam, Lee Boroson, Marley Dawson, Jae Ko, Barbara Liotta, Regi Müller, Bettina Pousttchi, Bernardí Roig [fig. 83], Arlene Shechet, Ranjani Shettar [fig. 84], Alyson Shotz, and Jeanne Silverthorne), and multimedia installations (Sanford Biggers, dBfoundation, Helen Frederick, Los Carpinteros, John F. Simon Jr., Richard Tuttle, and Xavier Veilhan).[11]

In each of these projects, meaning and interpretation were contextual: they stemmed not from individual works, whether historic or newly commissioned, but rather from their interrelationship and their connection to the site. By and large, Intersections projects have brought installation art into the museum, highlighting the art-making process along with a more immersive, corporeal experience of art. The series takes a collaborative approach to the curator's role, replacing curatorial authorship with artist-curator teamwork. In these ways, Intersections is aligned with a significant shift in the museum field over the past two decades: a gradual turn from traditional visual narratives of predominantly Western art toward multisensory and multimedia artistic practices and an engagement with important current political and social issues, as well as broader audiences.

At a time when museums have been shifting from being places for objects to being places for people—diversity, inclusion, participation, collaboration, civic engagement—we should proudly recall Duncan Phillips's words, "We stand for open-mindedness and tolerance of different points of view,"[12] and realize them. In today's highly polarized society, his idea of art as a "universal language, breaking down artificial barriers of nationality and race, a language which never differs in essentials however varied the local, national, racial and historical manifestations"[13]—dismissed by postmodern art theories as outmoded essentialism and universalism—offers a possibility of revaluing the importance of beauty and the meaning of art as a way of coming together and finding what connects us rather than divides us; commonalities rather than differences. The Phillips's centennial

fig. 83 (left)
Installation of Bernardí Roig's *The Man of the Light*, 2005. Intersections: *NO/ Escape* by Bernardí Roig (October 25, 2014–April 5, 2015), The Phillips Collection.

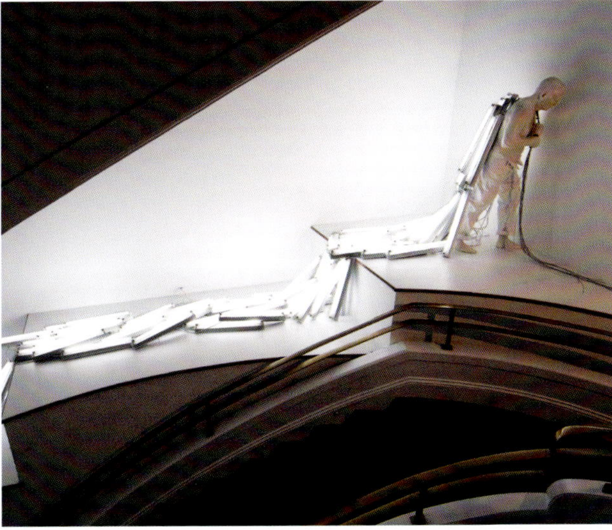

fig. 84 (right)
Installation of Ranjani Shettar's *MOHANA (Thread and Wax)*, 2019. Intersections: *Ranjani Shettar: Earth Songs for a Night Sky* (May 16–August 25, 2019), The Phillips Collection.

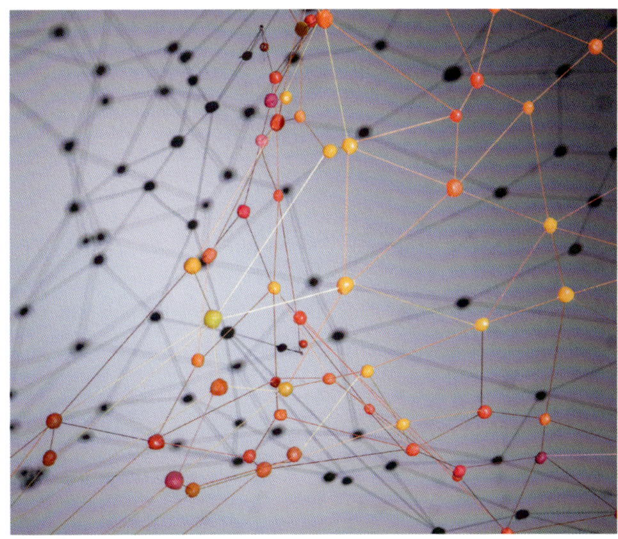

represents a significant moment for reflection—especially amid the massive fear, anxiety, and social distancing caused by the COVID-19 pandemic, as well as civil unrests and protests that emerged recently over racial rifts throughout the United States—on fundamental questions about the museum's existence and social relevance, present and future; the experience and content it provides, physical and digital; its audience; and the responsibilities of a contemporary art curator as a socially engaged and critically responsive cultural producer.

1 Duncan Phillips, "The Phillips Collection and Related Thoughts on Art," radio address, originally presented as "The Pleasures of an Intimate Art Gallery," Washington, DC, WCFM, February 24, 1954.

2 Phillips, "The Phillips Collection and Related Thoughts on Art."

3 Laib's *Wax Room* was commissioned in 2013; Kelly's sculpture *Untitled (EK 927)* was commissioned for the museum's new courtyard in 2005; and Bulloch's sculpture *Heavy Metal Stack: Fat Cyan Three* was commissioned in 2018 for the corner of Twenty-first and Q Streets.

4 In addition to the Intersections series, other programs that speak to the museum's engagement with living artists are the One-On-One exhibition series, as well as a series of public programs called Conversations with Artists. The full list of exhibitions from 1999 to the present is included in The Phillips Collection Exhibition History, see Appendix in this volume, p. 339.

5 Duncan Phillips, "Introduction," in *An Exhibition of a Selected Group of Paintings from the Phillips Memorial Gallery* (Washington, DC: Phillips Memorial Gallery, 1930).

6 Duncan Phillips, *A Collection in the Making* (New York: E. Weyhe; Washington, DC: Phillips Memorial Gallery, 1926), 9.

7 The terms "modern" and "contemporary" were largely interchangeable in critical debates of the 1940s and 1950s. Nowadays, "contemporary" refers to the *now* that historically follows the modern past but also indicates a shift in artistic production and discourse.

8 Phillips, *A Collection in the Making*, 6.

9 Phillips's concept, dating back to 1926, is borrowed from Alfred Stieglitz's term "experiment laboratory," which stressed that the museum should be an "experiment station," like a laboratory, as opposed to a collection that was fixed or frozen. See William C. Agee, "Duncan Phillips and American Modernism: The Continuing Legacy of the Experiment Station," in Erika D. Passantino and David W. Scott, eds., *The Eye of Duncan Phillips: A Collection in the Making* (New Haven, CT: Yale University Press; Washington, DC: Phillips Collection, 1999), 376 and n. 5.

10 See Brian O'Doherty, *Inside the White Cube: The Ideology of the Gallery Space* (Berkeley, Los Angeles, London: University of California Press, 1999) for a discussion of the modernist obsession with the "white cube" gallery space—square or rectangular, with white walls, and ceiling-mounted lighting, resulting in a neutral space, devoid of historical or social context, as an elitist, quasi-religious setting for art. This aesthetic approach, first described by O'Doherty in a series of three articles in *Artforum* in 1976, still dominates museums and galleries of contemporary art.

11 In the summer of 2020, the Phillips launched Digital Intersections, a virtual off-shoot of Intersections featuring newly created works in dialogue with the museum collection that do not inhabit physical spaces but rather live on the Phillips website, Facebook, and Instagram. The inaugural project was by Luca Buvoli, entitled *Picture: Present* (An Episode from "Astrodoubt and the Quarantine Chronicles" in 12 Scenes) July 20–December 1, 2020.

12 Phillips, "Introduction."

13 Phillips, *A Collection in the Making*, 13.

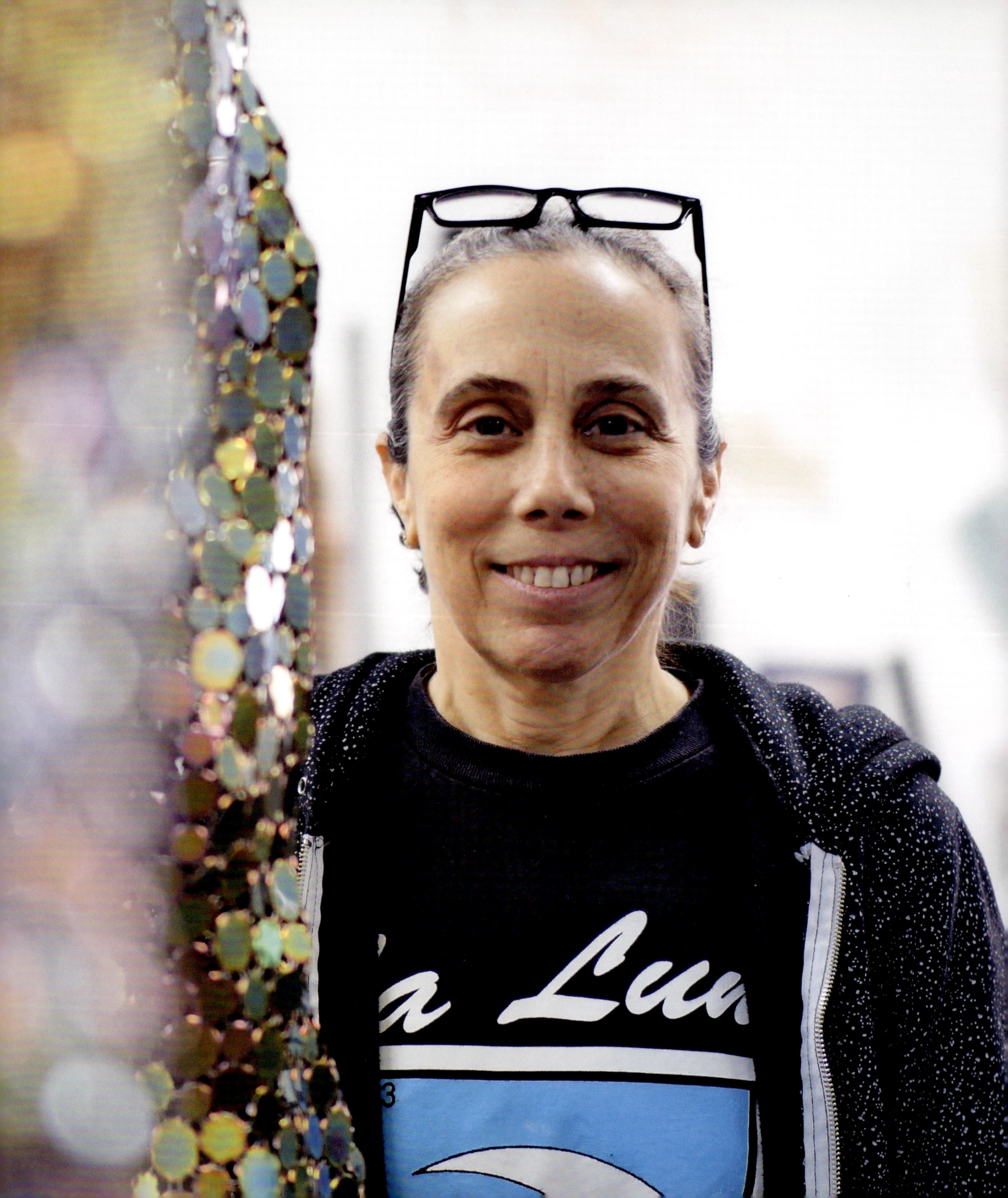

IN CONVERSATION WITH

ALYSON SHOTZ

Adapted from an interview with Vesela Sretenović that took place in the artist's Brooklyn studio on March 9, 2020.

Vesela Sretenović: I've just realized that it has been more than fifteen years since we first met, and, looking around your studio, I'm once again so surprised by your new work. It almost seems as though you're a different artist, but the truth is that your work evolves continuously.

Alyson Shotz: Yes, this work is really different than my work of the past few years, but it's related. In the past months, I really struggled over how I was going to remake my sculpture in response to the political climate. Making light, ethereal work was almost impossible, and I wanted to make something heavier and darker. I became attracted to used bicycle inner tubes; I found some on the street, and then I asked the owner of my local bike shop if he could collect them for me. I gave him a laundry basket and he started to throw them in there. Every few weeks, I'd pick up a load of tubes, and gradually I ended up with a lot. I began by folding the inner tubes, getting a density that's like a very dark, solid negative space. After that, I started adding copper that I had around the studio, creating an interplay of light and shadow. Then, suddenly, these new pieces started to feel more like my older work; the light moving across the copper is in constant flux, like so many of my other sculptures—*Object for Reflection*, for example. Recently, I've also noticed that they have an interesting relationship to Byzantine icons.

VS: Because the shimmering copper resembles the golden background of Byzantine icons?

AS: Yes, and also the light takes on a performative aspect as it does with the Byzantine icons. I see these as "twenty-first-century icons" that encompass distance as well as light. There are many miles contained in the tires themselves, there are the hours in those miles, and there is light acting on them through time.

> IN THE PAST MONTHS, I REALLY STRUGGLED OVER HOW I WAS GOING TO REMAKE MY SCULPTURE IN RESPONSE TO THE POLITICAL CLIMATE.

VS: There is a lot of weight here that wasn't in your previous work. At the same time, there is still a lot of weightlessness and transparency. It seems that, no matter what, light always finds its way into your work.

AS: Yeah. It's funny, because you always end up coming back to yourself in some way, but from a different angle.

VS: Talk about the process of making these works. You start by cutting and folding the inner tubes, right?

AS: Yes. After I clean the inner tubes and cut them down the middle, I nail them to a wood panel backing and they become folded in the process of nailing them. Initially, I used wood panels because I wanted them to emanate a feeling of great heaviness.

VS: Looking at them, I see paintings, which reminds me that you started as a painter.

AS: Yes, I studied painting as an undergraduate at RISD [Rhode Island School of Design], and then as a graduate at the University of Washington. However, at the same time, I was also exploring sculpture and photography in both of those places. Once I graduated and moved to New York, I continued making paintings, but I wasn't happy with the square format, the flat surface, the limitation of materials. I wanted to break out of that pictorial space and I started making sculptures, moving away

Alyson Shotz in her Brooklyn studio, March 2020.

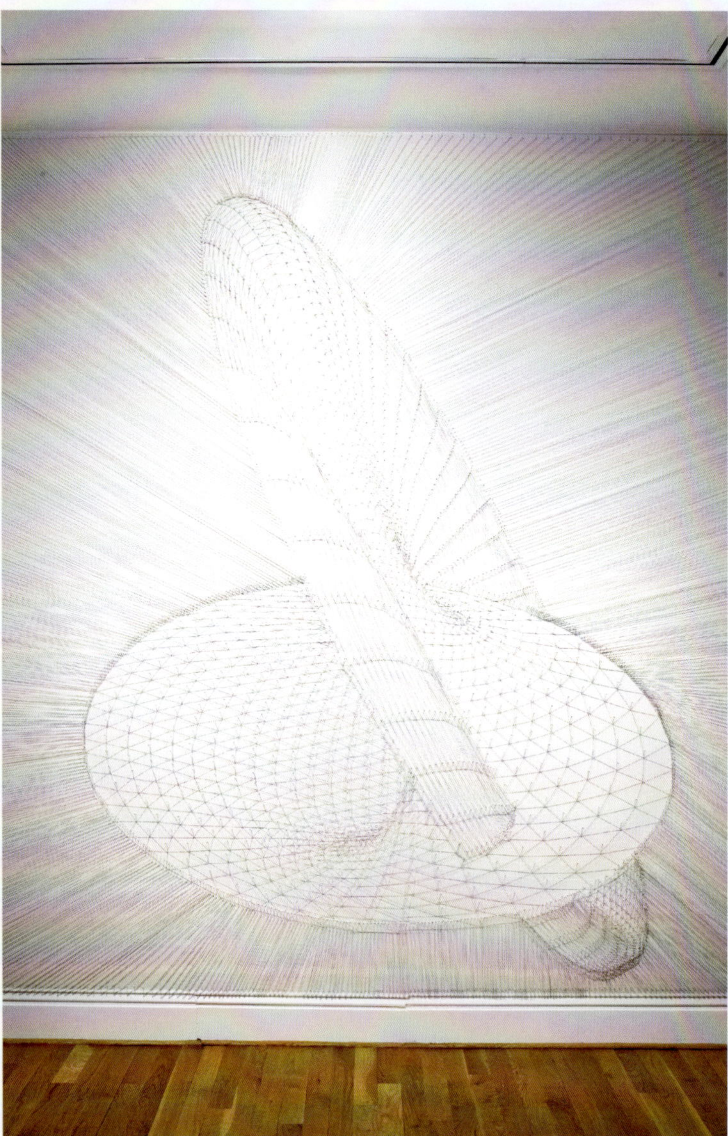

fig. 85
Installation of Alyson Shotz's *Ecliptic*, 2012. Intersections: *Ecliptic* by Alyson Shotz (February 16–May 27, 2012), The Phillips Collection.

from the canvas onto the wall, and then it went on from there. Now, I'm returning, in my own way, to the square or the rectangle of painting. Similarly, my string drawings were also a quasi-return to flatness. So, whenever I go back to painting, it's never really a true painting, because it has a sculptural aspect to it.
VS: In addition to these heavy icon-like paintings, you have a lot of filigree-like sculptural pieces suspended from the ceiling. They feel light and almost ethereal. What are they made of?
AS: This group is called *Intricate Metamorphosis* and they're made of plated steel. I design specific shapes that will fit together as a whole and have them punched industrially, out of sheet steel, then I connect the pieces with stainless steel rings. Each piece has to be individually folded onto the rings, and the whole thing, completed, becomes like a fabric made out of metal. The electroplating gives it its color.
VS: They glitter as they rotate. How do you get this kind of finish?
AS: Well, the finish took a couple of years of testing to figure out, like much of my work. I worked closely with a factory in the Midwest to create this color. With all of my work, there's a testing and refining process—which type of metal is best, and which thickness is best, and which finish. There's also a randomness inherent in the plating process that I really like: depending on the temperature and composition of the bath, as well as the temperature of the room, the color will vary. You don't know exactly how it's going to come out. So because of that, I don't do the finishing all at once—I send in pieces for plating and then connect them afterwards. The shape of the sculpture as a whole is greatly influenced by the material I've created and by gravity itself. I act as a kind of facilitator, guiding this new material into the sculpture it wants to be.
VS: Looking at *Intricate Metamorphosis* makes me think of your previous works exploring space, light, gravity, and time. How did you become interested in those phenomena?

WITH ALL OF MY WORK, THERE'S A TESTING AND REFINING PROCESS.

AS: At college, I studied geology; I was interested in the way glaciers move and behave. That led me to explore space and gravity, and naturally I turned to physics. At the same time, I was taking art classes, and in my initial drawing classes we learned about the concept of negative space. The question of space began to fascinate me, and it continues to fascinate me today.
VS: Clearly, light and volume, air and weight, material and immaterial have always been part of your work, physically and metaphorically. *Allusion of Gravity* (pl. 111), which the Phillips acquired in 2014, is literally about weightlessness and volume without mass.
AS: Yes, *Allusion of Gravity* is exactly about that. At the time, I was reading Einstein's *Theory of General Relativity,* which shows how gravity works through mass bending the space around it. I was really intrigued with the idea that the mass of the Earth or any planet or star can bend space, and

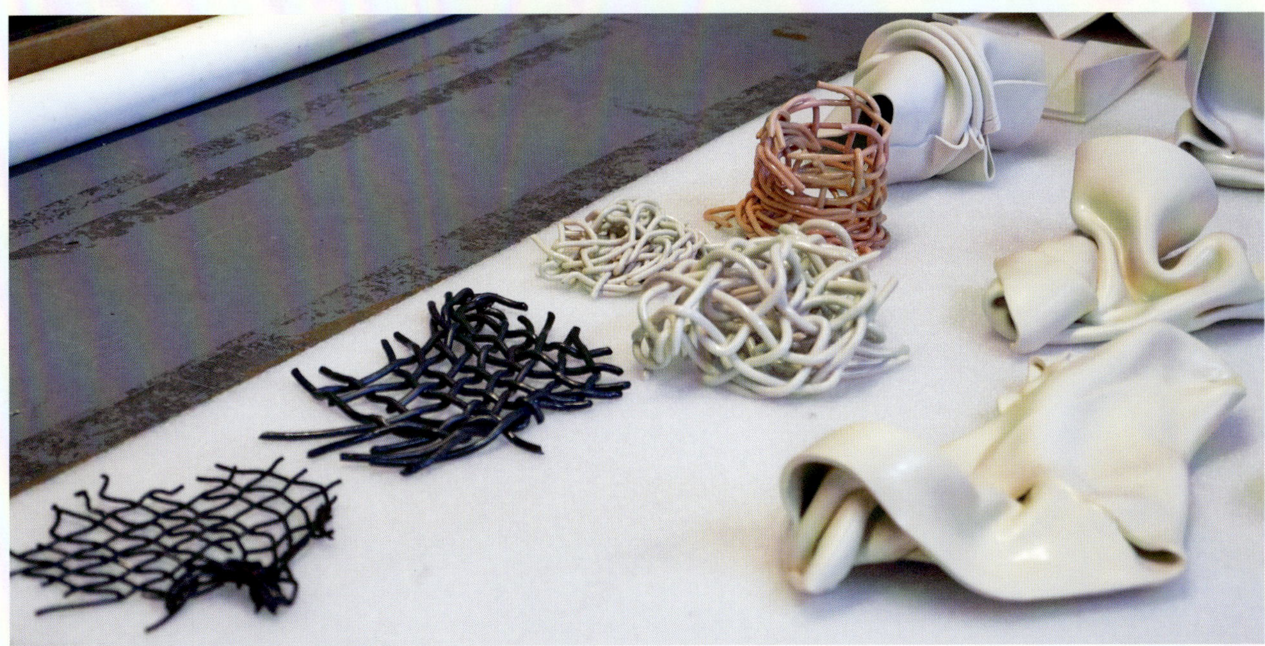

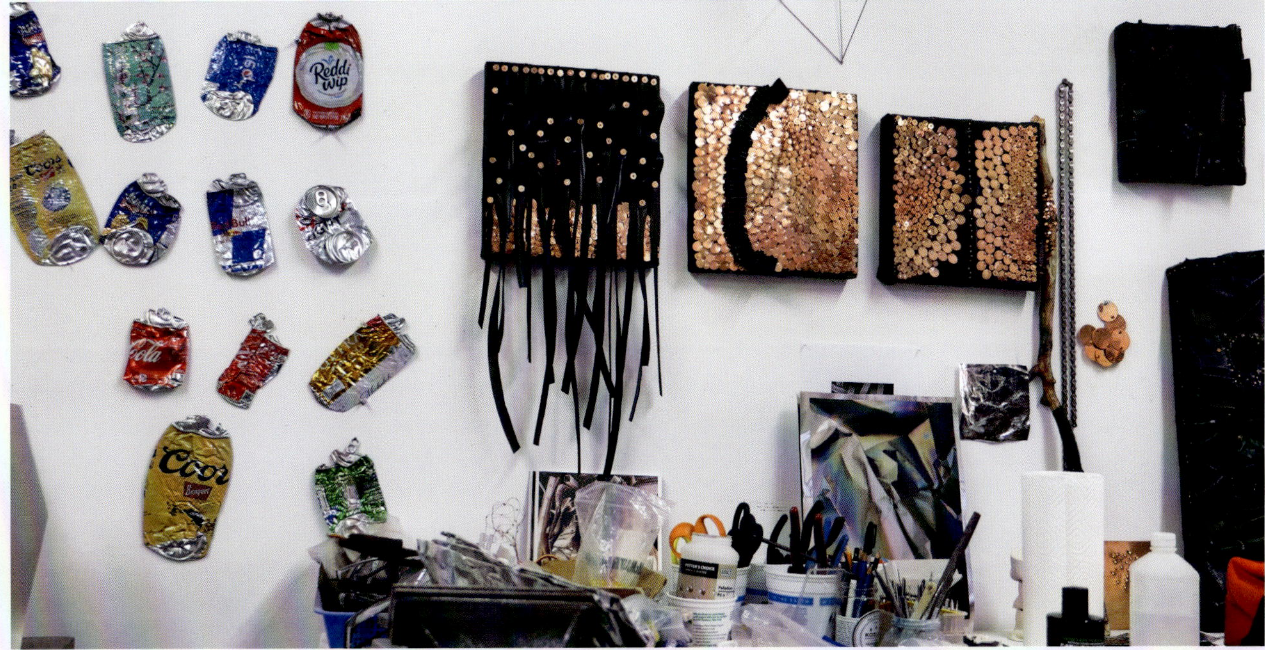

figs. 86 & 87
Alyson Shotz's Brooklyn studio, March 2020.

I was trying to capture it in my sculpture. The steel wire in that work is like the grid of space, while the beads act like space itself, being pushed down by an invisible mass.

VS: *Allusion of Gravity* has a strong interactive aspect. As people walk around it, the piece moves, the beads shimmer, reflecting light and casting shadows in space.

AS: I was trying to create a sculpture with very little density, made of light and shadow. I've always been interested in making sculptures that have a weightless quality, that also can encompass change in a natural way—through light and through movement of the viewer. The clear glass beads work to facilitate this. Each bead reflects the light differently and creates its own shadow. The space around the sculpture is reflected inside each individual bead like a miniature universe.

VS: In some other earlier works, more specifically in *The Shape of Space* (2004) in the Solomon R. Guggenheim Museum collection, you used plastic lenses in a similar way. I still vividly remember the work and how much I loved its labyrinthine structure that you can walk through and see through. It was such a magical and playful perceptual environment.

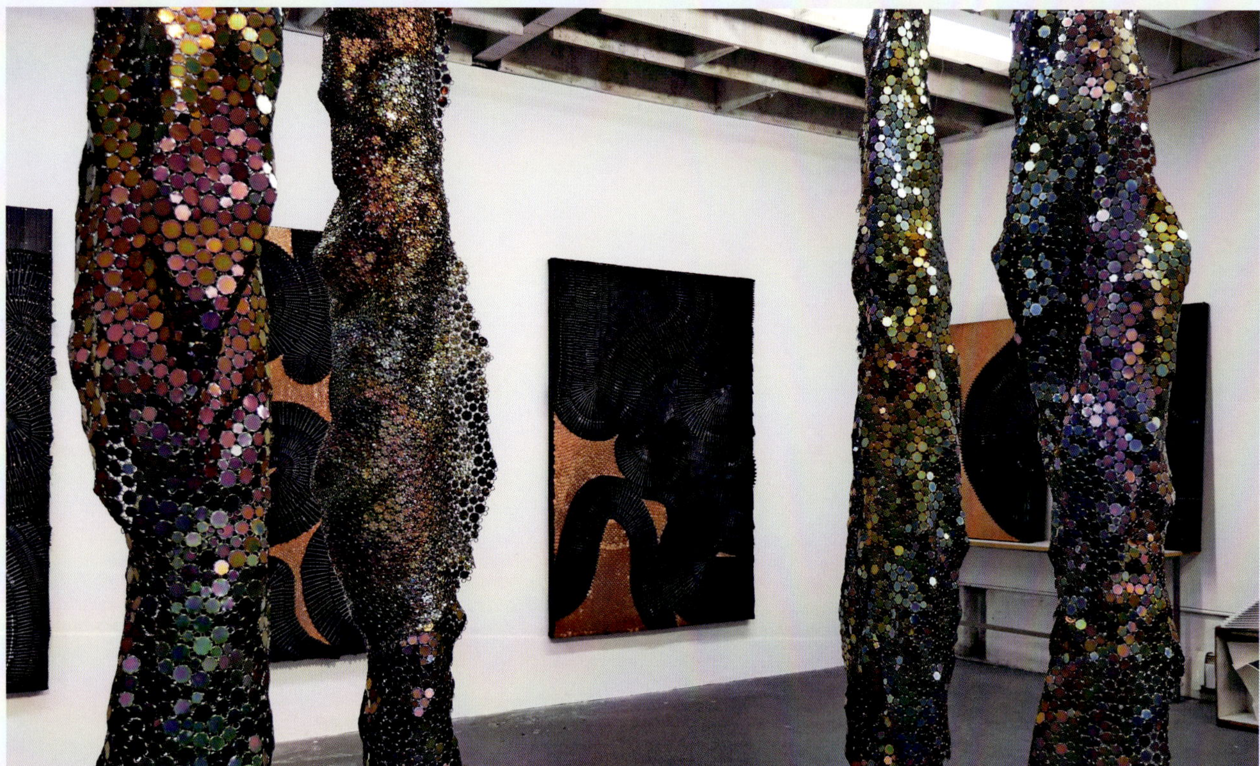

figs. 88 & 89
Alyson Shotz's Brooklyn studio, March 2020.

AS: Yes. Both this work and the Phillips's *Allusion of Gravity* change with light, and that's a big part of my work—incorporating natural light—so that the pieces look different upon each viewing and for each viewer.

VS: Since we've touched on The Phillips Collection, I'll bring up the 2012 exhibit that was part of its Intersections series of contemporary art projects. The show was called *Ecliptic* and comprised three interrelated large-scale drawings made of blue and white yarn looped over thousands of nails that occupied the space much as planets occupy the cosmos (fig. 85). Again, this work was at once different and not so different from your earlier work or, indeed, your current work (figs. 86–89). The line, the space, and the use of nails recurred. And although the work looked two-dimensional, it had a strong sculptural quality typical of your art. Looking back, what can you tell us about *Ecliptic*?

AS: Well, the shapes were elliptical, orbital, so they referenced space and time. The project started with an idea of making paintings/drawings in a new way. I didn't want them to be rectangular. I didn't really even want a drawn line, so I considered how to make a line without drawing one, and that's what gave me the idea of building a drawing using thread. The thread could create a shadow line on the wall. The drawings were raised two inches off the wall by large pins, so technically they were not flat but dimensional. There was also an illusionistic dimensionality in the thread drawing itself. From close up, they appeared flat, and as you moved past them they changed because of the density of thread and the way the shadows shifted. I conceived and worked on these as a trio of painting-like wall objects in relationship to the Phillips's outstanding painting collection.

THAT'S A BIG PART OF MY WORK—INCORPORATING NATURAL LIGHT—SO THAT THE PIECES LOOK DIFFERENT UPON EACH VIEWING AND FOR EACH VIEWER.

VS: Your work, in a tucked-away gallery that turned out to be perfect for creating its own little cosmic feeling, responded to the museum's interior architecture and not to the collection itself. What are the works at the Phillips that speak to you most?

AS: When I was a student, I visited The Phillips Collection, and fell in love with Arthur Dove's work. There's one painting in particular, *Me and the Moon*, that I absolutely adore because it tells a story about the mystery of the universe through natural abstracted forms. He abstracted the nature we see and feel, and I'm making art about the part of nature that we don't see, but it's very similar.

Albert Pinkham Ryder's *Moonlit Cove* (see fig. 31), Alexander Calder's mobiles,

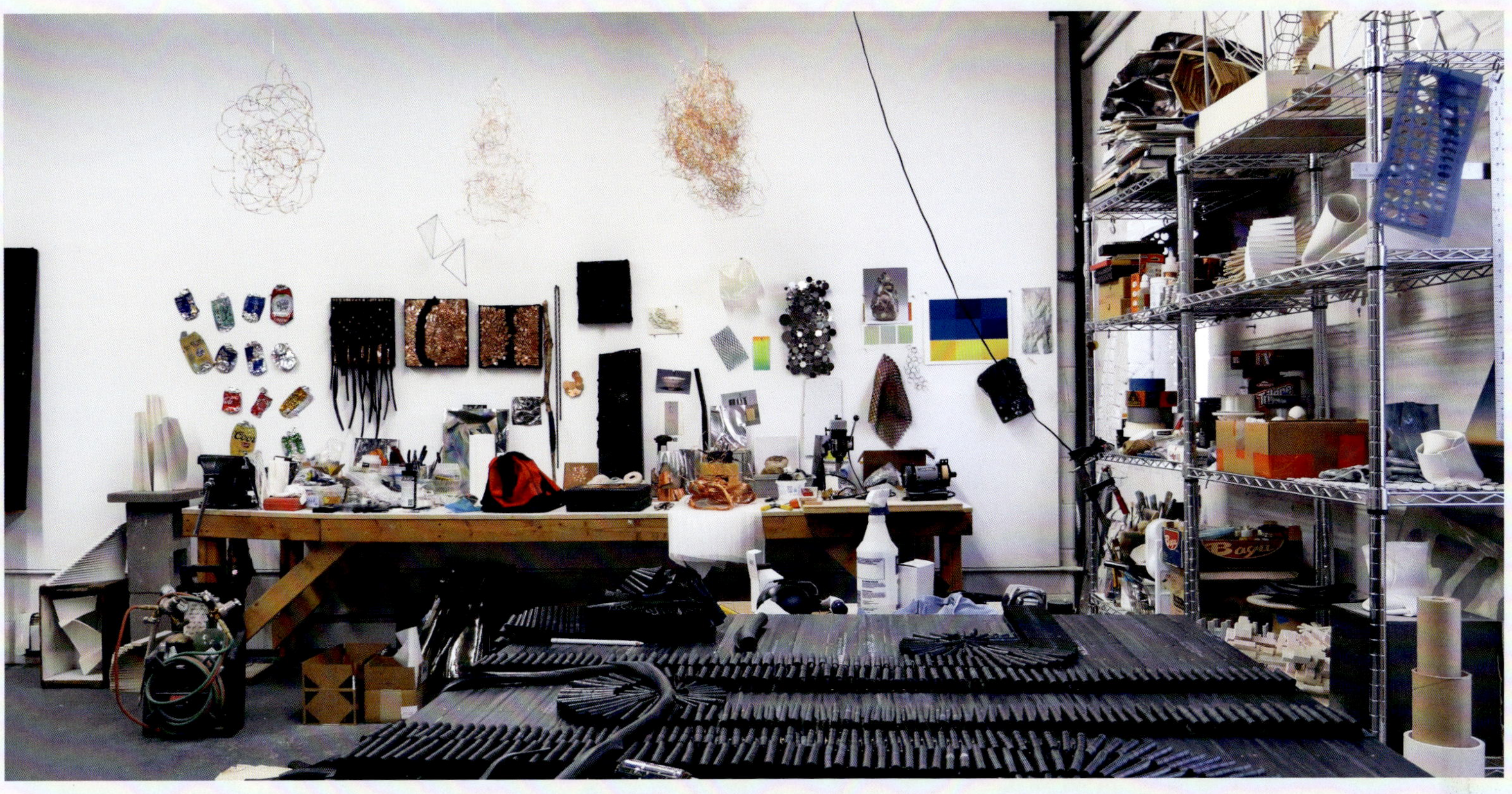

and Giorgio Morandi's small canvases have also been really influential. Morandi's use of negative space is so solid, so present. And his jars have equal presence. Sometimes they switch back and forth, so you're not really sure what's a jar and what's negative space. That question of space versus solidity has been a theme running through my work since the 1990s.

VS: Beyond the Phillips, which artists do you feel most connection with? Whose works inspire you the most?

AS: This is a really hard question, as there are so many. The artists that have inspired me most, though, have been women—Louise Bourgeois, Eva Hesse, Lygia Clark, Yayoi Kusama, Ana Mendieta. They really showed me a way to be an artist, and that was very important when I was starting out. Other artists who share my deep interest in space and light are, of course, James Turrell, Dan Flavin, Fred Sandback, Tony Smith.

VS: Do you think that the field of sculpture has changed in the past few decades?

AS: Definitely. The field is so much more diverse now. It's more accepting of different ways of making things, and of incorporating different media and, more importantly, of recognizing women artists. For example, when I started out, sewing, beading, and other "female" ways of making art were not accepted. I've been quietly championing that way of working for a long time by using those types of fabrication methods.

VS: So do you feel that there has been significant progress in terms of inclusion and recognition of other women artists in the art world?

AS: Yes, absolutely. We still have a long way to go, but we've definitely made progress. When I was in school, only a few women were mentioned in the history books. Now, when young female artists are coming up, they have so many more references, and that's got to make a huge difference.

VS: We look forward to featuring your *Allusion of Gravity* again during the Phillips Centennial exhibition in 2021. As we approach our hundredth anniversary, do you have a wish for the Phillips?

AS: I hope that the Phillips continues to show its beautiful permanent collection, and to connect it with artists of the present. I read somewhere that Duncan Phillips and his wife, Marjorie, wanted the museum to be dedicated to the art of their time, but also to be a museum that would encourage visual conversations among artists and artworks of all periods and styles. I find those connections between artists through time to be incredibly meaningful and I hope that the Phillips will continue to connect artists, linking the past with the present.

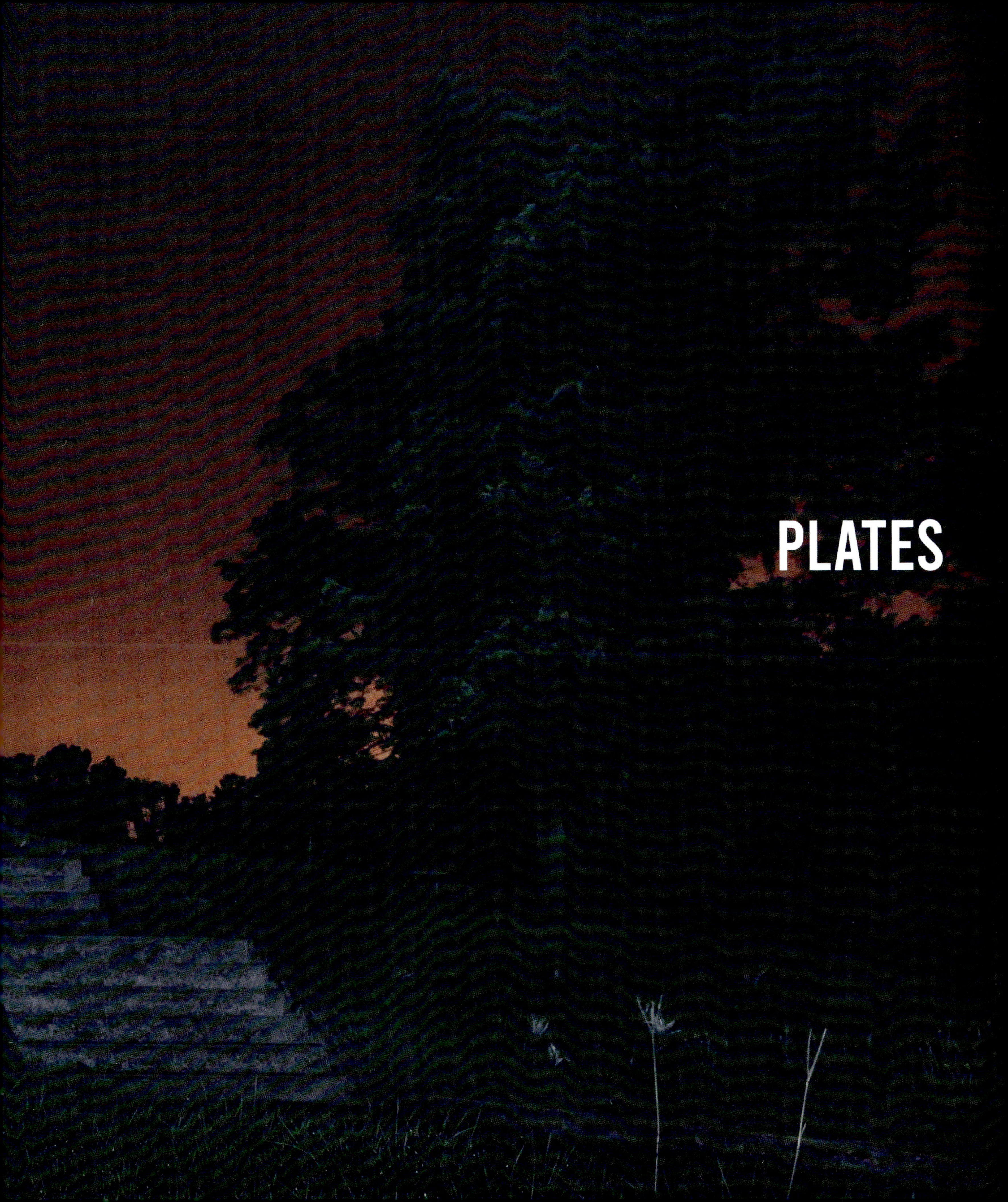

PLATES

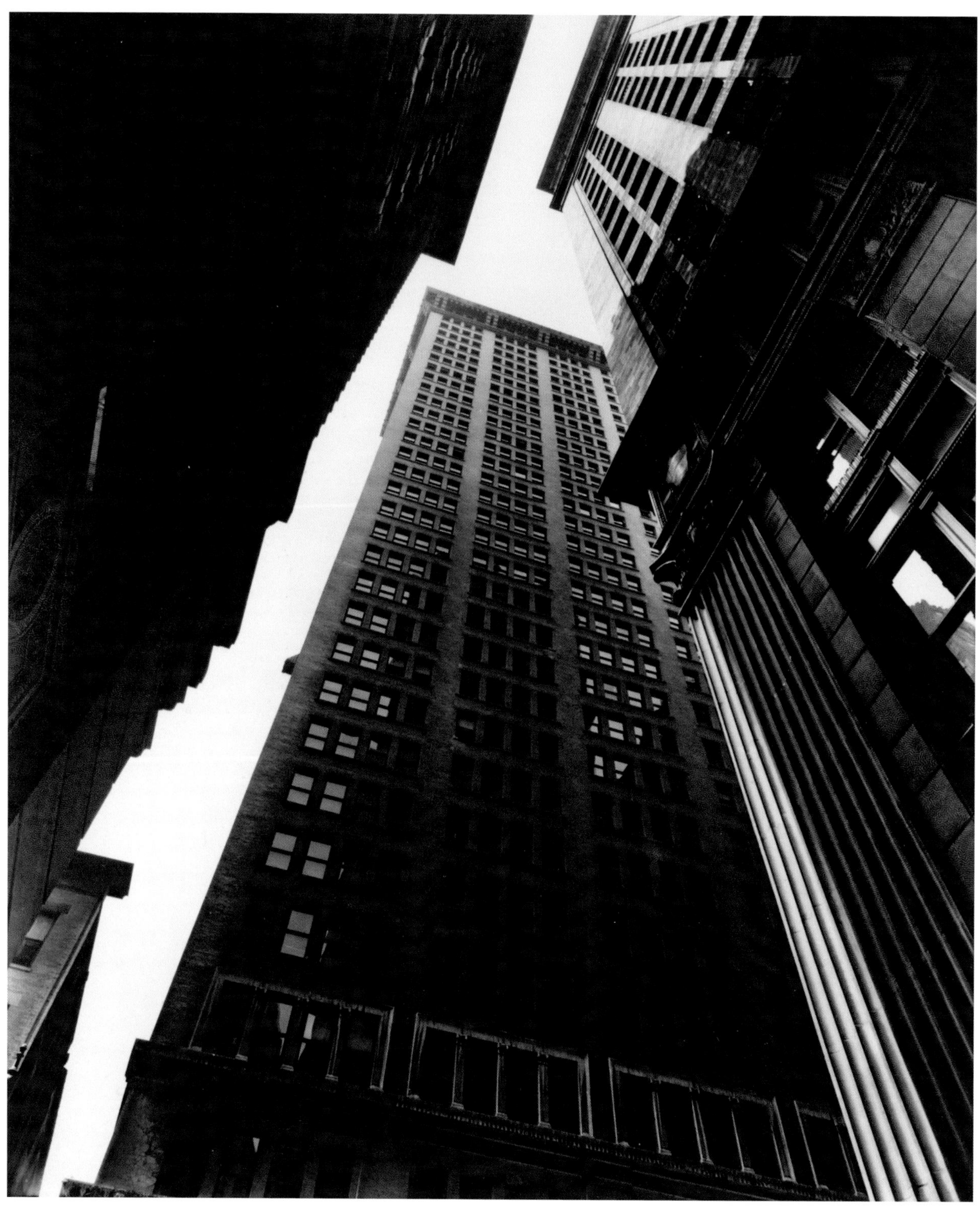

1
Berenice Abbott
Canyon: Broadway and Exchange Place, **1936**
Gelatin silver print,
9 3/8 × 7 1/2 in.
The Phillips Collection, Washington, DC,
Gift of the Phillips Contemporaries, 2001.

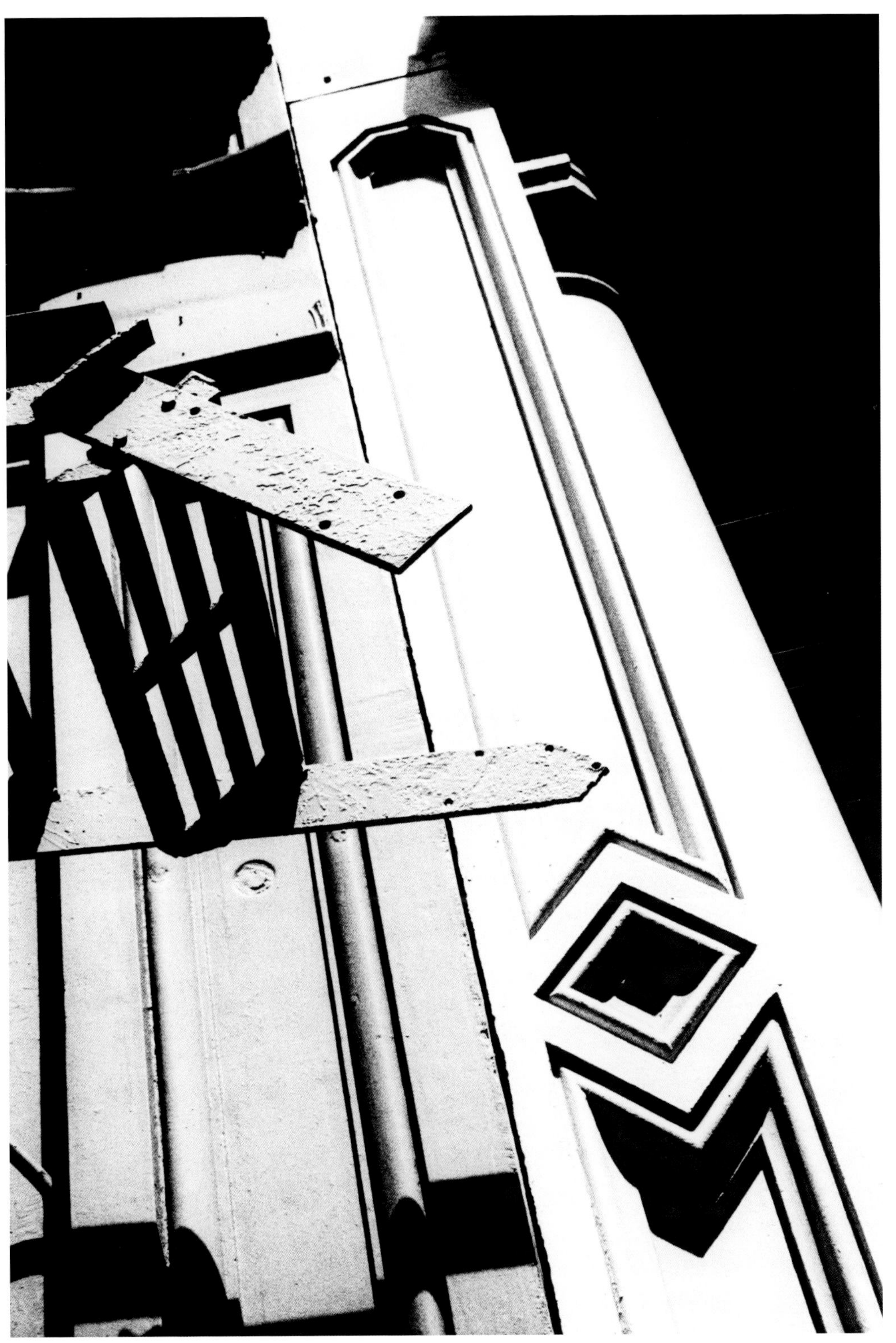

2
Ralph Gibson
***Untitled*, 2012**
Gelatin silver print,
14 × 11 in.
The Phillips Collection, Washington, DC,
Gift of Michelle and Stan Kurtz, 2015.

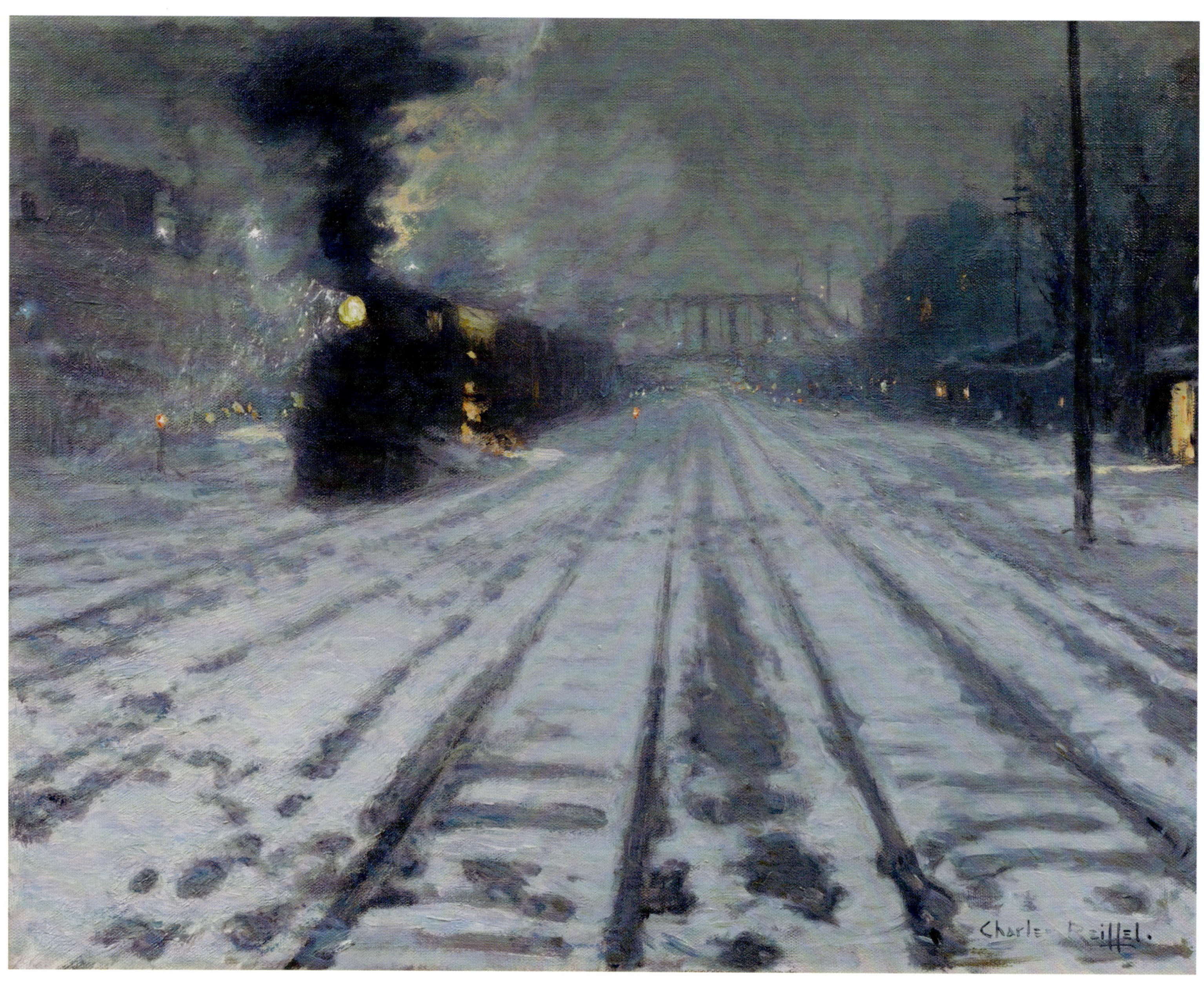

3
Charles Reiffel
Railway Yards-Winter Evening, ca. 1910
Oil on canvas,
18 1/8 × 24 3/16 in.
The Phillips Collection, Washington, DC,
Gift from the Trustees of the Corcoran Gallery of Art, 2018
(Museum Purchase, Gallery Fund).

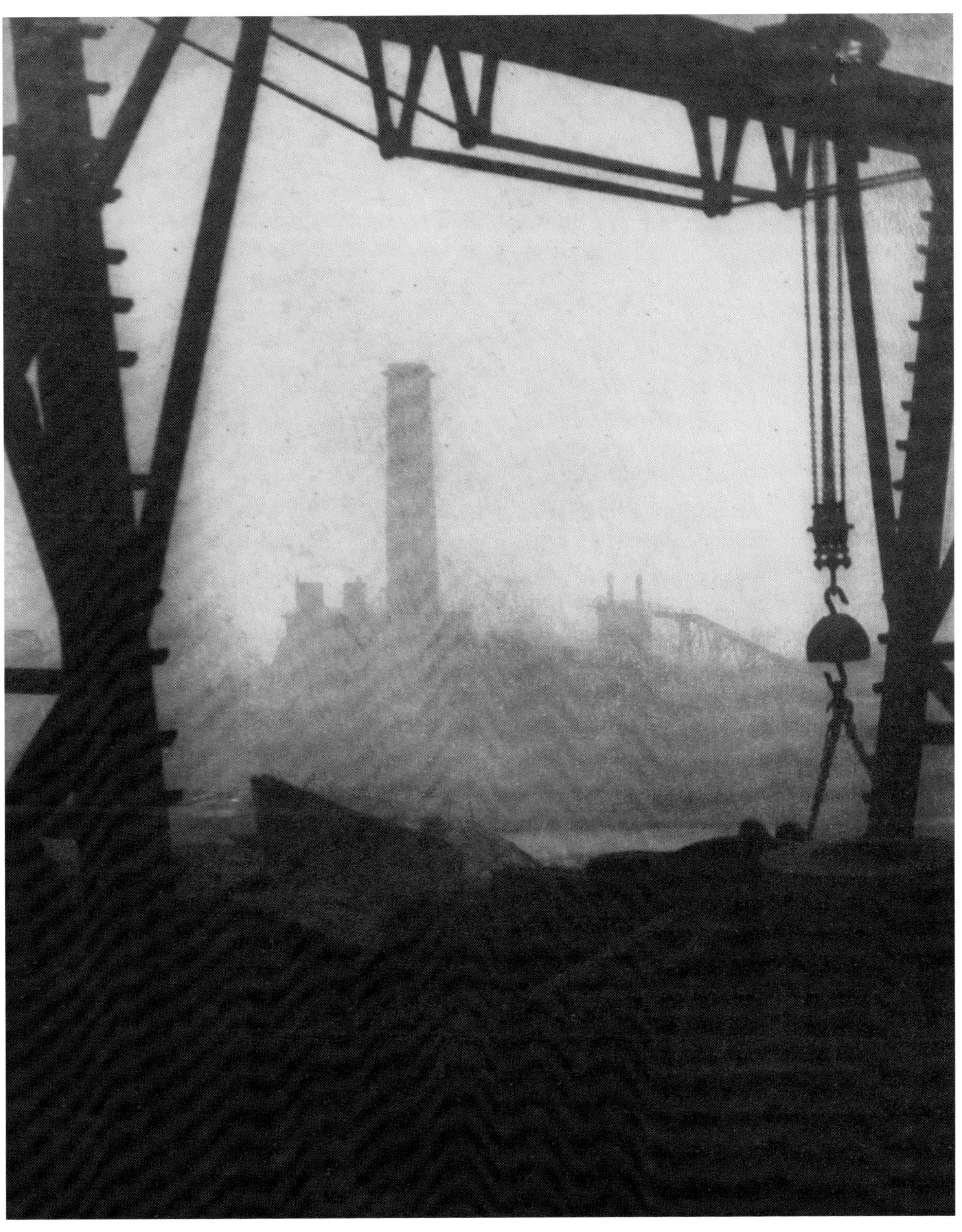

4
Alvin Langdon Coburn
***The Edge of Black Country*, undated**
Photogravure,
8 1/2 × 6 3/4 in.
The Phillips Collection, Washington, DC,
The Raymond Machesney Coburn Collection. Gift of
Raymond Machesney, initiated 2008, completed 2012.

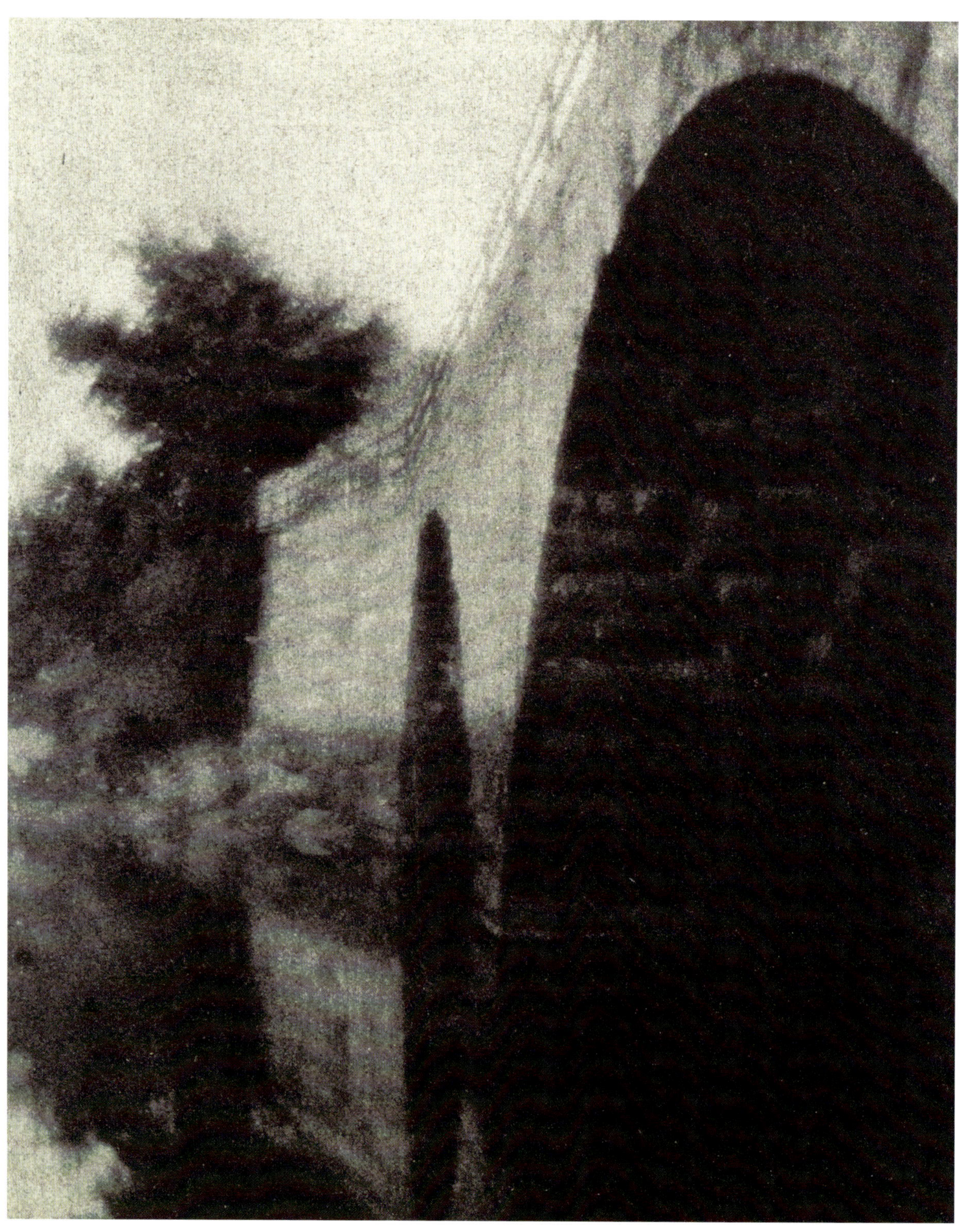

5
Alvin Langdon Coburn
The Bridge-Ipswich, 1904
Photogravure,
7 3/4 × 6 in.
The Phillips Collection, Washington, DC,
The Raymond Machesney Coburn Collection. Gift of
Raymond Machesney, initiated 2008, completed 2012.

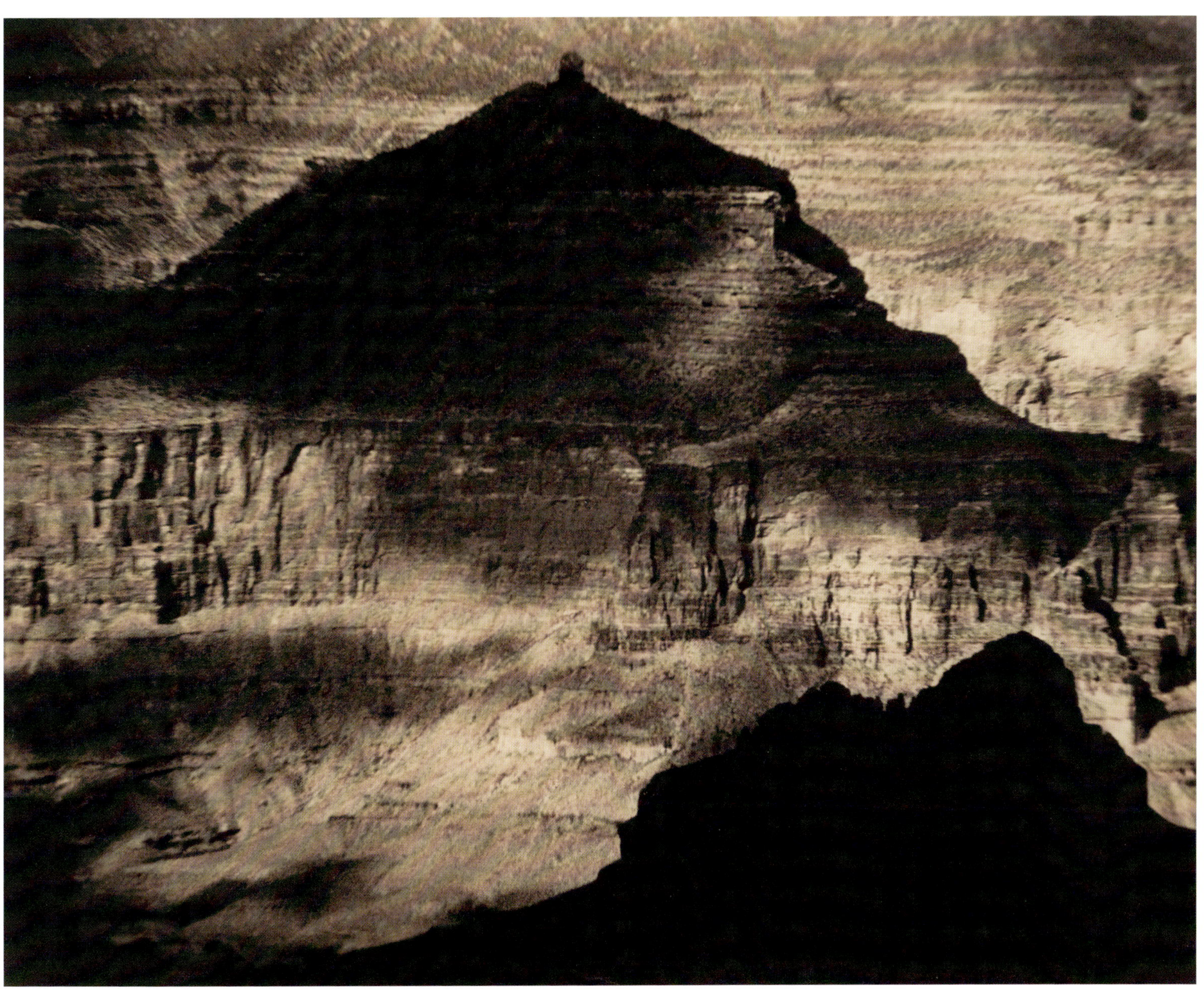

6
Alvin Langdon Coburn
The Great Temple, Grand Canyon, 1911
Gelatin silver print,
13 × 15 1/2 in.
The Phillips Collection, Washington, DC,
Gift of the Phillips Contemporaries, 2006.

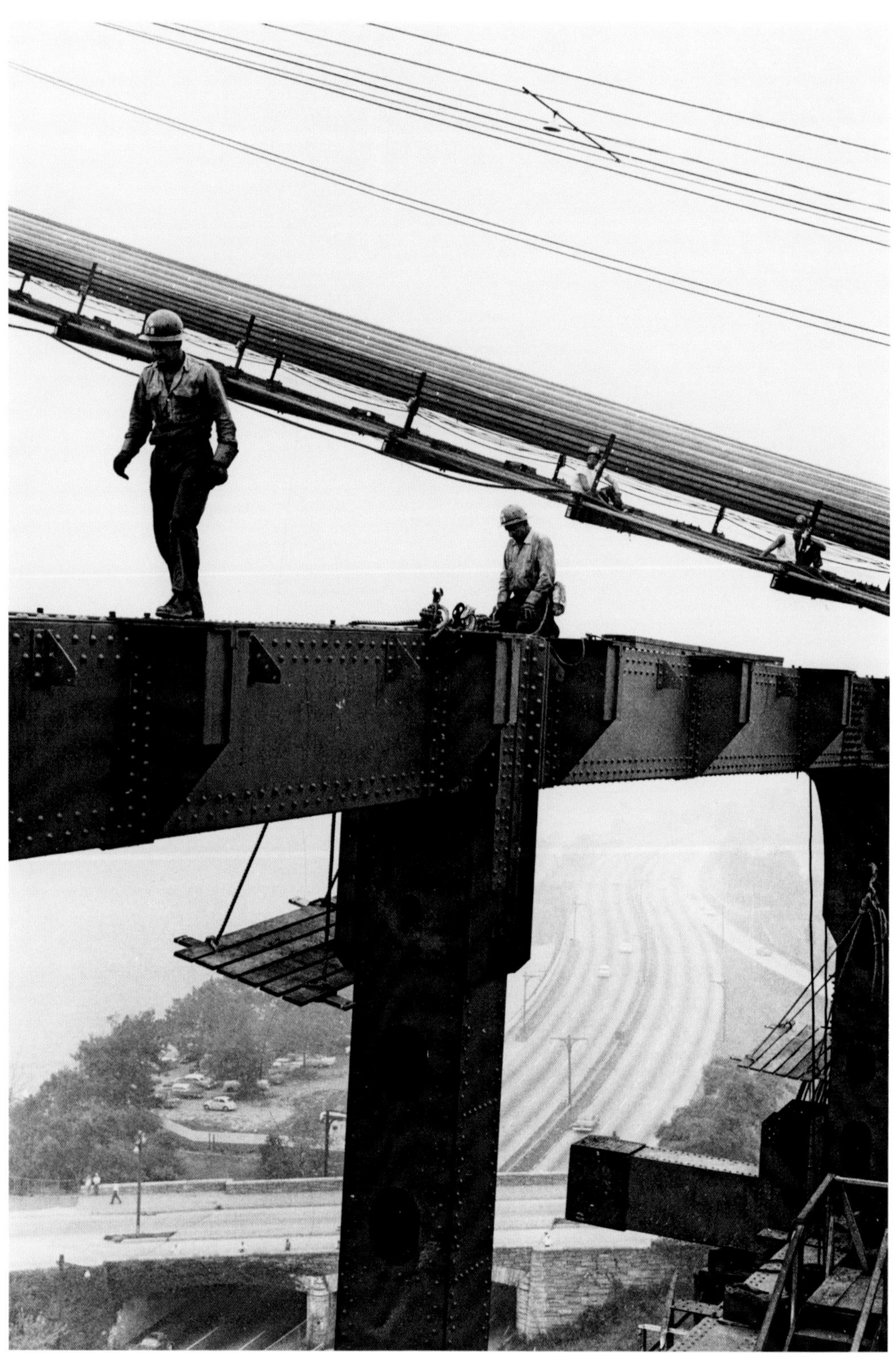

7
Bruce Davidson
Workers Balancing on Bridge (*The Bridge* series), 1963
Gelatin silver print,
14 × 11 in.
The Phillips Collection, Washington, DC,
Gift of Randy Kohls, 2013.

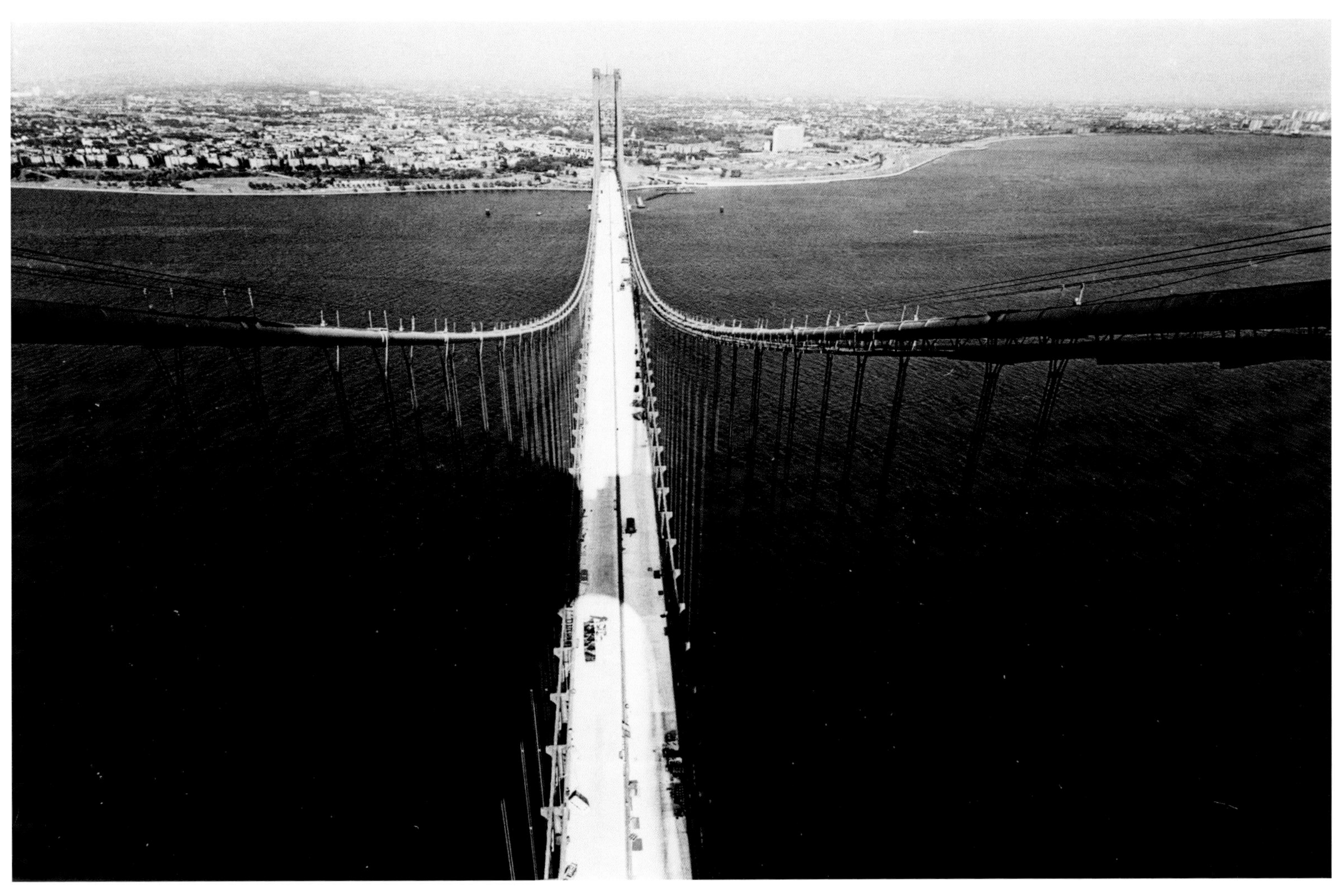

8
Bruce Davidson
Sweeping View of Bridge from Above (*The Bridge* series), ca. 1958
Gelatin silver print,
16 × 20 in.
The Phillips Collection, Washington, DC,
Gift of Robert and Kathi Steinke, 2013.

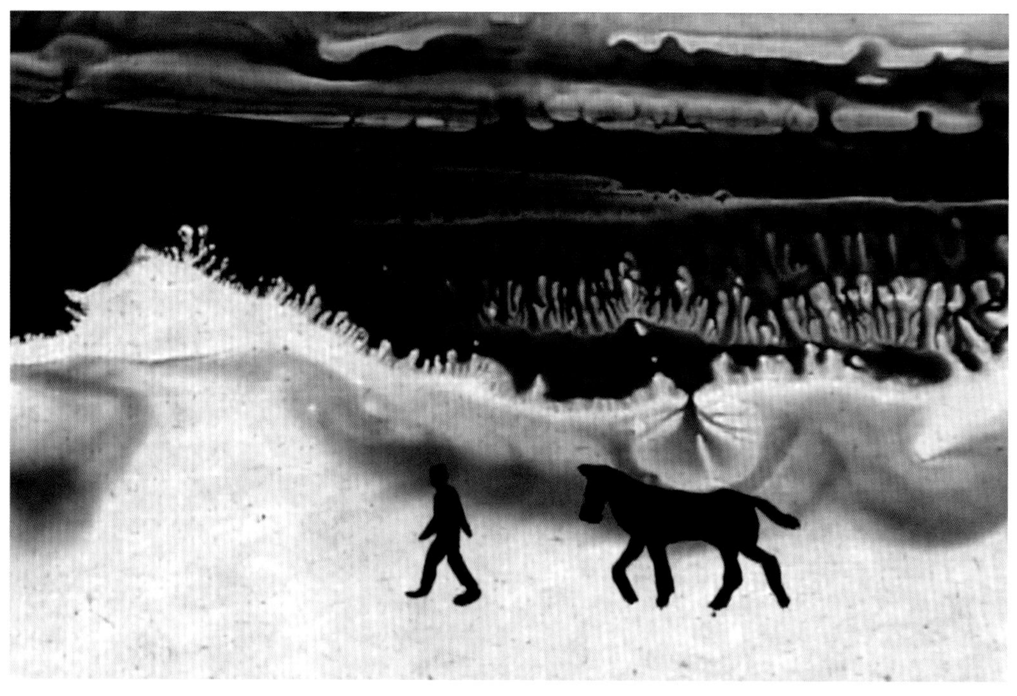

9
Jennifer Wen Ma
***Brain Storm*, 2009**
Single-channel video (color, sound).
Duration: 10:40 min.
The Phillips Collection, Washington, DC,
The Dreier Fund for Acquisitions, 2014.

JENNIFER WEN MA
BRAIN STORM, 2009

Jennifer Wen Ma

A long, narrow, vertical painting hangs in my New York studio. It is a set of twelve images of a man and a horse, painted in ink and brush on rice paper. I hang few artworks in the studio, but this has occupied its place on the wall for over a decade.

The twelve images make up the first animated sequence at the start of the video *Brain Storm* (2009). Set to a walking cadence by the animation, the pair walk onward steadily, unwaveringly, silently, and seemingly with contentment. I love the way the horse's tail swings once in a while. It gives a small clue to her personality and a glimpse of her inner mind. Initially the background of the video is paper-white, then, quickly, ink droplets, lines, washes, and splashes drip down or swell up to form an ever-changing abstracted landscape.

The making of the video took a couple of years, and had several iterations before its final form in *Brain Storm*. I would have no idea at the time that this work would propel me on a decade-long investigation into Chinese ink and ways to read and dissect literati landscape painting. I have undertaken projects that used more than three tons of ink to paint live plants in nature or manmade nature. I laser-cut 300,000 square feet of paper-like materials to create sculptural landscapes that are three-dimensional paintings people can walk through and explore. I made an opera that fused ancient *Kun* opera and Western opera singing voices, staged in an ebony garden set that could be opened and closed like a painting scroll. I continue to create luminous ink paintings on glass and mirrored surfaces that speak to collective and personal myths, stories, and symbology.

The genesis of this decade of exploration in a myriad of forms, scales, materials, contents, and concepts began with the ink play in *Brain Storm*. I have found that a deep dive into a material or an aesthetic tradition can be a source of unlimited creative energy when approached with the spirit of freedom and experimentation. These wells of inspiration can be found all around. Bolstered by the boundless richness, I press on in this adventure, like the horse in ink, putting one hoof in front of another, steadfast and resolute.

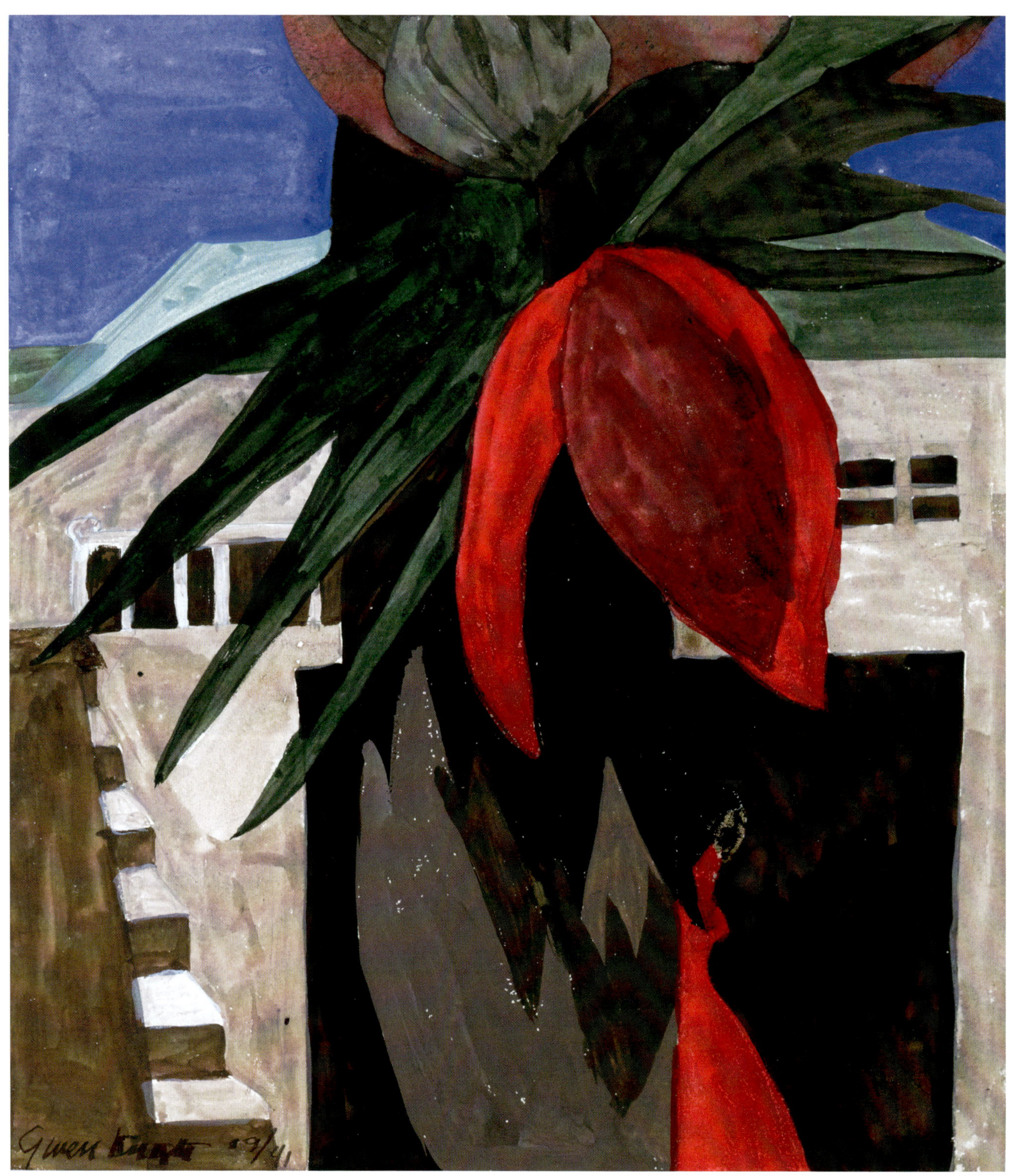

10
Gwendolyn Knight Lawrence
***Untitled* (*New Orleans* series), 1941**
Opaque and transparent watercolor over graphite pencil on paper,
14 1/2 × 12 3/4 in.
The Phillips Collection, Washington, DC,
Gift of the Phillips Contemporaries, 2001.

GWENDOLYN KNIGHT LAWRENCE
UNTITLED (NEW ORLEANS SERIES), 1941

Elsa Smithgall

Do works about the things you have experienced and your feelings about them; use your strengths. If you draw well, use drawing. If you are a colorist, use that skill.
—Gwendolyn Knight Lawrence

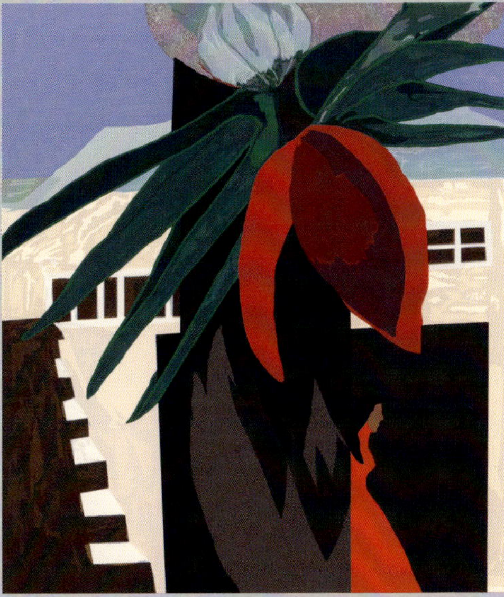

fig. 90
Gwendolyn Knight Lawrence
***Untitled (New Orleans* series), 2001–2**
Color screenprint on paper,
22 × 20 in.
The Phillips Collection, Washington, DC,
Gift of the Francine Seders Gallery, 2002.

This dazzling watercolor by Gwendolyn Knight Lawrence is among several works the artist made during her stay in New Orleans in 1941.[1] Newly wed to artist Jacob Lawrence, she set off with him for New Orleans that August in search of an urban "adventure." "We heard about New Orleans and its music, its drama, its romance," he later recalled.[2] It would be their first experience of the segregated South. Although Jim Crow laws meant she "couldn't go to the museum,"[3] Knight found artistic inspiration in New Orleans's colorful surroundings, creating charming street scenes, such as *New Orleans, Scene I (Back Porch)* and *New Orleans Scene II (Store)* (both in the collection of Jane Ellis and Jack Litewka), as well as landscapes, such as *Bayou* (Amistad Research Center, Tulane University).

In her watercolor, *Untitled (New Orleans Series)*, Knight creates a dynamic composition through the interplay of organic and geometric forms. In it she presents a magnified—bee's eye—view of a banana flower that fills the center of the composition and dwarfs the barely noticeable woman below. In monumentalizing the flower as its principal subject, Knight's image recalls the bold abstractions of Georgia O'Keeffe—works she would have seen during frequent visits to An American Place.[4] O'Keeffe had tackled the same subject in a series of charcoal drawings inspired by her trip to Bermuda in 1933–4.[5] Unlike O'Keeffe's stark rendering of a solitary banana flower in black and white, Knight's sun-drenched blossom, unfurling in shades of red and green against an azure sky, animates a theatrical backdrop of buildings, windows, and stairs. The elegant form of the silhouetted figure embodies the "linear beauty and economy of means" that Knight long admired in Asian drawing.[6]

Sixty years later, the artist decided to collaborate with printer Lou Stovall on a silkscreen print based on her earlier watercolor (fig. 90).[7] Exchanging proofs by mail, the two adapted the original composition into a slightly larger work that translated the aqueous media into solid blocks of color.
The resulting image is more graphic in sensibility while remaining faithful to the original in design. Completed the year after the death of her husband, the print beautifully evokes feelings of joy from a special time in Knight's life.

The epigraph is from Gwendolyn Knight Lawrence, cited in Thomas Riggs, ed., *St. James Guide to Black Artists* (New York: St. James Press, in association with Schomburg Center for Research in Black Culture, 1997), 303.

1 As Barbara Earl Thomas has suggested, New Orleans's hot and humid climate may have reminded the artist of her native Barbados. See also Sheryl Conkleton, "Gwendolyn Knight: A Life in Art," in Sheryl Conkleton and Barbara Earl Thomas, *Never Late for Heaven: The Art of Gwen Knight* (Seattle: University of Washington Press, in association with Tacoma Art Museum, 2003), 25.

2 Jacob Lawrence, in an interview with Jackson Frost, 2000, transcript, The Phillips Collection Archives, Washington, DC.

3 Gwendolyn Knight Lawrence, in an interview with Jackson Frost, 2000, transcript, The Phillips Collection Archives.

4 Knight called Alfred Stieglitz's gallery "a favorite of ours." Interview with Jackson Frost, 2000. While she claimed Arthur Dove among her favorites, Gwen also professed she "admired O'Keeffe, though her work was cold." Gwendolyn Knight Lawrence, cited in Conkleton, "Gwendolyn Knight: A Life in Art," 28.

5 In 1935, five of Georgia O'Keeffe's charcoal drawings of banana flowers were featured in *Georgia O'Keeffe at 'An American Place,' 44 Selected Paintings 1915–1927*. See Barbara Buhler Lynes, *Georgia O'Keeffe, Catalogue Raisonné* (New Haven, CT: Yale University Press; Washington, DC: National Gallery of Art; Abiquiu, NM: The Georgia O'Keeffe Foundation, 1999), 516–18.

6 Gwendolyn Knight Lawrence, cited in Riggs, *St. James Guide to Black Artists*, 303.

7 Knight first began making prints in the 1990s. Stovall had also made prints for Jacob Lawrence.

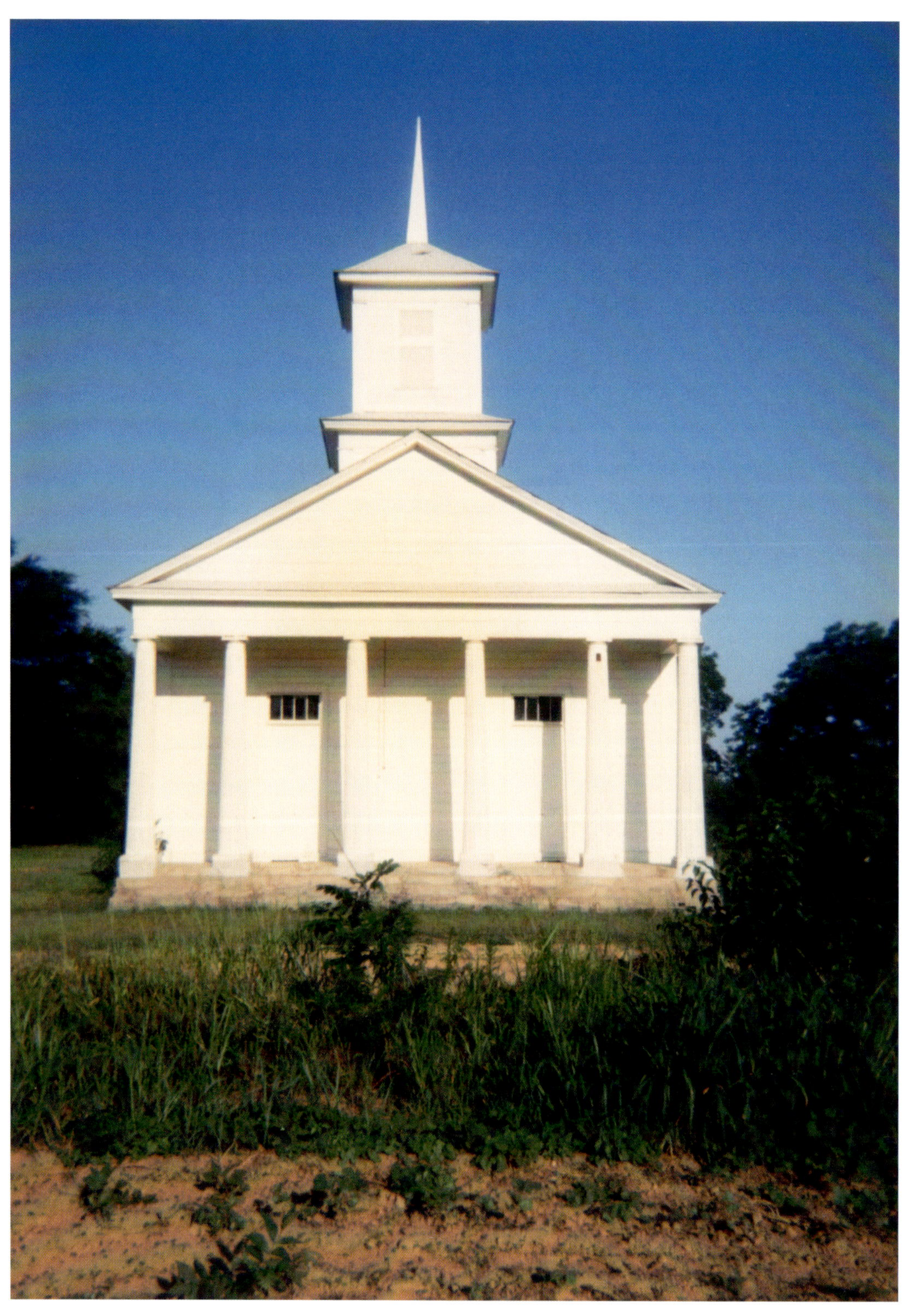

11
William Christenberry
Church across Early Cotton (Vertical View), Pickinsville, Alabama, **1964 (printed 2000)**
Chromogenic print,
5 × 3 1/2 in.
The Phillips Collection, Washington, DC,
Gift of Lee and Maria Friedlander, 2002.

WILLIAM CHRISTENBERRY
CHURCH ACROSS EARLY COTTON (VERTICAL VIEW), PICKINSVILLE, ALABAMA, 1964

Alexander Nemerov

Can a photograph really possess some small portion of the world, really claim it as a thing seen? The Phillips Collection owns thirty-one photographs by William Christenberry, most taken in his home region of west-central Alabama from the 1960s to the 1980s. As a student painter driving around with a small Kodak Brownie camera, Christenberry at first really did aim to take practical possession of what he saw. Finding a building that might figure in one of his paintings, he would stop to make a photograph, fixing the site into permanent form as a reference.

But something in these photographs implies possession in a more mysterious sense. In *Church across Early Cotton (Vertical View), Pickinsville, Alabama*, of 1964, the earliest of Christenberry's works at the Phillips, the church imprints itself on the viewer's eye, insisting that anything so bright and sharp could never be forgotten. The double glow of the building and the southern sunshine make a solar buzz, an intensity of light that burns the columns' shadows into the facade. A razor clarity of edges—the triangular pediment and stacked geometries of the tower, culminating in the toothpick spire—implies an eye cutting a form from its surroundings like scissors excising a pattern from paper. The building remains in place but feels *taken away*, as if Christenberry were a carpenter-magus moving the structure, board by board, from its actual location to a private place of his own.

To do so, he took care to make the church pocket size. This photograph and many others in the collection are small—roughly five by three inches. The intimate size turns the buildings into toys the mind can hold as a hand would: little structures that would not be out of place by the side of model railroad tracks in the playset of an imaginative child. (It makes sense that Christenberry painstakingly built models of some of the buildings he photographed.) Childhood is an era of possession, yes, a time when we might jealously guard our playthings, our collections (of matchboxes, postage stamps, and trading cards, all of which Christenberry's photographs evoke). But more beautifully, childhood is a time *when the world possesses us*, when it sometimes alights on our being and stays there, glowing like a winged insect drinking sweat from the back of our hand.

What kind of time unfolds in that experience? The time of the *Is*. Christenberry's photographs abound in it. The time of the *Is* does not explode upon the eye. It does not teeter in delicacies of suspended time, hushes of cessation, disclosing a hidden reality. The time of the *Is* endures us. It waits us out, waits until we see that the buildings we behold are nothing special, waits so that we drop any pretense of being a breathless tour guide to their vernacular loveliness, waits until we recognize their drowsy boredom with themselves in the light of another long day. These structures *are* and *are* and *are*—and in that slowness, burning on the eye, they become signs of the little we take away.

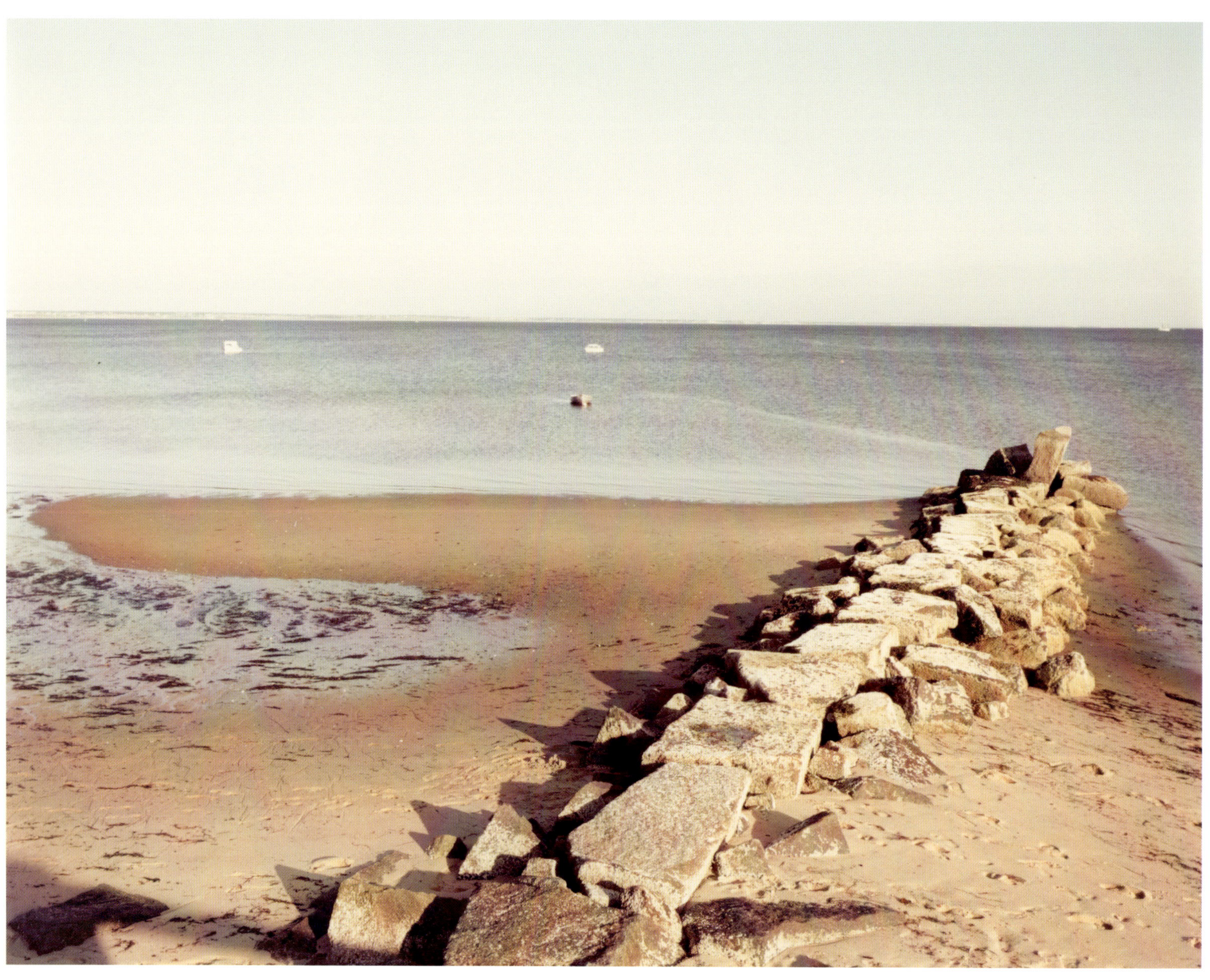

12
Joel Meyerowitz
Bay/Sky/Jetty, 1983
Chromogenic print,
11 × 14 in.
The Phillips Collection, Washington, DC,
Gift of Jordan and Devinah Finn, 2014.

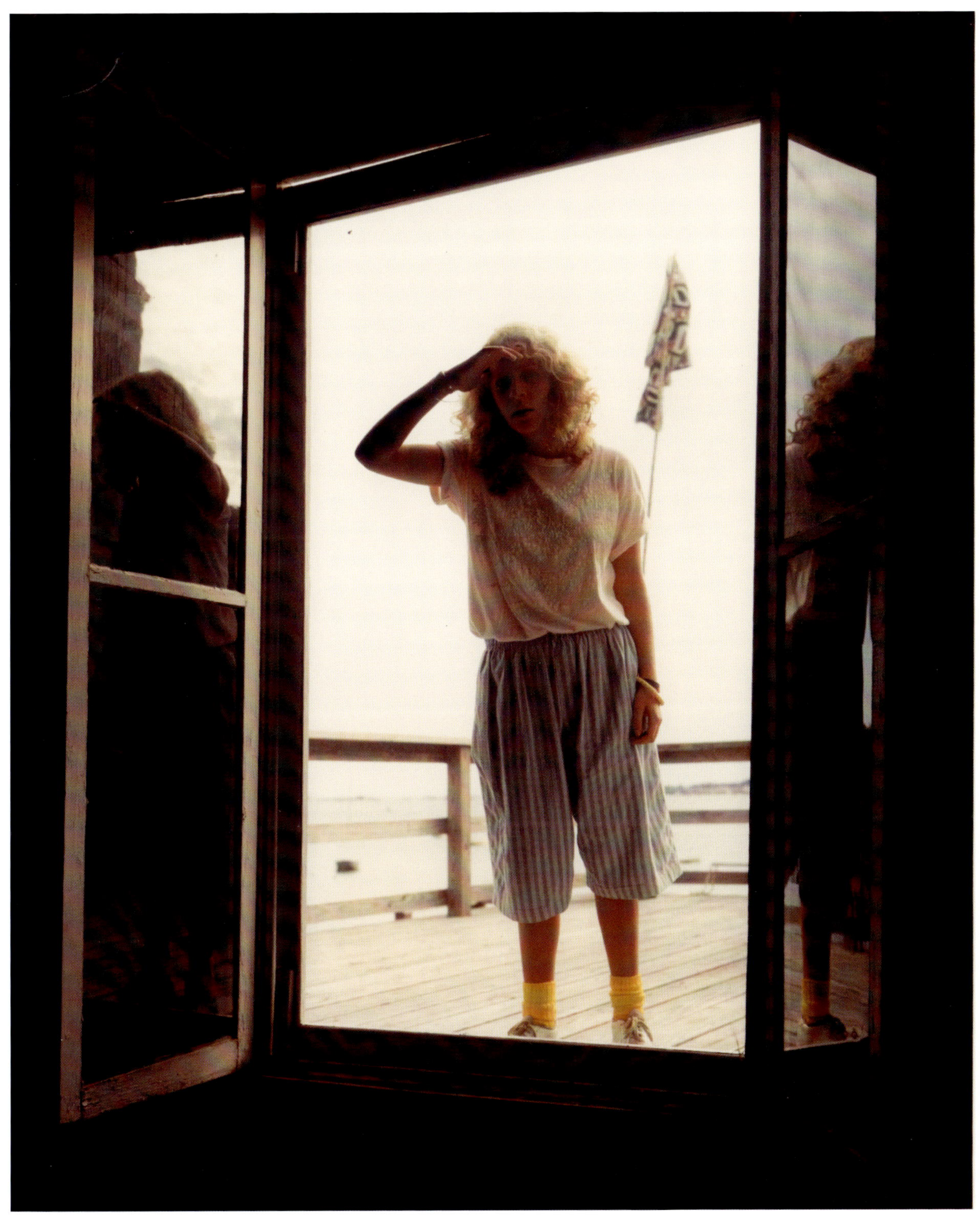

13
Joel Meyerowitz
Carrie, 1985
Chromogenic print,
14 × 11 in.
The Phillips Collection, Washington, DC,
Gift of Lisa Finn, 2017.

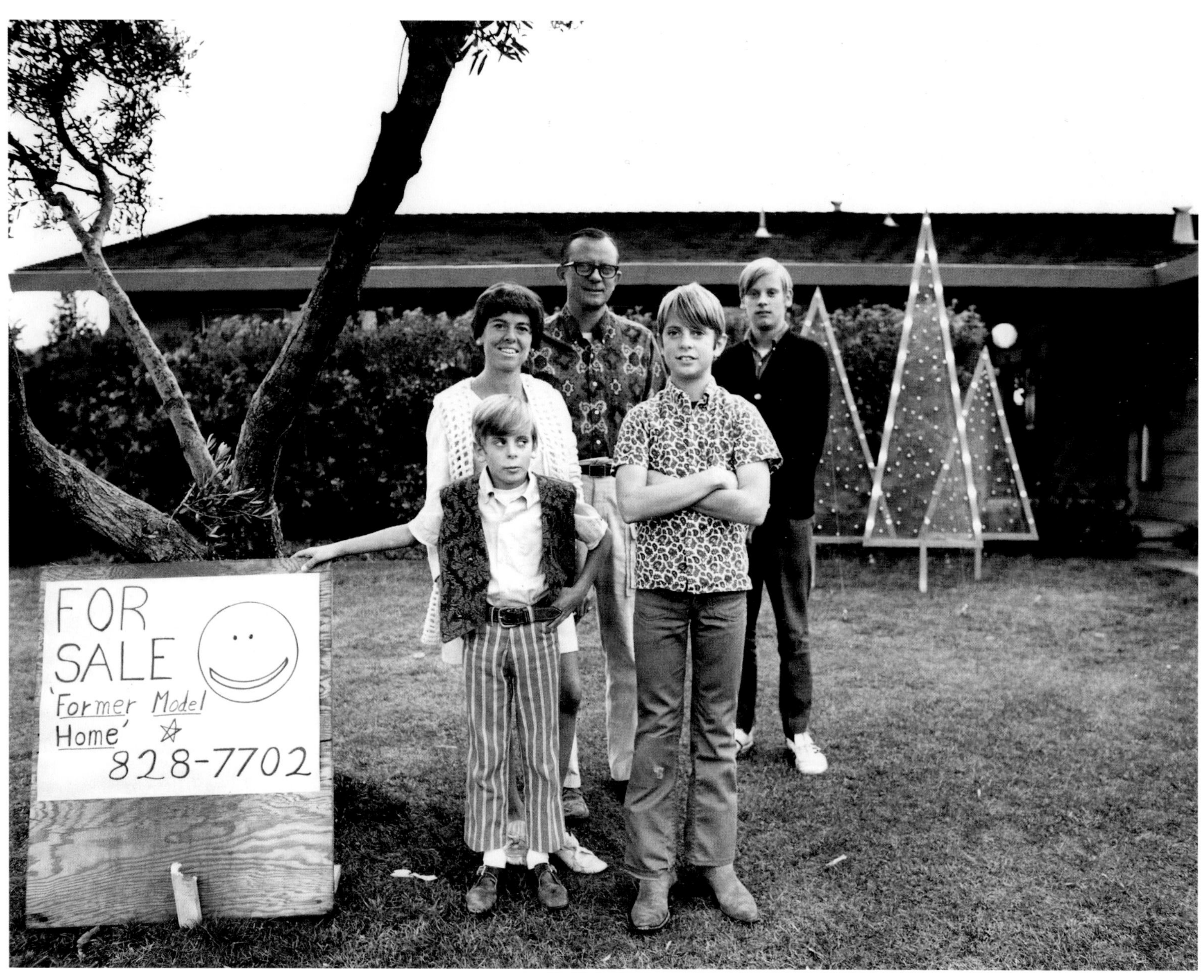

14
Bill Owens
***We have to move. My husband's been transferred to Southern California (Suburbia series)*, 1971**
Gelatin silver print,
8 × 10 in.
The Phillips Collection, Washington, DC,
Gift of Robert Shimshak and Marion Brenner, 2020.

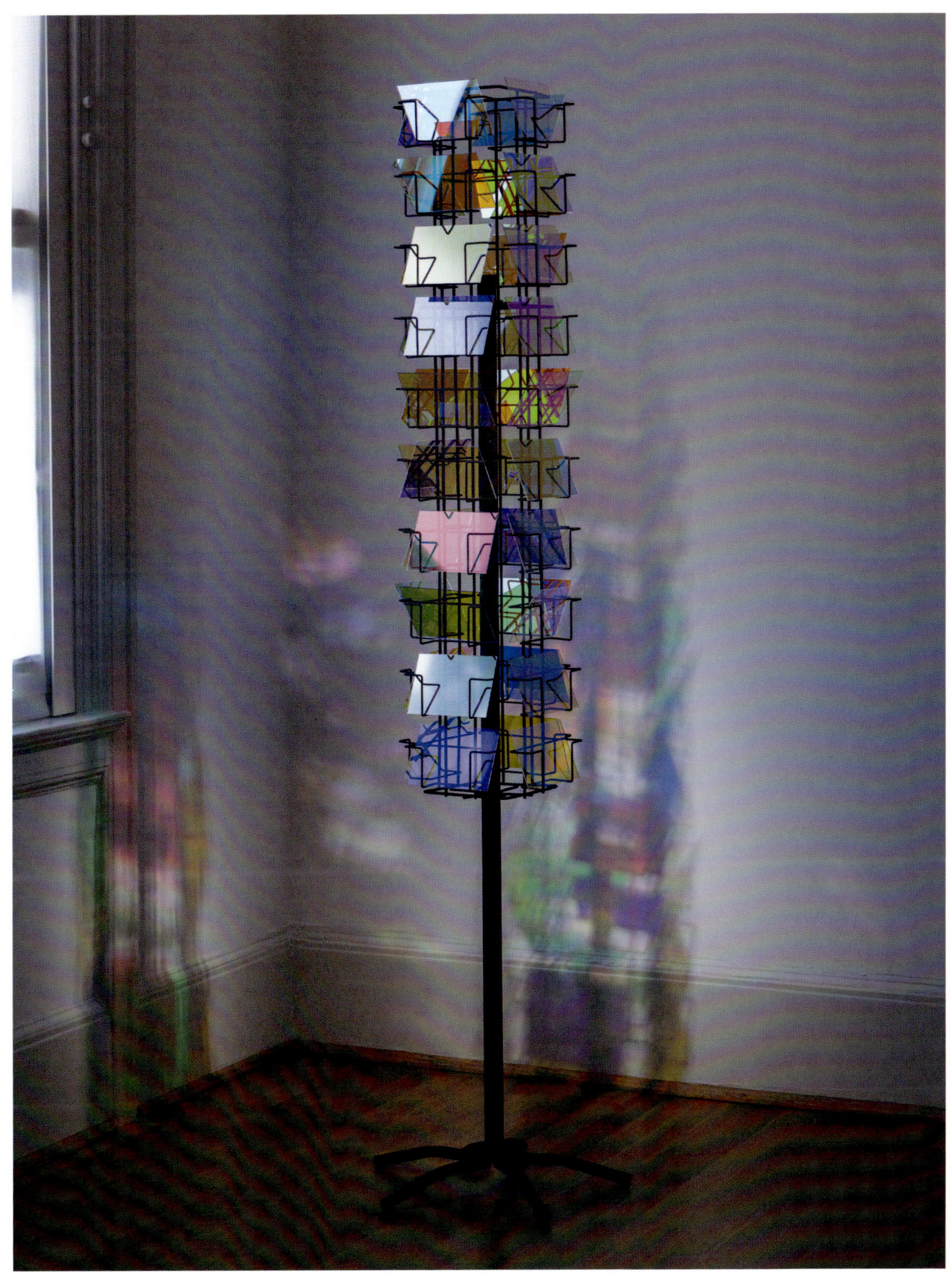

15
Stephen Dean
Prayer Mill, 2007
Metal and dichroic glass,
71 1/2 × 18 × 28 in.
The Phillips Collection, Washington, DC,
Gift of Tony and Heather Podesta Collection, 2019.

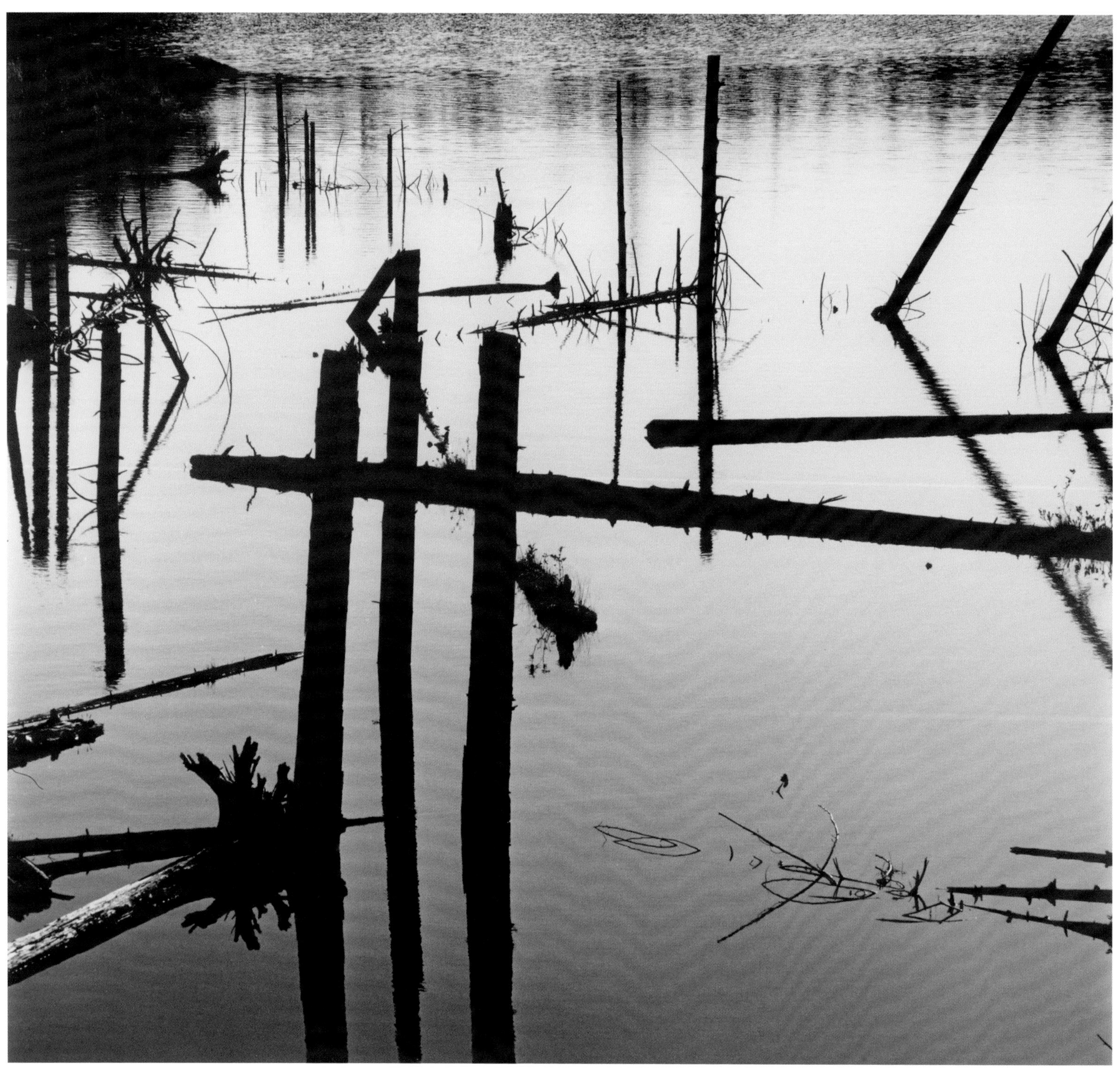

16
Brett Weston
High Sierra, ca. 1970
Gelatin silver print,
11 × 14 in.
The Phillips Collection, Washington, DC,
Gift of the Brett Weston Archive from the
Christian K. Keesee Collection, 2006.

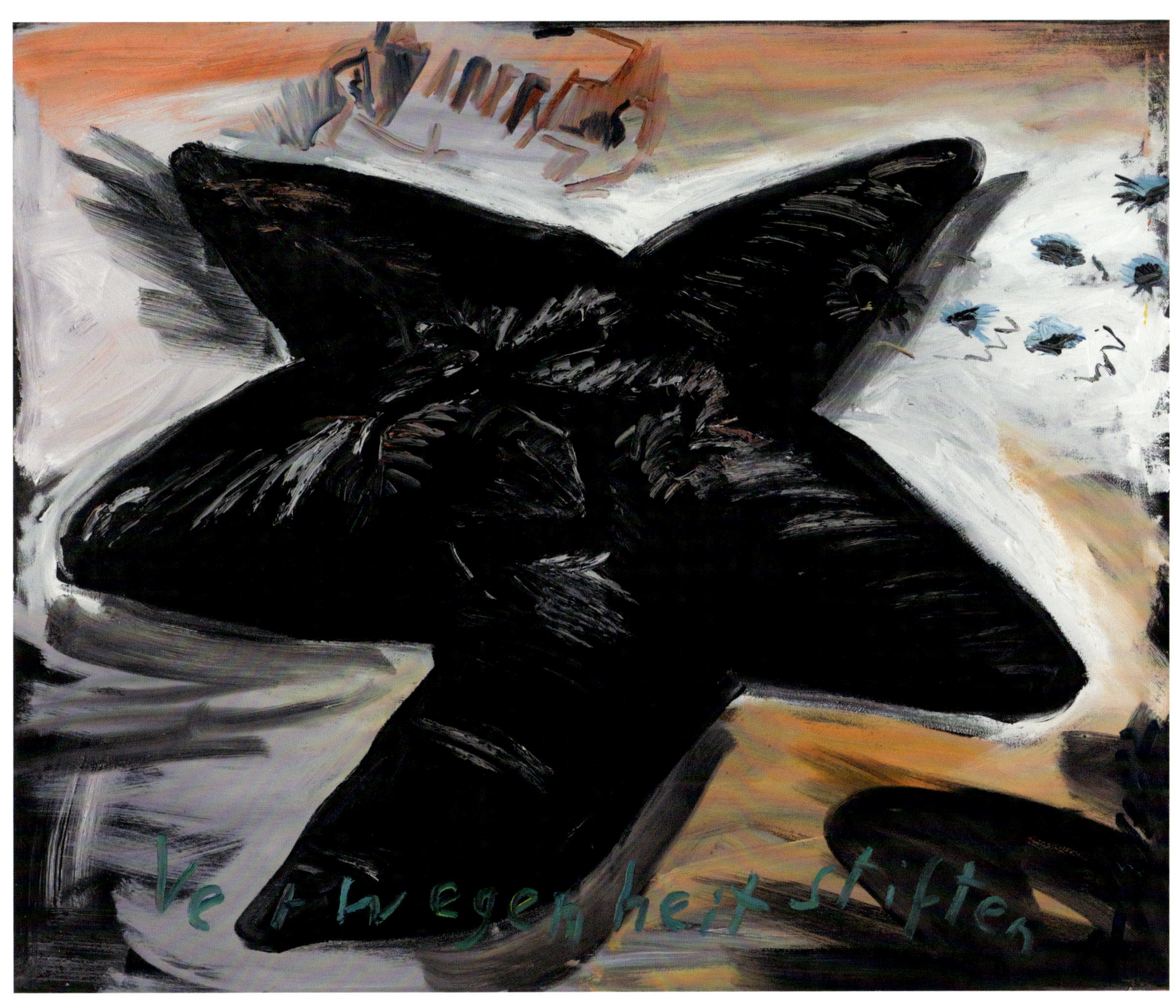

17
Jörg Immendorff
Verwegenheit stiften (Bestowing Audacity), 1982
Oil on canvas,
43 1/4 × 51 1/4 in.
The Phillips Collection, Washington, DC,
Gift of Michael Werner, 2015.

18
Ching Ho Cheng
Untitled, 1985
Charcoal and graphite on two pieces of torn rag paper, 42 1/2 × 72 1/2 in.
The Phillips Collection, Washington, DC, Gift of the Ching Ho Cheng Estate, 2018.

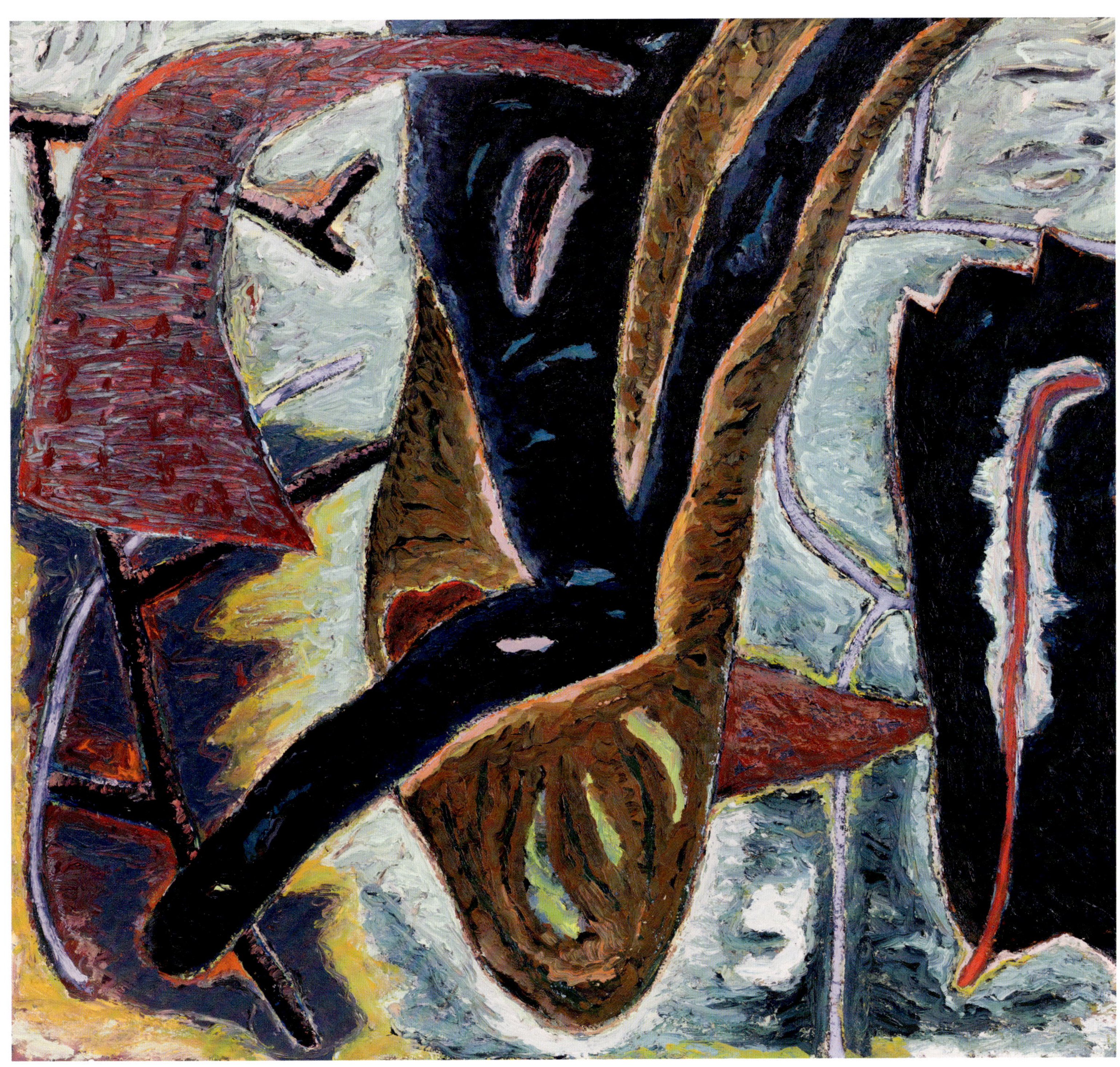

19
Gregory Amenoff
Trinity (for Van), 1982
Oil on canvas,
75 × 79 in.
The Phillips Collection, Washington, DC,
Gift of John Raimondi and Ralph T. Cantin, 2016.

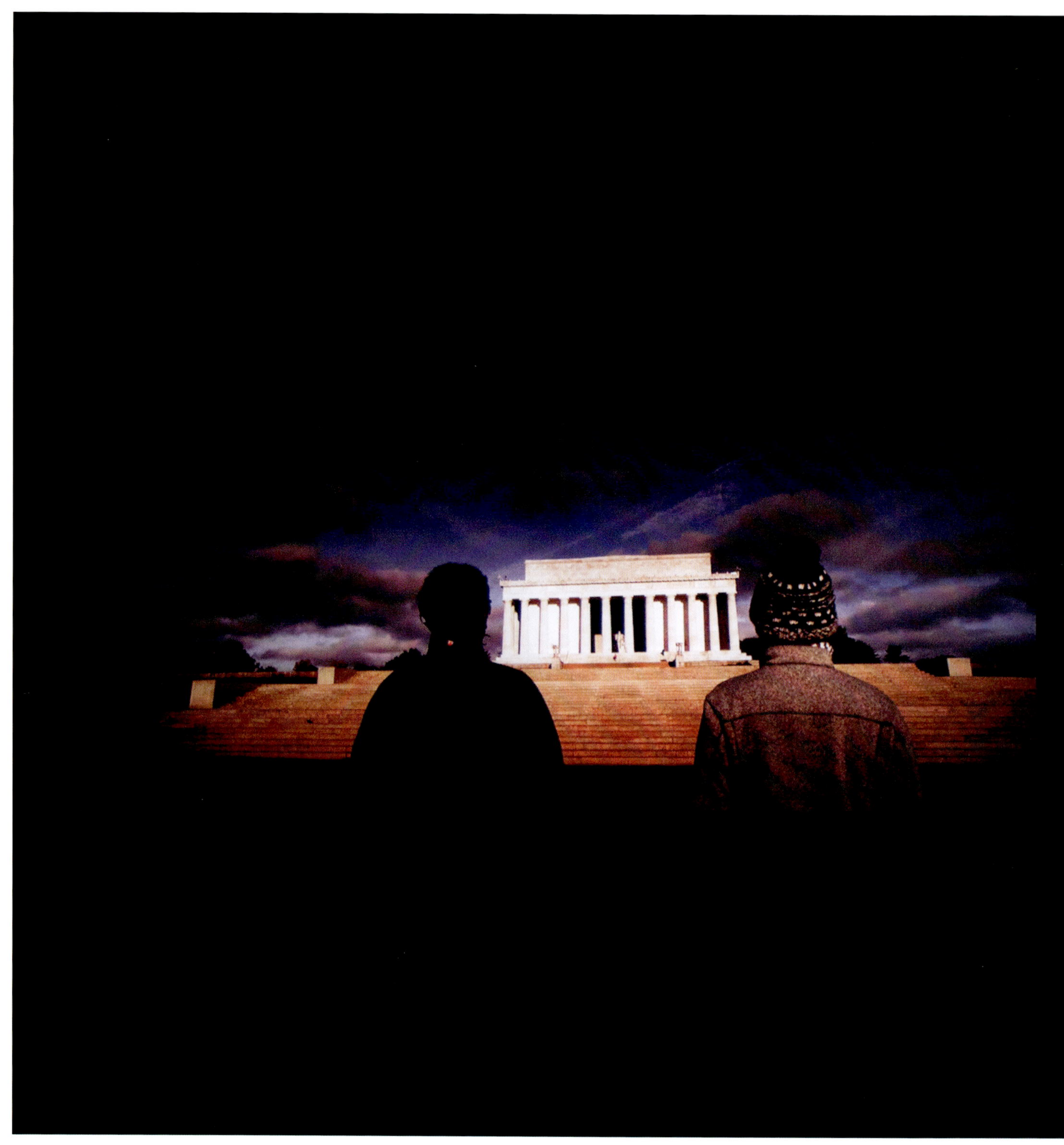

20
John Akomfrah
Transfigured Night, 2013
Two-channel HD color video installation (color, 5.1 sound).
Duration: 26.31 min.
The Phillips Collection, Washington, DC, The Dreier Fund for Acquisitions, 2019.

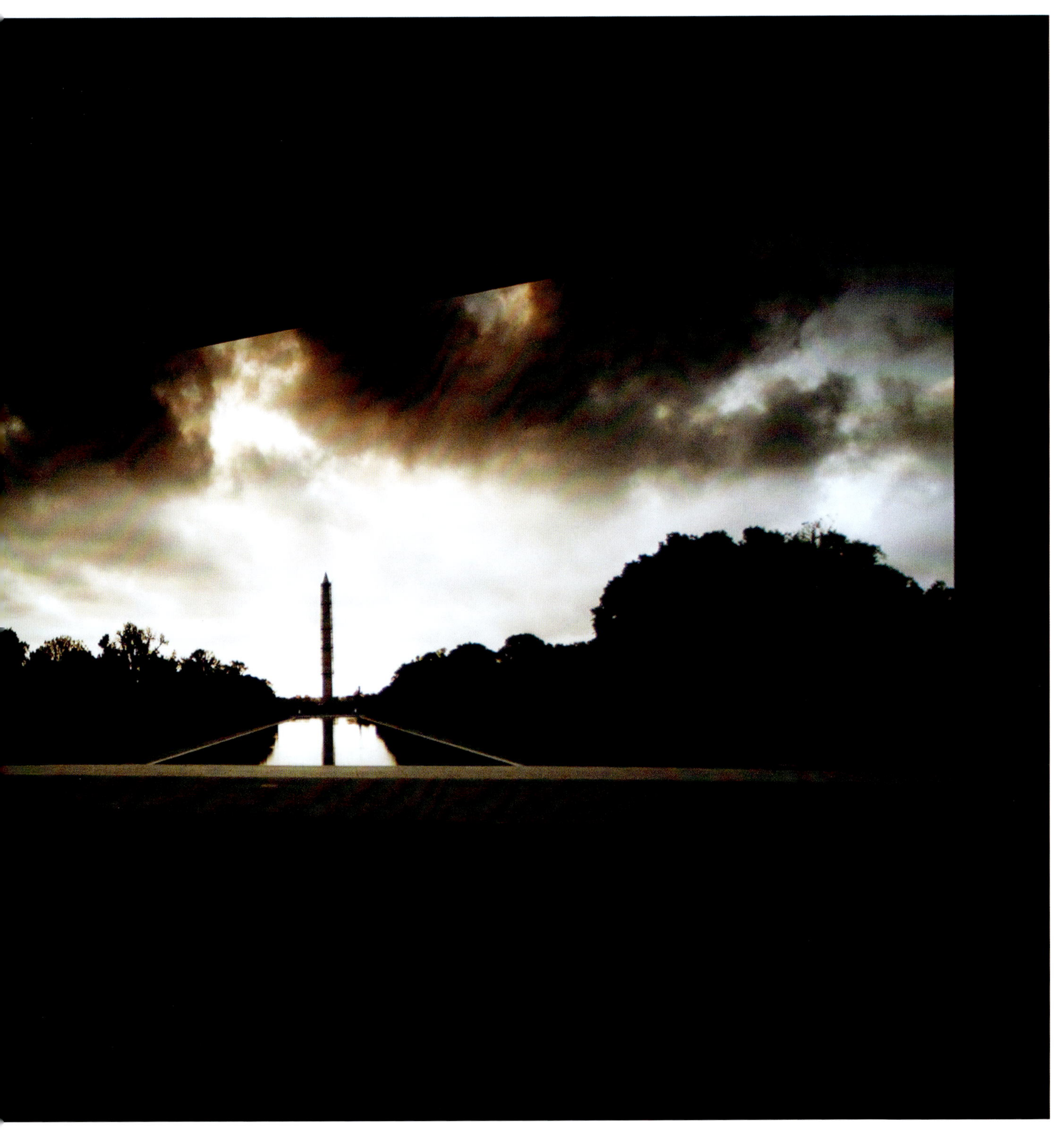

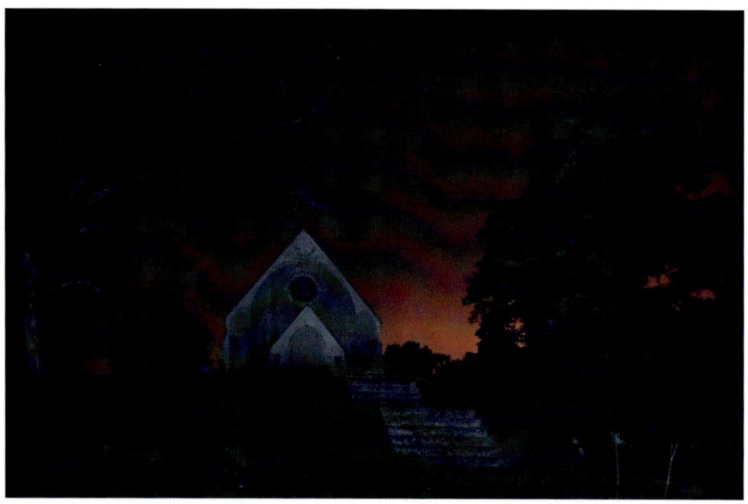

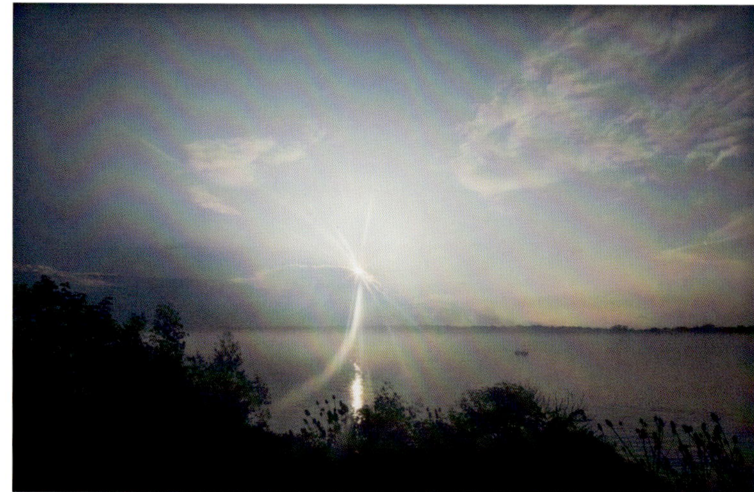

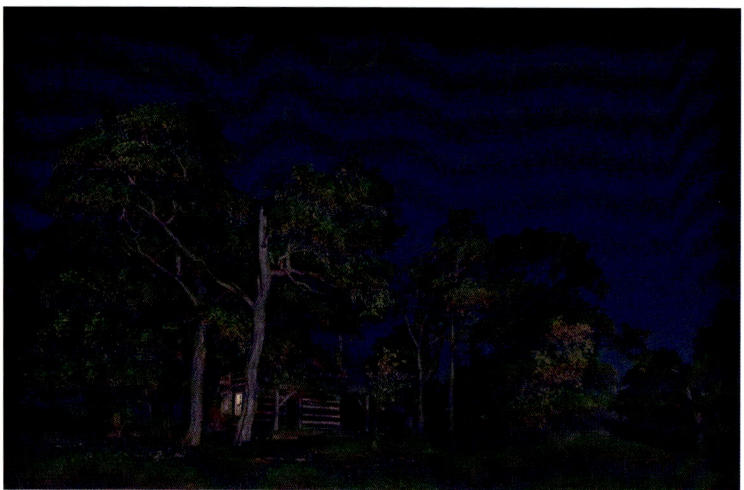

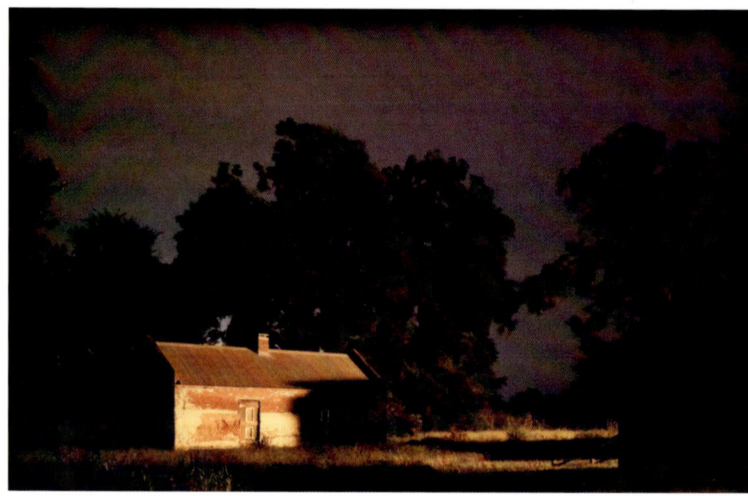

21 (top left)
Jeanine Michna-Bales
Resting Place, Church Hill, Mississippi (*Through Darkness to Light: Photographs Along the Underground Railroad* series), 2014
Chromogenic print,
12 1/2 × 18 in.
The Phillips Collection, Washington, DC,
Gift of Julia J. Norrell in memory of John Dingell, 2019.

22 (bottom left)
Jeanine Michna-Bales
On the Safest Route, James and Rachel Sillivan cabin, Pennville (formerly Camden), Indiana (*Through Darkness to Light: Photographs Along the Underground Railroad* series), 2014
Chromogenic print,
12 1/2 × 18 in.
The Phillips Collection, Washington, DC,
Gift of Julia J. Norrell in memory of John Dingell, 2019.

23 (top right)
Jeanine Michna-Bales
Within Reach, Crossing the St. Clair River to Canada south of Port Huron, Michigan (*Through Darkness to Light: Photographs Along the Underground Railroad* series), 2014
Chromogenic print,
12 1/2 × 18 in.
The Phillips Collection, Washington, DC,
Gift of Julia J. Norrell in memory of John Dingell, 2019.

24 (bottom right)
Jeanine Michna-Bales
Decision to Leave. Magnolia Plantation on the Cane River, Louisiana (*Through Darkness to Light: Photographs Along the Underground Railroad* series), 2013
Chromogenic print,
12 1/2 × 18 in.
The Phillips Collection, Washington, DC,
Gift of Julia J. Norrell in memory of John Dingell, 2019.

JEANINE MICHNA-BALES
THROUGH DARKNESS TO LIGHT: PHOTOGRAPHS ALONG THE UNDERGROUND RAILROAD

Jacqueline E. Lawton

When I first opened Jeanine Michna-Bales's photographic essay, *Through Darkness to Light*, I was struck by the haunting quality of the photographs. They are dark, foreboding, and provocative. I contemplated each image in awe and wonder. As a Black woman playwright, I felt the images evoke countless untold stories of enslaved people fighting for freedom and to be seen as human beings.

Each slave was considered to be only three-fifths of a human being for purposes of legislative representation and tax responsibility. Slavery was dehumanizing in every possible way, and the subsequent erasure of the stories of our forebears from history only further discounts our own life experiences and our role in society. These photos bring the stories of my ancestors to light.

Michna-Bales grew up in the Midwest, where the Underground Railroad provided passages to freedom for people fleeing slavery. She began her research with a curiosity about the landscape that surrounded her. She imagined the journey a fugitive might make under the cover of darkness, trusting the path would lead to deliverance.

Her series, thirteen images from which are owned by The Phillips Collection, grew out of a breadth of rich primary resources, including song lyrics; quotes from abolitionists; slave narrative texts; and images of maps, advertisements by slaveholders for the sale and exchange of enslaved people for goods and cash, abolitionist pamphlets and newspapers, illustrations, and minutes taken from anti-slavery meetings.

But the true power of this body of work is how it teaches us to see and examine our surroundings. The photographs were taken in the evening, at night, and during the early dawn. You have to adjust your eyes to see them, to make out the shape, to judge the distances, and to determine depth. Michna-Bales is undoubtedly skilled and knowledgeable at her craft. But when I saw the image of *Within Reach* (pl. 23), I caught my breath. The way the sun peeks out from behind the clouds feels like the embodiment of hope. I was impressed by how she captures such rich tones and colors with so little light.

Taken as a whole, her images reminded me that history is not merely a series of dates that lead to culminating events. History is a complex and complicated, interconnected web of lived experiences. Like the photos that require us to adjust our eyes to see them clearly, we have to sit with our history and wrestle with our understanding of the world in order to understand and appreciate it.

The searing beauty of Michna-Bales's photographic essay is that it reveals just how treacherous the journey toward freedom was. These images speak of a time when strangers of different races collaborated in the common struggle for freedom. The people who made up the Underground Railroad believed that all human beings deserved a chance to be free and that freedom was worth any sacrifice. More than anything, Michna-Bales's photos help to weave the stories of the Underground Railroad into our history in a concrete and nuanced way.

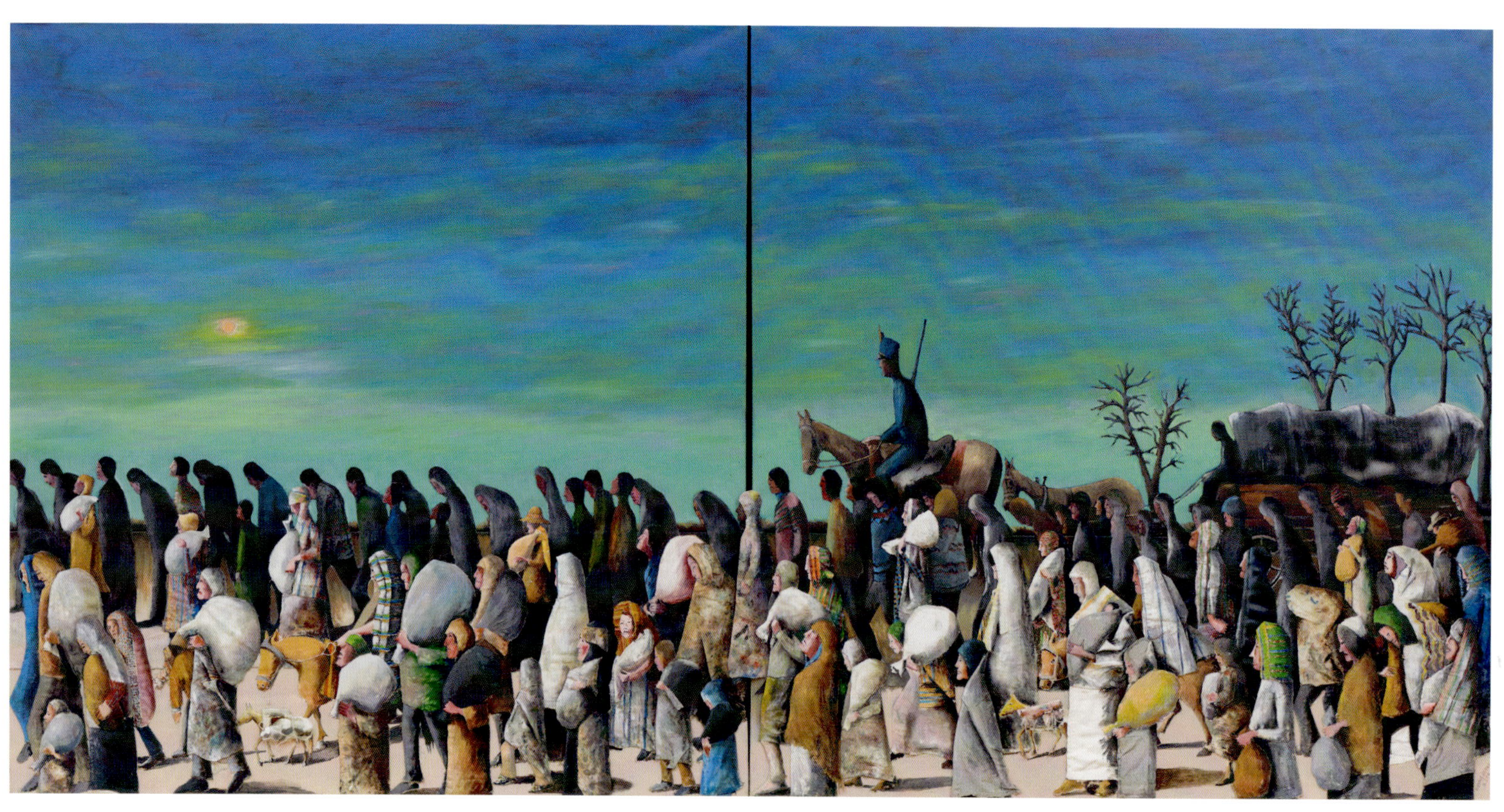

25
Benny Andrews
***Trail of Tears*, 2005**
Oil on four canvases with mixed media, painted fabric, and string collage,
76 × 145 × 1 in.
The Phillips Collection, Washington, DC,
Gift of Agnes Gund, 2019.

BENNY ANDREWS
TRAIL OF TEARS, 2005

heather ahtone

Migrants and refugees are the disadvantaged humans made victims of deliberate forces. Their stories are found in every epoch, a reflection of the political will of the day. Each story is composed of nameless individuals, families, and generations. They are violently displaced from their homes, from all that is familiar, and reduced to bodies acting on an inner determination to survive. Benny Andrews's *Trail of Tears* speaks to one such story, the involuntary removal of almost a hundred thousand of our Native American ancestors. Their forced relocations began at the eastern seaboard. The expulsion from their homelands continued, stretching from the Gulf Coast to the Great Lakes, and they were pushed beyond the Mississippi River.

For many Americans this story is an unfortunate moment in the founding of the United States. For Andrews, who was part Scottish and part Indian, and who self-identified as an African American,[1] it had to have been a story he heard as a child growing up in Georgia. Georgia is the homeland of the Cherokee Nation, which was at the center of the national struggle in 1830. The tribe protested the congressionally approved Indian Removal Act all the way to the Supreme Court, which decided in the Cherokee Nation's favor. Defying the decision, President Andrew Jackson sent the military to forcibly remove the Cherokee people. Many were flushed from their burning homes at gunpoint. The violence of this expulsion remains in the memory of the land; the same land where Andrews picked cotton as the child of a sharecropper.

The bodies in the foreground are materialized by collaged fragments of paper and cloth. Each fold of the material laid down on the surface serves to shroud the body; inferring vulnerable lean bodies and suggesting the burden of emotional weight carried by the refugees. The space between each figure is accented by short shadows, adding depth to the surface but also serving as a metaphor for the fracturing relationships. The threatening stormy sky weighs heavily above the group, pushing them forward. Most of the heads are bowed against this weight and the sorrow of their plight. The face of one child, just left of center, looks out to the viewer, engaging them as witness to the tragedy. They are driven forward by a stalwart soldier riding his horse. He rides above their heads, the shadow of a rifle pinning him to his position atop the horse. Even the trees are stripped of their leaves, perhaps a metaphor for how the people are stripped of their dignity.

Andrews's *Trail of Tears* defies a particular time or location, speaking to the plight of all who become migrants at the hands of oppressors. While the title may place these figures in the nineteenth century, they could just as easily be the refugees fleeing the gangs in Central America or the Syrian military. Andrews leaves the figures anonymous, but that child calls us to account for the tragedy in front of us.

---

1 Benny Andrews, "An Interview with Benny Andrews," Staniski Media, 2003, http://www.bennyandrews.com/about-benny. Accessed April 2020.

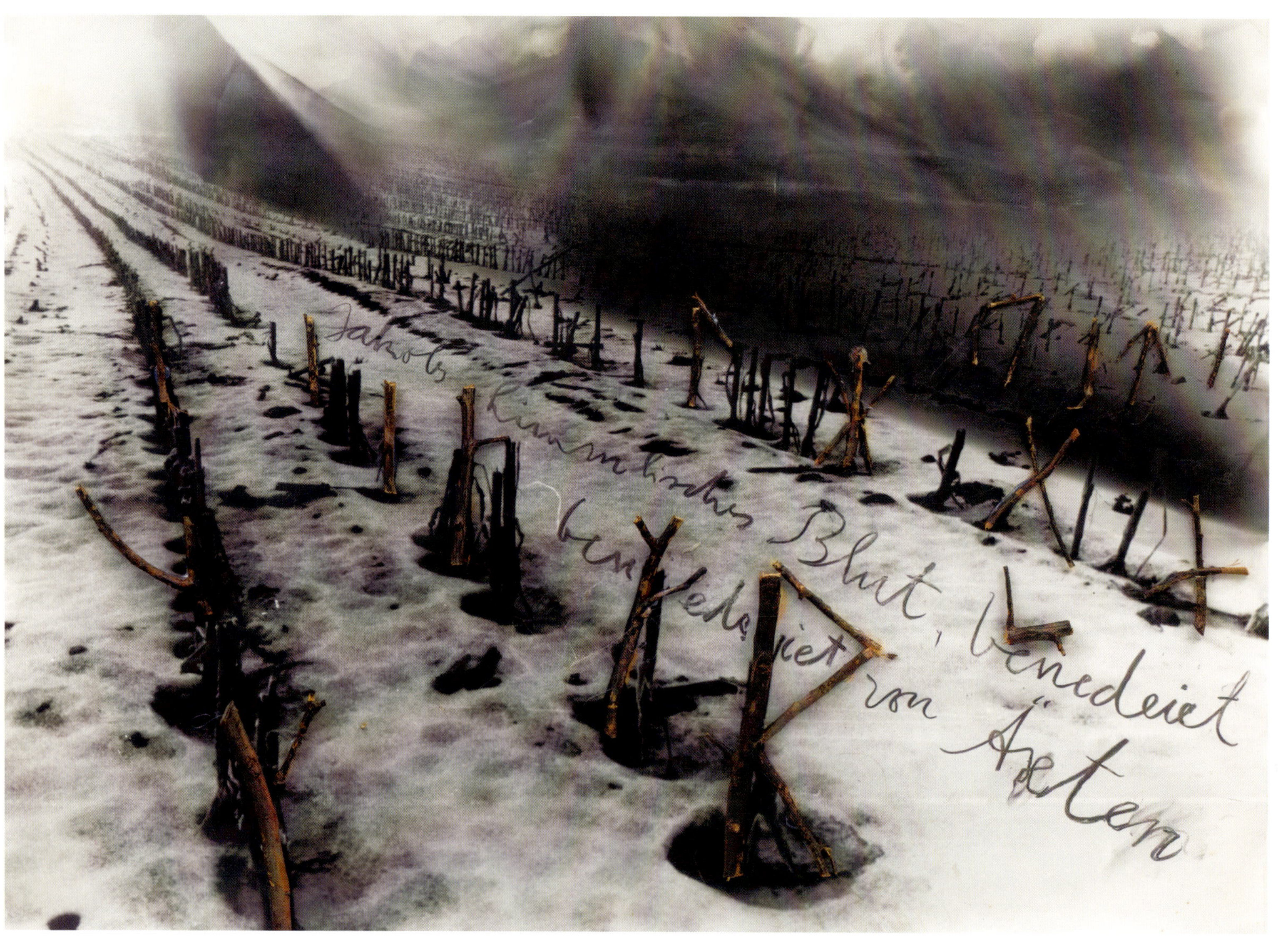

26
Anselm Kiefer
***Jakobs himmlisches Blut benedeiet von Äxten (Jacob's Heavenly Blood Blessed by Axes)*, 2005**
Charcoal and wood twigs on gelatin silver print,
25 × 33 1/2 in.
The Phillips Collection, Washington, DC,
Gift of Harry Grubert, 2018.

ANSELM KIEFER
JAKOBS HIMMLISCHES BLUT BENEDEIET VON ÄXTEN (JACOB'S HEAVENLY BLOOD BLESSED BY AXES), 2005

Bernardí Roig

The image is heartrending. A devastated, frozen landscape, the perspective entirely warped to the left, dominated by a disobedient vanishing point. It is an optical illusion that is incapable of containing a habitable space; the image of a place with no harvest, farmland with no future.

In a landscape of infinite mourning, suffering rolls across the image of scorched trunks that are wrapped around other, real trunks. Crucified, in fact, upon them. A hybrid print that produces a new visual labyrinth and bears the guilt and atonement of a culture that has razed its logocentric edifice. Light no longer prevails, but rather becomes a thick smoke that obscures any gaze. Next comes a snowfall of ash, ash from the incineration of Shulamith, the Jewish woman evoked by Paul Celan in "Todesfuge" (Death Fugue). But Shulamith is no longer there; she has been engulfed by a ruthless night. In her place is Jacob, son of Isaac, grandson of Abraham, father of Joseph.

The title of Kiefer's collage alludes to Hebrew antiquity, to blood and steel, and it does not forget that death is a master from Germany, as described by Celan, a poet who wrote in the language of the enemy and whose work is critical to understanding Kiefer's mind.

... your golden hair Margarete
your ashen hair Shulamith he plays with
the serpents[1]

Meanwhile, the land remains a coagulated void, unsettled by a flurry of blackness. We can hear the woodworms in those trunks affixed to the photo. The linearity of time is nothing more than an accumulation of expectations.

Jacques Rancière says that there are no stories.[2] They were all told in the Old Testament. We are in the time after all stories. Now is not the time to craft beautiful phrases to compensate for the emptiness of all waiting, but the time to take an interest in the wait itself. It is a time of absence and desolation that doesn't allow us to expect anything from the landscape. In fact, we are no longer able to even occupy it, as it has ceased to be a place at all; it has become a void.

That void has fallen silent; its sound is a merciless, smoky wind that batters what remains of the landscape as its absence spreads. As it spreads, it blankets that absence, because the experience of silence is the experience of delayed death. That silence is an avaricious mirror that shows us not the image of absence, but the image of death, which, ultimately, are one and the same.

This piece, guilty with the heritage of horror, is grounded in a return to Jewish mysticism and Kabbalah. Painting is the epic from trauma.

But this work, too, spares us the anecdotal. It retains its icy beauty in the storehouse of the visible, just before the epiphany. The question is: where will the white go when the snow melts?

---

1 Paul Celan, "Fugue of Death" (first published 1948; reprinted 1952), translation by Christopher Middleton, https://poets.org/poem/fugue-death. Accessed April 2020.

2 Jacques Rancière, *Béla Tarr, The Time After* (Minneapolis: University of Minnesota Press, 2015), 63.

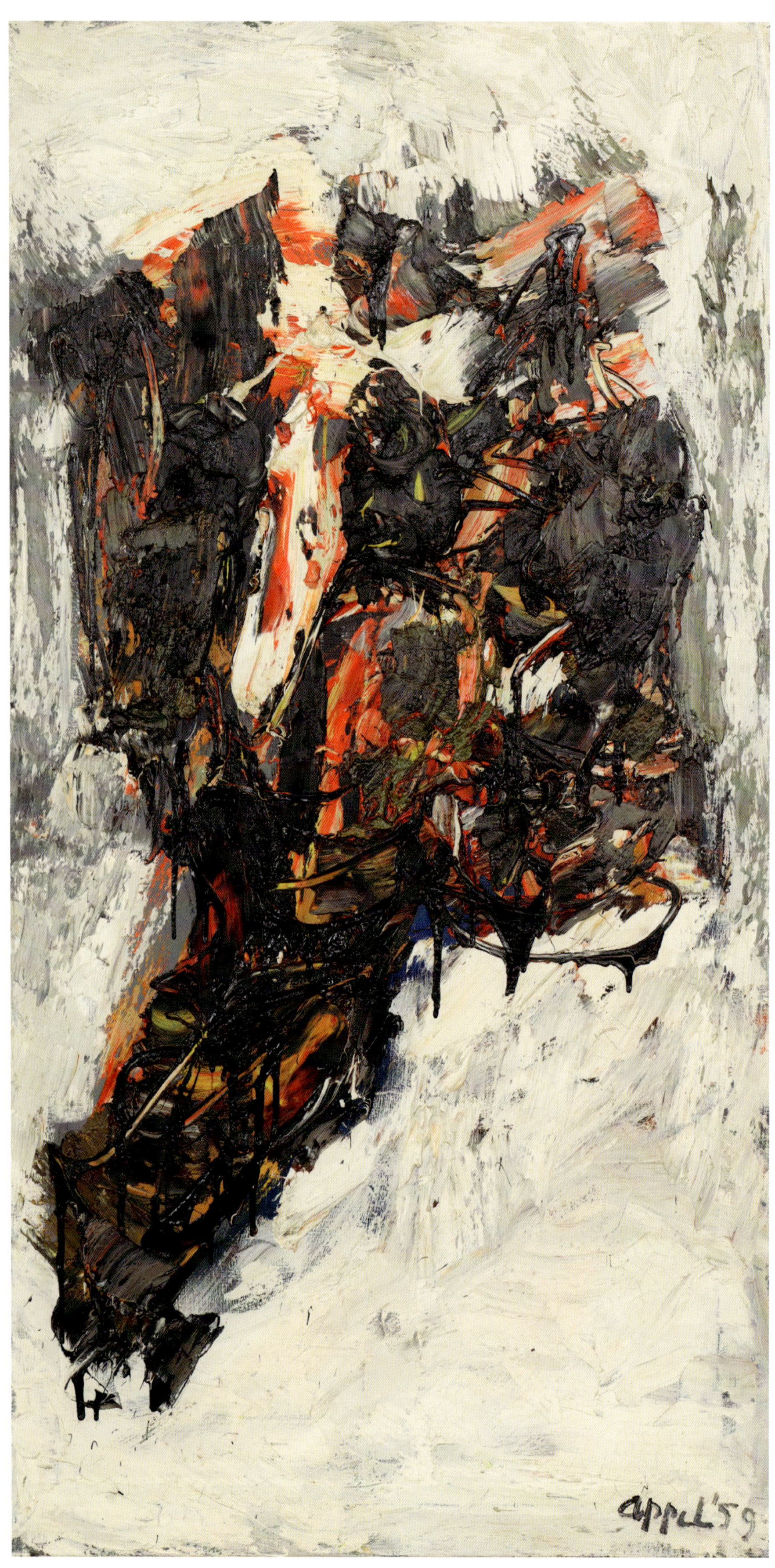

27
Karel Appel
***Tête comme un arbre (Head as a Tree)*, 1959**
Oil on canvas,
76 3/4 × 38 1/8 in.
The Phillips Collection, Washington, DC,
Gift of the Karel Appel Foundation, 2016.

KAREL APPEL
TÊTE COMME UN ARBRE (HEAD AS A TREE), 1959

Franz W. Kaiser

Karel Appel's *Head as a Tree* might bring to mind certain paintings of the 1980s and 1990s by Georg Baselitz or Markus Lüpertz (see fig. 91), but it was painted in 1959. At the time, Appel was at the peak of his international fame. Of Dutch origin, he had been living in Paris since 1950, where he had moved as a member of the international avant-garde group CoBrA. *The Elephant,* also in The Phillips Collection, is based on a small plaster sculpture made the same year, belonging to a group of sculptures of the artist's CoBrA period.

Moving to Paris seemed natural for an ambitious artist: the city was still considered the international capital of modern art. The CoBrA group dissolved in 1951, however, and of all its members, only Appel succeeded in his international breakthrough from Paris—as an artist associated with art informel.[1] Michel Tapié, the French art impresario who coined the term, included Appel in his pathbreaking show *Un art autre* (1952). He also brought important collectors, museum directors like James Johnson Sweeney, and the gallerist Martha Jackson to Appel's studio. Starting with his first visit to New York on the occasion of his second show at Martha Jackson Gallery in 1957, Appel spent some time in the United States every year. As far as the Parisian art world was concerned, he had "disappeared" to America,[2] while in fact his main home remained Paris; when in the United States, he would routinely introduce himself as a European painter living in the French capital.[3] In a sense, he belonged to everywhere and to nowhere. This might be considered a handicap, but it certainly played out to his advantage when New York took over from Paris as the international art capital.

An avid observer, Appel took his inspiration from what he saw in the streets and from what was going on in the international art world. The Phillips's *Woman with Flowers No. 1* (fig. 92) obviously took inspiration from nouveau réalisme, the French version of pop art. Always on his guard against getting stuck in a particular style, Appel made painterly experiments that could take him far afield—an example being *Landscape with Wheel* (The Phillips Collection). Constructed from small, repetitive brushstrokes, this painting is representative of Appel's quite atypical style of around 1980, which was originally inspired by an extreme enlargement of a detail from a Van Gogh painting.[4]

Continuing to live in Europe and in the United States, Appel kept on the move until an advanced age—from the 1990s on—between five studios on both sides of the Atlantic. He died on May 3, 2006, in Zurich, and is buried at the Père Lachaise cemetery in Paris.

---

1 This was Markus Lüpertz's perception in the early 1960s, as stated in an interview that I conducted with him. Franz W. Kaiser, *Markus Lüpertz—In't God'lijk Licht/In Divine Light* (The Hague: Gemeentemuseum, 2011), 33.

2 Testimony of Michel Ragon, whom I interviewed for Franz W. Kaiser, *Appel Retrospective* (The Hague: Gemeentemuseum, 2016), 24.

3 Cathérine van Houts, *Karel Appel—de biografie* (Amsterdam: Uitgeverij Contact, 2000), 239.

4 Information provided by the artist.

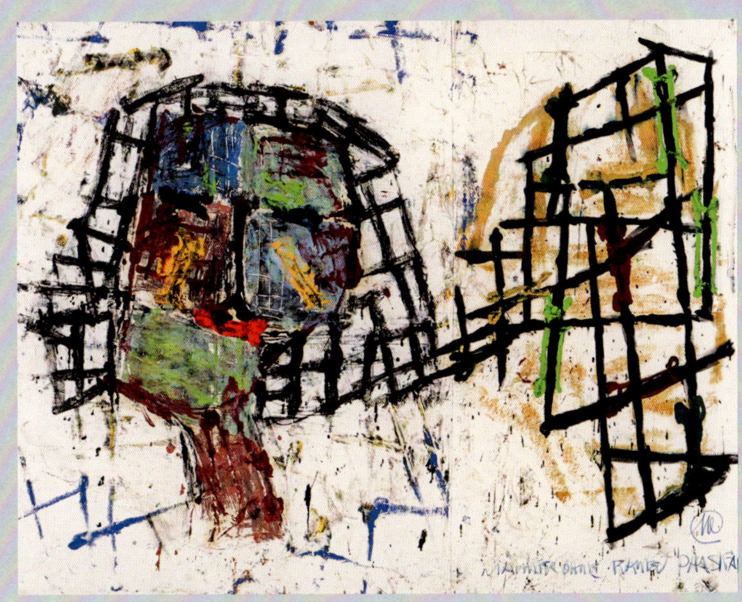

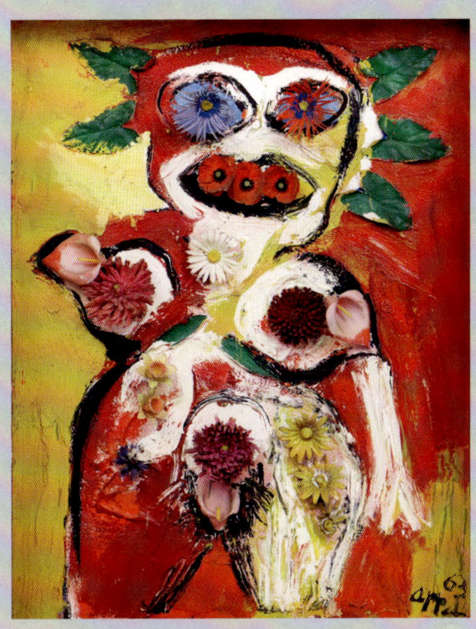

fig. 91 (left)
Markus Lüpertz
***Männer ohne Frauen, Parsifal*, 1994**
Tempera and oil on linen, 78 3/4 × 98 1/2 in.
Galerie Michael Werner, Märkisch Wilmersdorf, Cologne & New York.

fig. 92 (right)
Karel Appel
***Woman with Flowers No. 1*, 1963**
Oil on canvas with plastic flowers,
45 1/4 × 35 3/8 in.
The Phillips Collection, Washington, DC,
Gift of the Karel Appel Foundation, 2016.

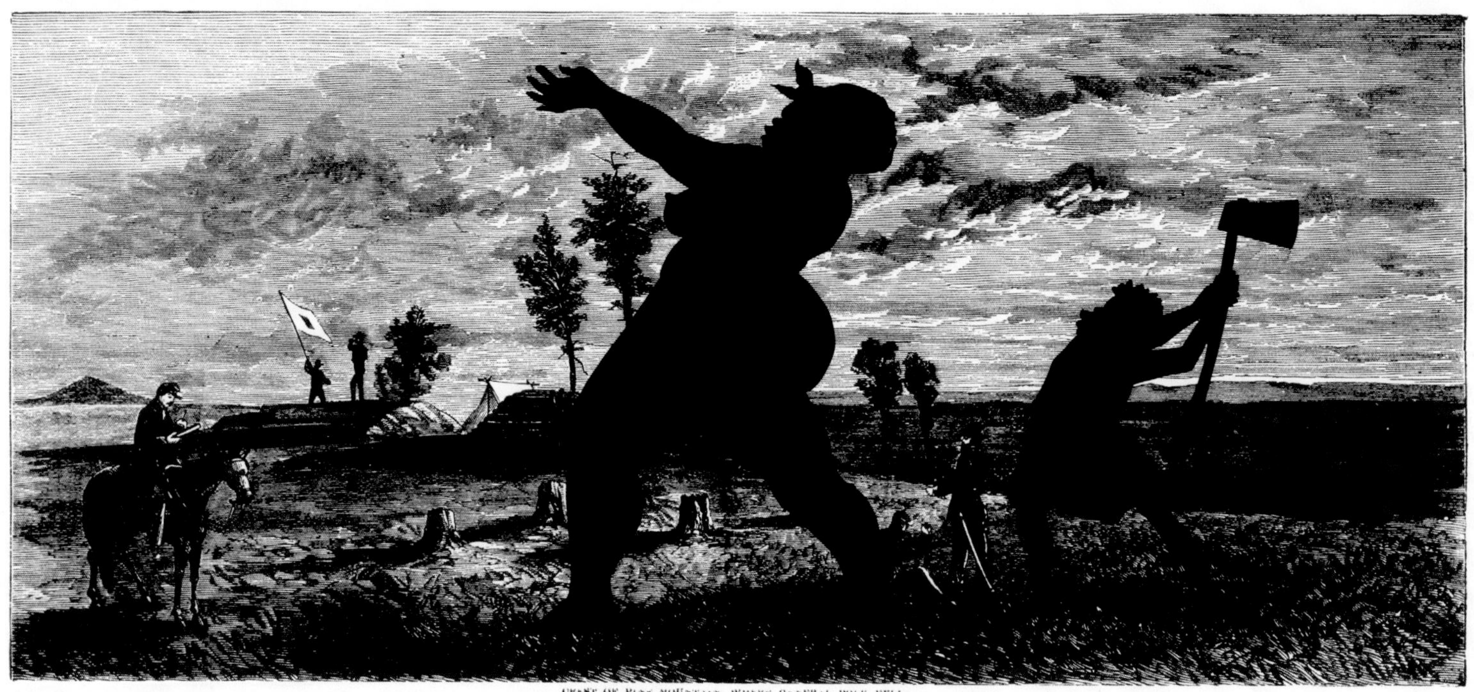

28
Kara Walker
Crest of Pine Mountain, where General Polk Fell, 2005
Offset lithograph with screenprint,
sheet: 39 × 59 in.
The Phillips Collection, Washington, DC,
Gift of Julia J. Norrell, 2015.

KARA WALKER
CREST OF PINE MOUNTAIN, WHERE GENERAL POLK FELL, 2005

Elsa Smithgall

It's that feeling of needing to make this offering as a form of truth telling, no matter how awful it is.
—Kara Walker

Like all of Kara Walker's creative work, *Crest of Pine Mountain, where General Polk Fell* is a form of truth telling, a vehicle through which she calls out and dispels myths and misrepresentations of our shared past. The print is one of fifteen lithographs and silkscreen prints that comprise her 2005 series *Harper's Pictorial History of the Civil War (Annotated)*. Interjecting new meaning into the images that illustrated the original two-volume book published in 1866, Walker's annotated version weaves past and present, myth and fantasy. Each image is the result of a two-part process: first through offset lithography, Walker creates an enlarged print of a given woodcut plate in Harper's book; then, onto its surface, she overlays silhouetted figures rendered in solid black silkscreen.

The Civil War was not a new subject for Walker. In 1994, she produced her first wall-sized installation, *Gone: An Historical Romance of a Civil War as It Occurred b'tween the Dusky Thighs of One Young Negress and Her Heart*. Unlike the complacent views of happy, ignorant slaves in the antebellum South perpetuated by Margaret Mitchell's novel *Gone with the Wind* (1936), on which her installation was partially based, Walker portrayed the brutality, sexual assaults, and suffering the enslaved people endured at the hands of their white owners.

In returning to the subject of the Civil War, this time in print form, Walker marshalled her signature silhouetted figures to infiltrate one of its first comprehensive primary accounts. In doing so, she challenged the editors' claim that the 836-page text illustrated with one thousand images represented an "impartial" view that sought to "narrate events just as they occurred." Catering to its predominantly white readership, the images glorified the heroic battle scenes and rarely showed the presence of the slaves.

In *Crest of Pine Mountain, where General Polk Fell*, Walker reimagines the original scene from Harper's publication depicting a decisive moment in the war's Atlanta campaign, when the Confederate Lieutenant General Leonidas Polk was killed by a cannon ball during a skirmish with Union forces in June 1864. By inserting two forceful female Black figures into the foreground of a landscape laced with shadows of human destruction, Walker gives voice to the suppressed undercurrent of slavery lurking on the political battleground. Walker's female figures push the white-dominant narrative off center, forcing the viewer to "uncover the often subtle and uncomfortable ways racism, and racist and sexist stereotypes influence and script our everyday lives."[1]

Layering is built into Walker's physical act of making each image and becomes a metaphor for the buried truths in front of our own eyes waiting to be excavated from the deeply encrusted strata of our changing world.

The epigraph is from an interview with Kara Walker, "The Melodrama of 'Gone with the Wind'", https://art21.org/read/kara-walker-the-melodrama-of-gone-with-the-wind/. Accessed April 2020. This interview was originally published on PBS.org in September 2003 and was republished on Art21.org in November 2011.

1 Walker, interviewed by Hans Ulrich Obrist, in *Kara Walker: Safety Curtain 1998/99*, exh. cat. (Vienna: Art Pool, Museum-in-Progress, and Vienna State Opera, 1998), cited in Darby English, *How to See a Work of Art in Total Darkness* (Cambridge, MA: MIT Press, 2010), 85, n. 17.

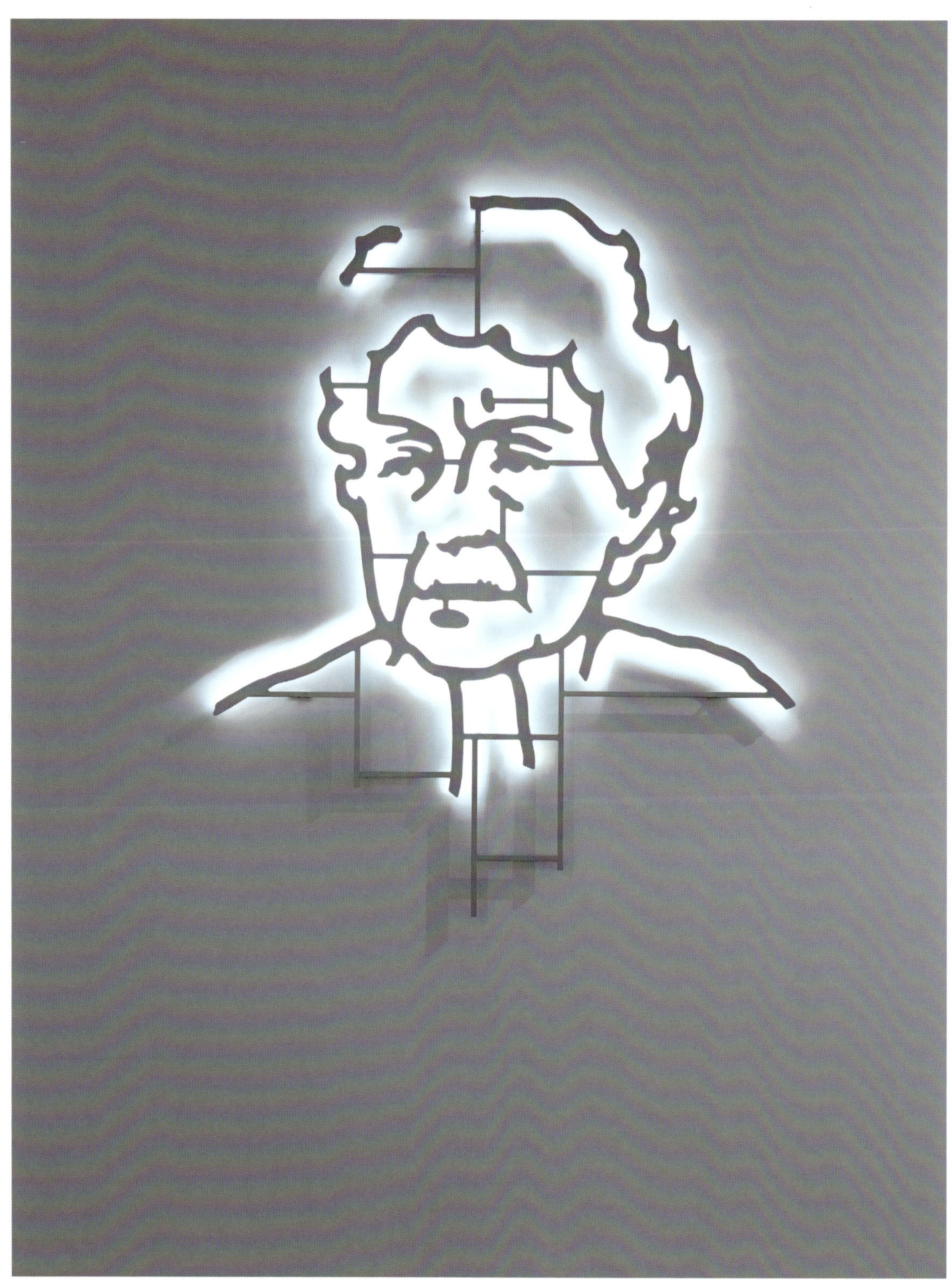

29
Los Carpinteros
Cachita, 2013
Powder-coated aluminum and LED lights,
75 1/2 × 61 × 2 in.
The Phillips Collection, Washington, DC,
Gift of Aaron and Barbara Levine, 2020.

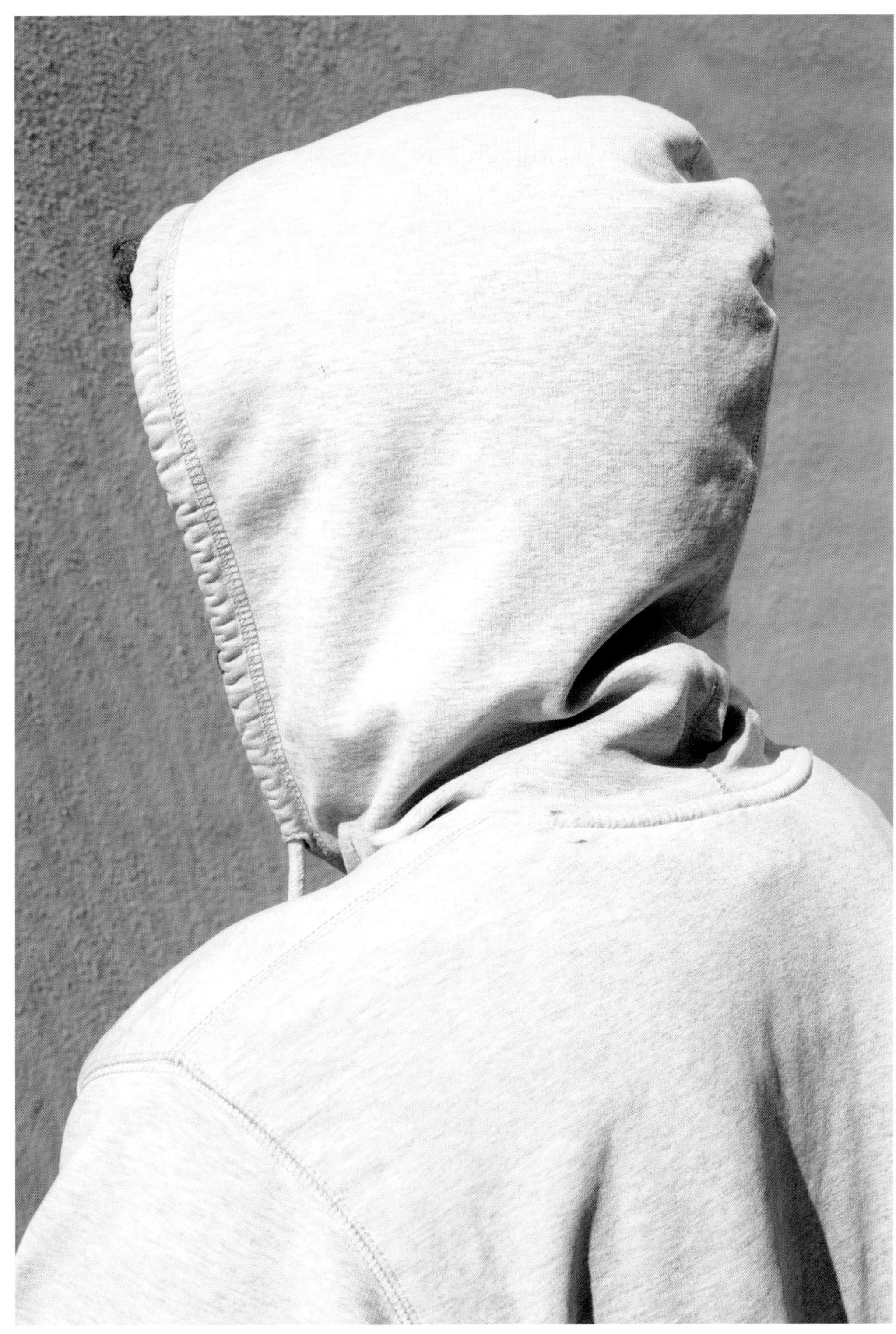

30
John Edmonds
Untitled (Hood 2), 2016
Pigment print,
20 × 14 in.
The Phillips Collection, Washington, DC,
Promised Gift of Vittorio Gallo.

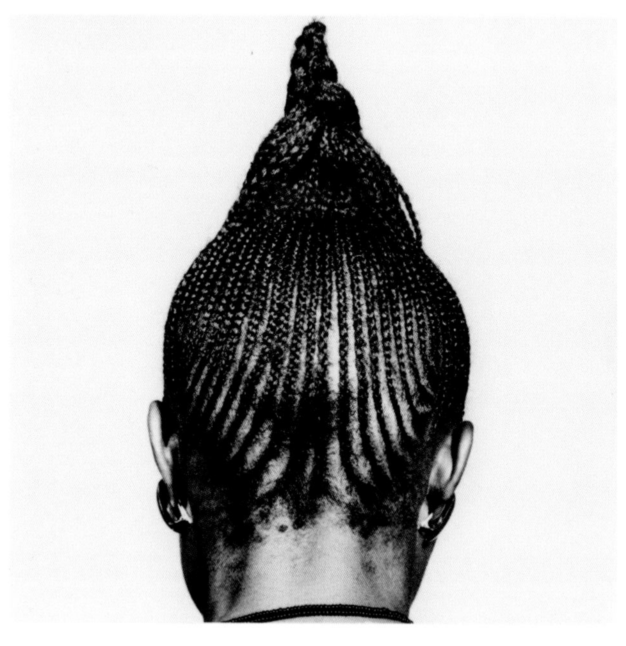

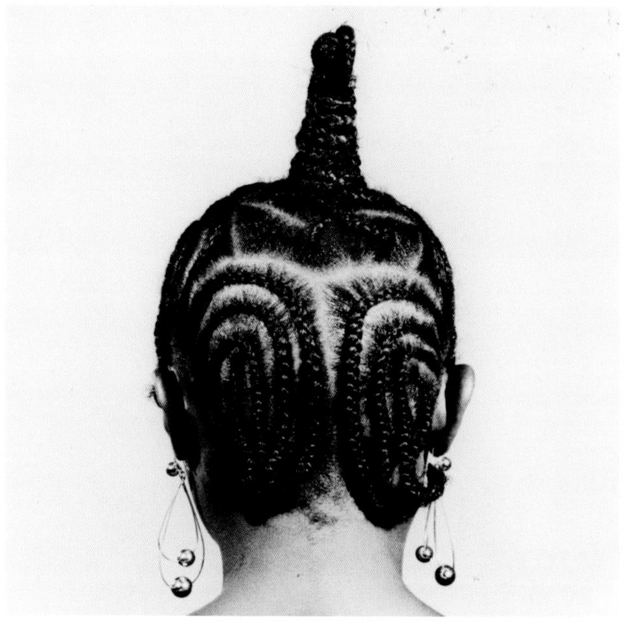

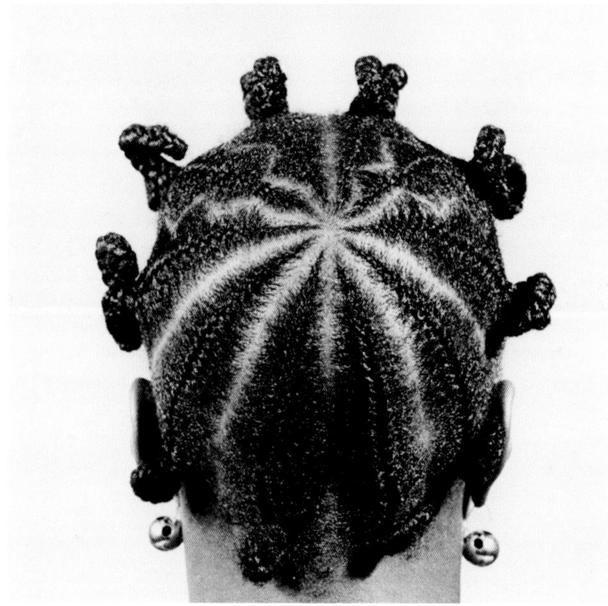

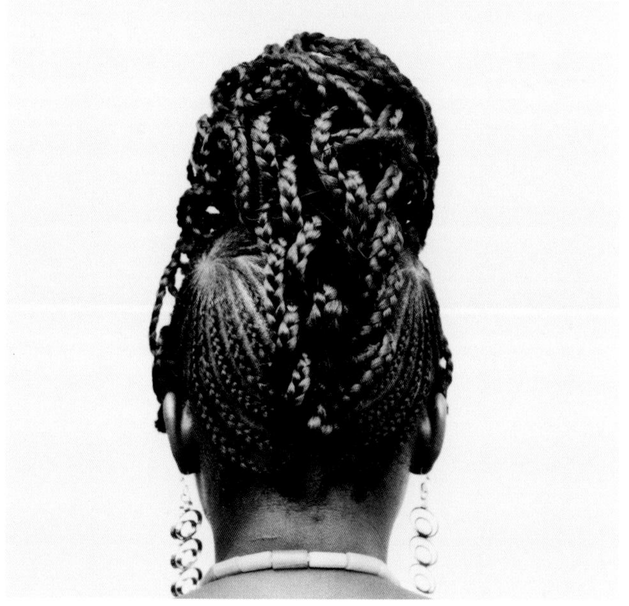

31 (top left)
J. D. 'Okhai Ojeikere
***Star Koroba HD 229/71* (*Hairstyles* series), 1971**
Gelatin silver print,
3 7/8 × 3 7/8 in.
The Phillips Collection, Washington, DC,
Gift of Julia J. Norrell, in memory of the victims of the shooting at Tree of Life Synagogue, Pittsburgh, 2018.

32 (bottom left)
J. D. 'Okhai Ojeikere
***Beri Beri HD 557/74* (*Hairstyles* series), 1974**
Gelatin silver print,
3 7/8 × 3 7/8 in.
The Phillips Collection, Washington, DC,
Gift of Julia J. Norrell, in memory of the victims of the shooting at Tree of Life Synagogue, Pittsburgh, 2018.

33 (top right)
J. D. 'Okhai Ojeikere
***Ife Bronze HD 323/72* (*Hairstyles* series), 1972**
Gelatin silver print,
3 7/8 × 3 7/8 in.
The Phillips Collection, Washington, DC,
Gift of Julia J. Norrell, in memory of the victims of the shooting at Tree of Life Synagogue, Pittsburgh, 2018.

34 (bottom right)
J. D. 'Okhai Ojeikere
***Abebe HD 849/75* (*Hairstyles* series), 1975**
Gelatin silver print,
3 7/8 × 3 7/8 in.
The Phillips Collection, Washington, DC,
Gift of Julia J. Norrell, in memory of the victims of the shooting at Tree of Life Synagogue, Pittsburgh, 2018.

J. D. 'OKHAI OJEIKERE *HAIRSTYLES*, 1968–75

Nontobeko Ntombela

Following Nigeria's independence in 1960, traditional hairstyles made a significant comeback, adapting to the new cosmopolitan lifestyle that accompanied the nation's ascendant oil economy. Between 1968 and 1975, the critically acclaimed Nigerian photographer J. D. 'Okhai Ojeikere systematically documented Nigerian women's hairstyles, through studio practice, producing an unprecedented archive of over a thousand negatives.

In Ojeikere's photographs, hairstyling is seen as an artistic, cultural, material, and social process, forming part of the unfolding African postcolonial modernity. The term for many of the hairstyles he documented is *Onile-Gogoro*—a Yoruba expression meaning "stand tall"—which was used to refer to the multi-story buildings then sprouting in Nigerian cities, and popularized through the music that defined the language and social movements of the 1960s.

The Onile-Gogoro hair designs, achieved through a technique called *olowu* (meaning "done with thread"), involve wrapping sectioned hair into locks that are then intricately woven into a design. Through the photographs, we can see new developments in styling, including the incorporation of hair extensions and wool into traditional weaving and plaiting.

These are not conventional portraits: they disrupt the "self-imaging" of the sitters whose hairstyles are shown, since we cannot see their faces. Shot against neutral monochromatic backgrounds, the photographing of the back or side of the head draws attention to the architectural and sculptural presentation of the hairstyle. The ingenious mastery and the skill of the hairstylist is accentuated by Ojeikere's commanding lighting. The range of complexity of the coiffures speaks to the labor that went into their making. Some designs have cultural, ethnic, and class significance. In *Ife Bronze* (pl. 33), the coiffure alludes to the incised striations on the face of the *Ife Head* (British Museum, London), one of a group of twelfth-century copper alloy heads discovered in 1938 at Ife, Nigeria. The vertical plaited horn of hair in Ojeikere's photograph echoes the horn on the sculpture, said to signify the power to communicate with the spiritual world.

The titles of Ojeikere's photographs are often quite literal. For example, in *Abebe* (pl. 34), the word *abebe* refers to a hand-held fan—evoked by the coiffure—traditionally an upper-class and royal accoutrement in the Yoruba-speaking community, suggesting the social status of the sitter.

Ojeikere's photographs define a particular moment in Nigeria that, in turn, formed part of the national identity. In some sense, they also document the future of hairdressing— some of the hairstyles are still plaited today across Africa and the globe, in this way coming to symbolize cross-border conversations. They also symbolize self-determination.

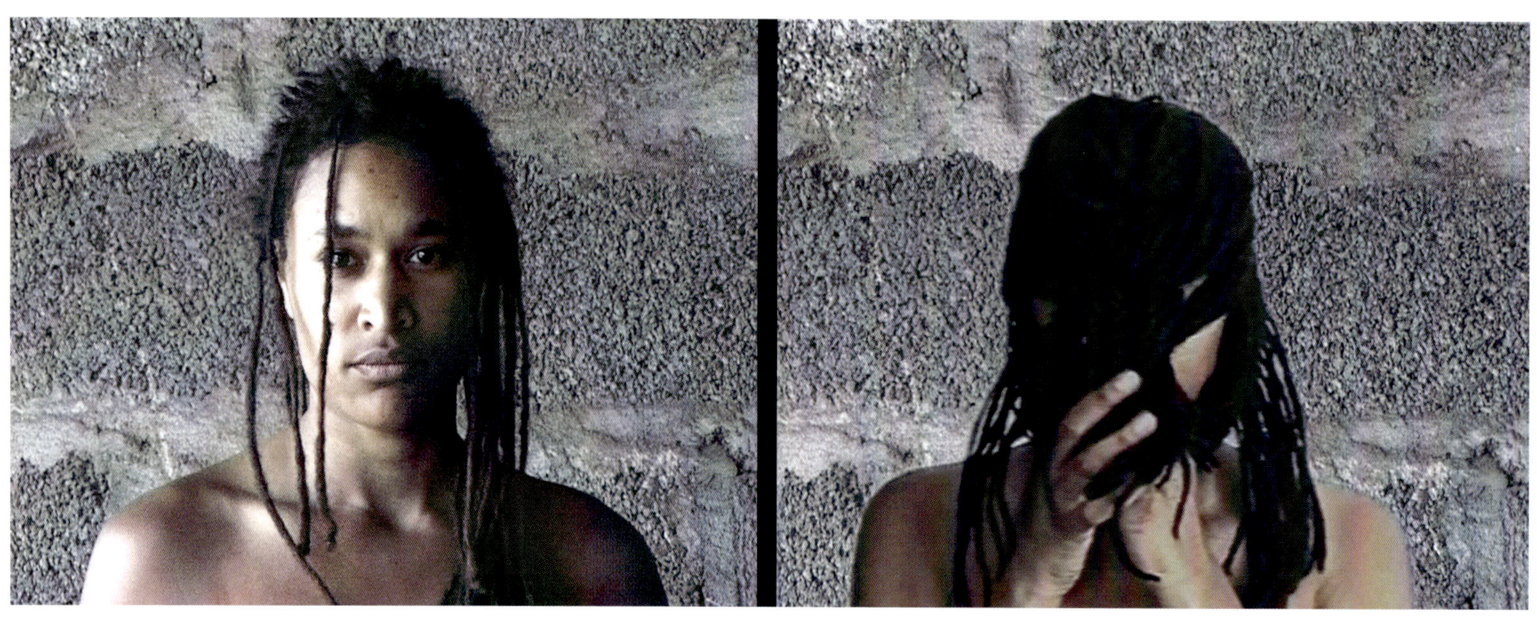

35
Mwangi Hutter
Cutting the Mask, 2003
Two-channel video (color, no sound).
Duration: 17:04 min.
The Phillips Collection, Washington, DC,
Gift of the Heather and Tony Podesta Collection,
Washington, DC, 2017.

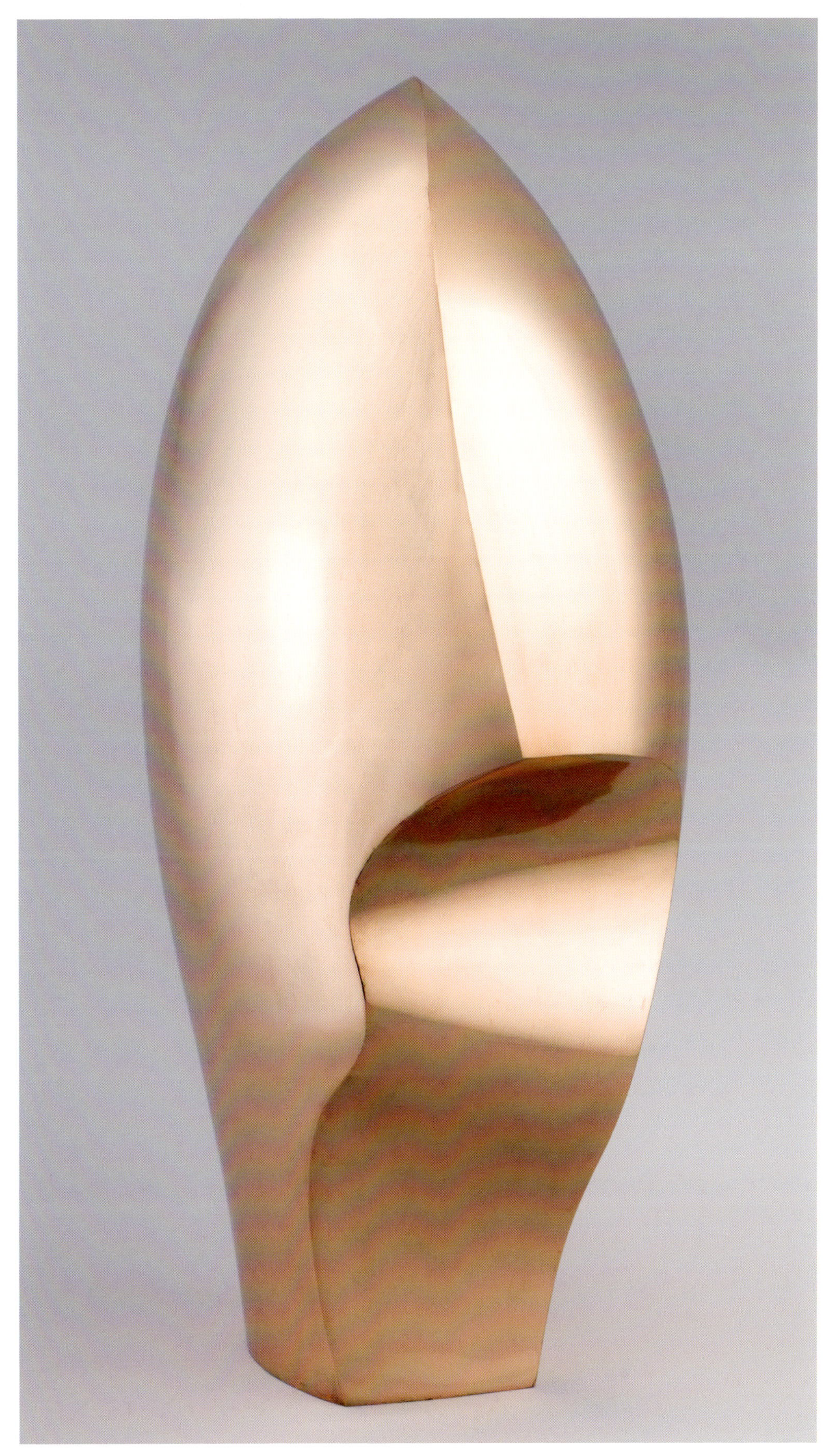

36
Hans (Jean) Arp
***Tête Heaume II (Helmeted Head II)*, 1959**
Bronze,
overall: 22 in.
The Phillips Collection, Washington, DC,
Gift of John and Joy Safer, 2003.

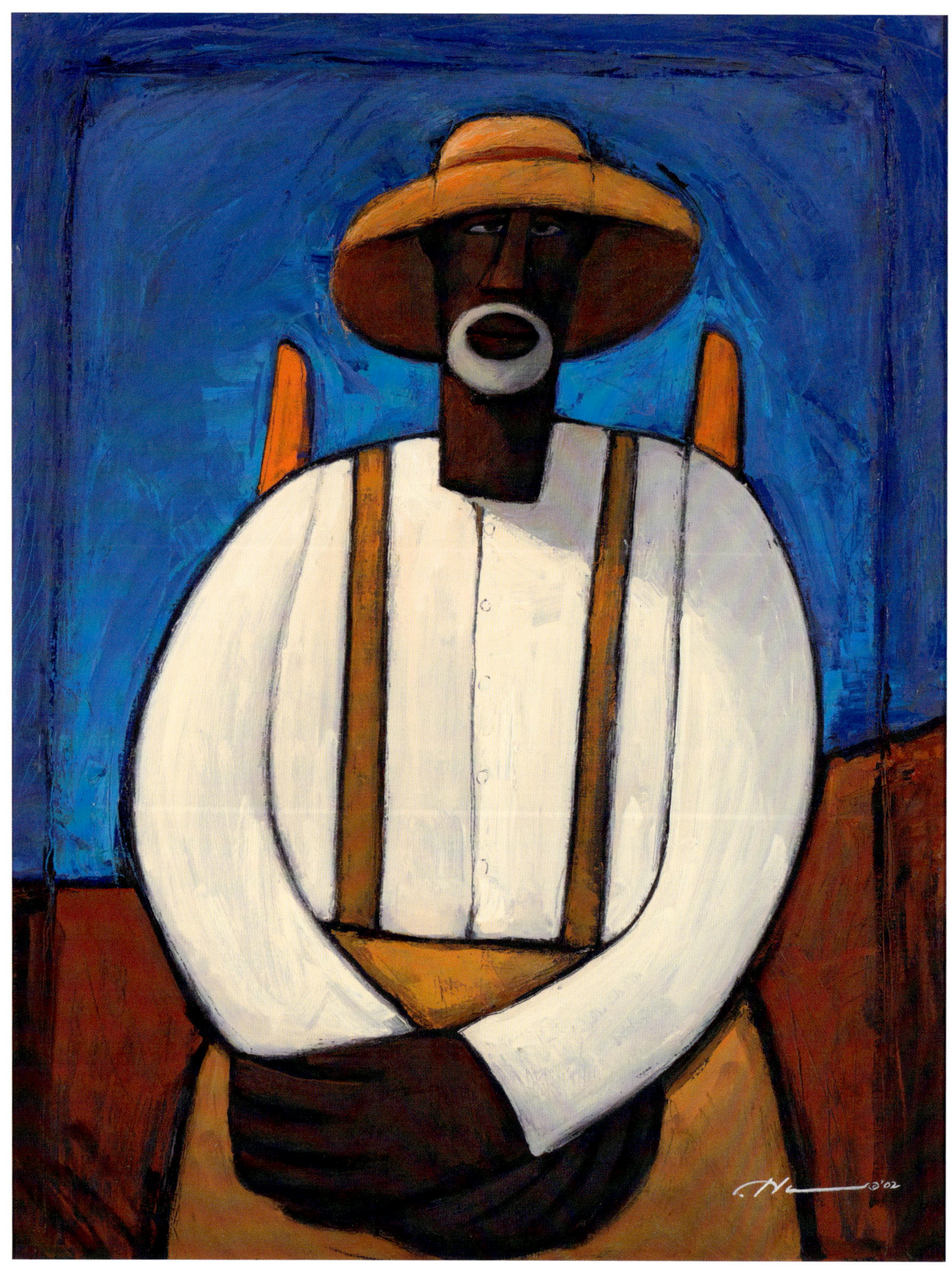

37
Joseph Holston
The Elder, 2002
Oil on canvas,
40 × 30 in.
The Phillips Collection, Washington, DC,
Gift of Joseph and Sharon Holston, 2014.

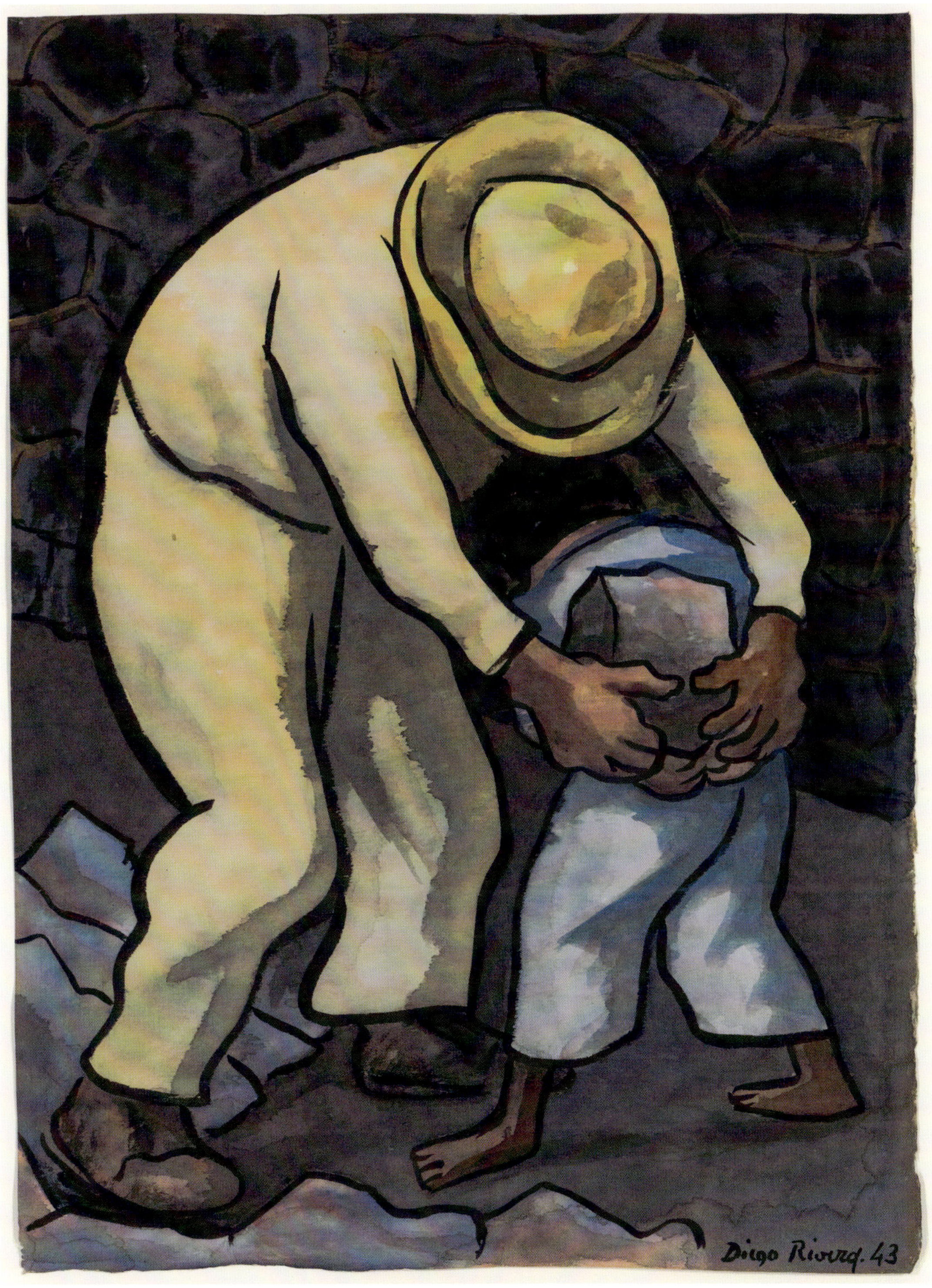

38
Diego Rivera
Untitled, 1943
Opaque and transparent watercolor on Japanese paper,
overall (uneven cut): 14 3/4 × 10 5/8 in.
The Phillips Collection, Washington, DC,
Gift of Kerry H. Stowell, 2012.

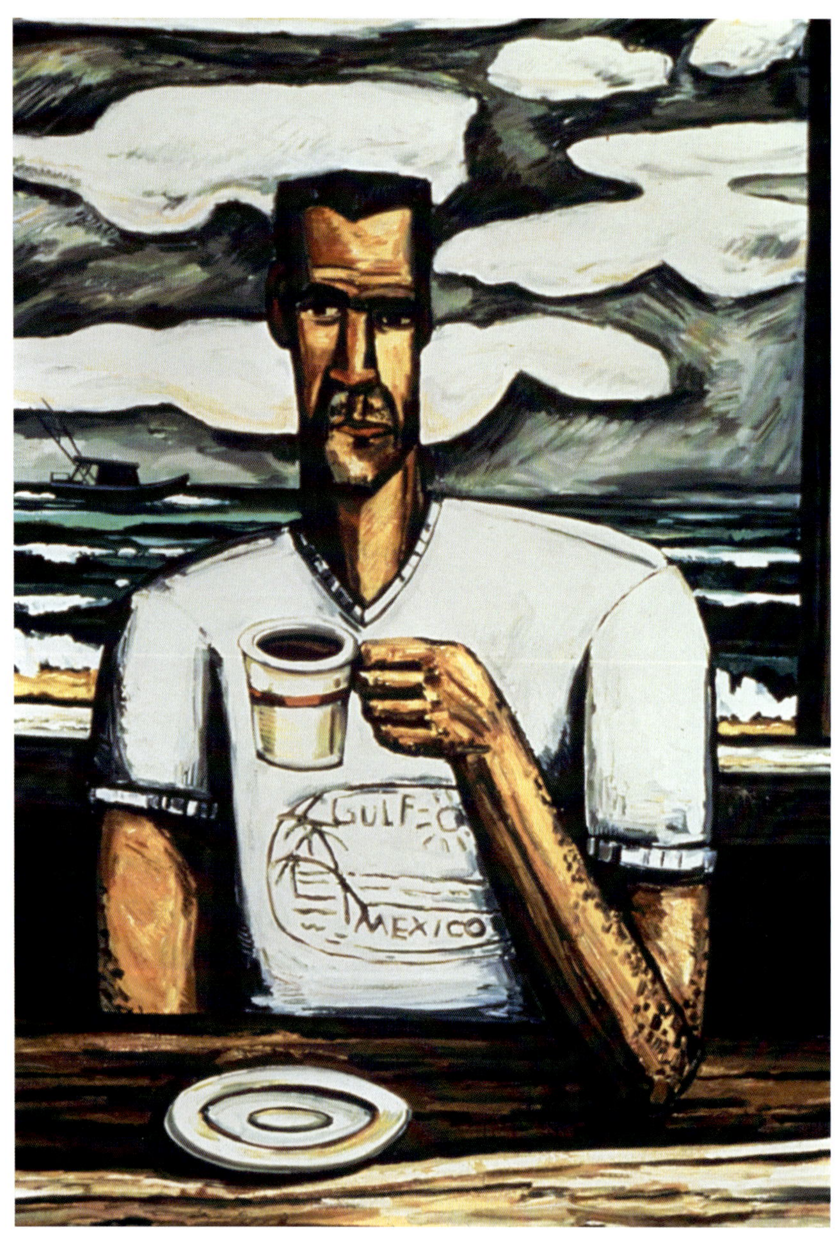

39
David Bates
The Gulf of Mexico, 1990
Oil on canvas,
76 × 52 in.
The Phillips Collection, Washington, DC,
Partial and promised gift of Patti and Jerry Sowalsky,
Potomac, MD, 2006.

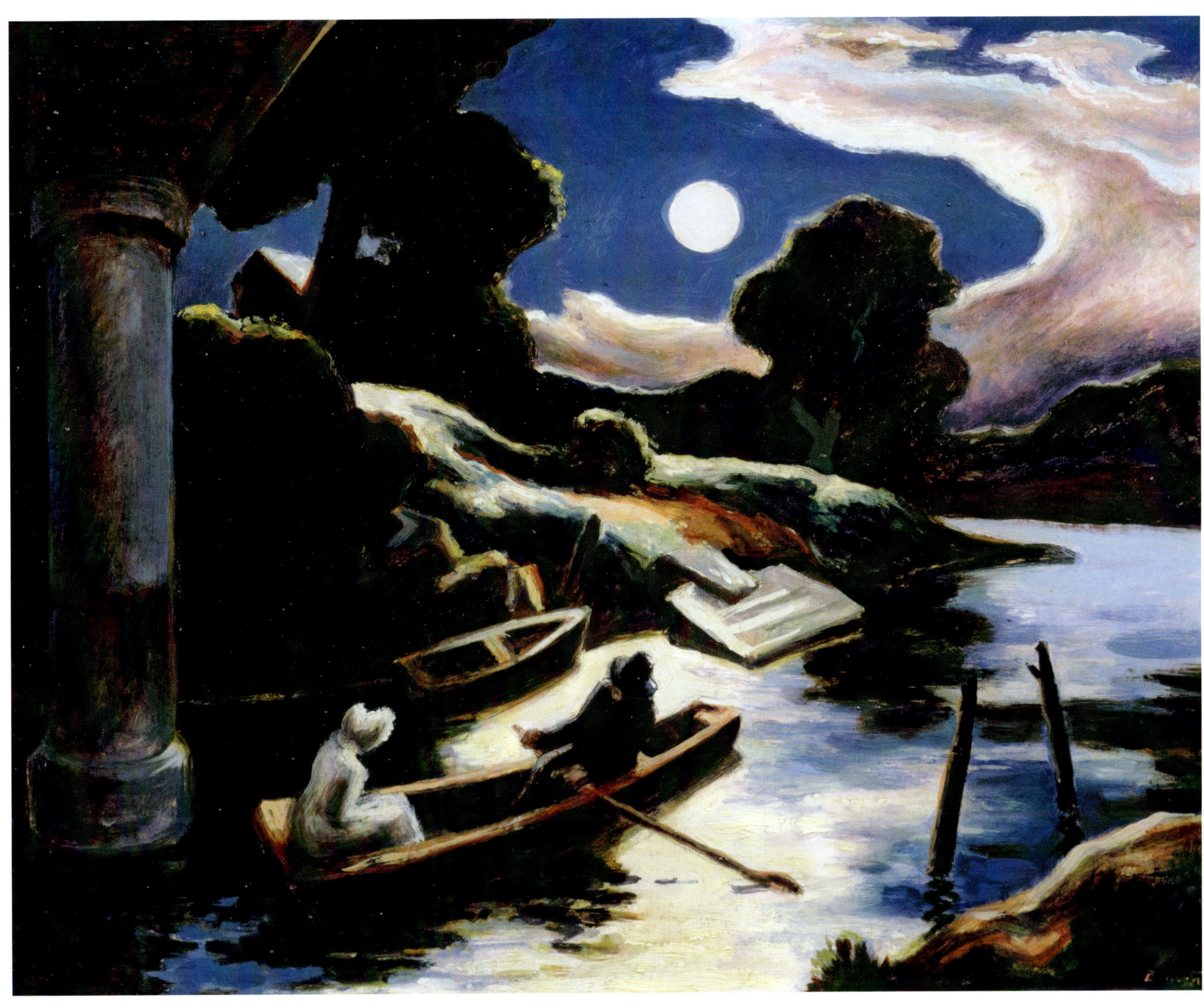

40
Thomas Hart Benton
Moonlight on the Osage, 1938
Oil on wood,
14 × 17 1/4 in.
The Phillips Collection, Washington, DC,
Partial and Promised Gift of Linda Lichtenberg Kaplan, 2001.

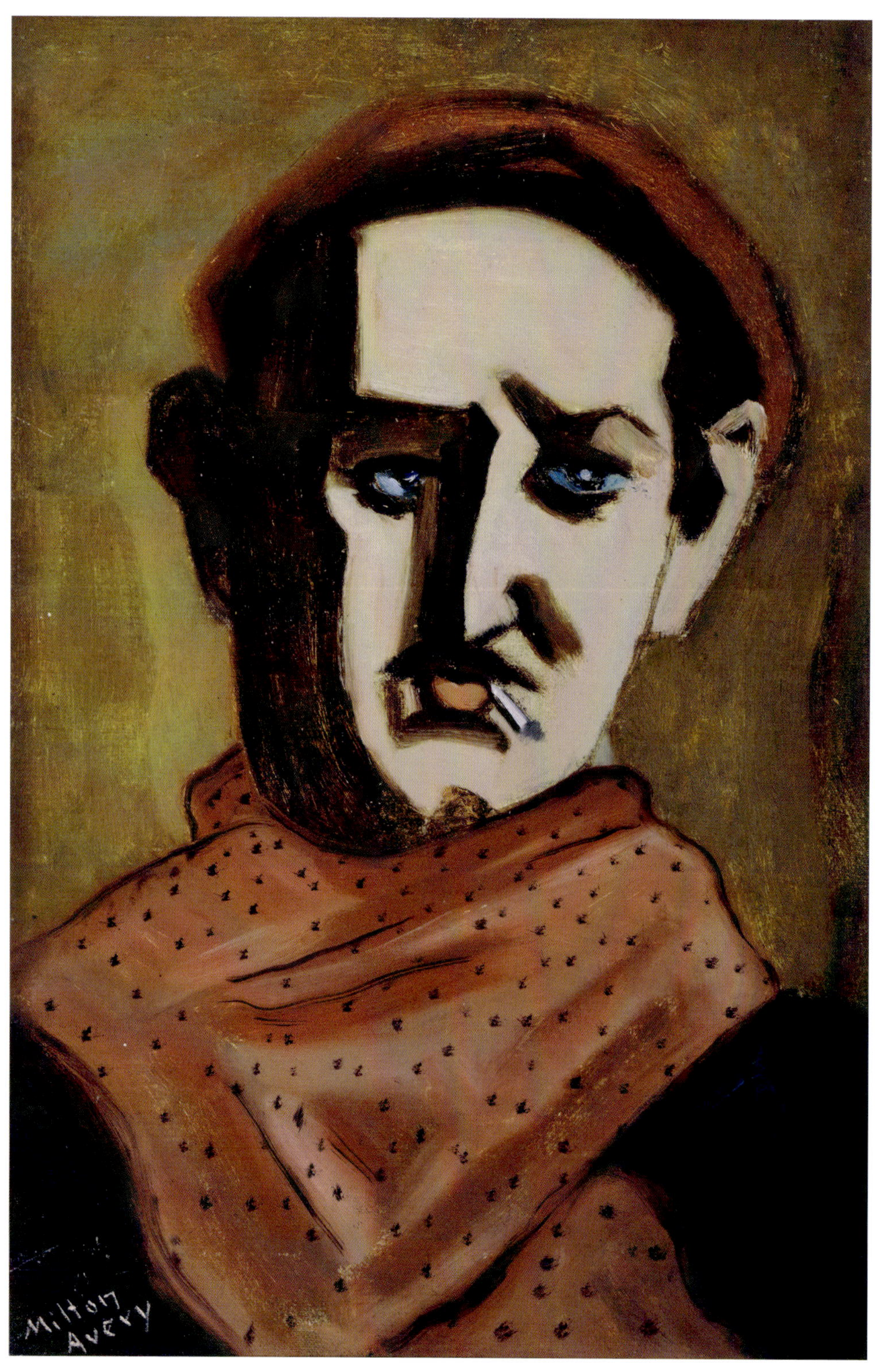

41
Milton Avery
Self-Portrait with Red Tam and Scarf, 1938
Oil on canvas,
22 × 14 in.
The Phillips Collection, Washington, DC,
Gift of Louis and Annette Kaufman Trust, 2008.

MILTON AVERY
SELF-PORTRAIT WITH RED TAM AND SCARF, 1938

Renée Maurer

Milton Avery immersed himself in the art world after he moved to New York City in 1925, attending numerous museum and gallery exhibitions, absorbing ideas from art periodicals, and developing his own style. He enrolled in classes at the Art Students League and drew landscapes and portraits of friends. After seeing Henri Matisse's art at the Valentine Gallery in 1927, Avery pursued a more modern aesthetic defined by simplified, flat color fields. His work caught the eye of patron Louis Kaufman, an accomplished violinist, who befriended Avery in 1928 and went on to acquire twenty-nine of the artist's paintings, including this example.

Through Kaufman, Avery met Mark Rothko, who introduced him to Adolph Gottlieb and Barnett Newman. Beginning in the 1930s, the group gathered at Avery's New York apartment to discuss painting and hold sketching sessions; they shared art-filled summers in Gloucester, Massachusetts. Avery became their mentor. He inspired them to experiment with various pigment combinations and make their art more abstract.

Joining the Valentine Gallery in 1935 encouraged Avery to challenge himself. No longer constrained by naturalistic hues, he explored the emotional and compositional effects of a bolder, more saturated palette. By compressing shapes and reducing details, his figures became even more abstract. He would later explain: "I eliminate and simplify, leaving apparently nothing but color and pattern.... [T]he purity and essence of the idea expressed in its simplest forms."[1]

The year *Self-Portrait with Red Tam and Scarf* was painted, Avery worked for the Easel Division of the WPA Federal Art Project. Although he was grateful for the stipend, his modernist approach was at odds with the program's promotion of representational art. This self-portrait, distinguished by its unmodulated color layers and sharply outlined forms, shows Avery's interest in the art of Matisse and Pablo Picasso. Facing the viewer, a cigarette between his lips, in this bust-length portrait Avery presents himself as a bohemian. He wears a red tam o' shanter, a traditional Scottish wool hat, and a large patterned red scarf wrapped around his neck. Dramatic lighting and shading carve expressive features into his sculpted face; his contemplative gaze does not engage with the viewer.

Five years after this canvas was painted, Duncan Phillips hosted Avery's first solo museum exhibition. Like Kaufman, Phillips had supported Avery's career early, acquiring in 1929 the first work by the artist to enter a museum collection, *Winter Riders* (1929). Phillips went on to assemble a distinguished unit of eleven works by Avery and organized three more solo shows for the artist. Phillips admired his independence, associating him with other artists in the collection like Arthur Dove and John Marin. Today, the museum owns over twenty-five works by Avery.

---

1 In Edward A. Aiken, *Milton Avery Revisited: Works from the Louis and Annette Kaufman Collection* (New York: Syracuse University Art Collection, 1999), 6.

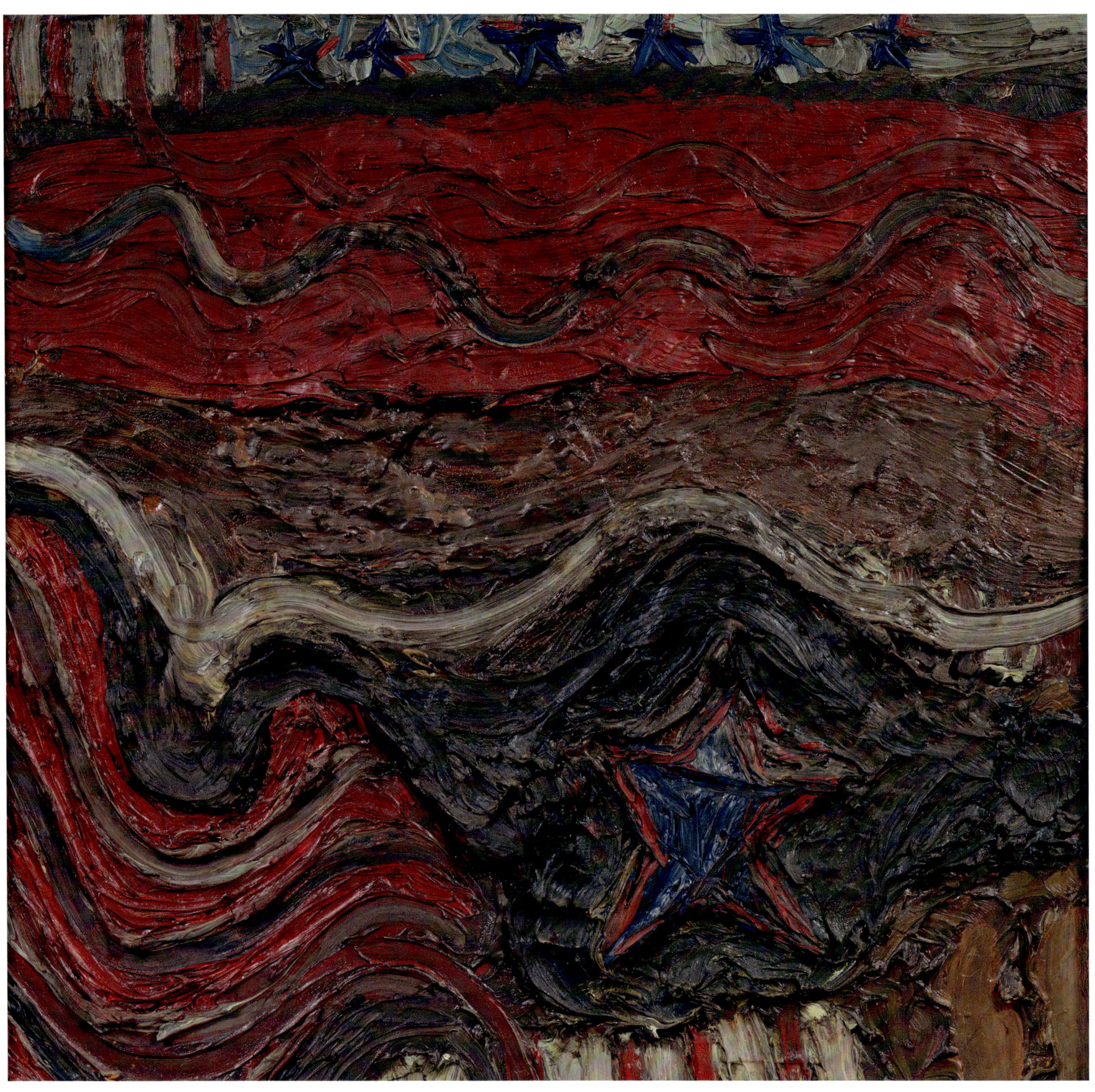

42
Jake Berthot
***Little Flag Painting*, 1961**
Oil on canvas,
20 × 20 in.
The Phillips Collection, Washington, DC,
Bequest of The Estate of Jake Berthot, 2015.

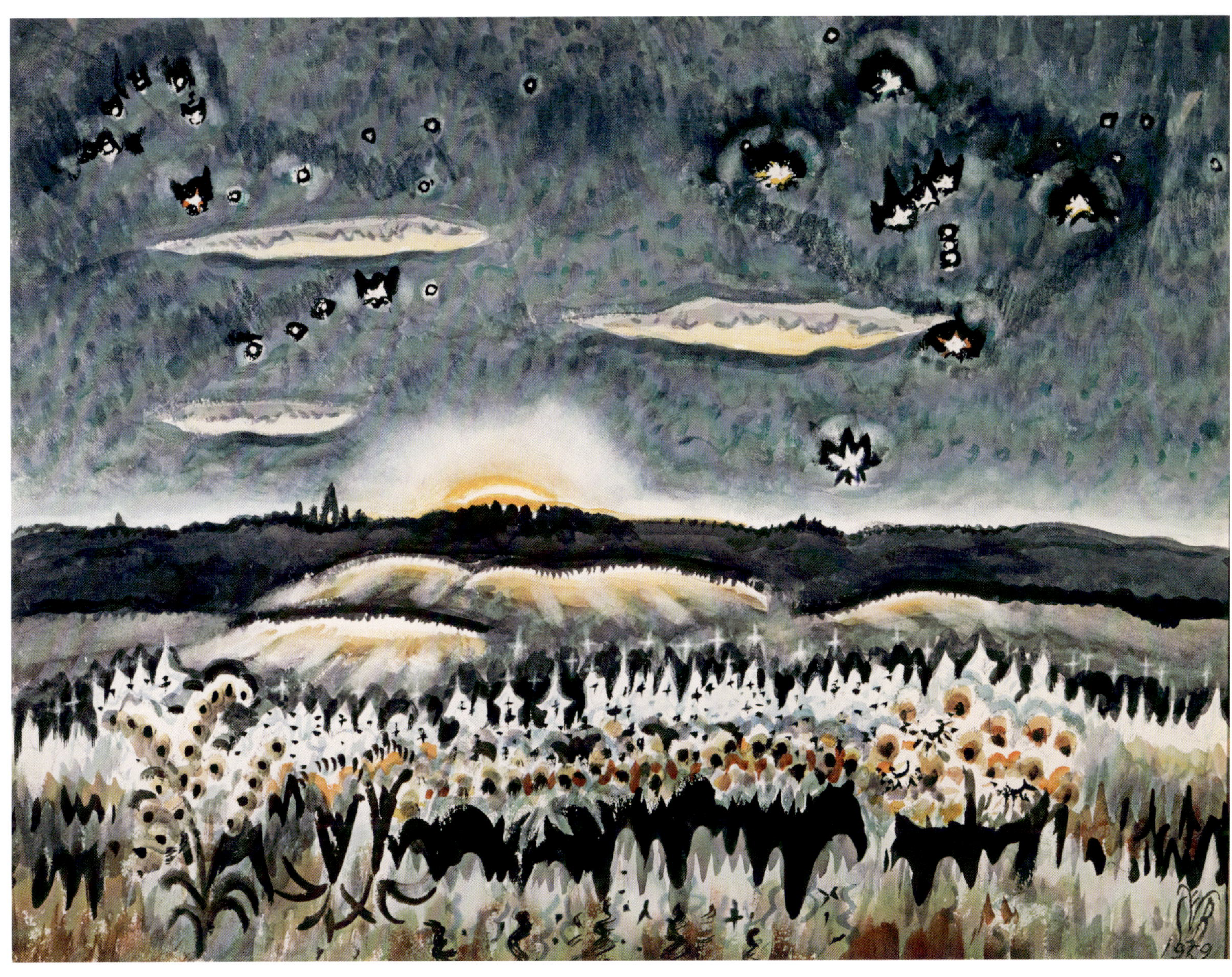

43
Charles Burchfield
December Moonrise, 1959
Watercolor on paper,
30 × 36 in.
The Phillips Collection, Washington, DC,
Gift of B. J. and Carol Cutler, 2009.

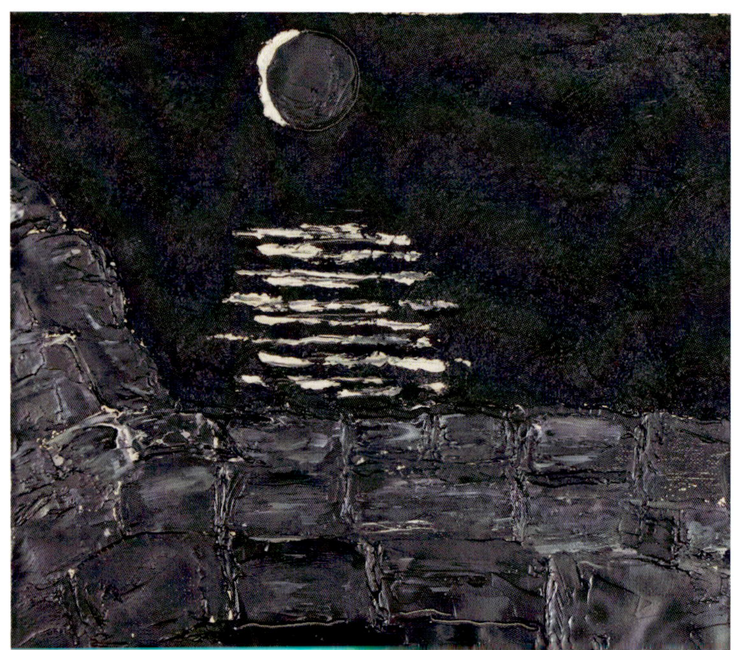

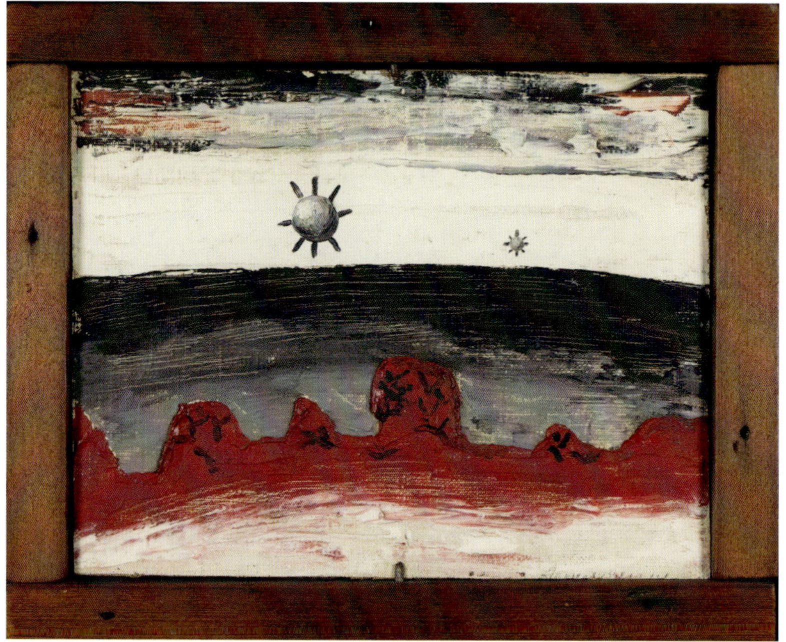

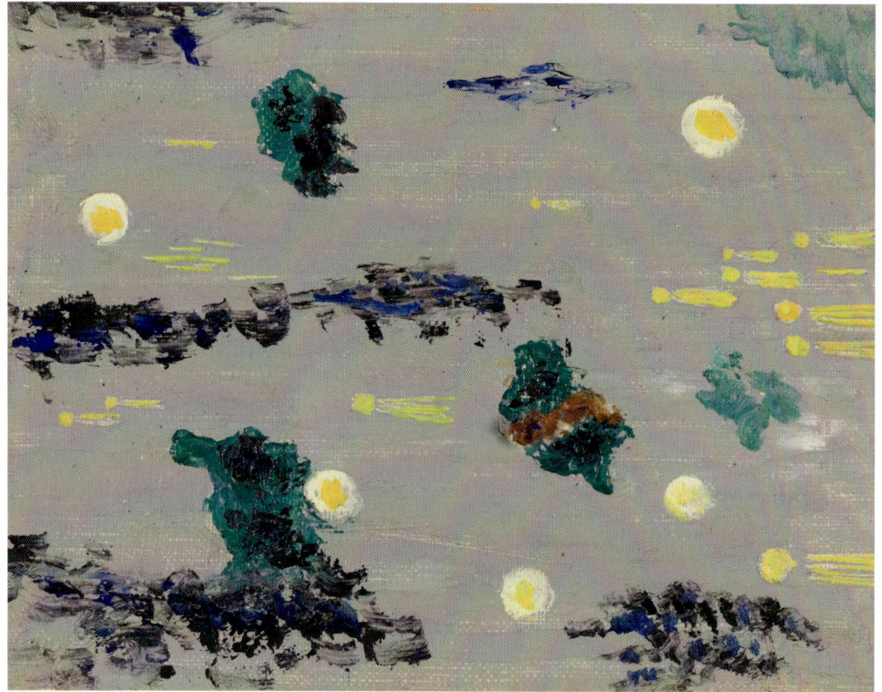

44 (top left)
Forrest Bess
Untitled (Black Seascape with Moon), 1951
Oil on canvas,
9 × 10 3/4 in.
The Phillips Collection, Washington, DC,
Promised Gift of Miriam Schapiro Grosof.

45 (top right)
Forrest Bess
Prophesy, 1949
Oil on canvas mounted on wood panel,
6 × 7 1/2 in.
The Phillips Collection, Washington, DC,
Gift of Miriam Schapiro Grosof, 2014.

46 (bottom)
Forrest Bess
The Asteroids #1, 1946
Oil on canvas mounted on wood panel,
8 × 10 in.
The Phillips Collection, Washington, DC,
Gift of Miriam Schapiro Grosof, 2014.

FORREST BESS
UNTITLED (BLACK SEASCAPE WITH MOON), 1951

Enrique Martínez Celaya

"A country hick—first class" was how Forrest Bess described himself in "Snooky," the journal he started as an autobiography, and there was something of that hickness in all of his paintings. They have an elemental presence and connection to tool chests and fish bait that feels far away from museums and auction houses. Bess's paintings don't avoid the material that burdens their shoulders as the work of a sophisticated New Yorker like Barnett Newman sometimes does, and their visionary presence reminds me as much of a lovingly crafted trout mount as they do the theological messages of the Swede Hilma af Klint. And yet, I can't think of another self-described hick who carved himself into a pseudo-hermaphrodite, showed his work at vanguard galleries, and corresponded with eminent intellectuals from around the world. Forrest Bess lived and worked in the in-between, and his liminality helped spring the alchemical birth of his paintings and protected their transcendent aspirations. He was a Texan Icarus, more sensible than the Greek one, who perhaps by being a first-class hick knew to fly close enough to the ground to avoid the high-altitude air that suffocated his fellow Betty Parsons Gallery artists, Jackson Pollock and Mark Rothko.

The painting *Untitled (Black Seascape with Moon)* (pl. 44) is a good example of his mastery of the in-between. Once I get over its monolithic, roofing-tile quality, the painting invites me to look at the sea over the wall. As soon as I do, it brings me back to the coagulated oil in the shape of bricks moved around crudely with a palette knife. The painting has the viscosity, dreaminess, and symbolism of an Albert Pinkham Ryder but without allowing the reprieve of a fairy tale. What am I looking at? Is that shape in the foreground in fact a wall, or is it a rocky part of the shore at Chinquapin? The only reason I know there is a sea is because there are nine gashes of white cut across wet black paint that recall reflections on dark waves. The whitish scar at the top is where the invisible horizon must be, and above it, the sky is a void etched with a reminder of the moon. A smear of white stands for the sunlit portion, but barely, as if the urgency of marking the arc of light was more important than its appearance. What things look like is not what matters here. The reflection on the water doesn't correspond to this particular moon, but to another, brighter moon, perhaps from a night when the void was not echoing as deeply within Bess. The mismatched reflection on the nervous sea has the longing of Edvard Munch without "the lonely ones" standing at the shore looking at the horizon for a way out. Forrest Bess didn't need stand-ins. His decaying body, his gaze toward the dome of heaven, and his loneliness were enough.

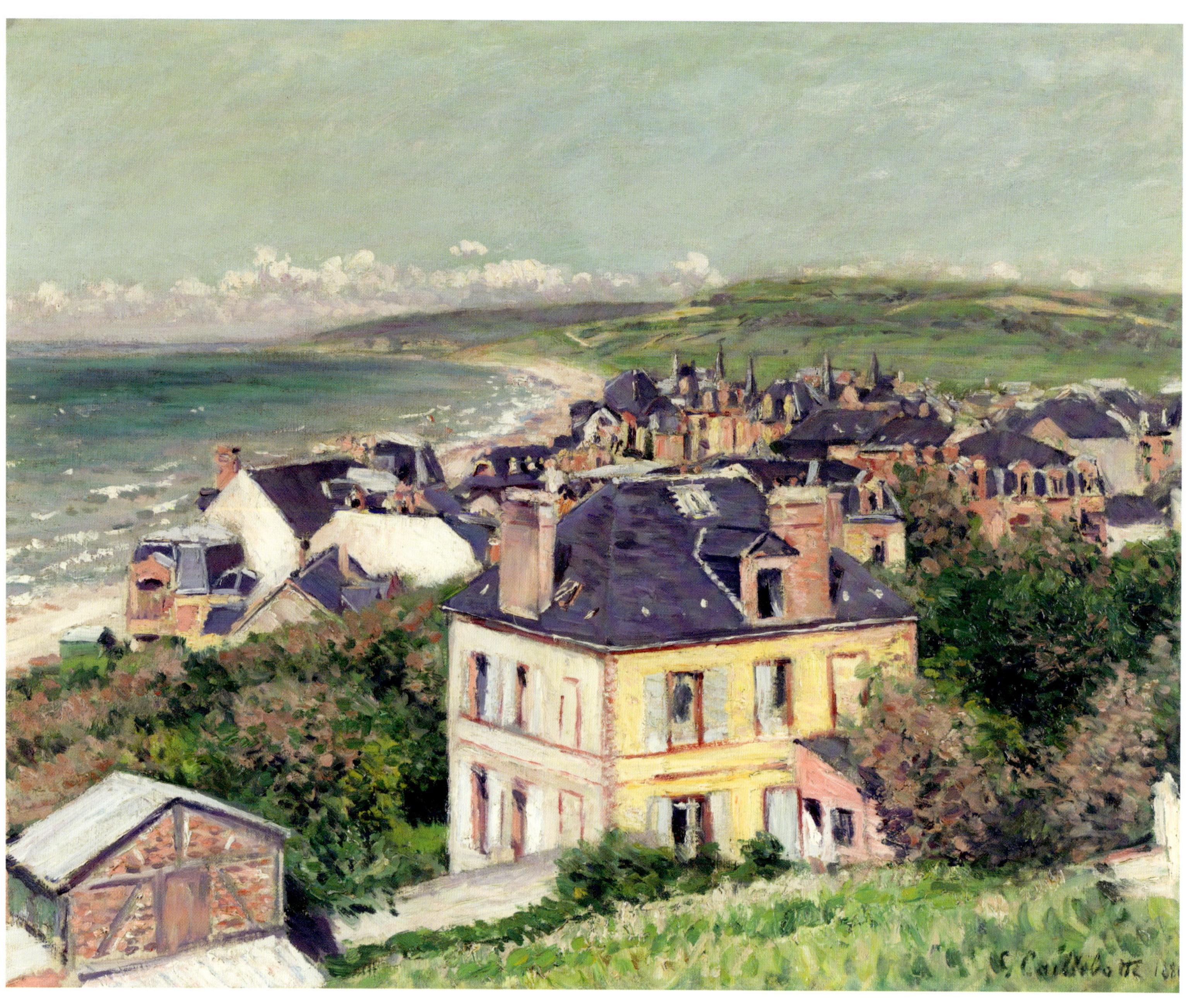

47
Gustave Caillebotte
Villers-sur-Mer, 1880
Oil on canvas,
23 1/2 × 28 in.
The Phillips Collection, Washington, DC,
Promised Gift of Mr. and Mrs. Duane Vieth.

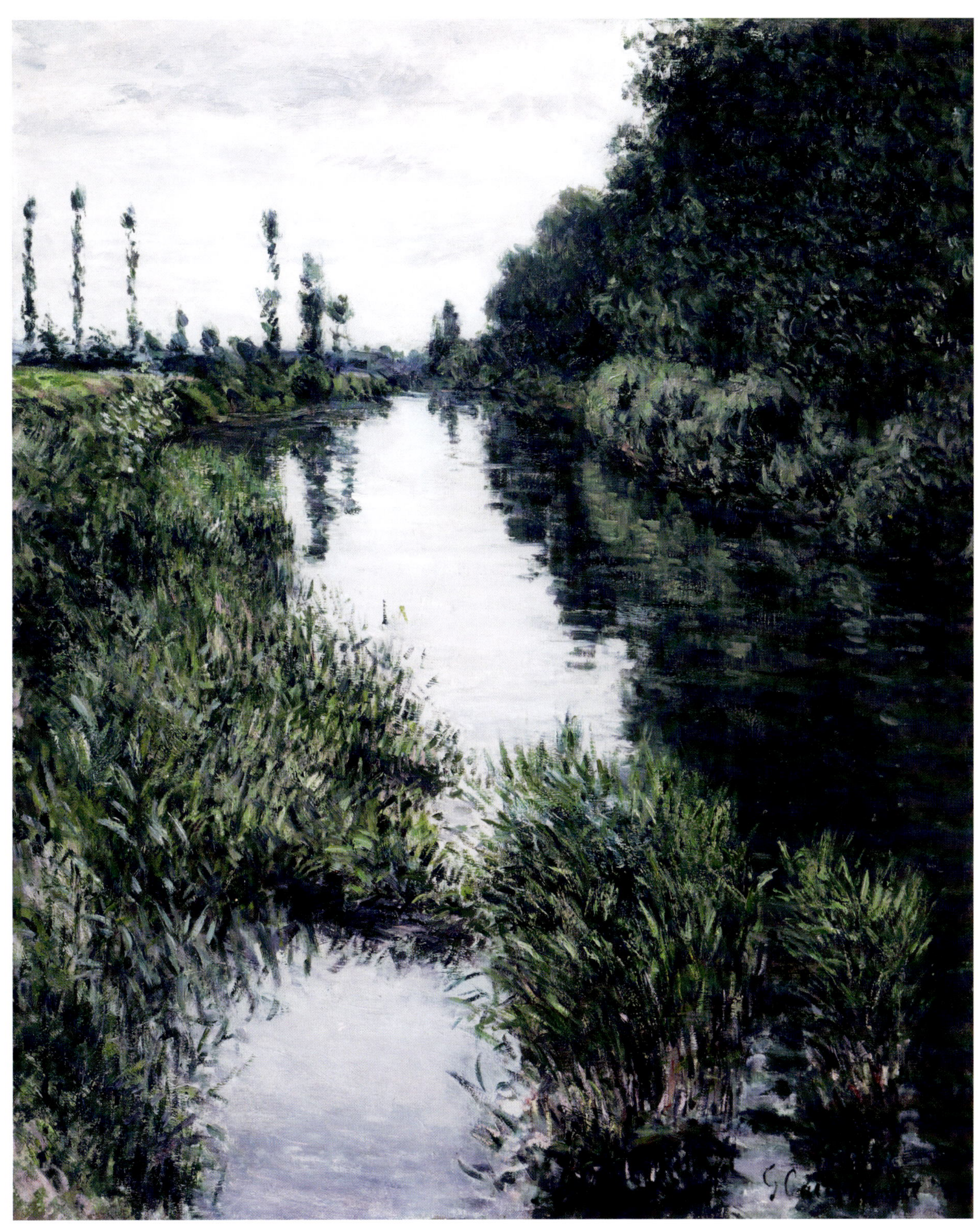

48
Gustave Caillebotte
Le petit bras de la Seine à Argenteuil
(*Small Tributary of the Seine at Argenteuil*), 1884
Oil on canvas,
36 3/16 × 29 1/2 in.
The Phillips Collection, Washington, DC,
Gift of Mary E. Weinmann, initiated 2007, completed 2019.

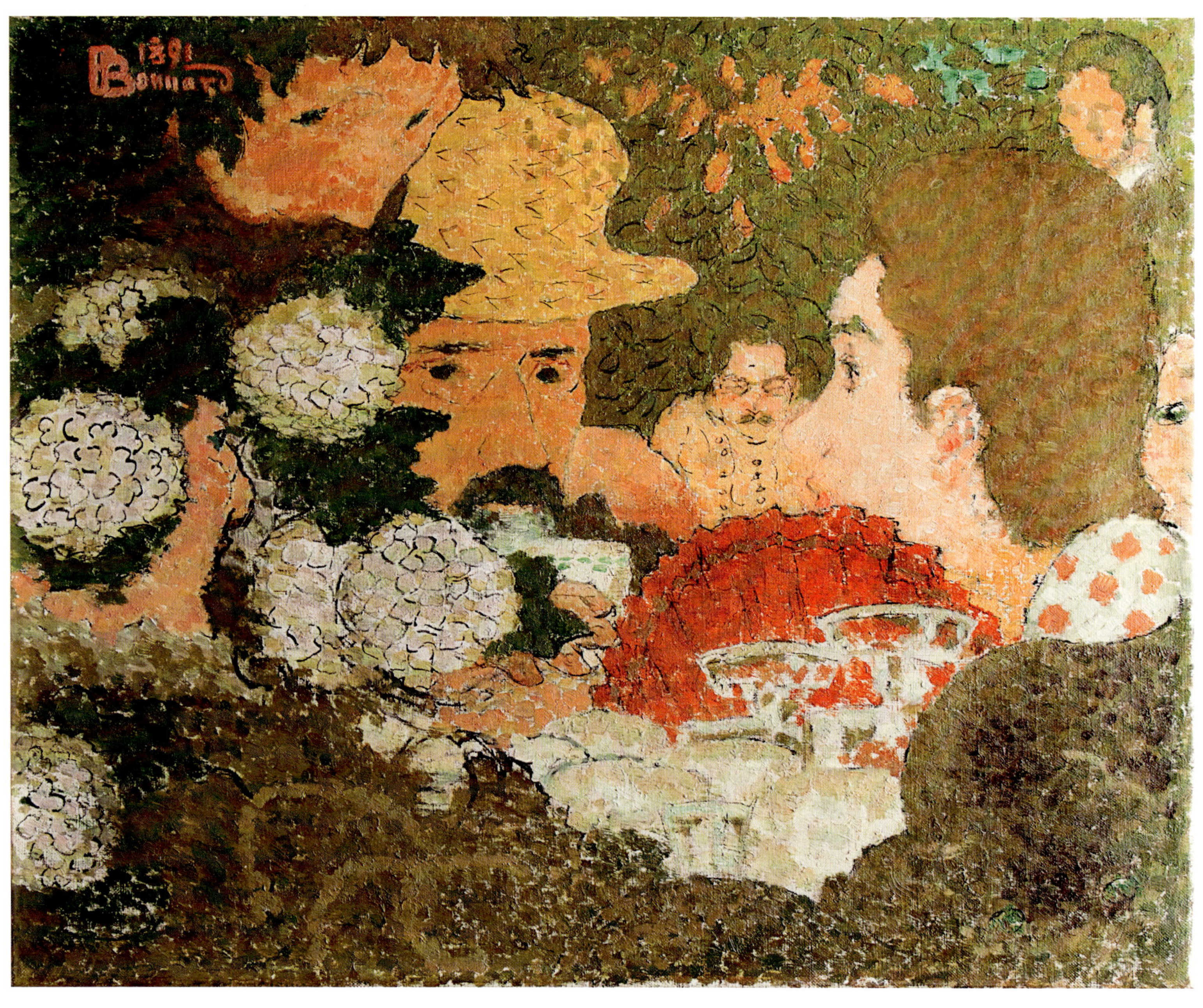

49
Pierre Bonnard
Afternoon in the Garden (Après-midi au jardin), 1891
Oil and black ink on canvas,
14 3/4 × 17 3/4 in.
The Phillips Collection, Washington, DC,
Promised Gift of Vicki and Roger Sant.

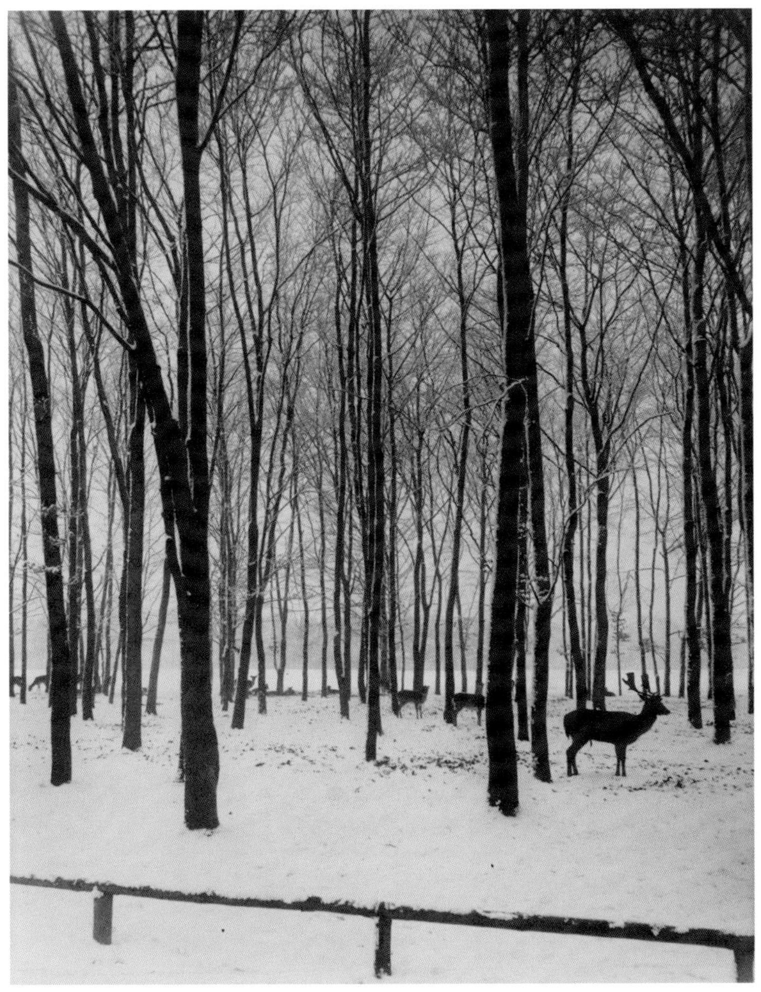

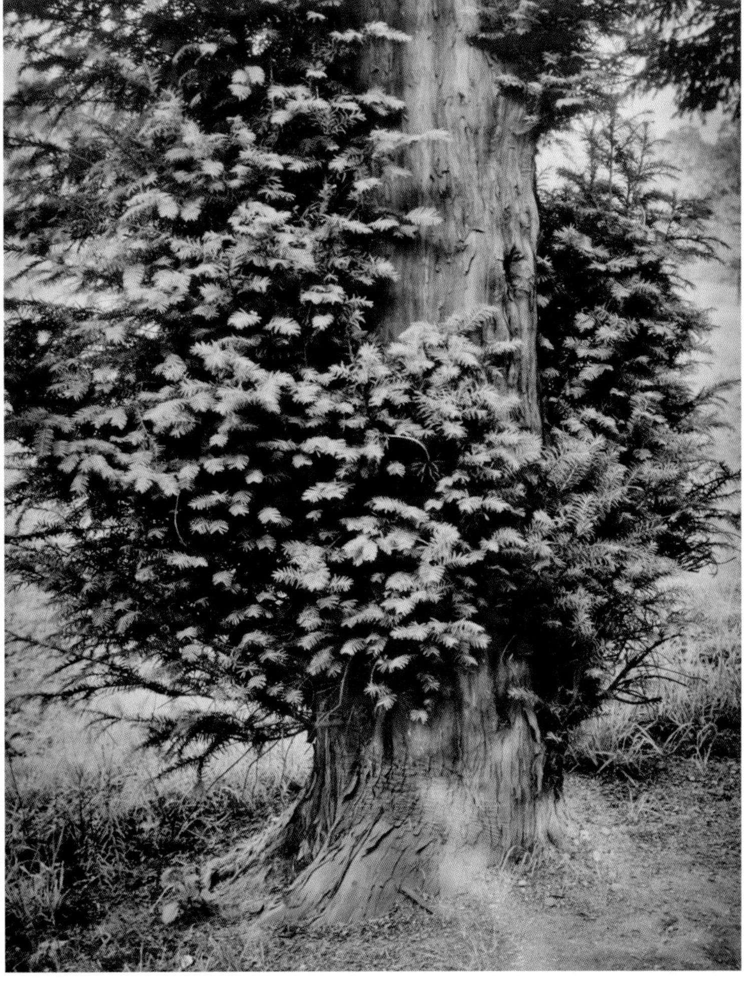

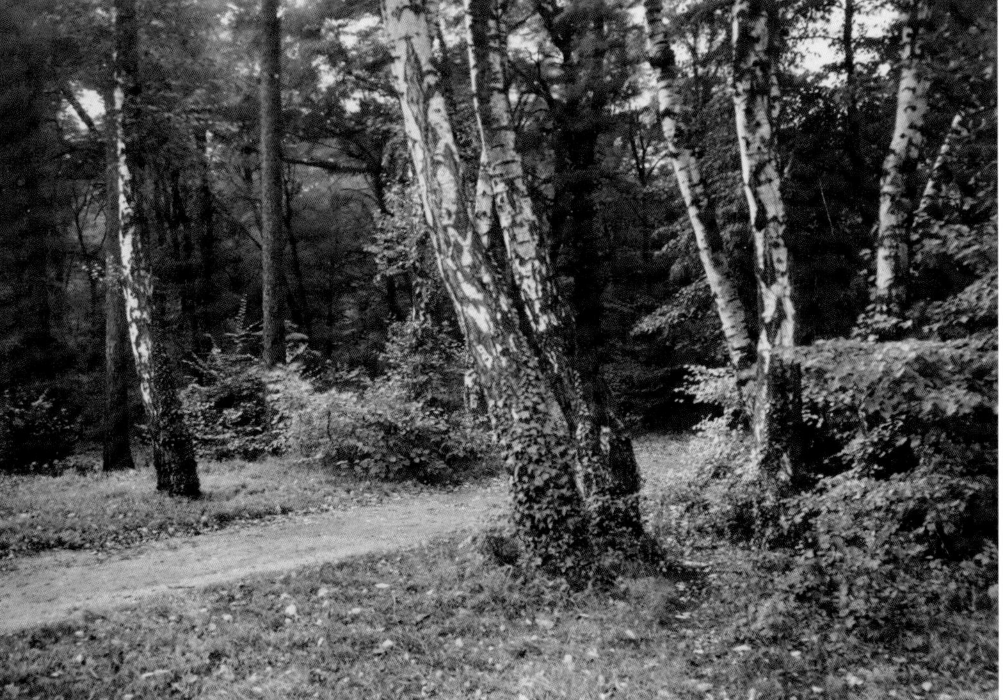

50 (top left)
August Sander
***Deerpark, Cologne*, 1938**
Gelatin silver print,
9 3/16 × 6 15/16 in.
The Phillips Collection, Washington, DC,
Gift of Kent and Marcia Minichiello, 2006.

51 (top right)
August Sander
***Yew in Spring*, 1930s**
Gelatin silver print,
9 1/4 × 6 13/16 in.
The Phillips Collection, Washington, DC,
Gift of Kent and Marcia Minichiello, 2006.

52 (bottom)
August Sander
***Birches in the Woods*, 1930s**
Gelatin silver print,
6 5/8 × 9 in.
The Phillips Collection, Washington, DC,
Gift of Kent and Marcia Minichiello, 2006.

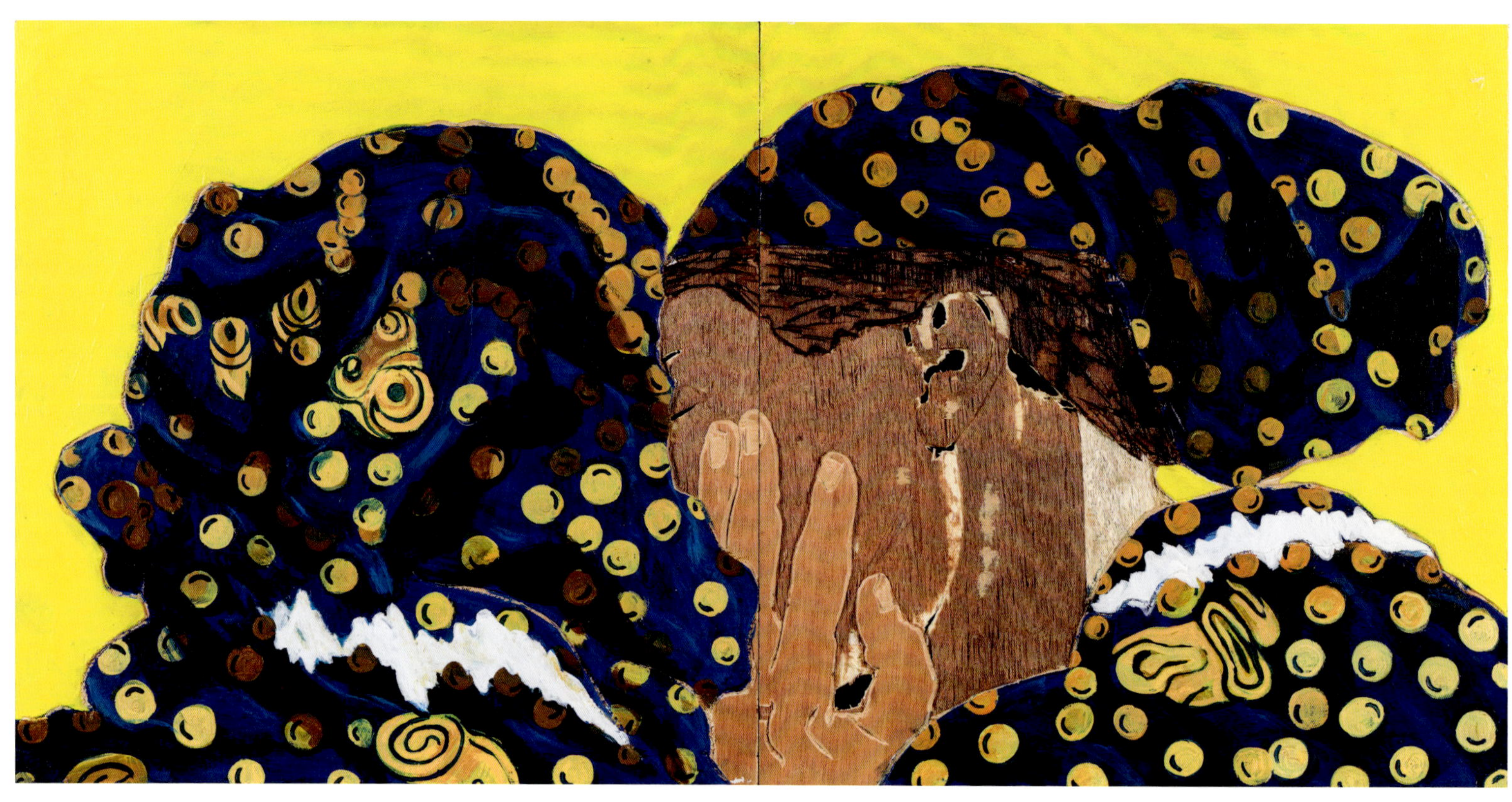

53
Aimé Mpane
***Mapasa*, 2012**
Acrylic and mixed media on two wood panels,
each: 12 1/2 × 12 in.
The Phillips Collection, Washington, DC,
The Dorothy and Herbert Vogel Award, 2012.

AIMÉ MPANE
MAPASA, 2012

Kate Cowcher

Kinshasa is a megacity of multiple identities. Perched above the Congo River, it was originally Léopoldville, capital of the Belgian Congo, sharply divided between grand colonial boulevards and a vast, informal *cité* for the indigenous population. Following independence, the hopeful era of Patrice Lumumba was swiftly extinguished by Mobutu Sese Seko's corrupt dictatorship. For thirty years, Mobutu's failure to provide services bred a culture of *débrouillez-vous* (fend for yourself); the city's popular nickname shifted from *Kin la belle* (Kinshasa the beautiful) to *Kin la poubelle* (Kinshasa the trash can). Despite many challenges, Kinshasa is renowned as dynamic and creative: the birthplace of Congolese rumba, of the sharp-dressing *sapeur* subculture, and of the "Popular Painters," who have narrated Congolese experiences in frank, comic-strip-style vernacular modernism. Kinshasa's street scene is matched by a rich intellectual culture; it is home to one of Africa's oldest art schools, the Académie des Beaux-Arts. Aimé Mpane is a son of this city. An Académie graduate, he has anchored his work, conceptually and materially, in Kinshasa's complex realities.

Mapasa consists of two square wooden panels painted in a deep, primary palette that recalls the graphics of Kinshasa's street painters. Where the latter strive for clarity, however, *Mapasa* is enigmatic: on a vivid yellow ground are two intermingled figures. An oblique face is hacked out of the wood's layers; some gouges are so deep that small holes gape. This is a familiar mode for Mpane, who uses such squares to create three-dimensional portraits roughly hewn from plywood's manufactured layers. Mpane has spoken explicitly of the material correspondence of plywood with skin, the tonal subtleties of the former mirroring the complexities of the human epidermis and condemning racism's false reductions. Plywood, however, also connects to Mpane's hometown, where it is ubiquitous in informal housing. Its mobilization here gestures toward Kinshasan resourcefulness; the most functional of materials is repurposed to bring to the fore questions about Congolese history and identity.

Mpane's method is as significant as his material. He carves plywood with an adze, a historic woodworking tool used across Africa for both practical and ceremonial purposes, and widely collected by European colonial ethnographers. The adze does violence to the wood's surface. In early series, such as *Ici on crève* (2006–8), that violence spoke explicitly to the recent and historic suffering of Kinshasa's population. In *Mapasa*, however, the adze's attack does not reveal a face. Unlike the subjects of Mpane's earlier work, *Mapasa*'s subjects turn away. They resist being seen, even as the adze hacks at an ear.

Mapasa is the Lingala word for "twins." As in other African societies, twins have historically held special status in the Lower Congo. In the BaKongo worldview, twins are sacred; they possess the powers of the *bisimbi* spirits and can communicate between earthly and ancestral realms. They are a mixed blessing: burdensome in the nourishment they require, yet revered as a phenomenon, as one entity in two. Mpane paints bold, graphic drapery to cloak his twins as one. The adze reveals a limited profile, whose hand further shields shared secrets. In the inaccessibility of its subjects, *Mapasa* speaks to Mpane's interest in refuting simplistic, primitivizing stereotypes of his homeland. It revels in the complexities of Congolese society, complexities that are only amplified by the humility of the material into which they have been carved.

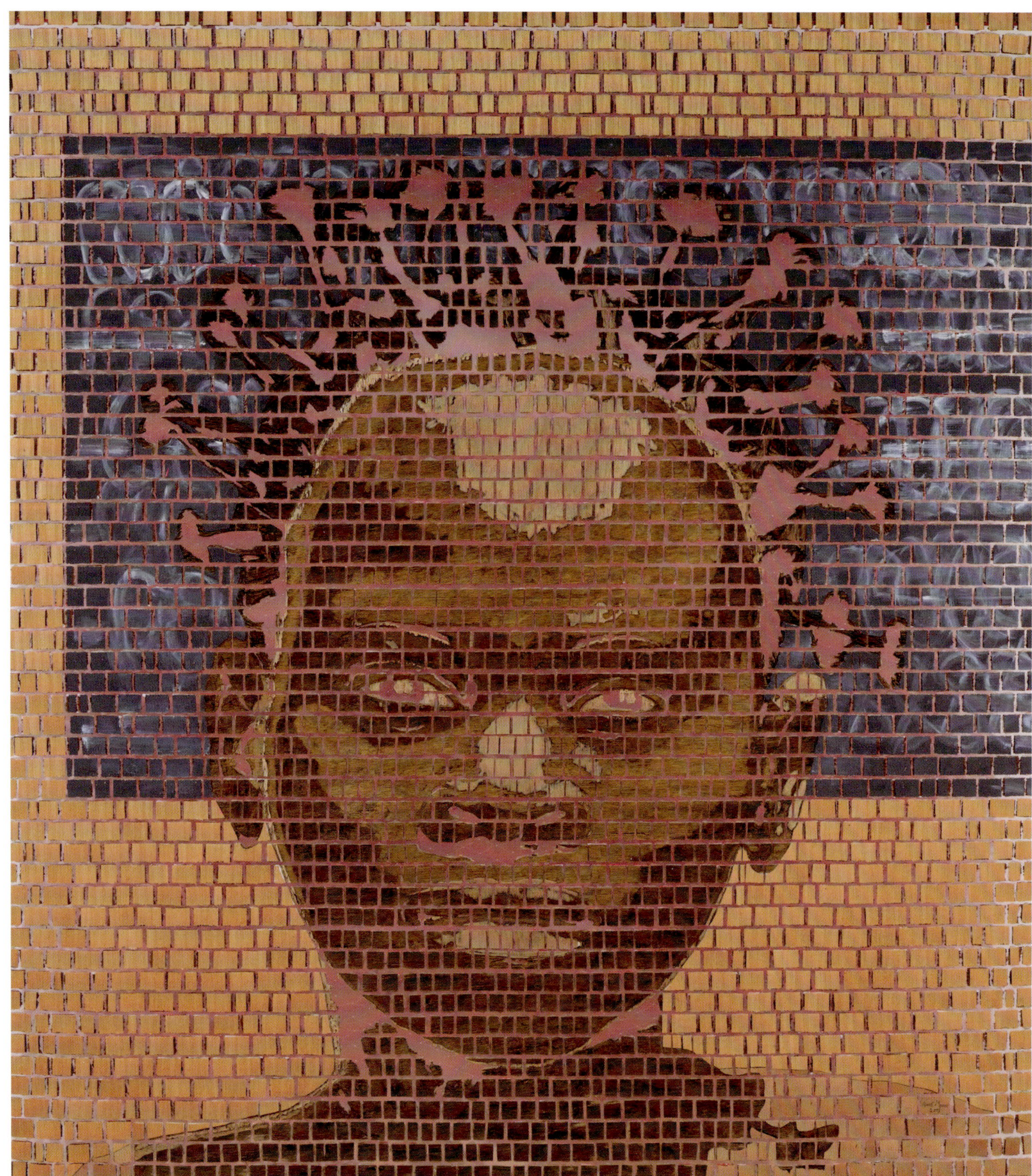

54
Aimé Mpane
Maman Calcule, 2013
Acrylic and mixed media on pieces of wood with monofilament,
83 × 73 in.
The Phillips Collection, Washington, DC,
The Dreier Fund for Acquisitions, 2019.

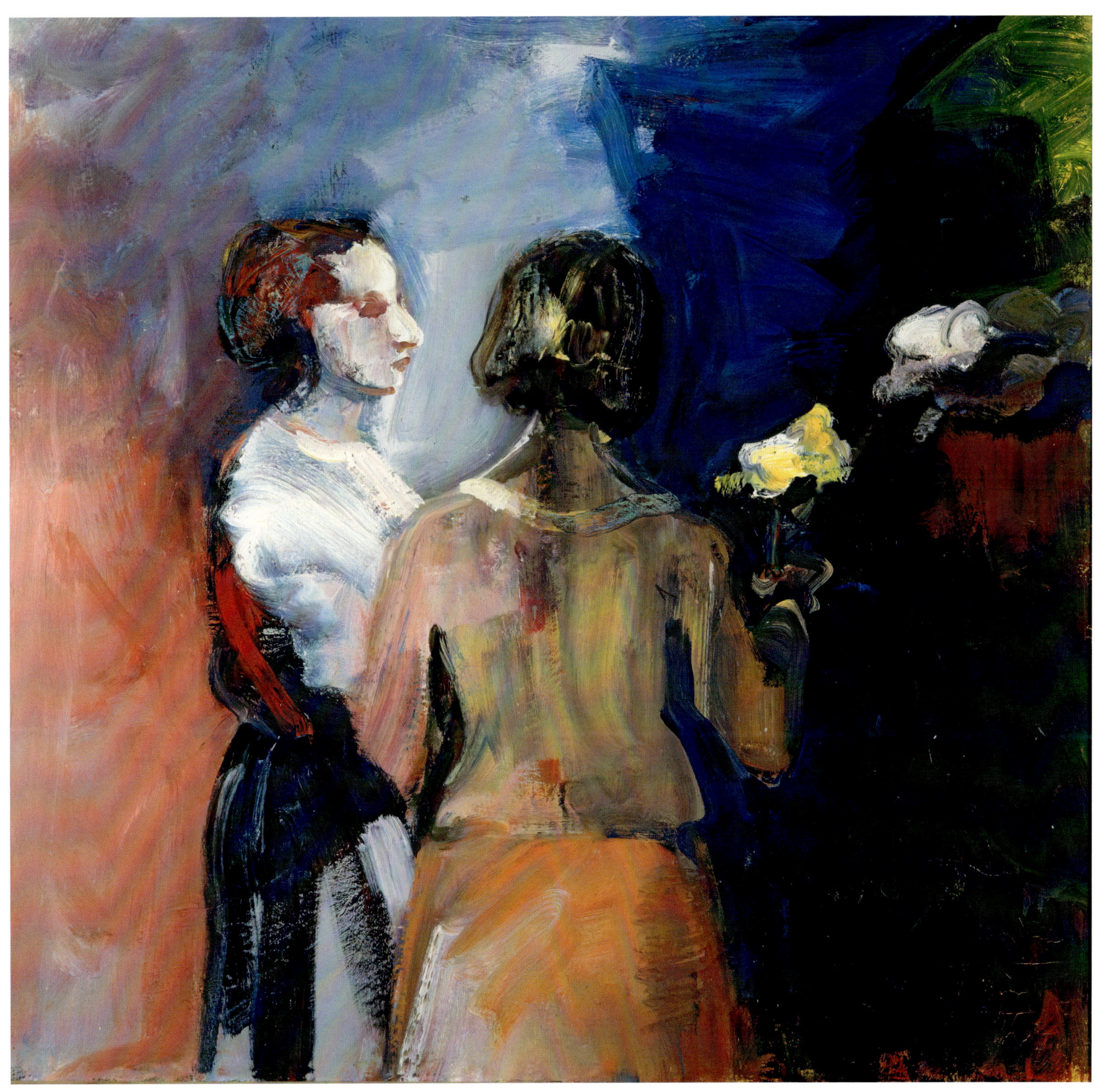

55
Elmer Bischoff
Figures: Back and Profile, 1960
Oil on canvas,
54 1/4 × 54 1/8 in.
The Phillips Collection, Washington, DC,
Gift of Mrs. Walter S. Salant, initiated 1994,
completed 2001.

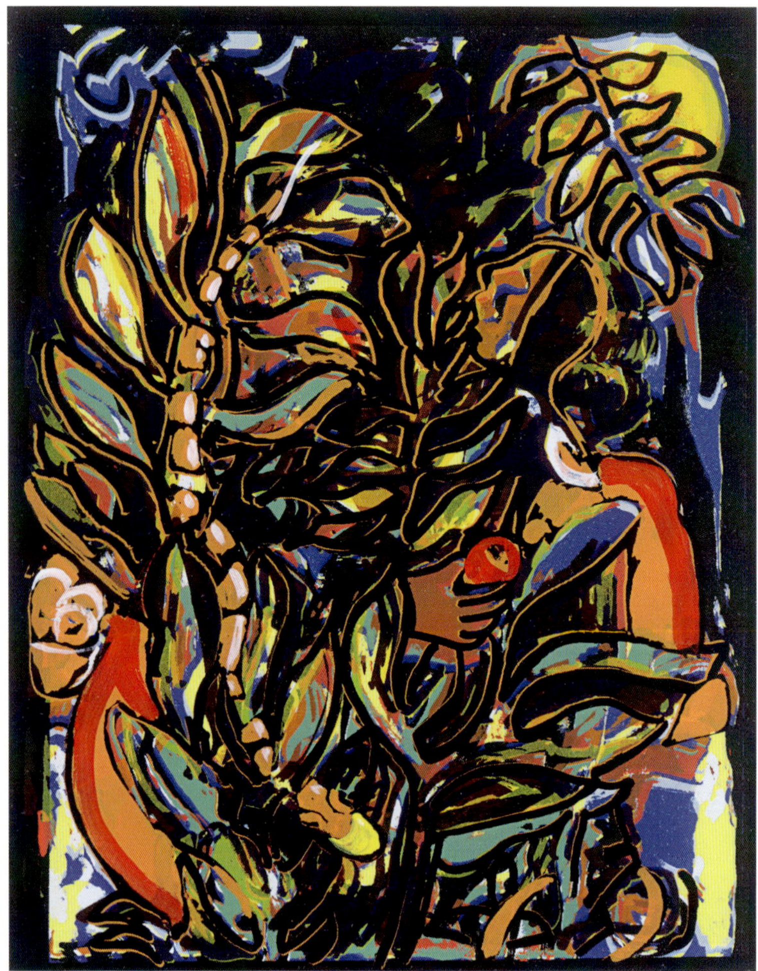

The seer arrived on the third wednesday of the afternoon, her voice the voice of the dead. Sparrows fled as if a hawk were near. As evening settled in our village, she asked us men to share our simplest tale. Because it was she who asked, it needed to be a tale without fear, a tale without hope....

56
David Driskell
Temptation in the Garden, 2009
From the *Doorway* portfolio, with poetry by Michael Albert
Color screenprint,
overall: 15 × 12 in.
The Phillips Collection, Washington, DC,
Purchase, The Hereward Lester Cooke Memorial Fund, 2009.

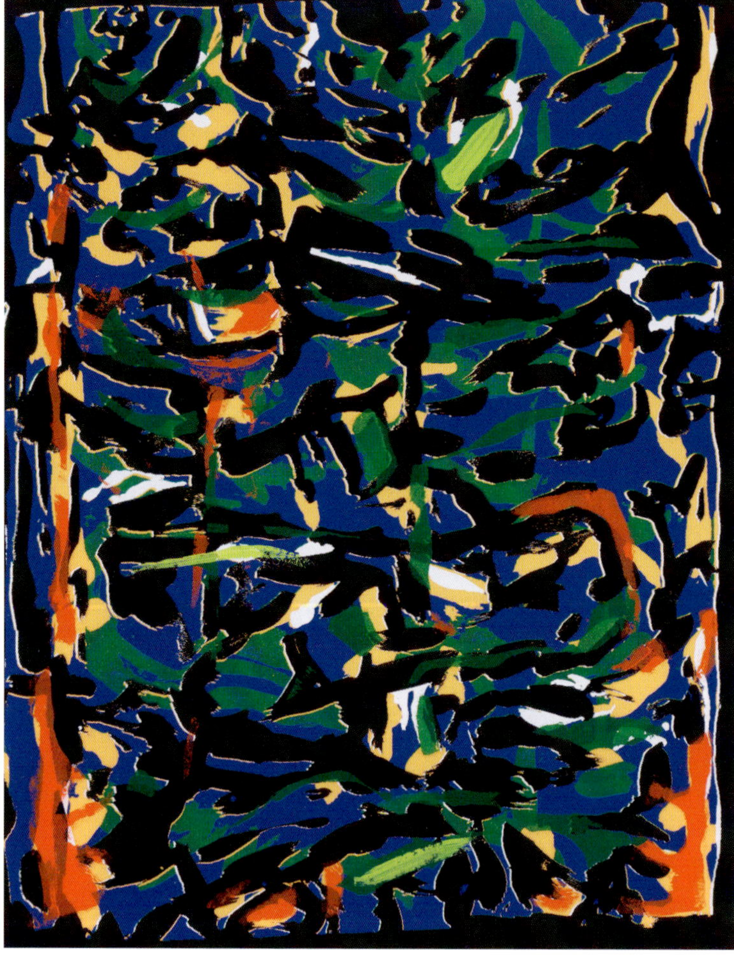

Their branches are our wings. They carry the weight of our sadness. They left our sorrow to their canopy in the sky. They are fragile and whole. They dance wildly at night. Their ecstasy is what we long for, what we most need, what we once were.

57
David Driskell
Pine Trees at Night, 2009
From the *Doorway* portfolio, with poetry by Michael Albert
Color screenprint,
overall: 15 × 12 in.
The Phillips Collection, Washington, DC,
Purchase, The Hereward Lester Cooke Memorial Fund, 2009.

DAVID C. DRISKELL
DOORWAY, 2009

Elsa Smithgall

David C. Driskell was skilled not only as a painter, but also as a printmaker who created innovative prints in a range of media, from woodcuts to lithographs to monoprints.[1] His 2009 *Doorway* portfolio is distinctive as a visual essay that combines twelve hand-pulled serigraphs with the evocative prose of Michael Albert. Printed by Curlee Holton at Cardinal Point Press, the project developed out of a close collaboration between the artist and writer: "Michael did not intend to provide a narrative that describes the images. Neither do the images illustrate the text. Nevertheless, something quite magical happens when the images and prose are viewed together," noted Cardinal Point Press's president, Howard Greenberg.[2]

Loosely based on compositions in collage, mixed media, and oil, the prints are a glowing testimony to Driskell's love of overlapping surfaces and vibrant, multi-colored forms. To create each image, Driskell choreographed a palette averaging twenty different colors, applying them one by one to build up brilliant surfaces. As the colors and forms meld into one another like molten liquid, their fluid edges ebb and flow in undulating rhythms. Image and prose are richly interwoven into a tapestry that sings of nature and its spiritual, inner life.

In *Pine Trees at Night* (pl. 57), Driskell explores a favorite subject that was the focus of his master's thesis at Catholic University in 1962. Over the ensuing years, the "massive pines towering towards the sky" outside his studio window in Maine afforded the artist much artistic sustenance.[3] His interest in the landscape went beyond naturalistic concerns. "I saw it as part and parcel of something larger ... everlasting life, eternity," the artist later explained.[4] Driskell's image is also distinguished by its nighttime setting. "You don't stop seeing because night comes," the wise artist once said.[5]

In the titular image for which the portfolio is named, the artist suggests the doorway as a passage between two worlds—interior and exterior, material and spiritual, real and imagined. In the *Doorway* prints, as in all of Driskell's work, one feels his divine connection to nature and the joy he derived from the creative act of making art. Driskell's everlasting spirit lives on in the soulful reverie of these and all his artistic expressions.

---

1 For more on Driskell's printmaking, see Adrienne L. Childs, *Evolution: Five Decades of Printmaking by David C. Driskell* (San Francisco: Pomegranate Press, 2007).

2 Howard Greenberg, in an email to Elsa Smithgall, August 14, 2009.

3 David Driskell, in "A Conversation between David Driskell and Bruce Brown," *David Driskell: Painting Across the Decade 1996–2006* (New York: DC Moore Gallery, 2006), n.p.

4 Driskell, in Oral History Interview with Cynthia Mills, 2009, n.p. Archives of American Art, Smithsonian Institution.

5 See "Artist Conversation with David C. Driskell and Elsa Smithgall" in this volume, p. 50.

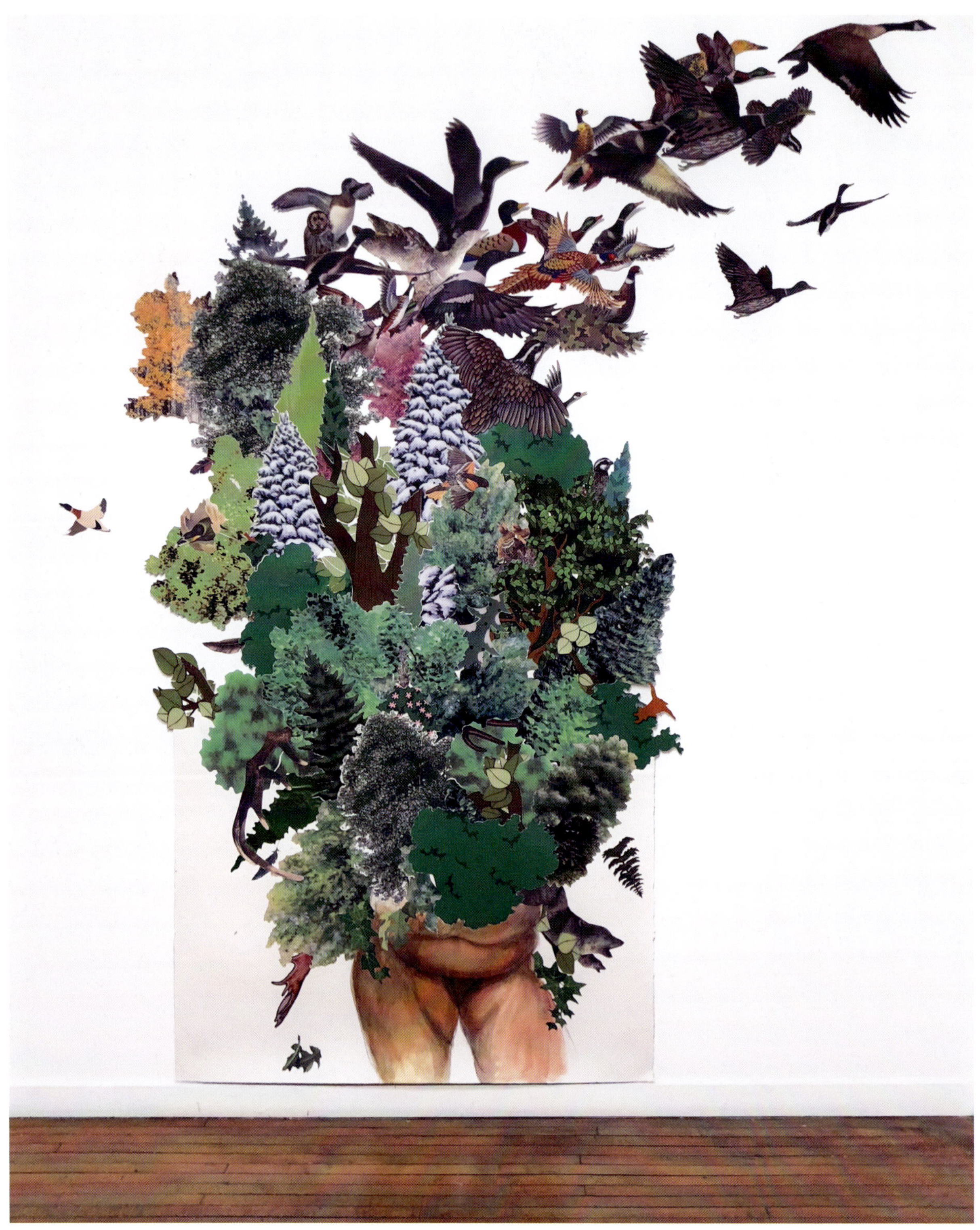

58
Zoë Charlton
***The Country A Wilderness Unsubdued*, 2018**
Graphite and acrylic on paper with collaged printed paper on matboard,
112 × 55 in.
The Phillips Collection, Washington, DC, Contemporaries Acquisition Fund, 2019.

ZOË CHARLTON
THE COUNTRY A WILDERNESS UNSUBDUED, 2018

Jessica Stafford Davis

"You don't find community, you build community in collaboration with others," is something Zoë Charlton said when introducing her work at the unveiling of *The Country A Wilderness Unsubdued* (2018) at The Phillips Collection.

The Country A Wilderness Unsubdued is a collage-based mixed-media work on paper. It is anchored by the core of a large, ample Black woman as its foundation. Only the thighs and stomach of the female nude are visible; the chest and head are covered by dense layers of branches and trees. Through the foliage, you can make out small portions of African tribal masks. The piece crescendos with birds flying out of the treetop and up into the air, seemingly chasing or following the lead bird in a kind of release.

When I look at this artwork, I feel a heaviness, the burden that one feels when having to carry the weight of others. The figure is carrying so much weight that she is unable to see clearly. The trees and leaves are lush and rich, thriving even as their weight may be too heavy to hold.

The work takes on a different meaning when I learn that Charlton's grandmother was its inspiration. She was a Black woman who lived in the south of the United States, in Tallahassee, Florida, a place known for its inequality and racist attitudes toward Black people, especially Black women. She was creative in coming up with ways to afford the land. She sold soup, worked as a domestic servant, and sharecropped the property well into the 1970s. She leaned on her community, and her community leaned on her. What I once viewed as a weight, I now see as fertile ground: the Black woman, who continually makes space for others. The layering of the branches and leaves reminds me of the universal family tree—the future generations that are seeded and grow from the rootstock of one who took a chance. Future generations will thrive because of her ingenuity.

The effort Charlton puts into her community is something I have seen first-hand. While her ethos inspires this work, it is evident in who Charlton is as a person. She is always interested in engaging and connecting; you find yourself leaving her presence more informed and more aware, wanting to share what you have learned. You want to continue to build the community. That is how I feel when engaging with one of her pieces, and when looking at *The Country A Wilderness Unsubdued*.

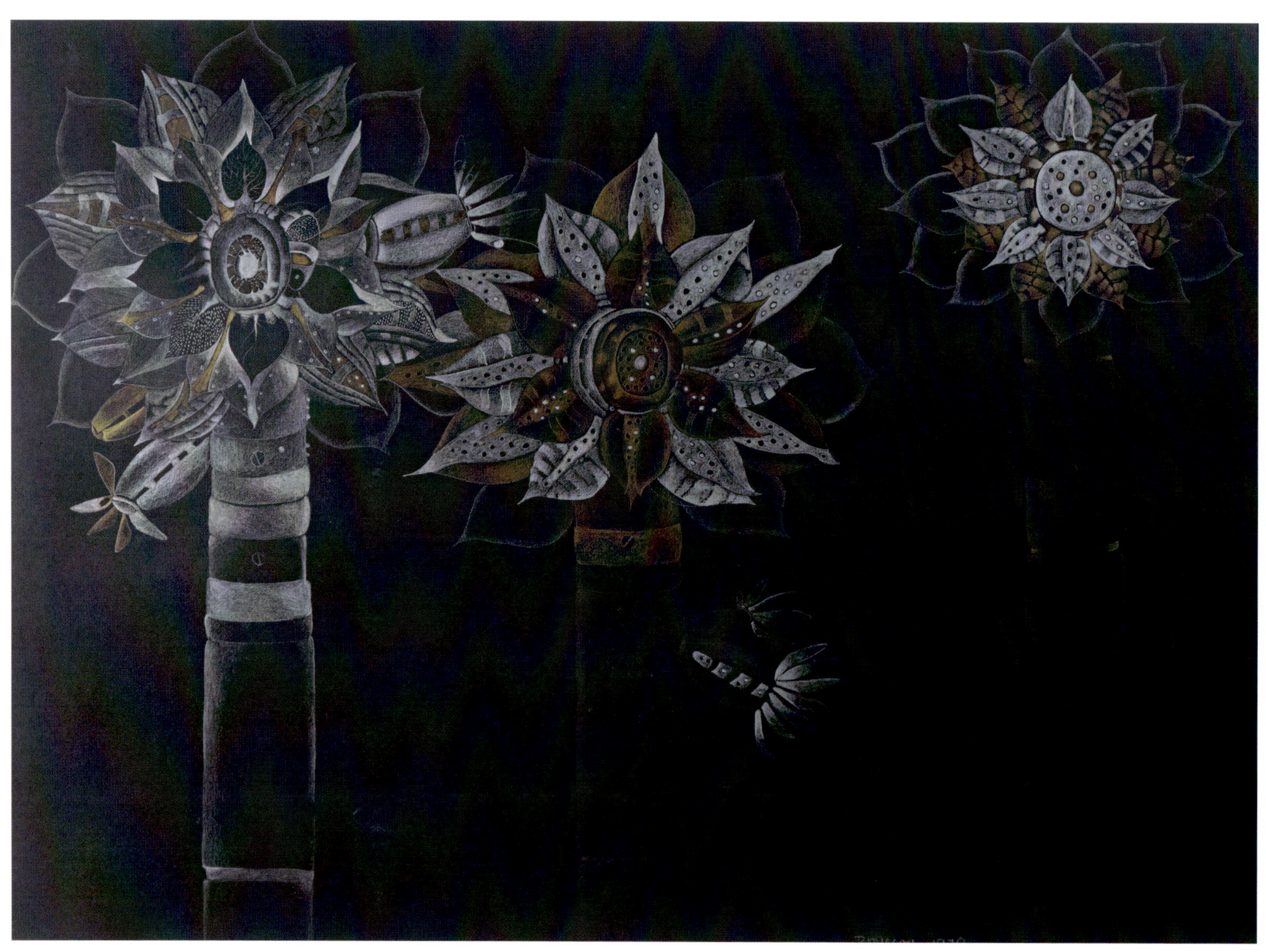

59
Lee Bontecou
Untitled, 1970
White and colored pencils on paper prepared with a black ground,
17 15/16 × 23 15/16 in.
The Phillips Collection, Washington, DC, Promised Gift of Linda Lichtenberg Kaplan.

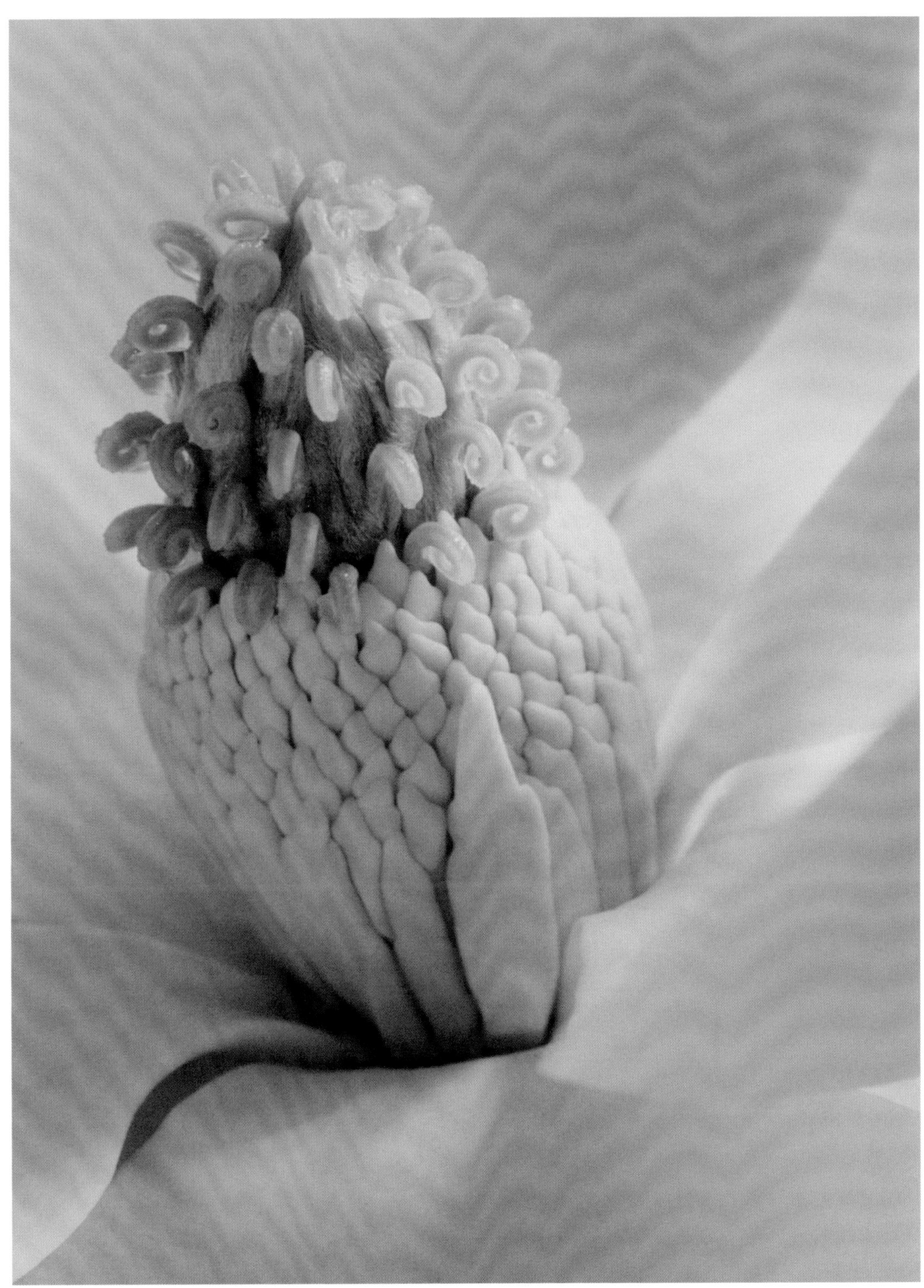

60
Imogen Cunningham
***Tower of Jewels*, 1925**
Gelatin silver print,
12 1/2 × 9 1/4 in.
The Phillips Collection, Washington, DC,
Gift of The Joseph and Charlotte Lichtenberg Collection,
initiated 2005, completed 2016.

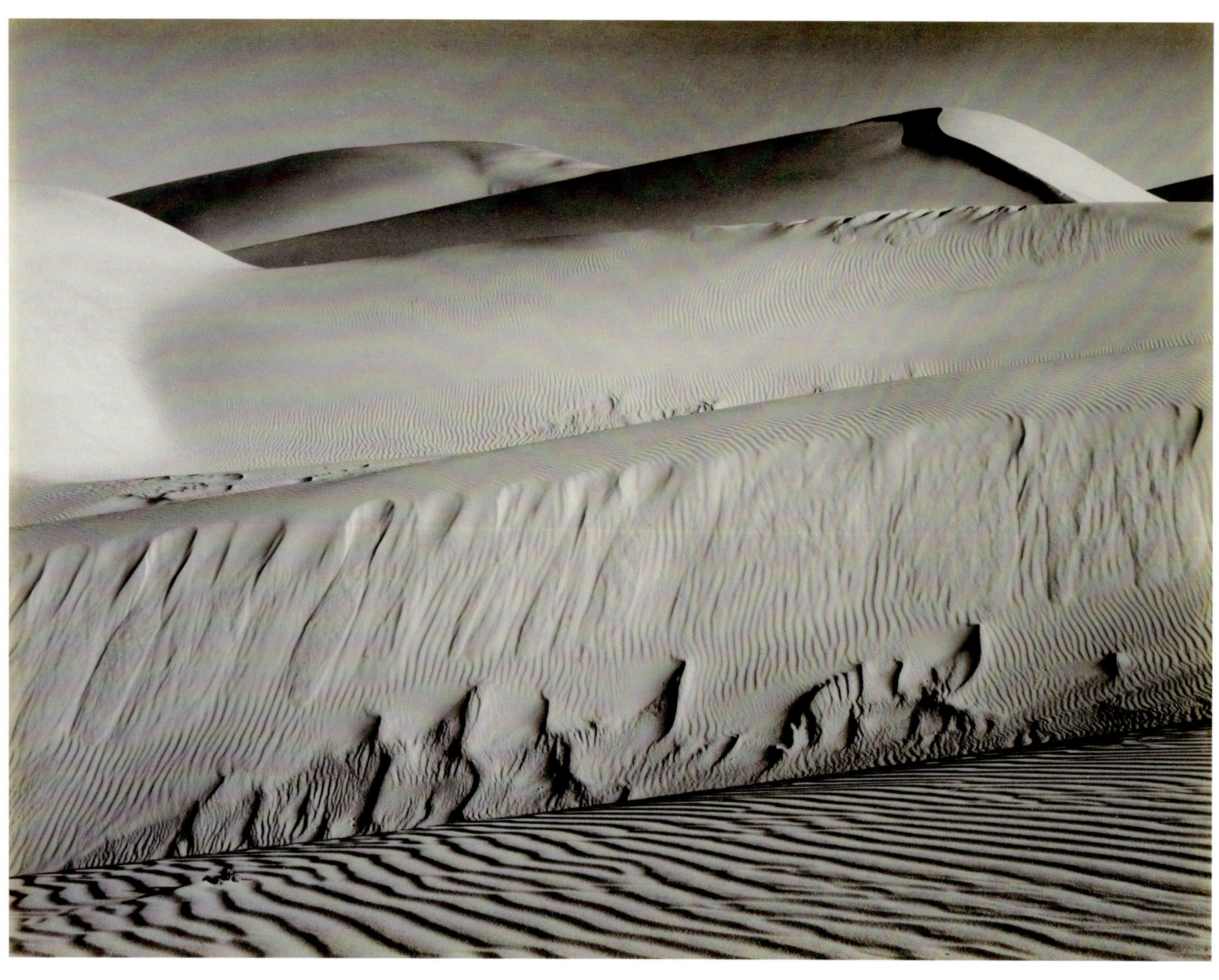

61
Edward Weston
Dunes, Oceano, 1936
Gelatin silver print,
8 × 10 in.
The Phillips Collection, Washington, DC,
Gift of The Joseph and Charlotte Lichtenberg Collection,
initiated 2005, completed 2016.

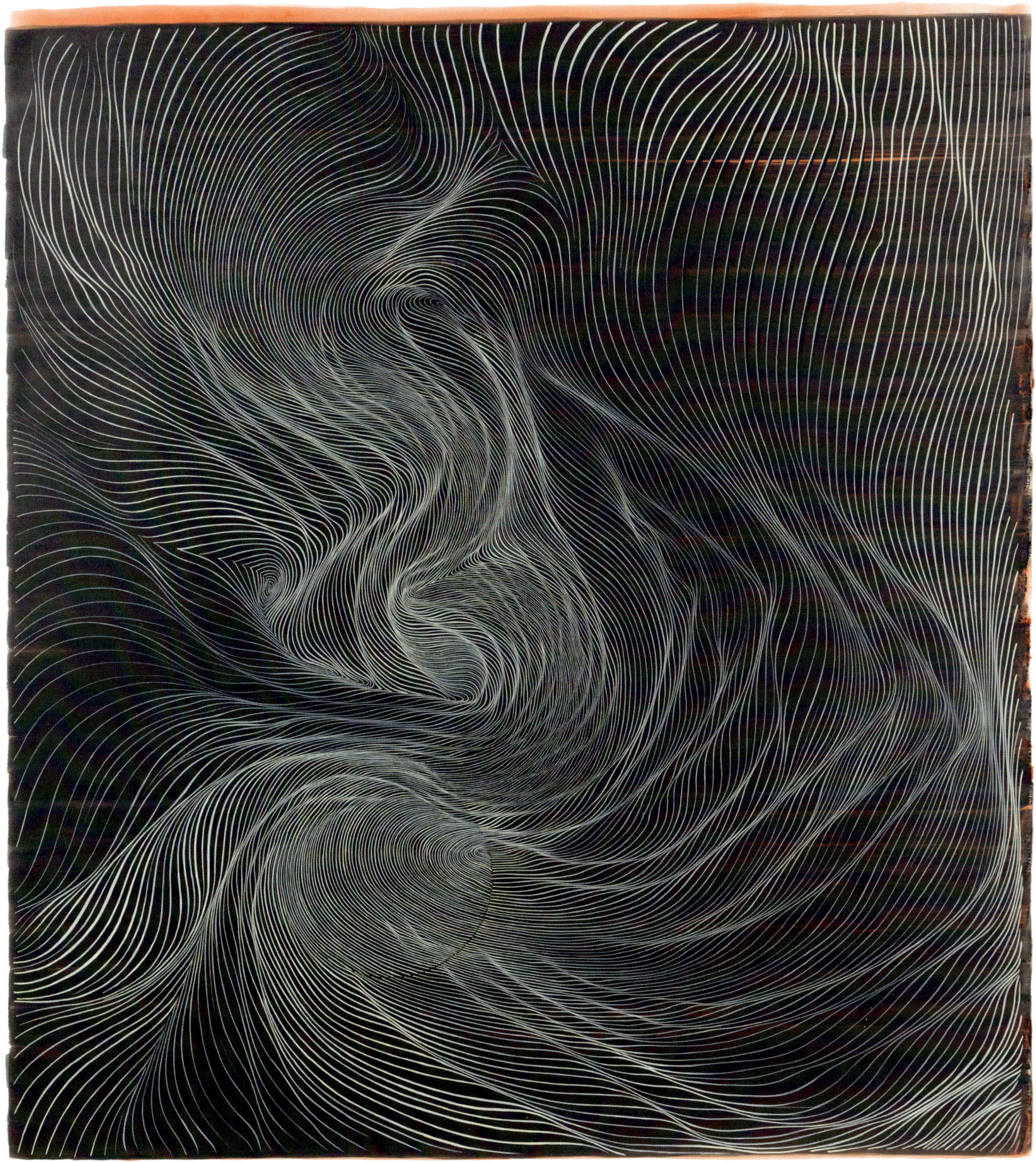

62
linn meyers
***Untitled*, 2014**
Acrylic ink on polyester drafting film,
42 × 39 in.
The Phillips Collection, Washington, DC,
Gift of Lucinda and Carlos Garcia, 2015.

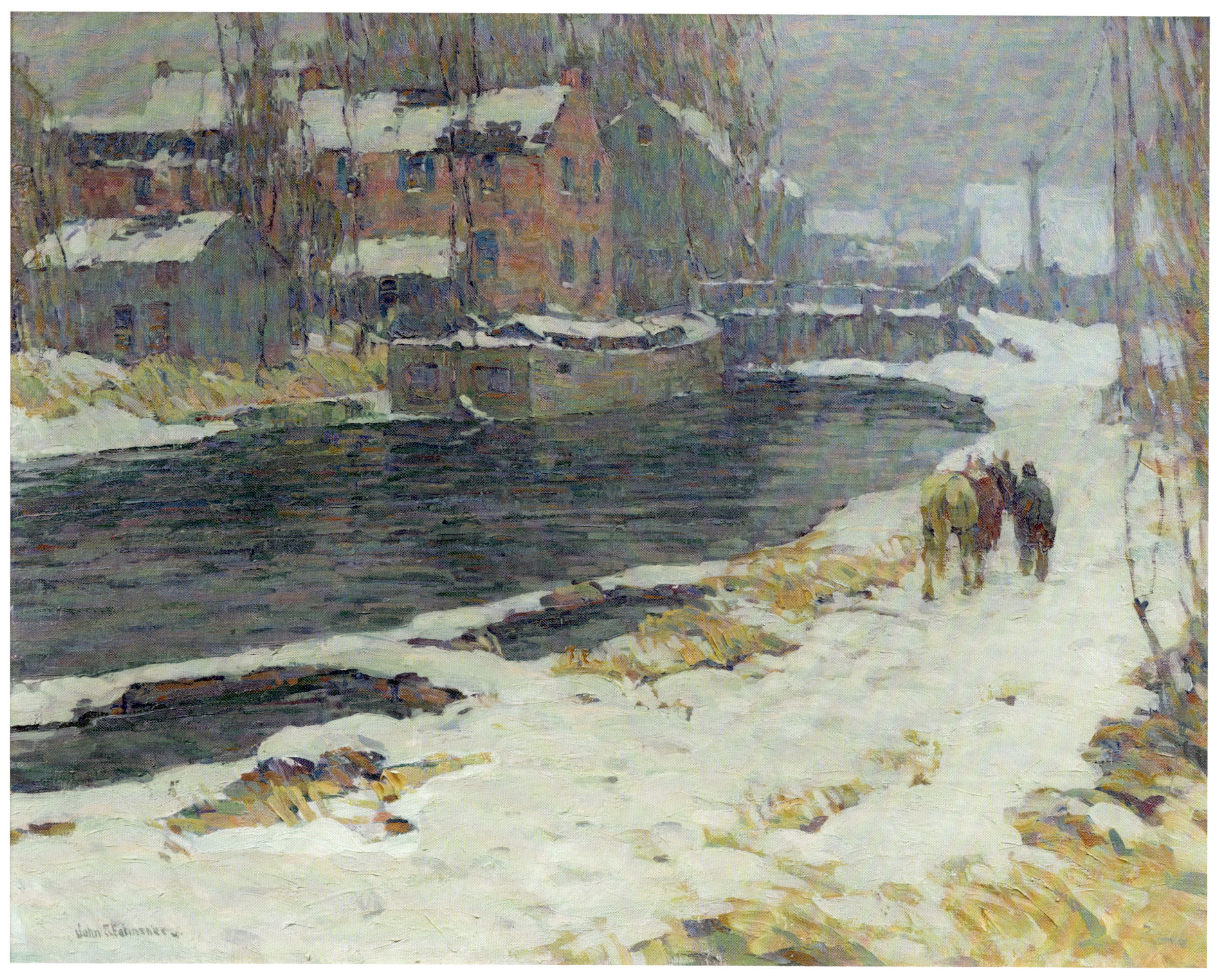

63
John Folinsbee
***Grey Thaw*, 1920**
Oil on canvas,
32 1/4 × 40 1/2 in.
The Phillips Collection, Washington, DC,
Gift from the Trustees of the Corcoran Gallery of Art,
2018 (Museum Purchase, Gallery Fund).

JOHN FOLINSBEE
GREY THAW, 1920

Susan Behrends Frank

Grey Thaw is a recent gift to The Phillips Collection from the Corcoran Gallery of Art. Awarded the Third William A. Clark Prize at the 8th Corcoran Biennial (1921–22), it is a standout work in the Phillips's small collection of New Hope (Pennsylvania) impressionist pictures. Duncan Phillips was introduced to John Folinsbee's work in 1916 at the Corcoran's 6th Biennial (1916–17), from which he bought the artist's large exhibition canvas *The Bridge at New Hope* (1916). By 1921, the year he opened his museum, Phillips had reluctantly exchanged his big Folinsbee for a smaller work by the artist, *Along the Canal* (1919–20), which remains a valued early acquisition in the collection. Through the Corcoran's gift, the Phillips is once again the holder of a major early work by this distinguished American artist, whom Phillips admired from the outset of his journey as a collector of American painting.

Folinsbee developed a sense for capturing light and atmosphere early in his career from his studies with Birge Harrison and John Carlson in Woodstock, New York. In 1916 he moved to New Hope, some forty miles north of Philadelphia on the Delaware River. By the second decade of the twentieth century, this small village in Bucks County had developed into a year-round artists' colony. Its leading artists—Daniel Garber, William Lathrop, Edward Redfield, and Robert Spencer—had been embraced by the critics as the embodiment of the populist spirit of America. With the exception of Lathrop, they primarily painted out-of-doors and were especially well known for their winter scenes.

Folinsbee's early New Hope years were spent exploring the rivers, canals, and bridges that defined this rural community. The Delaware, Lehigh and Raritan canal systems, which date from the 1830s, were still active, with mules towing canal boats and barges along the towpaths until 1932. Although a committed plein air painter, Folinsbee, who was confined to a wheelchair because of childhood polio, could not accommodate large canvases outdoors. Thus, works like *Grey Thaw* are studio paintings developed from oil sketches, drawings, and notes about color and light crafted into final compositions that speak not only to place, but also to emotional memory and response. In *Grey Thaw*, Folinsbee presents the grand sweep of the snowy towpath alongside the New Hope canal, where a solitary man walks with his mule through heavy snow. One of the many barges can be seen tied up on the opposite bank. The village's tightly clustered buildings are pushed to the top third of the composition. In the distance, a small snow-covered bridge links the towpath to the village. Even with its large scale, *Grey Thaw* retains the sense of place and intimacy that Duncan Phillips valued as the essential hallmarks of the New Hope school.

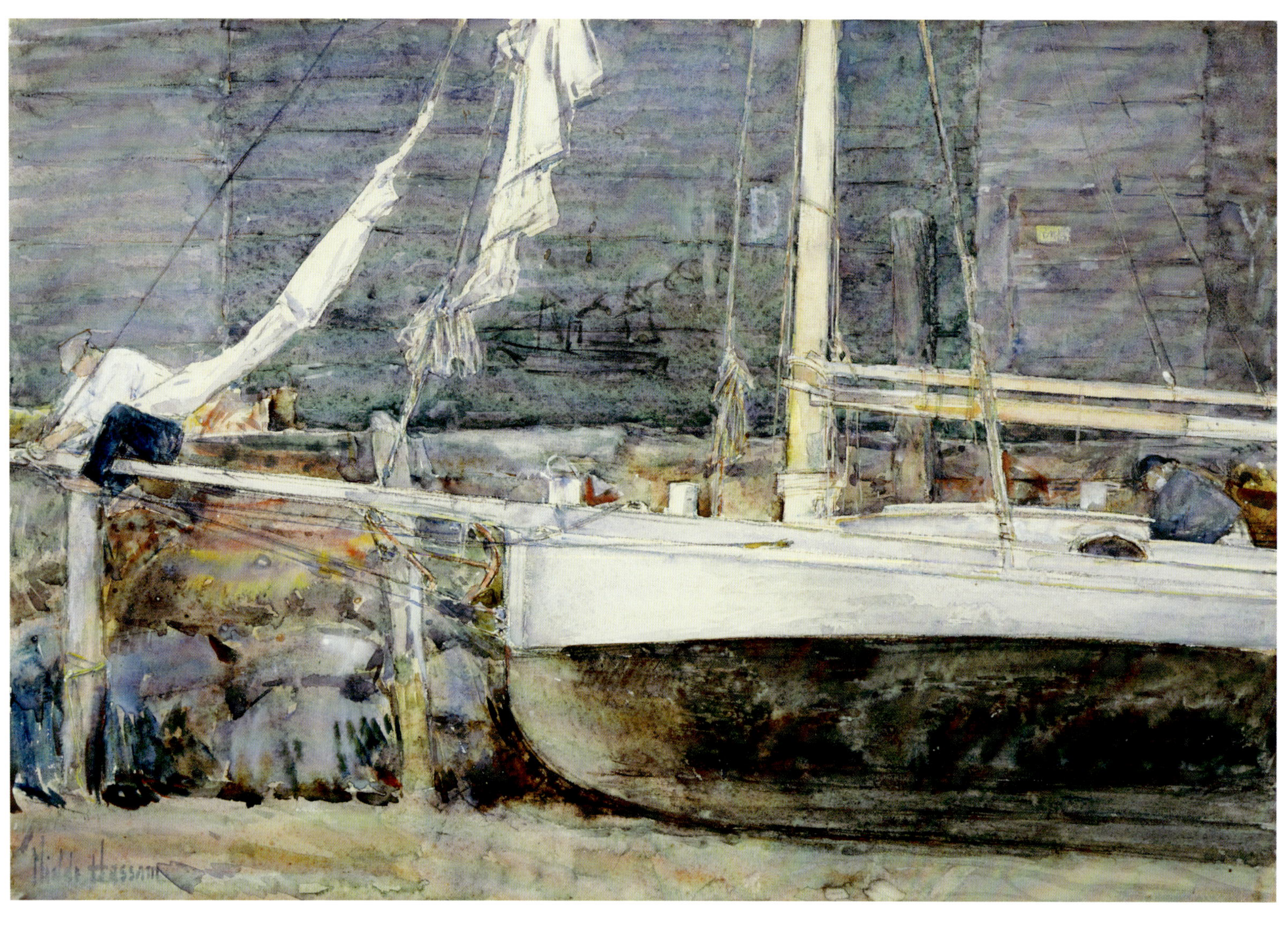

64
Childe Hassam
Drydock, Gloucester, ca. 1890s
Watercolor over ink and graphite pencil on paper,
13 3/16 × 19 1/2 in.
The Phillips Collection, Washington, DC,
Gift of Sandra Payson, 2004.

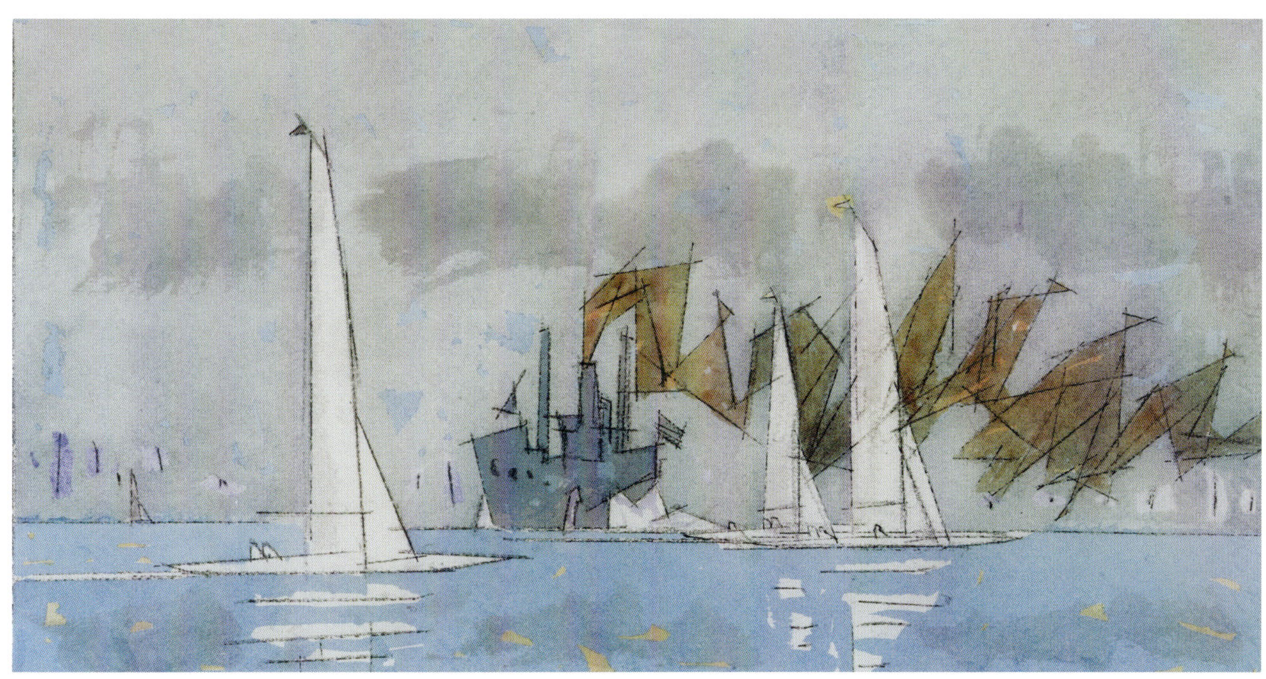

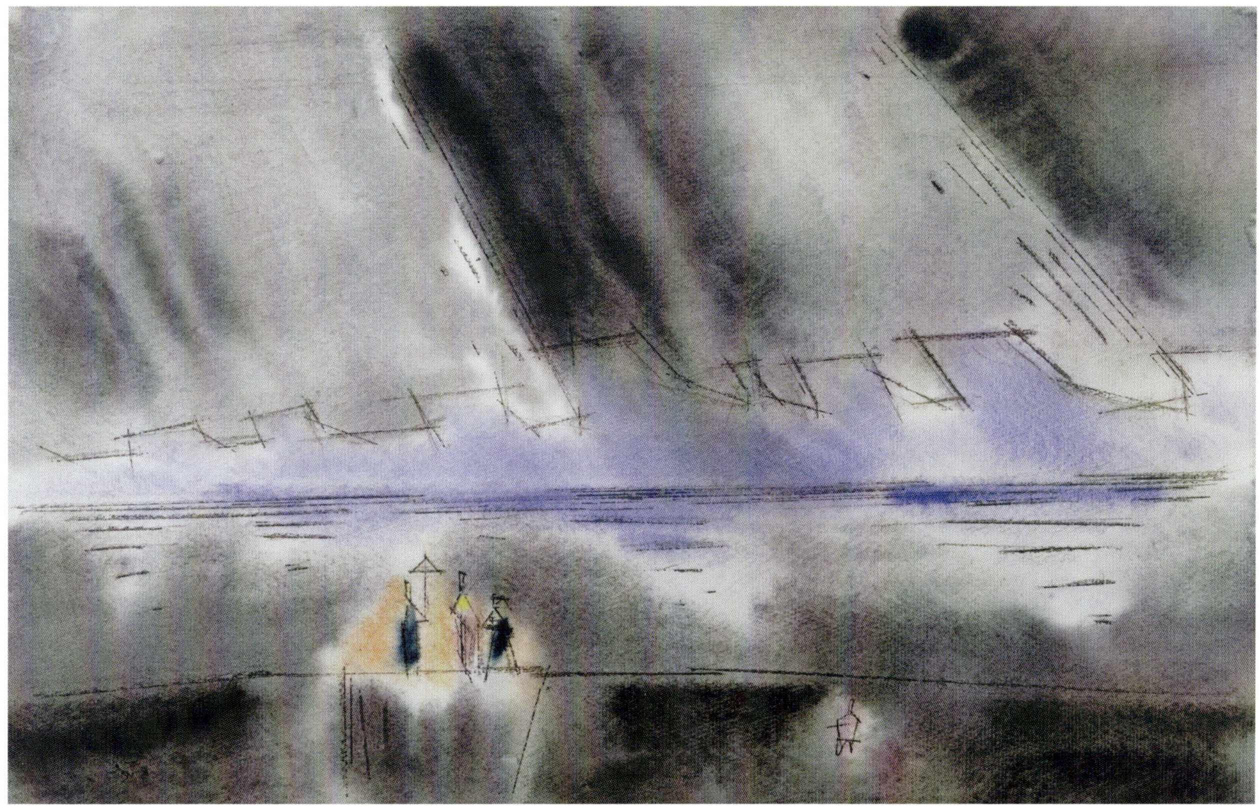

65 (top)
Lyonel Feininger
***Schiffe* (*Ships*), 1943**
Watercolor and pen and black ink on paper,
11 × 18 7/8 in.
The Phillips Collection, Washington, DC,
Gift of Bernhard and Marlene Witkop, initiated 2005,
completed 2010.

66 (bottom)
Lyonel Feininger
***Perfume and Sweet Candy*, 1948**
Watercolor and pen and black ink on paper,
12 1/4 × 18 1/4 in.
The Phillips Collection, Washington, DC,
Gift of Bernhard and Marlene Witkop, initiated 2005,
completed 2010.

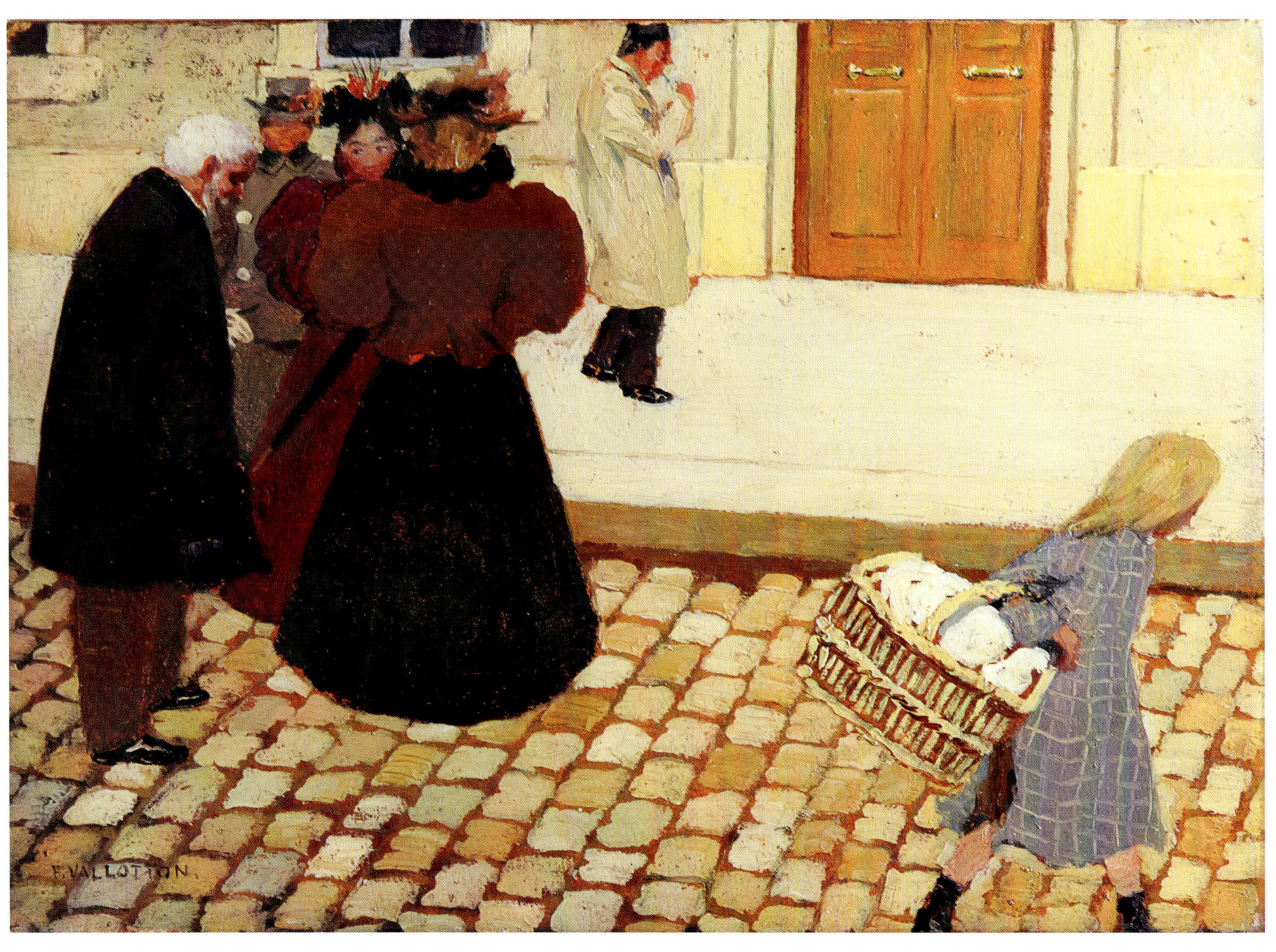

67
Félix Vallotton
***Scène de rue (Street Scene)*, ca. 1895**
Oil on cardboard,
10 1/14 x 13 3/8 in.
The Phillips Collection, Washington, DC,
Promised Gift of Vicki and Roger Sant.

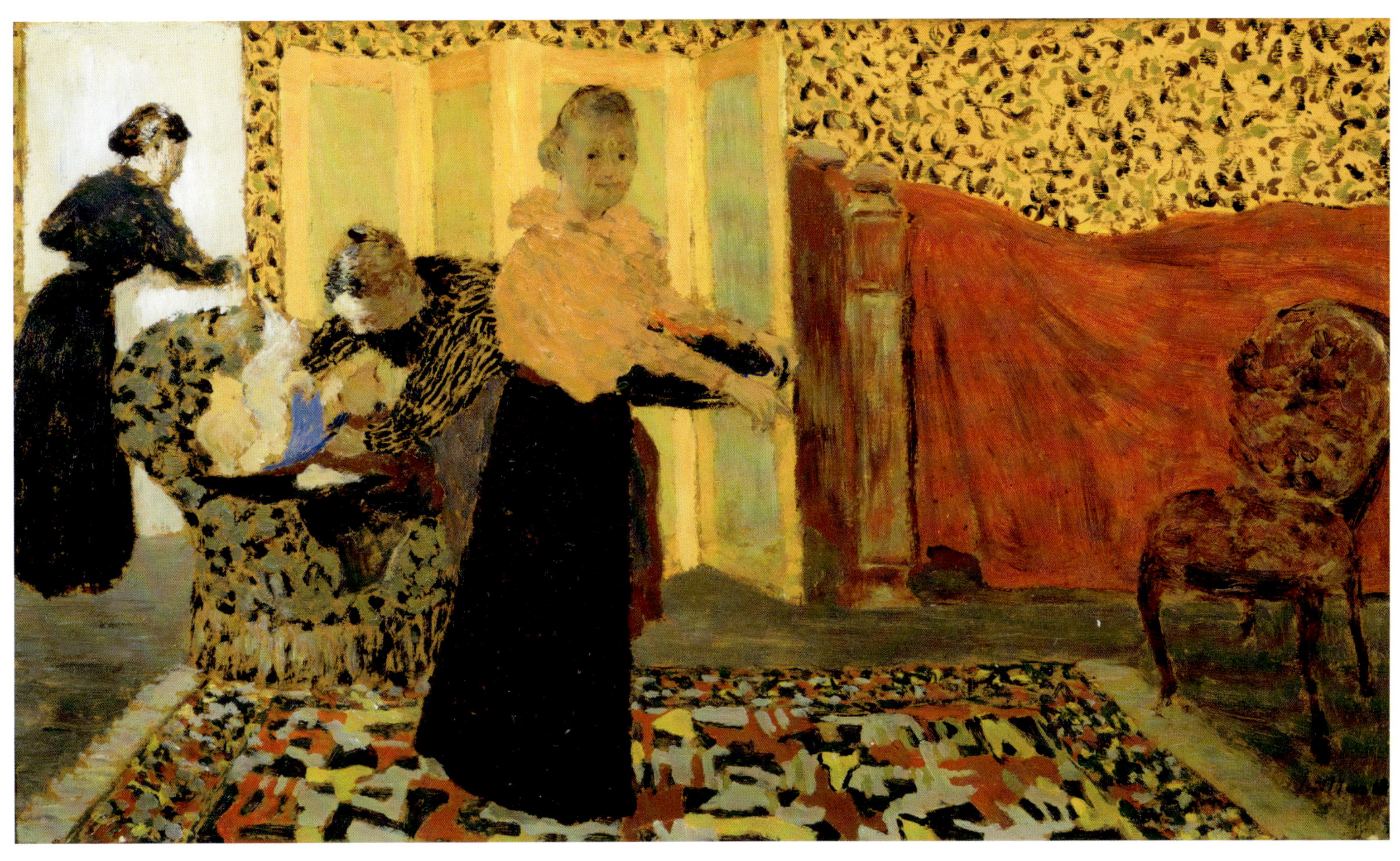

68
Édouard Vuillard
Intérieur au lit rouge ou *La Chambre nuptial (Interior with a Red Bed* or *The Bridal Chamber)*, 1893
Oil on cardboard mounted on cradled panel,
12 13/16 × 20 7/8 in.
The Phillips Collection, Washington, DC,
Promised Gift of Vicki and Roger Sant.

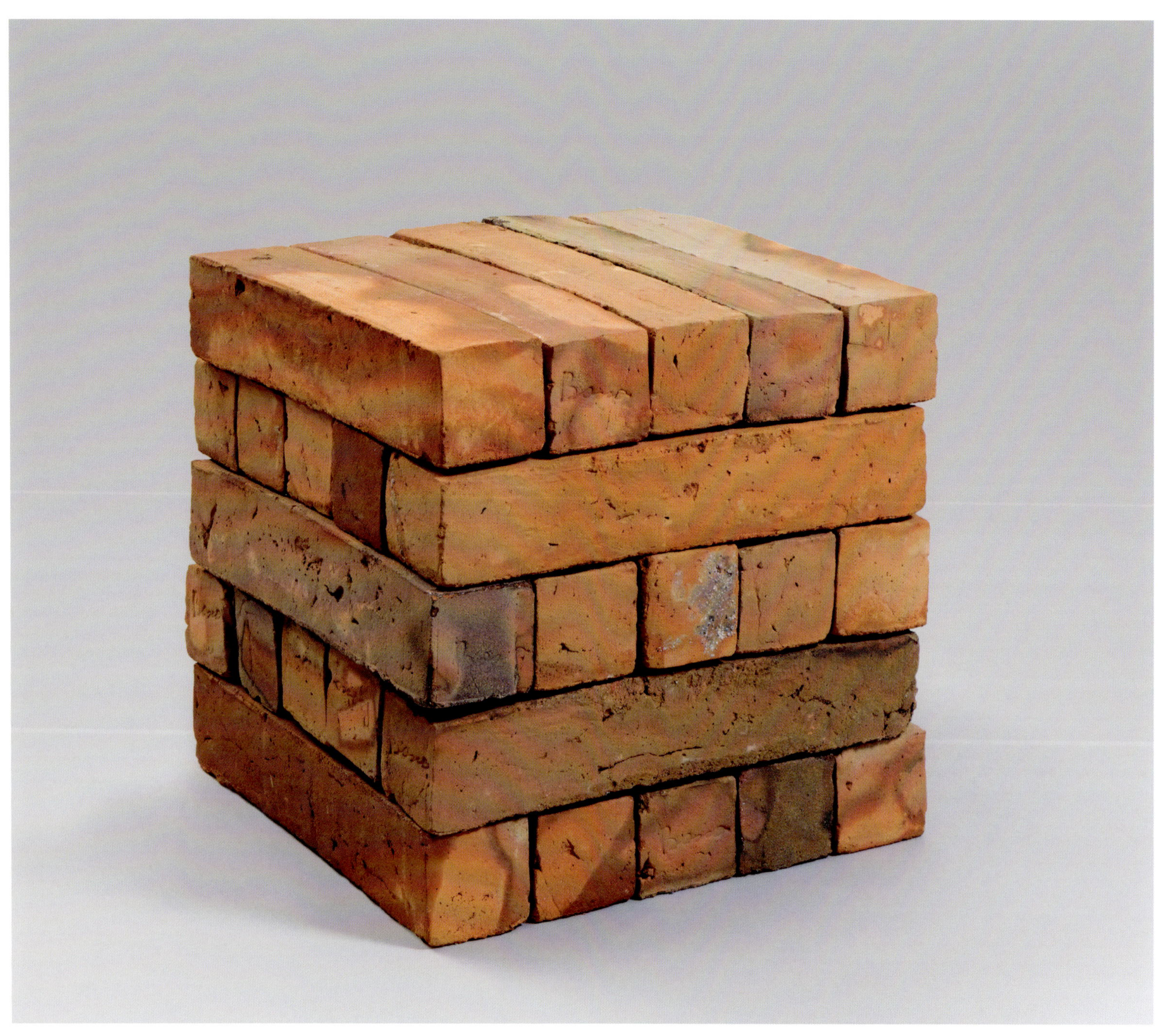

69
Bosco Sodi
***Muro*, 2017**
25 clay timbers,
each: 3 3/4 × 7 5/8 × 3 3/4 in.
The Phillips Collection, Washington, DC,
Gift of Bosco Sodi and Paul Kasmin Gallery, 2017.

BOSCO SODI
MURO, 2017

Vesela Sretenović

Mexican artist Bosco Sodi, who splits his time between studios in Brooklyn, New York, and Oaxaca, Mexico, is best known for highly textured, brightly colored, and often large-scale paintings with monumental presence. Using natural materials—such as wood pulp, sawdust, organic fibers, and raw pigments mixed with glue—and working intuitively, building up surfaces with layers of this mixture, he gives his monochromatic abstract paintings a rough, sensual appearance. Sodi deliberately leaves most of his works untitled, distancing them from any linguistic associations and focusing instead on their textural and gestural materiality. He has described his creative process as "controlled chaos" that makes "something that is completely un-repeatable."[1] The physical density and brute energy of his work bring to mind art informel and the work of Antoni Tàpies and Jean Dubuffet.

In recent years, Sodi has turned to sculpture. Following the traditions of his Mexican heritage, he makes his own clay—mixing raw earth with water and sand—at his studio in Oaxaca, shaping it by hand to form a series of smooth, solid cubes. Prior to their firing in a traditional brick kiln, they are left to dry in the sun. During this process, the hue and texture change, giving each one its own finish. When stacked into columns, the cubes form solemn minimalist sculptures that resemble caryatids.

Related to this sculptural body of work is Sodi's first public art project, *Muro* ("wall" in Spanish), created in 2017. A temporary wall, six feet high and twenty-six feet long, it comprised 1,600 clay timbers made in Oaxaca with the assistance of local craftsmen, many of whom had, at some point, entered the United States illegally. Timbers were then transported by truck along the same route taken by migrants who pass into Texas from the town of Nuevo Laredo. In the artist's words, this was his political action,[2] performed on September 7, 2017, in Washington Square Park after President Donald Trump threatened a government shutdown if Congress would not fund his proposed border wall between the United States and Mexico. With the help of friends and a group of Mexican-born New Yorkers, Sodi constructed the wall in the early morning. Later in the day, he invited the public of any nationality to participate in dismantling the wall one timber at a time. Afterwards, each timber was given a protective coating and signed by the artist, and participants were encouraged to take a part of the artwork home. *Muro* endures as a communally owned work of art, speaking to the hope that people, united, have the power to dismantle obstacles.

By acquiring a segment of the wall—twenty-five clay timbers—the Phillips became one of eight museums to participate in the public sharing of Sodi's art and his political message.[3]

---

1 See https://www.kasmingallery.com/artist/bosco-sodi. Accessed April 2020.

2 See https://www.kasmingallery.com/news/bosco-sodi--at-washington-square-park. Accessed April 2020. https://www.kasmingallery.com/__data/20d8fd632d6c886bc9f3fa67d3ce29ef.pdf. Accessed April 2020.

3 Other museums that have accepted portions of the wall are: the Museum of Contemporary Art San Diego, New Orleans Museum of Art, Des Moines Art Center, Wadsworth Atheneum Museum of Art, Nasher Sculpture Center, Walker Art Center, and Harvard Art Museums.

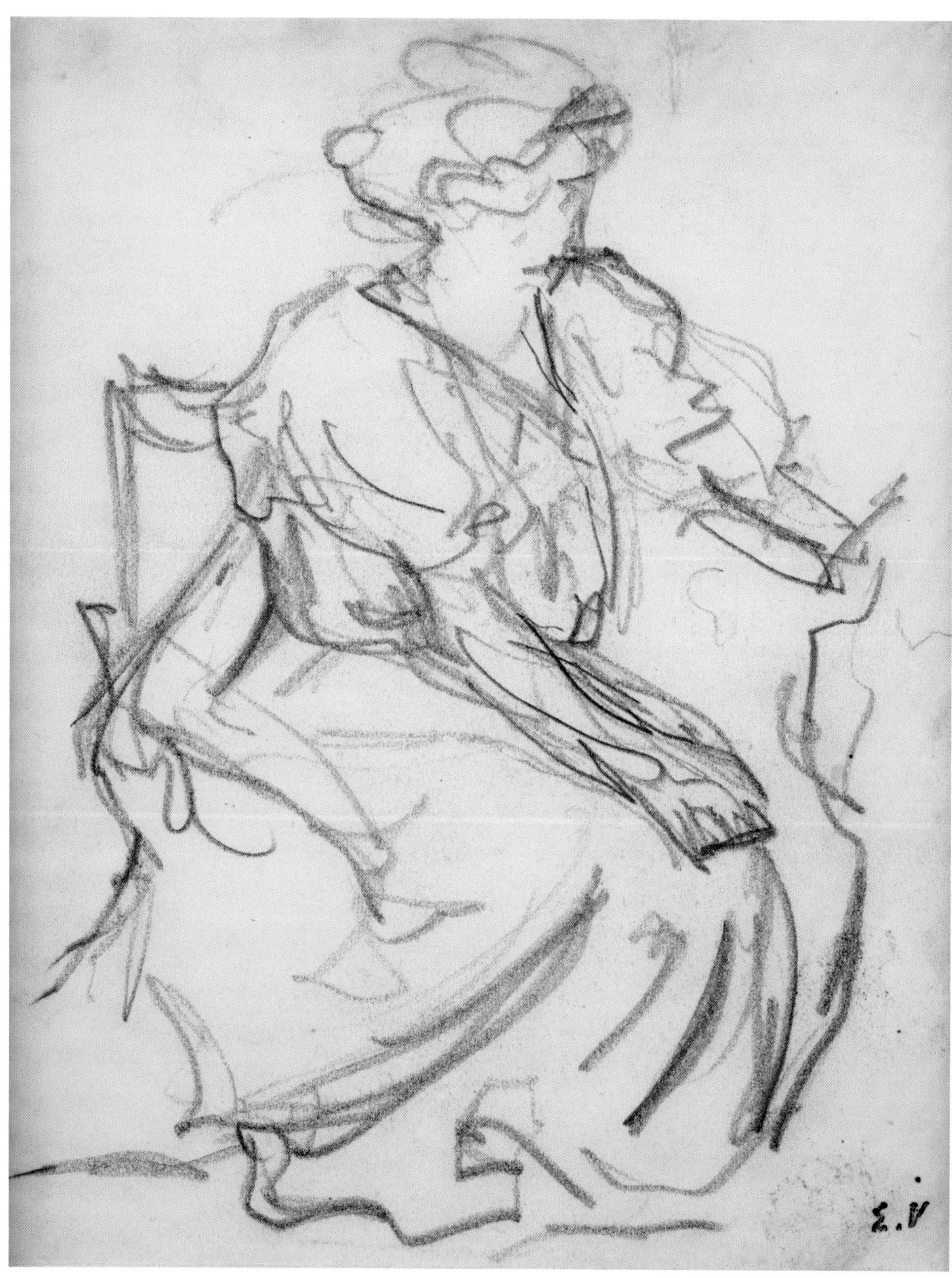

70
Édouard Vuillard
Lucy Hessel Seated in an Armchair, ca. 1912
Black pencil on paper,
5 1/2 × 4 3/8 in.
The Phillips Collection, Washington, DC,
Promised Gift of Jonathan and Roseann Aaronsohn.

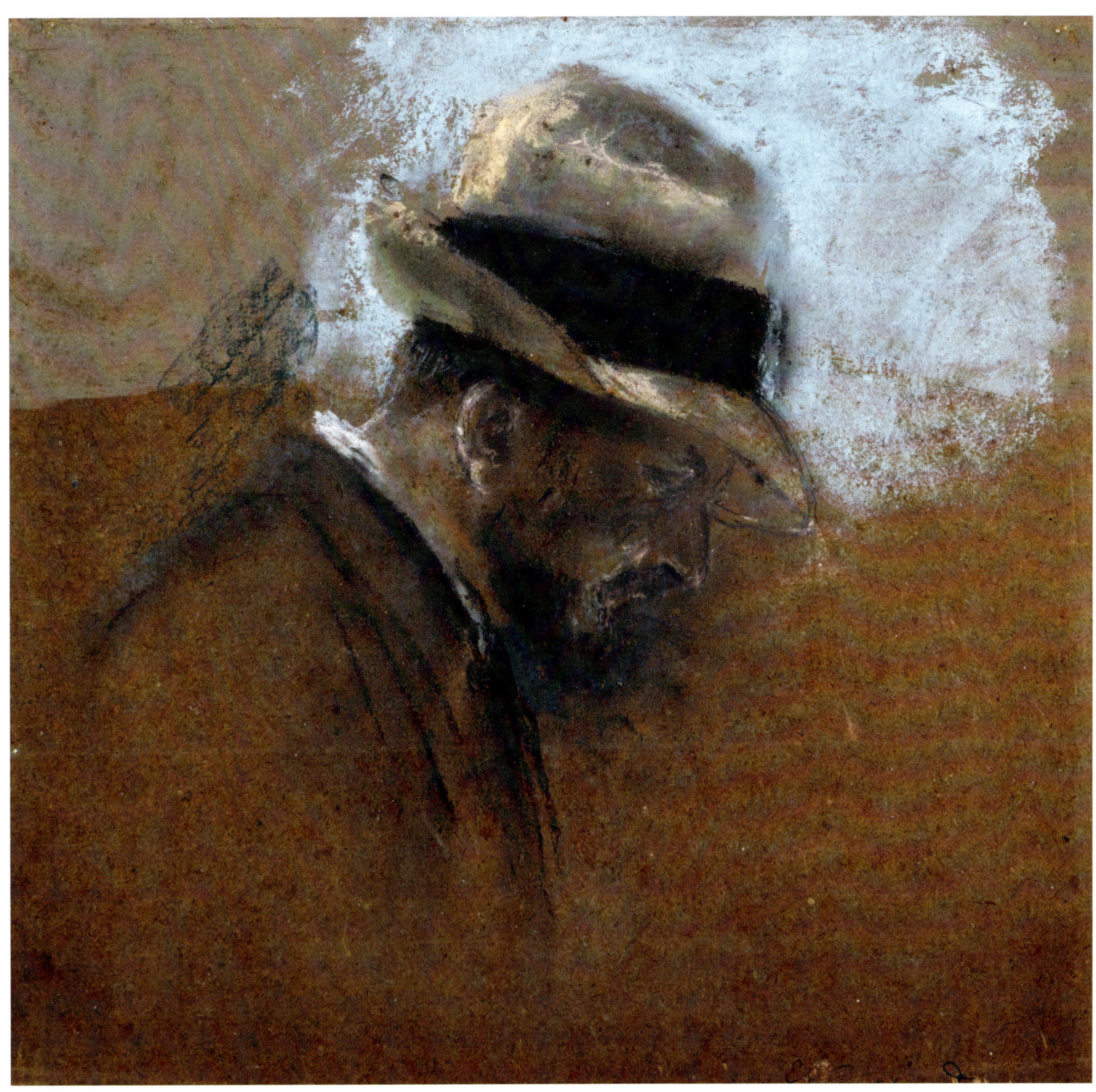

71
Édouard Vuillard
***Alexandre Natanson Seen in Profile*, 1907**
Pastel on brown paper,
10 1/4 × 9 7/8 in.
The Phillips Collection, Washington, DC,
Bequest of Seymour and Janet Rubin, 2003.

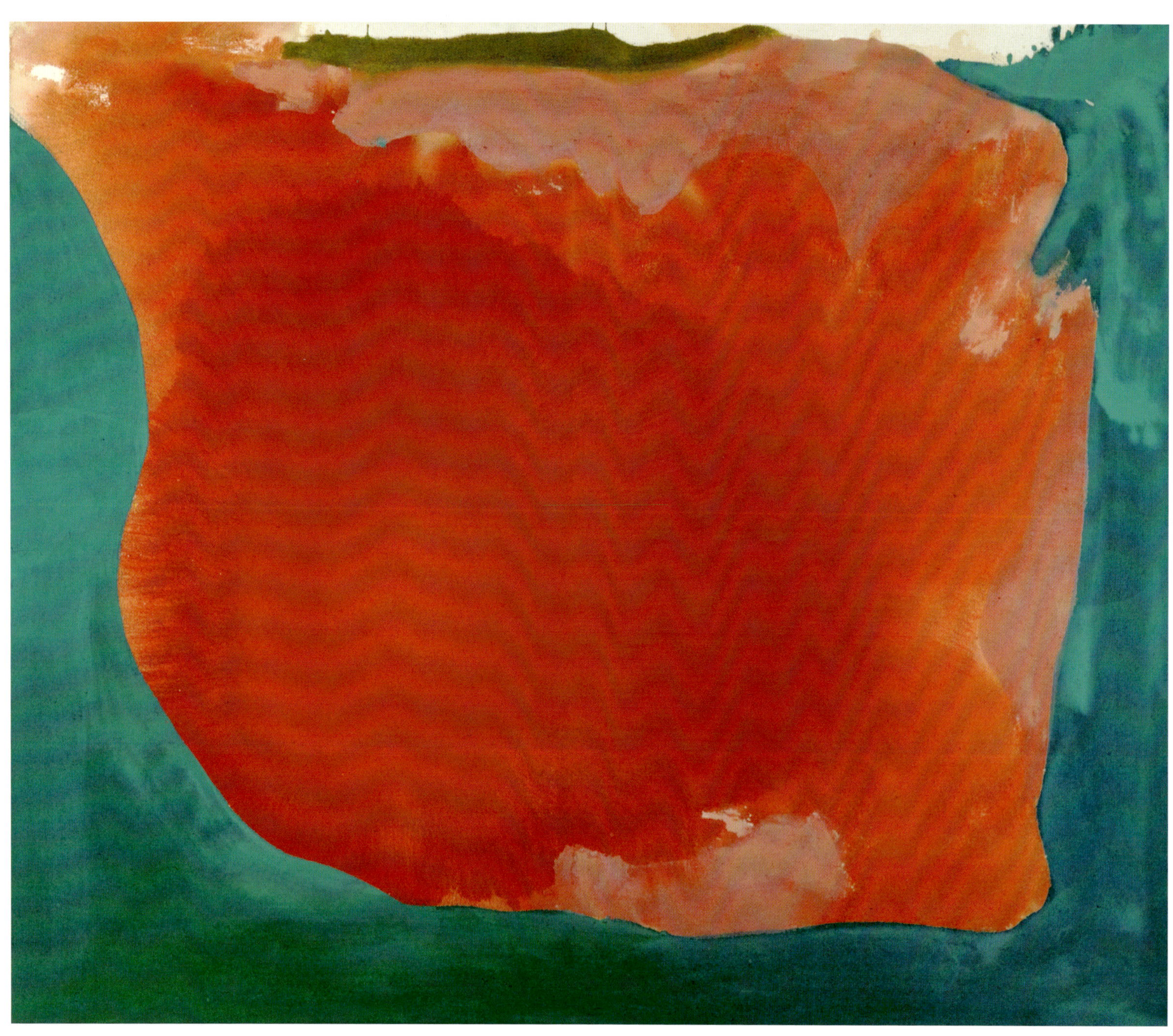

72
Helen Frankenthaler
***Canyon*, 1965**
Acrylic on canvas,
44 × 52 in.
The Phillips Collection, Washington, DC,
The Dreier Fund for Acquisitions and funds
given by Gifford Phillips, 2001.

HELEN FRANKENTHALER
CANYON, 1965

Renée Maurer

At fifteen, Helen Frankenthaler spent hours at the Museum of Modern Art advised by artist Rufino Tamayo, her teacher at The Dalton School. After studying painting at Bennington College, Vermont, Frankenthaler met, in 1950, critic Clement Greenberg and several artists from the New York school, including David Smith, Jackson Pollock, and her future husband, Robert Motherwell. Exposure to Pollock's art prompted Frankenthaler to jettison the easel and place the canvas on the floor to paint. In 1952, elements from nature began to permeate Frankenthaler's abstractions, as her memories from summer travels to Nova Scotia were absorbed and translated onto the canvas. That year, she produced the stained painting *Mountains and Sea* by pouring thinned oil paint onto raw, unprimed canvas. The process generated transparent, layered color fields that appear simultaneously flat and three-dimensional. Her compositional approach informed the work of Morris Louis, Kenneth Noland and others associated with the Washington Color school.

In 1963, Frankenthaler experimented with thinned acrylic paints, which dry quickly and without the turpentine residue of thinned oils. For Frankenthaler, acrylics were easier to control, and she could use them to create crisp edges between densely painted and transparent color areas.[1] Her explorations led to large-scale work that presented the dramatic interplay of vibrant hues. During 1964-65, Frankenthaler flooded primed canvases with poured acrylics, moving paint with brushes, rollers, sponges, and squeegees. In *Canyon*, hot oranges and reds pool and flow, while cool bluish greens curve and enclose the central fiery form. The chromatic saturations of this compact cropped image intensify and surge beyond the picture plane. Like earlier works, *Canyon* may evoke a sense of place, perhaps a confluence of memories from 1965—a trip northeast of Bennington following the death of David Smith, and excursions to the Greek islands and Croatia. More likely, *Canyon* reflects Frankenthaler's return to earlier compositional concerns like a reengagement with canvases such as *Tangerine* (1964, private collection), larger in scale but similar in color scheme.

In 1966, Frankenthaler was one of four artists chosen to represent the United States in the Venice Biennale. The following year, Andre Emmerich Gallery loaned *Canyon* to the International Council of the Museum of Modern Art's 1967 "Art in Embassies" exhibition in Montreal at the residence of General Richard Hawkins Jr., Consul General of the United States. In the brochure for the exhibition, Frankenthaler described her process: "A really good picture looks as if it's all happened at once.... I think very often it takes ten of those over-labored efforts to produce one really beautiful wrist motion that is synchronized with your head and heart, and you have it, and therefore it looks as if it were born in a minute."[2] *Canyon* was the first painting by the artist acquired by the Phillips; other important examples supplement the collection, including an early oil, a complex woodcut (see pl. 172), and a later print.

---

1 E. C. Goossen, *Helen Frankenthaler* (New York: International Council of the Museum of Modern Art, 1969), 13-14.

2 Quoted by Michelle Harvey, Museum of Modern Art, New York, in a letter to Jessie Fertig, The Phillips Collection, Curatorial Department, January 27, 2003, object file, Phillips Collection Archives, Washington, DC.

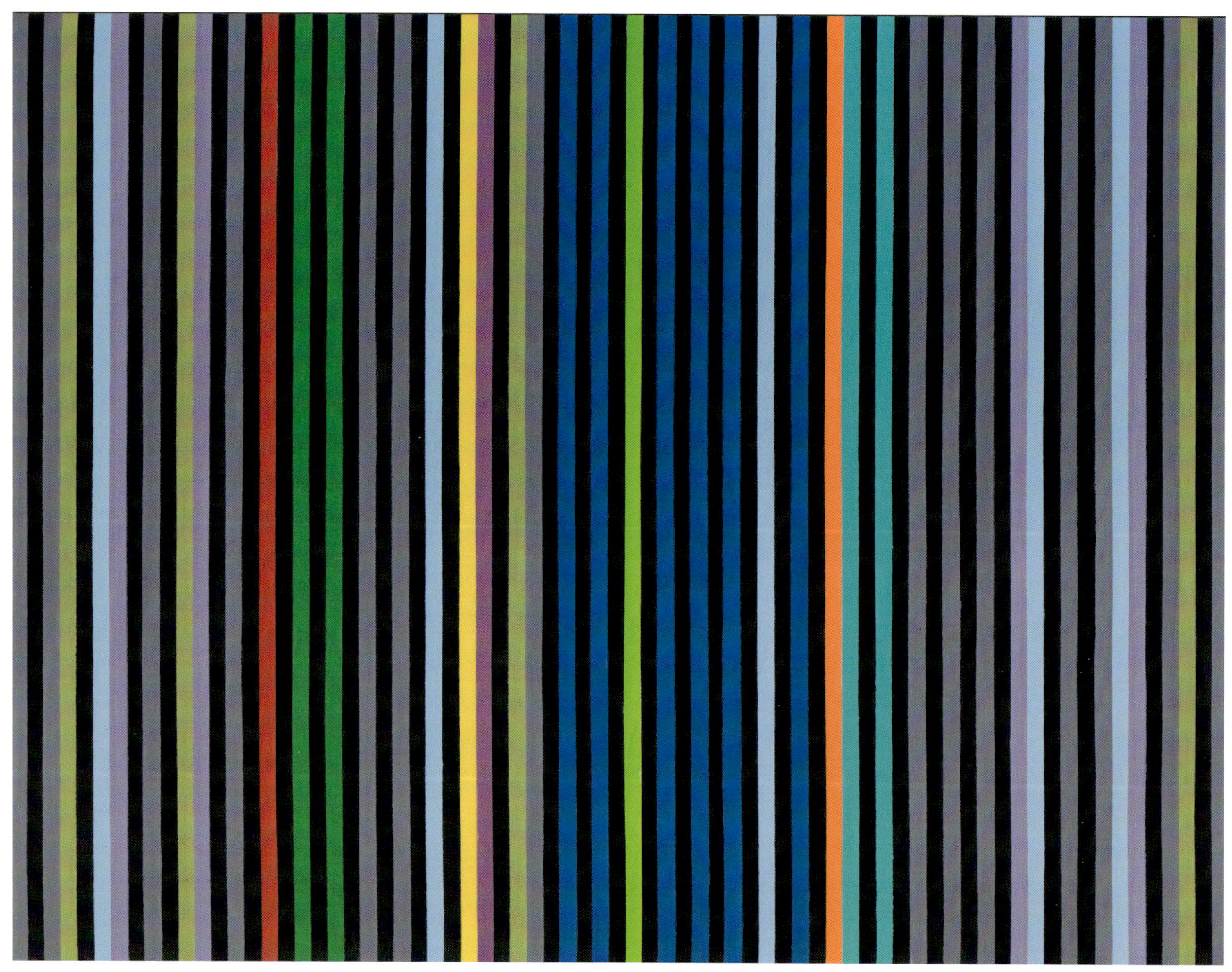

73
Gene Davis
65-2, 1965
Acrylic on canvas,
58 1/4 × 74 in.
The Phillips Collection, Washington, DC,
Gift of Richard E. Thompson, 2017.

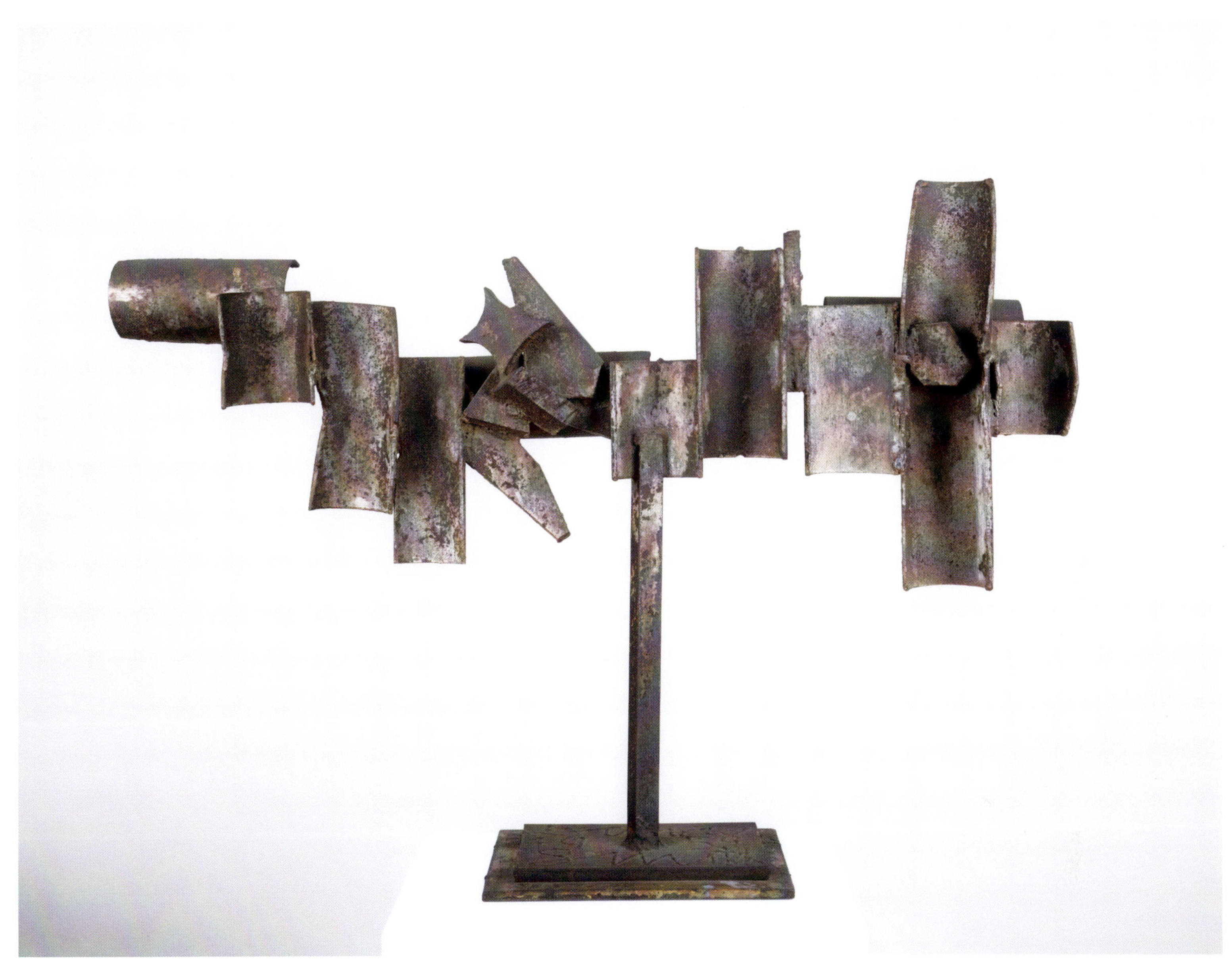

74
David Smith
Bouquet of Concaves, 1959
Steel with paint,
27 1/2 × 38 1/2 × 8 in.
The Phillips Collection, Washington, DC,
Gift of Gifford and Joann Phillips, 2008.

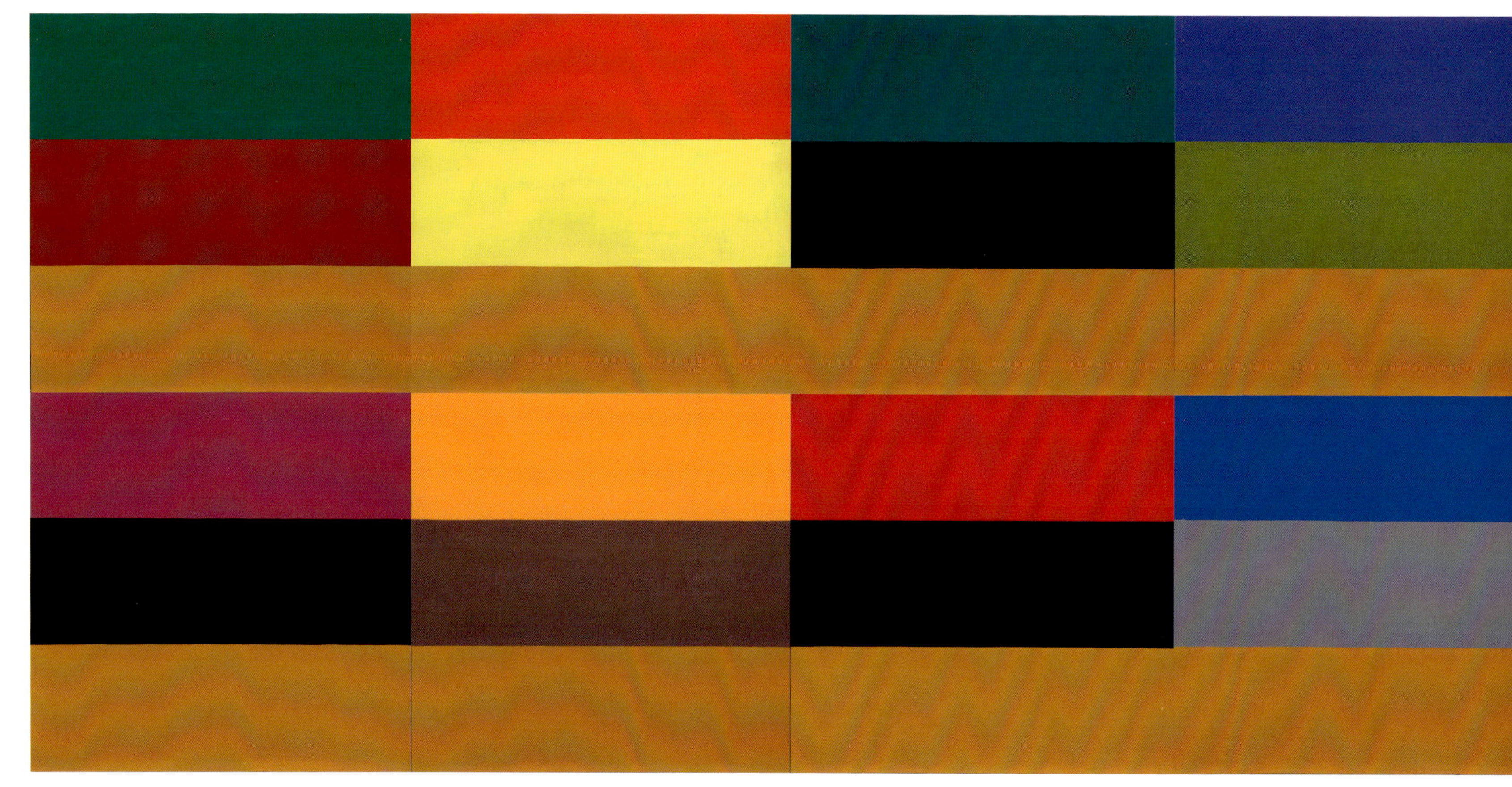

75
Poul Gernes
***Untitled (stripe series with ochre as recurring color)*, 1965**
16 enamel on hardboards,
each: 48 × 48 in.
The Phillips Collection, Washington, DC,
Acquired in 2019 with support from the Ny Carlsbergfondet.

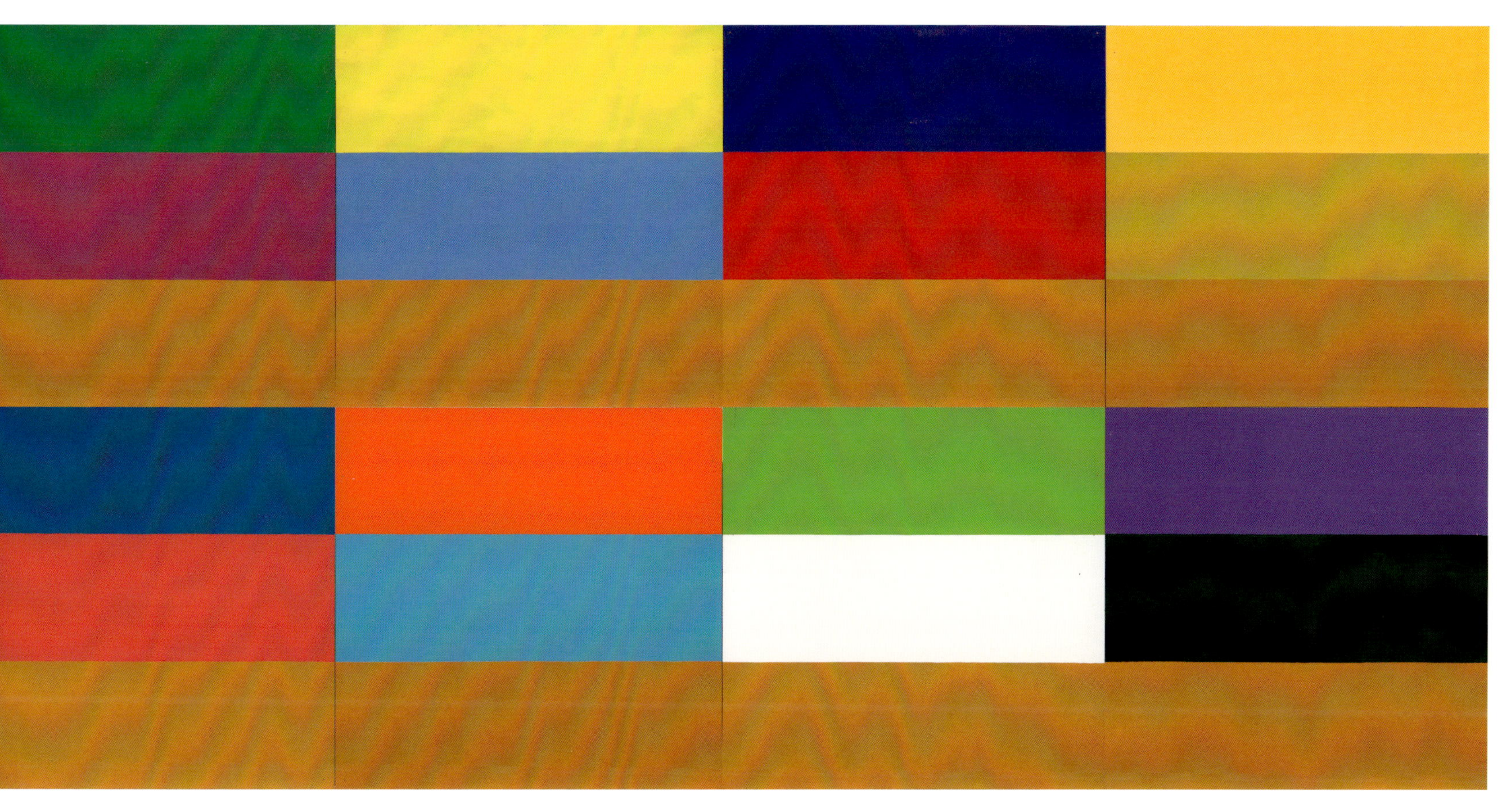

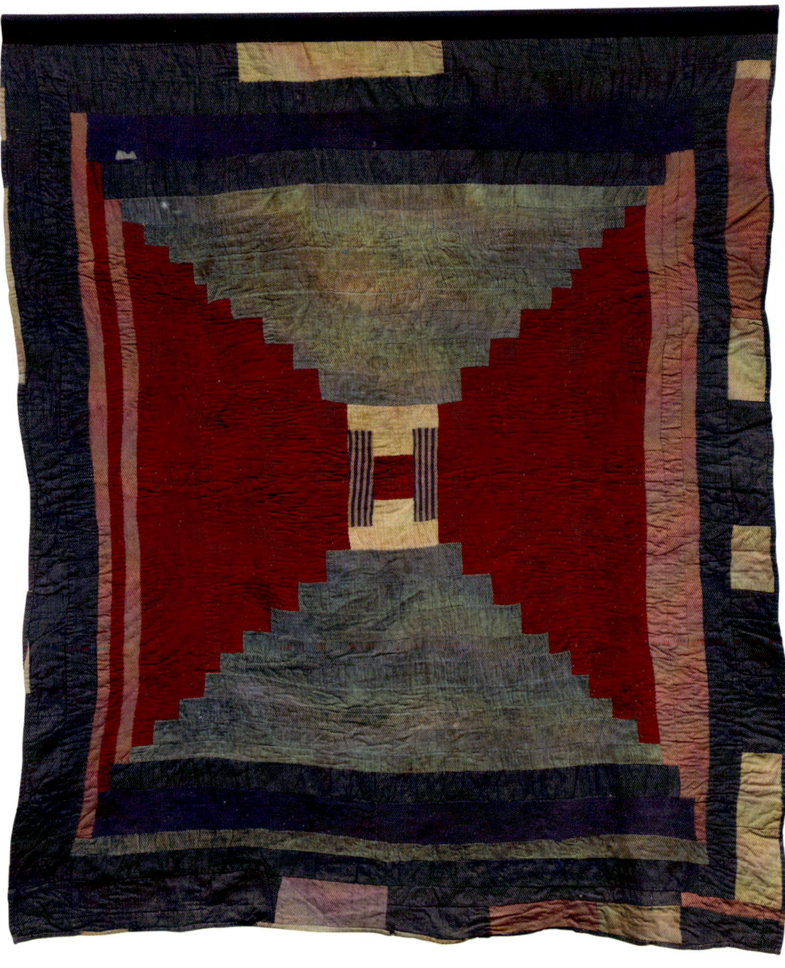

76
Lucy T. Pettway
***Two-sided quilt: blocks and strips and "Bricklayer,"* 1960s**
Double-sided quilt: blue denim cotton, red cotton, white cotton and wool fabrics,
81 × 73 in.
The Phillips Collection, Washington, DC,
Museum purchase, and gift of the Souls Grown Deep Foundation from the William S. Arnett Collection, 2019.

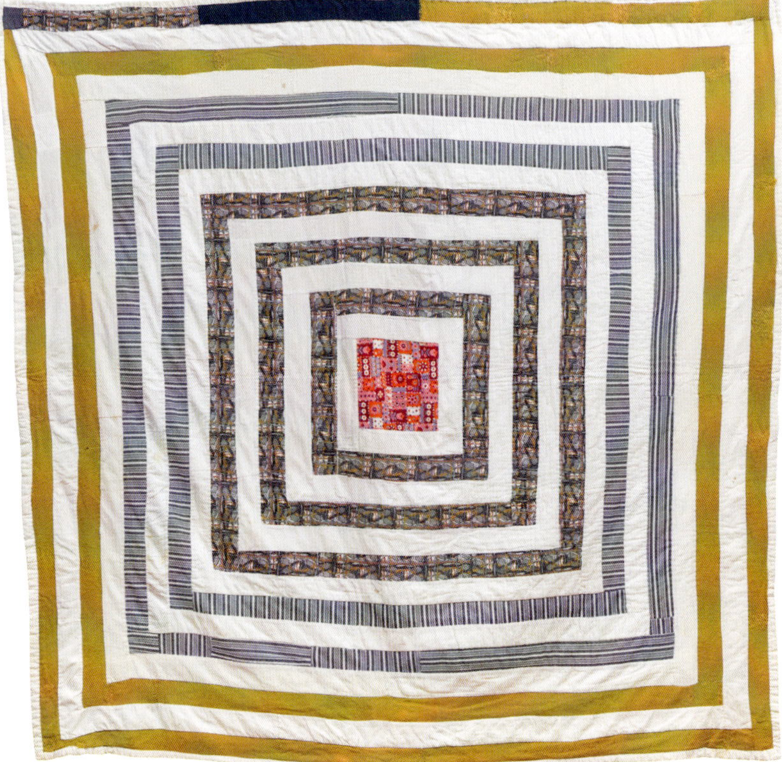

77
Malissia Pettway
***"Housetop,"* ca. 1960**
Printed cotton, cotton corduroy, cotton knit, polyester and damask fabrics with cotton flour sack cloth backing,
81 × 81 in.
The Phillips Collection, Washington, DC,
Museum purchase, and gift of the Souls Grown Deep Foundation from the William S. Arnett Collection, 2019.

LUCY T. PETTWAY
TWO-SIDED QUILT: BLOCKS AND STRIPS AND "BRICKLAYER," 1960s

Raina Lampkins-Fielder

Situated on the banks of the Alabama River, Gee's Bend resembles an inland island, surrounded as it is on three sides by water. This geographically isolated community has given rise to generations of African American quiltmakers possessed of peerless creative talents unparalleled in American art. It was within this rich artistic environment that Lucy T. Pettway distinguished herself as a master quiltmaker.

Always with a pencil and paper at hand, from a young age Lucy was a keen observer, sketching patterns and forms that would later serve as inspiration for her quilt designs. She studied her craft under the tutelage of her aunts, Martha Jane Pettway and Arie Pettway, both serious practitioners of the art form, and other members of the collaborative quilting community in Gee's Bend. This alternative academy has nourished over a century of talented quiltmakers—with porches and kitchens acting in place of traditional studios and lecture halls—and is a testament to the ingenuity born of necessity and scarcity.

Although Pettway eschewed confining her work to one specific style, *Two-sided quilt: blocks and strips and "Bricklayer"* (pl. 76) is a remarkable example of the locally named "Bricklayer" pattern, one of the preferred styles of the women of Gee's Bend.

On the top side of the quilt, Pettway pieces her fabric to mesmerizing effect as she builds the Bricklayer pattern out from the central block, aligning horizontal lines of faded blue denim with vertical red- and rose-colored strips. While her color palette was diverse, she was particularly drawn to red and pink hues. The internal push and pull—a visual call and response—seduces the eye with its perspectival play.

The bottom side of the quilt further demonstrates the improvisational impulses of the artist, where blocks and strips break free from the architectural symmetry of Bricklayer and are here deconstructed into their component parts. The lone strip of pink—perhaps a nod to the dominant conversation on the top side—illustrates the visual patchwork poetry in Pettway's work.

Mining the creative potential of discarded materials, Pettway's use of disused and recycled cloth, characteristic of many Gee's Bend quilts, is a bricolage of sorts, composed of clothing worn laboring in fields and factories and the remnants of ragged shirts and dresses. Mary Margaret Pettway, the artist's daughter and a third-generation quiltmaker, recalled receiving parcels of clothing from relatives in New York, noting that the pink material came from a childhood dress. The blue strips were cut from the jeans of her cousin; the quilt itself covered his bed for many years.

Both as functional objects to warm the family during harsh winters in unheated homes and as masterful works of art, Lucy T. Pettway's work acts as an extended family portrait, with ancestral echoes detected in shirt tails and faded knees. In *Two-sided quilt: blocks and strips and "Bricklayer"* and other quilts, Pettway has transformed these relics into some of the most compelling abstract art in any tradition.

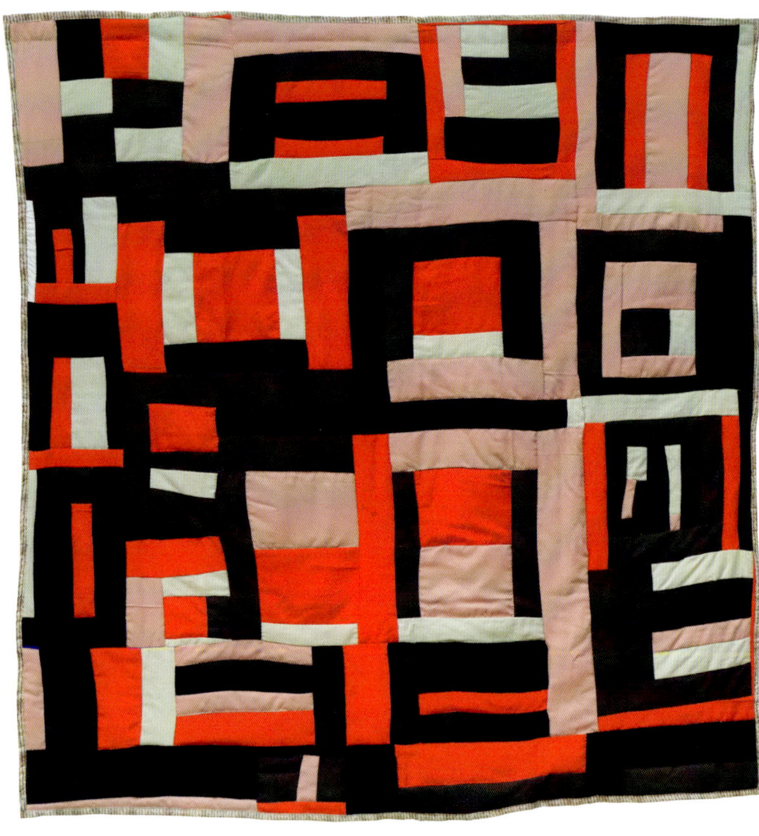

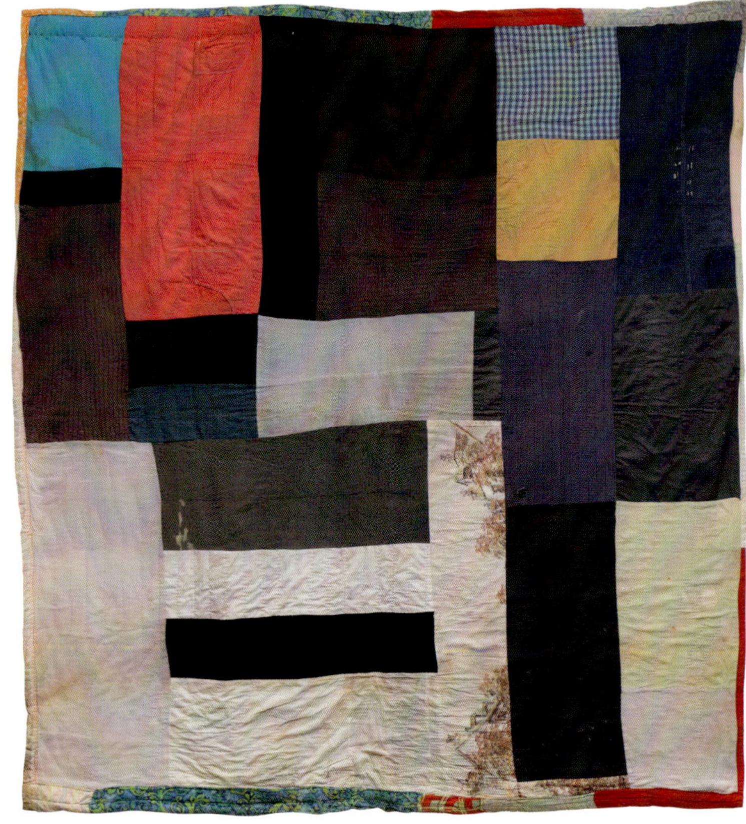

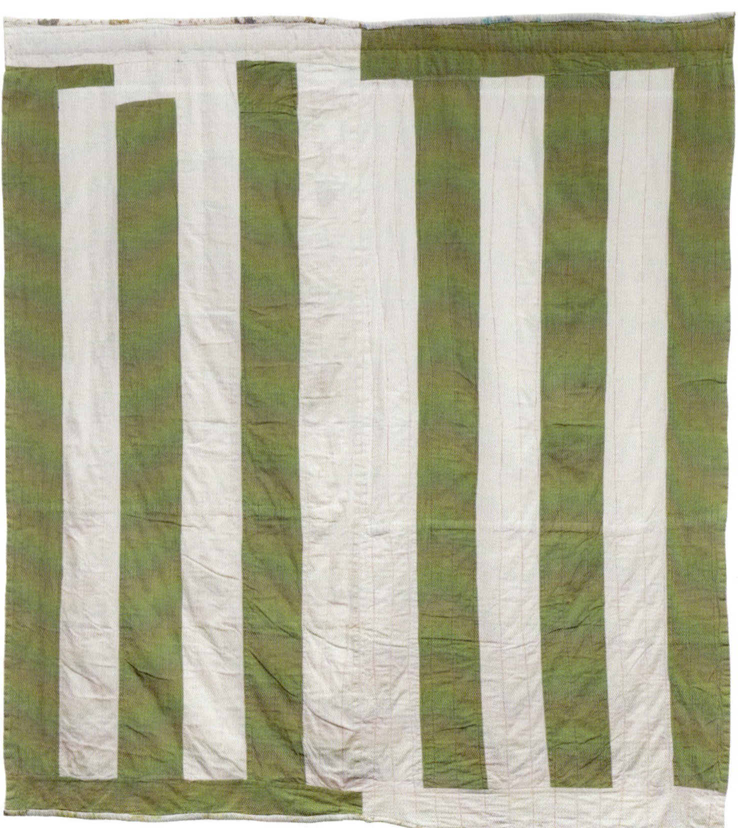

78 (top left)
Mary Lee Bendolph
***"Housetop" variation*, 1998**
Printed and multicolored cotton and wool fabrics, 72 × 76 in.
The Phillips Collection, Washington, DC, Museum purchase, and gift of the Souls Grown Deep Foundation from the William S. Arnett Collection, 2019.

79 (top right)
Aolar Mosely
***Blocks*, ca. 1955**
Cotton denim, red cotton overalls, used work clothes, muslin and other miscellaneous fabrics, 75 × 83 in.
The Phillips Collection, Washington, DC, Museum purchase, and gift of the Souls Grown Deep Foundation from the William S. Arnett Collection, 2019.

80 (bottom)
Arlonzia Pettway
***"Lazy Gals" ("Bars")*, ca. 1975**
Cotton corduroy fabrics with polyester fabric backing, 89 × 81 in.
The Phillips Collection, Washington, DC, Museum purchase, and gift of the Souls Grown Deep Foundation from the William S. Arnett Collection, 2019.

GEE'S BEND QUILTS, 1950S–1990S, AND MCARTHUR BINION, *DNA: BLACK PAINTING: 1*, 2015

Makeba Clay

For me, the power of art lies in its capacity to tell and share stories across time, place, and context. In a recent article,[1] I discussed the restorative impact art can have when it truly resonates with the core of our humanity. The quilts of Gee's Bend (pls. 76–80) and McArthur Binion's work *DNA: Black Painting: 1* (pl. 81) underscore the power of connecting memory, belonging, identity, and personal narrative through art.

The quilts of Gee's Bend feature memory, personal identity, and narrative. For Gee's Bend, the tradition of the patchwork quilt was born of scarcity and resourcefulness, arising when shortages of cloth called for the inventive salvaging of fabric scraps and remnants.[2] The transformation of mundane and overlooked objects into extraordinary things is a practice of conversion that Binion too has mastered.

Similarly, Binion intertwines autobiography and personal experience with the fiber of his creations. In works such as *DNA: Black Painting: 1*, he employs grids, hand-drawn lines, and photocopied versions of his birth certificate. Though his work is deeply personal, incorporating numbers from his phonebook and other private ephemera, Binion's biographical insertions create access points for others. For example, the materiality of his birth certificate, which designates his race as Black, calls forth the "one-drop rule"[3] and sheds light on the social conditions and perspectives that shaped his life and the lives of millions of others.

In these ways, the Gee's Bend community's and McArthur Binion's works speak to a universal experience of Black people in the United States, stressing the ways racial boundaries were enforced and understood, the ways people survived and even thrived despite that system.

The interplay of medium and narrative in the work of Gee's Bend and of Binion exemplifies how objects and simple forms can create language.[4] As the chief diversity officer of The Phillips Collection, I fix on language as the entry point for larger conversations that our society needs to have about race, equity, and community. We need artists to catalyze these conversations by creatively infusing humanity into topics that are often nuanced and messy, that require us to look at our history and actions critically, and to take responsibility for things we would much sooner forget.

Stories have been found to trigger chemical responses in our brains that are associated with empathy.[5] Now more than ever, we need that empathy to bridge the divides in our communities and remind us of all that unites us. Binion and the quiltmakers at Gee's Bend, alongside many others whose work is exhibited at The Phillips Collection, help us to do just that.

---

1 https://www.aam-us.org/2020/02/05/the-transformative-power-of-inclusive-storytelling-in-museums/. Accessed April 2020.

2 See https://www.soulsgrowndeep.org/gees-bend-quiltmakers. Accessed April 2020.

3 According to the one-drop rule, a social and legal principle of racial classification historically prominent in the United States in the twentieth century, a person with even one ancestor of African heritage ("one drop" of Black blood) is considered Black. Extensive literature on the one-drop rule attests to its persistence today.

4 See https://www.artspace.com/magazine/interviews_features/qa/in-a-predominately-white-art-world-mcarthur-binion-had-to-make-himself-up-to-succeed-54340. Accessed April 2020.

5 See https://hbr.org/2014/10/why-your-brain-loves-good-storytelling. Accessed April 2020.

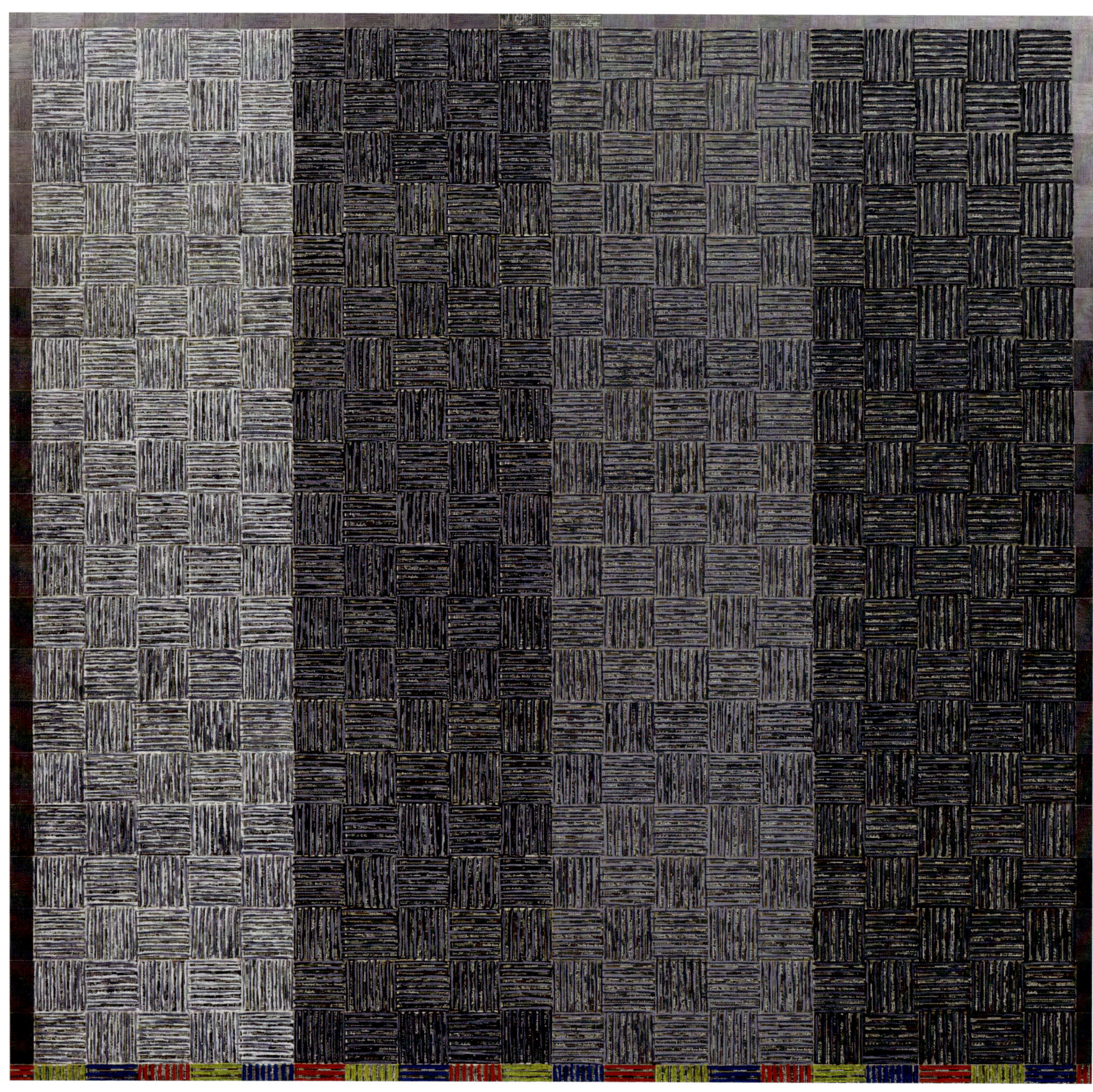

81
McArthur Binion
***DNA: Black Painting: 1*, 2015**
Paint stick, graphite, and collaged paper on board,
84 × 84 in.
The Phillips Collection, Washington, DC,
Director's Discretionary Fund, 2016.

MCARTHUR BINION
DNA: BLACK PAINTING: 1, 2015

Jenna Wortham

Fractals are seductive, dynamic systems defined by repetition. Gazing into them shifts your perception, inducing new neural frequencies. Landscapes reassemble, birthing hidden symmetries. The abstract starts to become familiar, like a mirror, showing new shapes and logic. New truths. This is the mystery and enigma that many of McArthur Binion's DNA grids invoke. They may appear minimalist, but they are laden with information rendered invisible. Encoded. Binion calls this the "under conscious"[1] of the work.

In *DNA: Black Painting: 1*, the terrain of the painting is made up of several equally sized parts and subparts, ad infinitum. The oil slick strokes create squares that grow into columns, which, in turn, create a large map on canvas that is a recapitulation of the original marks. The labor is immediately apparent, invoking awe at the time and process required. But the work doesn't stop there. The strokes are interwoven with shards of Binion's handwriting, lifted from an old address book, an intimate interlacing, which is only revealed to those who come close enough to see. Leaving traces of these intimate geographies and personal histories in one's work is an invitation. Labor begets labor. The more time you spend with the work, the likelier you are to unearth a map to Binion's memories. Of the intentional obfuscation, Binion says, "you are going to have to look really hard to see it under the paint. This is not about race, this is about history and images, about saying more with a lot less."[2]

In this way, the work itself is recursive, its own variant of fractal, discreet marks with the ability to become something else, something human. Binion often says he "made himself up,"[3] and in the work, he spreads himself out, too, by creating holy patterns of repetition that erect data about humans when they're complete, like DNA itself. It would be a mistake to see these works as merely an abstraction, though Binion allows for that entry-level reading, even as he complicates the concept, adding emotion by burying crucial and fraught personal information beneath all that sanguineness. The end result is being drawn in by the patterns, and awakened, sharply, by what lies beneath. Black artists are overburdened with responsibility—to explicate Black identity, and to tell the truth about America, to be its teachable moments. Binion refuses that responsibility. The work is both about that resistance, and a reminder that with the work, as with our country, if you want to look, it's all right there, in plain sight. The work reminds me of the poet Samiya Bashir, who also commandeers known laws of nature and mathematics, and reroutes them for her own use. In "Field Theories," she asks, "what is a thing of beauty / if not us? Repeat."[4]

---

1 https://frieze.com/article/mcarthur-binion. Accessed April 2020.

2 https://noma.org/mcarthur-binions-dna-painting-highlight-venice-biennale. Accessed April 2020.

3 https://www.artspace.com/magazine/interviews_features/qa/in-a-predominately-white-art-world-mcarthur-binion-had-to-make-himself-up-to-succeed-54340. Accessed April 2020.

4 https://poets.org/poem/field-theories. Accessed April 2020.

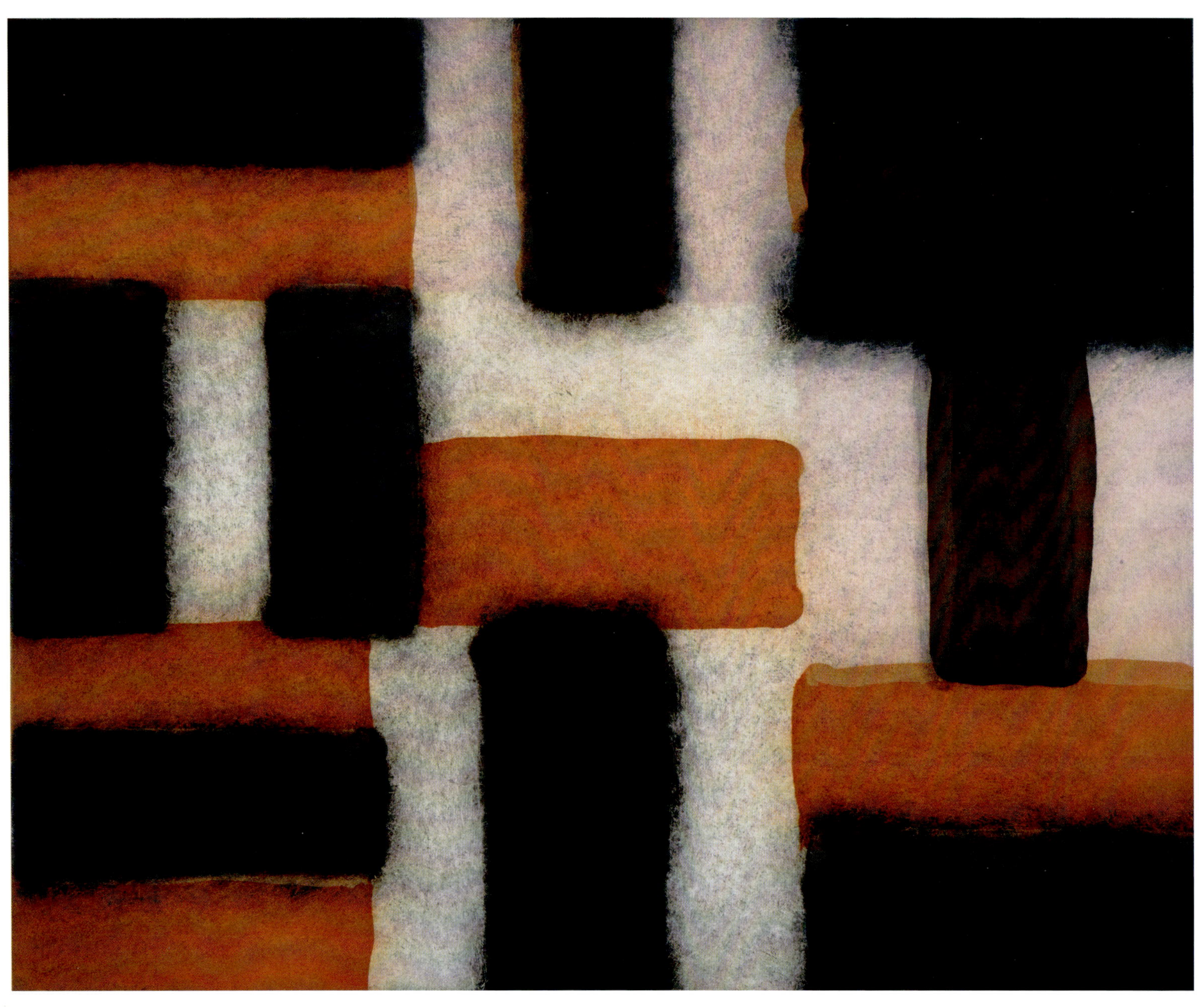

82
Sean Scully
***Day*, 2005**
Color aquatint with lift-ground and spit-bite, overall: 22 1/2 × 25 in.
The Phillips Collection, Washington, DC, Gift of the artist, 2005.

SEAN SCULLY
DAY, 2005

Renée Stout

Sean Scully: Twenty Years (1976–1995), a traveling exhibition installed in its second venue at the High Museum of Art in Atlanta, Georgia, in the fall and winter of 1995–1996, was my first encounter with the works of the painter. I recall walking through the elegant galleries feeling curious but somewhat detached from the hulking abstractions, with their wide swaths of subdued color. I left the museum that day, at the time unfazed by what I had seen. Yet for years to come, those works would remain someplace at the periphery of my mind. A mystery at the time, but in hindsight it had everything to do with the way certain works of art can speak to our core on a subconscious level, even as we consciously tell ourselves that they are "not our cup of tea."

As time passed, Sean's works would resonate more each time I discovered one in a museum in whichever city I found myself. I finally came to understand, but remained unable to articulate the depths of emotion the work seemed to stir within me. These same pangs of wistfulness would occur whenever I viewed the works of Giorgio de Chirico, Edward Hopper, and Charles Burchfield, but even more so, Giorgio Morandi. I include Sean in this group I call "the painters of melancholy." That phrase came as I pondered their works and realized that images could evoke specific words and words could evoke specific images. There is a kind of conceptual beauty in the word "melancholy," in that it sounds and looks like the state it defines. Of all the words in the English language, it's the one I would choose to represent the human condition.

Sean Scully is a complex and pensive man, but in these dark and troubling times, the melancholy of his paintings is not dark or foreboding, but rather the conveyance of a feeling that someone, something, sometime or somewhere, that once brought so much happiness, peace and solace, is now locked irretrievably in the past. The feeling is persistent and haunting, because we can never fully recall or grasp the elusive source of that sense of bittersweet longing. I squint at Morandi still-life compositions and see the horizontals, verticals and squares of Sean's paintings. I look at *Day* and I envision my half-remembered memories, compartmentalized and stacked like secret rooms and doorways that remain inaccessible and tinged with nostalgia.

Perhaps the word that captures the essence of *Day* best is the Welsh word *hiraeth*. A common pronunciation of the word is "hear-eye-th," which roughly translates as the yearning and longing for, or the missing of, something you can never return to, or that never really was.

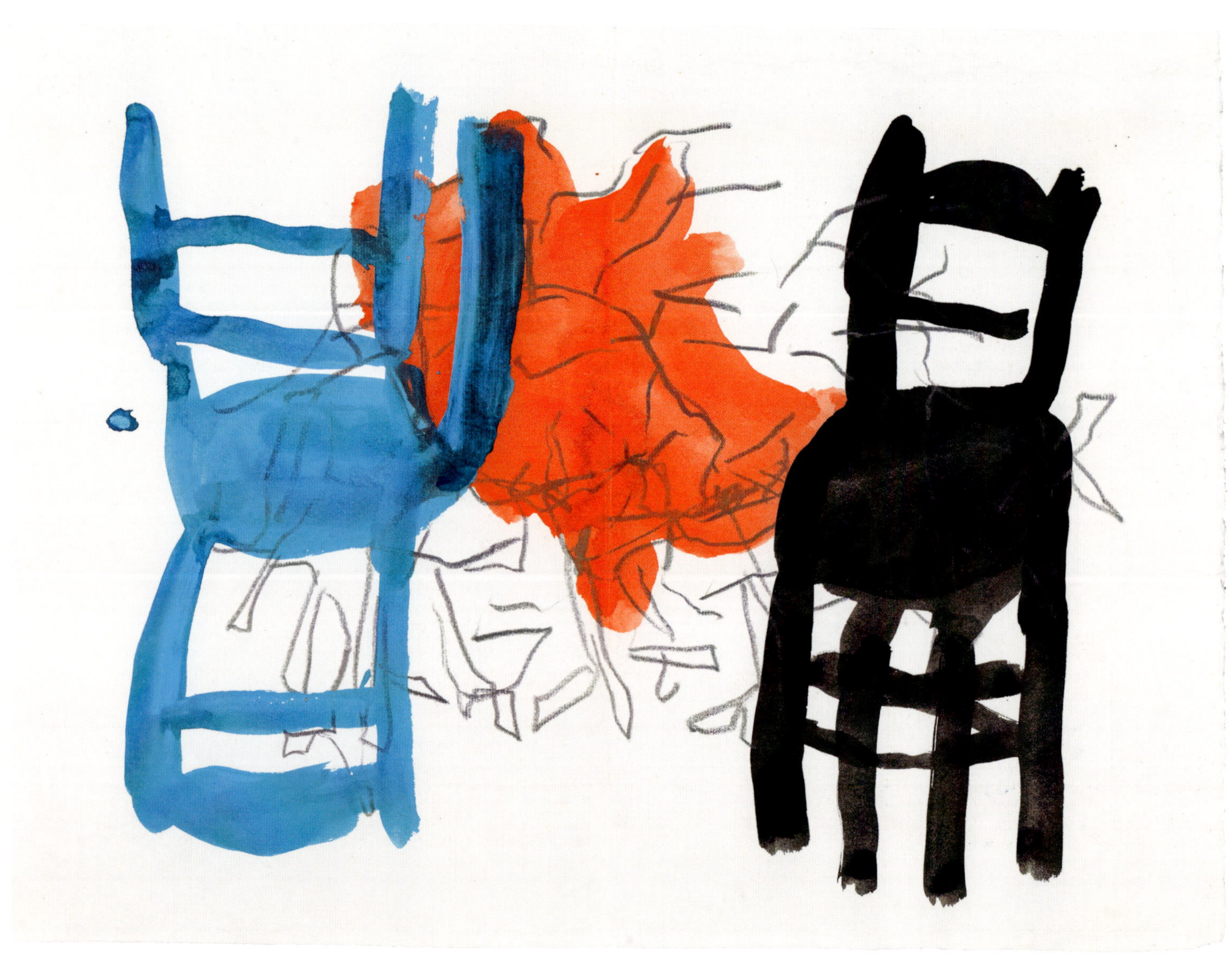

83
Georg Baselitz
***La sedia di Paolo*, 1988**
Opaque watercolor and black ink on Japanese paper,
13 3/4 × 18 in.
The Phillips Collection, Washington, DC,
Gift of Michael Werner, 2015.

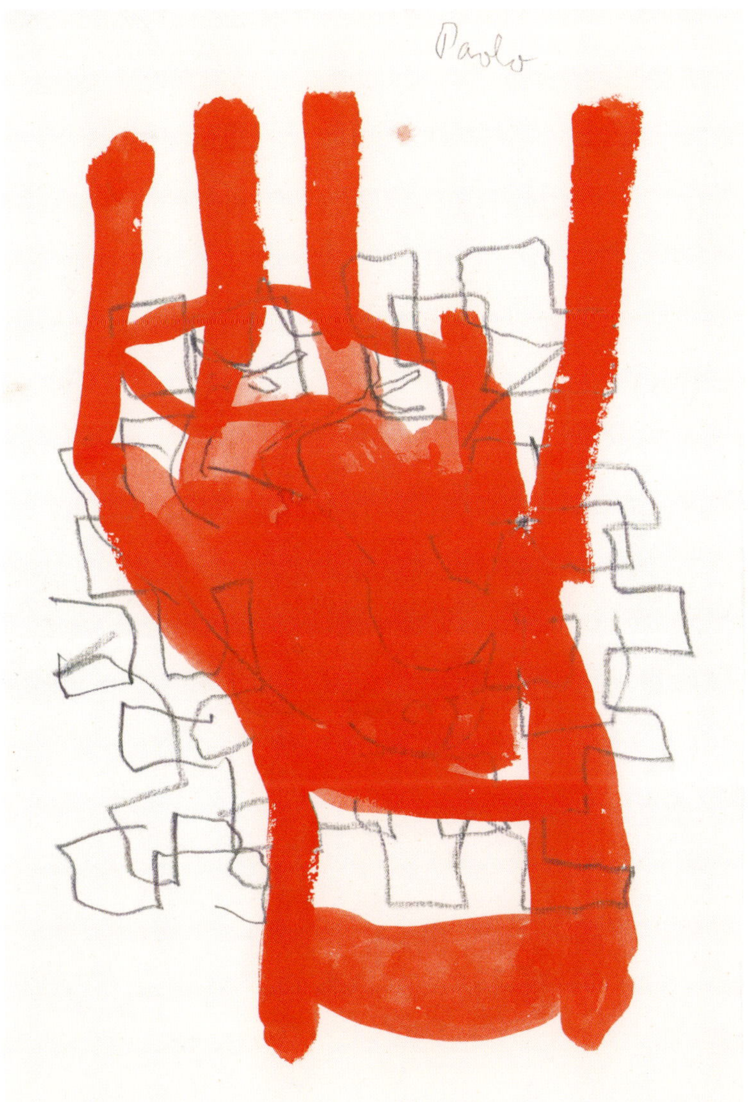

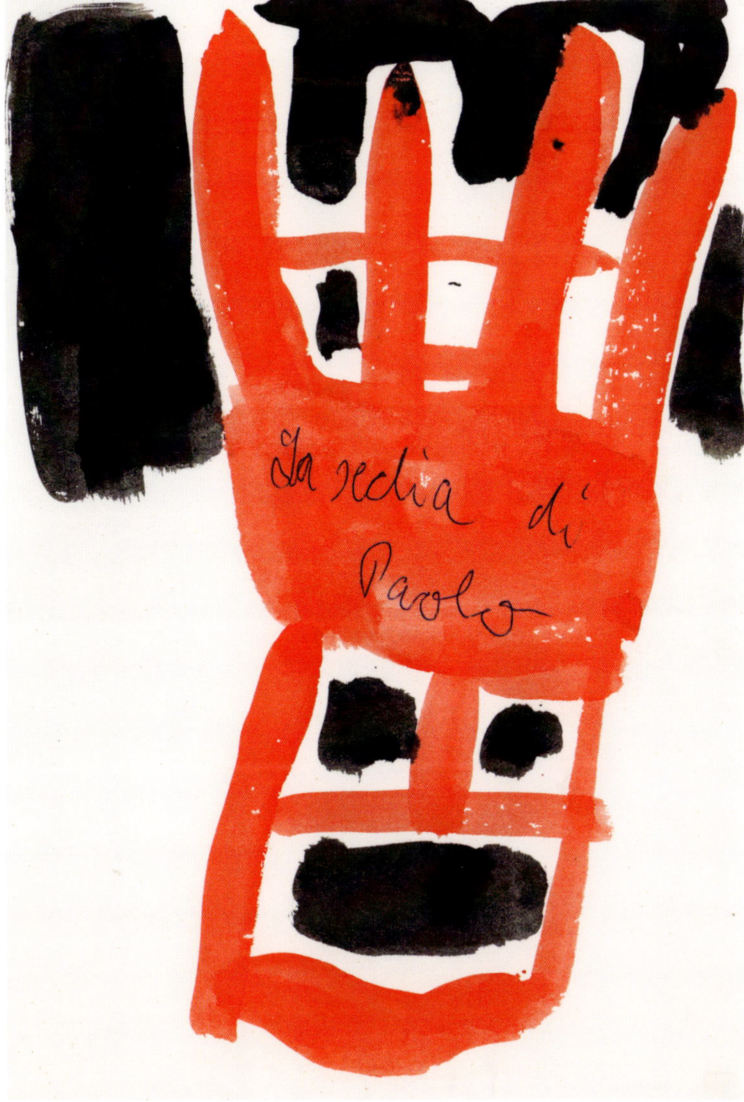

84
Georg Baselitz
***La sedia di Paolo*, 1988**
Opaque watercolor and black ink on Japanese paper, 13 3/4 × 9 1/4 in.
The Phillips Collection, Washington, DC, Gift of Michael Werner, 2015.

85
Georg Baselitz
***La sedia di Paolo*, 1988**
Opaque watercolor and black ink on Japanese paper, 13 3/4 × 9 1/4 in.
The Phillips Collection, Washington, DC, Gift of Michael Werner, 2015.

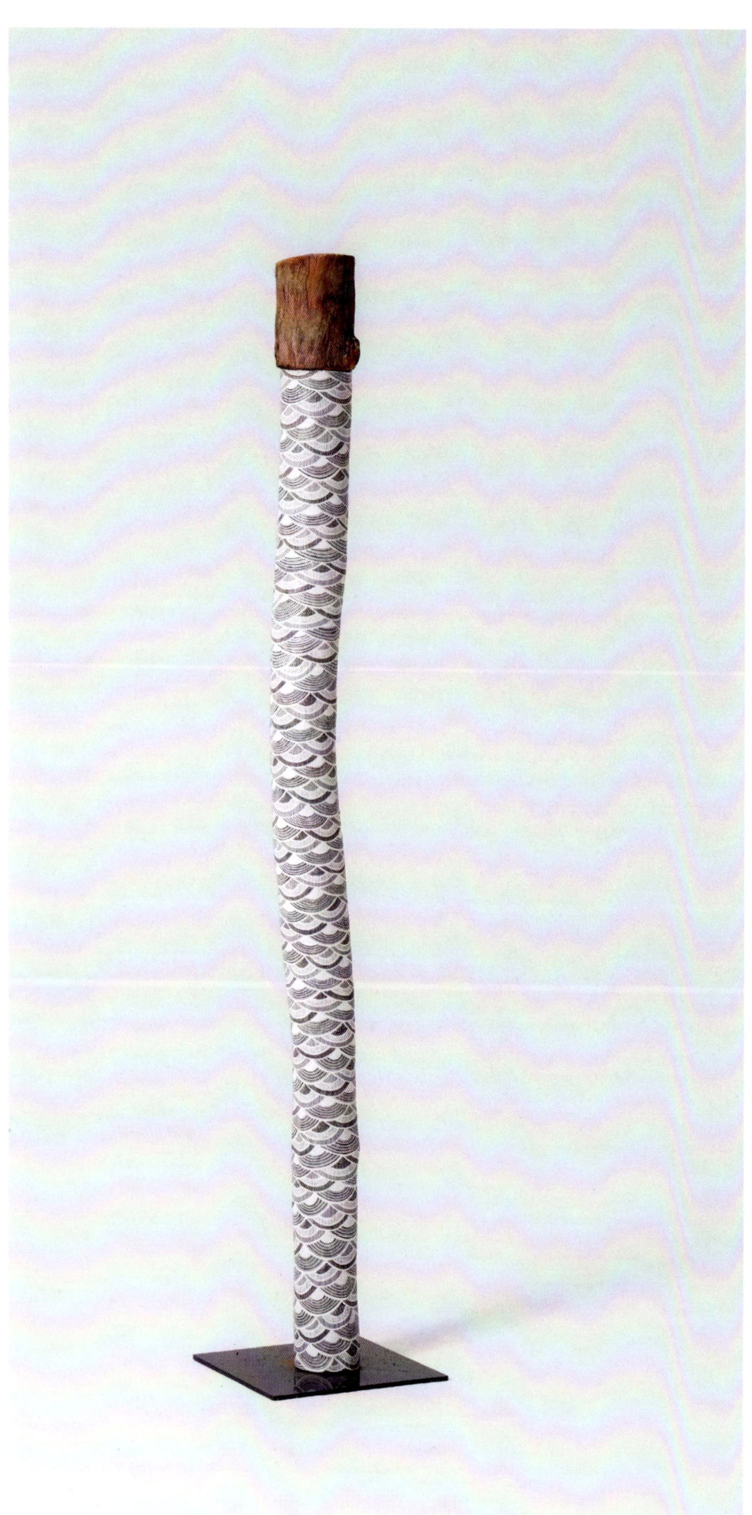

86
Dhurrumuwuy Marika
***Rulyapa*, 2018**
Natural earth pigments on hollow log,
90 1/2 in. high
The Phillips Collection, Washington, DC,
Promised Gift of Dennis and Debra Scholl.

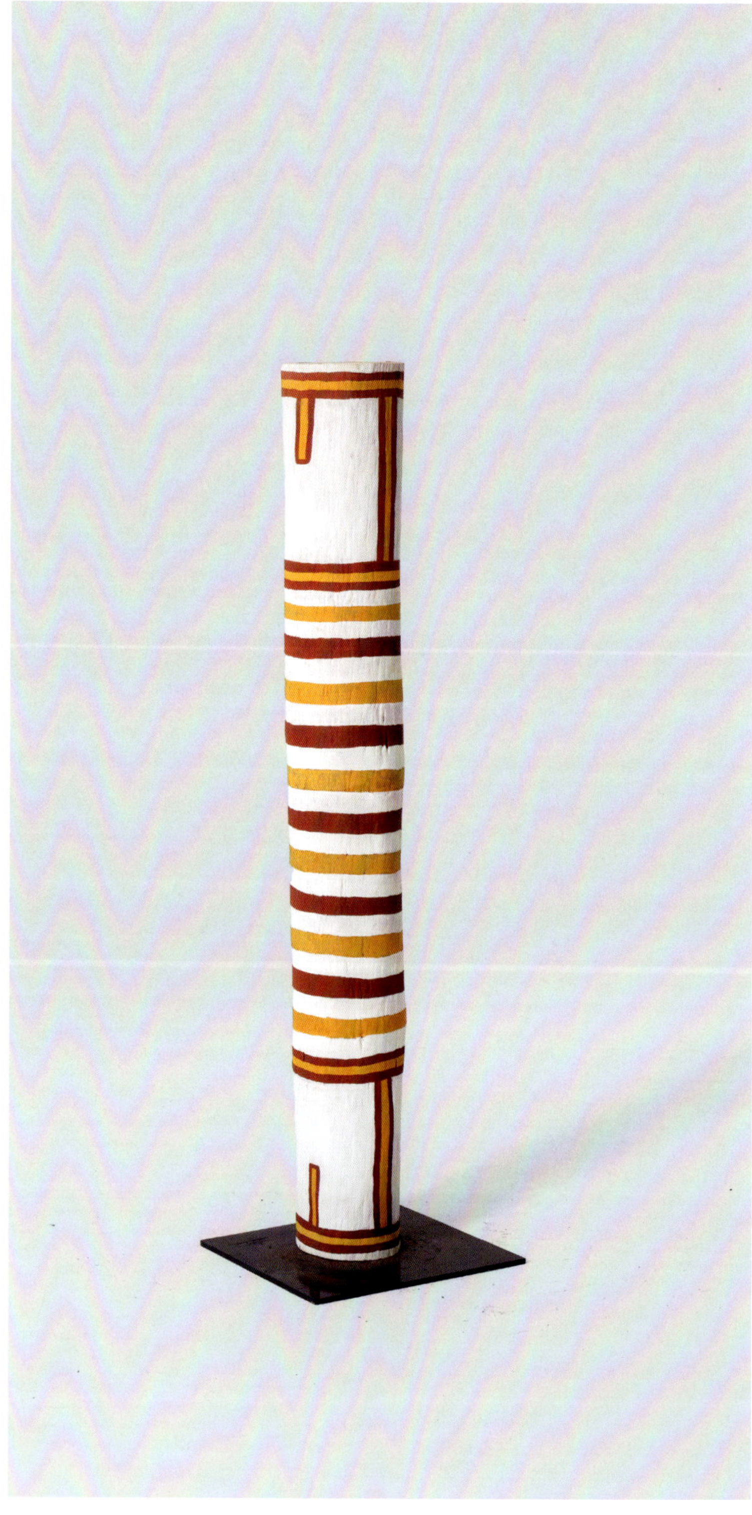

87
Nicky Djawutjawuku Garrawurra
***Garrawurra Body Paint Design*, 2018**
Natural earth pigments on hollow log,
59 7/8 in. high
The Phillips Collection, Washington, DC,
Promised Gift of Dennis and Debra Scholl.

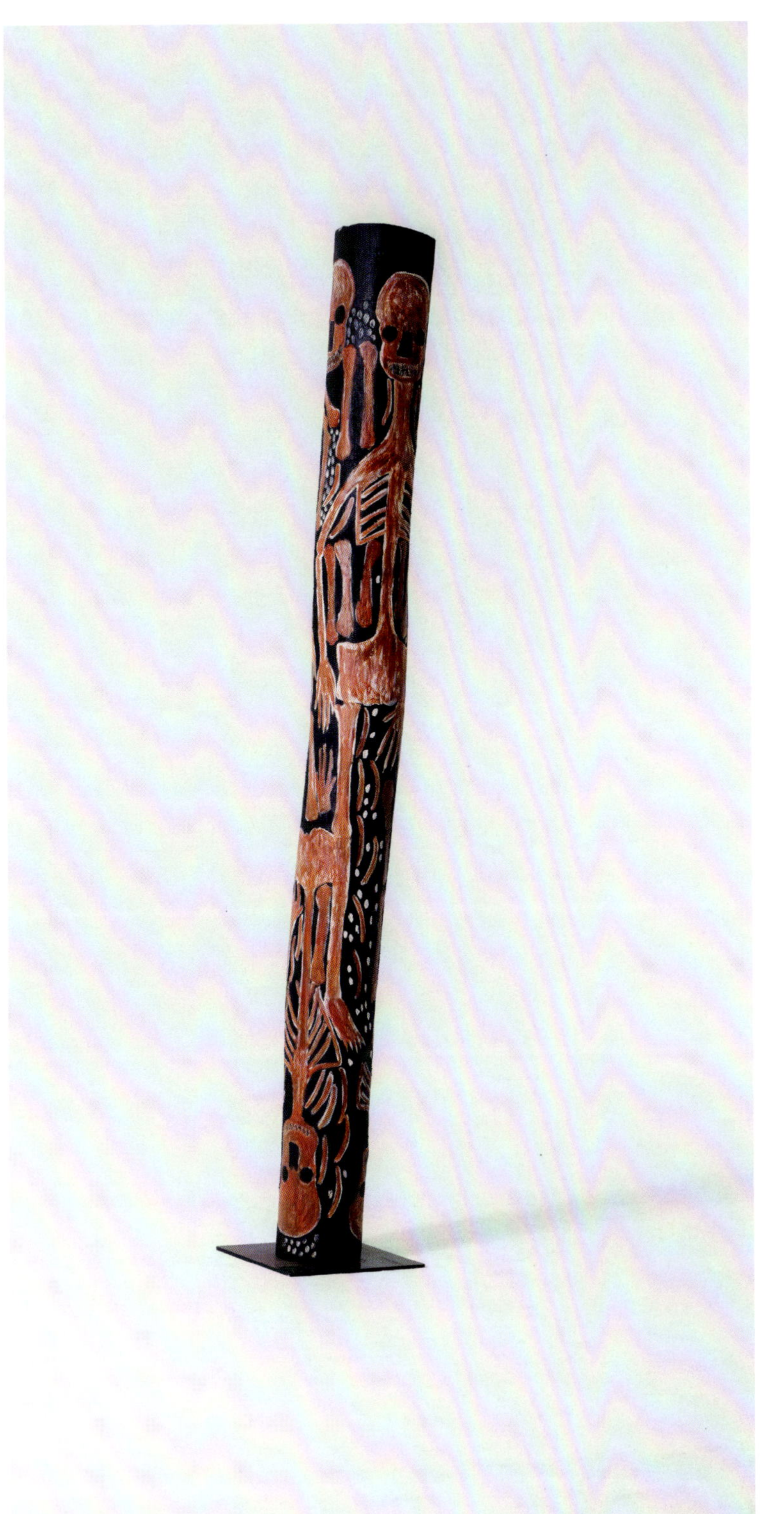

88
Joe Guymala
Lorrkon Story, 2018
Natural earth pigments on hollow log,
84 1/4 in. high
The Phillips Collection, Washington, DC,
Promised Gift of Dennis and Debra Scholl.

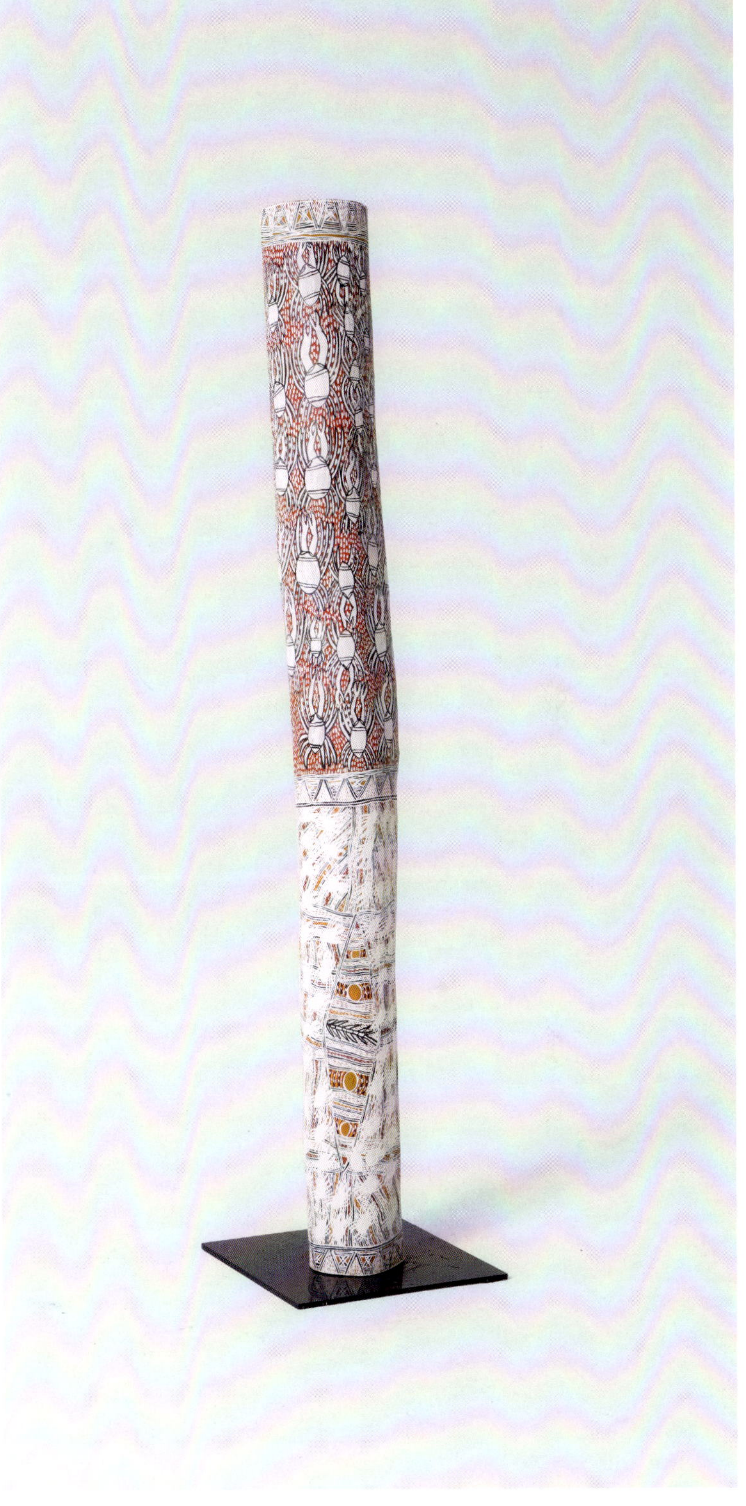

89
Galuma Maymuru
Ŋoykal, 2018
Natural earth pigments on hollow log,
180 in. high
The Phillips Collection, Washington, DC,
Promised Gift of Dennis and Debra Scholl.

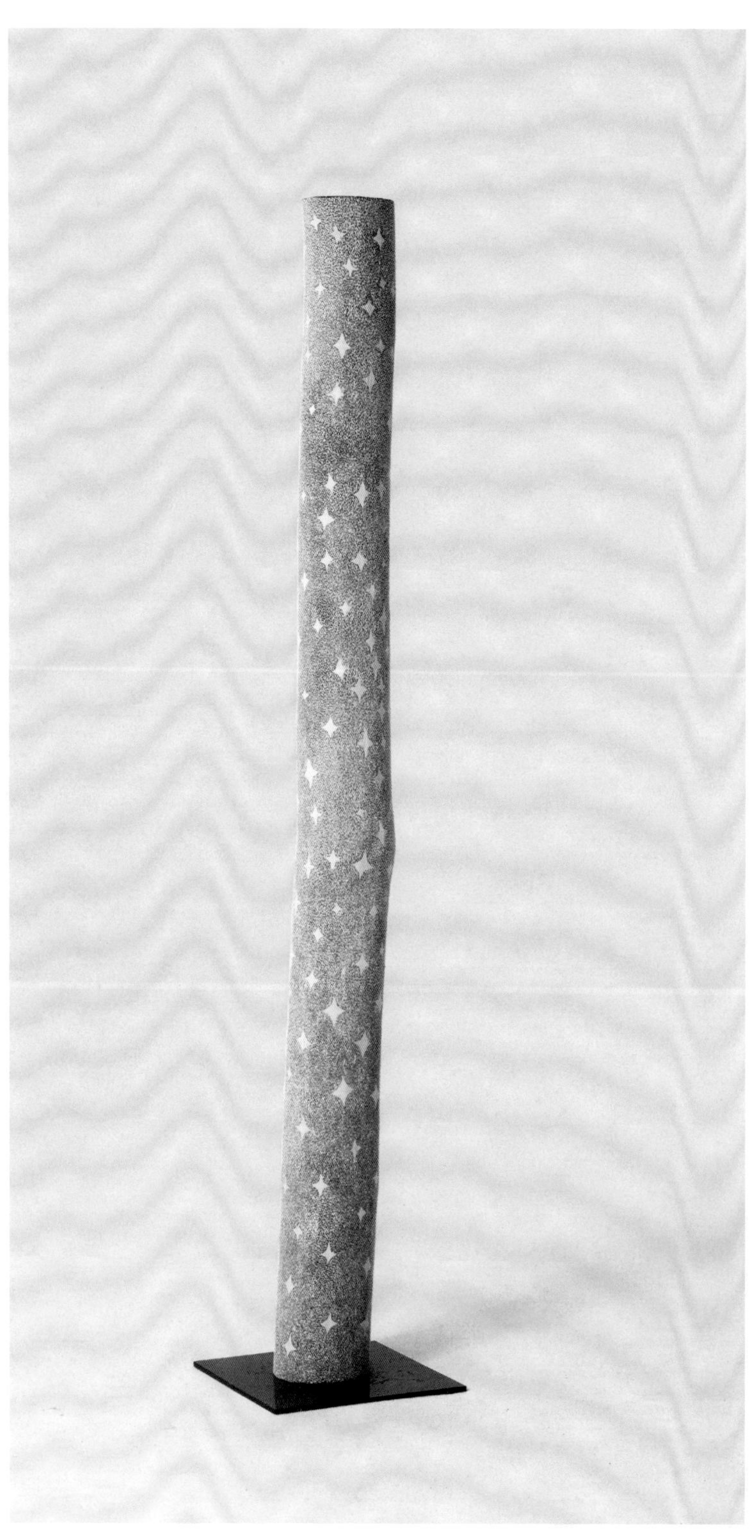

90
Naminapu Maymuru-White
***Milŋiyawuy*, 2018**
Natural earth pigments on hollow log,
162 in. high
The Phillips Collection, Washington, DC,
Promised Gift of Dennis and Debra Scholl.

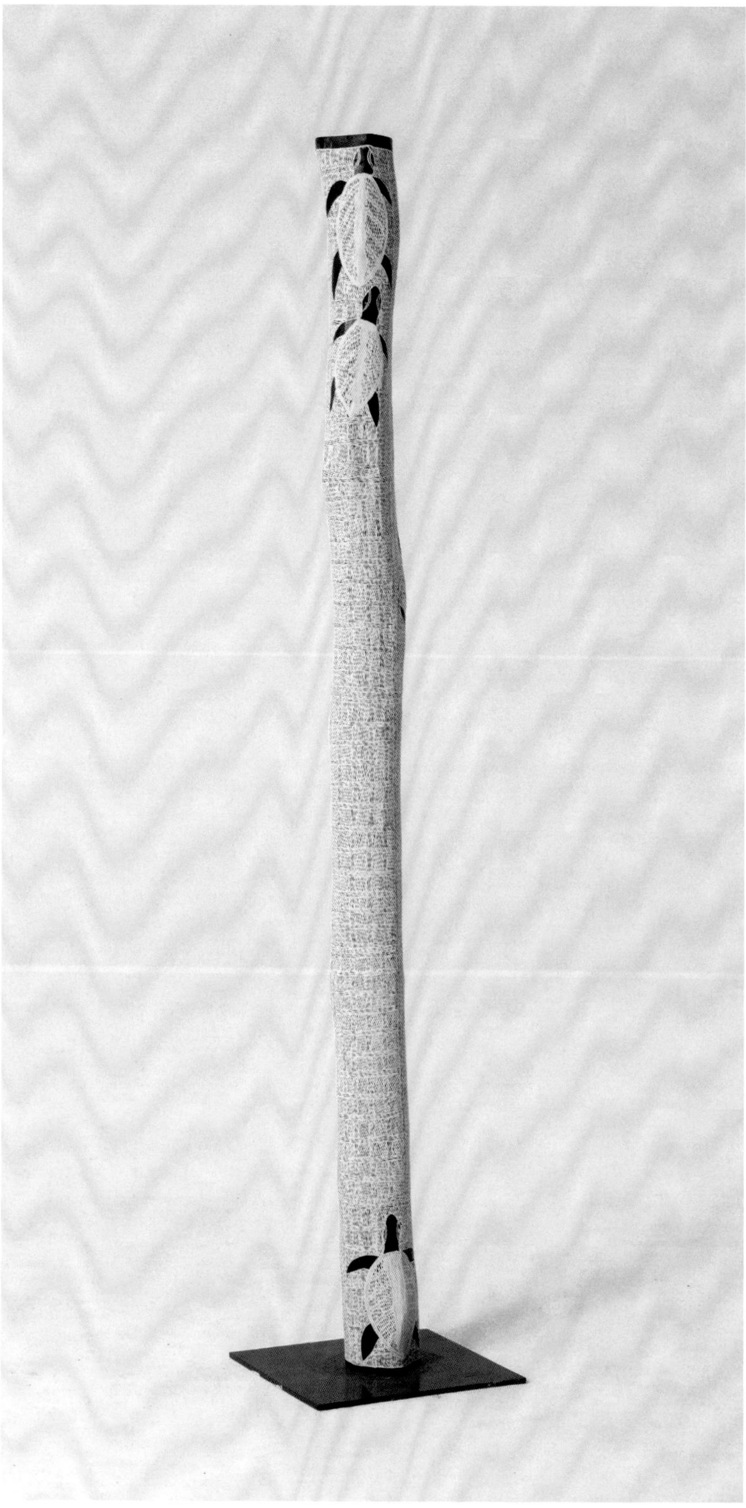

91
Marrnyula Mununŋgurr
***Djapu Larrakitj*, 2018**
Natural earth pigments on hollow log,
87 3/8 in. high
The Phillips Collection, Washington, DC,
Promised Gift of Dennis and Debra Scholl.

COLLECTION OF *LARRAKITJS*

Tina Baum

Standing as cultural sentinels, the traditional hollow burial poles or log coffins known as *larrakitj* or *lorrkon*[1] are powerful reminders of the important funerary practices of Aboriginal communities in Arnhem Land in the Northern Territory of Australia. Although the practices are no longer performed the "old way," due to the impact of Christianity and the introduction of government laws, burial poles are still produced as artistic expressions and are a reminder of the importance of cultural knowledge and ceremonial practices within communities today.

Traditionally, burial poles were an important component of a mortuary ritual that lasted days or weeks. Typically made from the stringybark tree (Eucalyptus tetrodonta), the burial poles were naturally hollowed out by termites. Specific family members or members of the community were chosen to paint designs on the log as part of the ceremony. After decaying for several years, the deceased's bones would be ceremonially ochred and interred in the log. Then the log would be placed upright at a specific site out in "Country," thereby ending the funeral ceremony. The log was left to decay naturally over time and return to the elements.

The time-consuming and logistical challenges to producing these works have not deterred artists from collecting logs and preparing and painting them for sale. Artists' individual styles are informed by cultural knowledge, transmitted through family designs that have been handed down or taught to them by elders or senior artisans, or through experimentation with different subject matter.

In recent years, contemporary artists have shown astounding creativity in producing these works (see pls. 86–91). Some artists have made use of new media, including song, dance, and imagery, to elaborate on or highlight a story associated with the work. Some have accentuated natural knots, gnarls, or organic bends in the wood, incorporating them into the overall design of the work, dynamically transforming a customary style. This variation can be seen in the impressive work, *Rulyapa*, by Dhurrumuwuy Marika (pl. 86), in which the natural curve of the wood is highlighted.

By painting the wood with distinctive natural red, brown, and yellow ochres, white clays, and black charcoal taken from the local environment, artists physically embed the tradition and knowledge of their Country in their art, reinforcing its cultural power. One example is Naminapu Maymuru-White's intricately painted white-on-black work *Milŋiyawuy* (pl. 90), an ethereal reminder of the importance of the stars to her Mangalili clan. It shows the complex constellations and stars associated with the Milky Way, and highlights their use in navigation and ancestral creation stories and at associated sacred sites in Country.

These significant *larrakitj* or *lorrkon* are powerful reminders and magnificent visual representations of each artist's strong cultural foundations, which drive their artistic expression and their ongoing connection to identity, community, and Country. They are remarkable time capsules that will remain formidable cultural markers for all future generations.

---

1 The terms *larrakitj* and *lorrkon* are linked to different communities in Arnhem Land.

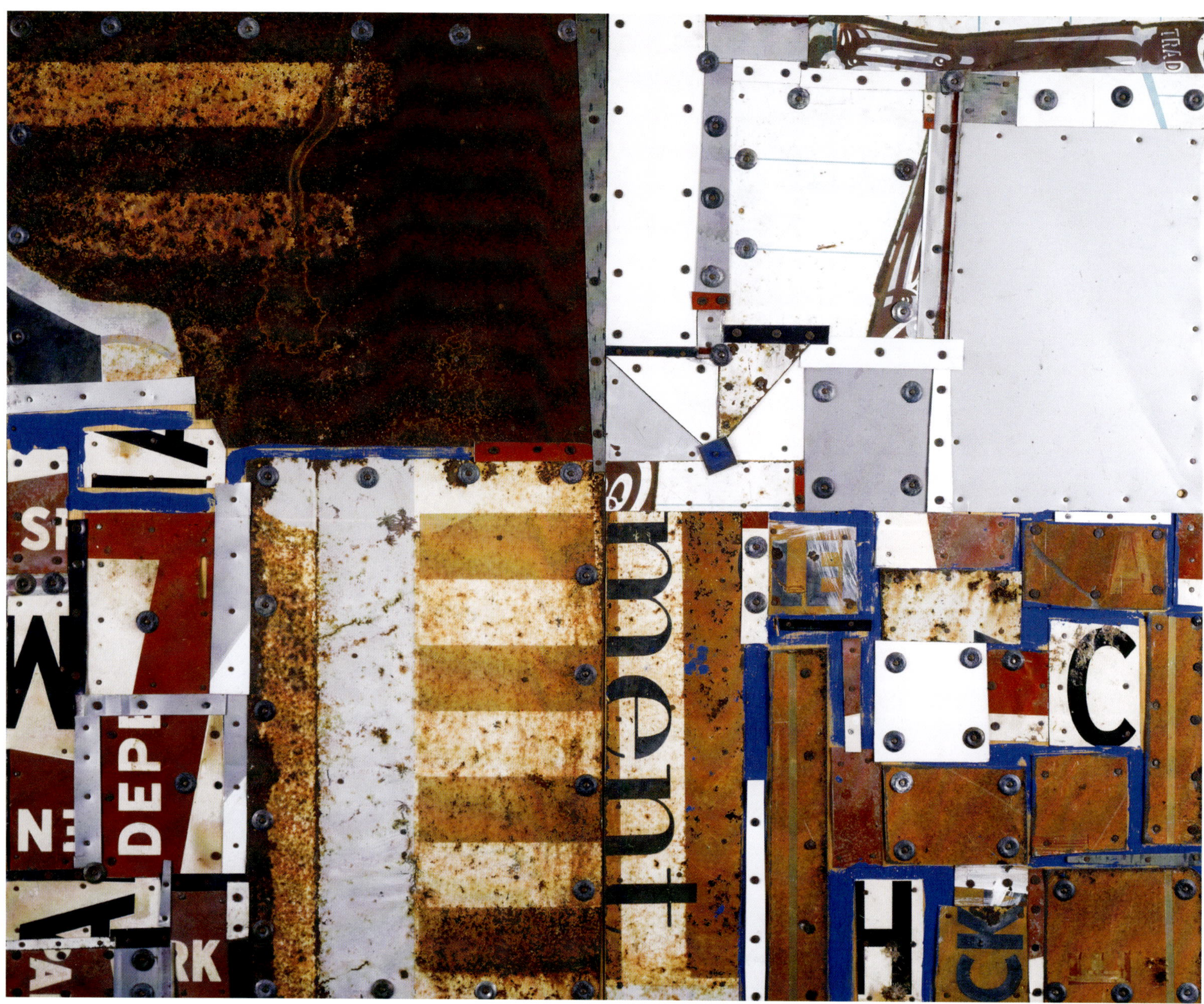

92
William Christenberry
***Wall Construction III*, 1985**
Painted metal signs, sheet metal, washers, nails, and tempera mounted on wood panel, 30 × 36 in.
The Phillips Collection, Washington, DC, Gift of Aaron and Barbara Levine, 2009.

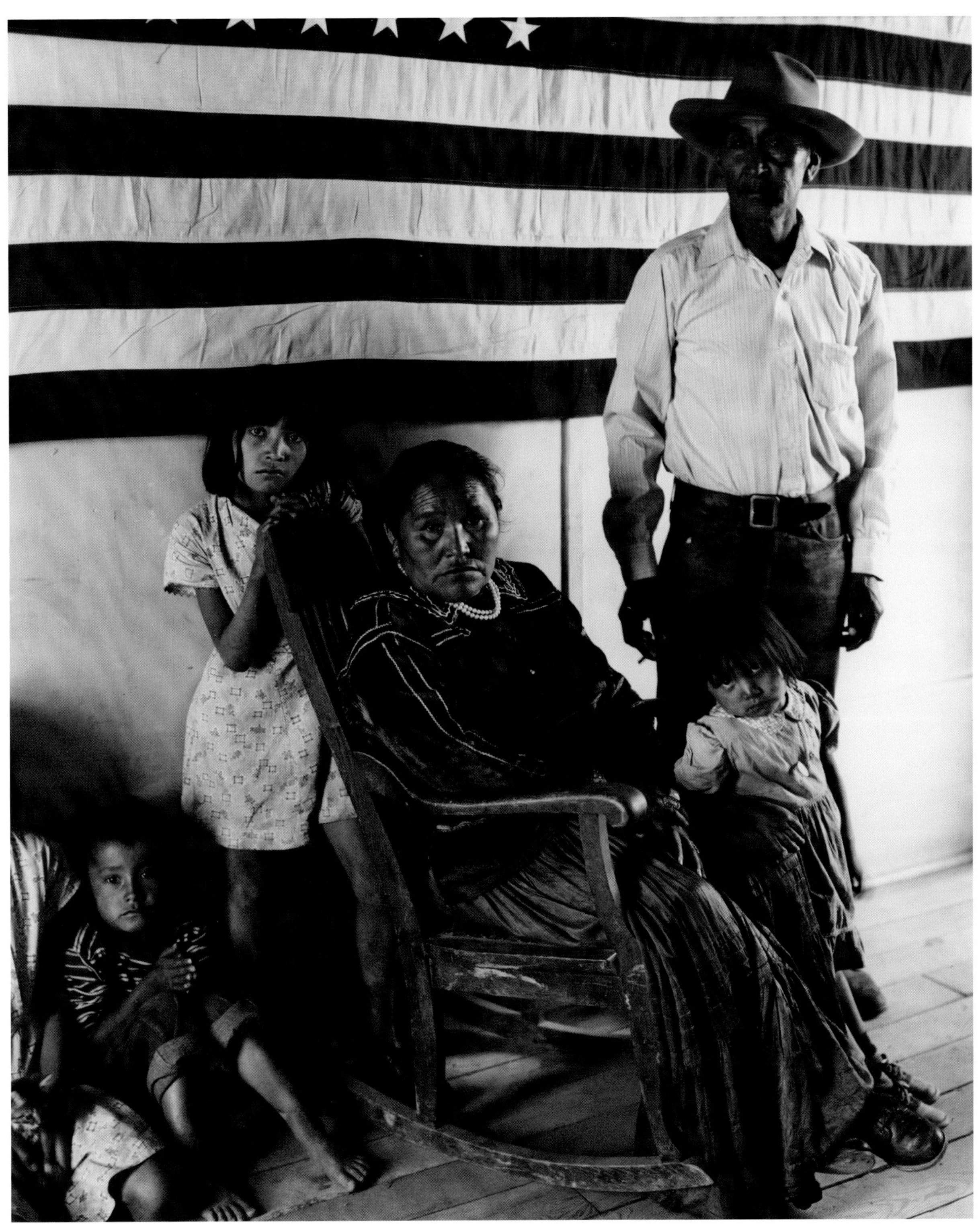

93
Laura Gilpin
Navajo Family (*Francis Nakai and Family, Red Rock*), 1950
Gelatin silver print,
20 1/4 × 16 1/4 in.
The Phillips Collection, Washington, DC,
Gift of Julia J. Norell in honor of Shelly Wischhusen, 2018.

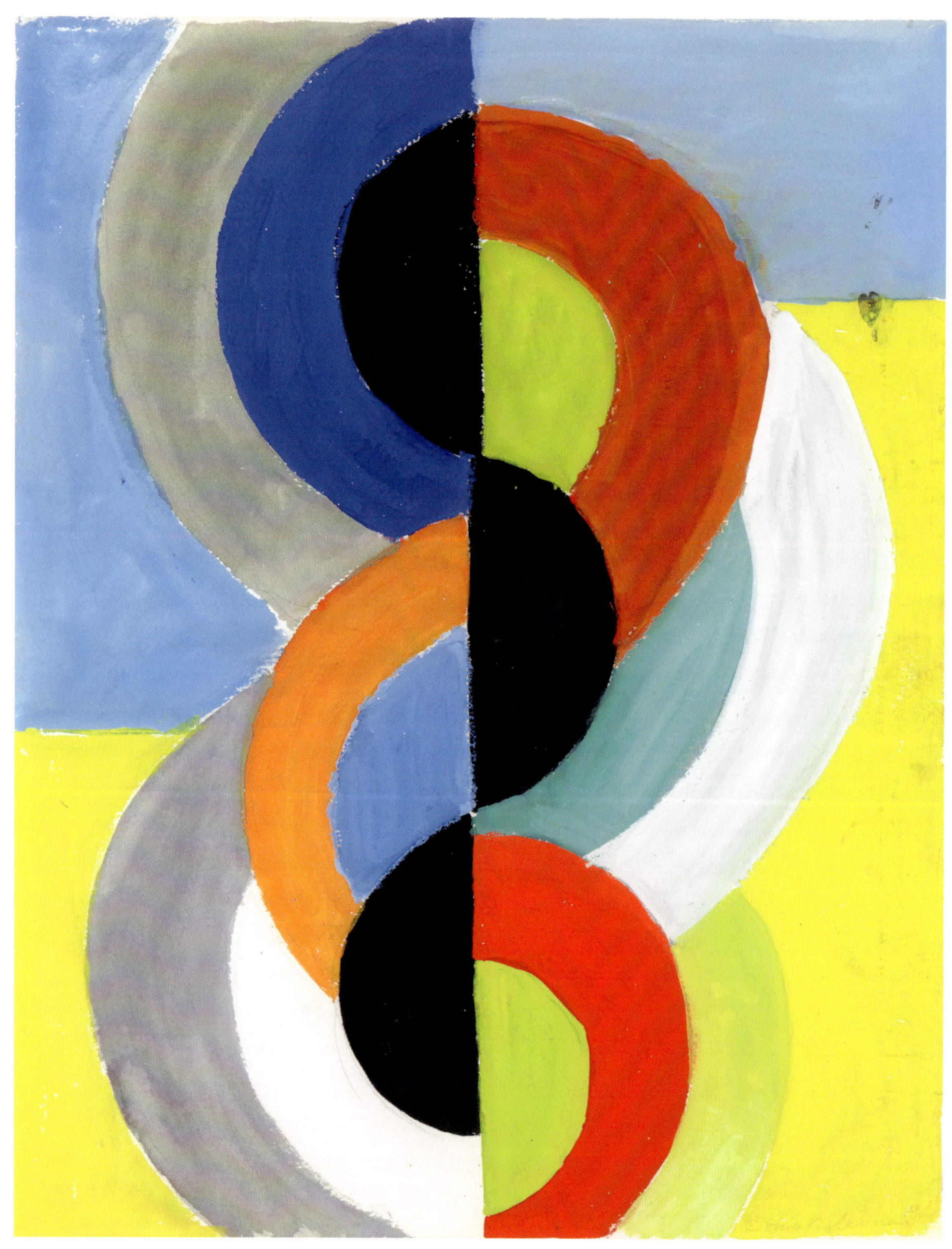

94
Sonia Delaunay-Terk
Rythme Couleur, 1961
Opaque watercolor over graphite pencil on paper,
25 5/8 × 19 3/4 in.
The Phillips Collection, Washington, DC,
Gift of Lilliane Litton, 2012.

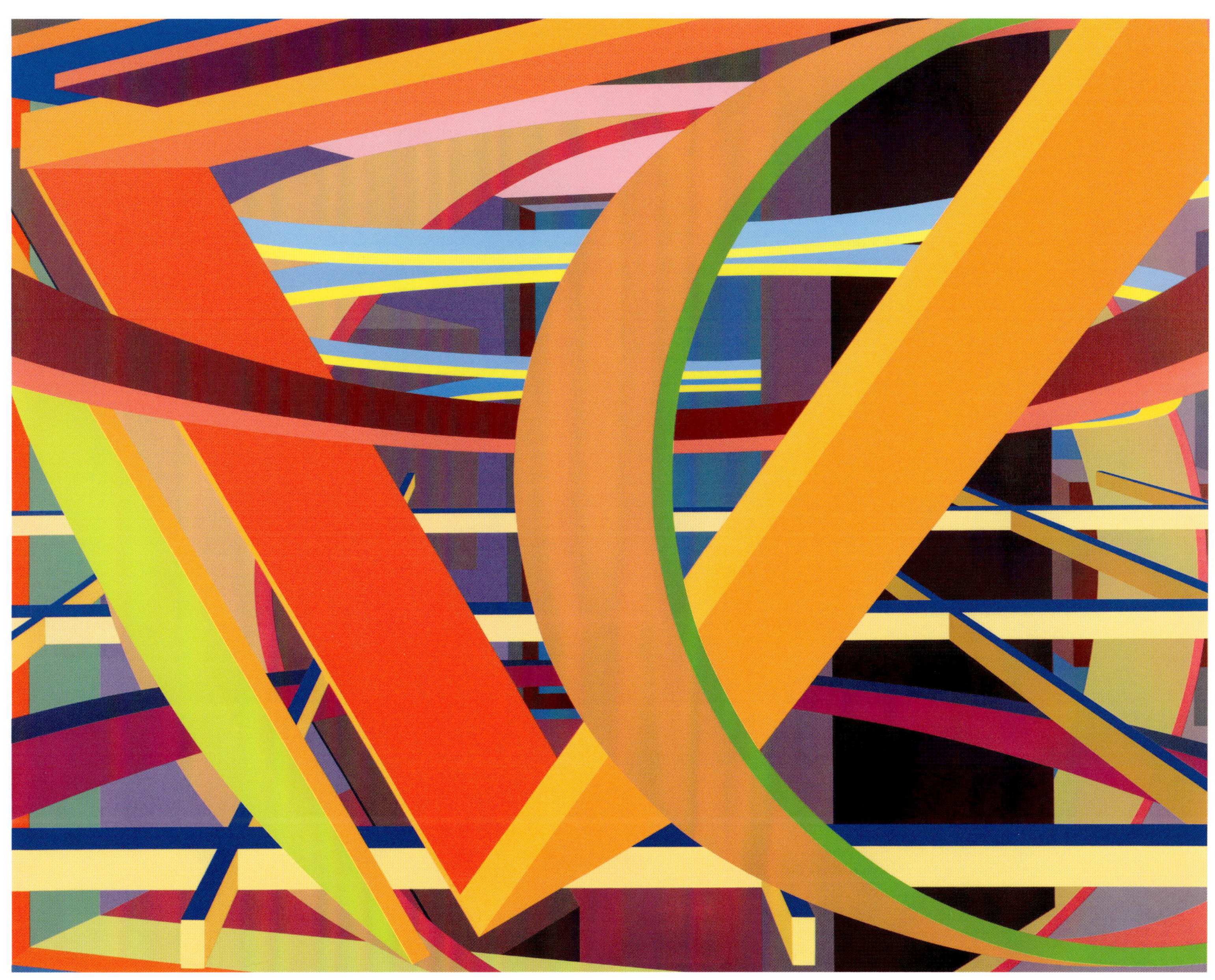

95
Al Held
***Pan North V*, 1985**
Acrylic on canvas,
48 × 60 in.
The Phillips Collection, Washington, DC,
Gift of Joseph Del Valle, Jr., 2013.

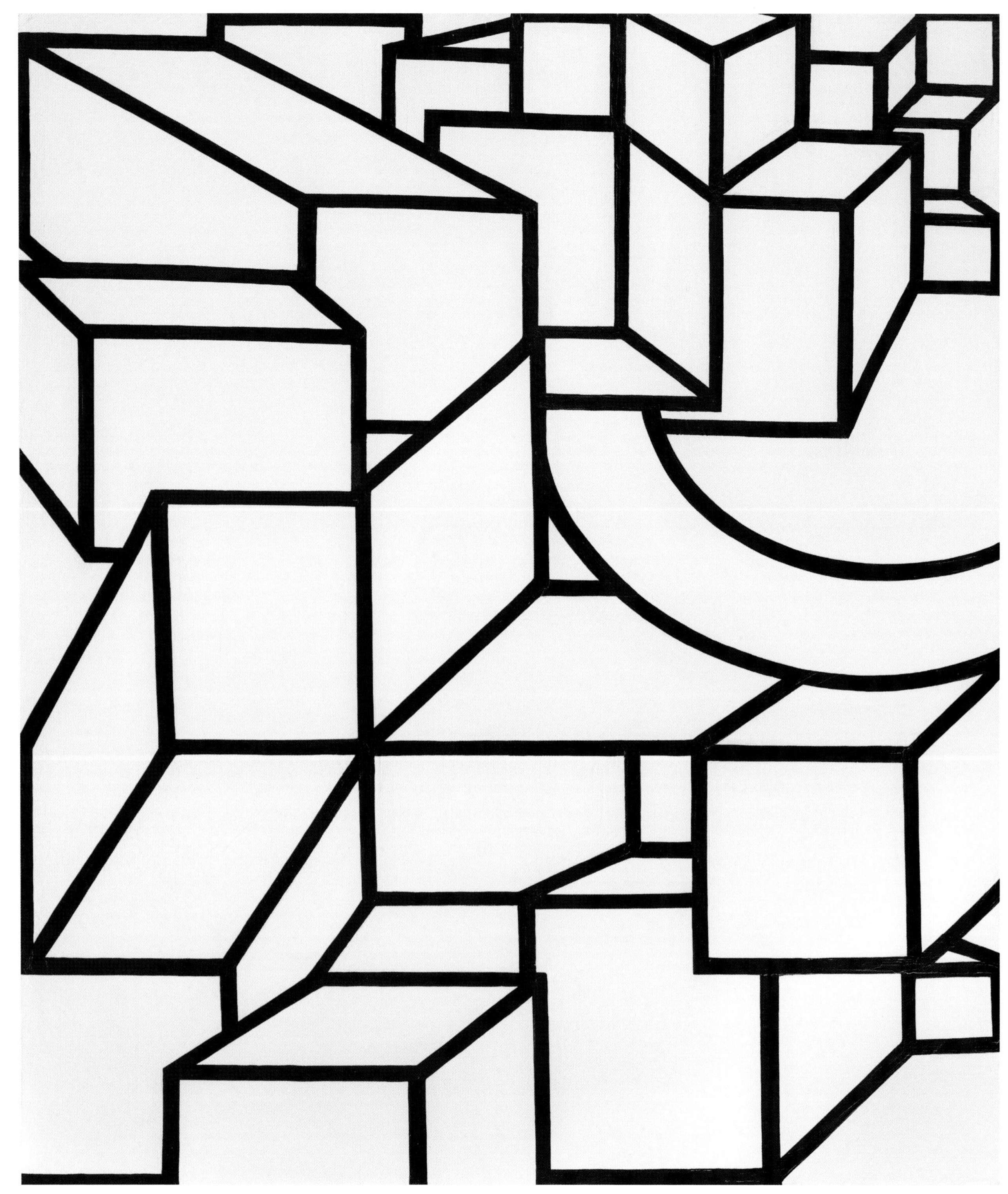

96
Al Held
***B/W XII*, 1968**
Acrylic on canvas,
60 × 50 in.
The Phillips Collection, Washington, DC,
Gift of Susan and Dixon Butler, 2019.

AL HELD
B/W XII, 1968, AND *PAN NORTH V*, 1985

Susan Behrends Frank

A prominent figure among the second generation of abstract expressionists, Al Held was part of the American expatriate circle in postwar Paris that included Sam Francis, Ellsworth Kelly, and Joan Mitchell. Although Held associated with Franz Kline and Mark Rothko in New York in the 1950s, his work in the mid-1960s moved away from an expressive formalism to a reductivist view concerned with spatial illusionism as a plastic experience with philosophical implications. The disciplines of mathematics and physics were poetic sources for Held's imagination as he sought to transform paradoxical reality into complex pictorial structures that could be experienced as ideal and harmonious spatial illusions. He expressed this view in 2003 as a desire "to show that chaos with its multiplicity of choices and possibilities can be viewed as a welcoming environment."[1] Two important examples of Held's work have entered The Phillips Collection in the past decade, each of which represents a significant transitional moment in the career of this seminal postwar American artist.

B/W XII is one of a series of paintings begun by Held in 1967 that relied on a restricted black-and-white palette to construct spare compositions focused exclusively on graphically defined geometric forms that create shifting perceptions of illusionary space. Boxlike geometric shapes and curved forms in *B/W XII* are created with uniform thick black lines that meet, stop, and start again, creating multiple perspectives and vanishing viewpoints. The composition is worked out on the canvas, where close viewing reveals subtle changes made by the artist. *B/W XII*, like other works in the series, evokes ideas of stability versus instability. Held remarked on this dichotomy in a 1977 essay: "[P]erceptions ... keep flowing back and forth in the same space.... The structure is continually in flux ... it's constantly coming together and coming apart and coming together and coming apart."[2]

In 1978, Held returned to using color in his work. A residency at the American Academy in Rome in 1981 further fueled his interest in color and architectural illusion as found especially in works of fifteenth-century Italian Renaissance painters such as Piero della Francesca and in the complex architectural prints of the baroque artist Giovanni Battista Piranesi. *Pan North V* (pl. 95) is part of a series of works begun in 1985 that reflect these interests. Contrasting colors, bold multi-directional movement, and tight cinematic cropping are distinguishing qualities of the series. In the Phillips's work, Held creates a screen of intersecting angles, arcs and circles beyond which a horizontal grid moves our eye into the distance to a window or a doorway into infinity. These complex visionary structures, where every line is trimmed with a razor blade and the surface sanded to flawless perfection, required Held to engage in a lengthy design process to work out in detail the composition and the colors in advance in order to achieve the final illusion of a mathematically conceived, ideal space.

---

1 Al Held, "Introductory Remarks," Lecture at Reed College, April 10, 2003. Archives, Al Held Foundation.

2 Al Held, "Al Held on His Work," in Galerie André Emmerich and Galerie Renée Ziegler, *Neue Bilder und Zeichnungen/Recent Paintings and Drawings; Frühe Werke/Early Works* (Zurich: Galerie André Emmerich; Galerie Renée Ziegler, 1977), n.p.

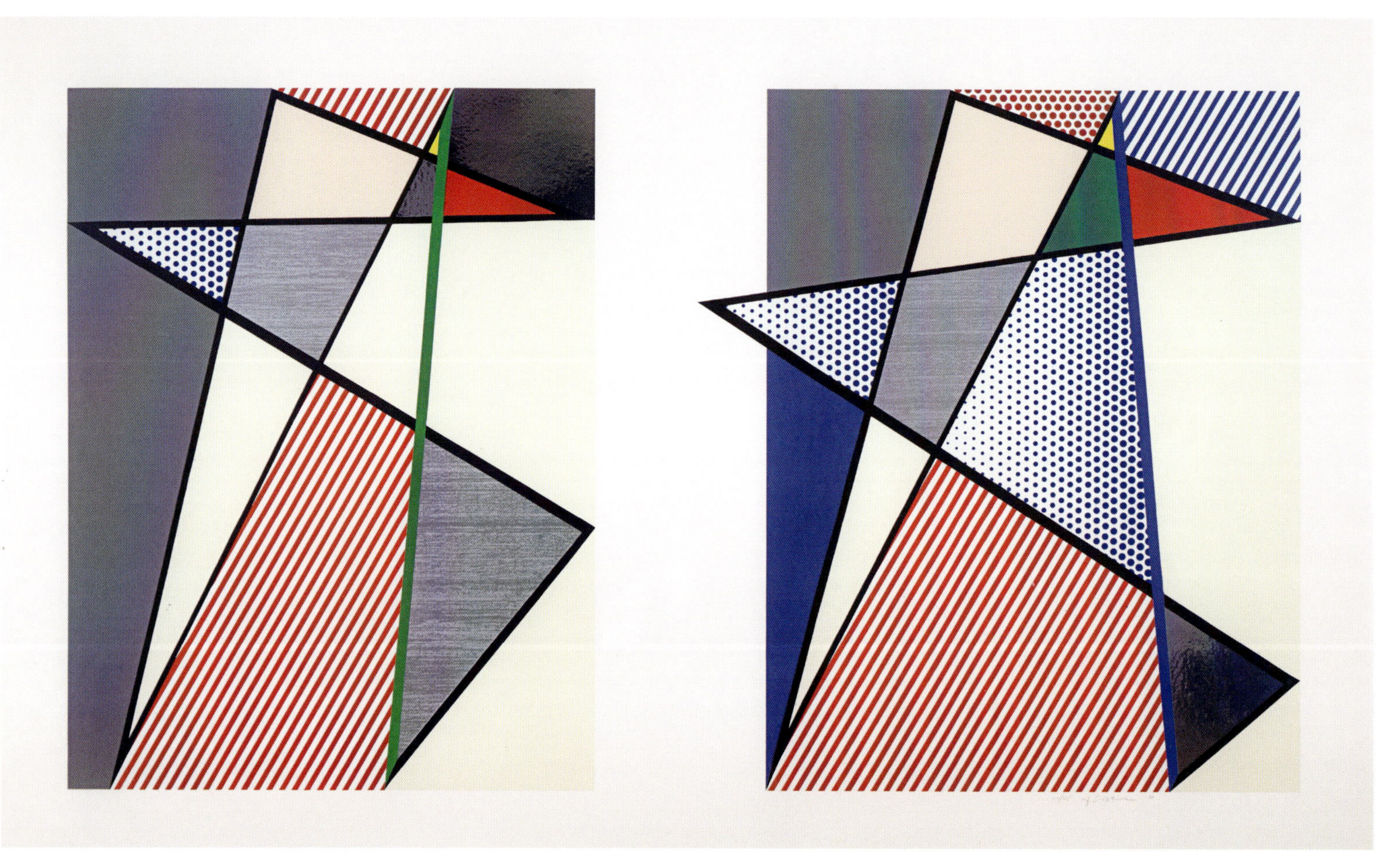

97
Roy Lichtenstein
Imperfect Diptych (*Imperfect* series), 1988
Color woodcut, screenprint, and collage on Archivart Museum Board,
overall: 57 7/8 × 97 3/4 in.
The Phillips Collection, Washington, DC,
Gift of Sidney Stolz and David Hatfield, 2009.

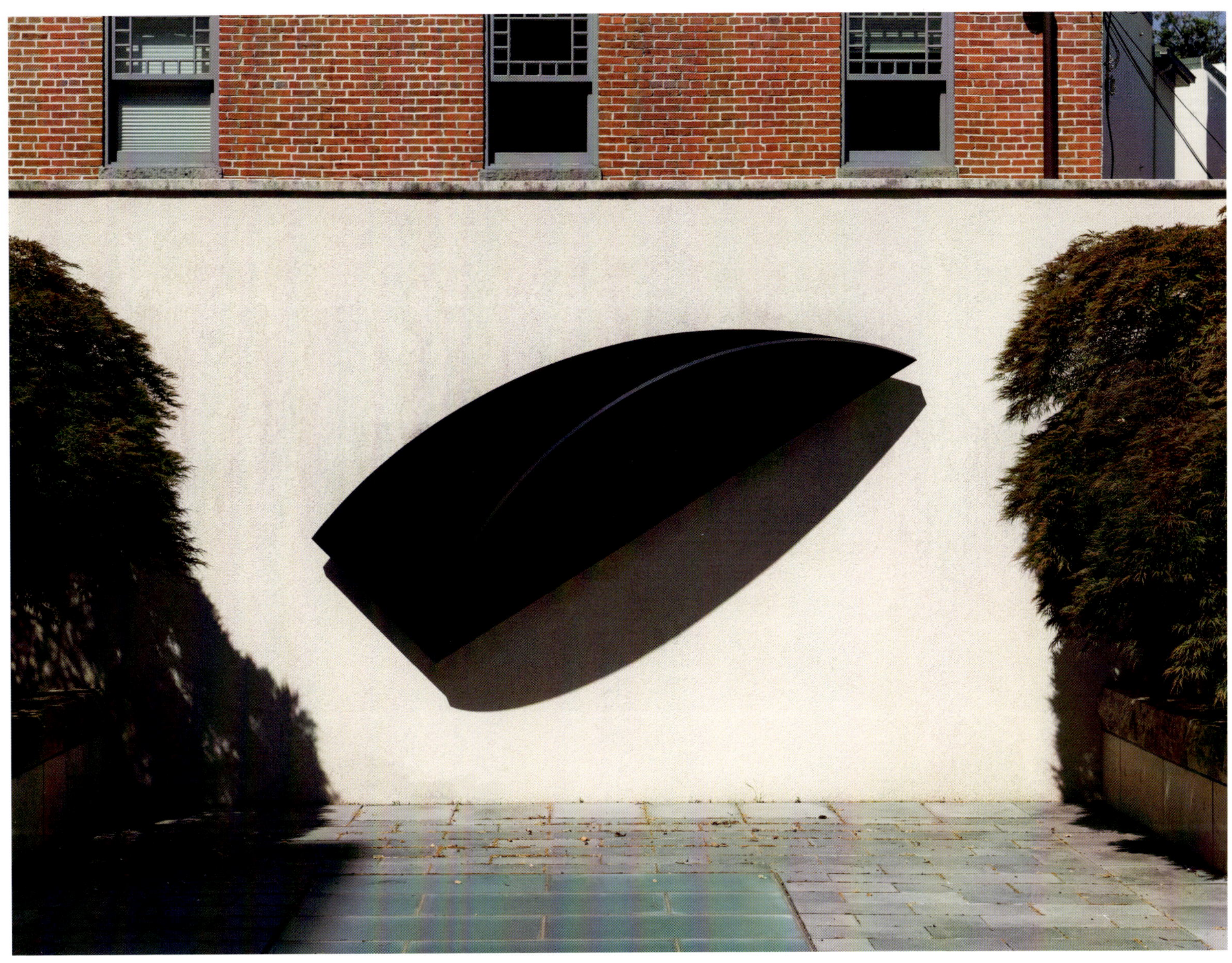

98
Ellsworth Kelly
***Untitled (EK 927)*, 2005**
Bronze,
117 × 63 3/16 × 1 in.
The Phillips Collection, Washington, DC, Hunter Courtyard,
Commissioned in honor of Alice and Pamela Creighton,
beloved daughters of Margaret Stuart Hunter, 2006.

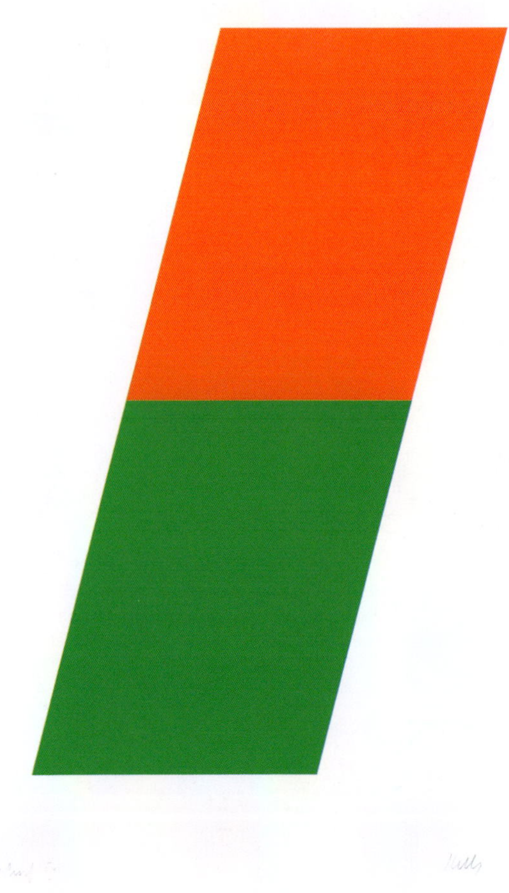

99 (top left)
Ellsworth Kelly
***Blue/Black*, 1970**
Two-color lithograph on Arjomari paper, overall: 36 × 34 in.
The Phillips Collection, Washington, DC, Gift of Fenner Milton, 2013.

100 (top right)
Ellsworth Kelly
***Yellow/Orange*, 1970**
Two-color lithograph on Arjomari paper, overall: 35 × 41 3/8 in.
The Phillips Collection, Washington, DC, Gift of Fenner Milton, 2013.

101 (bottom)
Ellsworth Kelly
***Orange/Green*, 1970**
Two-color lithograph on Arjomari paper, overall: 41 1/2 × 30 1/4 in.
The Phillips Collection, Washington, DC, Gift of Fenner Milton, 2013.

ELLSWORTH KELLY
UNTITLED (EK 927), 2005, AND *BLUE/BLACK*, *ORANGE/GREEN*, AND *YELLOW/ORANGE*, 1970

Vesela Sretenović

In 2006, The Phillips Collection unveiled Ellsworth Kelly's *Untitled (EK 927)* (pl. 98), commissioned for the museum's new courtyard.[1] Constructed of two flat bronze planes joined in a V at its base, this large sculpture rests elegantly on the courtyard's wall. Flanked by two Japanese maple trees on each side, its curvilinear, seemingly weightless, form points skyward, evoking a bird in flight.[2] It reflects Kelly's enduring interest in reductive, abstract shapes drawn from nature and architecture. His small *Maquette for EK 927* (fig. 93) reveals the creative process behind the full-scale work.

Kelly, an internationally acclaimed American painter, sculptor, and printmaker, is known for his geometric abstractions exploring dynamic relationships between shape, color, and space. Living in Paris from 1948 through 1954, he was influenced by historic architecture—especially Romanesque cathedrals—and European modern art, including that of Jean Arp, Constantin Brancusi, Alexander Calder, Henri Matisse, and Joan Miró. This exposure enabled him to abandon figuration and adopt abstraction, creating his signature vocabulary of simple geometric shapes in a spectrum of colors.

Returning to the United States in 1954 and settling in New York, Kelly rejected the subjective gestural and expressive language of the abstract expressionist movement, then at its height. The two- and three-dimensional works that he made for the rest of his career have been mistakenly related to minimalist art. In fact, Kelly's spare geometric abstractions differ profoundly from minimalism in making references to nature (plants, leaves, water) and architecture (facades, walls, windows), as well as by suggesting associative meanings.

After moving to rural Spencertown, New York, in 1970, Kelly's predominant output was shaped canvases and large sculptural works. He also turned to printmaking. In his prints, as in his paintings and sculptures, Kelly's focus was on interrelationships between flatness and depth, color and form, and literal and metaphorical meaning. In a long-lasting collaboration with the renowned Los Angeles printmaking studio and publisher Gemini G.E.L., Kelly completed more than two hundred original lithographs, silkscreens, aquatints, and etchings. The seven lithographs acquired by the Phillips are among the first he created at Gemini G.E.L. Naming the pieces for their color schemes—*Yellow/Orange*, *Red-Orange/Yellow/Blue*, or *Blue/Yellow/Red*, for example (see pls. 99–101)—Kelly called attention to their sheer visual presence, emphasizing the color-shape interplay. Working with master printer Kenneth Tyler, he produced each of the seven images in an edition of seventy-five, plus nine artist's proofs.

In 2013, in honor of the artist's ninetieth birthday, the Phillips organized *Ellsworth Kelly: Panel Paintings 2004–2009*,[3] an exhibition of Kelly's large-scale paintings—joined panels of solid color that blurred the boundaries between painting and sculpture.

1 The work was fabricated in 2005 and installed at the museum in spring 2006. The work's placement and installation were overseen by the artist. The commission was made possible through a generous gift from Margaret Stuart Hunter, a trustee of The Phillips Collection, in honor of her beloved daughters Alice and Pamela Creighton, and in celebration of the museum's newly created courtyard.

2 The piece weighs 1,500lbs.

3 The exhibition was accompanied by a catalogue: *Ellsworth Kelly: Panel Paintings 2004–2009*, by Vesela Sretenović (Washington, DC: Phillips Collection, 2013).

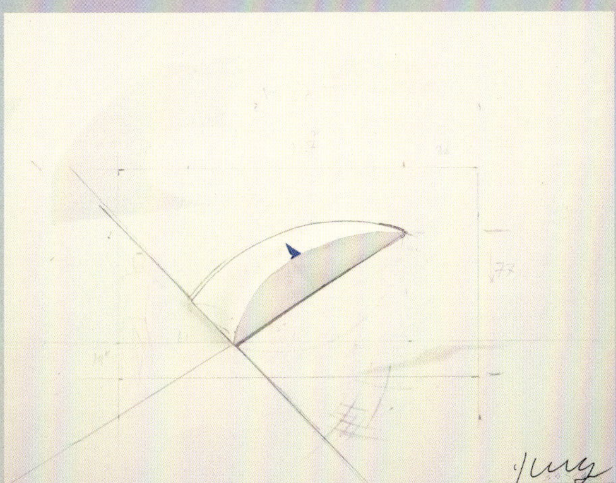

fig. 93
Ellsworth Kelly
***Maquette for EK 927*, 2005**
Graphite, pencil, and collage of cut paper on paper, 9 × 11 × 5/8 in.
The Phillips Collection, Washington, DC,
Gift of Margaret Stuart Hunter. Acquired 2006.

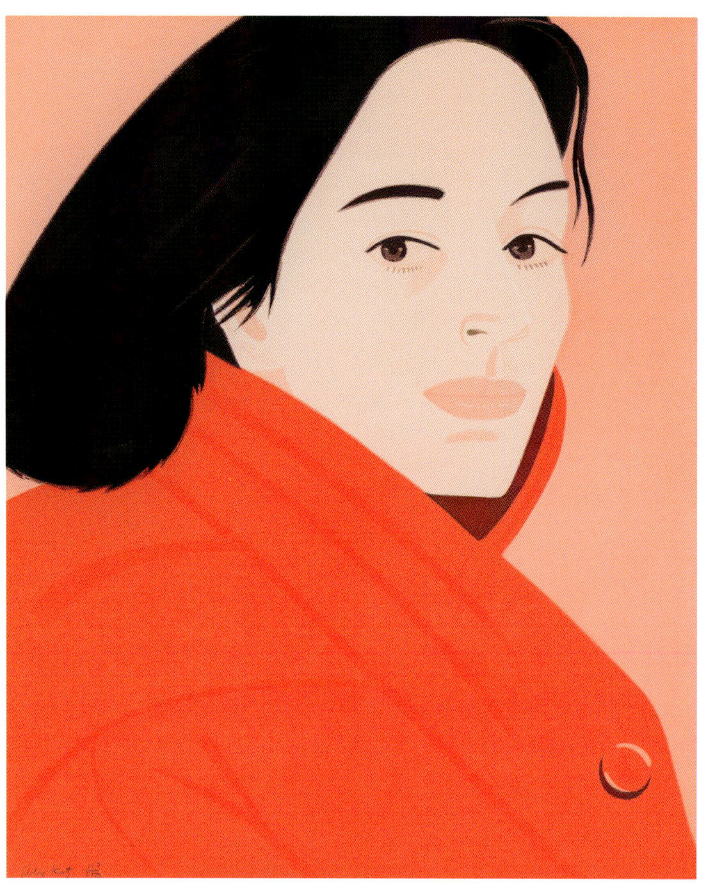

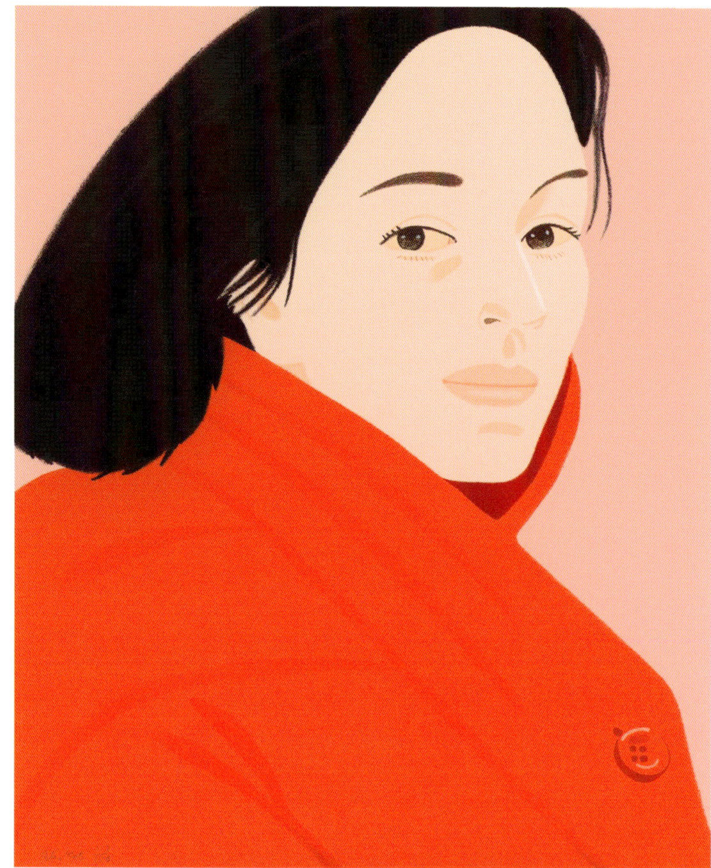

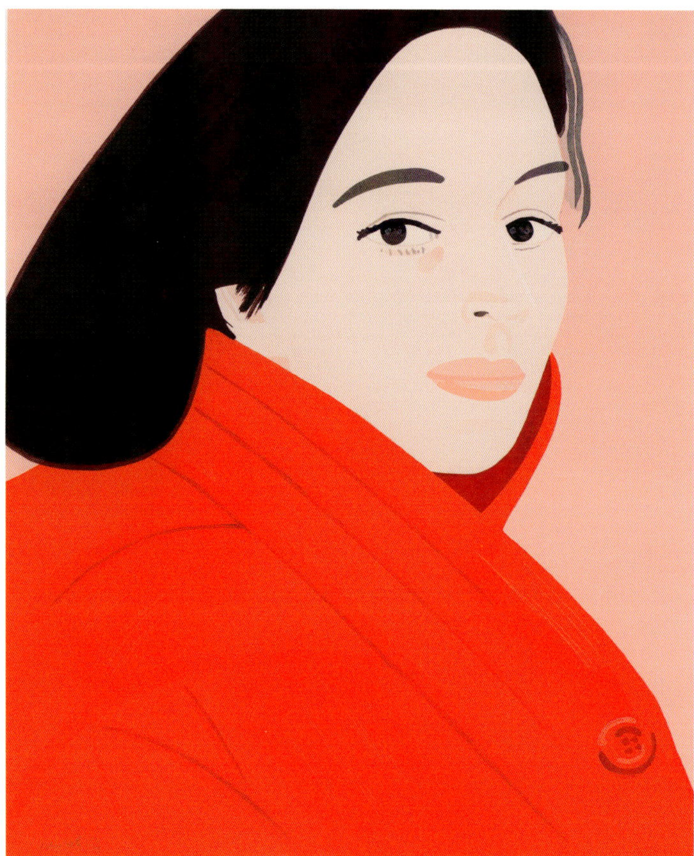

102 (top left)
Alex Katz
***Brisk Day*, 1990**
Aquatint,
overall: 35 3/8 × 28 1/2 in.
The Phillips Collection, Washington, DC,
Gift of Fenner Milton, 2013.

103 (top right)
Alex Katz
***Brisk Day*, 1990**
Silkscreen,
overall: 36 × 29 in.
The Phillips Collection, Washington, DC,
Gift of Fenner Milton, 2013.

104 (bottom)
Alex Katz
***Brisk Day*, 1990**
Woodcut,
overall: 36 × 29 1/8 in.
The Phillips Collection, Washington, DC,
Gift of Fenner Milton, 2013.

ALEX KATZ
BRISK DAY, 1990

Renée Maurer

In the 1950s, Alex Katz's large-scale realistic portraits and landscapes challenged the prevailing taste for abstraction that defined the New York school. Keenly interested in film, advertising, the art of Henri Matisse, and Japanese prints, Katz synthesized these influences into works that focused on his impressions of modern life. His ideas grew from ink drawings and then pencil sketches, which he enlarged to guide his paintings. Employing hard-edged lines and closely cropped forms, he posed stylish figures against flat fields of intense color.

Katz's approach to printmaking closely aligns with his interests in painting. Although he began experimenting with printmaking in the early 1950s, it became key to his practice in the mid-1960s. By manipulating color, line, and scale, his prints reexamine, distill, and pare down ideas first developed on canvas. He explained: "A lot of these things are experiments to where I have never been in the paintings.... I'm really trying to make things immediate."[1] Katz has produced dozens of print editions using a variety of techniques.

One of Katz's favorite subjects is his wife Ada, featured in over two hundred canvases and numerous drawings and prints. The three impressions that form *Brisk Day* (1990) repeat Ada in the same three-quarters pose, close-up, using three distinct techniques: woodcut, aquatint, and silkscreen (pls. 102–104). Katz wraps Ada in a bright red coat and positions her against a warm pink background. Her striking oval face is framed by her dark bobbed hair, and her large brown eyes engage with the viewer. Close examination reveals how Katz considered each technique and made adjustments to his images as he revised them through the printing process. He explained: "When you work on a print you start out and then after you get the first proof you change your ideas. You go with the material."[2] In its dramatic interplay between bold colors and flattened forms with distinct edges, the woodcut captures a youthful Ada with kohl-lined eyes, a seductive gaze, and pouting, full lips. In the aquatint, the colors are rosier and closer in hue. Ada's hair is darker, her features are more angular at the nose and chin, and slight lines appear by her eyes and mouth. In the silkscreen, shaded areas near her eyes, nose, mouth, and ear add modeled contours and volume to her face.

A small oil sketch of Ada in a gray coat was a point of departure for Katz's *Brisk Day*.[3] These three prints provide valuable commentary as to how Katz's practices in different media produce improvisations and variations on well-known themes.[4] The first works by Katz to enter the collection, these prints join two earlier lithographs, *Day Lily 1* and *Day Lily 2*, both from 1969.

---

1 Marietta Mautner Markhof and Klaus Albrecht Schröder, *Alex Katz Prints* (Vienna: Hatje Cantz, 2010), 31, 35.

2 Markhof and Schröder, *Alex Katz Prints*, 41.

3 David Cohen, "*Alex Katz Prints* by Marietta Mautner Markhof and Klaus Albrecht Schröder," *Print Quarterly* 28, no. 2 (June 2011): 220.

4 Cohen, "*Alex Katz Prints*", 222.

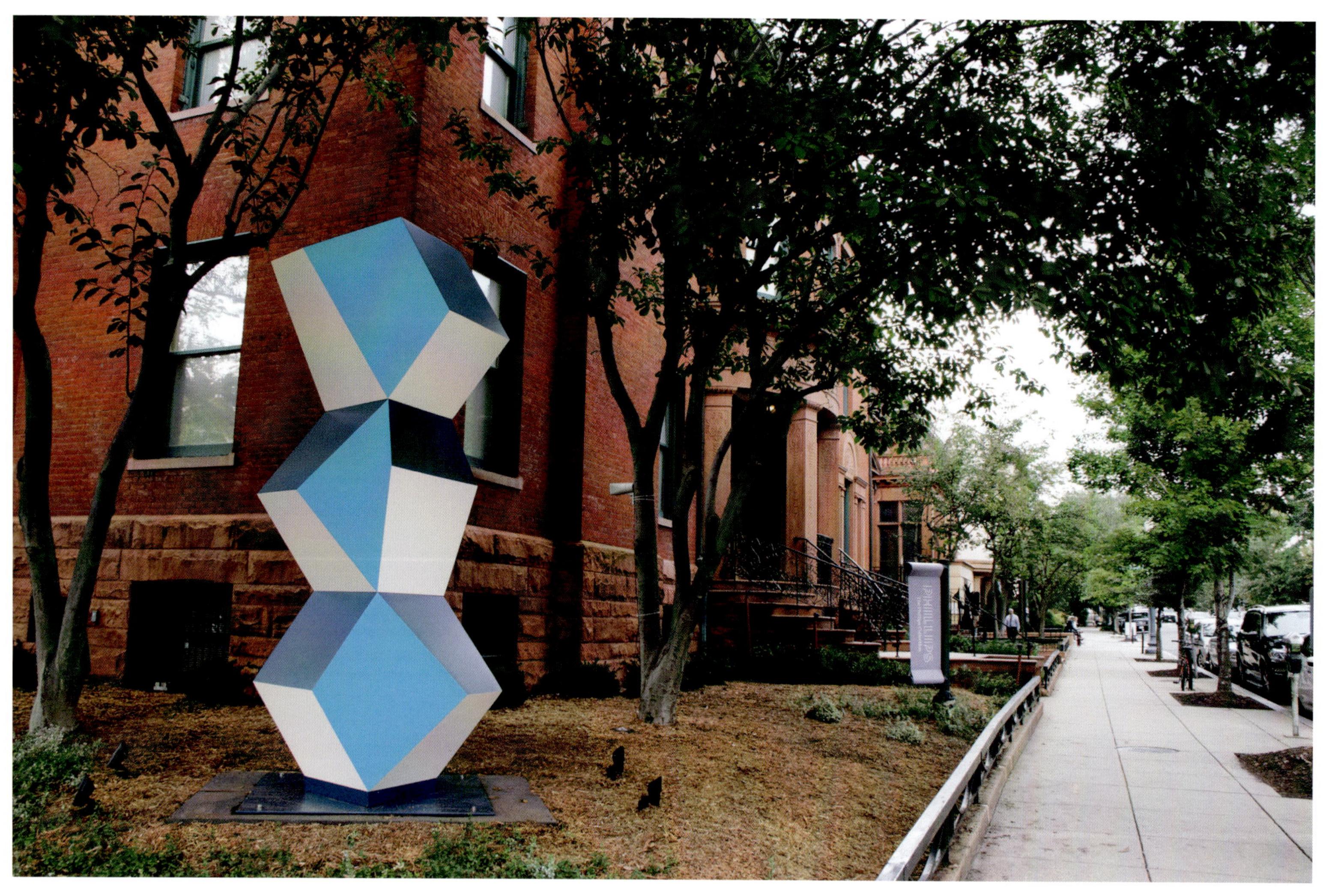

105
Angela Bulloch
***Heavy Metal Stack: Fat Cyan Three*, 2018**
Painted steel,
118 1/8 × 55 1/8 × 39 3/8 in.
The Phillips Collection, Washington, DC,
Made possible with support from Susan and Dixon Butler, Nancy and Charles Clarvit, John and Gina Despres, A. Fenner Milton, Erica Richter, Harvey M. Ross, George Vradenburg and The Vradenburg Foundation, 2018.

106 (top left)
Rudolf de Crignis
***Painting #02-25*, 2002**
Oil on canvas,
30 × 30 in.
The Phillips Collection, Washington, DC,
Gift of the Estate of Rudolf de Crignis, 2019.

107 (bottom left)
Rudolf de Crignis
***Painting #04-34*, 2004**
Oil on canvas,
30 × 30 in.
The Phillips Collection, Washington, DC,
Gift of the Estate of Rudolf de Crignis, 2019.

108 (top right)
Rudolf de Crignis
***Painting #03-14*, 2003**
Oil on canvas,
30 × 30 in.
The Phillips Collection, Washington, DC,
Gift of the Estate of Rudolf de Crignis, 2019.

109 (bottom right)
Rudolf de Crignis
***Painting #06-52*, 2006**
Oil on canvas,
30 × 30 in.
The Phillips Collection, Washington, DC,
Gift of the Estate of Rudolf de Crignis, 2019.

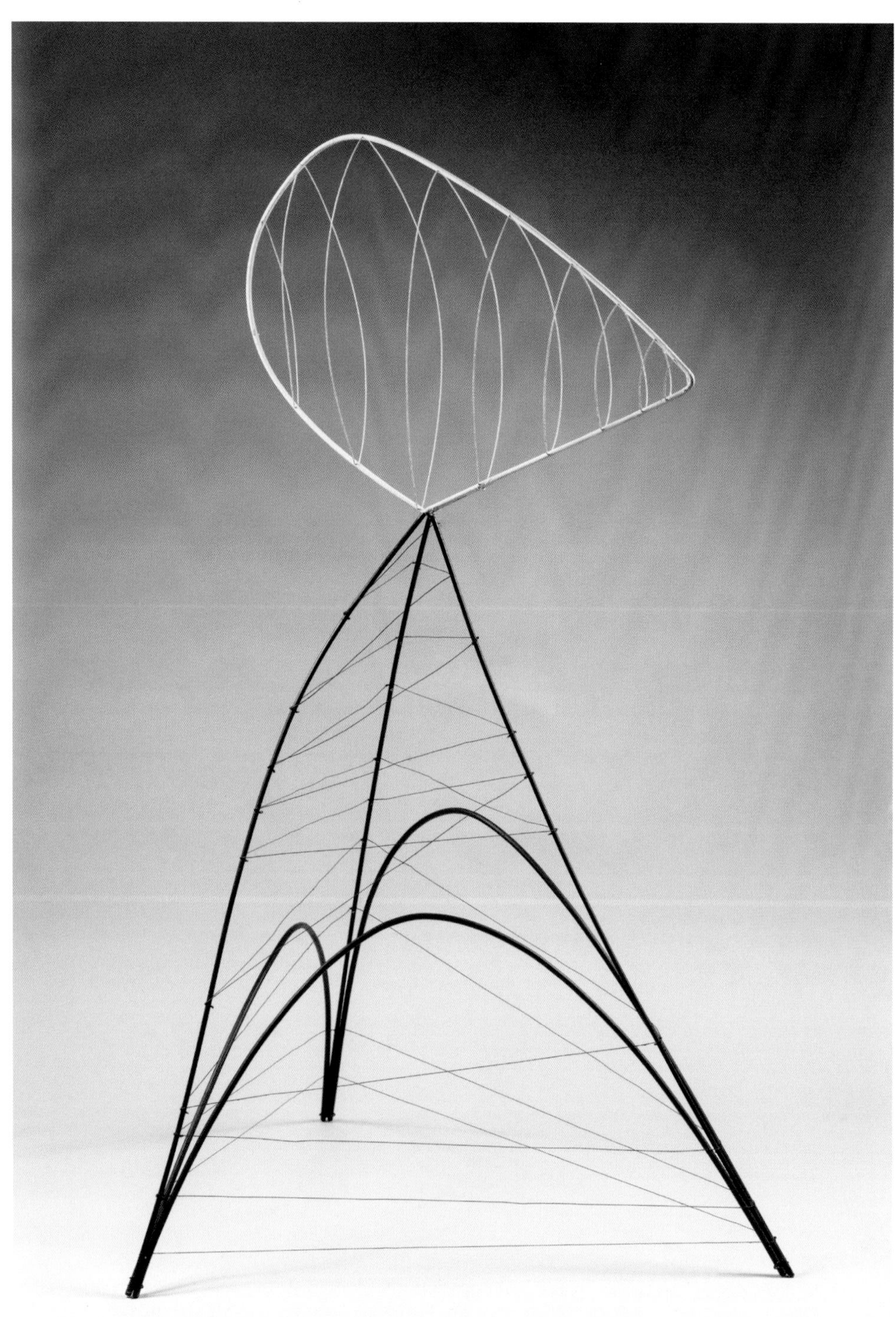

110
Alexander Calder
***Hollow Egg*, 1939**
Wire, metal rod, and paint,
54 × 39 1/2 × 38 1/8 in.
The Phillips Collection, Washington, DC,
Gift in memory of Betty Milton, a close friend of Louisa Calder, initiated 2001, completed 2018.

ALEXANDER CALDER
HOLLOW EGG, 1939

Elizabeth Hutton Turner

Framed by rods and modeled entirely in wire, *Hollow Egg* apprehends phenomena much as Calder described: "[O]bjects behind other objects should not be lost to view, but should be shown through the others by making the latter transparent. The wire sculpture accomplishes this in a most decided manner."[1] *Hollow Egg* also frames a visual paradox:[2] predominantly composed of space, the object disdains sculptural mass. Made to be seen, it is a reverie on transparency, barely distinguishable from its surroundings.

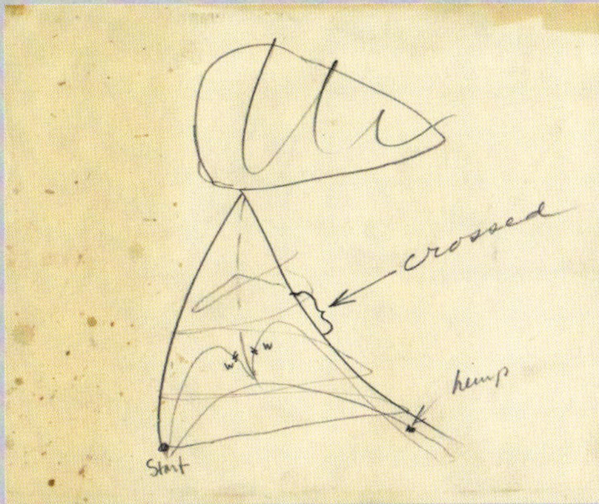

fig. 94
Alexander Calder
Untitled (Preliminary drawing for *Hollow Egg*), 1939
Pencil on paper,
8 1/2 × 11 in.
Calder Foundation, New York;
Mary Calder Rower Bequest, 2011.

James Johnson Sweeney, who included *Hollow Egg* in Calder's major retrospective at the Museum of Modern Art, New York (MoMA), in 1943, once observed that the aesthetics of transparency—what he called "visual lightness"—went hand in hand with Calder's practice in wire.[3] In the tension and resistance of bending wire, the artist found a fluency between thought and action that permitted his line drawing (fig. 94) to escape the page and launch into the air. This new wire line conferred sculptural properties of volume and shape on contours traced in space. Wire images communicated Calder's own energy, speed, and efficiencies, and tapped into the invisible realities of space-time physics, as an early statement by him concerning his motorized wire abstractions makes clear.[4]

In 1939, the year *Hollow Egg* was created, Calder was collaborating with architects working with transparency in steel and glass. *Hollow Egg* was one of five sculptural models for a proposed but unrealized African habitat designed by Oscar Nitzchke for the Bronx Zoo.[5] Among Calder's five models, *Hollow Egg* was distinguished by its self-contained ovoid shape and its lack of wire extensions, recalling another project of 1939, his model of two intersecting planes of Plexiglas—awarded first prize in a competition sponsored by manufacturers Rohm and Haas at MoMA. Calder admittedly wrestled with the medium and was dissatisfied with its aesthetic quality.[6] The serenely simple volumes of *Hollow Egg* offered an alternative solution to creating transparency in sculpture through a flexed and permeable architecture, enclosing volumes of open space while opening up the same enclosure to light and air.

Looking again at *Hollow Egg*, one explores the contours of its volumetric white rod frame loosely bound by loops of thin white wire, perched atop a dark tripod of arching black rods wrapped with thin black wire. The egg-shaped top engages the viewer at eye level, as if asking to be seen. Gazing into the empty frame, the sense of something pulsing or shifting within its contours invites free association between real shapes and imagined spatial dimensions. The ephemeral-looking structure leans forward like some kind of wind foil being pulled into the fourth dimension.[7] Alternatively, one imagines a two-dimensional creature springing into three dimensions by virtue of its own cast shadows. Ultimately, one finds *Hollow Egg* conjuring Calder himself performing his signature move, namely, "delineating space without filling it."[8]

---

1 Alexander Calder, "Statement on Wire Sculpture" (manuscript, 1929), Calder Foundation archives.

2 Calder's titles, usually bestowed as an afterthought, are not meant to denote representations. See Alexander S. C. Rower, "License Plates," in *Alexander Calder: Retrospective* (Humlebaek: Louisiana Museum of Modern Art, 1995), 33, 35.

3 James Johnson Sweeney, "Alexander Calder," in *Calder* (Saint-Paul de Vence: Fondation Maeght, 1969), trans. Margreth C. Schultz (Boston: Boston Book & Art, 1971), 6. For a discussion of Calder in relation to James Johnson Sweeney's curatorial philosophy, see Marcia Brennen, *Curating Consciousness* (Cambridge, MA: MIT Press, 2010), 2–29.

4 Alexander Calder, "Que ça bouge—À propos des sculptures mobiles" (manuscript, 1932), Calder Foundation archives. Translation courtesy Calder Foundation, New York.

5 For a discussion of the five models, see Alexander S. C. Rower, "Bronx Zoo Project," in *Calder Stories* (Santander: Centro Botín, 2019), 81. See also Calder's comment on metal "trees" for the Bronx Zoo in *Alexander Calder: Recent Gouaches-Early Mobiles* (New York: Perls Galleries, 1970).

6 Alexander Calder, *Calder: An Autobiography with Pictures*, edited by Jean Davidson (New York: Pantheon Books, 1966), 175.

7 My thanks to Alexander S. C. Rower for this observation. Thanks also to Susan Braeuer Dam for reviewing this entry.

8 Sweeney, "Alexander Calder," 1971, 6.

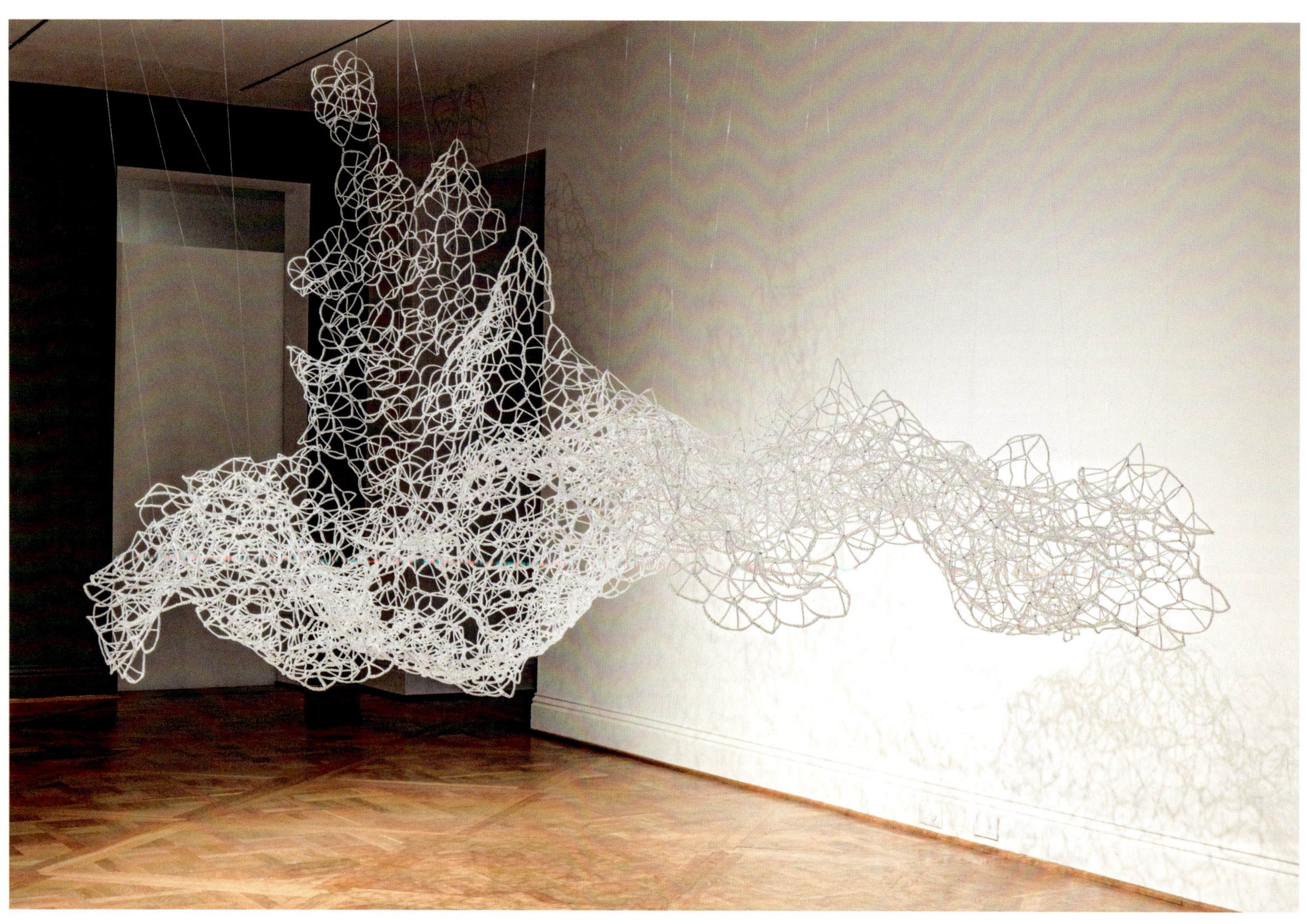

111
Alyson Shotz
***Allusion of Gravity*, 2005**
Clear glass beads and steel wire,
108 × 96 × 156 in.
The Phillips Collection, Washington, DC,
Gift of John and Sara Shlesinger, 2014.

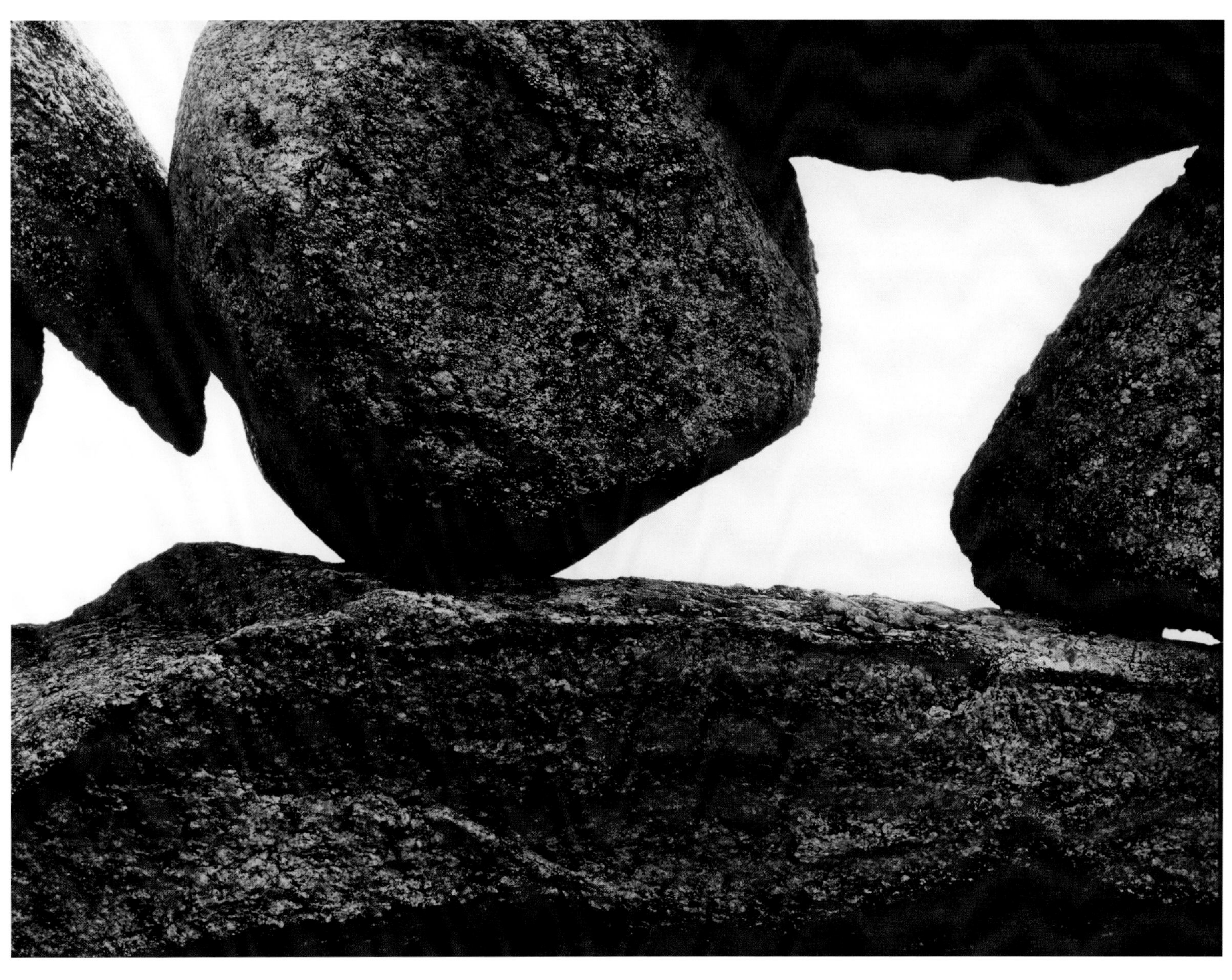

112
Aaron Siskind
***Martha's Vineyard 107 B*, 1954 (printed ca. 1980–84)**
Gelatin silver print, ed. 13/15,
36 × 50 in.
The Phillips Collection, Washington, DC,
Gift of the Phillips Contemporaries, 2003.

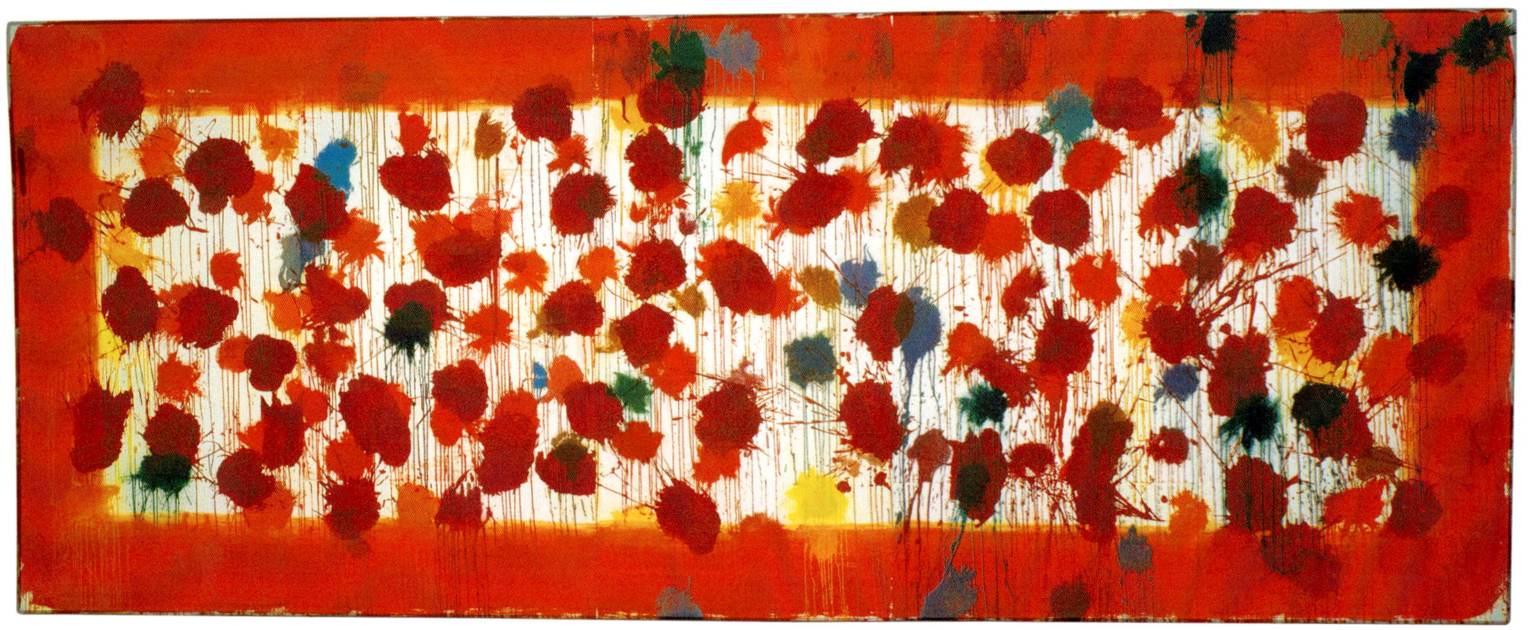

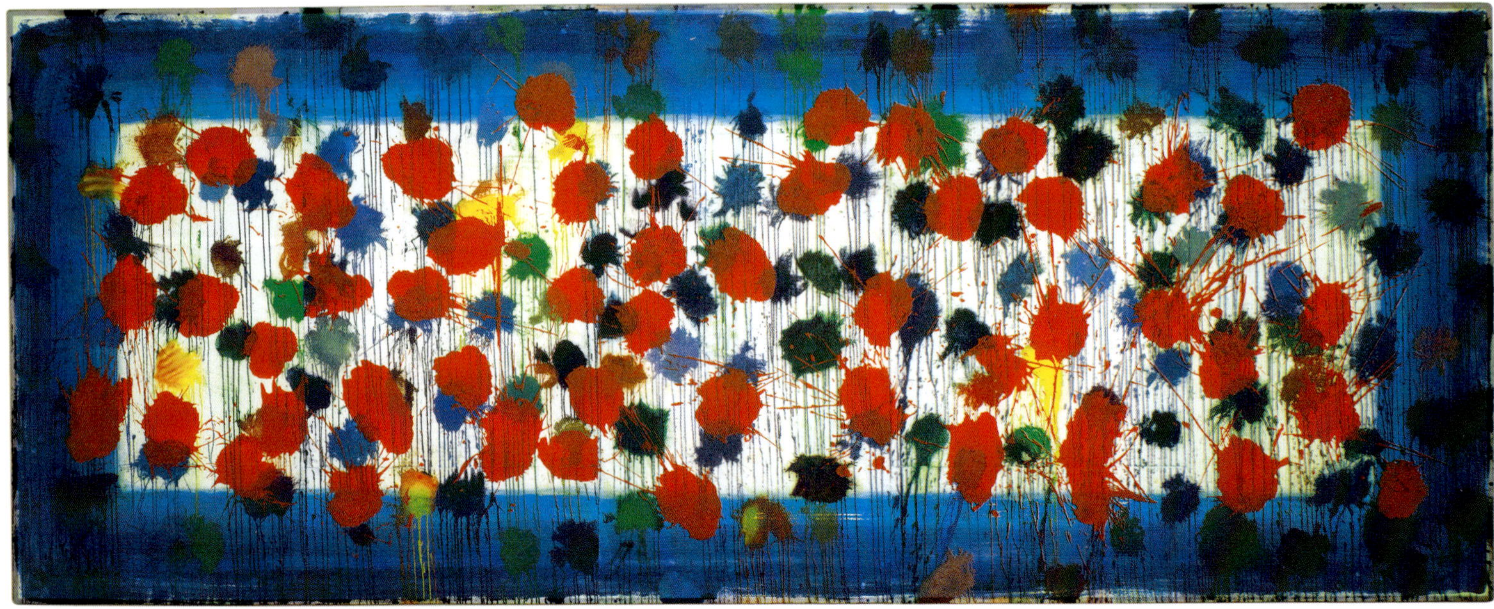

113 (top)
Howard Hodgkin
***As Time Goes By* (*red*), 2009**
Sugar-lift aquatint with carborundum relief and extensive hand-painting on five panels of 350 gsm handmade Moulin du Guè paper,
overall: 96 × 240 in.
The Phillips Collection, Washington, DC,
Gift of Luther W. Brady in memory of Laughlin Phillips, 2010.

114 (bottom)
Howard Hodgkin
***As Time Goes By* (*blue*), 2009**
Sugar-lift aquatint with carborundum relief and extensive hand-painting on five panels of 350 gsm handmade Moulin du Guè paper,
overall: 96 × 240 in.
The Phillips Collection, Washington, DC,
Gift of Luther W. Brady, Mr. and Mrs. C. Richard Belger, Marion Oates Charles, Dr. and Mrs. Brian D. Dailey, Mr. Léonard Gianadda, Linda Lichtenberg Kaplan, Mr. and Mrs. Marc E. Leland, Caroline Macomber, B. Thomas Mansbach, Dr. and Mrs. Ronald A. Paul, Gifford and Joann Phillips, and Trish and George Vradenburg in memory of Laughlin Phillips, 2010.

HOWARD HODGKIN
AS TIME GOES BY, 2009

Liesbeth Heenk

Although Howard Hodgkin was a Turner Prize winner in 1985 and was knighted in 1992, he never felt his painting and printmaking were properly understood in his native England; attractive work with luscious colors could not be taken seriously there.

In both mediums, paradox and ambiguity are paramount. Although the production of a print took up a lot of time, the result needed to appear effortless. Indeed, one never feels the agony of the printmaking process in Hodgkin's work. With the hand application of paint and framing devices, his prints are actually on the edge of being paintings. He loved the impersonal quality of the hand-painted marks that he applied to his prints from 1986 onwards.

As Time Goes By is the largest and most monumental set of prints Hodgkin ever made—possibly the largest intaglio prints ever undertaken. Preparing the plates was a tour de force for the 77-year-old artist. Feeling the chariot of time was creeping up on him, Hodgkin's sense of urgency increased, which may have been one of the reasons for the megalomanic nature of the undertaking.

Hodgkin was reluctant to disclose the meaning of a work. He insisted that each print, seemingly abstract, was firmly rooted in reality. These etchings carry a quote from a literal source: "As Time Goes By," from the film *Casablanca* (1942), a song about the eternal aspect of love in this ephemeral world. We will never know whether the title was planned or whether it was the afterthought of his partner, Antony Peattie. The prints allude to the lyrics but do not illustrate them.

Only when standing close to the prints, which were made with five successive layers, does one note their complexity. Jack Shirreff and Andrew Smith of the 107 Workshop had all the sheets of heavy paper laid out on the floor and applied the borders first, using special brushes. When the paper had absorbed the many liters of paint, they started the actual printing process. The surface displays an intricate interplay between painted and printed parts, with the carborundum embossing creating depth. The blobs are seemingly spontaneous, yet were actually carefully planned in relation to the plates. A medley of bold blotches and striations, the work looks decorative at first sight, but breathes an eternal freshness, reconciling the extremes of vibrant color with harmony.

It was the artist's wish to have the two five-panel prints (pls. 113, 114) displayed in the gallery without glazing. The monumental prints seem to float freely in space; the viewer is able to make an immediate connection without the hindrance of a Perspex layer.

As Time Goes By is a celebration of life and love, made by an artist who singlehandedly redefined the practice of English printmaking and stubbornly paved the path for more exuberance within it. He has enriched our world by inventing his own visual language based on an exquisite sense of color, which carries emotion and expresses joie de vivre.

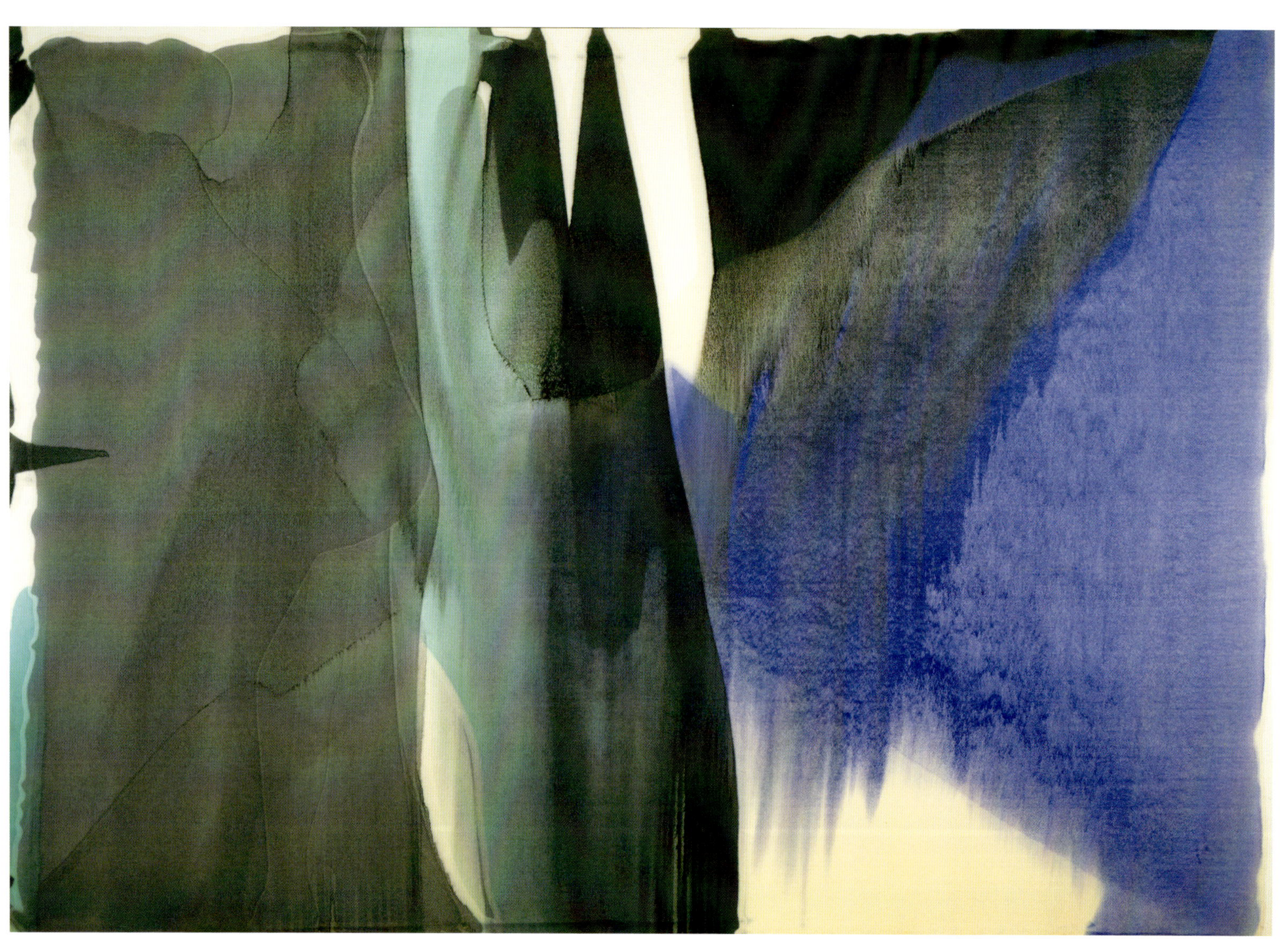

115
Morris Louis
***Seal*, 1959**
Acrylic on canvas,
101 1/8 × 140 3/4 in.
The Phillips Collection, Washington, DC,
Gift of Marcella Brenner Revocable Trust, 2011.

MORRIS LOUIS
SEAL, 1959

Renée Maurer

When he was not painting, Morris Louis wandered the galleries of The Phillips Collection, fueled by the colorful canvases of Pierre Bonnard and Henri Matisse and the abstractions of Arthur Dove and Mark Rothko. Louis taught nearby at the Washington Workshop Center of the Arts, where he befriended Kenneth Noland, an instructor. After a trip to New York in 1953 with influential art critic Clement Greenberg, Louis's style evolved. Having seen works by Franz Kline and Jackson Pollock, as well as Helen Frankenthaler's stained painting *Mountains and Sea* (1952, Helen Frankenthaler Foundation, New York),[1] Louis launched into rapid experimentation, dripping and pouring paints onto unprimed canvases. He declared Frankenthaler's art "a bridge between Pollock and what was possible."[2] For several weeks, the technically inventive Louis explored how to eliminate texture and pictorial depth from his compositions and painted without a brush.[3]

Louis worked in solitude on one canvas at a time in his twelve by fourteen-foot studio, the dining room in his Washington, DC home. He evaluated his paintings when they were stretched for exhibition and in 1957, after his first New York solo show, he destroyed several. He explained, "The more I paint, the more I'm aware of a difference in my approach."[4] Louis developed his *Veil* series by pouring thin layers of transparent color from the top of his canvas, allowing the paint to absorb and stain. He preferred Magna acrylics, which dried quickly and remained distinctly vibrant and fluid when diluted. After his critically acclaimed solo show at French and Company in New York in April 1959, a burst of productivity brought forth at least a hundred other large canvases, including the mural-sized *Seal*. Marked by sapphire, emerald, and ebony washes, its expressive color and impressive scale grew out of a response to earlier work. For *Seal*, Louis shifted the angle of his stretcher, the tautness of the canvas, and the viscosity and volume of his acrylics. He allowed his paints to flow in various directions, creating a type of drawing without the trace of a brush mark.

Seal was first featured at French and Company in March 1960, when Greenberg chose a range of *Veils* and variations for Louis's second solo exhibition there. Soon after, Greenberg heralded a new generation of American painters that formed the Washington Color school. Many of these artists found inspiration at The Phillips Collection, and Duncan and Marjorie Phillips championed their efforts by acquiring and exhibiting their work. *Seal* is the eighth work and the earliest painting by Louis to enter the collection.

---

1 The work is on extended loan to the National Gallery of Art, Washington, DC.

2 Quoted in James M. Truitt, "Art-Arid D.C. Harbors Touted 'New' Painters," *Washington Post*, December 21, 1961.

3 Michael Fried, "The Achievement of Morris Louis," *Artforum* 5 (February 1967): 34.

4 Quoted in Diane Upright, *Morris Louis: The Complete Paintings* (New York: Harry N. Abrams, 1985), 15.

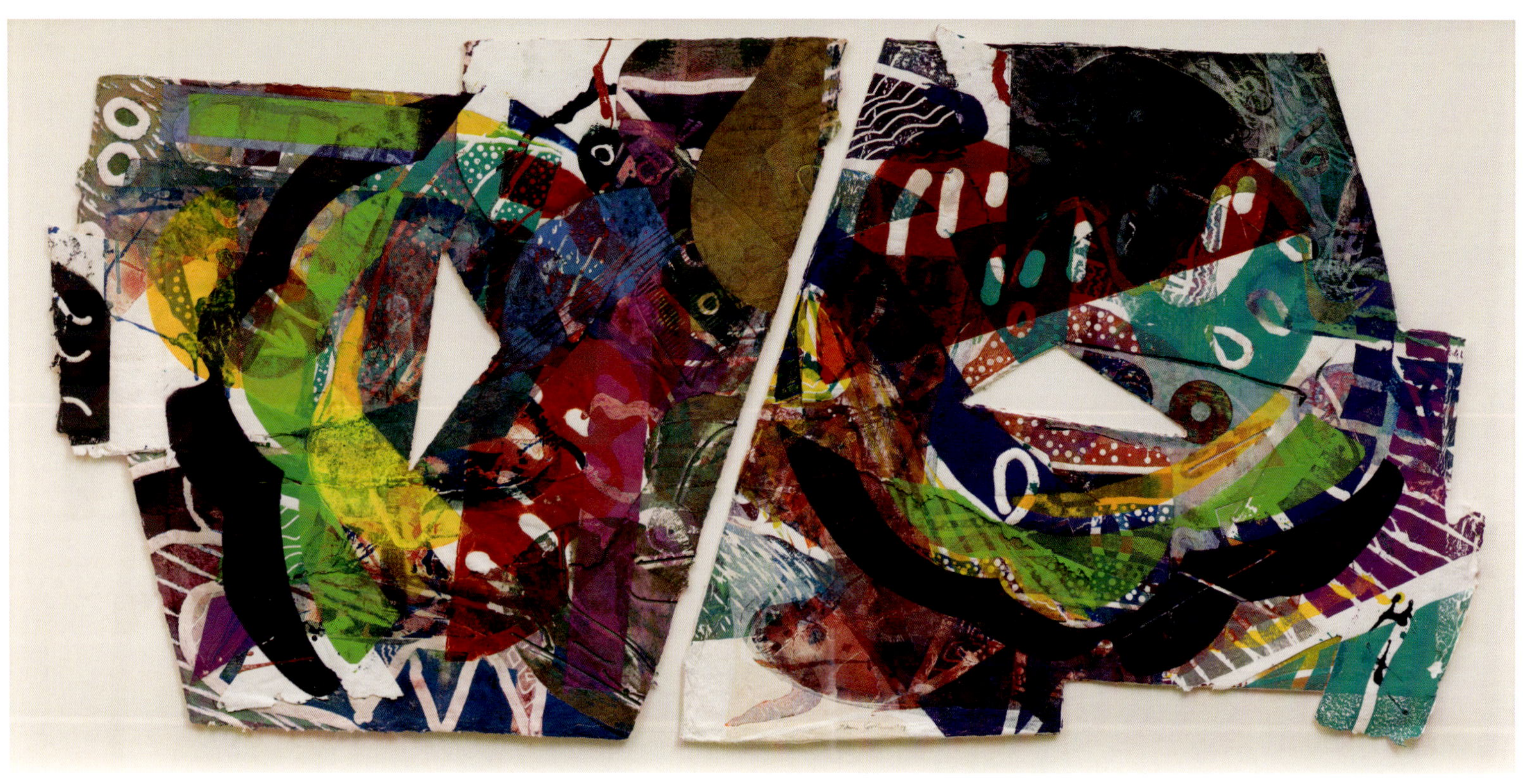

116
Sam Gilliam
Purple Antelope Space Squeeze, 1987
Diptych: Relief, etching, aquatint, collagraph, and painted collage on two pieces of handmade paper with embossing, hand-painting and painted collage, overall: 41 1/2 × 81 5/8 in.
The Phillips Collection, Washington, DC, Bequest of Marion F. and Norman W. Goldin, 2017.

SAM GILLIAM
PURPLE ANTELOPE SPACE SQUEEZE, 1987

Renée Maurer

After graduating from the University of Louisville, Sam Gilliam moved to Washington, DC, in 1962, where he discovered a flourishing art scene and the large stained abstractions of the Washington Color school, led by Gene Davis, Thomas Downing, Morris Louis, and Kenneth Noland. Gilliam frequented the galleries of The Phillips Collection and was inspired by the art of Pierre Bonnard, Georges Braque, and Arthur Dove.[1] In late 1966, Marjorie Phillips offered Gilliam his first museum solo exhibition, having seen his hard-edge geometric designs and early abstractions. Motivated by this opportunity, Gilliam searched for a new direction and reconsidered his poured and stained surfaces.[2] He discovered that by creasing, bunching, or crumpling paper, still wet with watercolor, he could create a structure and a type of drawing for his color combinations on canvas. In 1967, the Phillips purchased Gilliam's *Red Petals* and hosted his show, which was well received. Gilliam explained, "I think that *Red Petals* in a sense and the Phillips show were like the start of confidence."[3]

During this pivotal time, Gilliam's experimentations influenced his production of prints. As a visiting artist at the University of Wisconsin, Madison, in the early 1970s, Gilliam worked with William Weege, who encouraged him to be technically inventive. Later, in 1987, when Weege founded Tandem Press, Gilliam became the first artist to print there, and *Purple Antelope Space Squeeze* was Tandem's first editioned work. With its collage elements that shift in and out of relief, it embodies Gilliam's improvisational approach, where "the surface is no longer the final plane of the work. It is instead the beginning of an advance into the theater of life."[4]

To start this project, Gilliam sent Weege a drawing, and assistants cast a mold for the shape of the paper, which was printed with dense lithography inks transferred from carved woodblocks. According to Tandem Press, Gilliam then collaged and painted the paper pieces and produced prints using inked and un-inked metal relief plates, welded found objects, and steel and zinc etched and aquatinted plates.[5] Gilliam manipulated these elements on each sheet, altering colors as he went along, adding hand-painted details while the inks were still wet so that they mixed as the piece went through the press.[6] Each impression bears a unique pattern because the artist placed the printing elements in different positions and inked them in a variety of colors. Gilliam's innovative *Purple Antelope Space Squeeze* is a strong addition that enhances the twelve other works by the artist in the collection.

---

1 Gilliam created *Flour Mill* (2011), a stunning installation in the Goh Annex, a response to Dove's *Flour Mill II* (1938), which he remembered seeing on early visits to the museum.

2 Jonathan P. Binstock, *Sam Gilliam* (Washington, DC: Corcoran Gallery of Art, 2005), 26.

3 Conversation with the author in December 2010.

4 Sam Gilliam and Annie Gawlak, "Solids and Veils," *Art Journal* 50, no. 1 (Spring 1991): 10.

5 *Tandem Press: 25 Years of Printmaking* (Madison, WI: Chazen Museum of Art, 2013), xxi.

6 *Tandem Press: 25 Years of Printmaking*, xxi.

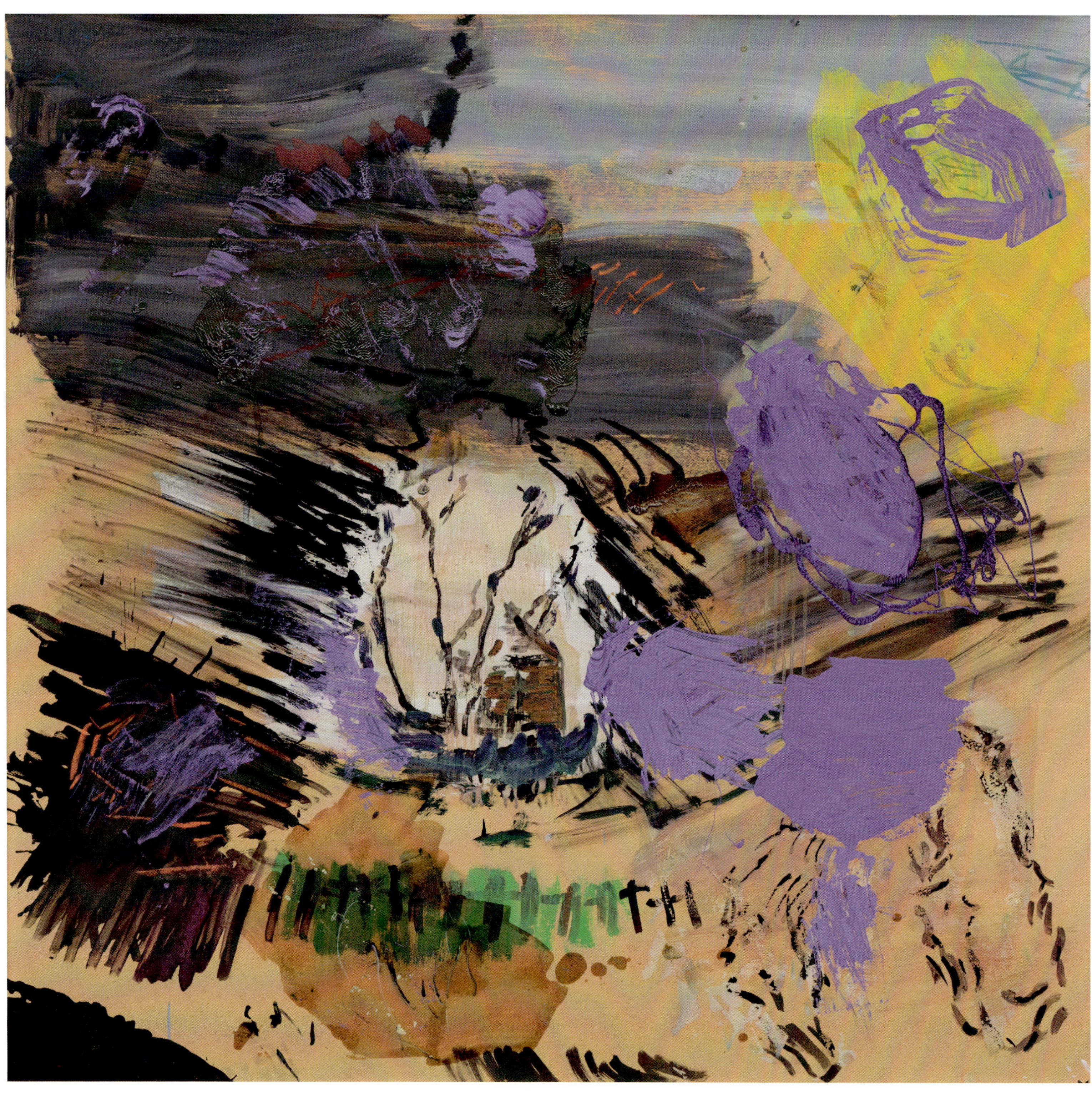

117
Per Kirkeby
Untitled, 2012
Mixed media on hardboard,
48 × 48 in.
The Phillips Collection, Washington, DC,
Gift of Lynne and Joe Horning, 2019.

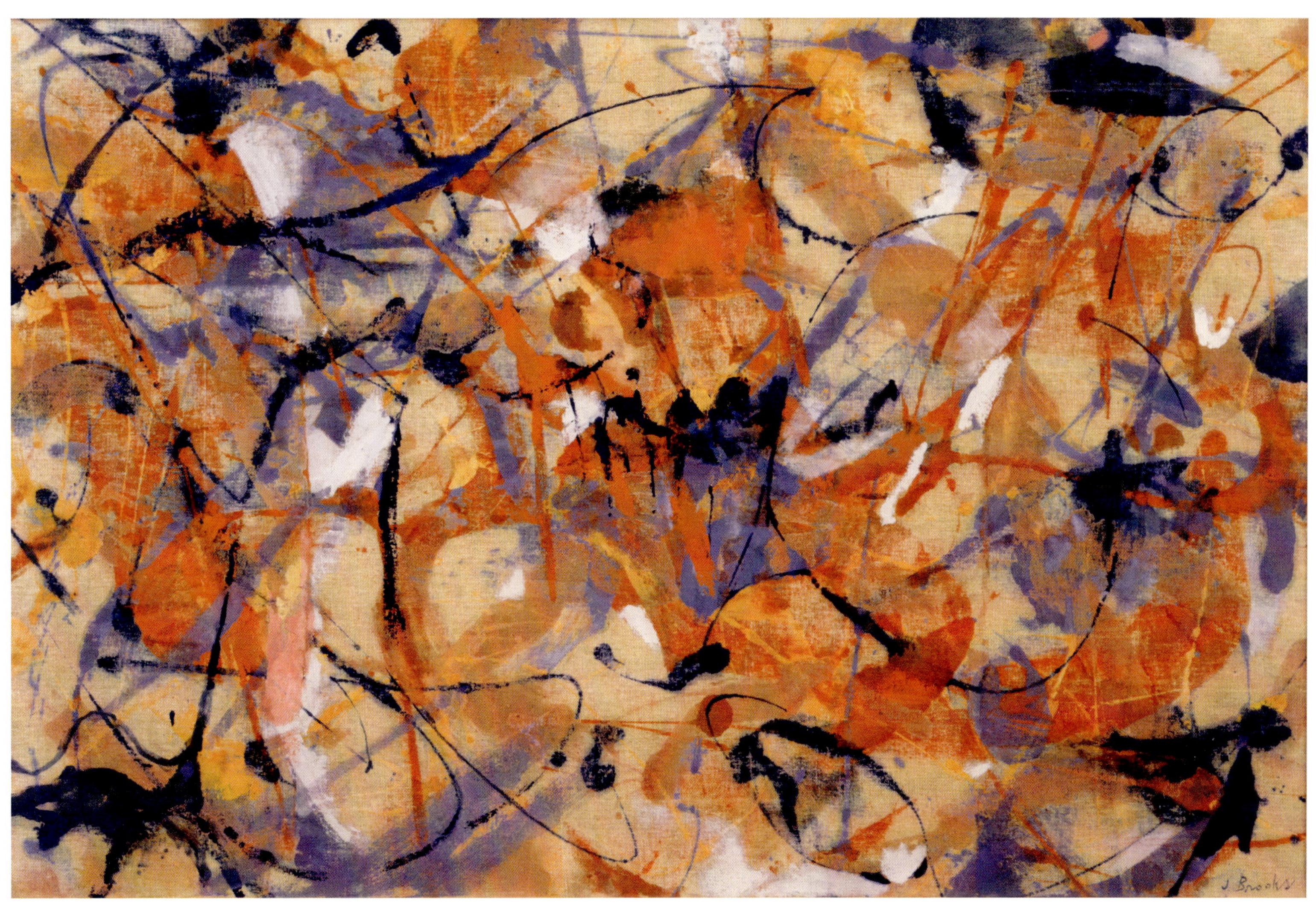

118
James Brooks
***G*, 1951**
Oil on canvas,
36 × 53 in.
The Phillips Collection, Washington, DC,
Promised Gift of Madeline and Stephen Anbinder,
Courtesy of John Raimondi.

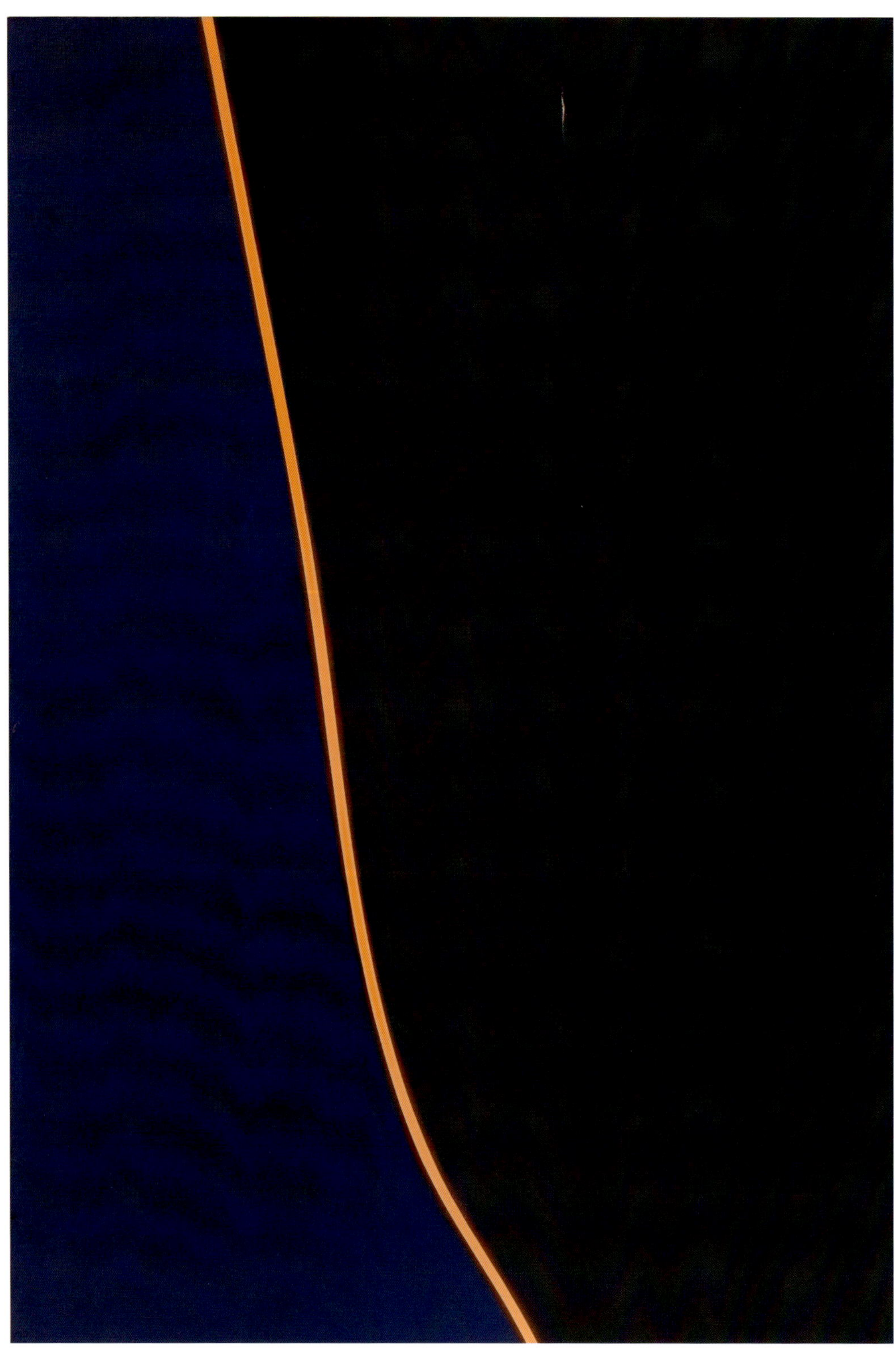

119
Lorser Feitelson
Untitled (March 14), 1972
Acrylic on canvas,
60 × 40 in.
The Phillips Collection, Washington, DC,
Director's Discretionary Fund, 2016.

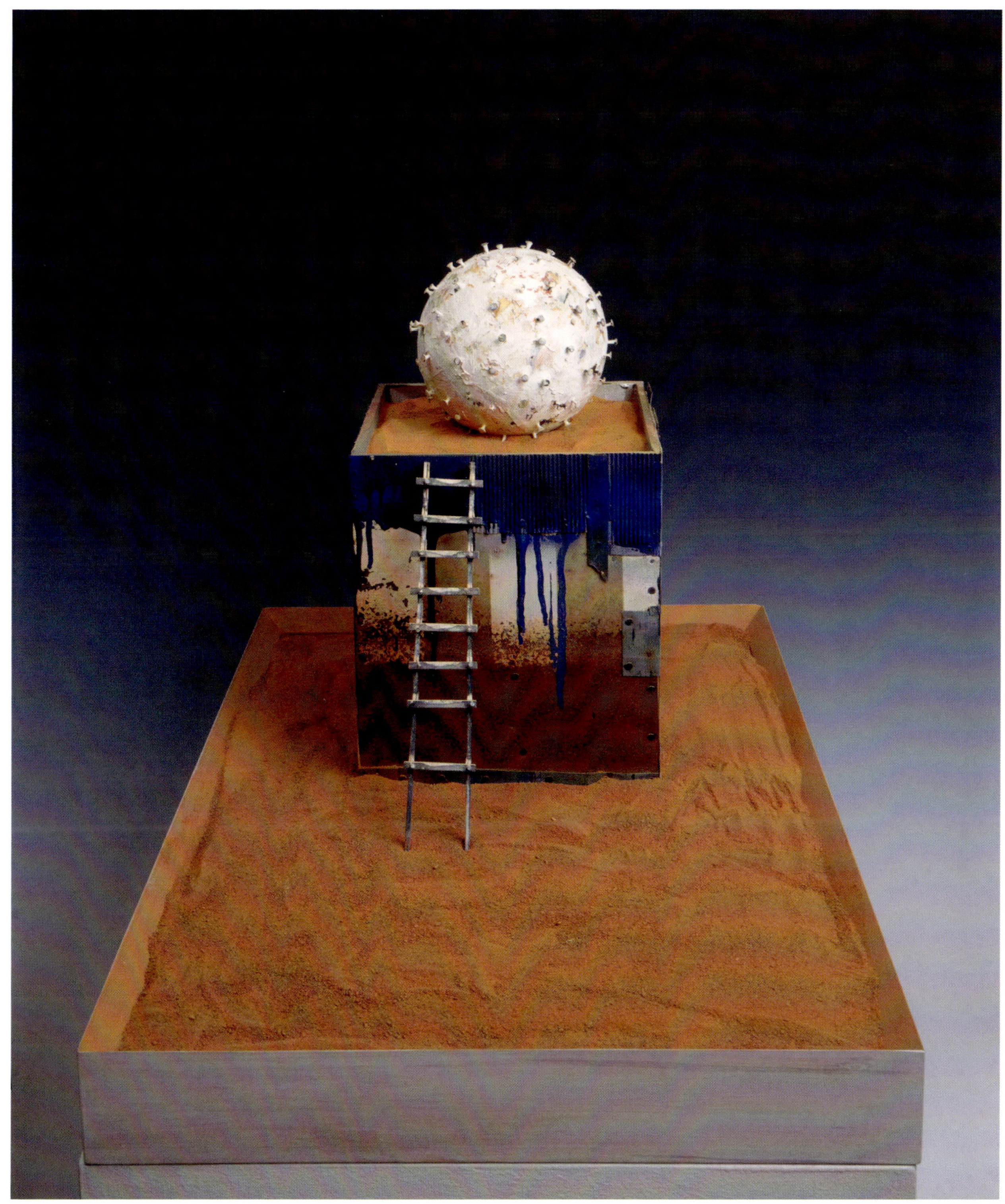

120
William Christenberry
Southern Monument XI, 1983
Mixed media, wood, sheet metal, metal signs, roofing materials, red soil and paint,
19 × 28 1/2 × 19 in.
The Phillips Collection, Washington, DC,
Gift of Philip M. Smith, 2004.

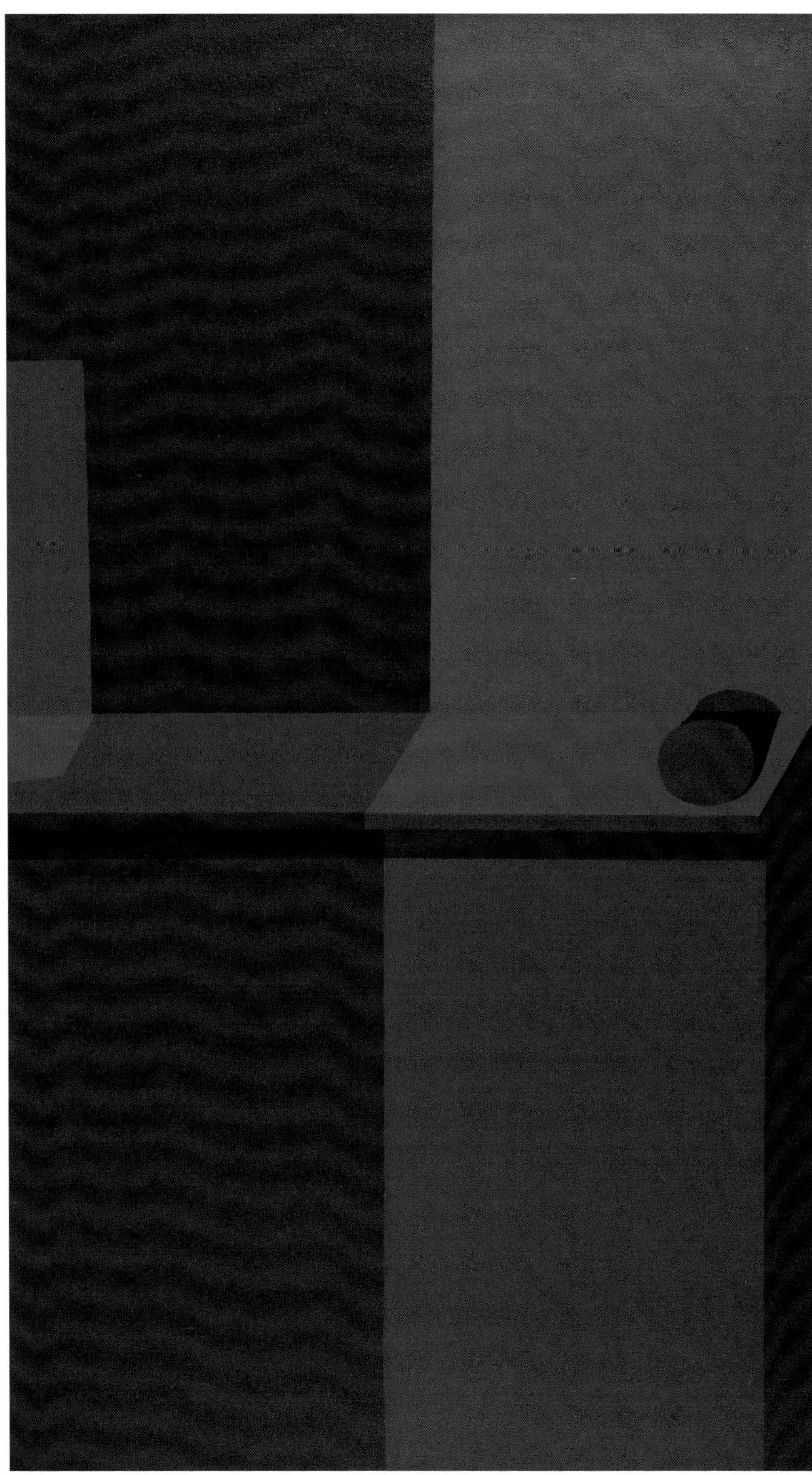

121
Helen Lundeberg
***Untitled*, 1961**
Oil on canvas,
36 × 20 in.
The Phillips Collection, Washington, DC,
Gift of The Feitelson/Lundeberg Art Foundation, 2017.

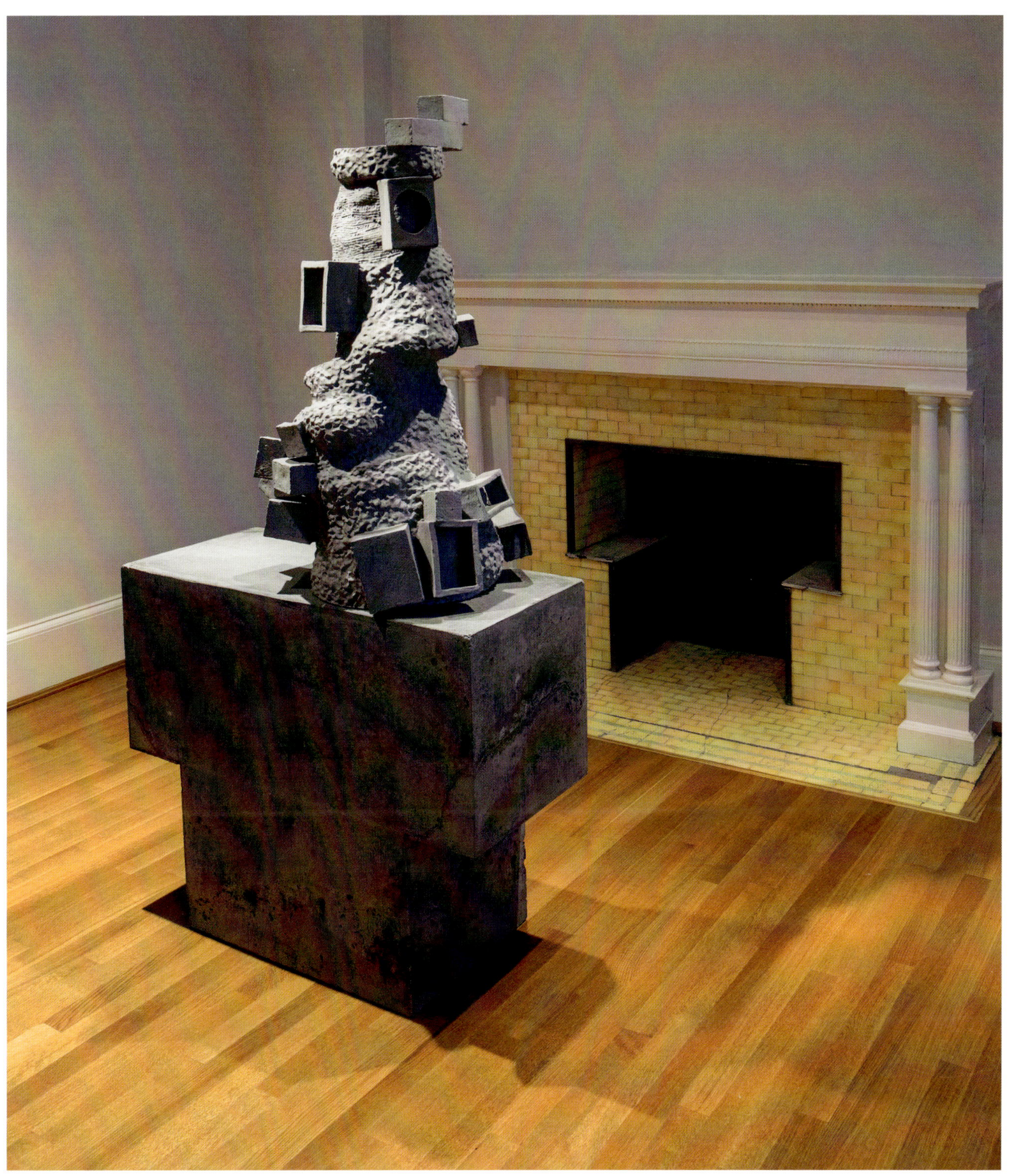

122
Arlene Shechet
***The Possibility of Ghosts*, 2013/2016**
Glazed ceramic and steel,
47 × 21 1/2 × 17 in.
The Phillips Collection, Washington, DC,
Purchased with funds given by Carolyn Alper,
Carol Brown Goldberg, Dani Levinas, Klaus Ottmann
and Leslie Tonkonow, and Wendy Makins, 2017.

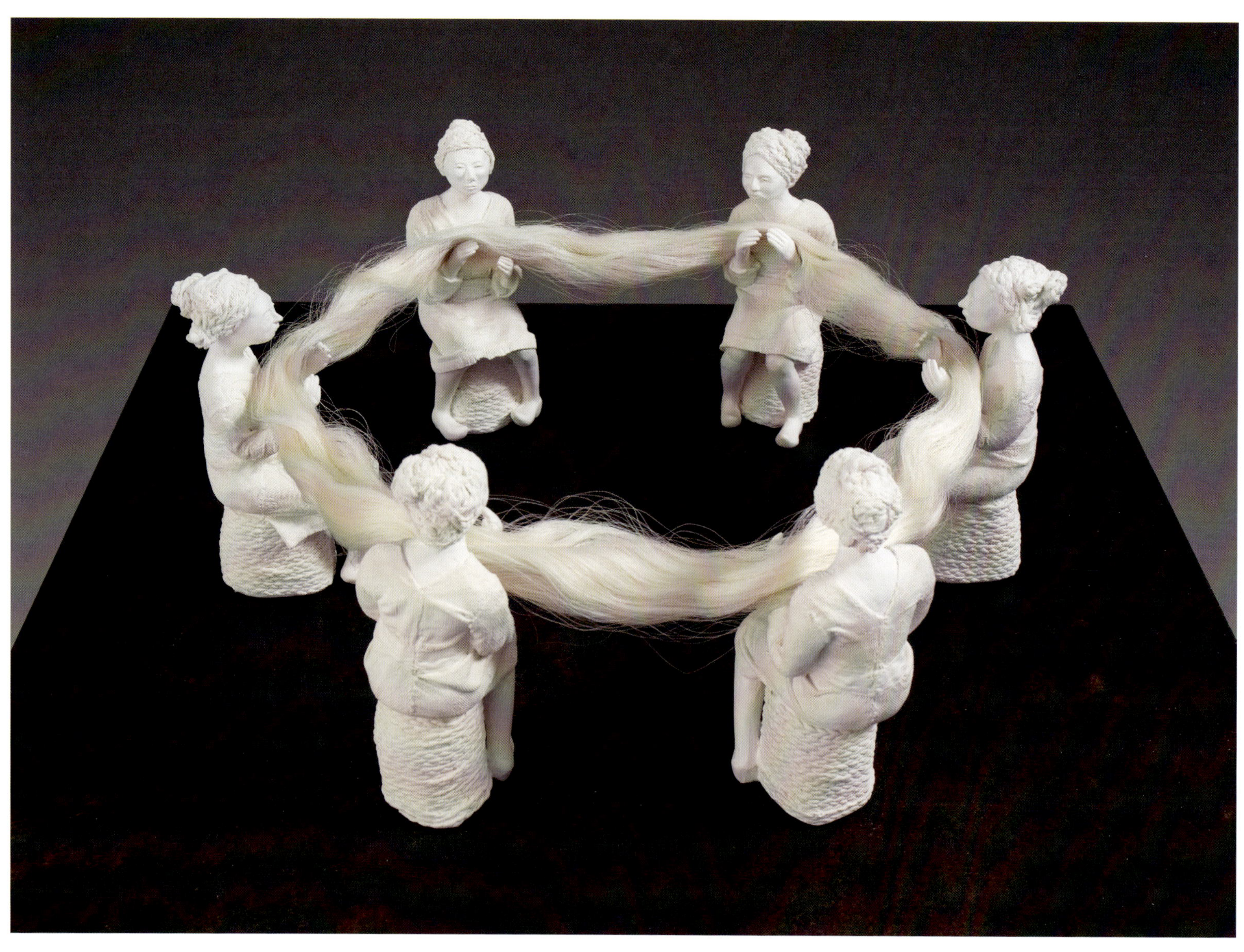

123
Amy Cutler
Idle Spinners, 2011
Hydrocal, silk, and steel,
8 × 24 × 24 in.
The Phillips Collection, Washington, DC,
Gift of Zöe and Joel Dictrow, 2020.

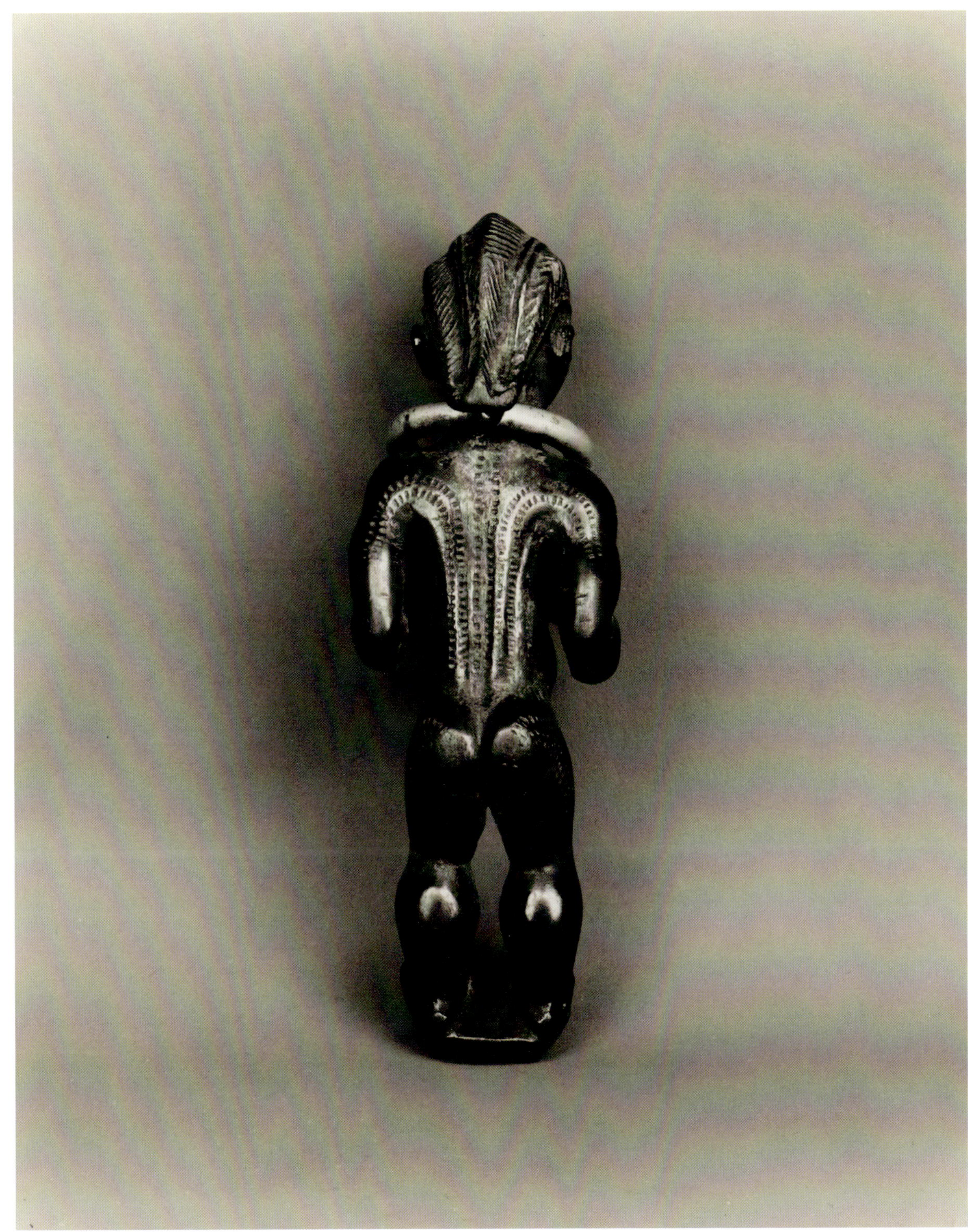

124
Walker Evans
Untitled, 1935
Gelatin silver print,
10 × 8 in.
The Phillips Collection, Washington, DC,
Gift of Samuel A. Stern, 2011.

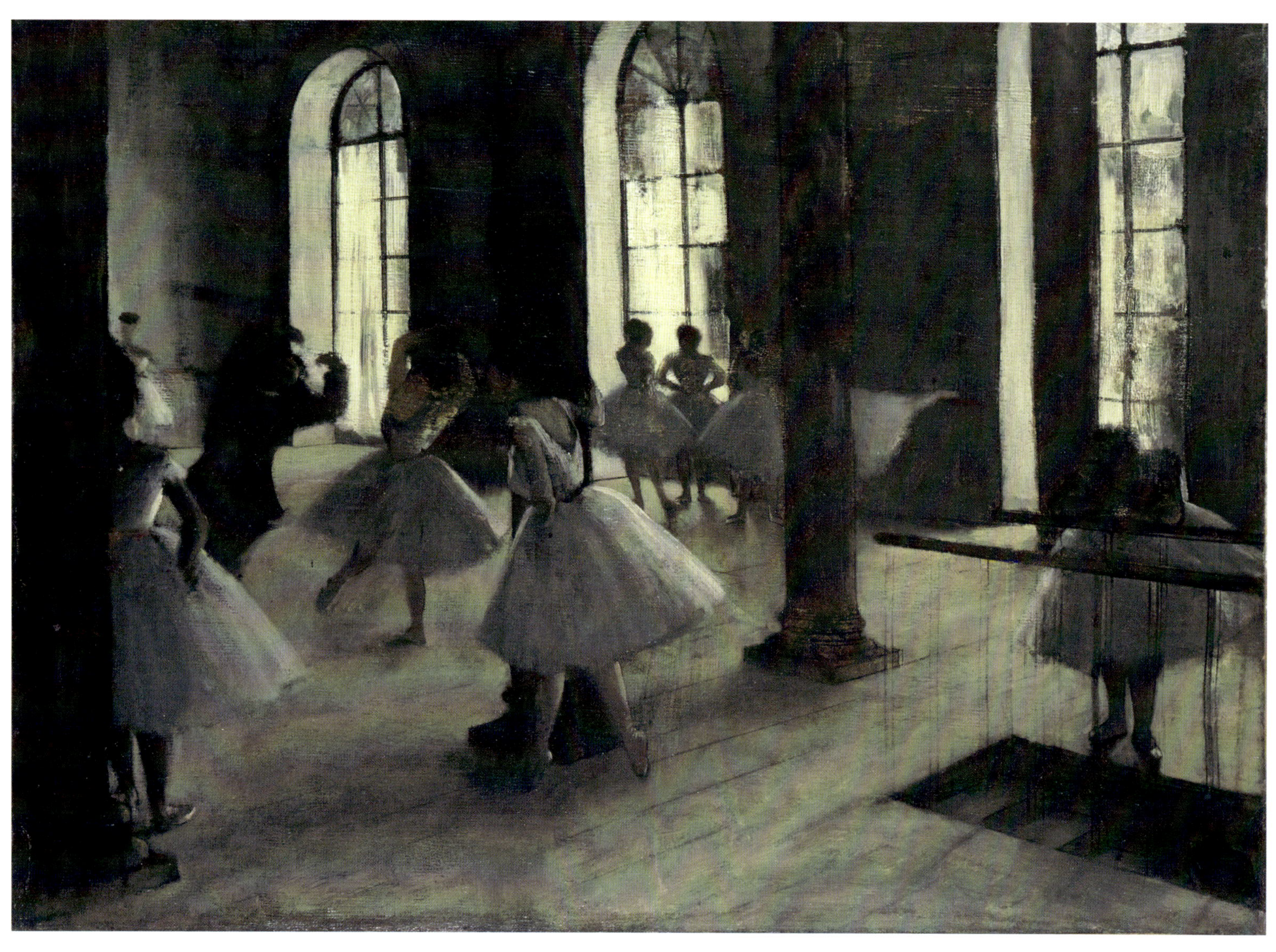

125
Hilaire-Germain-Edgar Degas
La Répétition au foyer de la danse (Dance Rehearsal),
ca. 1870–72
Oil on canvas,
16 × 21 1/2 in.
The Phillips Collection, Washington, DC,
Gift of anonymous donor, initiated 2001, completed 2006.

HILAIRE-GERMAIN-EDGAR DEGAS
LA RÉPÉTITION AU FOYER DE LA DANSE (*DANCE REHEARSAL*), CA. 1870–72

Eliza E. Rathbone

In both subject and execution, this painting speaks to many essential qualities of the art of Edgar Degas: observation, refinement, composition, balance, discipline, and ceaseless repetition that we also associate with the art of classical ballet—one of Degas's central subjects. For Degas, dance was a lifelong passion, the one to which he devoted the largest number of works—drawings, pastels, prints, paintings, and sculpture—and for which he was and remains to this day the unparalleled master. He believed, like the artists of classical antiquity, that the human figure was art's most important subject, and the dancers who spent their days practicing, rehearsing, resting, and performing at the Paris opera house offered a vast repertoire of poses, a seemingly infinite resource for the study of human, mostly female, anatomy. *La Répétition au foyer de la danse* (*Dance Rehearsal*) depicts a group of dancers practicing in a lofty room of the old Opéra on rue Le Peletier, and initiated a sequence of paintings in the 1870s of dancers in this space.[1] Although the old opera house burned down in 1873, around the time Degas painted this work, he continued to situate future dance rehearsal subjects in this same room, which he modified as freely as he rearranged the poses and groupings of dancers themselves.

In this almost colorless rendering, daylight enters the room through tall windows, arched at the top and extending to the floor, silhouetting figures against the light, an effect Degas favored at this time. To create these compositions he drew upon countless life studies. Contrasting exquisite line with blurred effects suggesting movement, he enlivened this grisaille image with the dancers' sheer fanned skirts and colorful sashes. The instructor demonstrates a step to a dancer, arms raised in arcs as he tilts his body back and to the side. Some architectural elements such as the railing and suggestion of stairs to a lower level appear to be an invention to give one of the dancers something to lean on, an element eliminated in later renderings of this space. One of two closely related paintings of dancers that Degas showed in the third impressionist exhibition in 1877, *La Répétition au foyer de la danse* reveals his preoccupation with compositional theme and variation that expanded during the 1870s. For all the informality and verisimilitude suggested by the painting, Degas's method underscores the combination of observation and invention in constant dialogue in his work. While this painting appears to have few revisions, it is painted over a previous image on the same canvas, a vertical portrait possibly of Degas's father.[2]

In the late 1870s, Degas suffered significant financial losses due to the bankruptcy of his uncle's business in New Orleans, and he badly needed buyers for his work. *La Répétition au foyer de la danse* was purchased by an English collector, Henry Hill of Brighton, then entered a private collection in America, and eventually became a gift to The Phillips Collection. It fills a gap made by Duncan Phillips himself, when in 1952 he gave to the Yale University Art Gallery (his alma mater) the very first Degas— another scene of a ballet rehearsal (*The Ballet Rehearsal*, 1885)— that he had acquired for his museum.[3]

---

1 Eliza Rathbone, "Degas's *Dancers at the Barre*: Years in the Making," in Eliza Rathbone and Elizabeth Steele, *Degas's Dancers at the Barre* (Washington, DC: Phillips Collection, 2011), 23–24, and n. 15.

2 Rathbone and Steele, *Degas's Dancers at the Barre*, 116–17.

3 Eliza Rathbone, "Degas in The Phillips Collection," in Rathbone and Steele, *Degas's Dancers at the Barre*, 105–6.

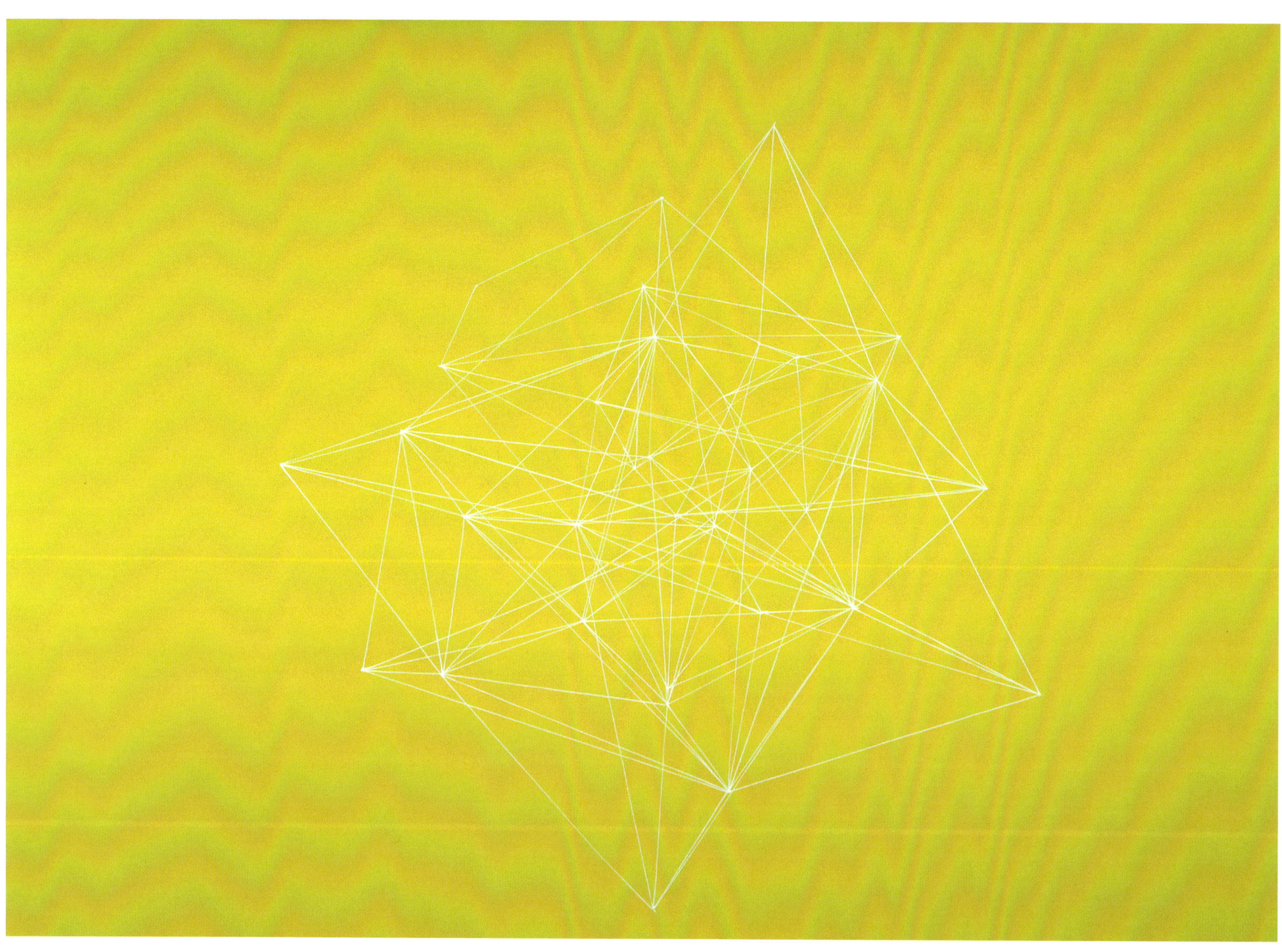

126
Kate Shepherd
***Chrysanthemum*, 2010**
Oil and enamel on wood panel,
28 × 38 in.
The Phillips Collection, Washington, DC,
Purchase, The Hereward Lester Cooke Memorial Fund
and Gift of C. Richard Belger and Evelyn R. Craft, 2010.

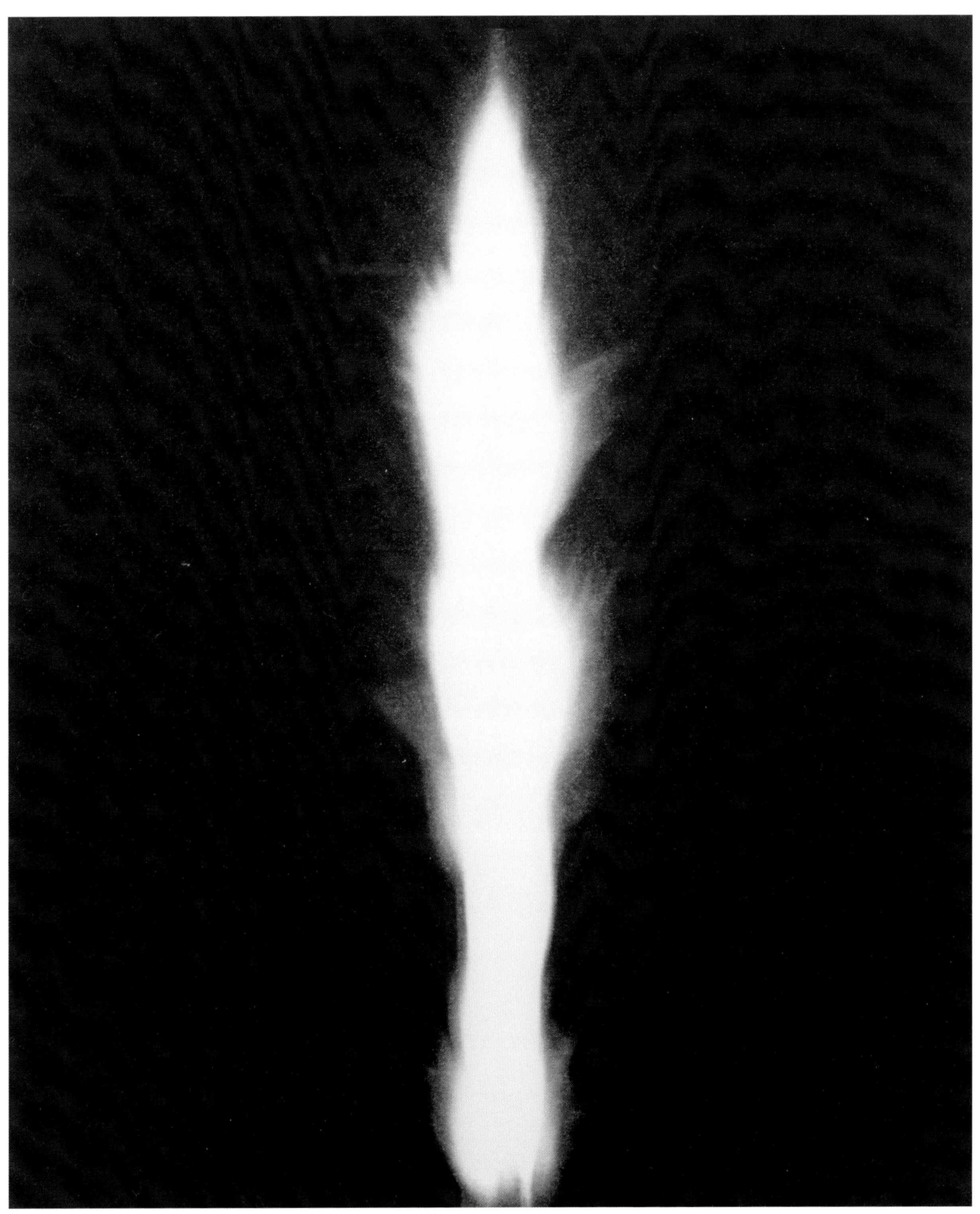

127
Hiroshi Sugimoto
In Praise of Shadows, 2003
Lithograph,
overall: 21 1/4 × 18 1/8 in.
The Phillips Collection, Washington, DC,
Gift of the Heather and Tony Podesta Collection,
Washington, DC, 2008.

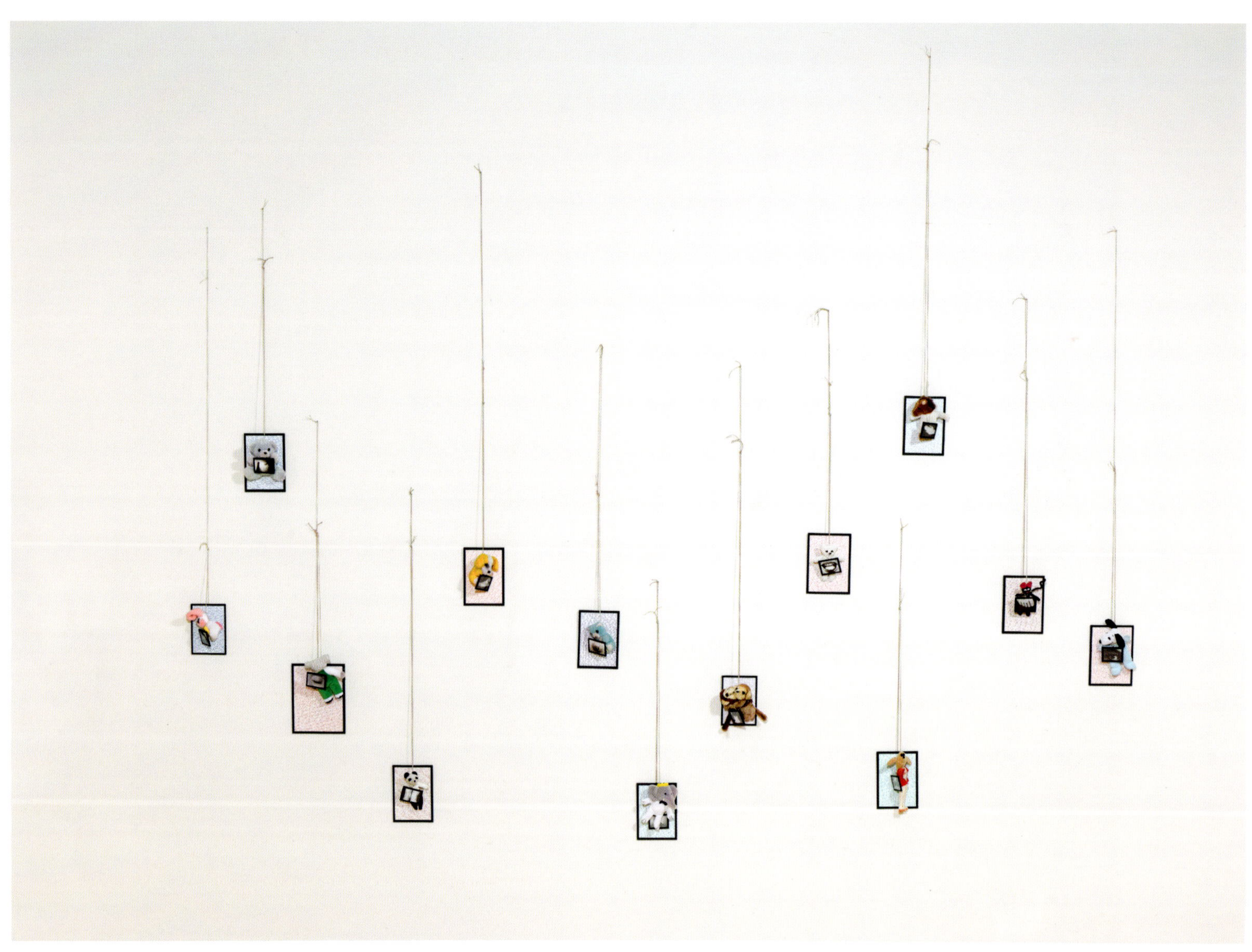

128
Annette Messager
***Mes petites effigies*, 1989–90**
13 plush toys, 13 framed gelatin silver prints, and 13 framed texts, dimensions variable
The Phillips Collection, Washington, DC,
Gift of Arthur and Carol Goldberg, 2014.

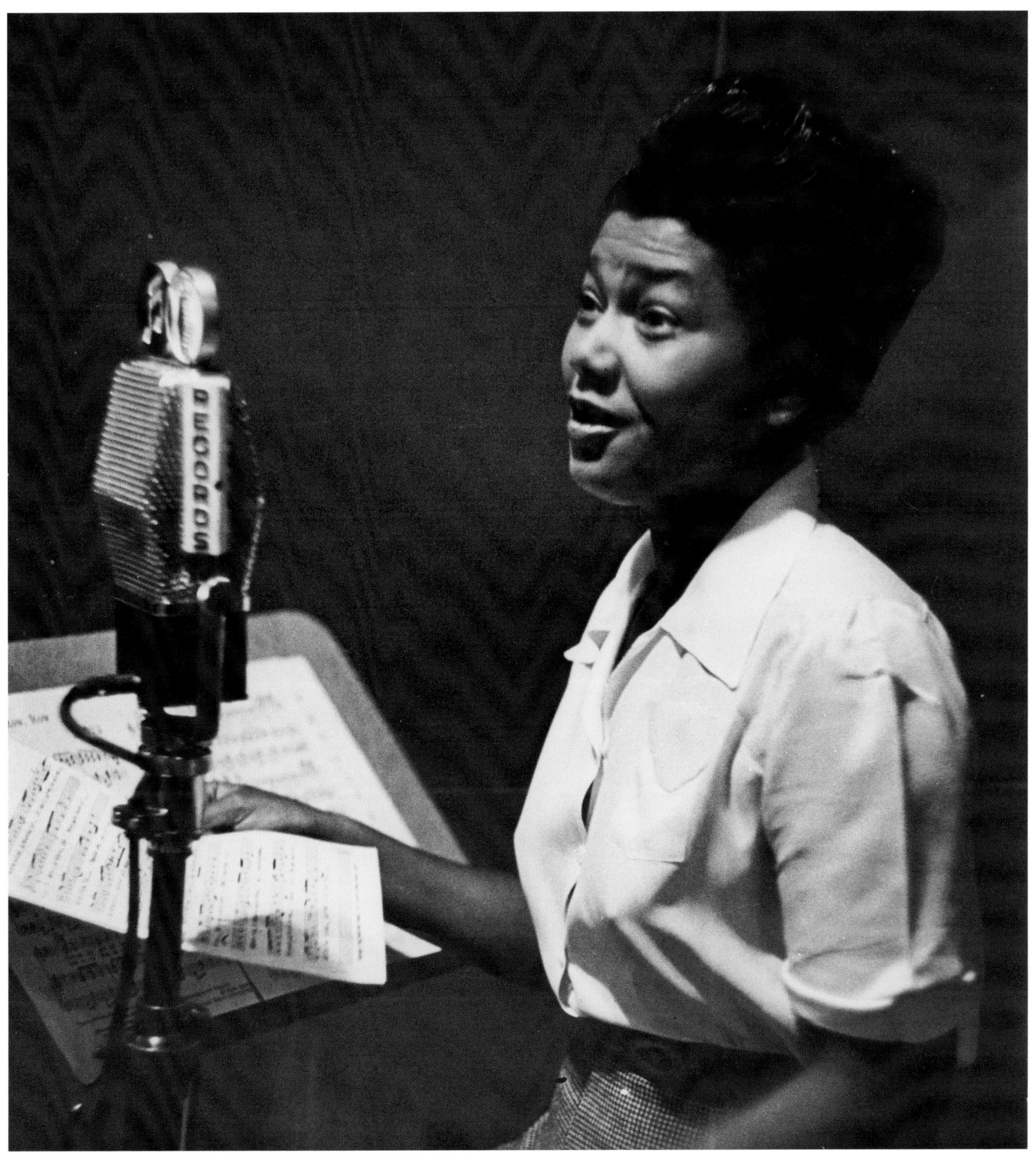

129
W. Eugene Smith
Pearl Bailey in a CBS Recording Session, ca. 1947
Gelatin silver print,
10 1/4 × 9 5/8 in.
The Phillips Collection, Washington, DC,
Gift of Michael and Joyce Axelrod, 2019.

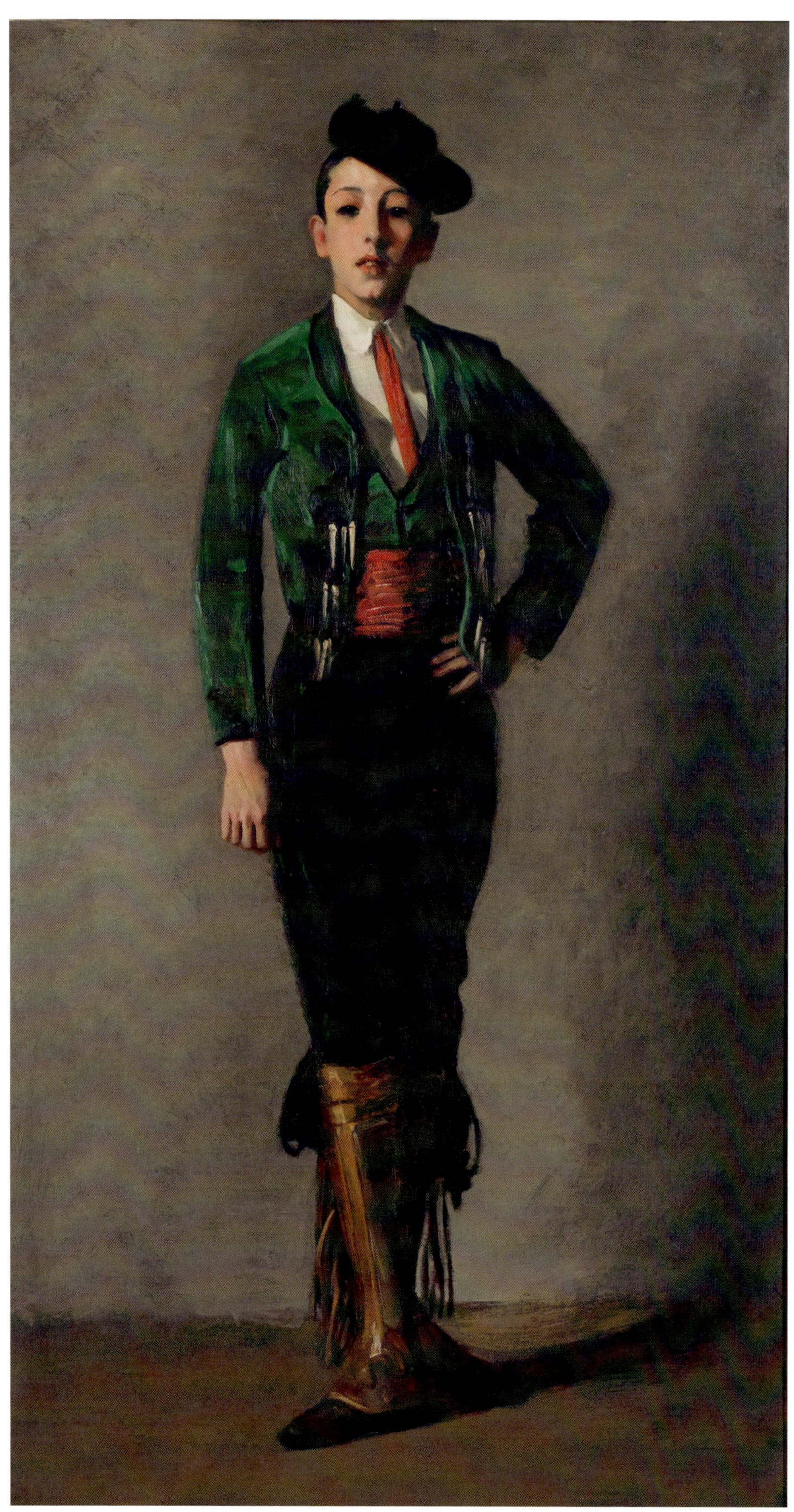

130
Robert Henri
***Spanish Dancer* (*Eduardo Cansino*), ca. 1910**
Oil on canvas,
75 × 42 in.
The Phillips Collection, Washington, DC,
Bequest of Armida B. Colt, 2012.

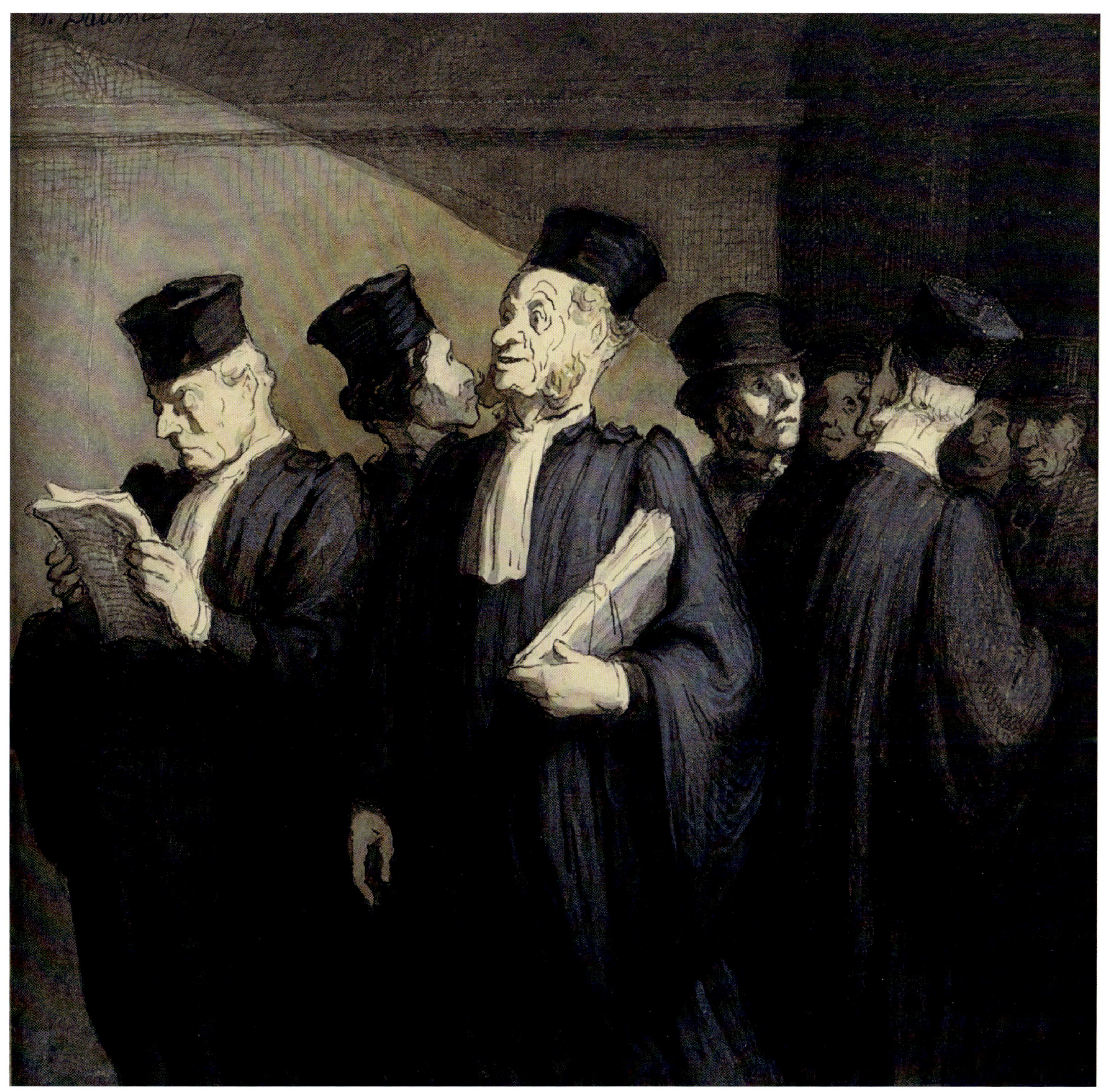

131
Honoré Daumier
Avant l'audience, 1860–65
Opaque and transparent watercolor, black and brown ink, black chalk, and graphite pencil on paper, 9 1/16 × 8 7/8 in.
The Phillips Collection, Washington, DC, Gift of Dawn Greene, 2009.

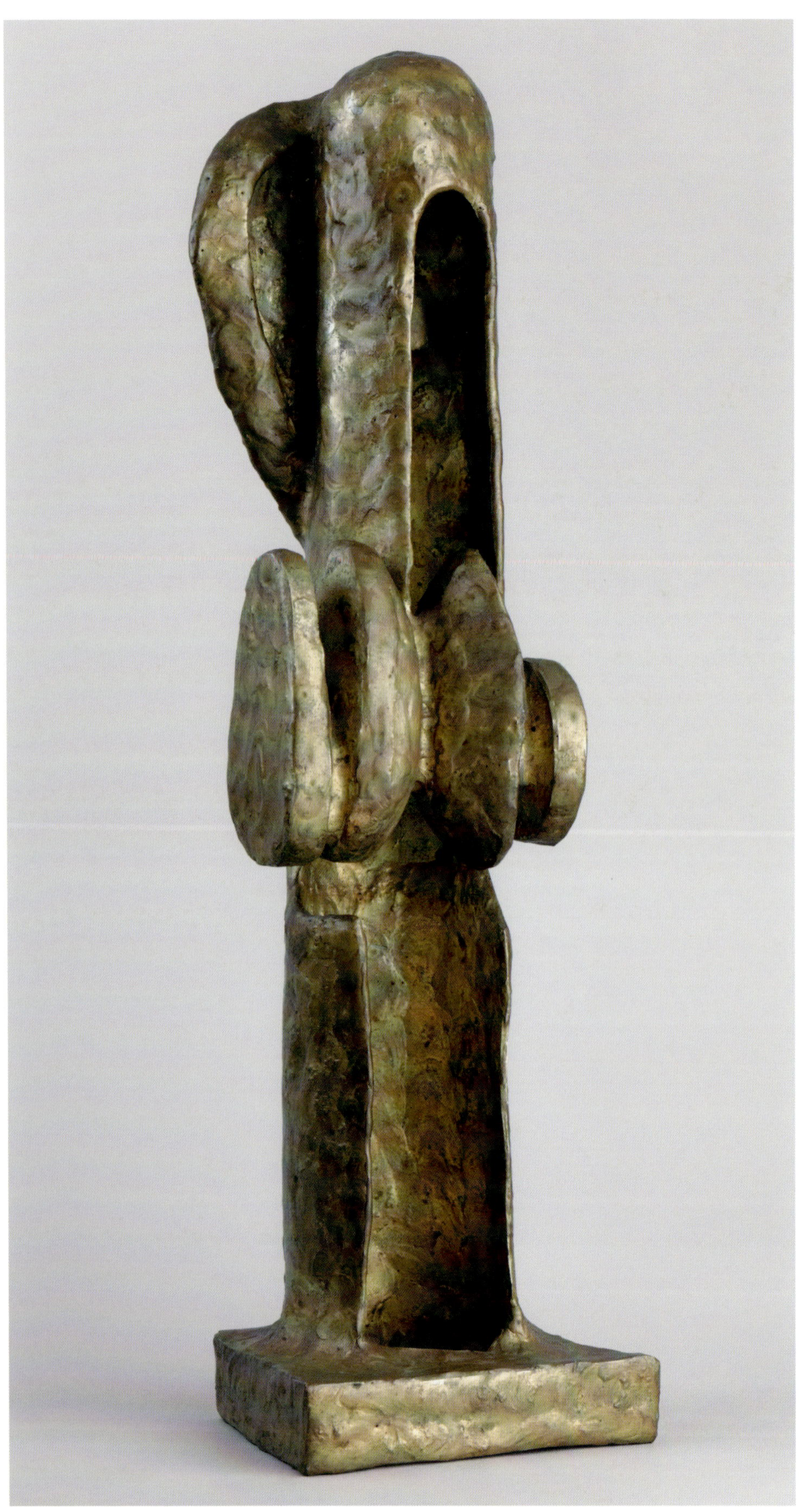

132
Seymour Lipton
***Model for "Oracle"*, 1965**
Nickel, silver, and bronze on Monel,
15 1/8 × 4 1/2 × 4 1/8 in.
The Phillips Collection, Washington, DC,
Gift of Alan Lipton, 2012.

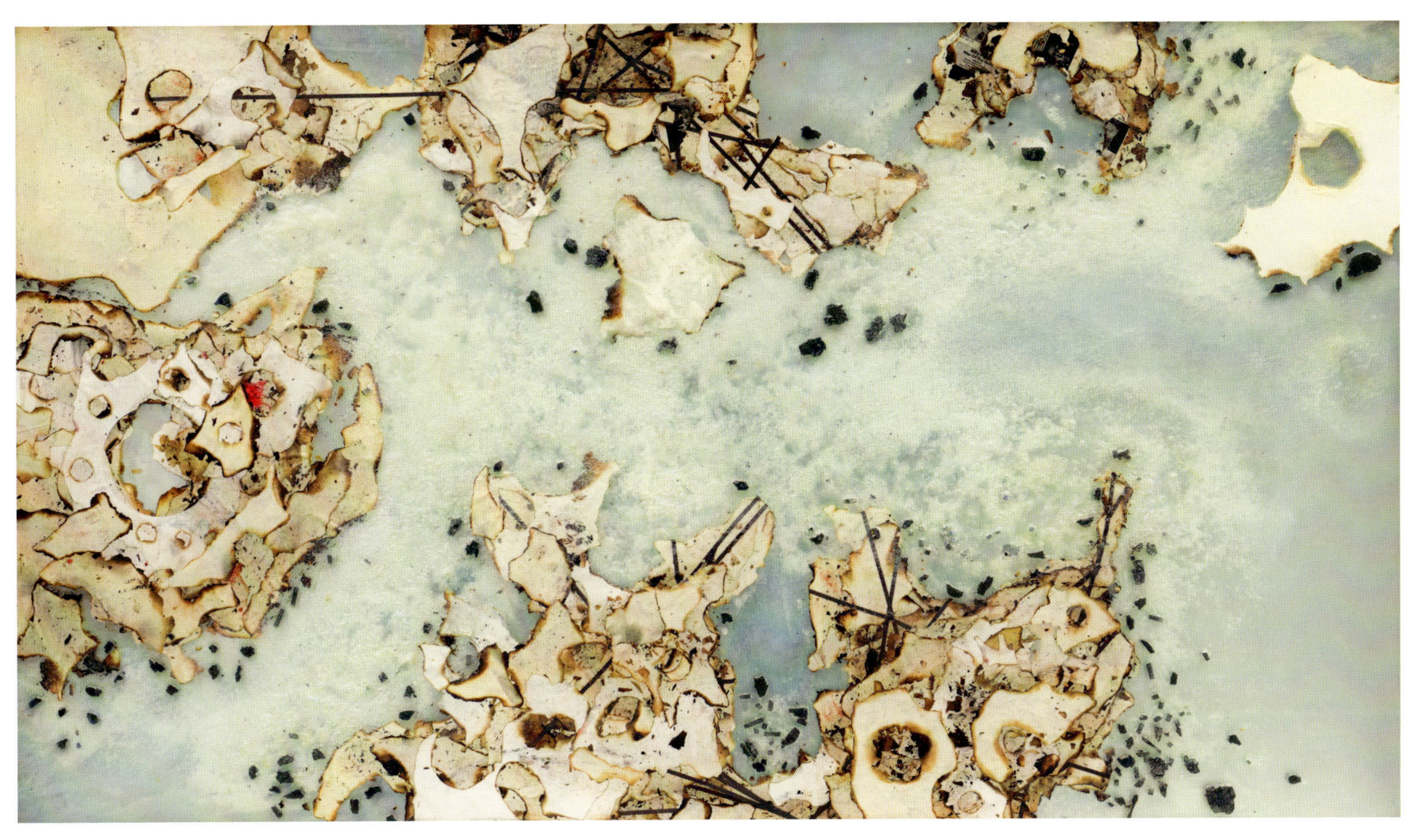

133
Ellington Robinson
***Never Forget on Ice*, 2013**
Acrylic, collage, found objects, glue and wax on framed mirror, 38 × 53 × 2 in.
The Phillips Collection, Washington, DC, Contemporaries Acquisition Fund, 2018.

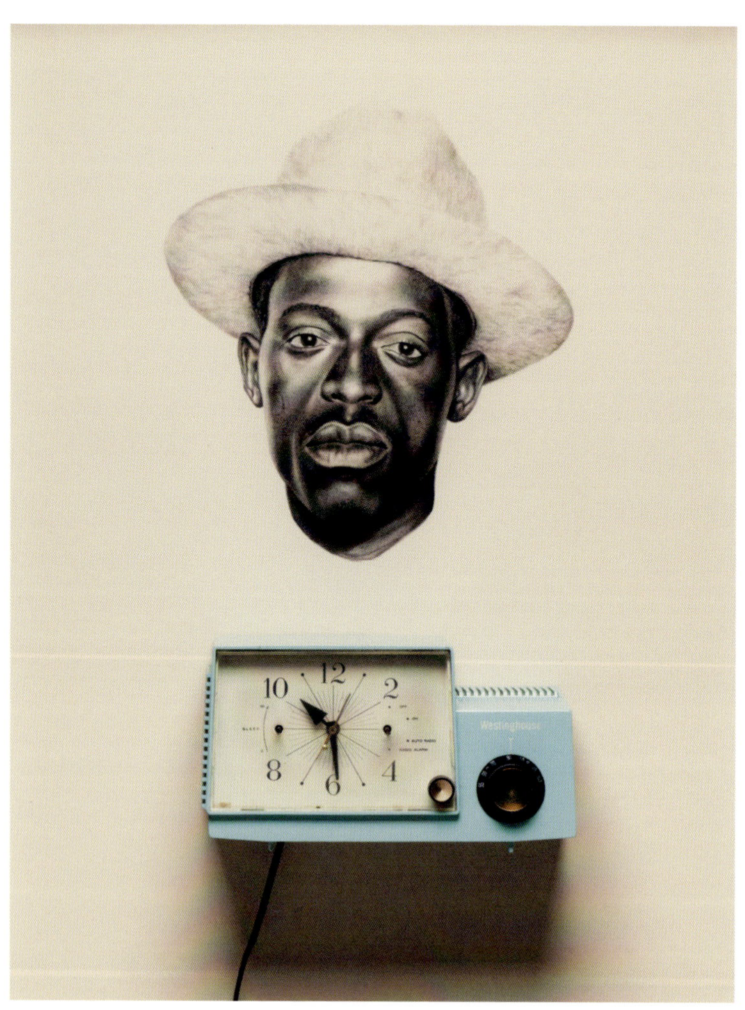

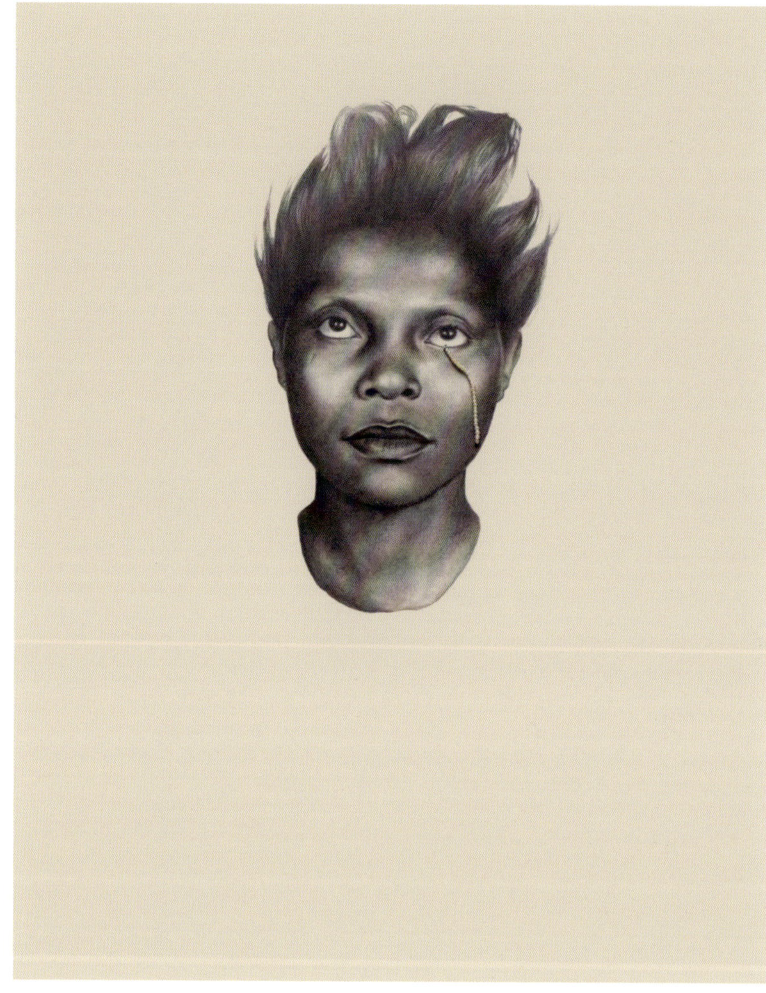

134
Whitfield Lovell
***Kin XXXV (Glory in the Flower)*, 2011**
Conté crayon on paper with vintage clock radio,
30 × 22 3/4 × 5 3/4 in.
The Phillips Collection, Washington, DC,
The Dreier Fund for Acquisitions, 2013.

135
Whitfield Lovell
***Kin XLV (Das Lied von der Erde)*, 2011**
Conté crayon on paper with string of pearls,
30 × 23 × 1/8 in.
The Phillips Collection, Washington, DC,
The Dreier Fund for Acquisitions, 2013.

WHITFIELD LOVELL
KIN XXXV (GLORY IN THE FLOWER), 2011

Ellington Robinson

With an exquisite, delicate hand, a pluralistic narrative in the diasporic galaxy is created with metaphoric planes and sfumato contours of the Southern human experience: the times of a segregated South, a map bifurcated by barbaric domestic policies and a frantic frequency of civil resolution. Whitfield Lovell's multimedia cocoons of graceful fluidity capture and freeze the in-between and bottom-of-the-stairwell happenings: the characters in the jook joint located at the crossroads, sipping on fiery brown liquids, as soulful 45-records spin in the Seeburg; the characters in the secret parlor upstairs, who bet their weekly earnings on the suit of spades. These venues are not listed in the Green Book and the faces inside are not in the history books of greatness next to Bayard Rustin or Fred Shuttlesworth. Lovell forages and obtains the IDs of these faces of David Ruffin's "Common Man"—everyday people, whom Lovell reframes, reforms, rejoices, repurposes, juxtaposes, and masters, making of these subjects masterpieces in dialogue with particular objects.

Kin XXXV (Glory in the Flower) (pl. 134) is a cosmology of Arabic numerals, a Sumerian sexagesimal system of time, symbolic and cosmic panache. The golden ratio is purposely skewed in an asymmetrical wonder. 10:29 is the catatonic time on the coral blue Westinghouse Tube Model H-78415. The color is soft, feminine, calming, and playful. The time captures a plethora of possibilities of a post-traumatic, high-cortisol fervor. There is a centripetal gestural dance with the hands of the clock and the numbers: never flush, they flirt. Over the location of the heart, the orbital dial appears like a stethoscope's chestpiece and bell. The T marker is to the right of the 9 and over the zero, indicating a 90.1 MHz frequency, perhaps. A horizon of furled dust lies on the floor of the radio: skin cells, fibers and particles from midcentury. With gravitational sensitivity, the electric cord falls past the bottom margin to the floor of the frame, coiled and extended like a cobra, balancing the intricate nuances of the lower half of the composition.

The handling of the chiaroscuro with the Conté is so masterfully invented, from the highlight on the nose to the cast shadow on the right, under the brim of the hat. The value shifts create superb plasticity, giving depth to the perspective. The values of the portrait parallel the local color and values of the clock, including its cast shadow. Thus, the portrait's forms, deceivingly, have as many planes as the actual three-dimensional clock, resulting in visual harmony of object and drawing. Textures of the hat, hair, and skin make for a painterly surface, more so than a photographic trompe l'oeil simulation. The delicate balancing act of the portrait echoes the gestural dance of the hands of the clock. The head gently leans to its left, the ear hovering over the speaker, Johnny Ace's "So Lonely" playing on 90.1. Tears border the lower eyelids, reflecting the light, reflecting bravado, reflecting deep pain. The lips remain poised, mirroring the lips of an Ife sculpture, in all its coolness.

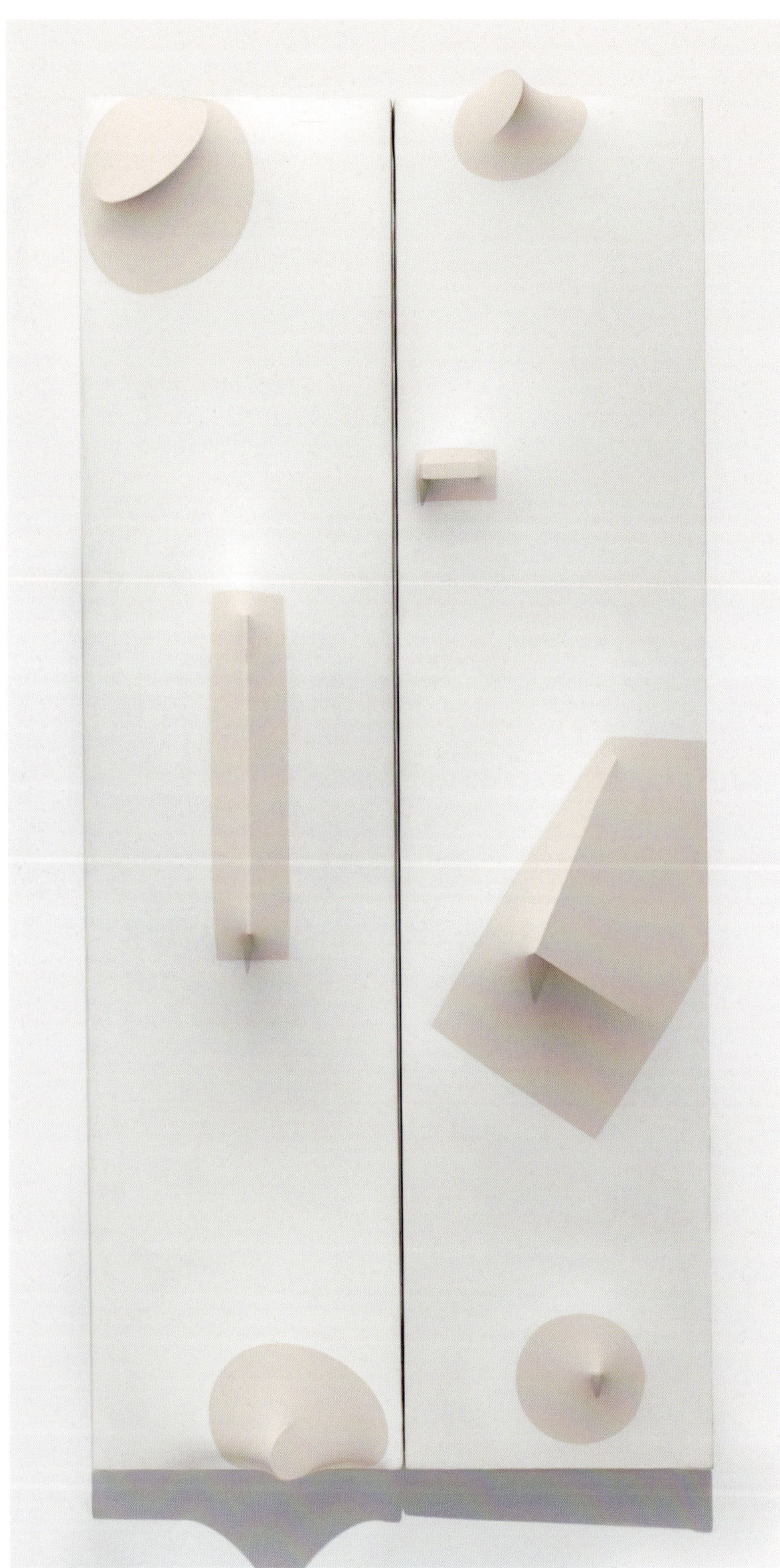

136
Zilia Sánchez
***Maquinista, diptico* (*Machinist, diptych*), 2008**
Acrylic on canvas,
each: 62 × 13 5/8 × 6 in.
The Phillips Collection, Washington, DC,
Director's Discretionary Fund, 2016.

ZILIA SÁNCHEZ
MAQUINISTA, DIPTICO (MACHINIST, DIPTYCH), 2008

Vesela Sretenović

After graduating from Havana's San Alejandro Academy in 1948, Zilia Sánchez started her career as a painter and theater set designer working in Cuban social and cultural circles associated with the pre-revolutionary, anti-Batista movement. During the mid- and late 1950s she traveled to Europe, including Madrid and Paris, and in 1960 she moved to New York City, where she lived among exiled Cubans and the city's Puerto Rican community. Since 1971, she has lived and worked in San Juan, Puerto Rico.

From the outset, Sánchez's artwork has been geared toward abstract language and themes of body and space. While her early paintings display characteristics of European postwar abstraction (Jean Dubuffet, Antoni Tàpies, Lucio Fontana), her later works feature canvases stretched over wood armatures, producing paintings with strong sculptural dimensions and fleshy sensuality. From the 1970s onward, she has referred to them as "erotic topologies."[1] Characterized by reductive, systematic forms, modular geometry, sequencing, and repetition, Sánchez's mature work has often been associated with minimalism and post-minimalism and their Latin American parallels, concretism and neo-concretism. However, with frequent references to female heroines and warriors from ancient mythology (Antigone, Amazons, and Trojans), and recurring motifs of lunar shapes, female forms suggestive of breasts, nipples, vaginas, or lips, and tattoo drawings that map physical and psychological topologies, her work resists specific categorization. Swelling from the wall, Sánchez's corporeal abstractions in neutral palettes of grays, blues, and pinks carry ambiguous content and metaphorical meaning.

Maquinista, diptico (*Machinist, diptych*) is a recent erotic topology in Sánchez's signature style, a canvas stretched over a hand-molded wooden armature. Made in two panels in acrylic in pale flesh colors, the piece is stern and restrained. Although it has a sensual elegance, the work is quite mechanized, or rather masculinized, underscoring a concept of duality typical of Sánchez's work. In fact, life for her exists only in "twos":[2] self and others, feminine and masculine, painterly and sculptural, personal and universal.

Maquinista was featured in *Soy Isla (I Am an Island)*, the artist's first museum retrospective, organized by the Phillips in 2019.[3]

---

1 Sánchez credits her close friend, exiled Cuban poet and artist Severo Sarduy (1937–1993), with coining the term "topologías eróticas" (erotic topologies), referring to her shaped canvases. This first appeared in his essay "Estructuras en secuencia" for the catalogue that accompanied her 1970 solo show *Las topologías eróticas de Zilia Sánchez* at Museo de la Universidad de Puerto Rico.

2 See https://www.phillipscollection.org/multimedia/2019-02-16-zilia-sanchez-documentary. Accessed April 2020.

3 The exhibition featured over sixty works tracing Sánchez's seventy-year career. The title, *Soy Isla*, referred to her experience as an islander, both connected to and cut off from the mainland and mainstream art currents. After its presentation at the Phillips (February 16–May 19, 2019), the exhibition traveled to Museo de Arte de Ponce, Puerto Rico (June 15–October 21, 2019), and to El Museo del Barrio, New York (November 20, 2019–March 22, 2020). It was accompanied by a comprehensive catalogue. See Vesela Sretenović, *Zilia Sánchez: Soy Isla* (New Haven, CT: Yale University Press; Washington, DC: Phillips Collection, 2019).

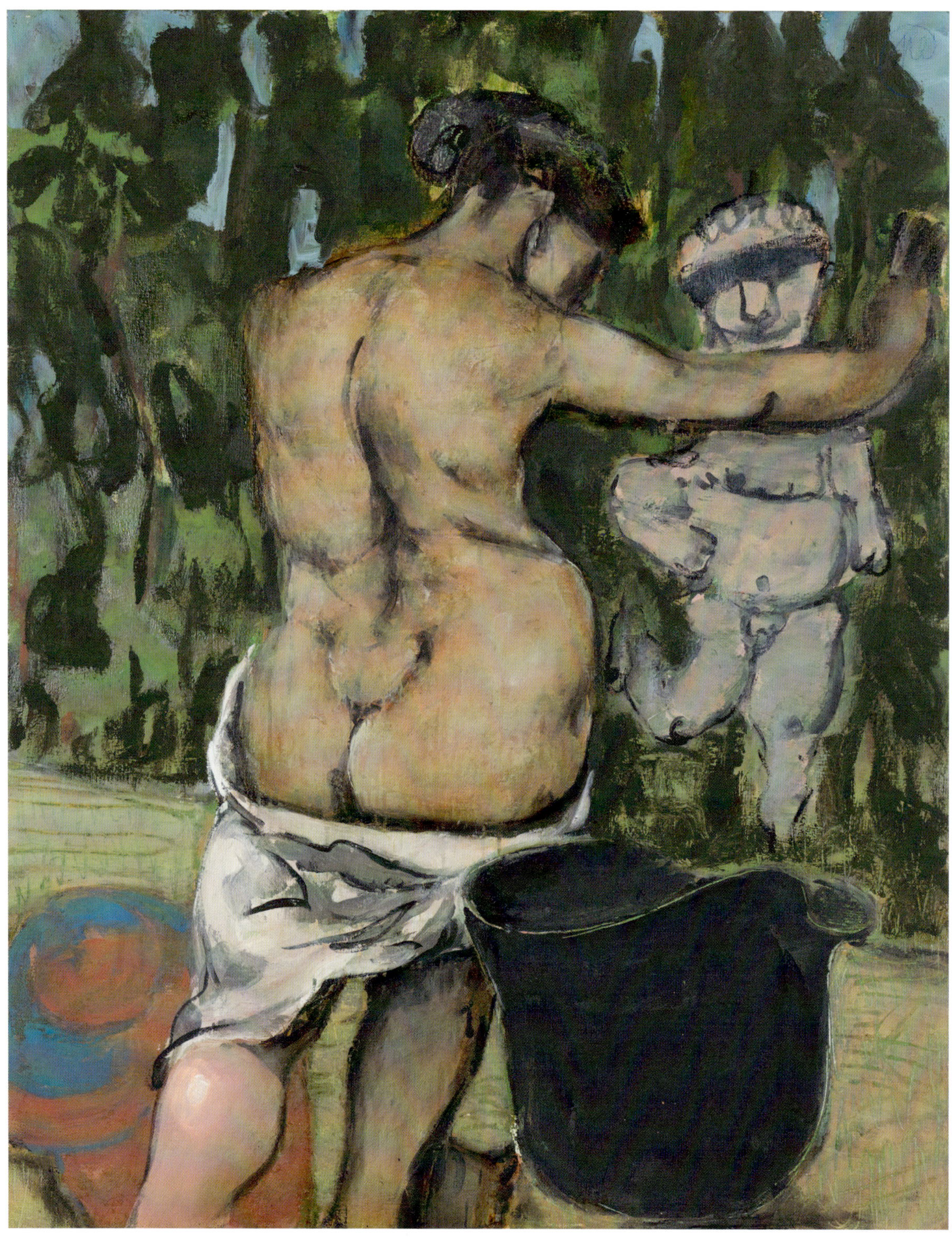

137
Markus Lüpertz
Kassandra I, 2013
Mixed media on canvas,
51 1/4 × 39 1/4 in.
The Phillips Collection, Washington, DC,
Gift of Michael Werner, 2015.

MARKUS LÜPERTZ
KASSANDRA I, 2013

Klaus Ottmann

Markus Lüpertz, a true titan of contemporary German art, emerged from the darkness of Germany after World War II. Unlike his postwar peers, Lüpertz did not abandon figuration, and in the early 1970s he embarked on his most controversial paintings, which prominently featured German military motifs. The *Stahlhelm*, the steel helmet worn by the German soldiers since World War I, occupies center stage in many of his early paintings, and reappears in paintings he has made since 2000, which are inspired both by Nicolas Poussin's *Et in Arcadia Ego* (fig. 96) and Alain Resnais's 1961 film *L'Année dernière à Marienbad* (*Last Year at Marienbad*). Poussin's painting depicts the moment when, according to Pliny the Elder, the art of painting was first discovered, but it is also a reminder that death rules even in Arcadia, the idyllic, unspoiled paradise praised by Virgil. Resnais's enigmatic, highly stylized film set in a fictional hotel and shot in various formal gardens in Germany, depicts actors and classical statues almost indistinguishably.

The connection between art and death made by Poussin is given a German slant by Lüpertz in paintings such as *Kassandra I* (2013) by juxtaposing a classical figure with a German military helmet in an Arcadian landscape setting. The central figure in *Kassandra I* is a partially draped female nude assumed to be Cassandra, the prophetic Trojan princess who not only foretold the fall of Troy but also her own death. Her figure is a faithful copy of Gustave Courbet's *The Bathers* (fig. 95), based in turn on an 1853 photograph of a female nude model by the Parisian photographer and lithographer Julien Vallou de Villeneuve. In front of Cassandra and to her right is the ubiquitous green steel helmet, oversized and upturned, which now functions as a decorative vessel. Facing Cassandra is a child-sized nude male, reminiscent of antique statues of Bacchus, like the one in the collection of the J. Paul Getty Museum (*Infant Bacchus*, 1st century AD).

Cassandra had received a gift of prophecy from the god Apollo in exchange for sexual favors, but after she rejected his advances, he condemned her to be forever disbelieved. Lüpertz here seems to draw a comparison between Cassandra's cursed prophetic gift and the gift of the artist to compel us to see representation as mere abstraction. Lüpertz insists that "in painting the truth can only be the canvas, the paint itself."[1]

Of all living painters, Lüpertz resembles most closely what in German is called a *Künstler-Philosoph*, an artist-philosopher. The term was first used by the German philosopher Friedrich Nietzsche with regard to his vision of art as metaphysical activity. For Nietzsche, art and philosophy are thus intertwined. He once said that "in all of philosophy, what is missing until now is the artist."[2] Lüpertz, who in his paintings and writings refers frequently to Nietzsche, has insisted that there is a distinction between philosophers and artists: the former question the world, the latter question themselves. Yet, like Nietzsche's expanded vision of art, Lüpertz's paintings straddle the Apollonian and the Dionysian, the idealized world of representation through form and beauty on the one hand, and the contradictions and pain of human existence on the other.

---

1 Markus Lüpertz, *Der Kunst die Regeln geben: Ein Gespräch mit Heinrich Heil* (Zurich: Amman Verlag, 2005), 30.

2 Friedrich Nietzsche, "Nachlaß," in *Kritische Studienausgabe*, ed. G. Colli and M. Montinari (Munich: Deutscher Taschenbuch Verlag, 1999), 13:14[170].

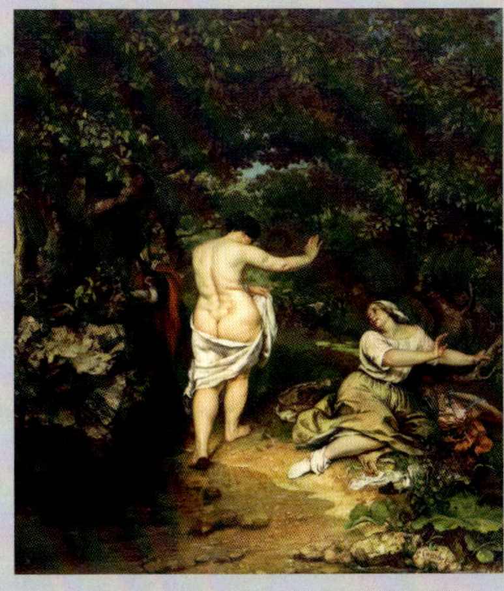

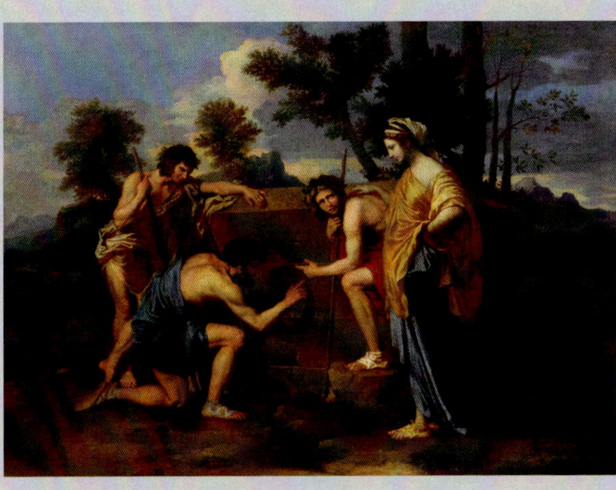

fig. 95 (far left)
Gustave Courbet
***The Bathers*, 1853**
Oil on canvas,
89 × 76 in.
Musée Fabre Montpelier Agglomération, 868.1.19.

fig. 96 (left)
Nicolas Poussin
***Et in Arcadia Ego*, 1637–38**
Oil on canvas,
33 1/2 × 47 1/2 in.
Musée du Louvre, Paris.

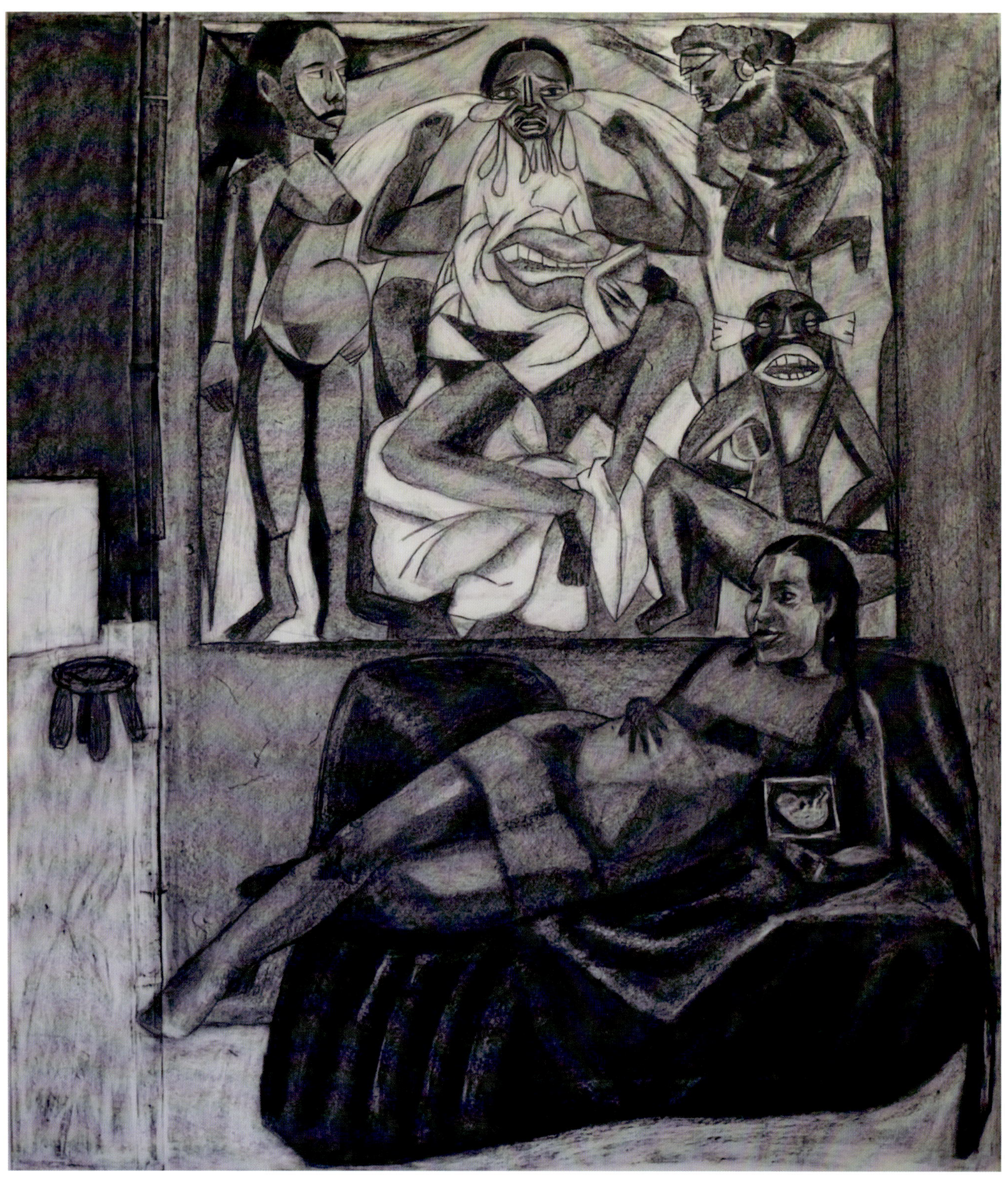

138
Mequitta Ahuja
Xpect, study, 2018
Oil-based charcoal on polyester drafting film,
32 1/2 × 28 in.
The Phillips Collection, Washington, DC,
The Dreier Fund for Acquisitions, 2020.

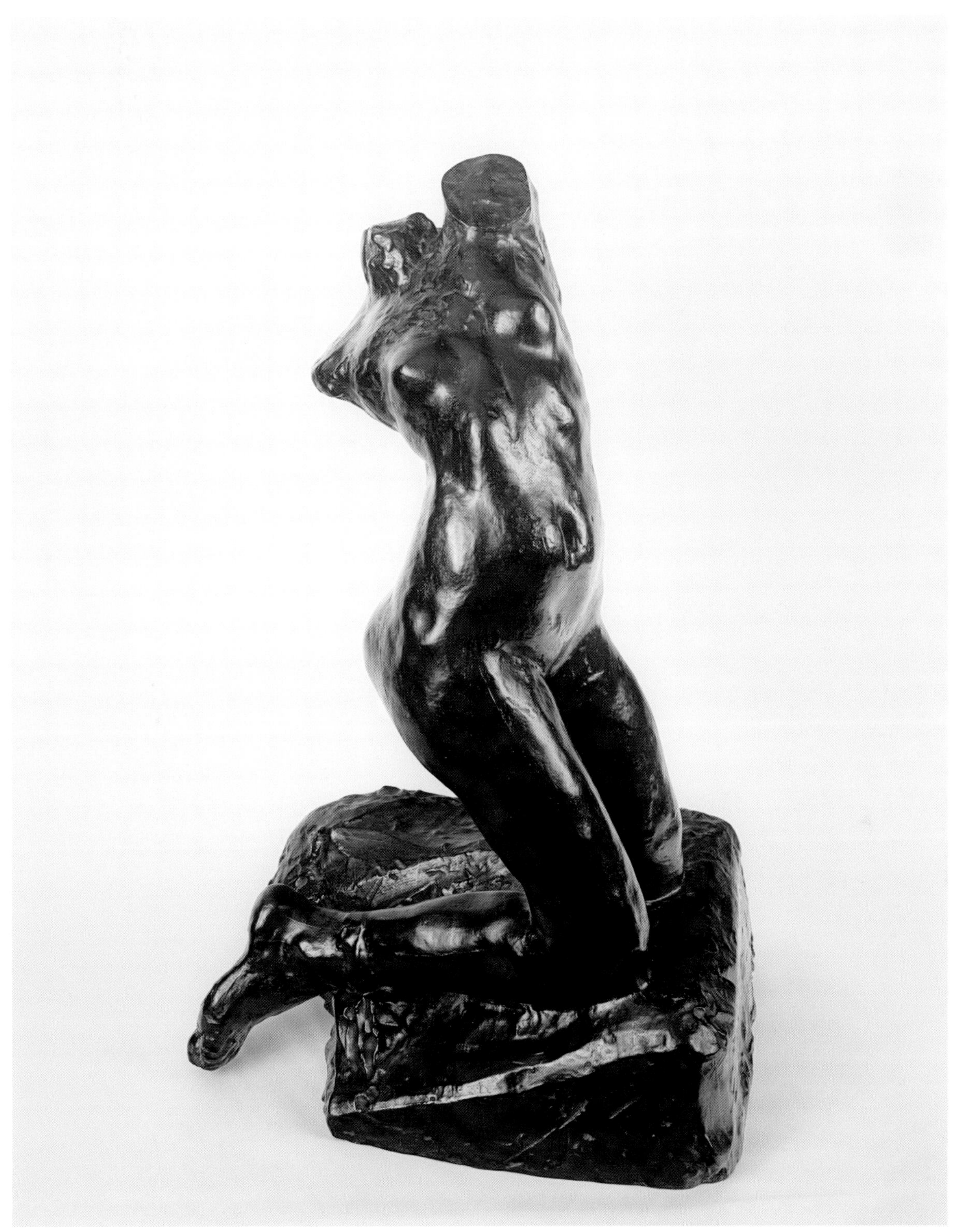

139
Auguste Rodin
Female Torso, Kneeling, Twisting Nude, **undated (cast 1984)**
Bronze,
23 3/4 × 12 5/8 × 13 3/4 in.
The Phillips Collection, Washington, DC,
Gift of Iris & B. Gerald Cantor Foundation, 2009.

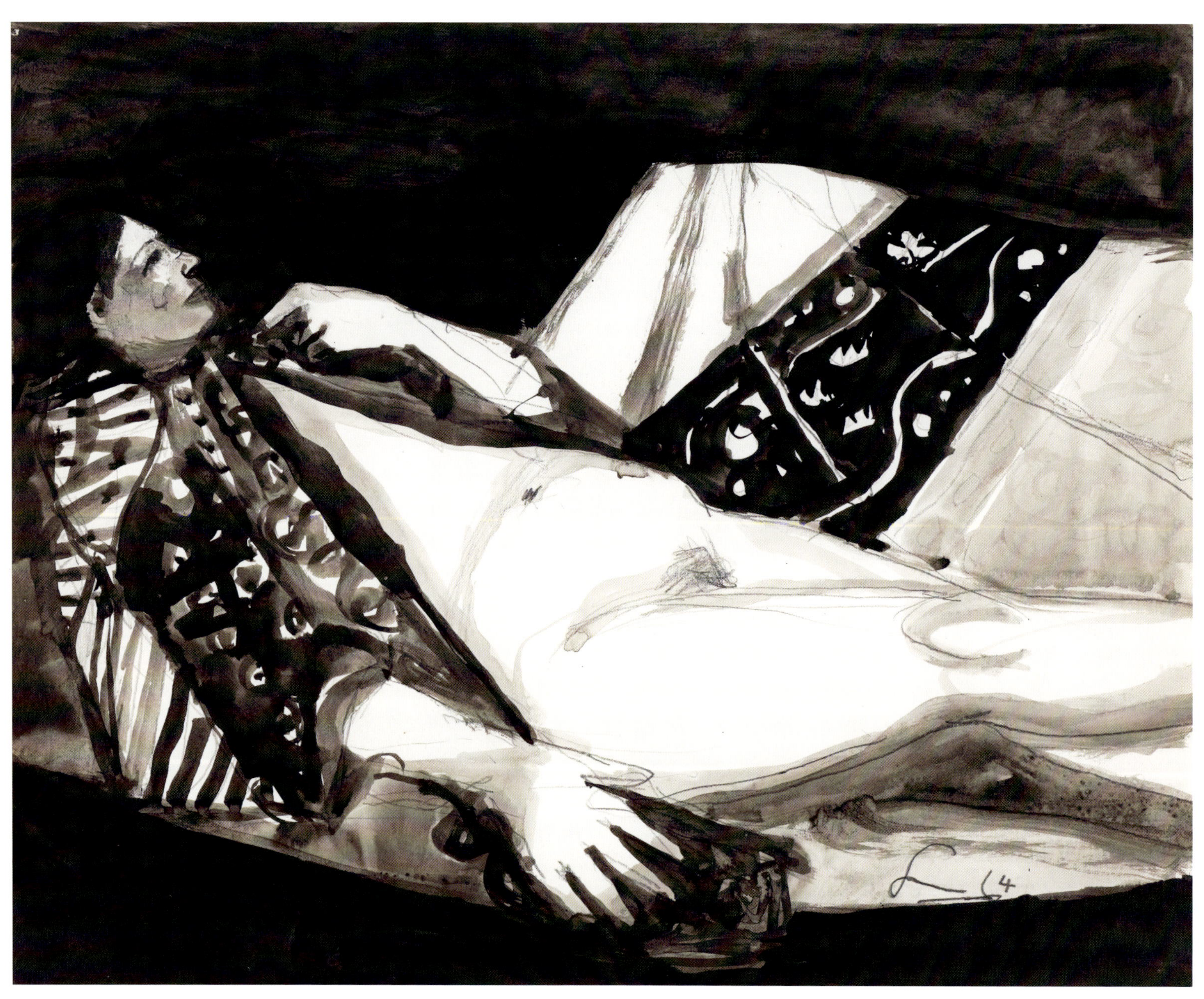

140
Frank Lobdell
***Figure Drawing Series No. 93*, 1964**
Graphite and ink wash over graphite pencil on paper,
14 × 17 in.
The Phillips Collection, Washington, DC,
Gift of Ann Kohs in honor of Eliza Rathbone, 2015.

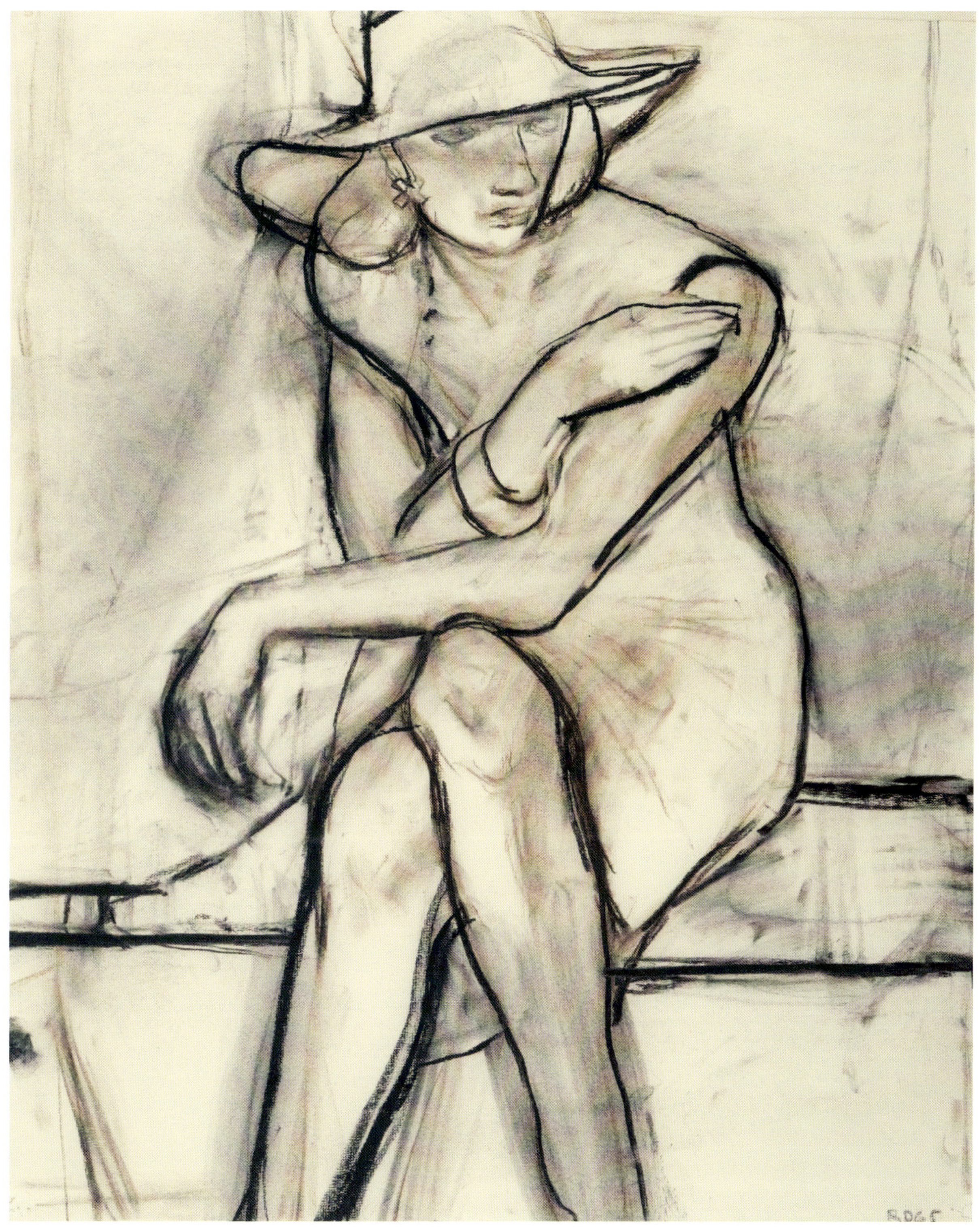

141
Richard Diebenkorn
Untitled (Seated Woman Wearing a Broad-brimmed Hat),
1965
Charcoal and brown chalk on paper,
23 1/2 × 19 in.
The Phillips Collection, Washington, DC,
Bequest of Anne S. Reich, in memory of Henry S. and
Anne S. Reich, 2009.

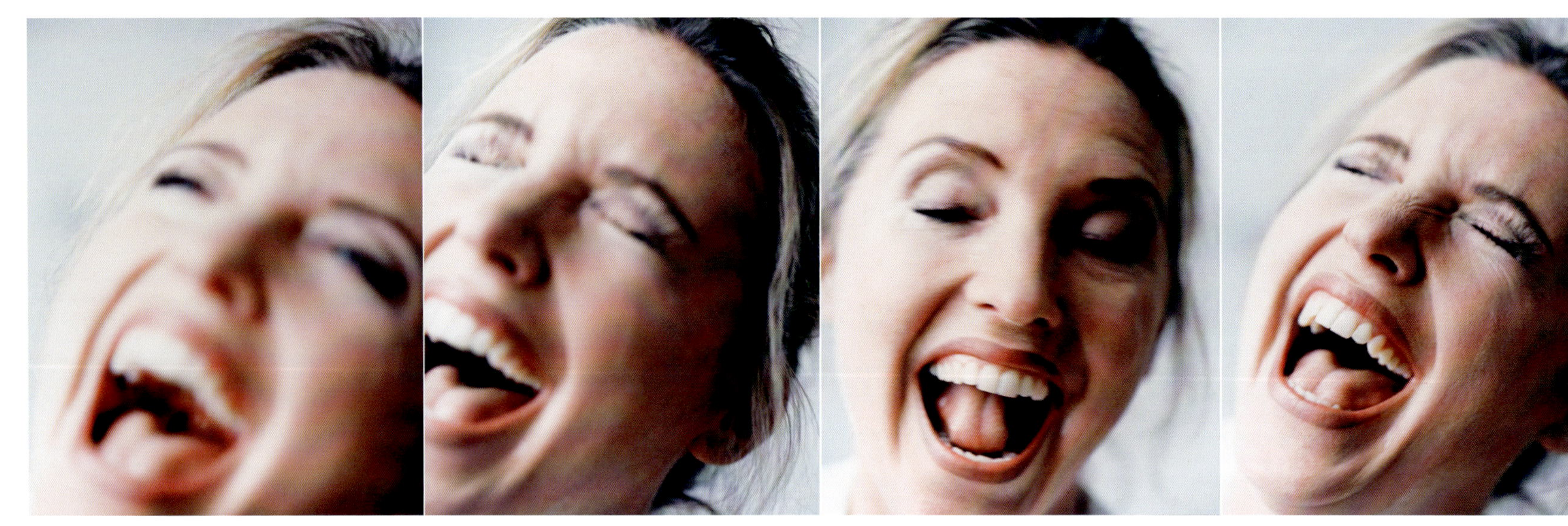

142
Sam Taylor-Johnson
Cry Laughing, 1997
8 Chromogenic prints on aluminum,
each: 16 × 12 in.
The Phillips Collection, Washington, DC,
Gift of the Heather and Tony Podesta Collection,
Washington, DC, 2011.

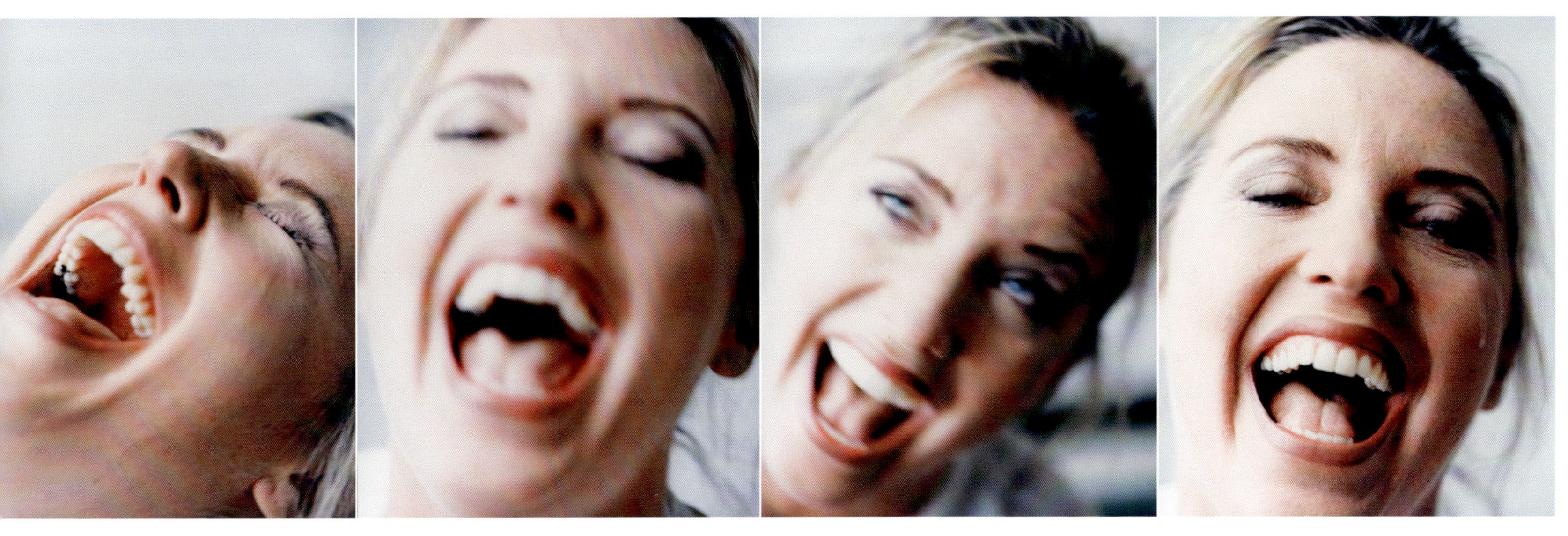

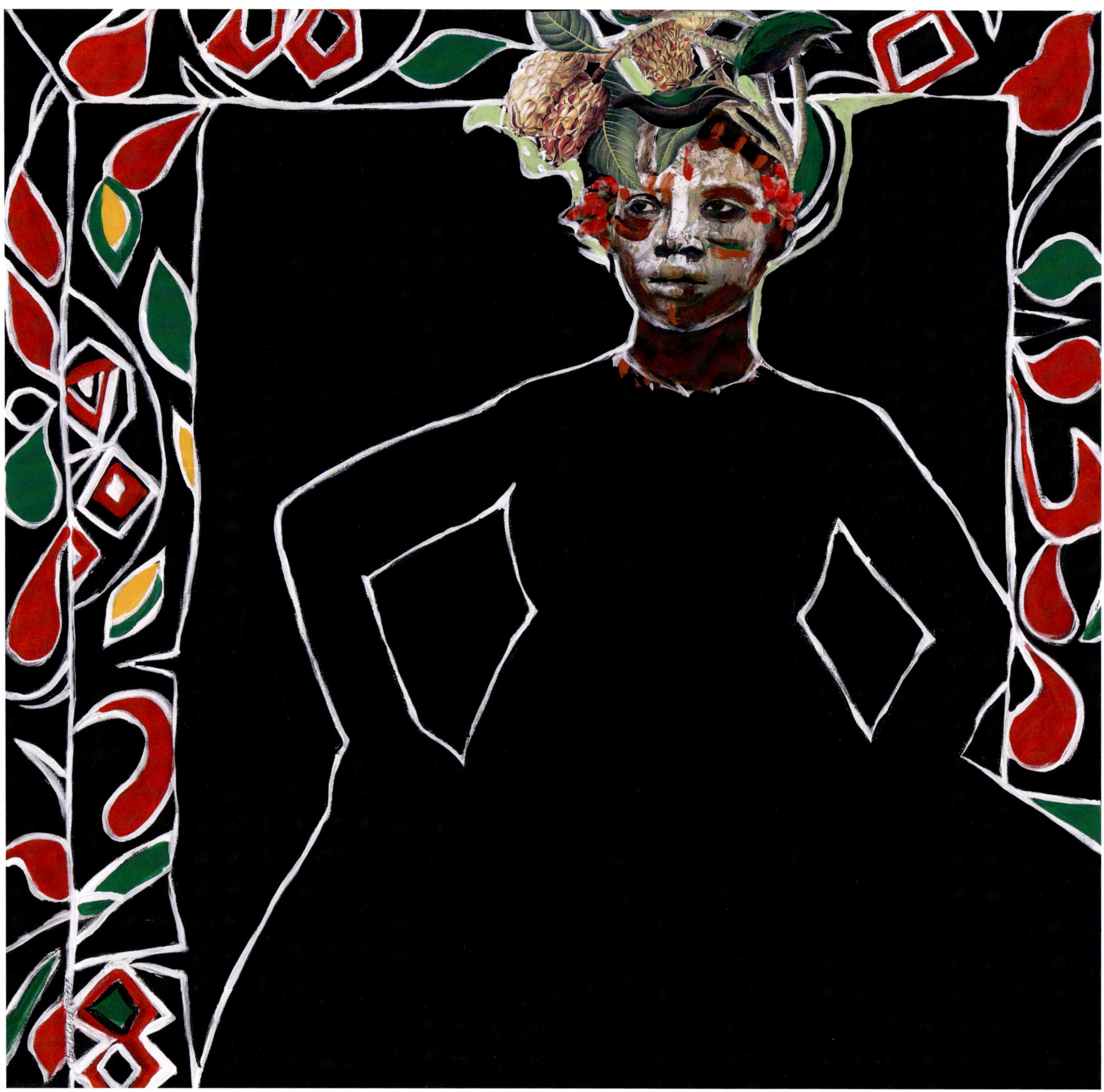

143
Janet Taylor Pickett
***And She Was Born*, 2017**
Acrylic on canvas with printed paper collage, 30 × 30 in.
The Phillips Collection, Washington, DC, The Dreier Fund for Acquisitions, 2020.

JANET TAYLOR PICKETT
AND SHE WAS BORN, 2017

Adrienne L. Childs

Painter and collagist Janet Taylor Pickett's artistic practice reflects her intimate life experiences as a daughter, mother, artist, and an African American woman. These intersecting identities fuel her creative energies and inform her paintings, collages and assemblages, a body of work wholly about women. The dress form, ubiquitous in her work, is an armature for Taylor Pickett's ideas, a vessel that provides the structure for her female-centric narratives. In her hands, the traditionally feminine garment is a vehicle for women's histories, a metaphor for memory, and a symbol of identity and personal expression. The domestic and interior lives of women of color throughout the globe are consistent concerns in Taylor Pickett's artistry. Her collages often combine contemporary images of Black women with images drawn from art history. Africa and Europe, past and present, coexist in her often-ornate collages and paintings, defying linear timeframes and logical geographic or cultural relationships.

Taylor Pickett is one of a cadre of African American artists who have cultivated a sustained dialogue with European art and iconography in the twenty-first century. By engaging canonical European art, these artists have challenged the exclusionary practices of the art world, and, like Taylor Pickett, claimed the right to enter into fruitful conversations with the "masters." The work of Henri Matisse has resonated with Taylor Pickett since the 1970s. Through quoting him, borrowing motifs, and channeling his decorative sensibilities she has been in a creative exchange with Matisse throughout her career. Her relationship to Matisse is a productive repartee in which she borrows elements of his work and filters them through her own concerns, memories, and traditions, often combining them with images of women and objects from the African diaspora. Taylor Pickett created *And She Was Born* for The Phillips Collection's 2020 exhibition *Riffs and Relations: African American Artists and the European Modernist Tradition*. Her signature dress form is drawn in a simple white line—inspired by the white line that defines Matisse's painting *The Red Studio* (1911). The dress form with arms akimbo (a power stance) supports the collaged and painted head of a Surma woman from the Omo Valley in Ethiopia. The source of the head with the elaborate botanical headdress is a photograph by Hans Silvester that was published in his book *Natural Fashion: Tribal Decoration from Africa*. The Surma men, women, and children artfully use nature for body adornment featuring elements such as flowers, leaves, and fruits. For Taylor Pickett, their non-Western notions of beauty and natural designs were consistent with her own visual vocabulary. The decorative border that surrounds the mostly black canvas incorporates a motif from Matisse's *Interior with Egyptian Curtain* (1948) in The Phillips Collection. Black dominates *And She Was Born*, as it does Matisse's canvas, unusual in the work of both artists. Taylor Pickett finds common ground in the beauty of the Surma woman and Matisse's decorative motifs and realigns them through her personal vision of the strength and beauty of Black women.

---

1 See Kathy Imlay, *Janet Taylor Pickett: The Matisse Series* (self-pub, Montclair, NJ, 2016).

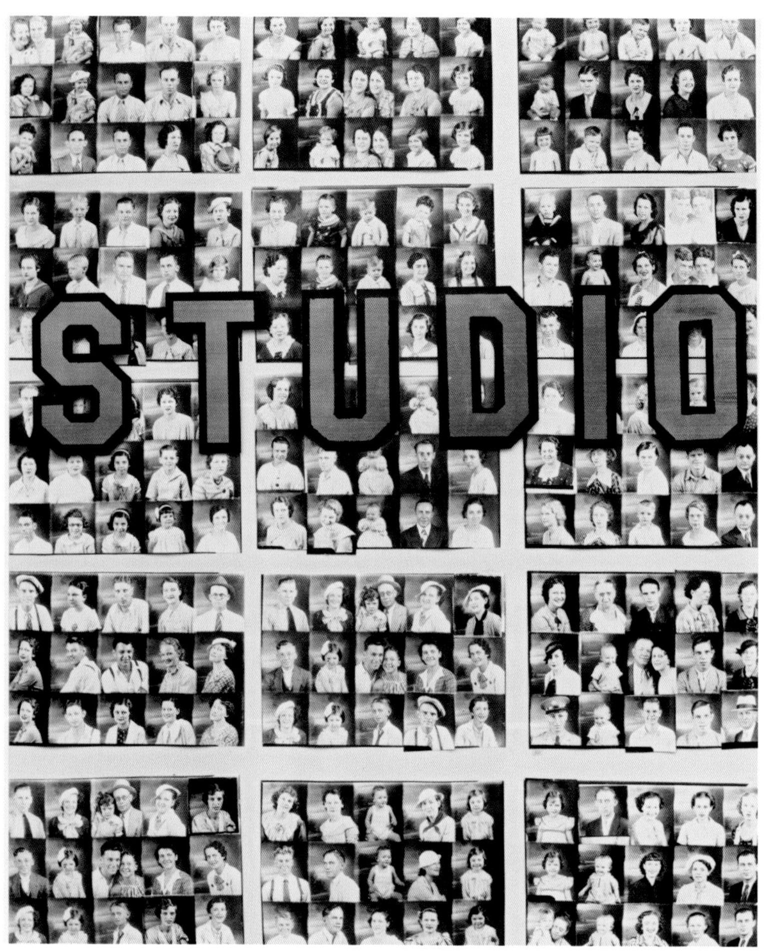

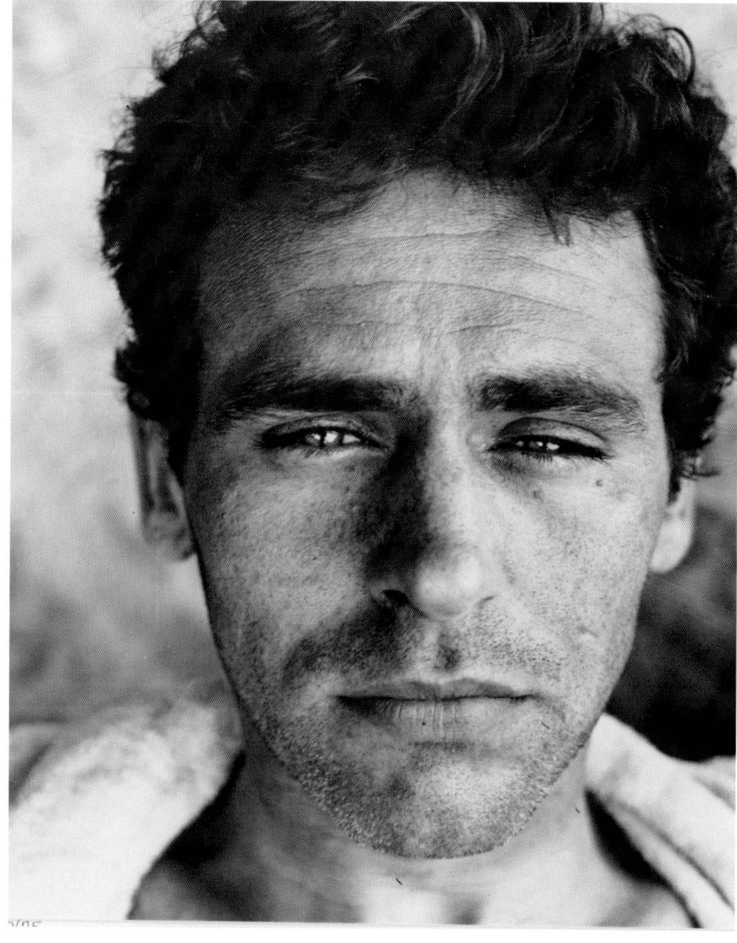

144
Walker Evans
Penny Picture Display, Savannah, 1936
Gelatin silver print,
12 7/8 × 10 1/4 in.
The Phillips Collection, Washington, DC,
Gift from the Trustees of the Corcoran Gallery of Art,
2018 (Gift of the Rev. Jo C. Tartt, Jr.).

145
Walker Evans
Portrait of James Agee, 1937
Gelatin silver print,
8 3/4 × 6 7/8 in.
The Phillips Collection, Washington, DC,
Gift from the Trustees of the Corcoran Gallery of Art,
2018 (Gift of the Rev. Jo C. Tartt, Jr.).

WALKER EVANS
PORTRAIT OF JAMES AGEE, 1937

Antony Gormley

This is the portrait of an artist with eyes that seem to look equally inside and out (pl. 145). It's difficult not to think that this picture was taken outdoors in the sharp light of the cotton fields of Alabama against which the shining eyes close, and yet that boxer's dressing gown, although out of focus, is suggestive of someone who has just come from a fight. James Agee went south with Walker Evans to meet the truth of the inherent injustices of America and internalized the guilt of that witnessing. *Let Us Now Praise Famous Men* (1941), the outcome of their journey, has become a pillar in American literature alongside Harriet Beecher Stowe's *Uncle Tom's Cabin* (1852) and James Baldwin's *The Fire Next Time* (1963). All three are indictments of the claim set forth in the American Declaration of Independence: maybe everyone has the right to pursue happiness and wealth, but not everyone gets to exercise it. How can we use prose and poetry—the act of witness and the act of reflection—to deal with the paradoxes of the American urge to self-realization and its total denial under cruel commercial conditions? Walker Evans's haunting portrait bears witness to the impossibility of pure creation in the context of human suffering.

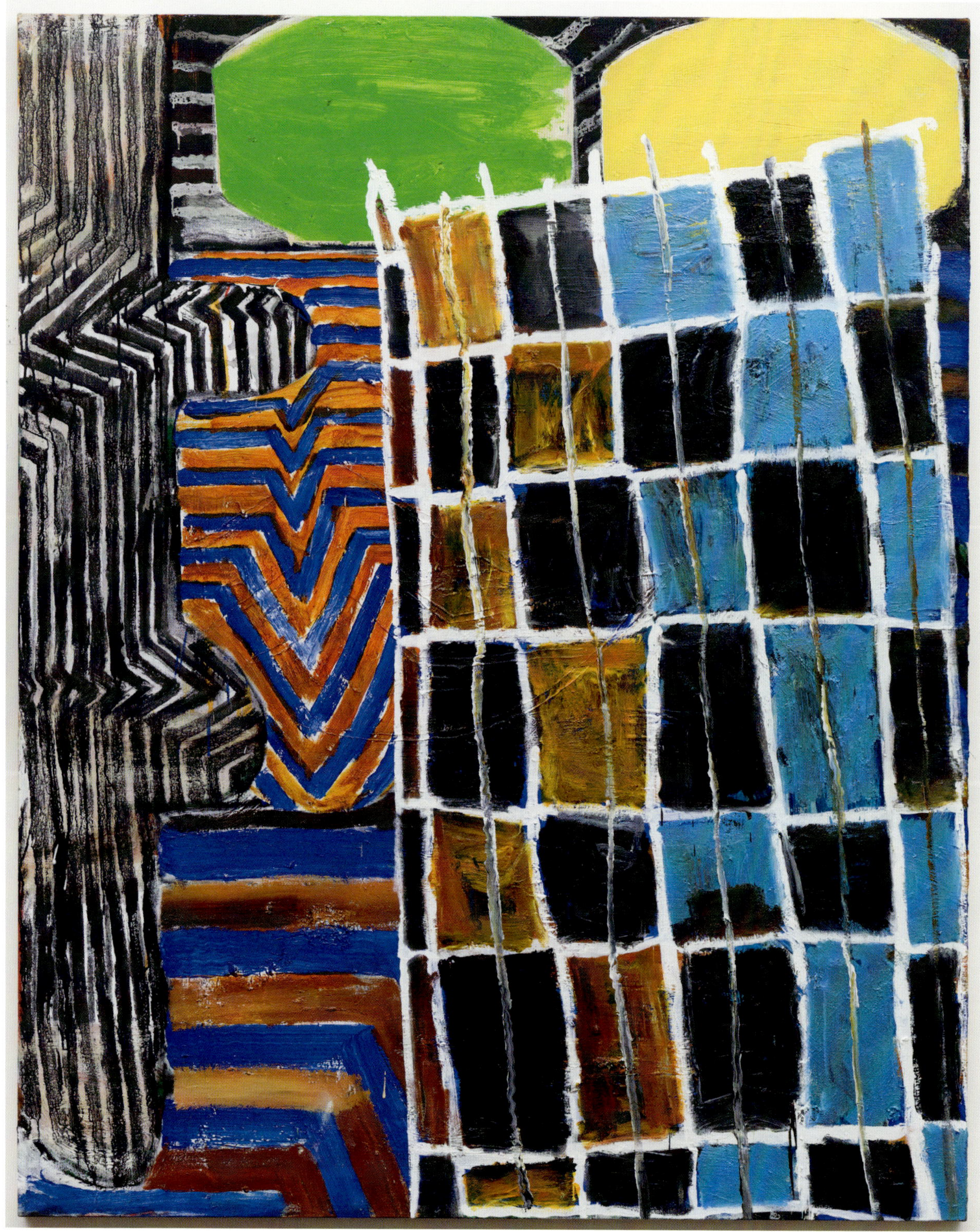

146
John Walker
***Stacked II*, 2018**
Oil on canvas,
84 × 66 in.
The Phillips Collection, Washington, DC,
Gift of Joe and Nancy Keithley with additional funds
from The Hereward Lester Cooke Memorial Fund, 2020.

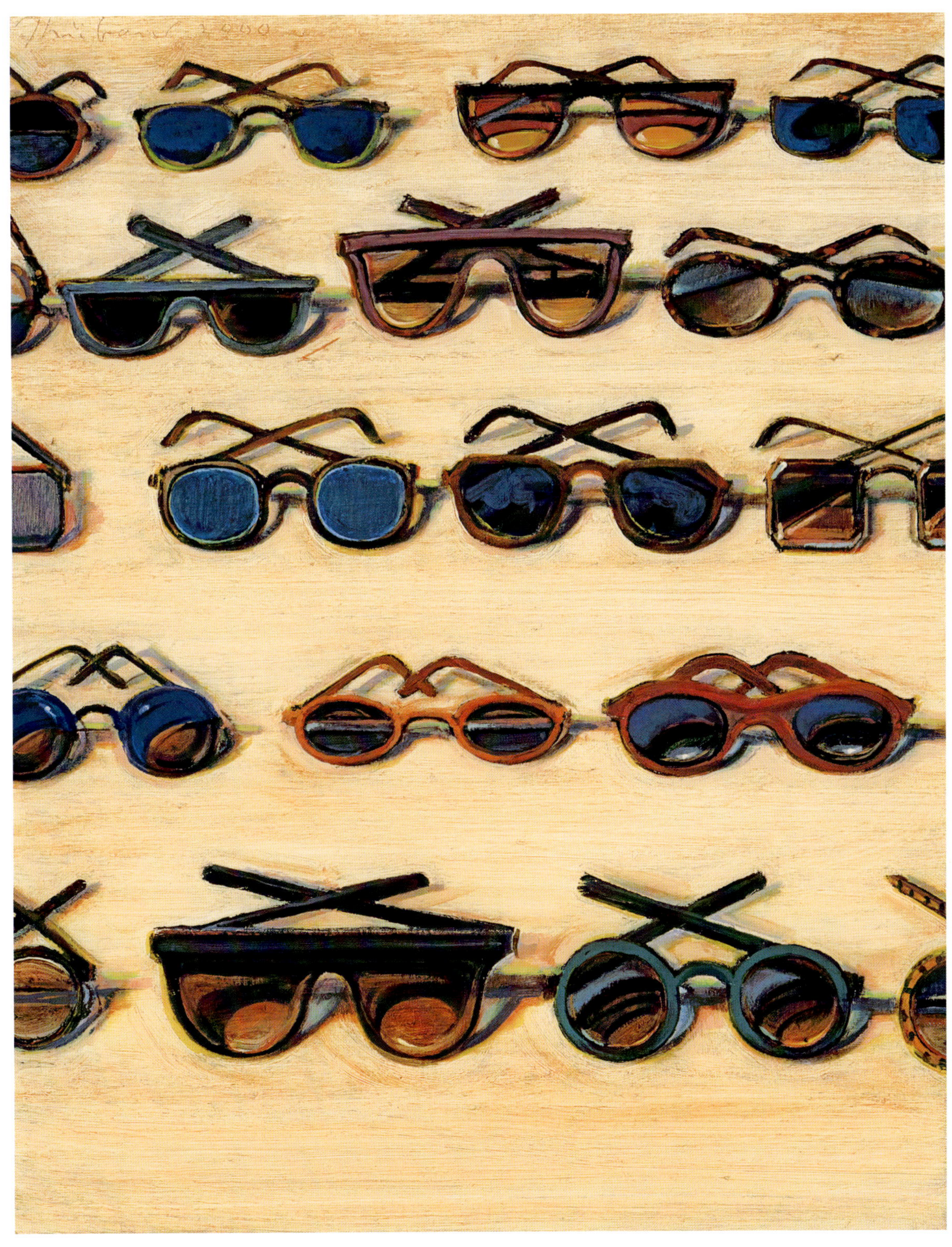

147
Wayne Thiebaud
Five Rows of Sunglasses, 2000
Oil on canvas,
20 × 16 in.
The Phillips Collection, Washington, DC,
Gift of the Thiebaud Family, 2001.

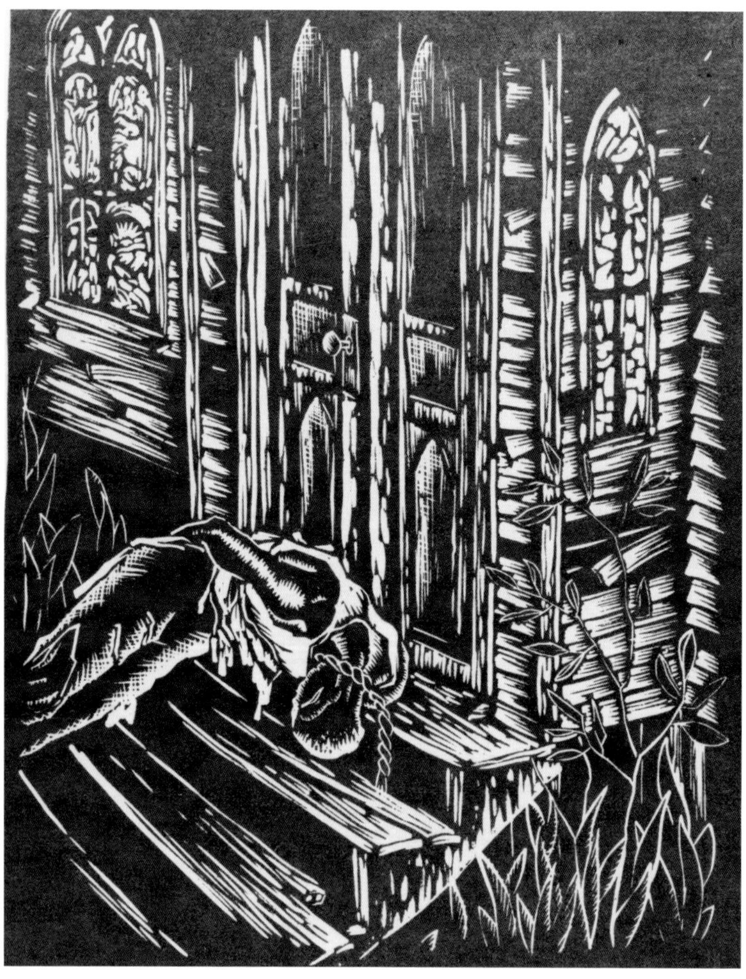

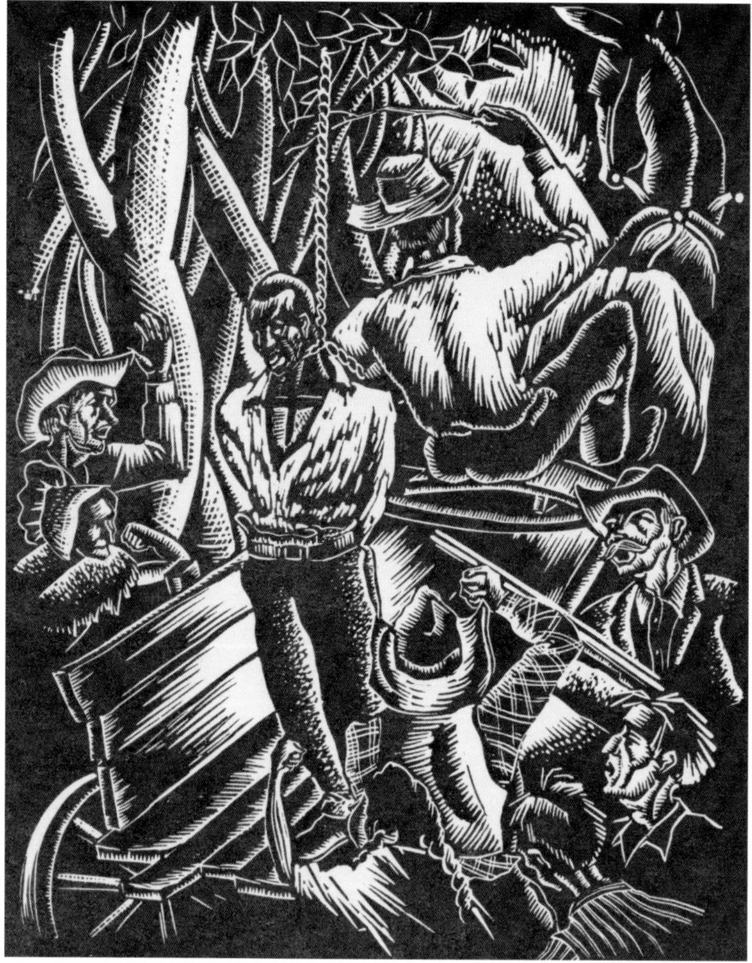

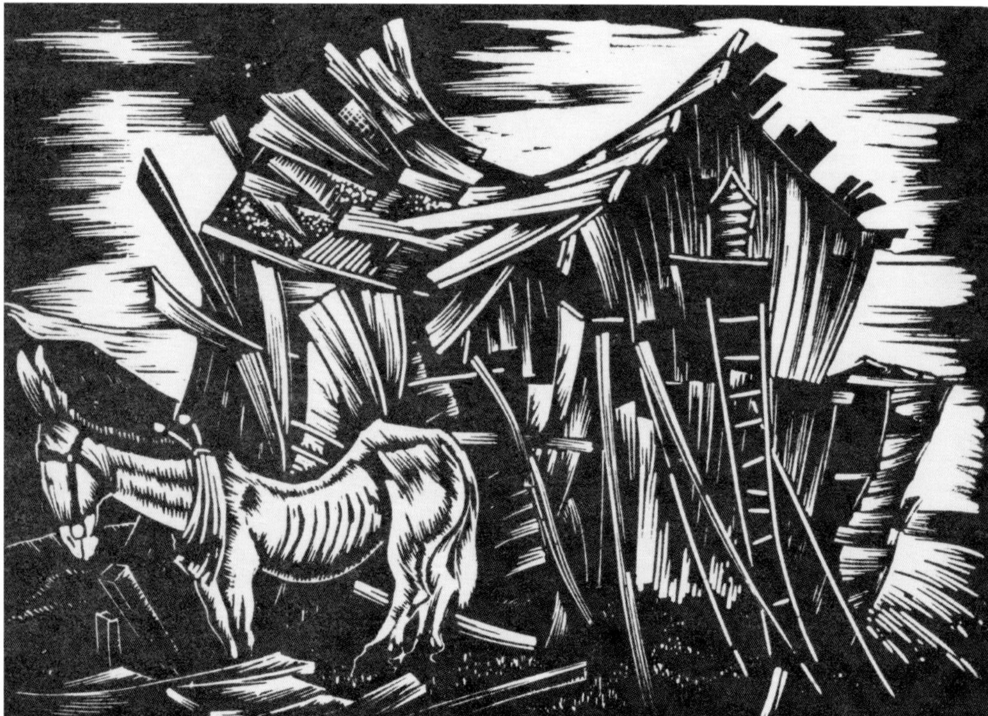

148 (top left)
Hale Woodruff
***By Parties Unknown*, 1931–46 (printed 1996)**
Linoleum cut print,
19 1/8 × 15 in.
The Phillips Collection, Washington, DC,
Gift of Auldlyn Higgins Williams and E.T. Williams Jr., New York, NY, in memory of Robert Grayson McGuire III, Washington, DC, 2015.

149 (top right)
Hale Woodruff
***Giddap*, 1931–46 (printed 1996)**
Linoleum cut print,
19 1/8 × 15 in.
The Phillips Collection, Washington, DC,
Gift of Auldlyn Higgins Williams and E.T. Williams Jr., New York, NY, in memory of Robert Grayson McGuire III, Washington, DC, 2015.

150 (bottom)
Hale Woodruff
***Relics*, 1931–46 (printed 1996)**
Linoleum cut print,
19 1/8 × 15 in.
The Phillips Collection, Washington, DC,
Gift of Auldlyn Higgins Williams and E.T. Williams Jr., New York, NY, in memory of Robert Grayson McGuire III, Washington, DC, 2015.

HALE WOODRUFF
ATLANTA PORTFOLIO, 1931–46

Elsa Smithgall

The black image can be the environment, it can be the problems that one faces, it can be the look on a man's face.... But if it's worth its while, it's also got to be universal in its broader impact and its presence.
—Hale Woodruff, 1968

Hale Woodruff's *Atlanta Portfolio* is at once inspired by his experiences in the Deep South and universal in its scope and enduring meaning in our twenty-first-century world. Comprising eight linocuts that the artist made during his years heading up the art department at Atlanta University, the portfolio is notable for addressing the poverty and toils of everyday African American life in the South during the 1930s (see pls. 148–150). That Woodruff chose to focus two of the prints on scenes of lynching is significant. His works answered a call from Walter White, executive director of the National Association for the Advancement of Colored People (NAACP), who was putting together an exhibition explicitly aimed at raising awareness and support in favor of an anti-lynching bill awaiting passage in Congress.[1] At a time when lynchings were at a record high, the Costigan-Wagner bill, named for its sponsors Sen. Edward P. Costigan (R-CO) and Sen. Robert F. Wagner (R-NY), brought renewed attention and urgency to a form of racial terror that had persisted long since the end of slavery.

Woodruff honed his graphic abilities and skillful command of line and patterns of dark and light as a political cartoonist at the *Indianapolis Edge*, where he got his start while pursuing his studies at the nearby John Herron Art Institute. In *Giddap* and *By Parties Unknown*, we see the fruits of the artist's incisive eye and hand in creating scenes that cut to the heart of an emotional subject. In one—*Giddap*—we bear witness alongside the spectators to a lynching that is about to unfold. In the other—*By Parties Unknown*—we see its painful aftermath in the lifeless body left on the steps of a run-down church. Woodruff's depictions evoke at once suffering and redemption, as Helen Langa has suggested.[2]

The deep pathos emanating from the slumped figure on the foot of the church steps in *By Parties Unknown* calls to mind a panel in Jacob Lawrence's *Migration Series*. In panel 15, Lawrence symbolizes the painful absence of the victim through an empty noose dangling from a tree branch with a crouched figure in mourning nearby. Lawrence's view of lynching shows its earlier manifestation as a leading cause of the Great Migration.[3]

Images such as these remind us of the legacy of lynching in the form of hate crimes today. It took a century, and over two hundred attempts, for Congress to pass two federal anti-lynching bills.[4] Upon the Senate bill's passage, its champion, Cory Booker, noted, "Today, we have ... taken corrective action that recognizes this stain on our country's history."[5]

The epigraph is from Al Murray, Oral History Interview with Hale Woodruff, November 18, 1968, Archives of American Art, Smithsonian Institution.

1 These were among 49 works by 37 artists included in *An Art Commentary on Lynching*, Arthur U. Newton Galleries, New York, February 15–March 2, 1935.

2 Helen Langa, "Antilynching: Art Exhibitions: Politicized Viewpoints, Racial Perspectives, Gendered Constraints," *American Art* 13, no. 1 (Spring 1999): 29.

3 *Panel no. 15: Another cause was lynching. It was found that where there had been a lynching, the people who were reluctant to leave at first left immediately after this.* (Original 1941 caption.)

4 The Senate passed their Justice for Victims of Lynching Act on December 19, 2018, and the House passed H.R. 35, The Emmett Till Anti-Lynching Act on February 26, 2020. At the time of writing, Congress has yet to reconcile the two versions, leaving the fate of a federal anti-lynching bill uncertain. The founding in 2018 of the National Memorial for Peace and Justice, in Montgomery, Alabama, marks the first national memorial to honor the victims of lynching and slavery.

5 Cory Booker, cited in Louis P. Masur, "Why it took a century to pass an anti-lynching law," *Washington Post*, December 28, 2018.

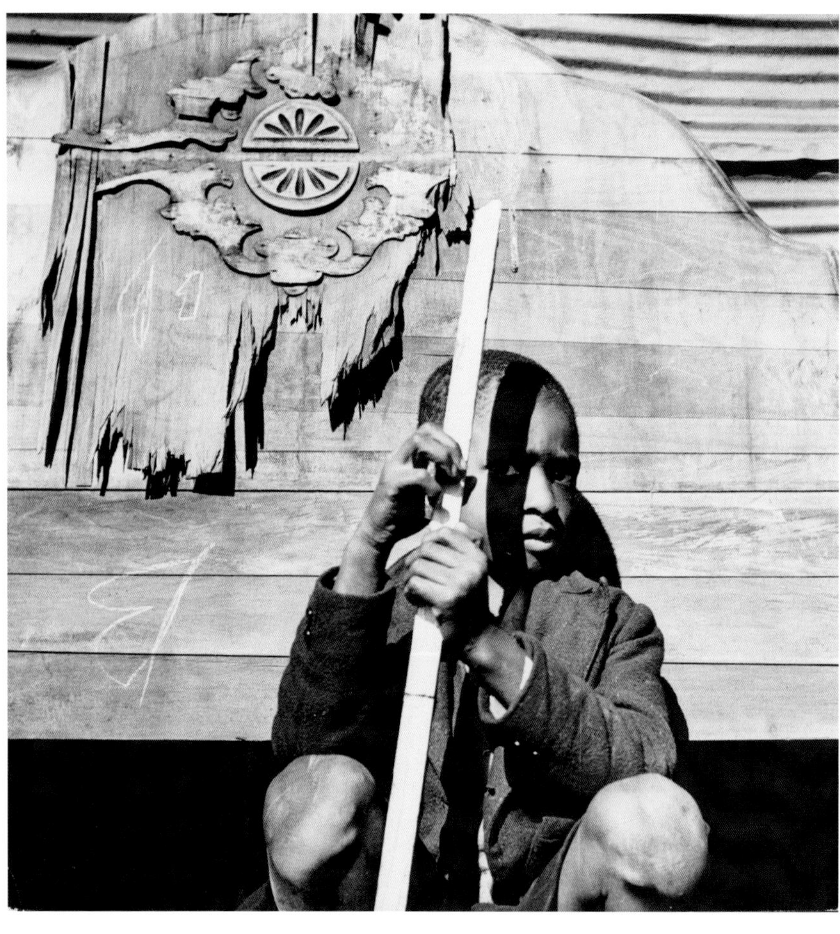

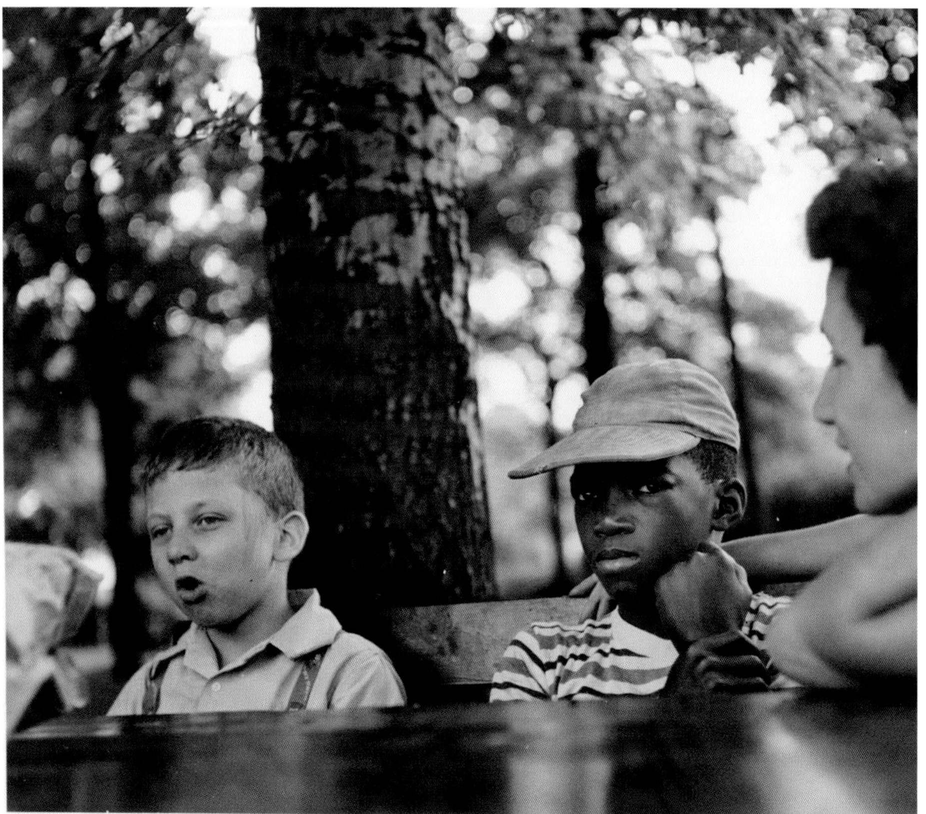

151 (top)
Esther Bubley
***A Child Whose Home Is an Alley Dwelling near the Capitol*, 1943**
Gelatin silver print,
10 7/8 × 10 1/8 in.
The Phillips Collection, Washington, DC,
Gift of Cam and Wanda Garner, 2012.

152 (bottom)
Esther Bubley
***Untitled (Two Boys on a Bench)*, 1951**
Gelatin silver print,
11 × 14 in.
The Phillips Collection, Washington, DC,
Gift of Cam and Wanda Garner, 2013.

ESTHER BUBLEY
A CHILD WHOSE HOME IS AN ALLEY DWELLING NEAR THE CAPITOL, 1943, AND *UNTITLED (TWO BOYS ON A BENCH)*, 1951

Renée Maurer

Esther Bubley was one of the most prolific photographers of her time. She was also one of the first women, in the US, to support herself as a freelance magazine photographer. Influenced by the documentary images taken for the Farm Security Administration (FSA), Bubley left the Midwest at nineteen in search of a career in the nation's capital. Unable to land a photography job, she moved to New York, briefly worked for *Vogue*, and then returned to Washington in the spring of 1942 to microfilm records for the National Archives. That year she met Roy Stryker, former FSA director and head of the photographic unit of the Office of War Information (OWI), a government agency that documented the US's mobilization during World War II. He hired Bubley as his darkroom assistant.

Stryker encouraged Bubley to go out and take photographs of her surroundings. Using a handheld Rolleiflex camera and a quick point-and-shoot style,[1] Bubley photographed the rhythms of city life. She unobtrusively framed the private moments of sensitive subjects. Her first project acknowledged the wartime housing shortage in Washington, and it led to her promotion to OWI field photographer.[2] Bubley photographed *A Child Whose Home Is an Alley Dwelling near the Capitol* (pl. 151) for her "Around Washington" series. This image depicts a young boy from one of the overcrowded settlements constructed in the DC alleys for poor and working-class families. These alley dwellings survived into the 1940s.

Bubley's ability to capture an honest portrait of her subjects brought her several magazine commissions. For *Pageant*'s serial story "A Matter of Love," Bubley detailed the life of Jackie Solomon, also known as "Tommy," an eight-year-old boy in therapy at the Pittsburgh Children's Guidance Clinic. Bubley spent a week in Jackie's home and accompanied his family on outings. *Untitled (Two Boys on a Bench)* (pl. 152) was featured in the December 1951 issue with the caption: "One day Tommy [shown speaking] stepped out of his shell.... On a picnic with his group from the Clinic, Tommy protests when kids tease a newcomer ... he identifies himself with the rejected stranger."

The Phillips holds the second largest collection of Bubley's photographs in the Washington area after the Library of Congress. These images showcase Bubley's extraordinary storytelling and her eye for the poignant details of everyday life.

---

1 Later Bubley used a 35-millimeter camera, which attracted less attention and required less light. See Bonnie Yochelson, *Esther Bubley: On Assignment* (New York: Aperture Foundation, 2005), 14.

2 Bubley contributed more than two thousand images to the OWI file. See Melissa Fay Greene, *The Photographs of Esther Bubley* (Washington, DC: Library of Congress, 2010), 7.

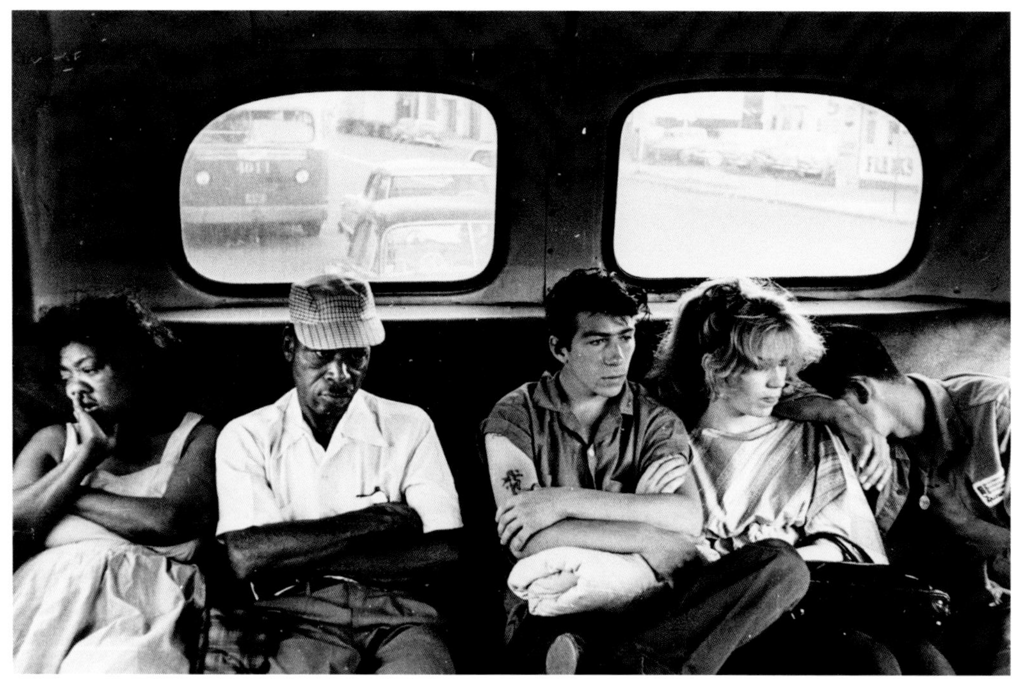

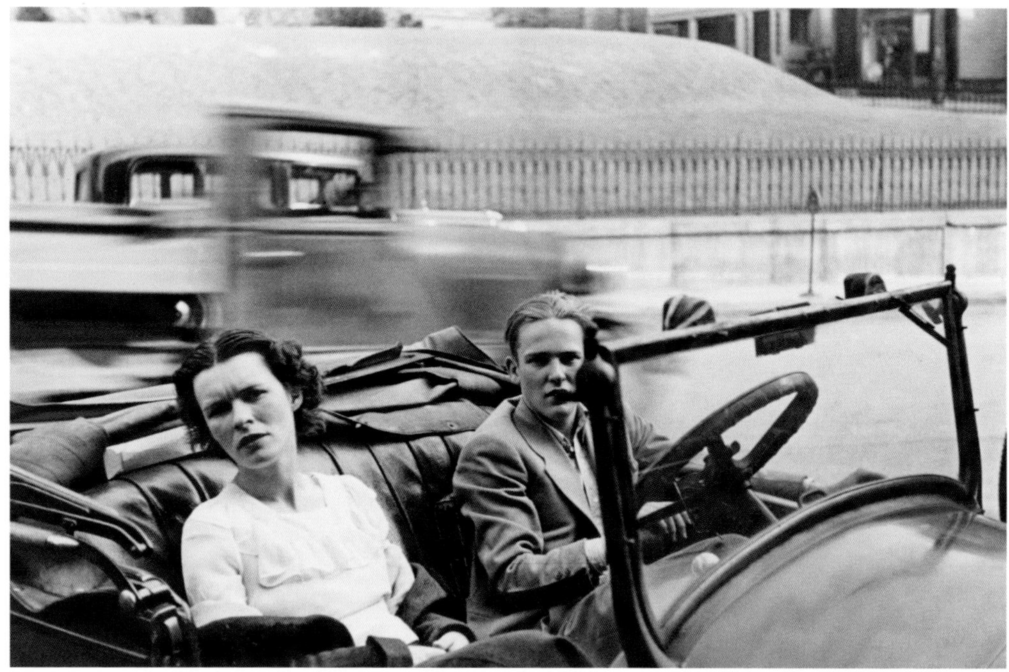

153 (top)
Bruce Davidson
Sitting in the Back of the Bus (*Brooklyn Gang* series), 1959
Gelatin silver print,
11 × 14 in.
The Phillips Collection, Washington, DC,
Gift of Saul E. Levi, 2013.

154 (bottom)
Walker Evans
Main St., Ossining, New York, 1932
Gelatin silver print,
12 × 15 1/2 in.
Gift from the Trustees of the Corcoran Gallery of Art, 2018
(Gift of the Rev. Jo C. Tartt, Jr.).

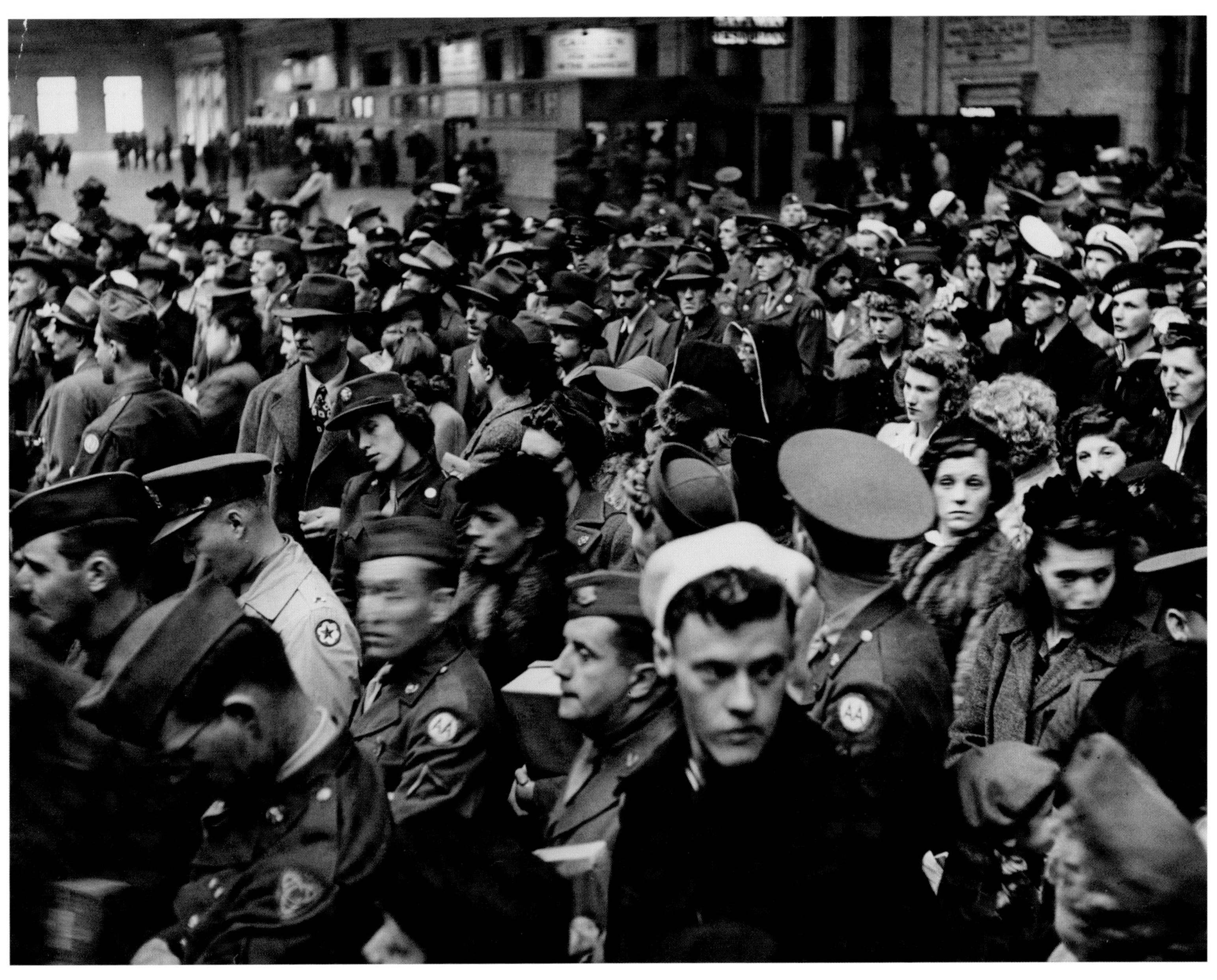

155
Alfred Eisenstaedt
Sunday afternoon crowd of passengers waiting for trains in Union Station, Washington, DC, 1934
Gelatin silver print,
10 5/8 × 13 1/4 in.
The Phillips Collection, Washington, DC,
Gift of Cam and Wanda Garner, 2014.

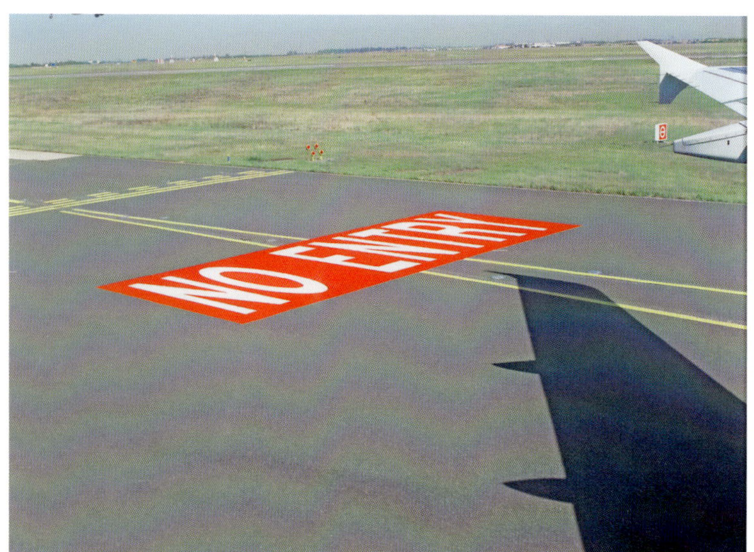

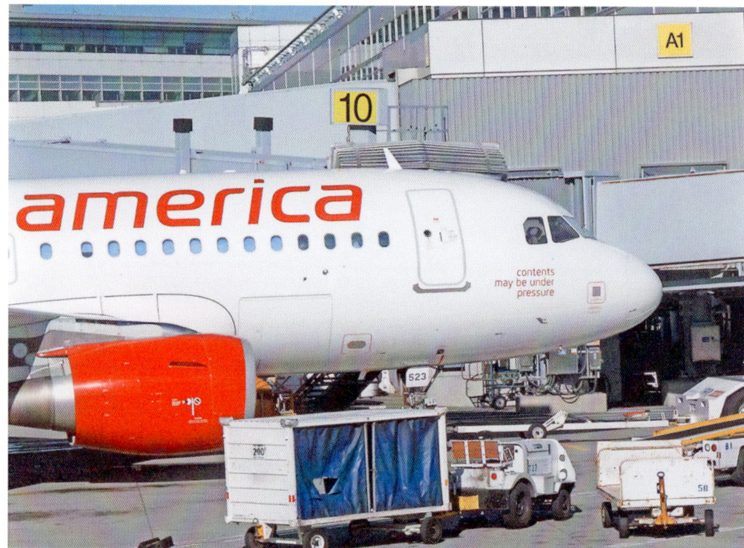

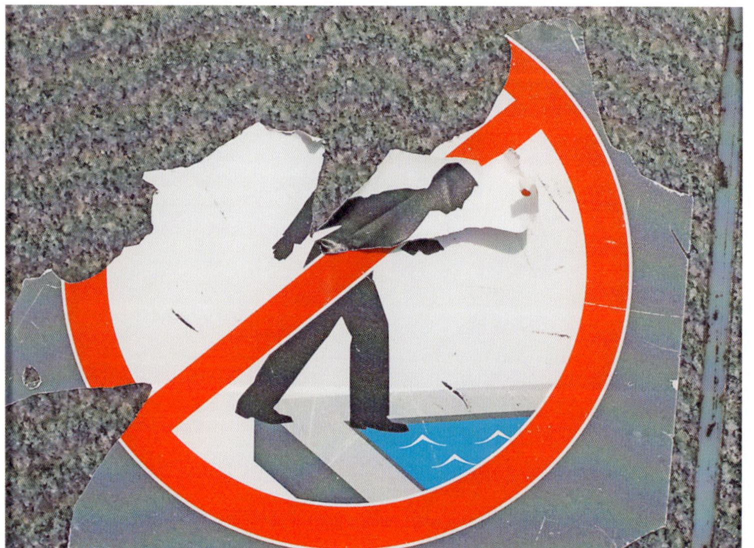

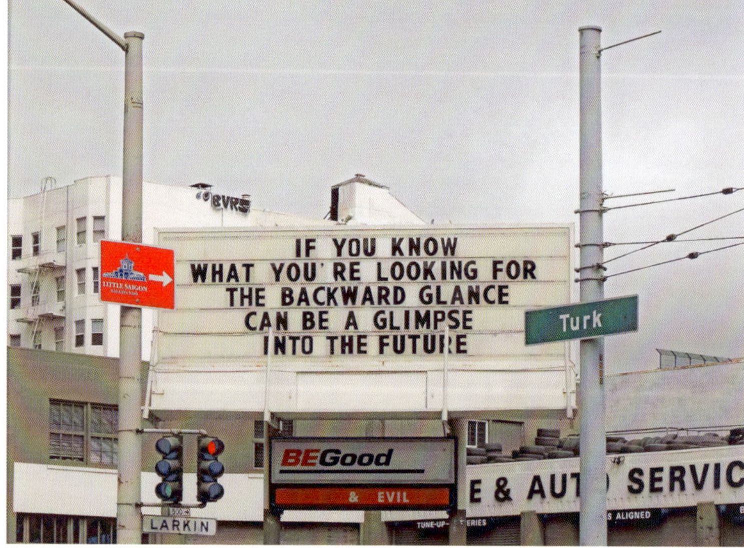

156 (top left)
Allan deSouza
***No Entry*, 2011**
Chromogenic print,
12 × 16 in.
The Phillips Collection, Washington, DC,
Purchase, The Hereward Lester Cooke
Memorial Fund, 2014.

157 (bottom left)
Allan deSouza
***Crossing*, 2011**
Chromogenic print,
12 × 16 in.
The Phillips Collection, Washington, DC,
Purchase, The Hereward Lester Cooke
Memorial Fund, 2014.

158 (top right)
Allan deSouza
***Pressure*, 2011**
Chromogenic print,
12 × 16 in.
The Phillips Collection, Washington, DC,
Purchase, The Hereward Lester Cooke
Memorial Fund, 2014.

159 (bottom right)
Allan deSouza
***Future*, 2011**
Chromogenic print,
12 × 16 in.
The Phillips Collection, Washington, DC,
Purchase, The Hereward Lester Cooke
Memorial Fund, 2014.

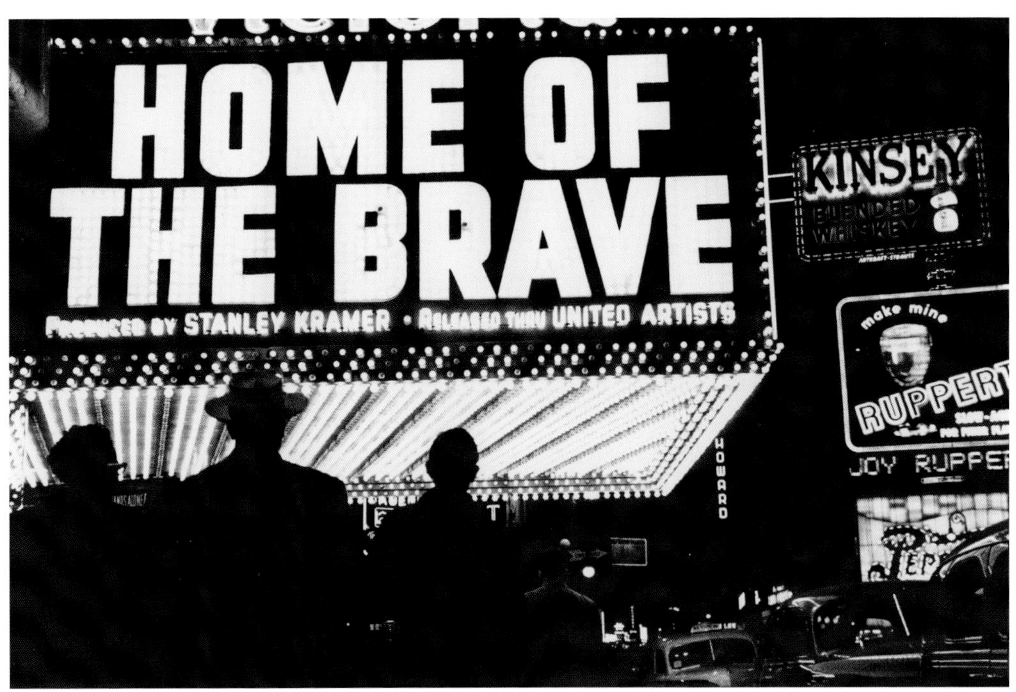

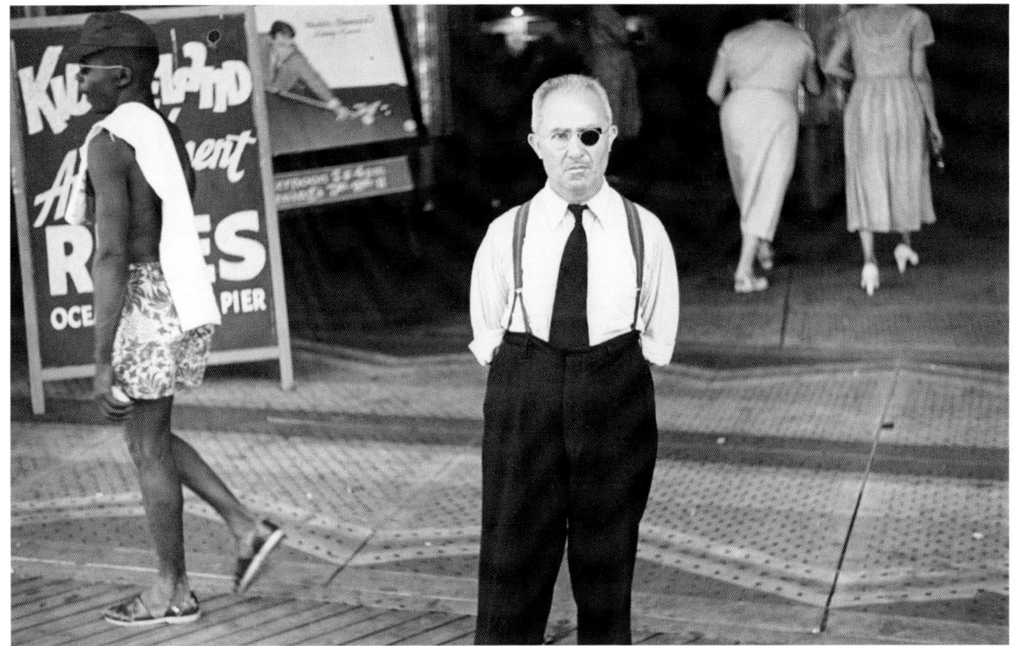

160 (top)
Louis Faurer
***Times Square, N.Y. (Home of the Brave),* 1950 (printed 1981)**
Gelatin silver print,
11 × 14 in.
The Phillips Collection, Washington, DC,
Gift of Steve LaMantia, 2013.

161 (bottom)
Louis Faurer
***Boardwalk, Atlantic City, N.J.,* 1937–38**
Gelatin silver print,
11 × 14 in.
The Phillips Collection, Washington, DC,
Gift of Leo and Nina Pircher, 2014.

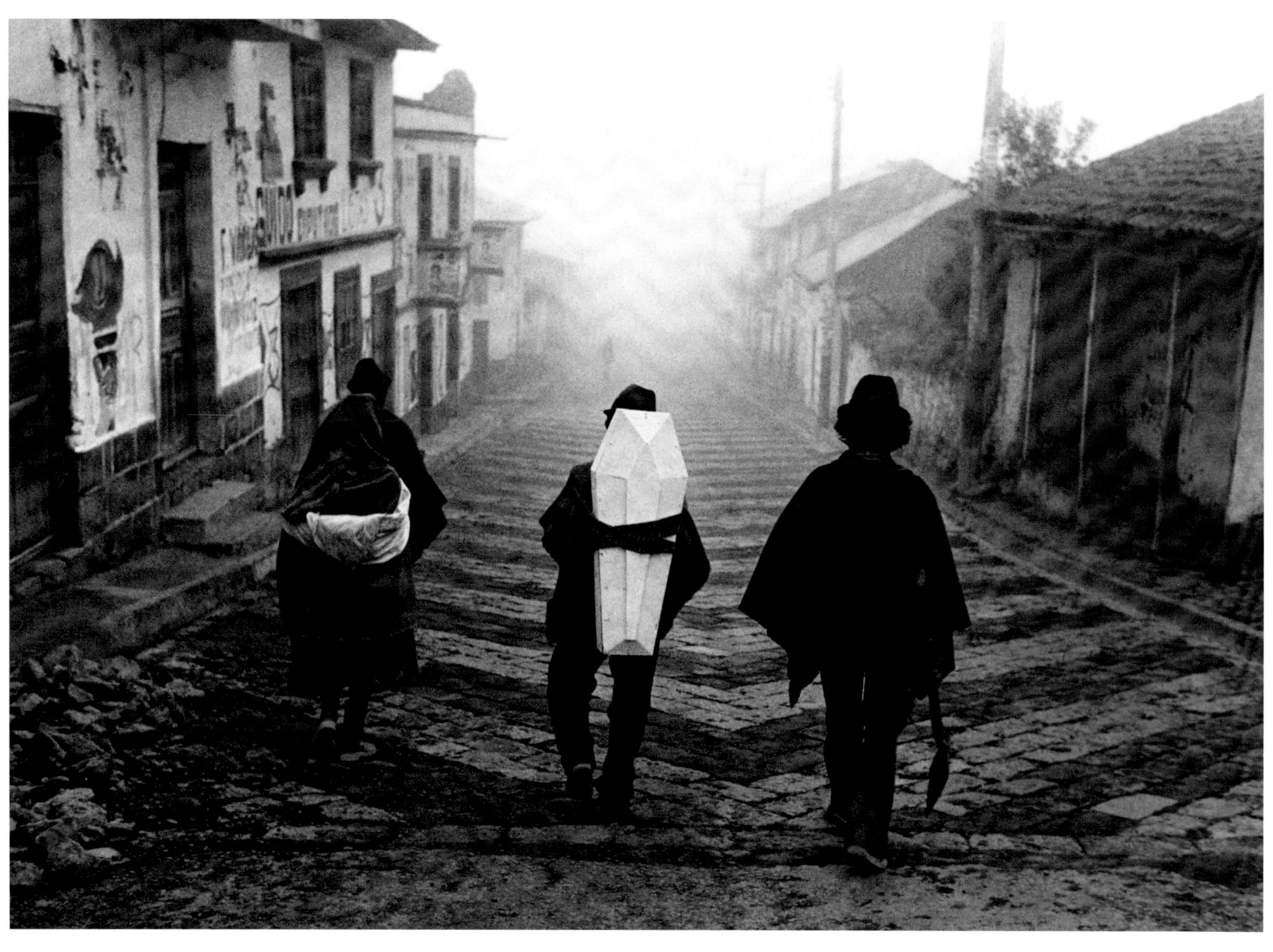

162
Flor Garduño
On the Way to the Cemetery, [Tixan] Ecuador, 1988
Gelatin silver print,
16 × 20 in.
The Phillips Collection, Washington, DC,
Gift from the Collection of Michael and
Joyce Axelrod, Mill Valley, California, 2013.

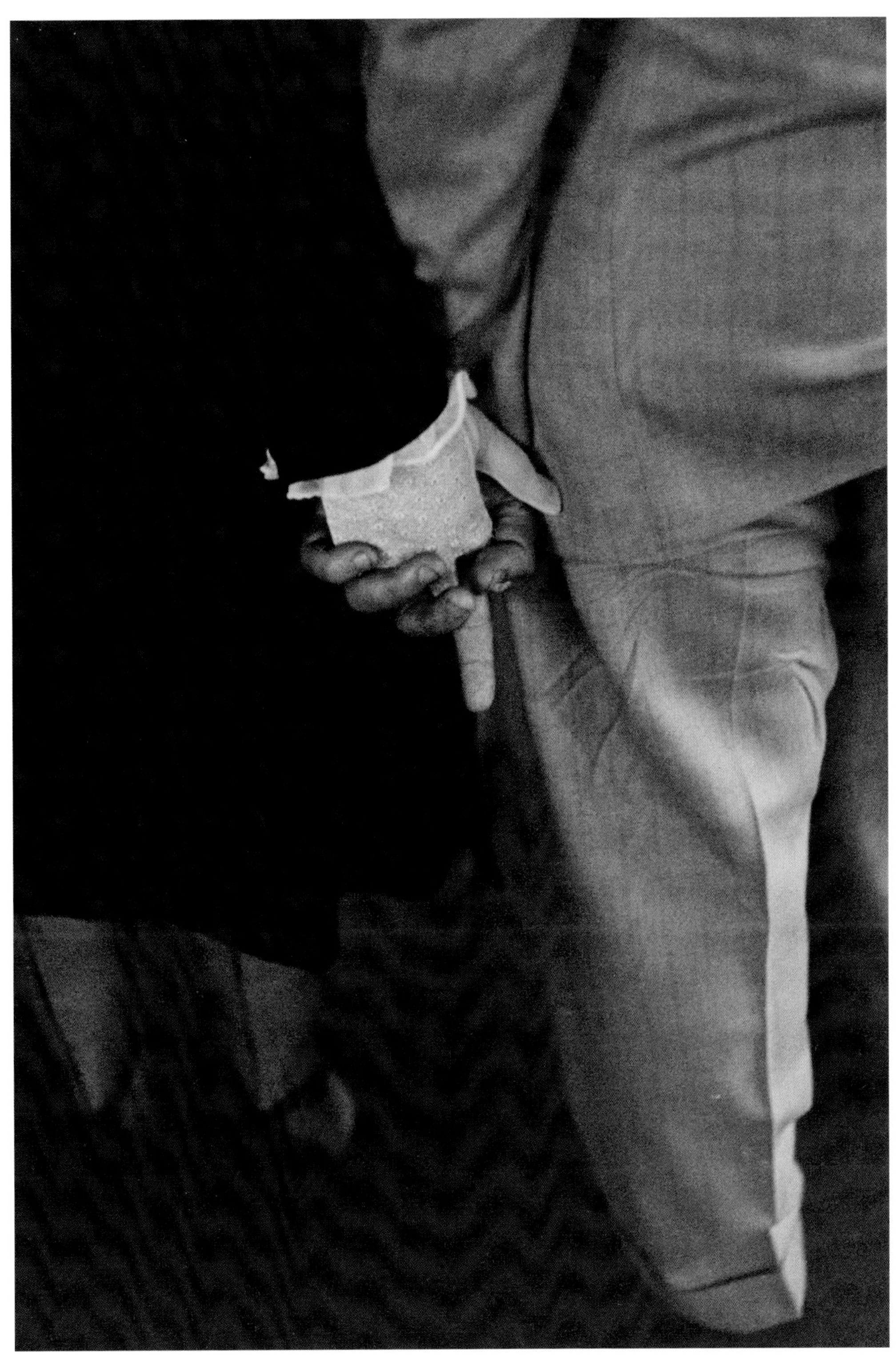

163
Louis Faurer
Freudian Hand Clasp, New York,
1946–49 (printed 1980)
Gelatin silver print,
14 × 11 in.
The Phillips Collection, Washington, DC,
Gift of Steve LaMantia, 2013.

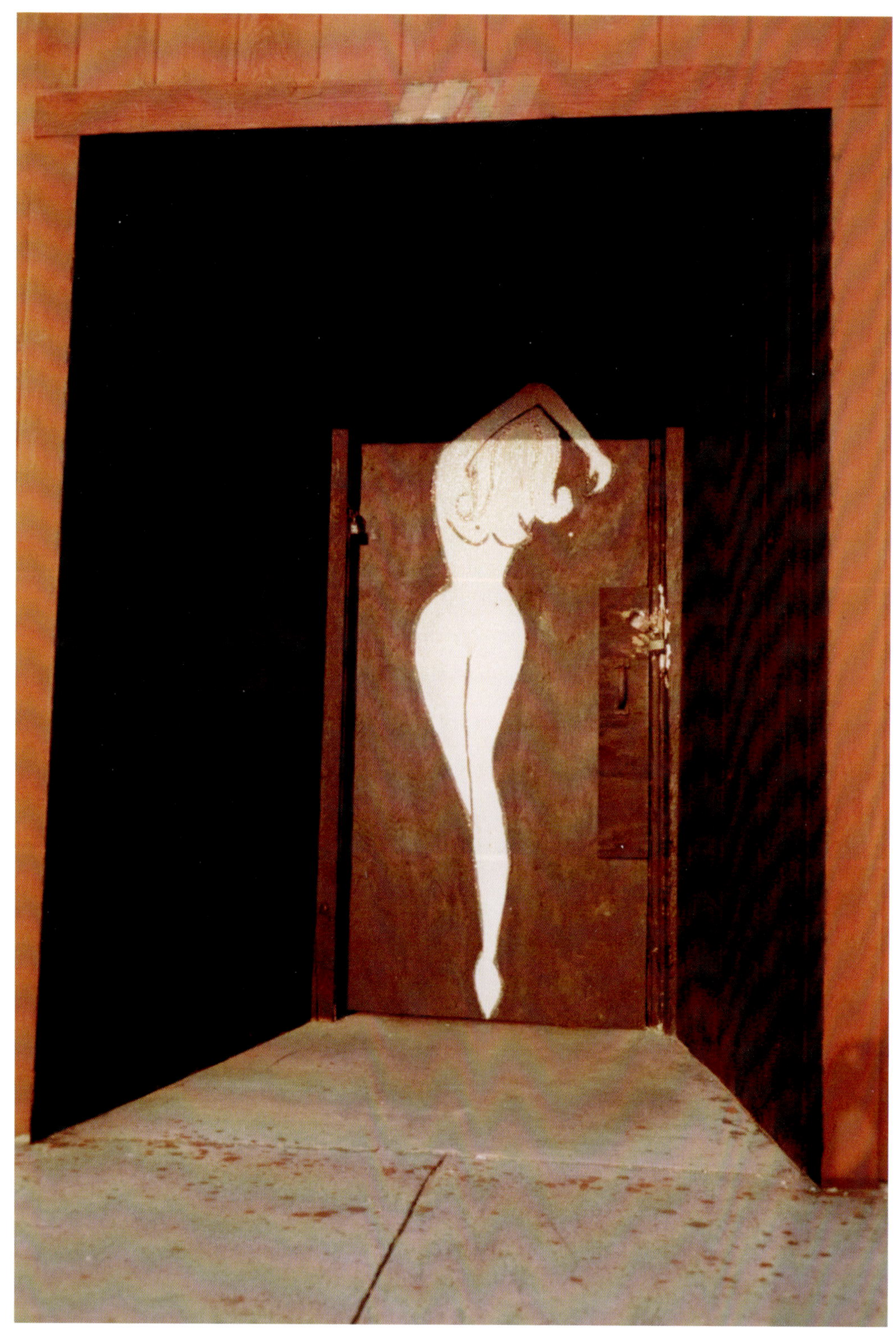

164
William Eggleston
***Topless Doorway*, 1972**
Chromogenic print,
13 × 9 in.
The Phillips Collection, Washington, DC,
Gift of Benjamin Nicolette, 2006.

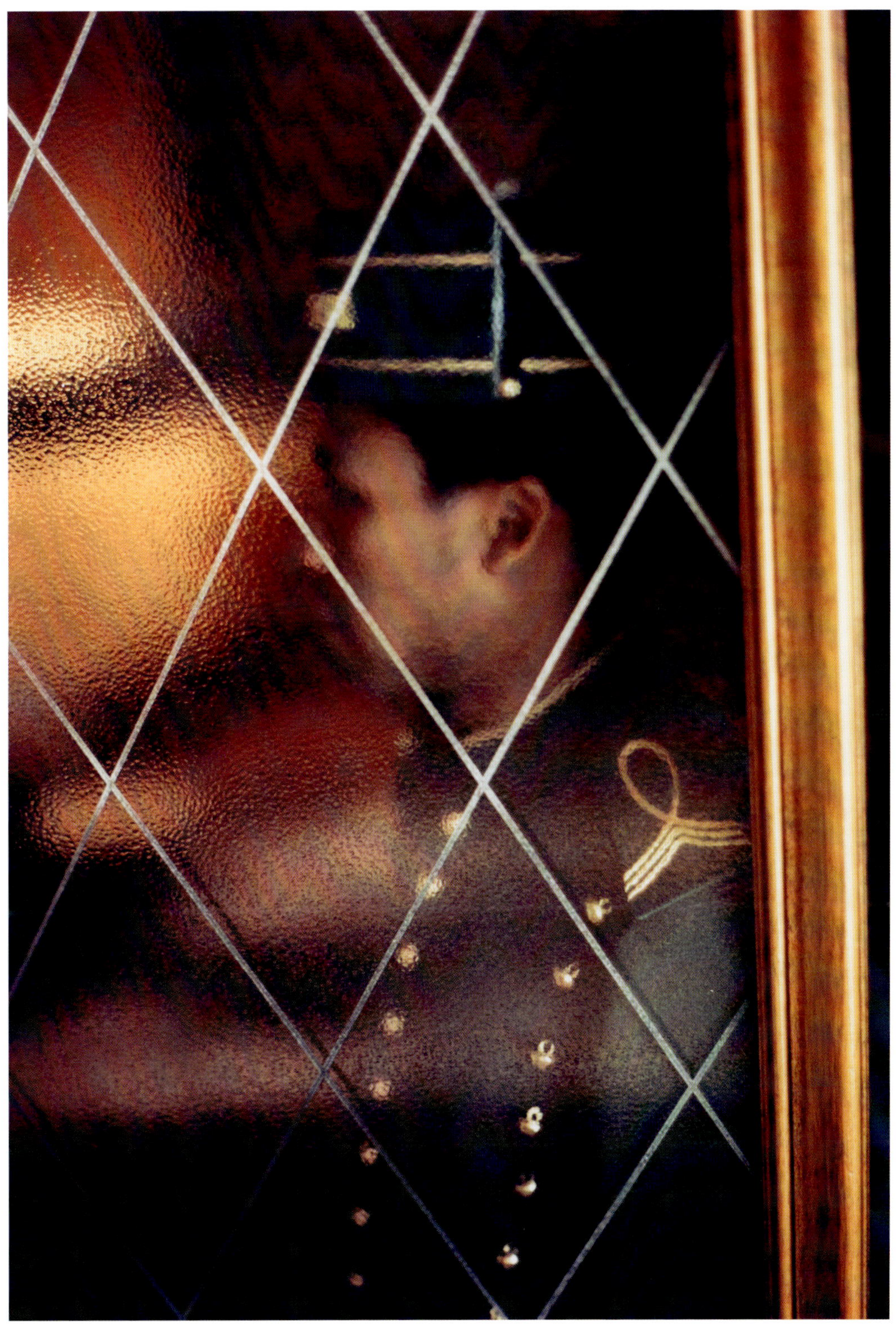

165
Ralph Gibson
Untitled, 1991
Chromogenic print,
20 × 16 in.
The Phillips Collection, Washington, DC,
Gift of Nina and Leo Pircher, 2018.

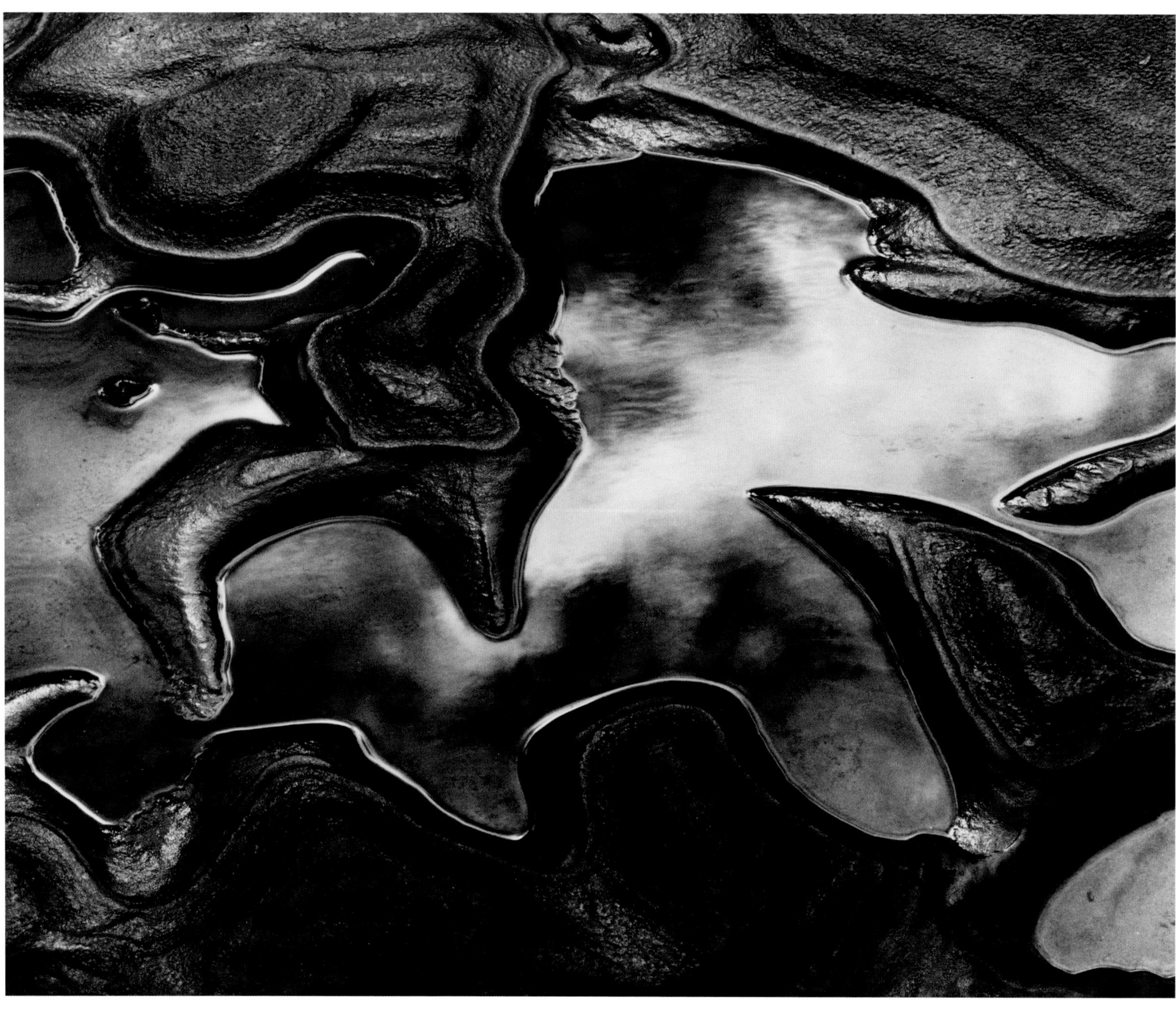

166
Brett Weston
***Glacial Silt, Alaska*, 1973**
Gelatin silver print,
11 × 14 in.
The Phillips Collection, Washington, DC,
Gift of the Brett Weston Archive from the
Christian K. Keesee Collection, 2006.

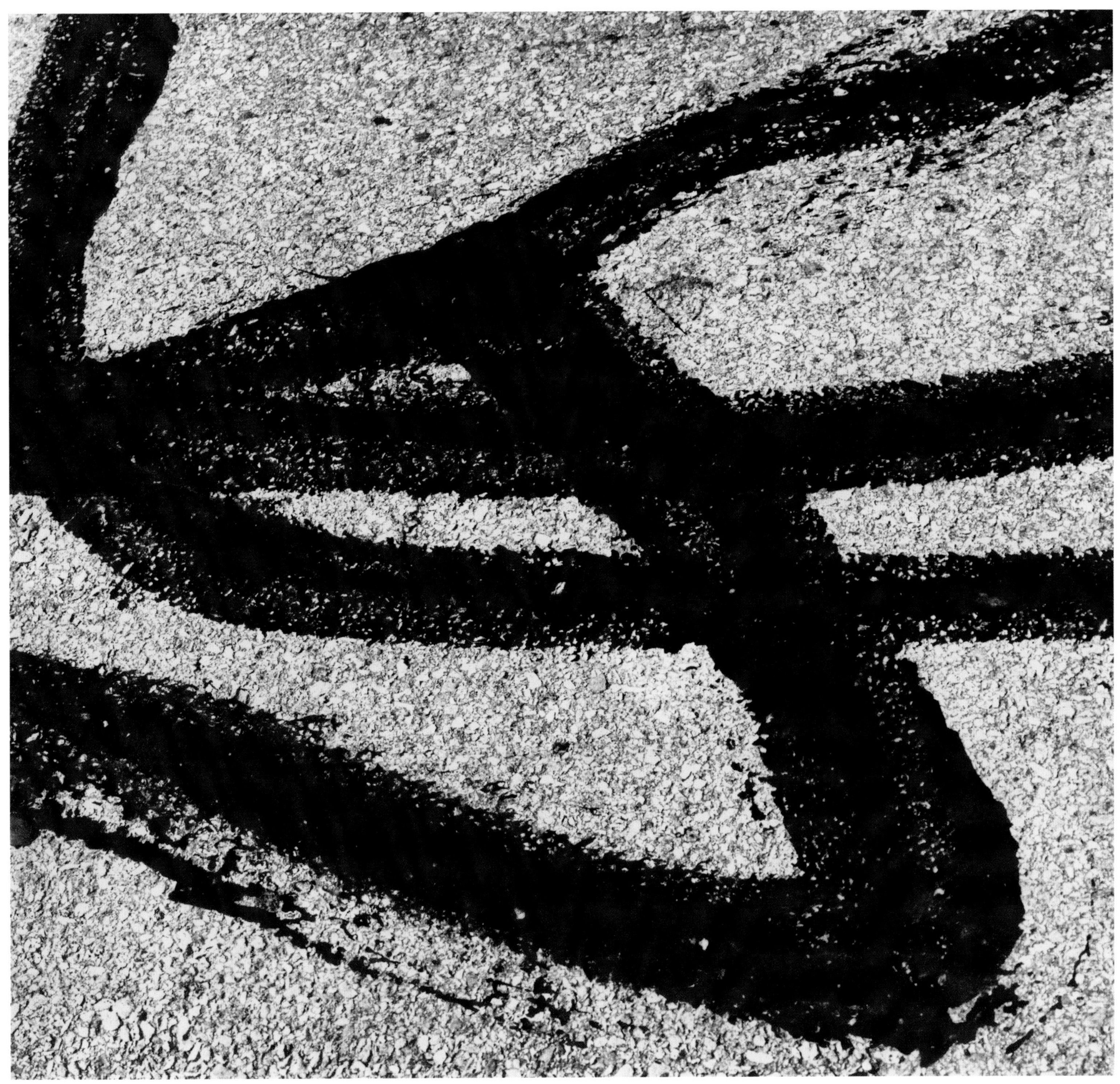

167
Aaron Siskind
Providence 68, 1986 (from Tar Abstracts Portfolio),
ca. 1989
Photogravure,
image: 13 5/8 × 13 5/8 in.
The Phillips Collection, Washington, DC,
Gift of Sandra and David Berler in honor of Ann and
Donald Brown, 2015.

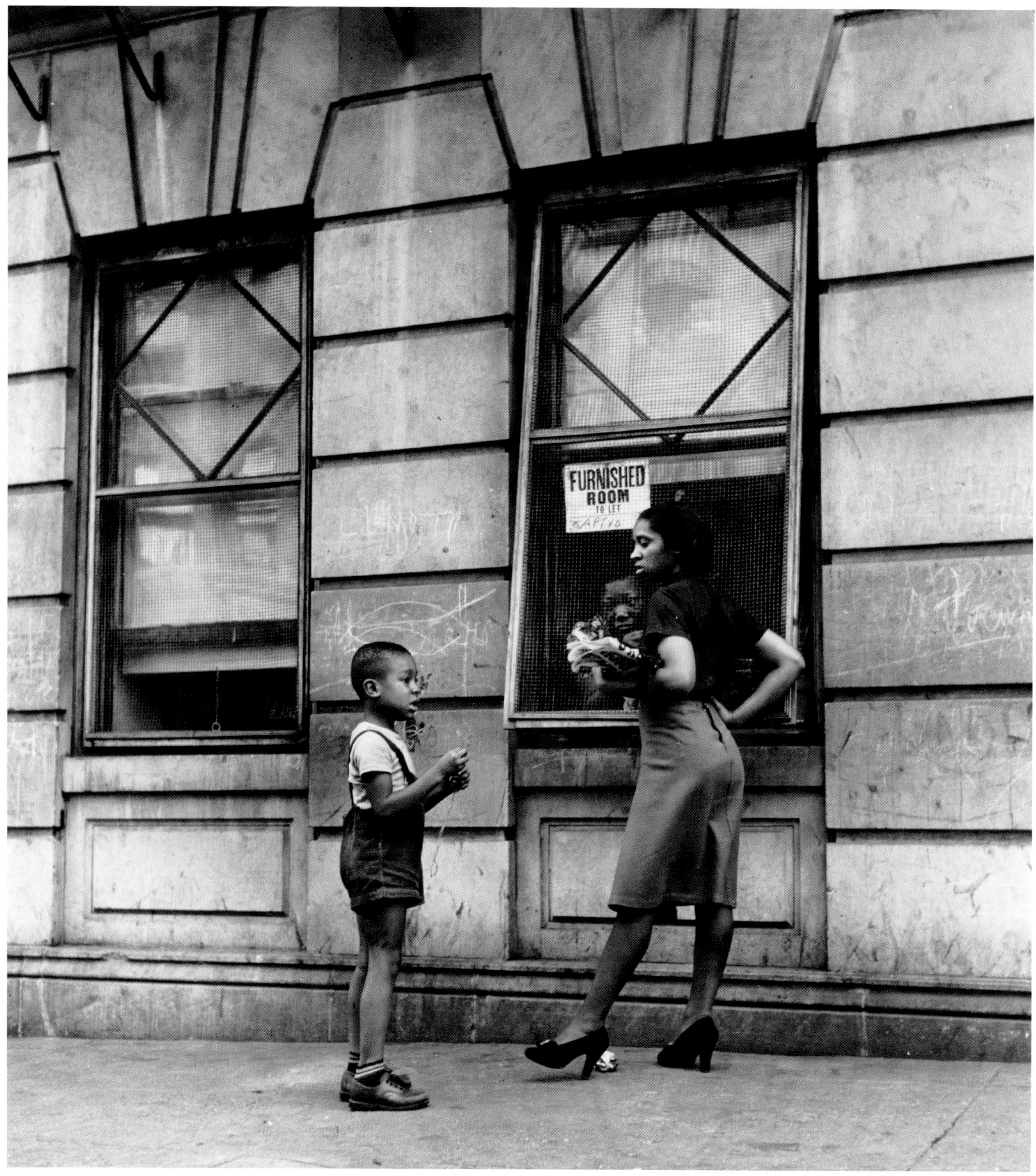

168
Aaron Siskind
Street Scene 2, Harlem, 1940 (printed 1981)
Gelatin silver print,
9 5/8 × 8 1/2 in.
The Phillips Collection, Washington, DC,
Gift of Peter Ocko and Kate Axelrod, 2016.

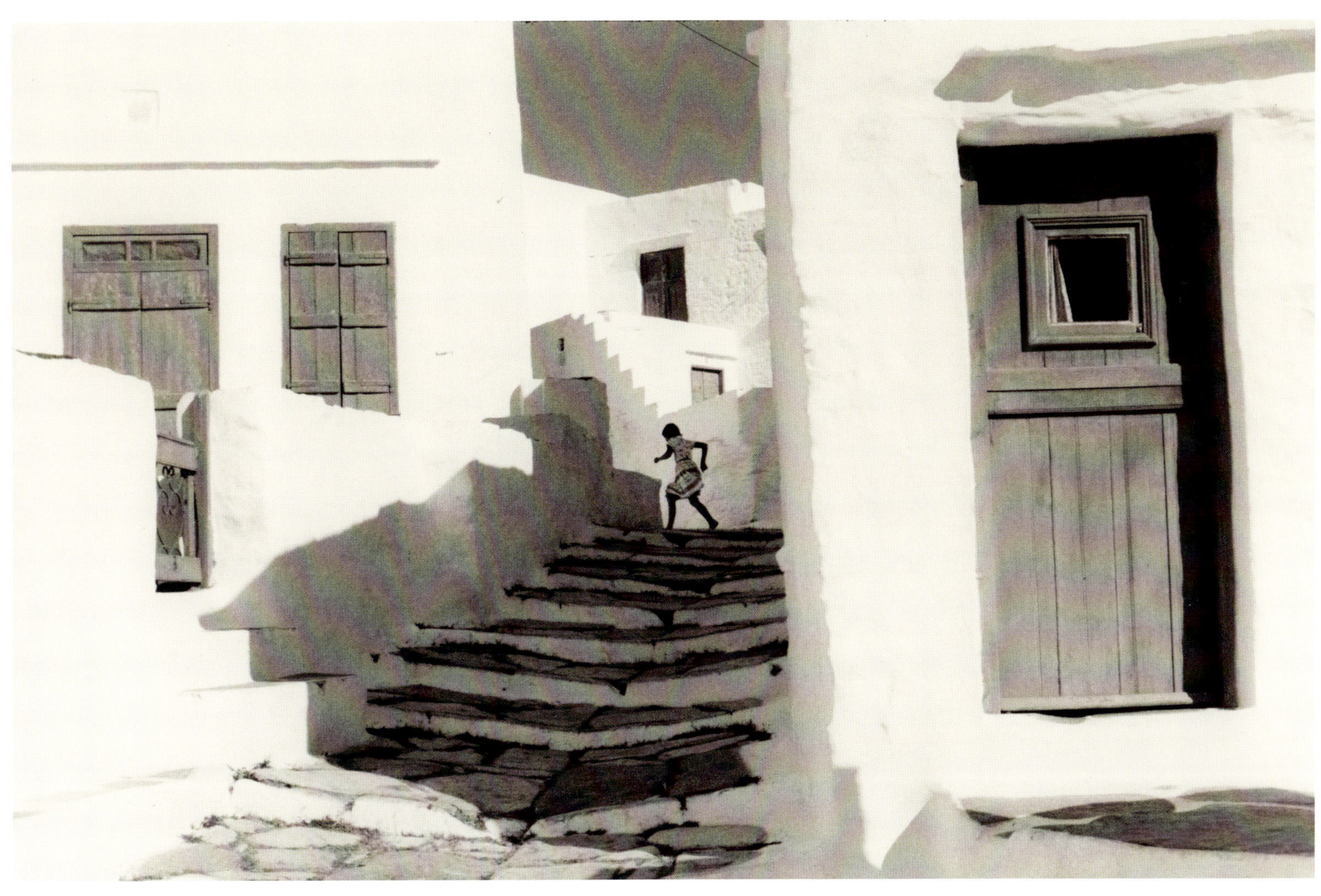

169
Henri Cartier-Bresson
***Siphnos, Greece*, 1961**
Gelatin silver print,
12 × 16 in.
The Phillips Collection, Washington, DC,
Gift of Kent and Marcia Minichiello, 2014.

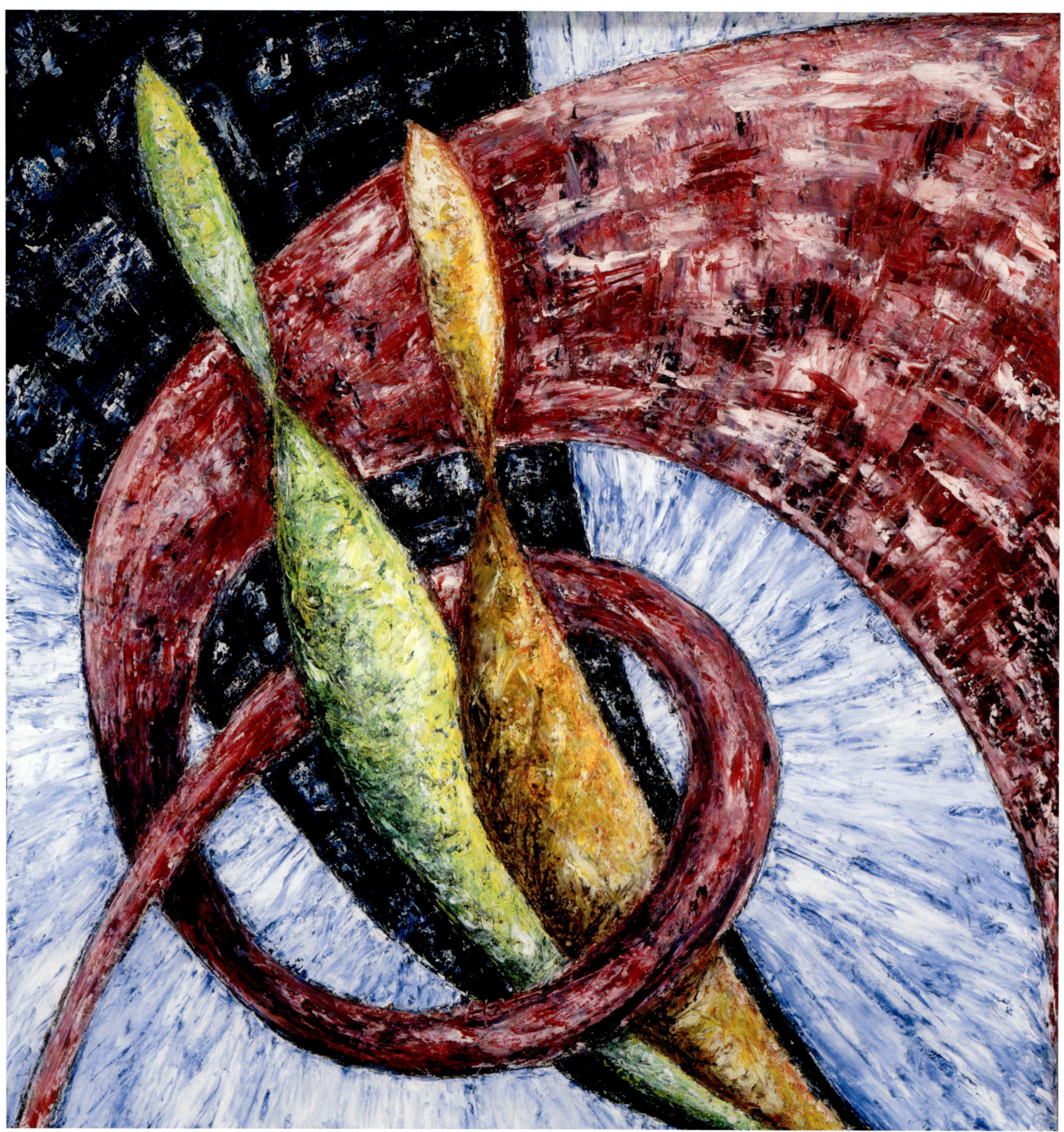

170
Bill Jensen
Deluge, 1980–81
Oil on canvas,
26 × 24 in.
The Phillips Collection, Washington, DC,
Gift of Gifford and Joann Phillips, 2009.

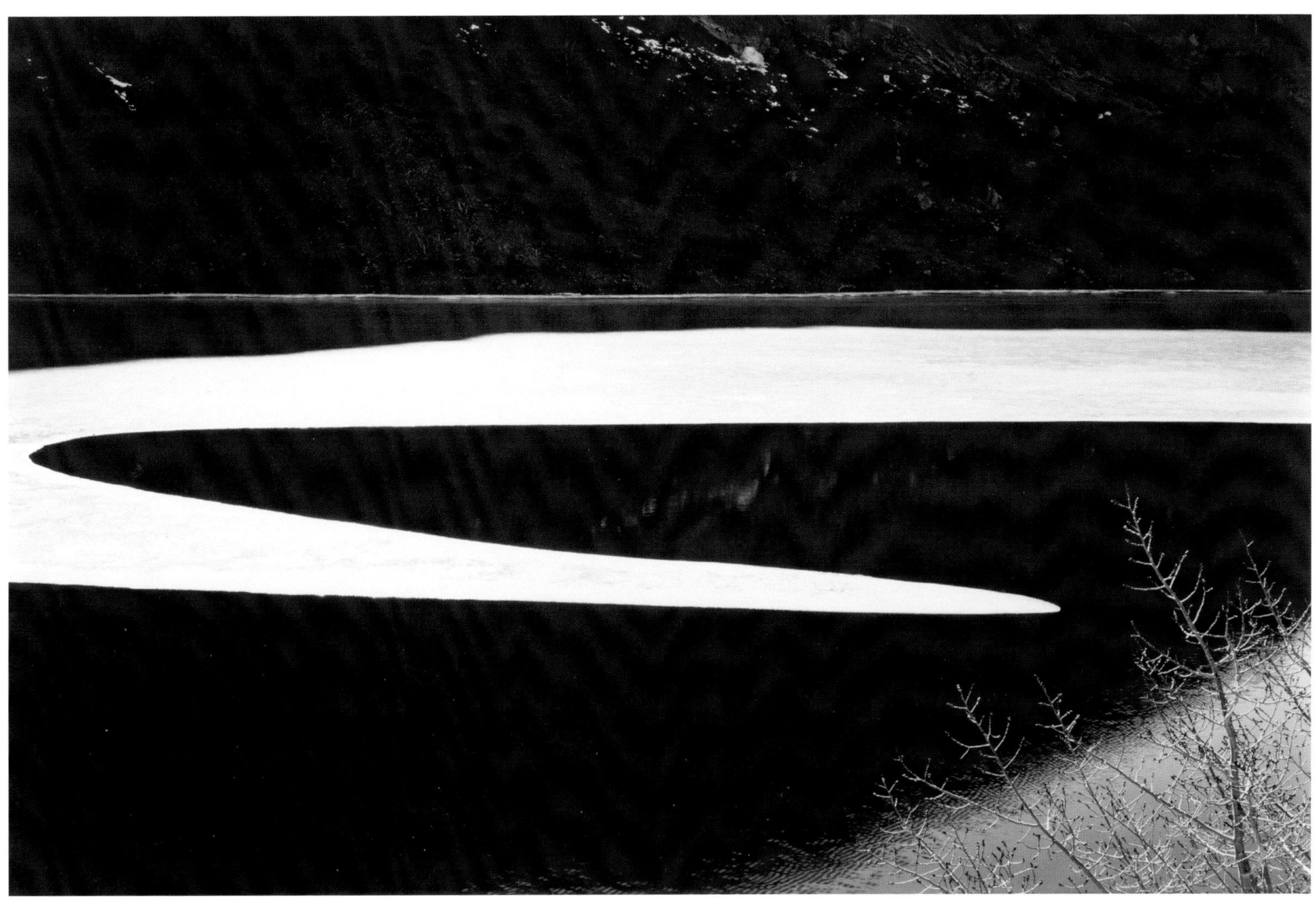

171
Ansel Adams
Ice on Ellery Lake, Sierra Nevada, California, ca. 1959
Gelatin silver print,
13 × 18 3/4 in.
The Phillips Collection, Washington, DC,
Gift of the Phillips Contemporaries, Caroline M. Macomber, Linda Lichtenberg Kaplan, Trish and George Vradenburg, Luther W. Brady, Bonnie B. Himmelman, and David W. Steadman, 2003.

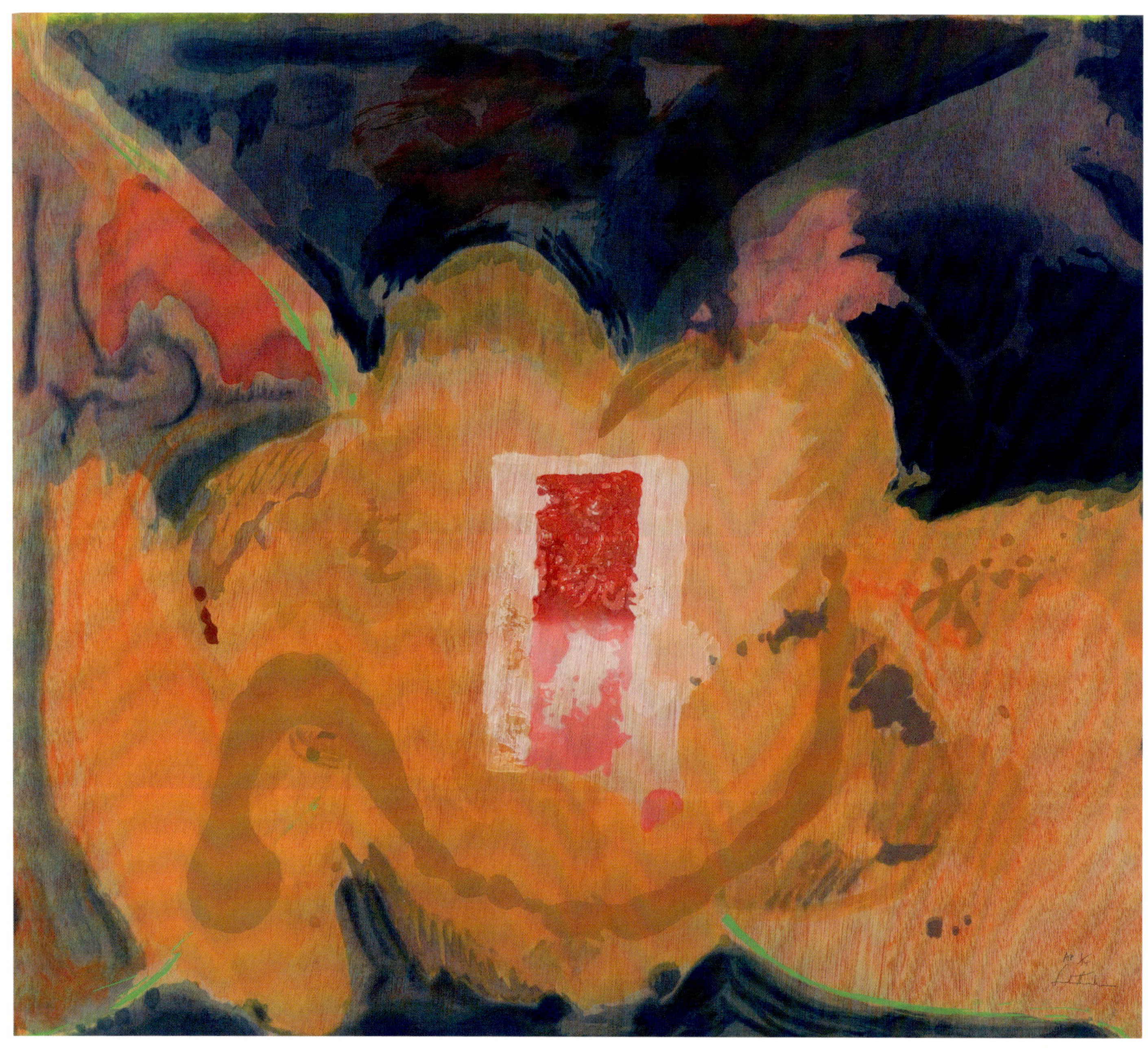

172
Helen Frankenthaler
***Tales of Genji V*, 1998**
Woodcut printed in 49 colors from 21 blocks, 42 × 47 in.
The Phillips Collection, Washington, DC, Promised Gift of Steve and Linda Weitz.

173
Joseph Marioni
Crimson Painting, 2009
Acrylic on canvas,
37 × 31 in.
The Phillips Collection, Washington, DC,
Gift of Wade Wilson, 2011.

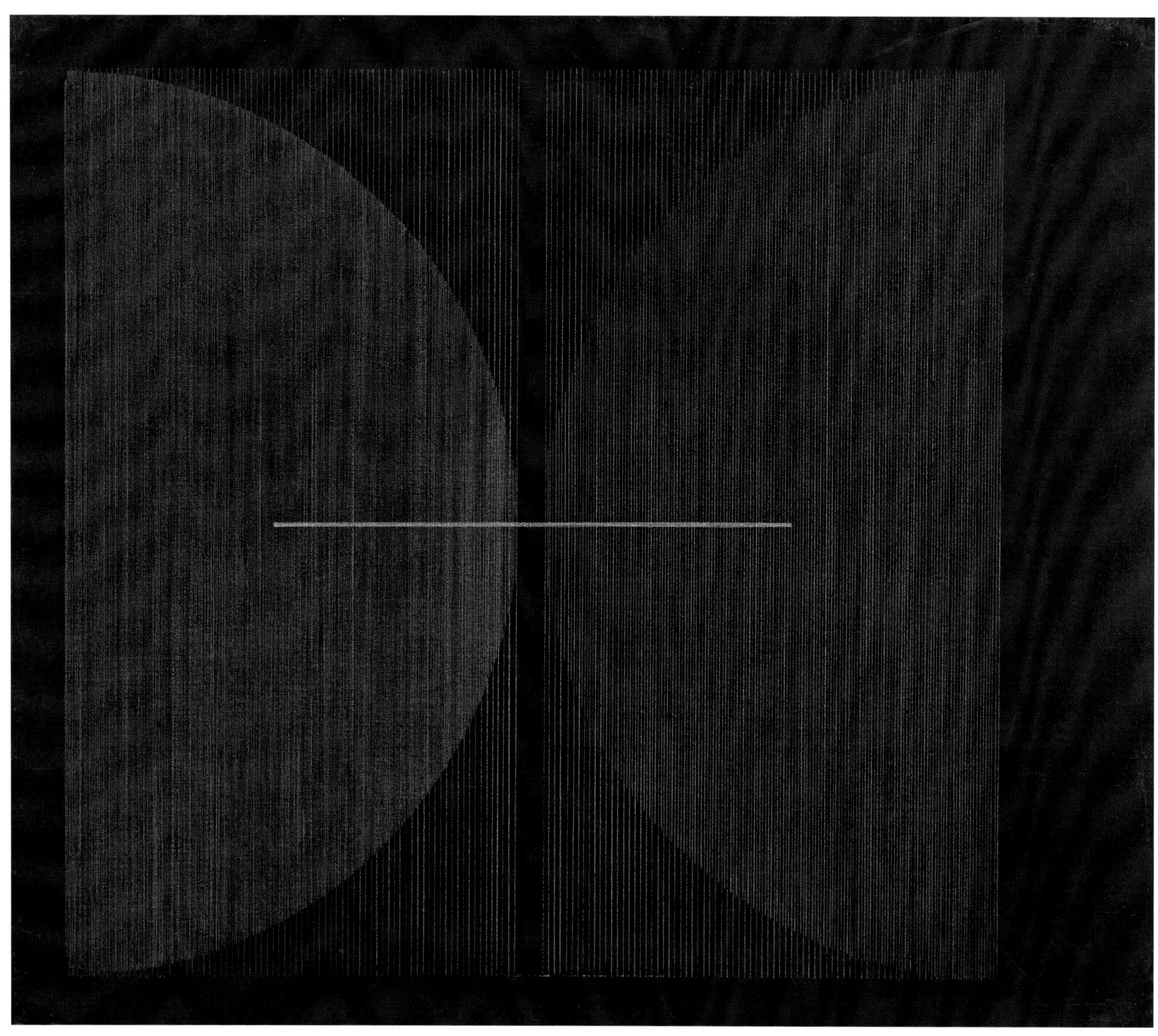

174
Bice Lazzari
***Measures and Signs (Misure e segni)*, 1967**
Tempera on canvas,
35 × 39 3/8 in.
The Phillips Collection, Washington, DC,
Gift of Mariagrazia Oliva Lapadula and the Archivio Bice Lazzari,
Rome, 2018, courtesy of the Embassy of Italy, Washington, DC.

BICE LAZZARI
MISURE E SEGNI (*MEASURES AND SIGNS*), 1967

Susan Behrends Frank

Born in Venice in 1900, Bice (Beatrice) Lazzari was a pioneer in postwar Italian art. For most women in the early twentieth century, there were limited opportunities to pursue a career in the fine arts, but in Italy it was especially difficult between the wars. Lazzari was compelled to find an alternative path. Although trained as a figure painter, she began her career in the late 1920s in the applied arts, designing ceramic tiles and some jewelry, as well as textiles for pillows, rugs, curtains, and embroideries. In the postwar years, she made her permanent home in Rome, where she found her unique artistic voice. Although her early work in the applied arts was often geometric in style, her paintings of the 1950s were expressive and abstract, while her works in the 1960s and 1970s, though increasingly reductive, involved experimentation with materials and a singular focus on rhythmic mark-making. *Measures and Signs*, with its emphasis on minimal gestures, demonstrates the artist's complete control.

Lazzari was not only a visual poet. She wrote equally expressively about her creative process in the pages of her notebooks:

> Everything is rhythm and obsession, and this interchangeability
> gives me the right measure of order and, at the same time,
> intensifies my thoughts...
> These light lines, that run over the canvas and stop at a
> predetermined point, that little by little inexorably thicken and
> break, create a measure that repeats itself or not depending on
> my decision to reject or accept on a day-to-day-basis.
> Because listening carefully to a day's rhythm is what works best.
> —Milan, 1967

In paintings and works on paper, Lazzari created poetic compositions that resemble graphs, maps, musical staffs, and notes. Later in her career she further simplified her imagery, as seen in *Measures and Signs*, creating grids, lines, rows of dots and dashes, and irregular shapes using a limited palette. Reflecting her lifelong passion for music and poetry, Lazzari's lines and forms create rhythms that interact with each other, making her works come alive in a manner akin to musical notation.

A romantic spirit fiercely dedicated to pushing the boundaries of her art with unwavering discipline, Lazzari made her lifelong project a precise and solitary quest for new codes, expressive means and visual languages within the framework of painterly abstraction. Although little recognized in her lifetime, she remains underappreciated for her contributions to twentieth-century abstraction even as she is today considered one of Italy's most revered modern artists. The Phillips Collection was only the second museum in North America to recognize Lazzari's unique voice and move to acquire her work.

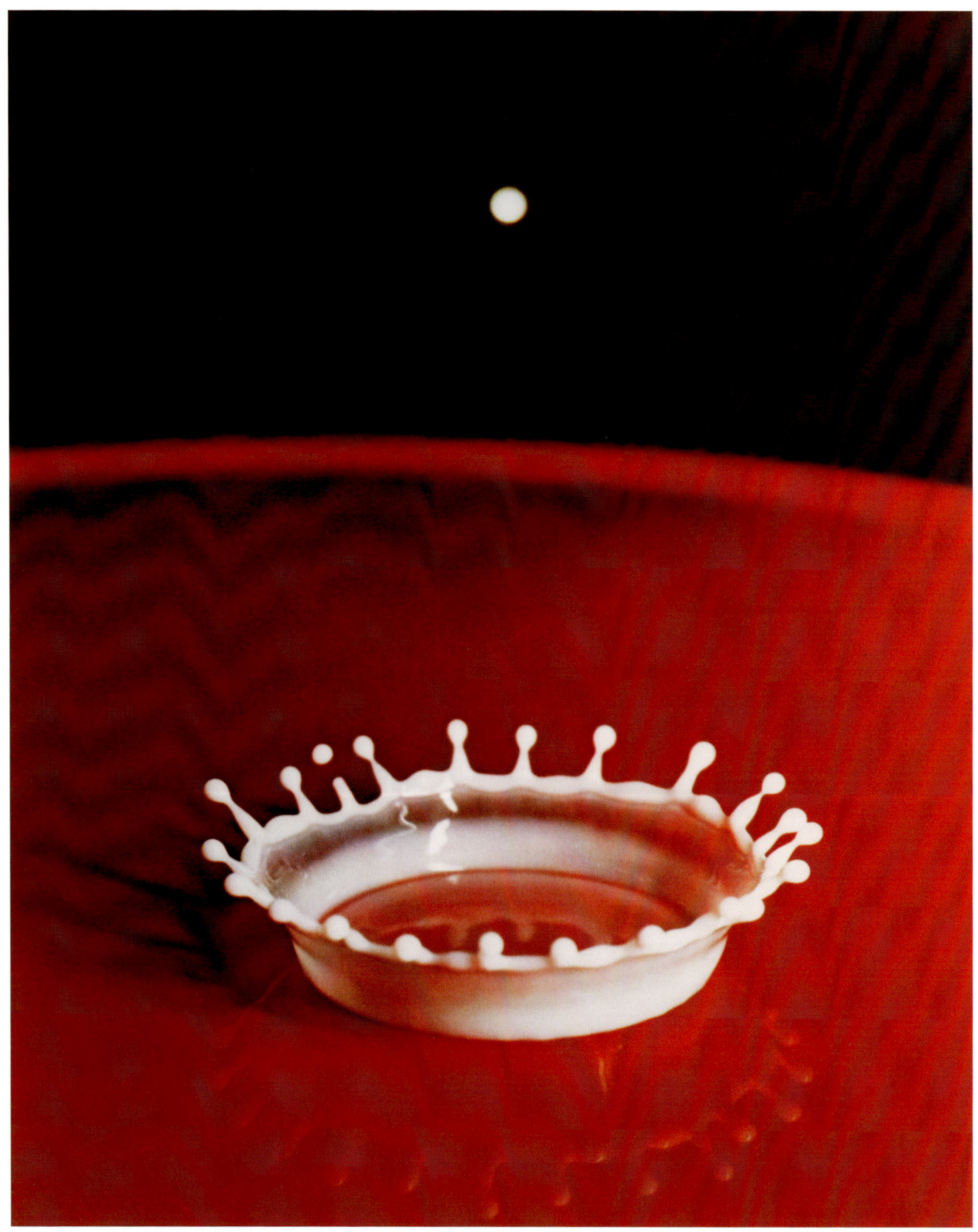

175
Harold Edgerton
Milk Drop Coronet, 1957
Dye transfer print,
overall: 14 × 11 in.
The Phillips Collection, Washington, DC,
Gift of The Joseph and Charlotte Lichtenberg Collection,
initiated 2005, completed 2016.

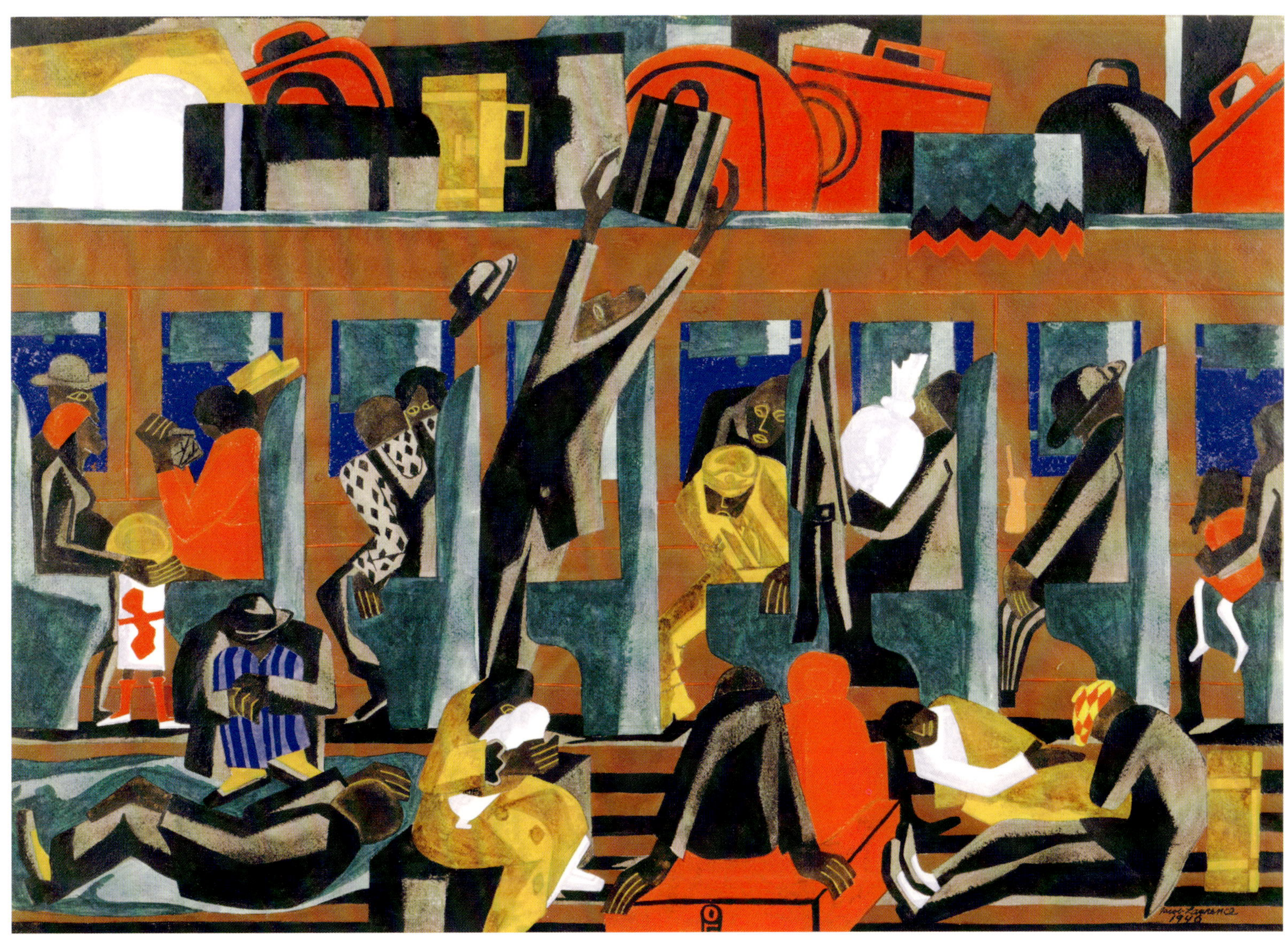

176
Jacob Lawrence
Going Home, 1946
Opaque watercolor on paper,
22 × 30 1/4 in.
The Phillips Collection, Washington, DC,
Promised Gift of Linda Lichtenberg Kaplan.

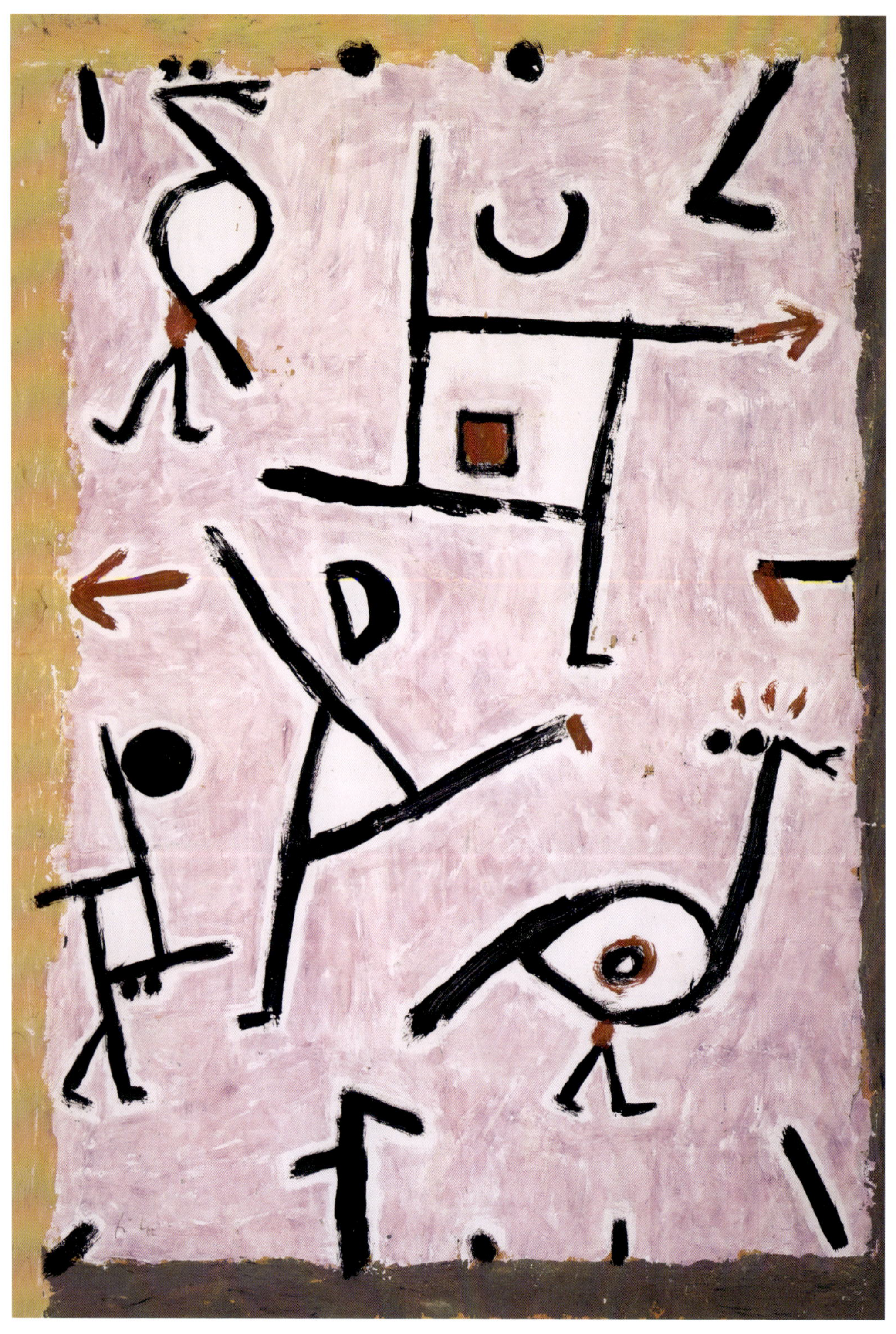

177
Paul Klee
Nach Rechts, Nach Links (*To the Right, To the Left*), 1938
Opaque watercolor on paper,
19 1/4 × 13 in.
The Phillips Collection, Washington, DC,
Gift of Elizabeth Klee, initiated 2005, completed 2017.

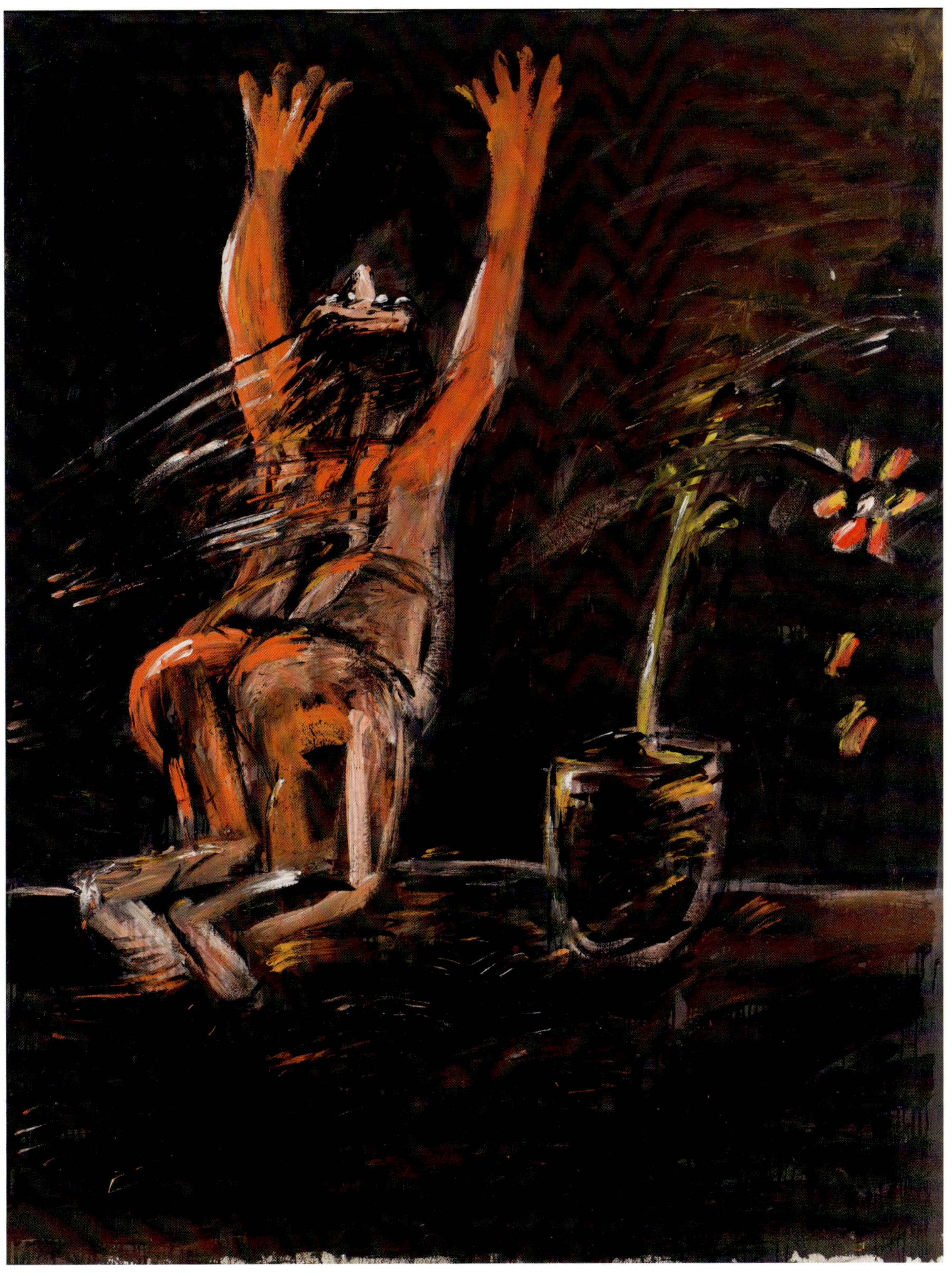

178
Walter Dahn
Trying to Look Like a Flower, 1983
Acrylic on canvas,
79 × 60 in.
The Phillips Collection, Washington, DC,
Gift of Arthur and Carol Goldberg, 2013.

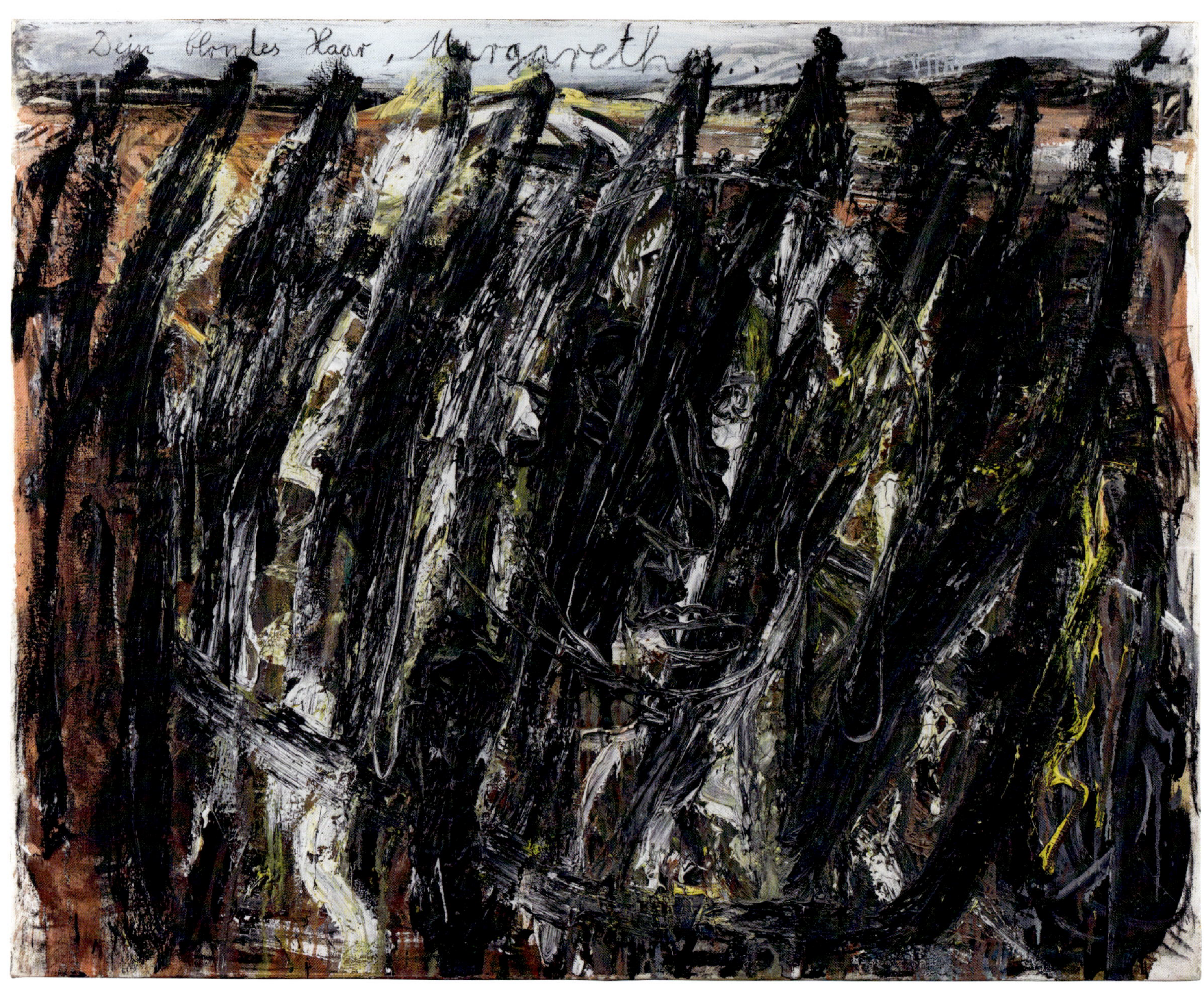

179
Anselm Kiefer
Dein blondes Haar, Margarethe
(*Your Blond Hair, Margarete*), 1981
Oil and straw on canvas,
46 1/2 × 57 in.
The Phillips Collection, Washington, DC,
Gift from the Family of Anita Reiner in her memory, 2014.

ANSELM KIEFER
DEIN BLONDES HAAR, MARGARETHE (*YOUR BLOND HAIR, MARGARETE*), 1981

Dominique Baqué

How can one be a German artist after Nazism and the destruction of "kultur"? This is the primary question Anselm Kiefer has asked himself, echoing the famous lines in Theodor Adorno's *Negative Dialectics* of 1955: "Auschwitz demonstrated irrefutably that culture has failed.... All post-Auschwitz culture ... is garbage."[1] Since then, how have we managed "after Auschwitz" or, more precisely, "following" Auschwitz? And yet ... Kiefer painted and continues to paint; others write, make movies, act, dance. Might kultur then be redeemed?

In 1981, Kiefer encountered the poetry of Paul Celan, the Austrian and Jewish poet who devoted his life and poetry to preserving the memory of the Shoah through works such as *Sand from the Urns* and *Poppy and Memory*, but above all through the inaugural text entitled "Death Fugue," written in Bucharest in May 1945, three months after the liberation of Auschwitz by the Red Army. This poem, which ends with the lines "Your golden hair Margarete / Your ashen hair Shulamith," would reorient the entirety of Kiefer's work and give rise to many paintings that function as "transformation groups," to use Claude Lévi-Strauss's concept, around the figure of Margarete. More than any other German artist, Kiefer would borrow many themes from Jewish tradition, showing the extent to which Jewish thought is inscribed in the very heart of German thought and its memory: it is about asserting that German Jews were an intrinsic component of German identity, before their extermination by the Nazis. Hence, the deep reading into Jewish mystics, Hassidism, and the Kabbalah: Jewish mythology is the only one that can save German kultur, which lies in a state of advanced decomposition, as relayed by Gershom Scholem and Isaac Louria. It would be the antidote to the ban put forth by Adorno. And so, Kiefer regularly compares Margareta and Shulamith: Margareta, a mythological figure in the German collective memory, embodies the Faustian blond wife, the perfect incarnation of the Aryan woman, while Shulamith is the Jewess from the Song of Songs. By comparing Margareta and Shulamith, Kiefer contributes to de-Nazifying the myths—such as those of Siegfried or Brunhilde—that were appropriated by National Socialism.

The paintings devoted to Margarete call for a new material, decisive in Kiefer's painting—straw, symbolizing the blondness of her hair—which he attaches directly to the canvas. About thirty works—paintings, watercolors, painted photographs—feature the figure of Margarete and her blond hair, including *Dein blondes Haar, Margarethe*. Here, the horizon line is situated as high and as far away as possible on the canvas: a gray, ashen sky, on which we see, in Kiefer's fine, careful, recognizable script, writing that acts as a "signature." The earth of German soil, *das Land*, is violently hatched with thick, black lines, like a geographical erasure, while a few wisps of straw connote Margarete's hair but struggle to brighten or illuminate the painting's darkness. It is as if a soldier, through the fractured lines and pictorial impasto, were defying German soil. And here the careful eye will note—an optical illusion? over-interpretation?—behind the enraged hatchings, the barely sketched outline of a face: the contour of the oval, eyes, mouth, nose perhaps, like a phantom, a dead/living apparition at the heart of the painting and the land. Could this be Margarete's "other" that we glimpse here? Shulamith, Margarete's double and opposite; Shulamith the Jewess perhaps; Shulamith, not with golden hair but with ashen hair....

Translated from the French by Jeanine Herman.

1 Theodor W. Adorno, *Negative Dialectics*, trans. E. B. Ashton (London: Continuum, 2007), 366–67.

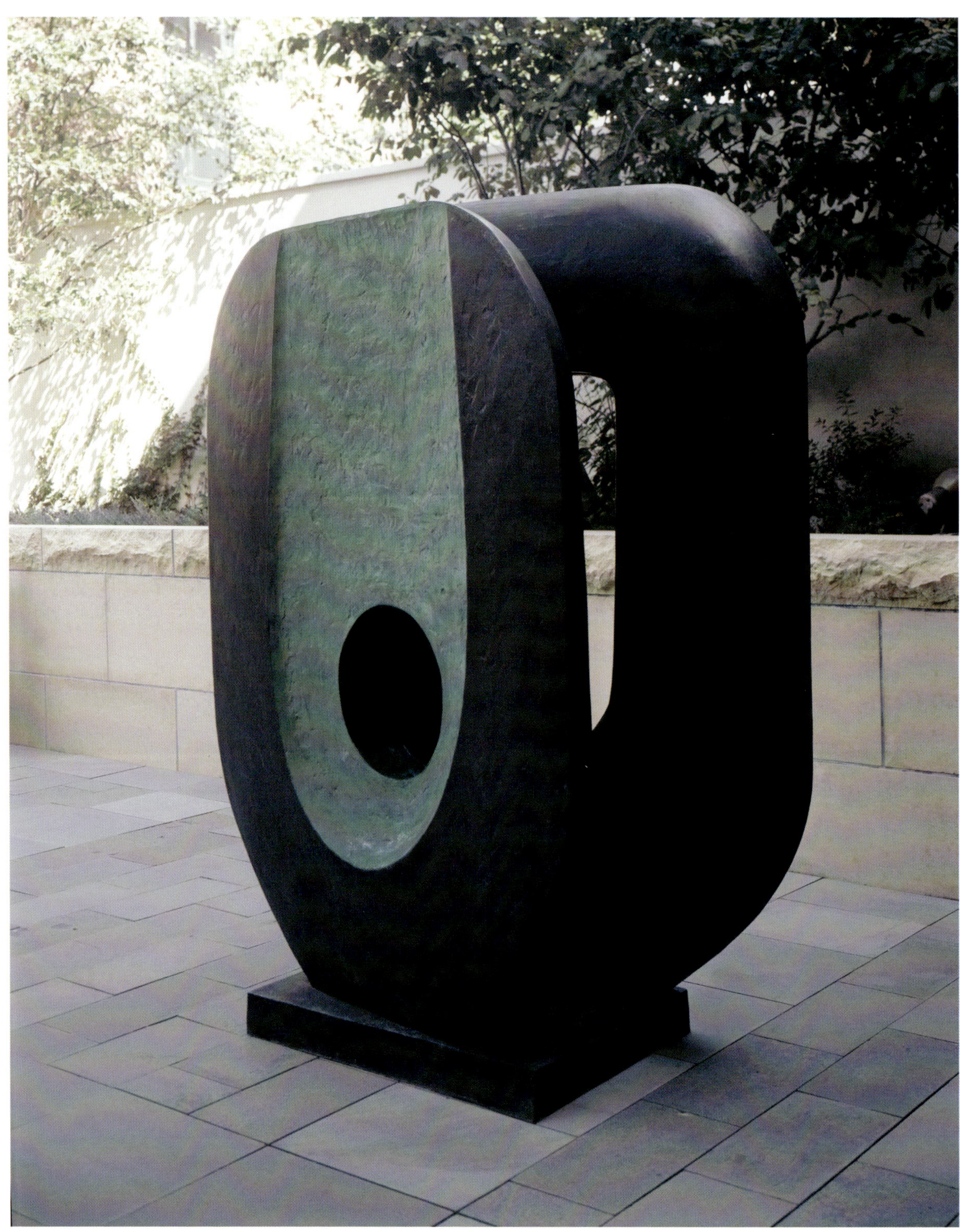

180
Barbara Hepworth
Dual Form, 1965 (cast 1966)
Bronze,
72 in. high
The Phillips Collection, Washington, DC,
Acquired with the Dreier Fund for Acquisitions and additional funds from Natalie R. Abrams, Alan and Irene Wurtzel, and a bequest from Nathan and Jeanette Miller, 2006.

181
Richard Serra
***Reykjavik*, 1991**
Paintstik over screenprint on handmade Japanese paper,
67 × 76 in.
The Phillips Collection, Washington, DC,
Gift of Sid Stolz and David Hatfield, 2018.

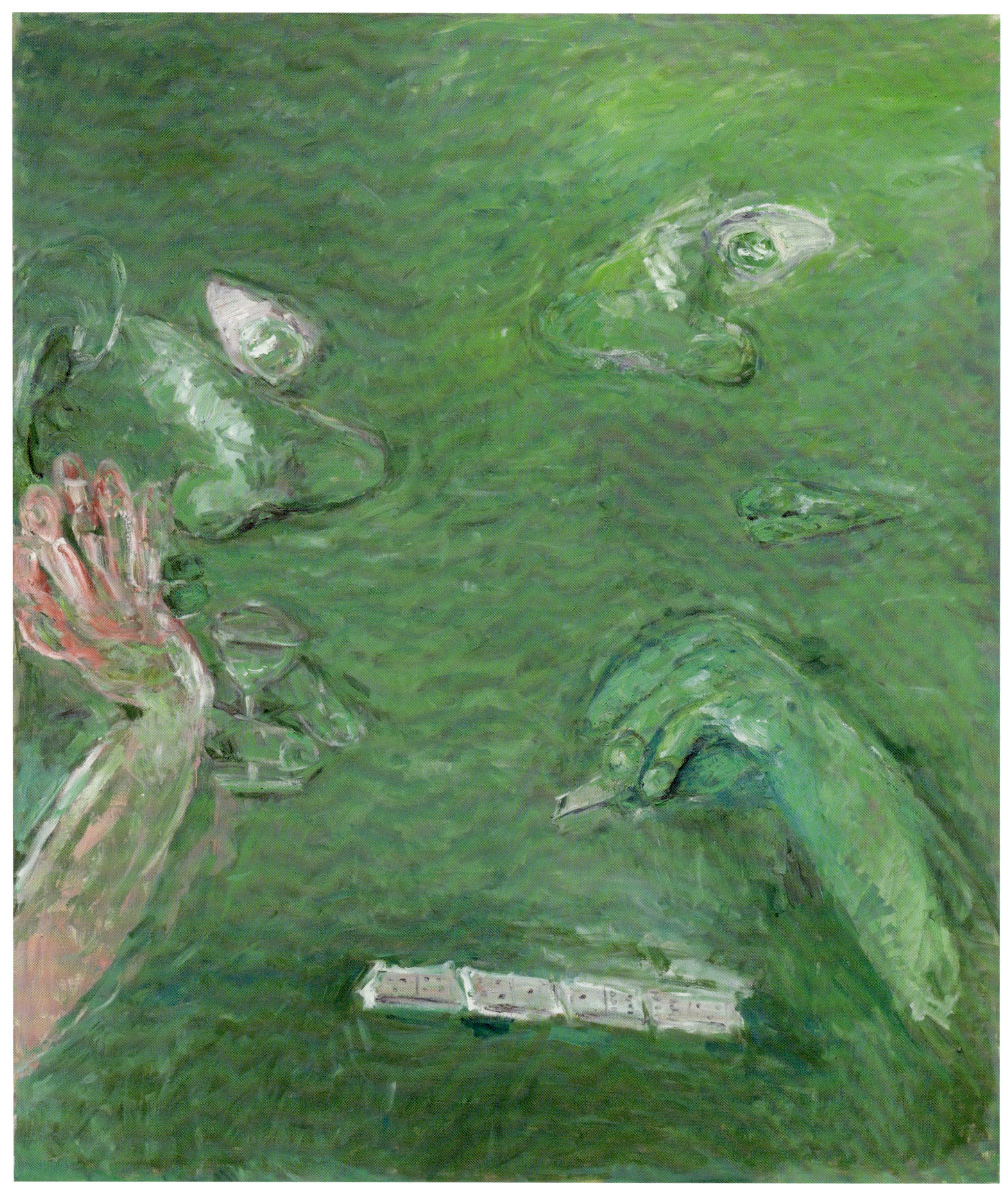

182
Susan Rothenberg
Dominos-Cold, 2001
Oil on canvas,
86 1/2 × 72 1/2 in.
The Phillips Collection, Washington, DC,
Gift of Alice Swistel, James L. Phillips and
Marjorie Phillips Elliott, 2019.

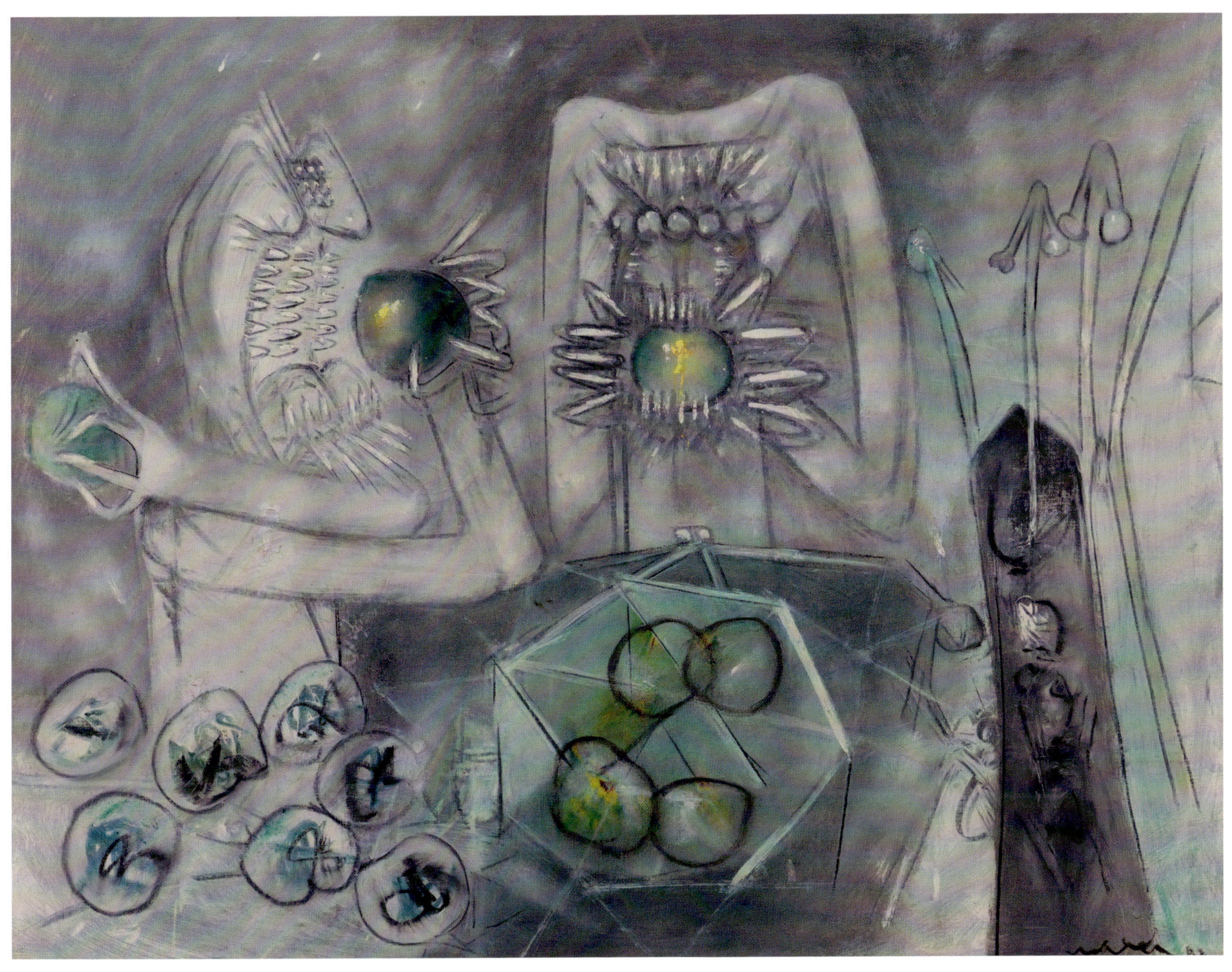

183
Roberto Matta
Being Beauteous (The Appletalists), 1952
Oil on canvas,
37 × 45 3/4 in.
The Phillips Collection, Washington, DC,
Gift of The Rosalind Gersten Jacobs and Melvin Jacobs
Collection, New York, 2018.

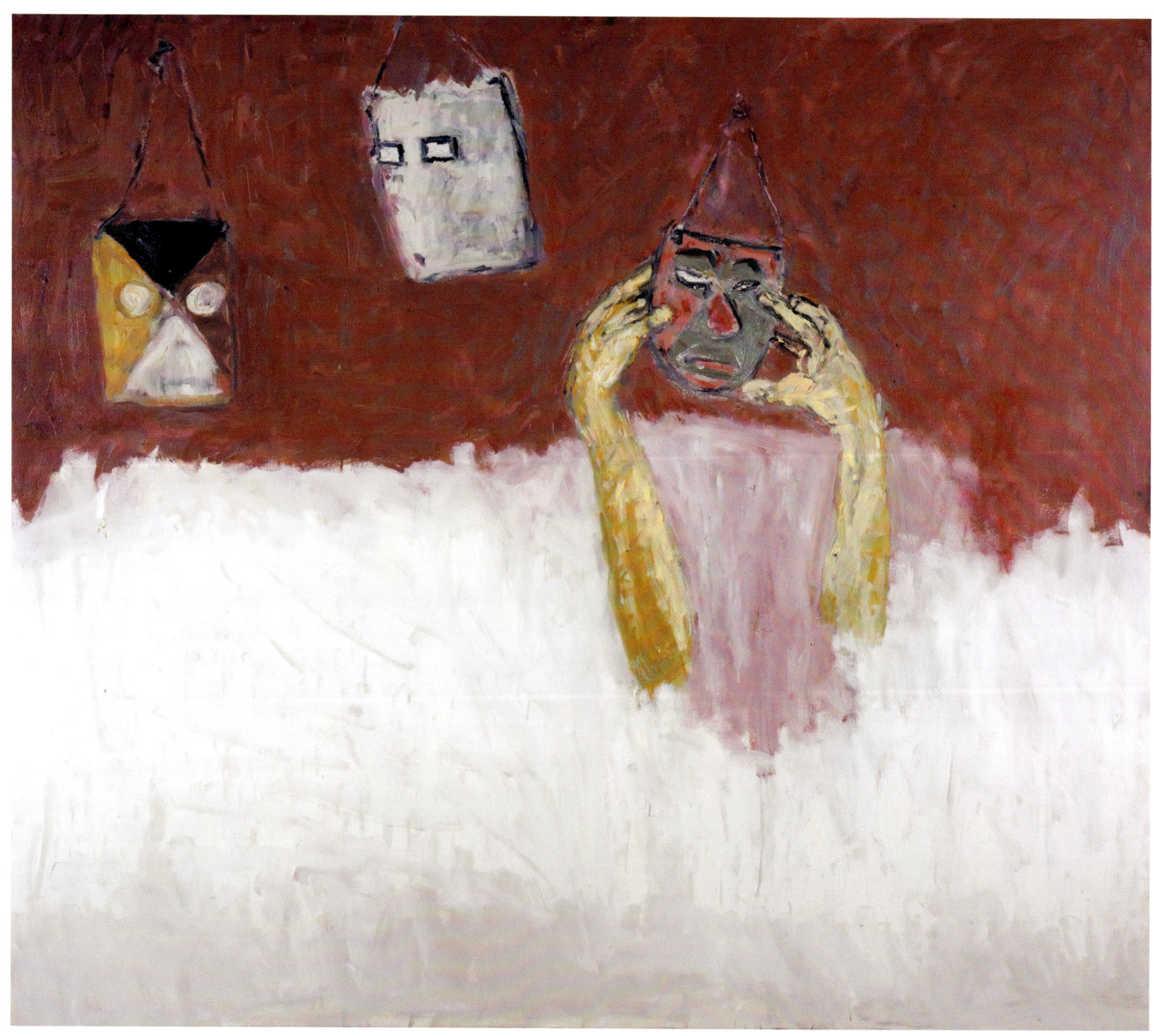

184
Susan Rothenberg
Three Masks, 2006
Oil on canvas,
59 3/16 × 66 1/8 in.
The Phillips Collection, Washington, DC,
The Dreier Fund for Acquisitions, 2007.

SUSAN ROTHENBERG
DOMINOS-COLD, 2001, AND *THREE MASKS*, 2006

Susan Rothenberg

I am afraid I am not a great explainer of why I do what I do.

The painting *Dominos-Cold* (pl. 182) is an expression of how I fell in love with green—a color I did not know well before I moved to New Mexico in 1990. Dominoes was a prominent game in our house. My husband, Bruce, and I played frequently, sometimes with friends. I used cold and warm versions of green to represent the felt-covered game table, the site of our favorite board game. I like the fact that the hands aren't anchored. They just float around the space of the painting. You really have to know that they are at a table. The hands are just these living things, moving around like the dogs or the horses.

When I painted *Three Masks* in 2006 (pl. 184), I was toying with the idea of paper bag masks like kids wear for Halloween. The masks are painted casually hanging on hooks. One is like the face in my *Self Portrait* (private collection) from the same year. You know the old saw that everything an artist does is a self-portrait? I think it's true. All of my work has a portrait element to it. But I still have a hard time allowing myself to make a complete human figure. So I guess it's kind of a broken portraiture. Sometimes masks, like my later paintings with disembodied parts or prosthetics, can be considered puppets or marionettes.

I would like to express my respect and gratitude to Eliza Rathbone, who curated my show at The Phillips Collection in the fall of 1985 and encouraged the acquisition of my work. Gifford and Joann Phillips bought *Dominos-Cold* from my 2002 show at Sperone Westwater, in which there were four domino paintings and four or five green paintings. Congratulations to the Phillips for a wonderful collection, and thank you for my place in it.

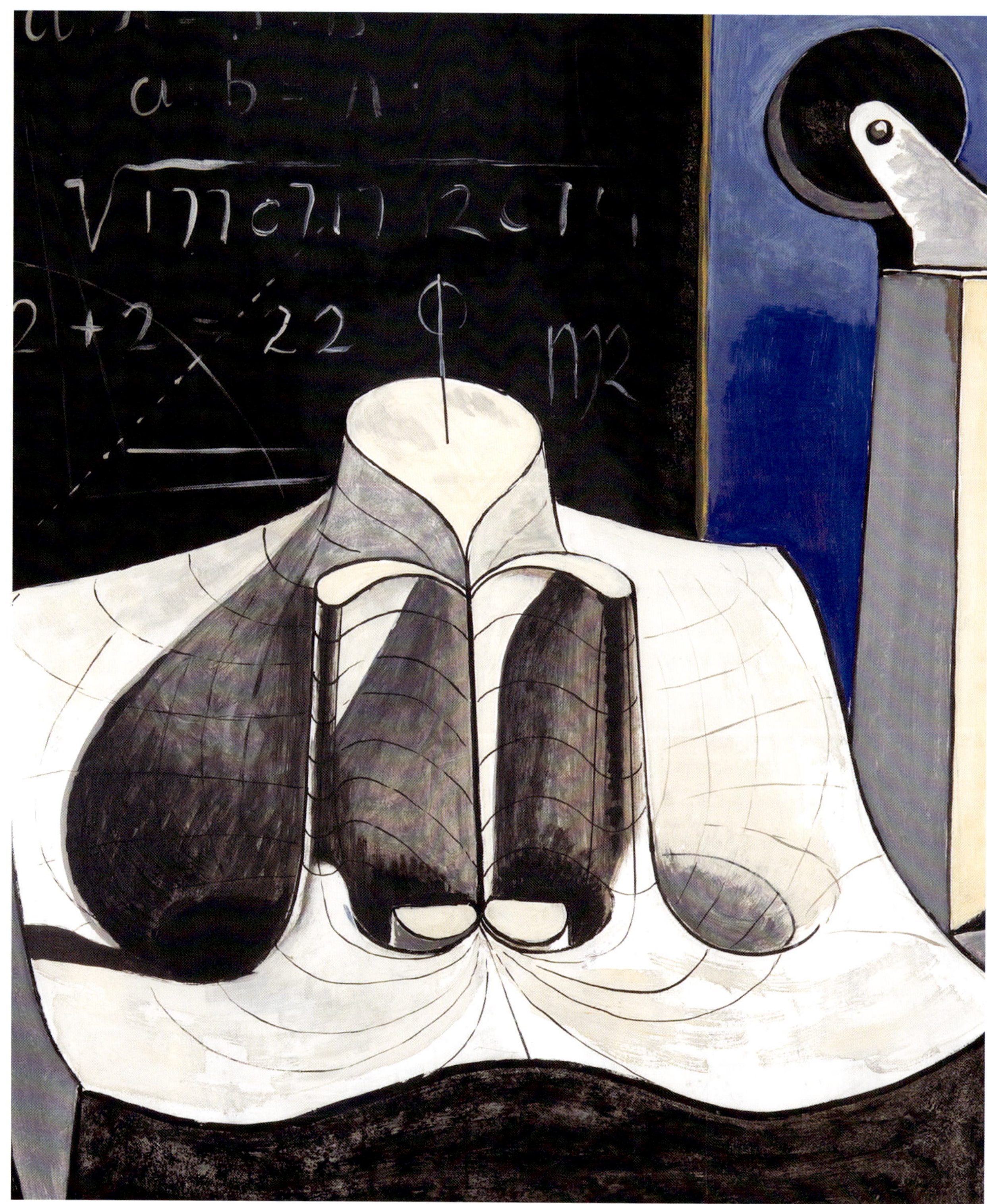

185
Man Ray
Shakespearean Equation, Julius Caesar, 1948
Oil on hardboard,
24 × 19 3/4 in.
The Phillips Collection, Washington, DC,
Promised Gift from The Rosalind Gersten Jacobs and Melvin Jacobs Collection, New York, in honor of Wendy Grossman.

MAN RAY
SHAKESPEAREAN EQUATION, JULIUS CAESAR, 1948

Wendy A. Grossman

Fie, fie on all tired jades,
on all mad masters, and all foul ways!
Was ever man so beaten? Was ever man
so ray'd?
—William Shakespeare
Taming of the Shrew, Act IV, Scene 1

How does one make sense of a purported link connecting mathematics, Shakespeare, and the artist Man Ray? The fortuitous encounter of "man so ray'd" in the Bard's *Taming of the Shrew* notwithstanding, could this trifecta be anything other than a surrealist riddle? Or a game of wits posed by the elusive trickster, Man Ray, an artist who reinvented everything about himself to suit his adopted avant-garde persona?[1] His inventive approach to humanizing mathematical models and translating them into enigmatic forms at the heart of this riddle is epitomized in *Julius Caesar*, a key work from the artist's *Shakespearean Equations* series.

Like the twenty-two other paintings that constitute this series, *Julius Caesar* is the culmination of a creative process that began in Paris in the 1930s with Man Ray's encounter at the Institut Henri Poincaré with a collection of plaster, wood, and wire mathematical models. Photographs he created of these objects (see fig. 97), which took on a life of their own within surrealist practice at the time,[2] provided the inspiration for the *Shakespearean Equations* paintings he created while living in Hollywood over a decade later.

Featured as a centerpiece of *Man Ray–Human Equations*, the 2015 exhibition at The Phillips Collection, *Julius Caesar* encapsulated the innovative and idiosyncratic vision that guided the artist's creative practice throughout his long career on both sides of the Atlantic.[3] In this composition, he mapped out the undulating lines defining the original mathematical model, casting the object as the central character in a theatrical tableau. Despite being a figurative, faithful rendition of the plaster model, the monumentalized object in this *Shakespearean Equation* is not immediately identifiable to the viewer, suggestive as it is of a headless torso. The painting's intriguing object is presented with dramatic lighting and shadows identical to those in his original photograph upon which the canvas is based, imbuing the form with a commanding presence evocative of the Roman general named in the painting's title. On the blackboard behind the model the artist scrawled both logical and seemingly illogical algebraic formulae, ranging from the rational "a : A = b : B" and "a : b = A : B" to the irrational and literal "2 + 2 = 22." In the space between these two relational formulations is the philosophical question and unsolved problem of the "square root" of Man Ray, the answer to and meaning of which is left for us to decipher.

This painting finds a fitting home at The Phillips Collection as a bookend of sorts complementing Man Ray's *The Black Tray* (1914), which was the first work by the artist to enter a museum collection when it was acquired by Duncan Phillips in 1927.

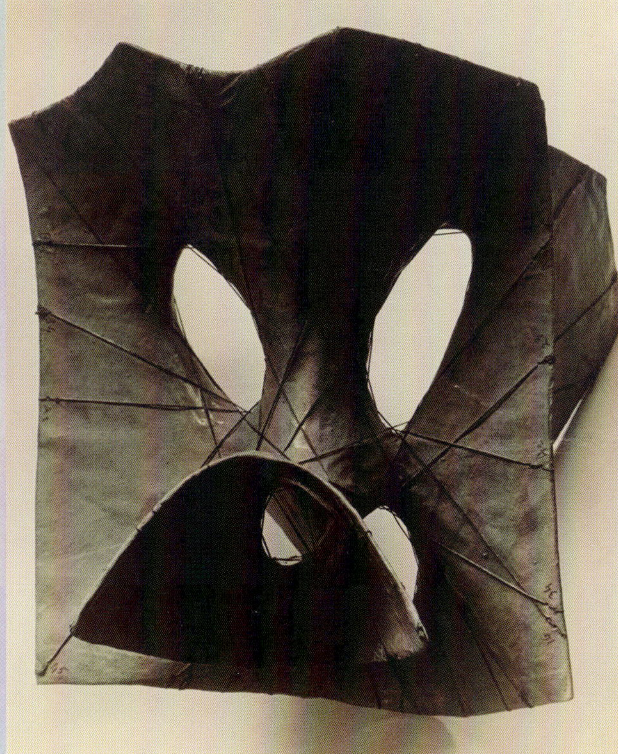

fig. 97
Man Ray
***Untitled (Mathematical Object)*, 1934–35**
Gelatin silver print,
11 3/4 × 9 1/2 in.
The Phillips Collection, Washington, DC,
Gift of Wendy A. Grossman and Francis Naumann, 2015.

---

1 Born Emmanuel Radnitzky in Philadelphia into a Russian émigré family, he and his family legally changed their last name to Ray in 1912 in the face of xenophobia and antisemitism. Shortening his nickname Manny to Man, the artist took on his new persona as Man Ray.

2 Man Ray's photographs were illustrated as full-page plates in the May 1936 issue of *Cahiers d'art* devoted to the "object," published to coincide with the *Exposition surréaliste d'objets* at the Galerie Ratton. They were reproduced to accompany articles by Christian Zervos, the magazine's editor, and André Breton.

3 See Wendy A. Grossman and Edouard Sebline, eds., *Man Ray. Human Equations: A Journey from Mathematics to Shakespeare* (Ostfildern: Hatje Cantz, 2015).

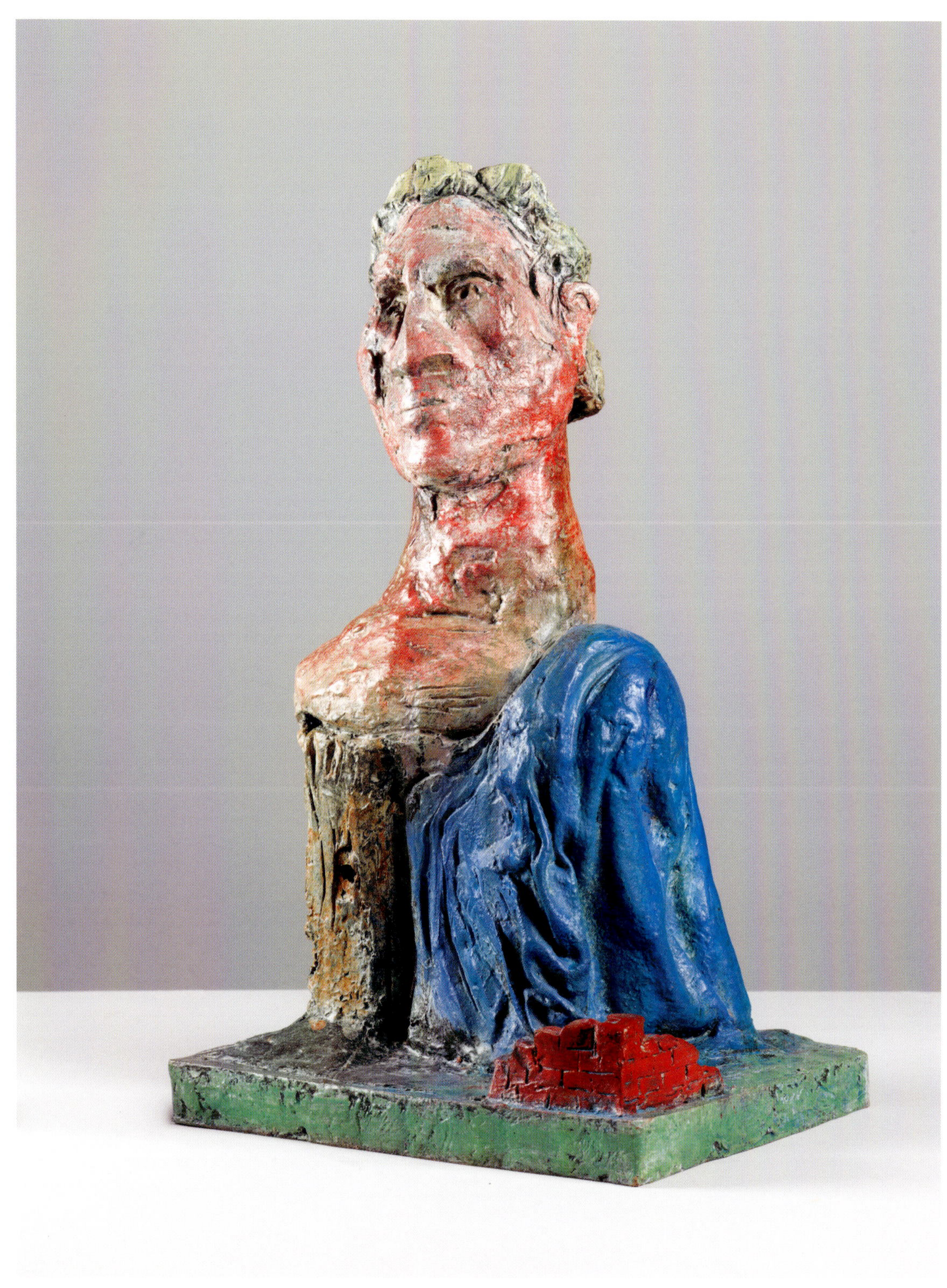

186
Markus Lüpertz
***Troja (Troy)*, 2004**
Painted bronze,
15 × 8 1/4 × 7 in.
The Phillips Collection, Washington, DC,
Gift of Michael Werner, 2015.

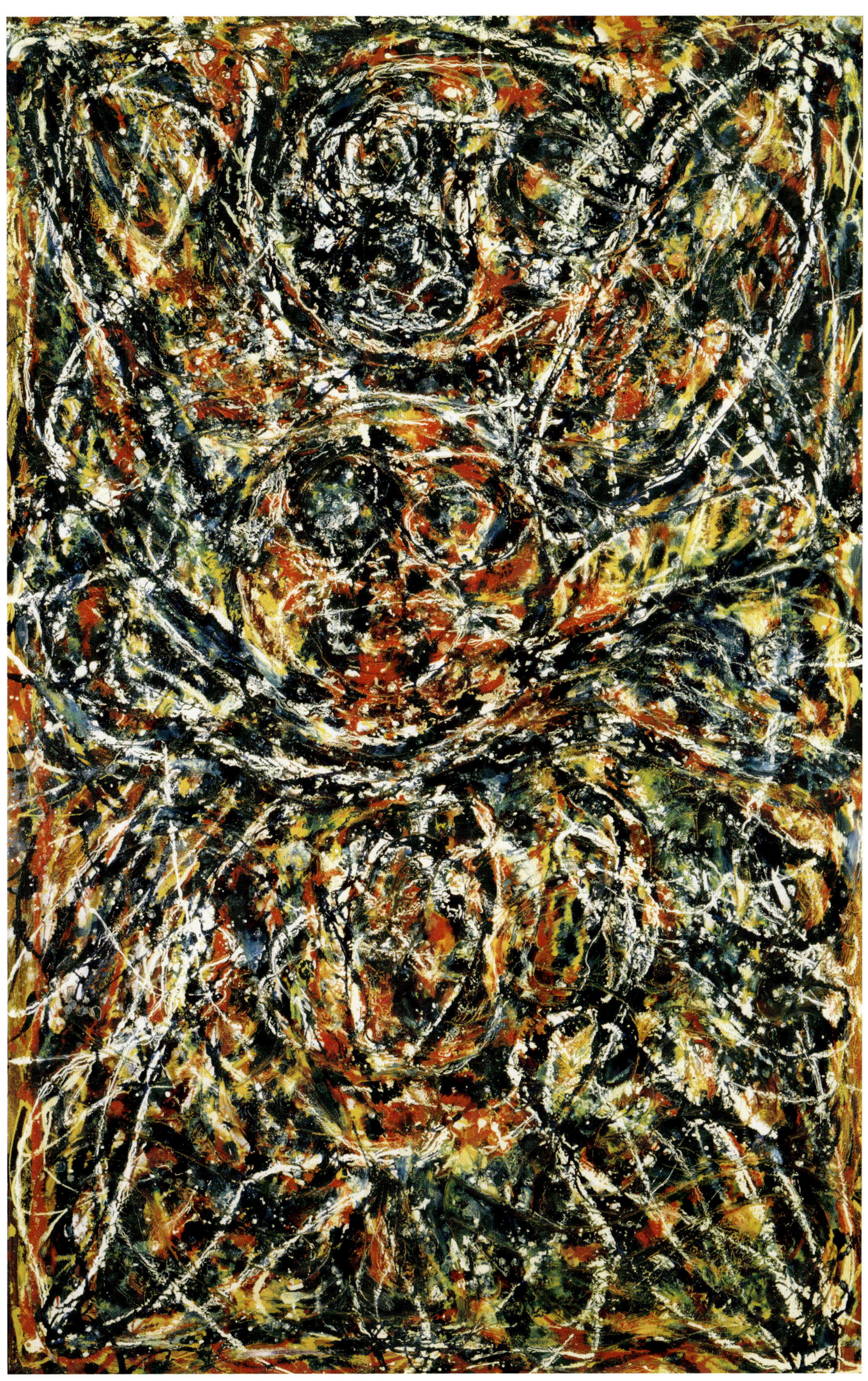

187
Alfonso Ossorio
***Mother and Child,* 1951**
Oil and enamel on canvas,
45 3/4 × 28 3/4 in.
The Phillips Collection, Washington, DC,
The Dreier Fund for Acquisitions, 2008.

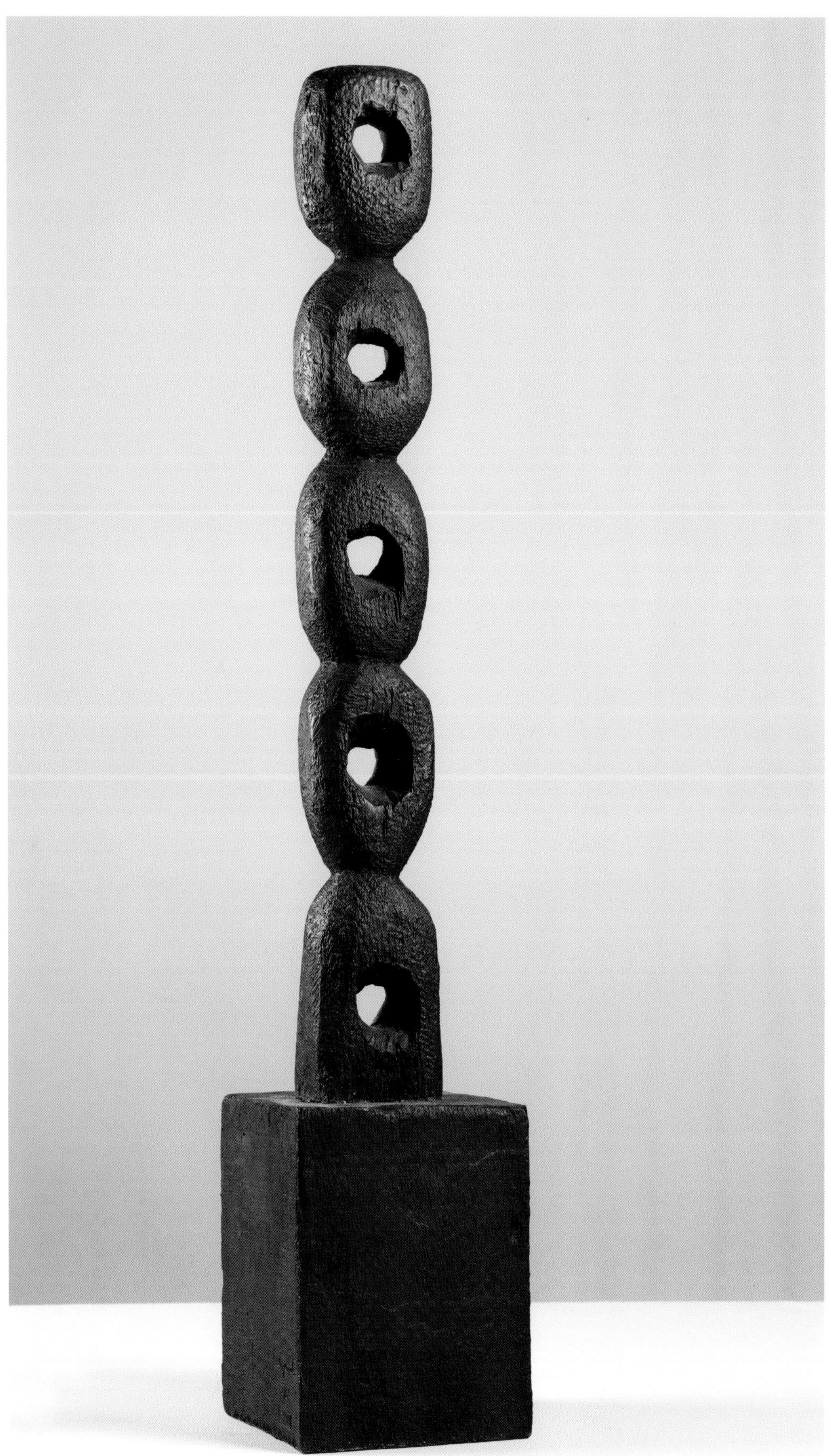

188
A.R. Penck
***Fünf (Five)*, 1987**
Bronze,
20 3/4 × 4 × 4 in.
The Phillips Collection, Washington, DC,
Gift of Michael Werner, 2015.

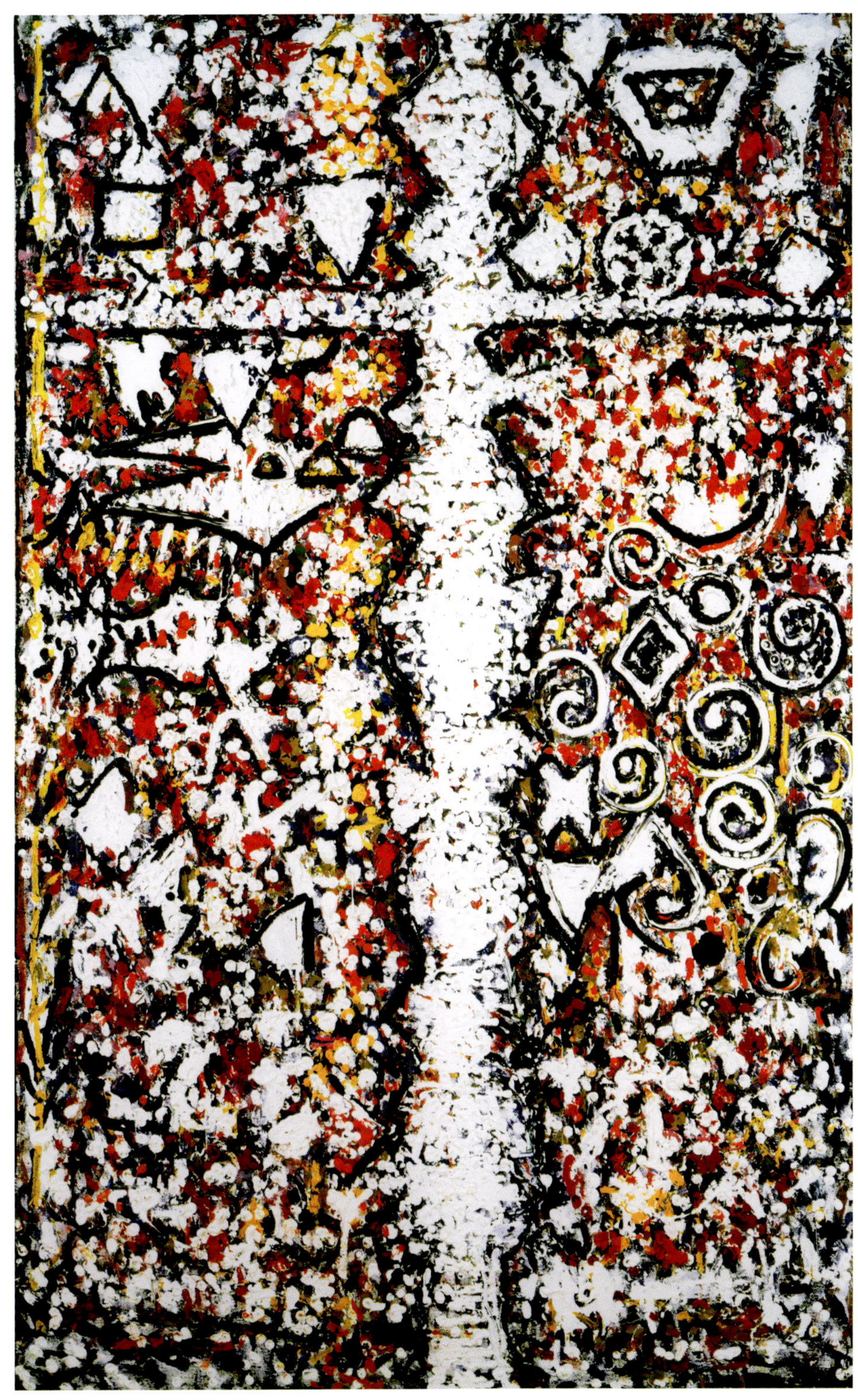

189
Richard Pousette-Dart
Totemic Transcendental, 1982
Acrylic on canvas,
80 × 48 in.
The Phillips Collection, Washington, DC,
Gift from the Estate of Richard Pousette-Dart, 2009.

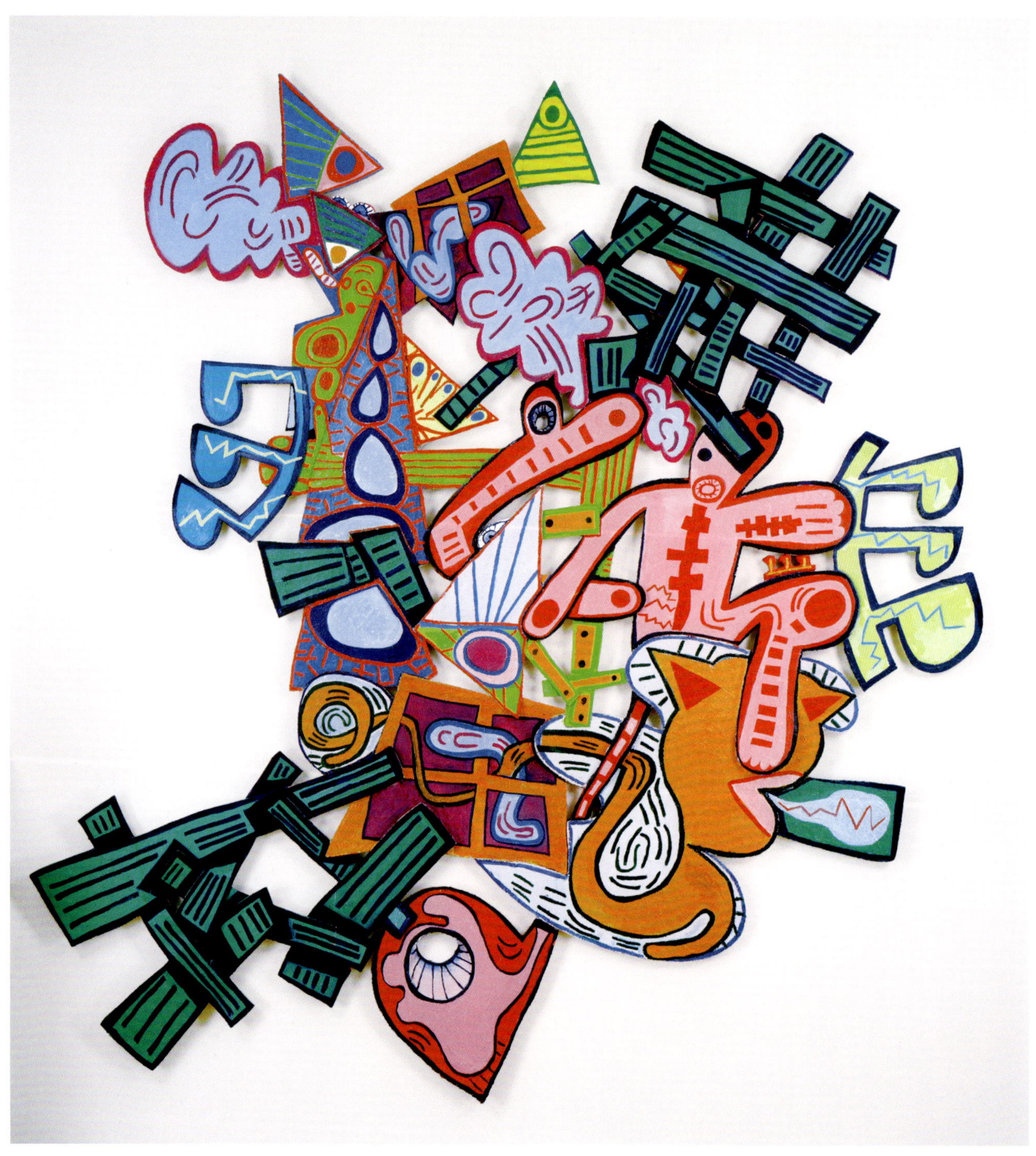

190
Elizabeth Murray
***The Sun and the Moon*, 2004–05**
Oil on panel mounted on wood,
117 × 107 1/2 in.
The Phillips Collection, Washington, DC,
Gift of Agnes Gund and Daniel Shapiro and
Gifford and Joann Phillips, 2006.

ELIZABETH MURRAY
THE SUN AND THE MOON, 2004–05

Renée Maurer

Painting is the ... determination of the mind and the act of the hand.... [R]ealizing where you cannot have control and where you have to have control ... that's the little bitty unknowing place where paintings come out of.
—Elizabeth Murray

Elizabeth Murray was always drawn to the color, graphic quality, and humor of comics. At the School of the Art Institute of Chicago and at Mills College in Oakland, California, she studied cubism, surrealism, and pop art, as well as the work of Paul Cézanne, Philip Guston, Jasper Johns, and Robert Rauschenberg. In the 1970s, Murray explored the sculptural quality of her canvases, determined to make her static objects move. In 1976, she freed her art from the two-dimensional flat surface to create puzzle-shaped painted pieces that jutted out into space. She began with a large drawing, then with a clay maquette, before assistants constructed the wooden armature that shaped her work.

The composition for *The Sun and the Moon* was planned before Murray was diagnosed with cancer. She explained: "I started painting it before I got sick. I was really having a lot of trouble with it, partly because I was starting to have these really terrible headaches.... And I put it all [in the] painting.... Then I started in on it a couple of weeks after I got back from the hospital.... I had to show myself that I could work. And it was hard.... But you still have to keep at it ... and gradually things start to sort themselves out. The thing that is interesting about the painting is that it shows how I had lost my mental coordination, how the forms connected."[1] Pushing ahead, she used whatever "came to hand ... adjusting the colors and marks later."[2]

Murray's intense jumble of abstract and cartoon-like shapes derives from her personal repertoire of symbols that evoke feelings of anxiety and struggle. The right side shows a pink figure, with arms and legs spread, overwhelmed by a smothering cluster of brightly painted, angular forms. The figure's limbs and chest are marred by red stitches. An oversized green hashtag sign, used in cartooning to indicate the force and sound of a punch, wedges through the figure's head. Smoke blows out of its mouth, and an orange cat, perhaps Murray's pet, Abraham, weaves around the figure's legs, yowling. The all-seeing eye of God hovers near an open window, musical notes appear cracked, form and color clash with sound. Life in *The Sun and the Moon* is not still; turmoil reigns. This large scale, dynamic work was the first painting by the artist to enter The Phillips Collection, later complemented by three sculptural prints.

This epigraph by Murray is from the audio guide transcription for *Degas to Diebenkorn: The Phillips Collects*, February 9–May 25, 2008, recorded when her work was acquired in 2006.

1 Phong Bui and Robert Storr, "Elizabeth Murray," In Conversation, *Brooklyn Rail*, October 2005: 12–14. See also https://brooklynrail.org/2005/10/art/in-conversation-elizabeth-murray-with-ro. Accessed April 2020.

2 In Carol Kino, "A Visit with the Modern's First Grandmother," *The New York Times*, October 2, 2005. See also https://www.nytimes.com/2005/10/02/arts/design/a-visit-with-the-moderns-first-grandmother.html. Accessed April 2020.

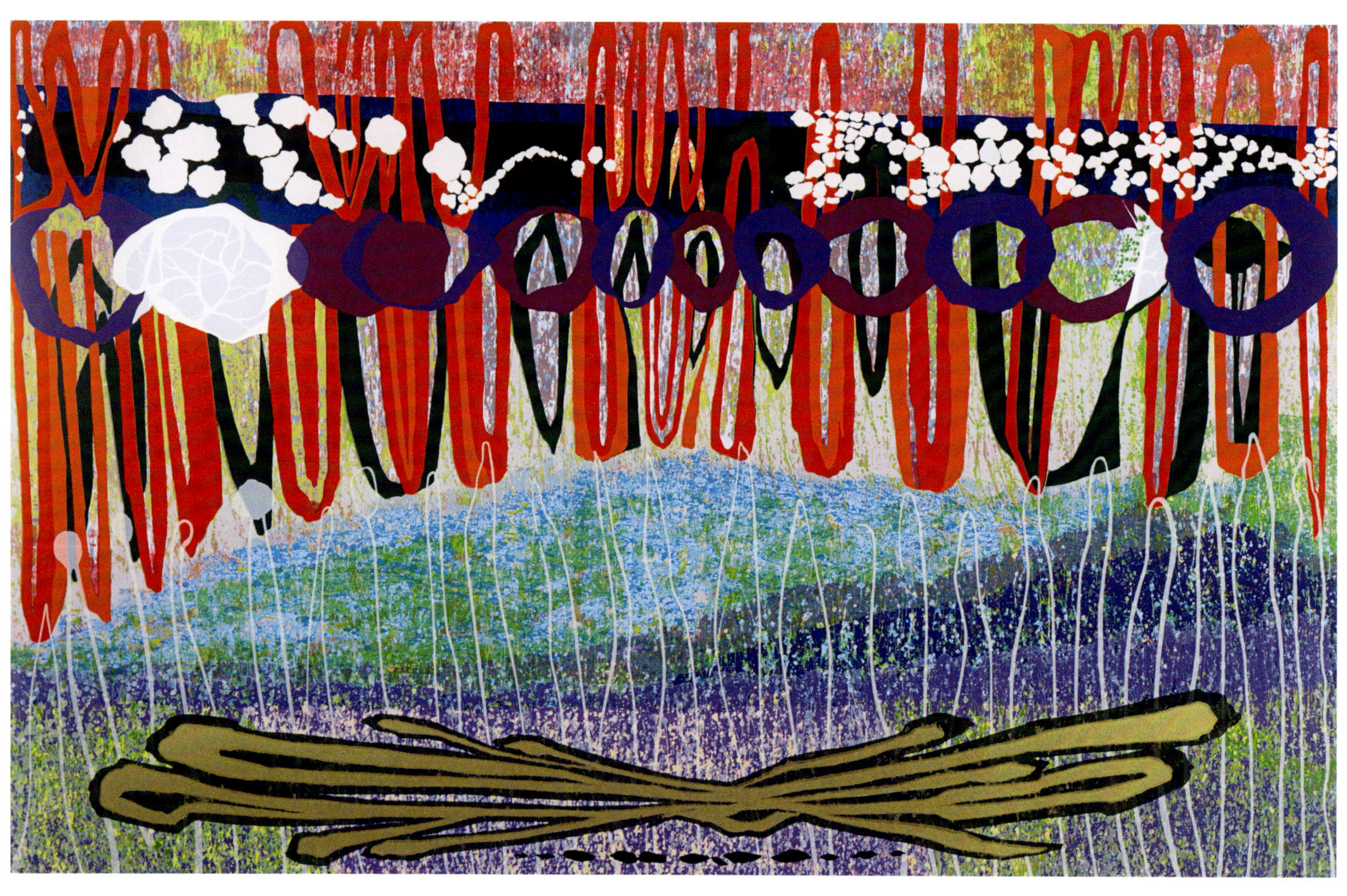

191
Lou Stovall
Suite for Sergei, 2007
Color screenprint on Bristol board,
overall: 26 1/8 × 40 in.
The Phillips Collection, Washington, DC,
Gift of The Honorable Ann and Donald A. Brown, 2009.

LOU STOVALL
SUITE FOR SERGEI, 2007

Lou Stovall

My infatuation with Sergei Rachmaninov's music led me to create a series of three silkscreen prints. *The Sixth Movement, The Sixth Movement II*, and *Suite for Sergei*, which is the third in my series, are each inspired by Rachmaninov's *The Four Piano Concertos*, as performed by Vladimir Ashkenazy with the Concertgebouw Orchestra and conducted by Bernard Haitink. The four piano concertos are arguably the most beautiful, difficult and practically impossible pieces of music to perform. Ashkenazy has long been considered one of the finest musicians to have mastered the awesome, beautiful, and technical demands of Rachmaninov's music. *Suite for Sergei* is not just a single piece of art; it builds upon my lasting appreciation of Rachmaninov's creativity.

Sergei Rachmaninov in his own words:

> In my own compositions, no conscious effort has been made to be original, or Romantic, or Nationalistic, or anything else. I write down on paper the music I hear within me, as naturally as possible. I am a Russian composer, and the land of my birth has influenced my temperament and outlook. My music is the product of my temperament, and so it is Russian music.... What I try to do, when writing down my music, is to make it say simply and directly that which is in my heart when I am composing. If there is love there, or bitterness, or sadness, or religion, these moods become a part of my music, and it becomes either beautiful or bitter or sad or religious.[1]

Like Sergei Rachmaninov, I have followed the instincts of my heritage to share with you the making of the silkscreen print *Suite for Sergei* from creative thought to realization. My perception is that Rachmaninov began with the notion to set down his feelings about his environment. He loves Russia, as I love America. Encouraged by his music and passion for his surroundings, I sought to set down my own feelings about my love of the American landscape.

Suite for Sergei is constructed as if from a dream, intersecting elements of landscape and invention from my imagination. I thought that Rachmaninov may have had some recognition of a favored landscape in what might have been a dreamlike state of mind as he wrote down on paper the music that he was hearing in his imagination. I began with the landscape in a horizontal creation with hills rising on the right and a sense of a lake and sky in the near background. I superimposed twelve black shapes under the landscape to symbolize the piano. Twelve is my number to signal universal truths, and I feel those truths play out in Rachmaninov's music. With gold flourishes outlined in black, I represented Rachmaninov conducting with his baton. The conducting of the orchestra is represented in gold ink, as I imagine his movements as golden moments. The orchestra and the instruments are represented by vertical, semi-elliptical lines in translucent white.

Our world is one of sound made beautiful with joyful thoughts of our environment. I represent this point of view with loops of color and visual pauses, just as pauses in music make space for artistic understanding. I have rendered the music as visual art in a free-flowing but ordered abstract composition which rises above the landscape. Many colors and shapes act as symbols and devices with which I hope to inspire in you, the viewer, a sense of wonder wrought of creativity. I use this method to suggest the action of making a foundation for thought and to further one's emotional response to the nature of creativity that builds upon what lies below. In other words, art rises above all.

---

1 Sergei Rachmaninov, interview by David Ewen, *The Etude*, vol. 12, no. 59, December 1941.

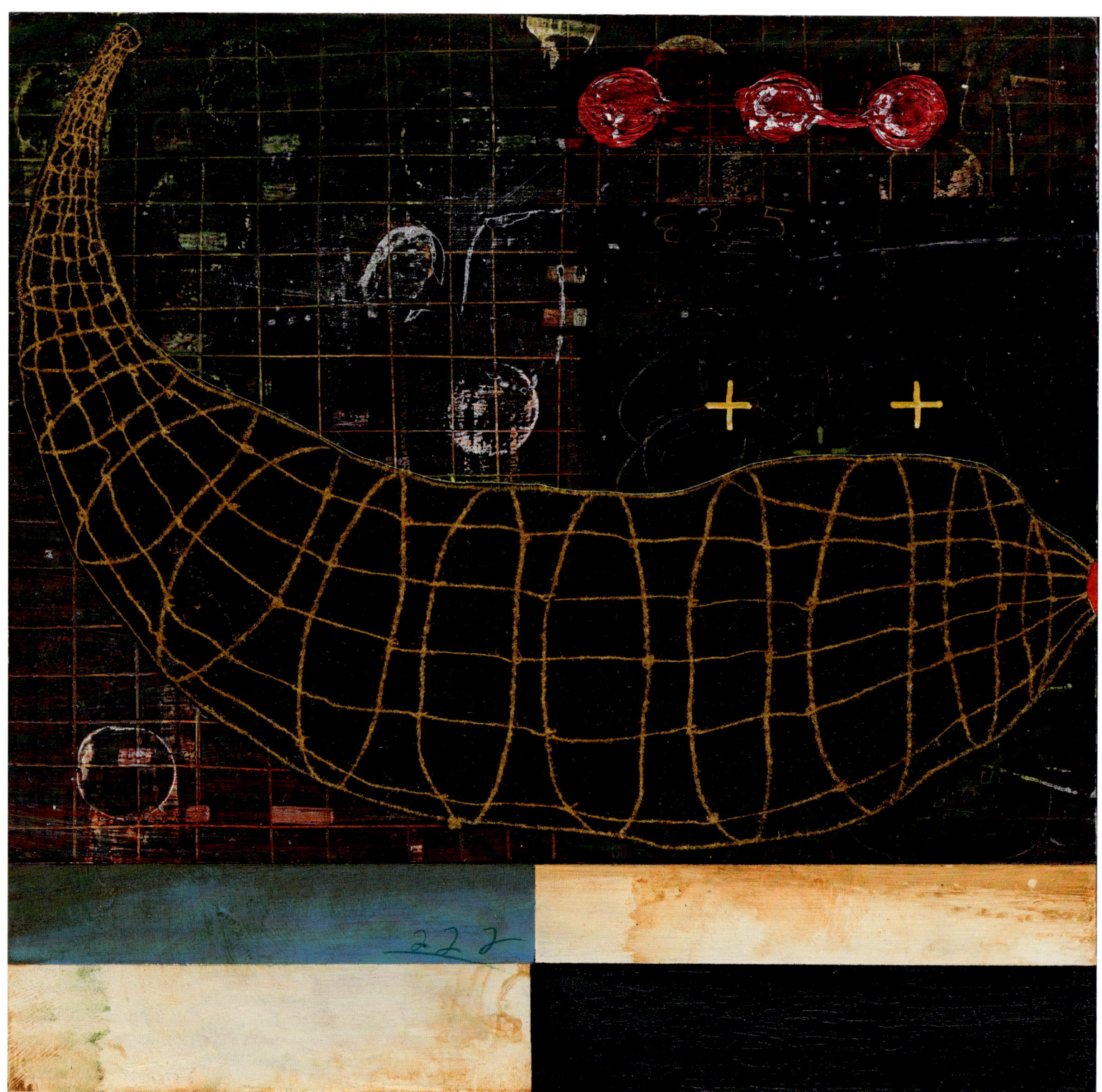

192
Renée Stout
Escape Plan A, 2017
Oil, acrylic, latex, and varnish with paper collage on wood panel,
22 × 30 in.
The Phillips Collection, Washington, DC,
Director's Discretionary Fund, 2018.

RENÉE STOUT
ESCAPE PLAN A, 2017

Sean Scully

I have known Renée through her Art, for a good decade. She was hanging in the house of a friend of mine, Stephen Phillips, the curator of *Wall of Light*, my 2005 exhibition, launched by The Phillips Collection. I saw, as I saw her paintings of café signs, that they had rough relationships with Street Art or Pop Art: I was fascinated because they seemed at once naïve and sophisticated. She painted beautifully. I asked Stephen who it was, and that's how I got interested in my friend Renée Stout. Her paintings subsequently distinguished themselves, and separated themselves from much other Art made in America. Because she includes shadow. The space between.

Her paintings, as in *Escape Plan A*, 2017, or in my *Life Readings (for Nathan Lyons)*, 2017, are kind of political, but only in the sense that they must be first Art. She is bothered, as am I, by what has happened to the fabric of political dignity in our country. And her disturbance motivates her Art. But it doesn't define it. In *Escape Plan A*, there is a net that can be seen as an exit tube, but it's also read, by me at least, as a trap. There's order trying vainly to re-establish itself at the bottom of the painting. But it's dirty. A dirty order one might say. Though above all, these elements that are simple and mysterious, are painted masterfully, and inhabit her world of the night, the painted night. The world of shadow, where nothing, including the value of escape, is that simple.

We have history, we have now, and out of those we try to fashion a future. In *Life Readings (for Nathan Lyons)*, possibilities and imperatives surface as graffiti only to recede back into time-worn shadow. As I pass my painting every day, which is hung on the wall next to my office, I am always wondering what it means. Indeed, in the last few years, I have wondered similarly about our country, and what it means. As much as the inspiration of a troubled imagination, these are strange and fascinating paintings, because above all: they are Art. A source of wonder.

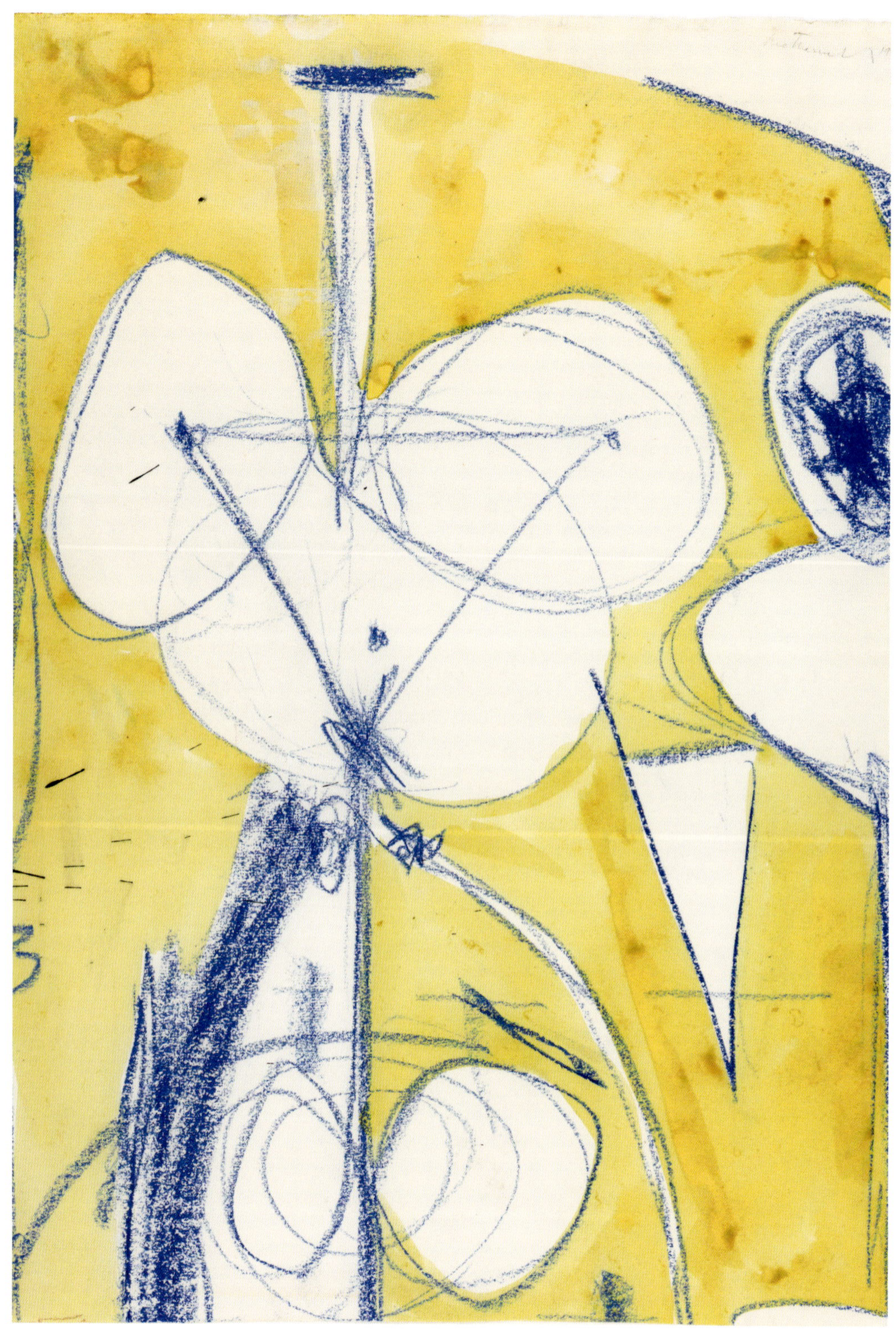

193
Robert Motherwell
***Concept of Woman*, 1946**
Watercolor, wax crayon, and black ink on paper,
19 1/16 × 13 3/16 in.
The Phillips Collection, Washington, DC,
Gift of Susan and Louis Stamberg, 2014.

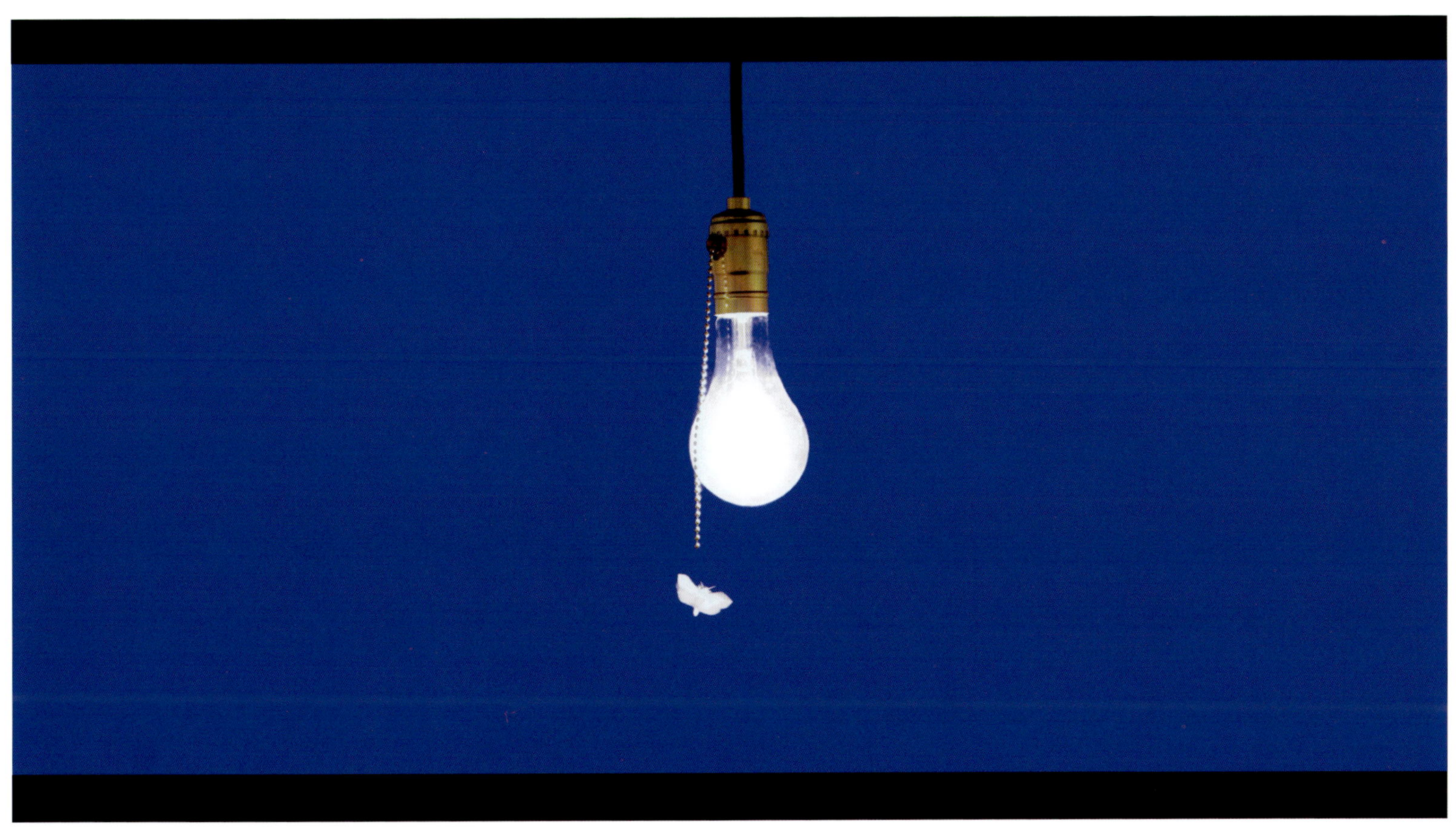

194
Brian Dailey
***Jikai*, 2013**
Single-channel video (color, sound).
Duration: 4:55 min.
The Phillips Collection, Washington, DC,
Acquired 2015.

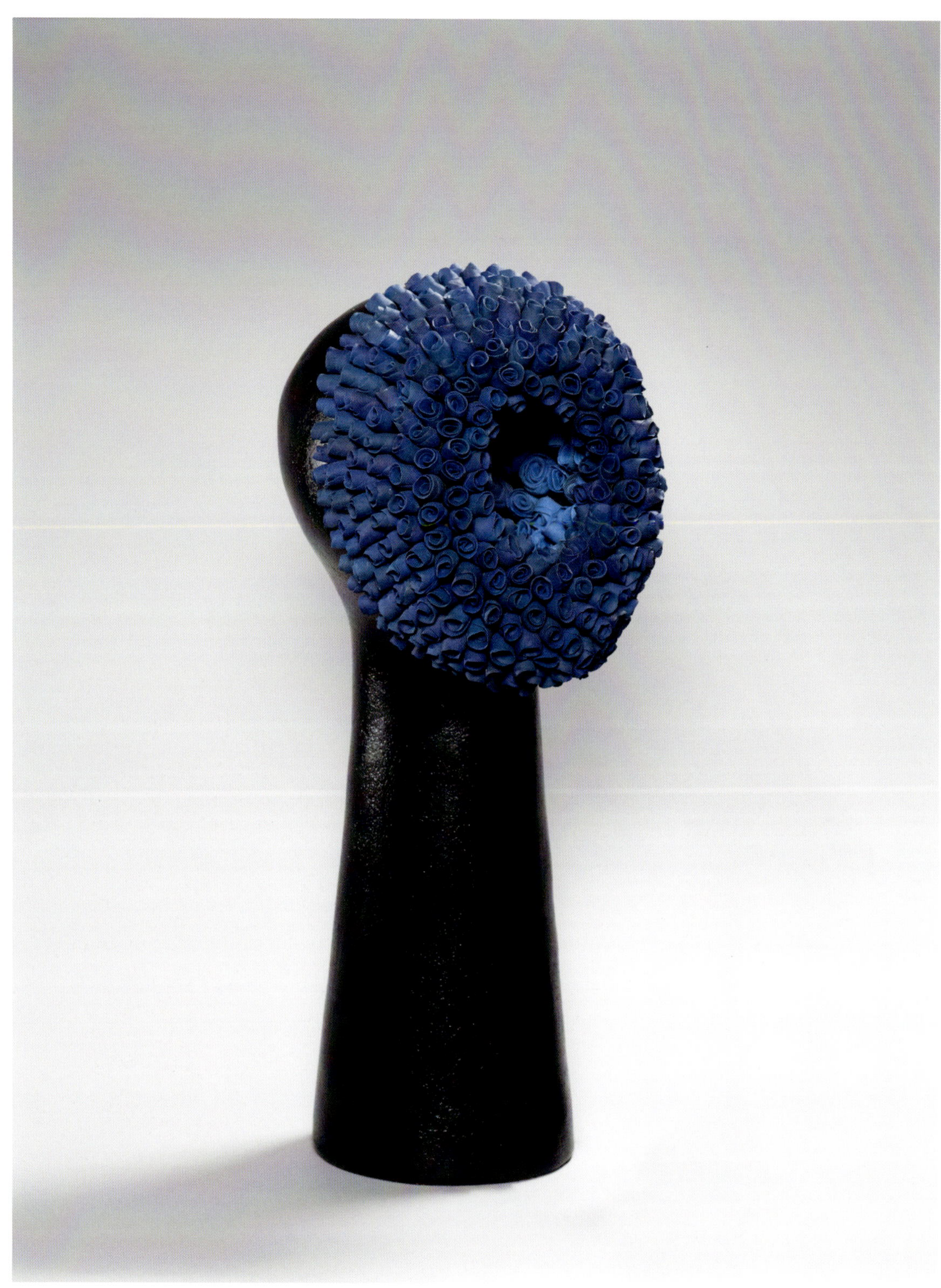

195
Simone Leigh
***No Face (Crown Heights)*, 2018**
Terracotta, graphite ink, salt-fired porcelain and epoxy,
20 × 8 × 8 in.
The Phillips Collection, Washington, DC,
Director's Discretionary Fund, 2019.

SIMONE LEIGH
NO FACE (CROWN HEIGHTS), 2018

Taylor Renee Aldridge

[T]he eyes set deep in the darkness of her face. They were not the eyes of a child. Something too old lurked in their centers. They were weighted, it seemed, with scenes of a long life. She might have been old once and now, miraculously, young again—but with the memory of that other life intact.
—Paule Marshall

The artist Simone Leigh has described her work as "auto-ethnographic,"[1] and she has sought to unearth a plethora of pioneering Black women through her multidisciplinary practice. As a ceramist and artist who brings social sensibilities to her work, Leigh creates objects and worlds that remark on architecture, womanhood, and abstract figuration. In *No Face (Crown Heights)*, a smooth, life-size black bust, an elongated neck accounts for the greater part of the object and supports a small round ball of a head. The comprehensible analogy to human anatomy ends there: a cluster of several dozen blue terracotta blooms appear on the plane where we might expect a face. The markers that allow us to determine finite descriptors of identity and personhood—face, nose, eyes, lips—are made indiscernible in this facial bouquet. What are we to make of their absence? Perhaps it is not a lack, but rather indicative of a figure turning inward to become whole. What freedoms could be gained if we went inside? This abstract face has become commonplace in Leigh's sculpture; a smooth black surface where eyes should be, lips unambiguously full, or absent altogether.

The reference to Crown Heights—a neighborhood in Brooklyn that was once referred to as "Weeksville," a haven for Black free people in the nineteenth century—gives the abstracted figure a geographic refuge and invokes an earlier social sculpture project by the artist, *Free People's Clinic*, a programmatic activation at the Stuyvesant Mansion that celebrated the lineage of Black female medical pioneers from nineteenth-century Weeksville, such as Dr. Susan McKinney Steward.

In the past, Leigh has focused on the tradition of unidentified African women potters, in which authorship is defined by the whole, so that one artist cannot be distinguished from the others. Her abstracted figures reflect this collective authorship, as in *No Face (Crown Heights)*, as well as in a group of other works by the artist, also titled "No Face." With their facial opacity, like the vessels made by the anonymous African women, they tend to exist outside time, thus invoking a seriality of memory and memorial as it pertains to Black female embodiment across time and space. Furthermore, the blooms on *No Face (Crown Heights)* suggest that there is the opportunity to germinate once we choose interiority, once a face cannot be captured. If we consider the history of Black women, as Leigh often seeks to do, it is understood that such histories are fraught with violence, escapism, and a matrilineage that has been plagued by the inheritance of bondage. In this case, breaking fugitivity—seeking a particular interior freedom—sometimes requires a fugitive hiding in plain sight.

The epigraph is from Paule Marshall, *Brown Girl, Brownstones* (1959; repr., Eastford, CT: Martino Fine Books, 2014), 2.

1 "Sculptor Simone Leigh finally gets her due." CBS This Morning, https://www.cbs.com/shows/cbs_this_morning/video/LB9sKvAsLnOZzYEMpPin1wEVrbqWnzKo/artist-simone-leigh-finally-in-the-spotlight-reflects-on-her-naysayers/. Aired April 27, 2019. Accessed April 2020.

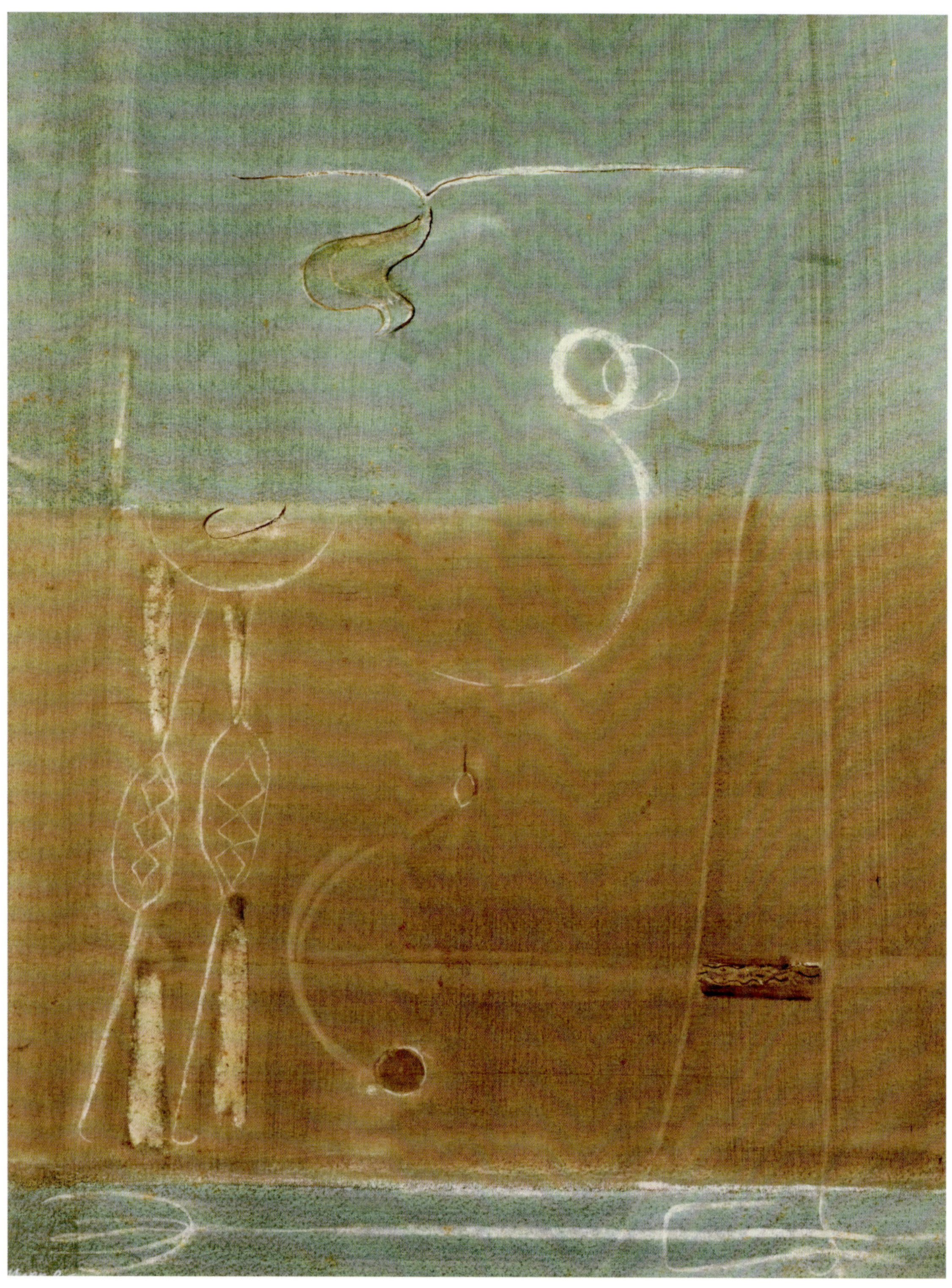

196
Mark Rothko
***Aubade*, 1944**
Opaque watercolor and ink with scraping on paper,
25 1/4 × 19 in.
The Phillips Collection, Washington, DC,
Gift of Rebecca B. and Julius W. Allen, initiated 1994,
completed 2001.

MARK ROTHKO
AUBADE, 1944

Bosco Sodi

I am in my studio in Oaxaca, Mexico, at Casa Wabi, quarantining myself amid the Coronavirus outbreak. During these worrisome times, in which the art world is becoming feeble, I have been reflecting on this beautiful painting.

Throughout time I have been convinced that one of the reasons I fell in love with the art world is because of the works of Mark Rothko. For me, this somber piece is without a doubt one of his most extraordinary works of art. *Aubade* reflects the troublesome circumstances of the world, as it was created in 1944 toward the end of World War II. The work invokes the existential battle of the current generation in an extremely complicated era. Simultaneously, in the rawness of the moment, the technique becomes similar to Arte Povera. It is a sort of collage on paper, utilizing basic elements and accidents created by the paper itself. Little by little, it separates itself from the representation and clearly exposes marks of what will be in the future the characteristic way of painting of Rothko. The transparencies, the rectangle as a pictorial object, morph into one exterior of reality. A new everything. In this new everything, in which color unquestionably dominates as the protagonist, a certain sensation is created, a distinctive phenomenon in which the piece becomes a single structure of color. This object which floats on the wall seems to separate itself from any restrictions, as if it were about to fly off at any moment.

The more I understand and familiarize myself with the works of Rothko, the more I begin to realize that he was not only important for abstract expressionism but also for other current movements such as American minimalism—this is evident in the works of Robert Irwin, Dan Flavin, and even Donald Judd. It is also evident in a great number of artists like Gerhard Richter, Richard Serra, and James Turrell, among others. Obviously, and without placing myself at the level of the artists named, Rothko has been an immense influence on my art. Donald Judd said it best when he intimated that Rothko had achieved nothing less than the creation of "a new reality and a new wholeness."[1]

---

1 Donald Judd, *Complete Writings* (Eindhoven: Van Abbemuseum, 1987), 42.

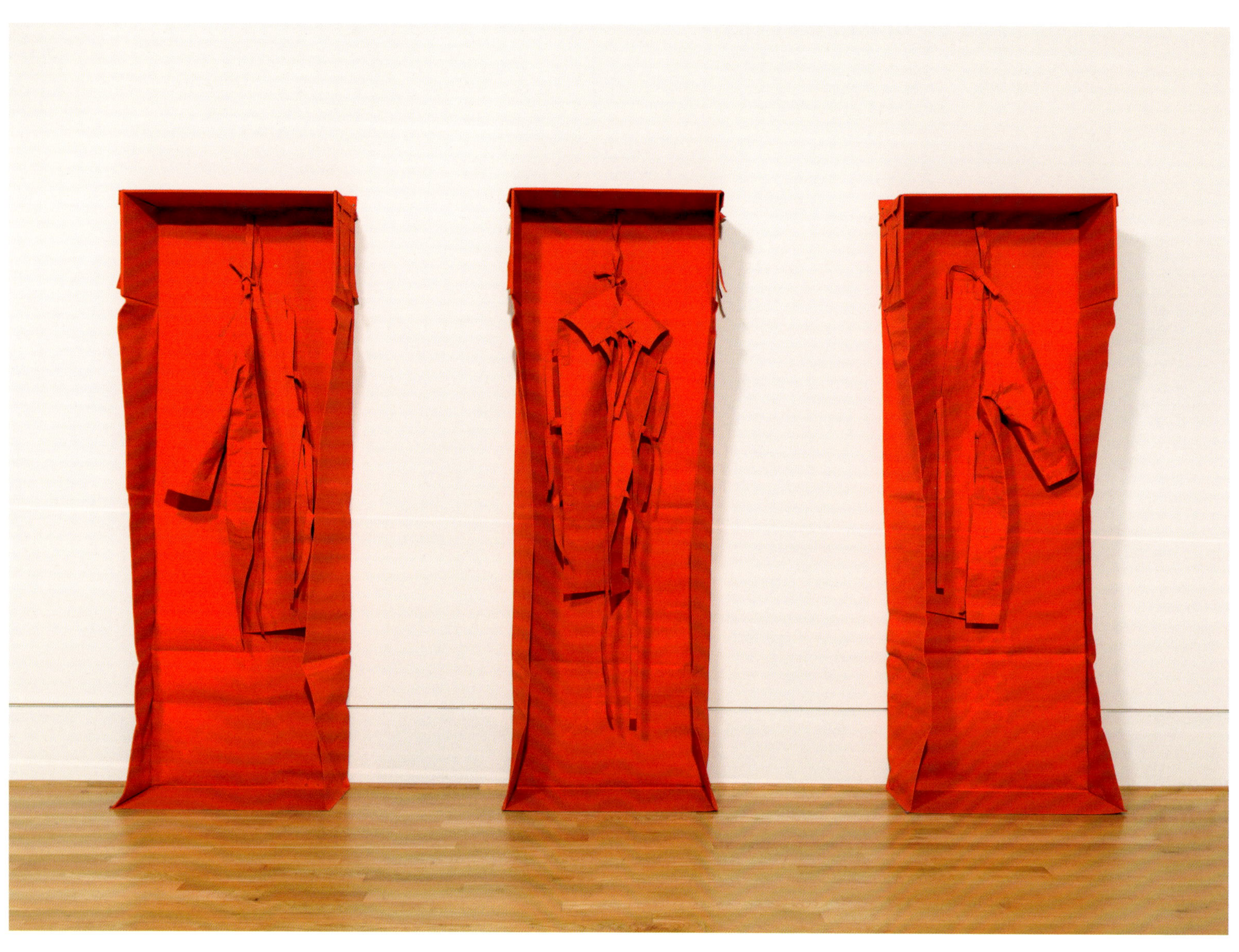

197
Franz Erhard Walther
***Roter Gesang* (*Red Song-Formation*), 1984**
Cotton fabric and wood,
each sculpture: 90 1/2 × 29 1/2 × 11 7/8 in.
The Phillips Collection, Washington, DC,
Gift of Arthur and Carol Goldberg, 2013.

FRANZ ERHARD WALTHER
ROTER GESANG (RED SONG-FORMATION), 1984

Klaus Ottmann

Since his *1. Werksatz* (First Work Set), 1963–69, comprised of fifty-eight dyed and undyed cotton pieces of cloth, Franz Erhard Walther has been creating sculptural objects made of heavy cloth and wood in collaboration with his wife, Johanna, who has been stitching together his works since then. Walther is considered one of the first proponents of participatory art. His objects or "instruments for process," as he prefers to call them, are meant to be hung on a wall, worn on the body, folded, stepped on, or otherwise manipulated.

Walther, recipient of the Golden Lion for best artist at the 2017 Venice Biennale, first gained recognition in the 1960s for his experimental sculpture and was included in such groundbreaking exhibitions of that era as Harald Szeemann's *When Attitudes Become Form* (1969, Kunsthalle Bern), *Spaces* (1969–70, Museum of Modern Art, New York), which featured site-specific installations by five artists and one artist collective, and *documenta* 5 (1972, Kassel).

Born in 1939 in Fulda, Germany, where he still lives, Walther studied at the Düsseldorf Art Academy. There, like many young postwar artists, he came under the influence of art informel, a European counterpart to abstract expressionism that emphasized the expressive instincts of the artist over defined subject matter. Walther developed his relational aesthetics while studying under K. O. [Karl Otto] Götz, who is best known for his bold, liquid abstractions that translate the gestural style of informel into relational actions. Influenced by the writings of the Canadian perception psychologist and experimental aesthetician Daniel E. Berlyne, Götz taught art by using methods of empirical psychology. Like the American artist James Lee Byars, who studied psychology, philosophy, and art, and in the late 1960s created a series of relational plays using communal silk garments, Walther has long challenged the limitations of traditional sculpture by mostly focusing on the relationship between physical and psychological perception.

Walther frequently uses the German word *Gesang* (song or chant) in its alternate meaning of "grouping or formation" to describe his often serial cloth arrangements such as his *Gesang der Schreitsockel* (*Song-Formation of the Stride Blocks*) (1975/77, Kunstmuseum Luzern). The Phillips's *Roter Gesang*, like its counterpart *Gelber Plastischer Gesang (einzeln zusammen)* (*Yellow Sculptural Song-Formation [Separately Together]*) (fig. 98), belongs to his series of Wall Formations, which he began in 1978 and which is characterized by the use of primary colors. Each of the three boxlike open spaces of red cloth contains a piece of red clothing. Together, the three pieces of clothing (left sleeve and shoulder, midsection, right sleeve and shoulder), which are meant to be worn individually, form a complete red coat. The work is only completed when activated by each viewer wearing a section of the coat and stepping into the sculpture. As Walther wrote for the *Spaces* catalogue in 1969: "The pieces are to be used ... everyone has to make use of his own abilities, to experience his own possibilities."[1]

1 Franz Erhard Walther, "Instruments for Processes, 1962–69," in Jennifer Licht, *Spaces* (New York: Museum of Modern Art, 1969), n.p.

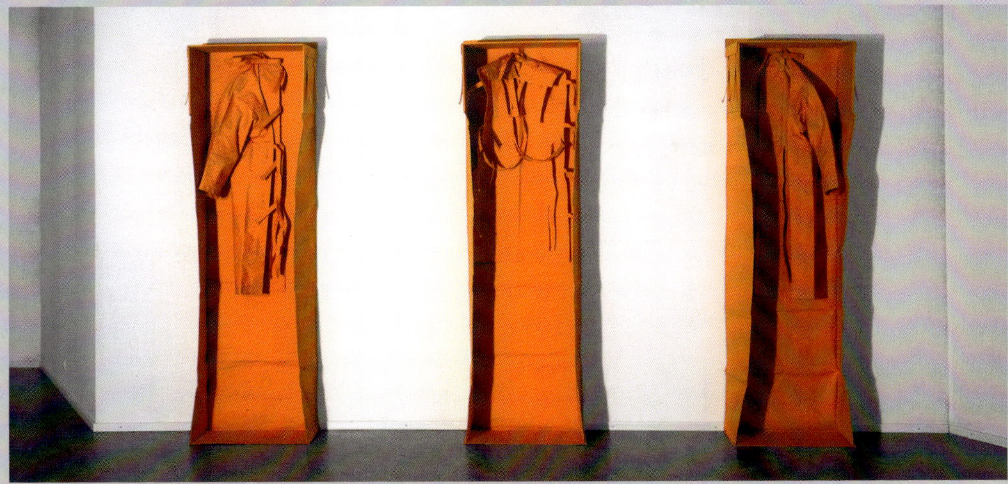

fig. 98
Franz Erhard Walther
***Gelber Plastischer Gesang (einzeln zusammen)*, 1984**
Textile and wood,
(3 ×) 83 7/8 × 24 5/8 × 12 3/8 in.
Collection Van Abbemuseum, Eindhoven, The Netherlands, Gift of the artist, 1984.

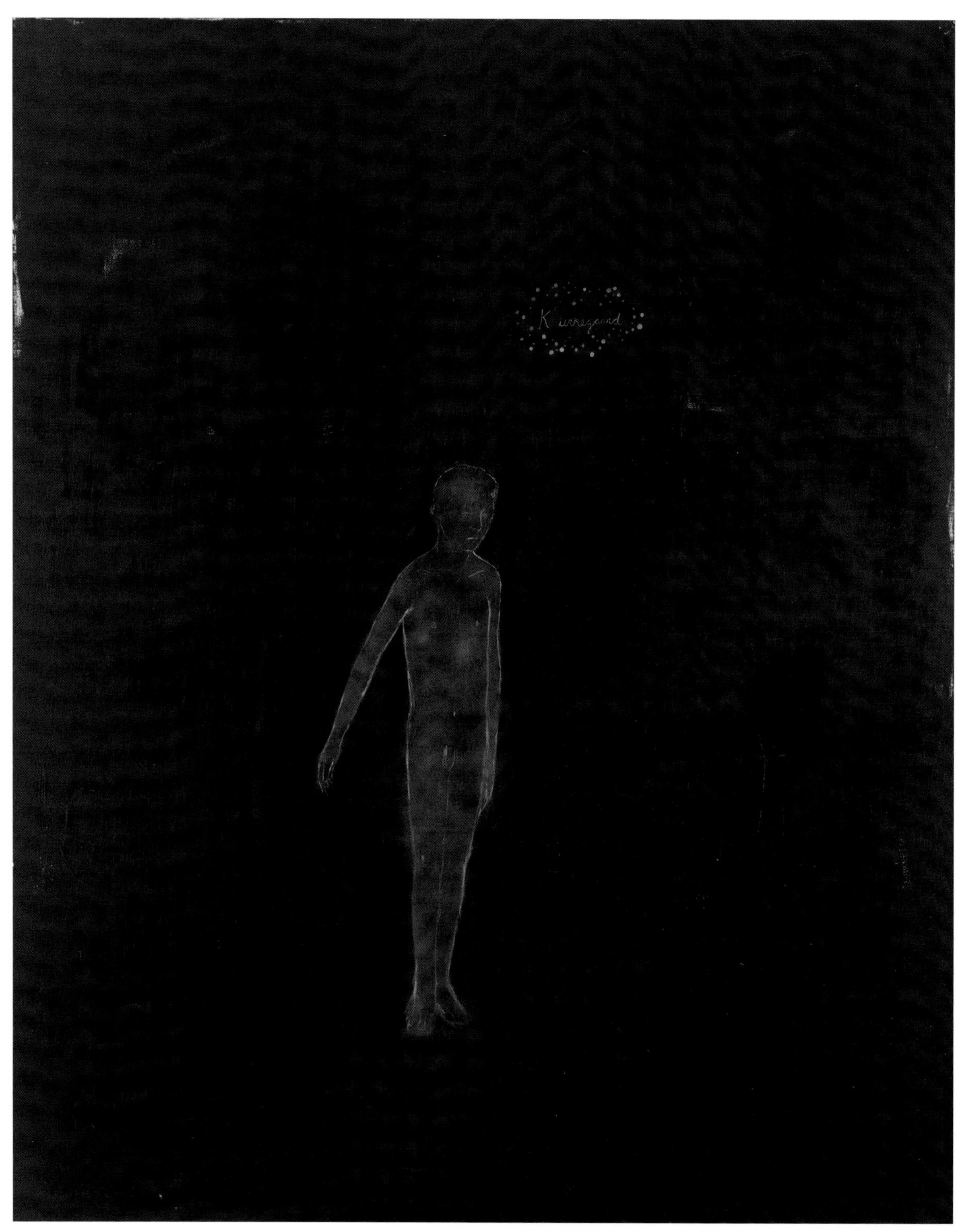

198
Enrique Martínez Celaya
The First Kierkegaard, 2006
Oil, wax and tar on canvas,
100 × 78 in.
The Phillips Collection, Washington, DC,
Gift of the artist in honor of Klaus Ottmann, 2015.

ENRIQUE MARTÍNEZ CELAYA
THE FIRST KIERKEGAARD, 2006

Klaus Ottmann

The Cuban-born American artist Enrique Martínez Celaya trained as a physicist as well as an artist. His paintings and sculptures examine the complexities and mysteries of individual experience, particularly in relation to nature and time, and explore the questions of the human condition through diverse knowledge systems as well as through literature, poetry, and art. With its emphasis on spirituality and transcendence, his work exemplifies aspects of the shift from modernism to postmodernity.

The nineteenth-century Danish philosopher Søren Kierkegaard has been a continual presence in Celaya's art. The biblical story of Abraham willing to sacrifice his son Isaac is central to Kierkegaard's philosophical work *Fear and Trembling* (1843), which examines the existential dimension of faith. Kierkegaard recognized in the story a paradox of faith, "that the single individual is higher than the universal, that [he] ... determines his relation to the universal by his relation to the absolute, not his relation to the absolute by his relation to the universal."[1] According to Kierkegaard, the single individual must be *unconditionally* willing to sacrifice. This sacrifice is situated in the in-between of nothingness and anxiety, between the imaginary and the symbolic, the "disquieting supervision of responsibility."[2]

In *The First Kierkegaard*, that single individual is represented by a nude adolescent boy painted in a glowing Rembrandtesque sienna, standing within a background of dark tar (bitumen), with his right arm slightly raised. The boy, who appears in many of Celaya's paintings and sculptures, and his gesture of humility, are meant as a reminder of our ethical imperative. Neither assertive nor submissive, it is meant as a contemplative and quiet proposition of the highest spiritual order. "What Kierkegaard, [Fyodor] Dostoyevsky, [Friedrich] Nietzsche, and most other prophets have in common is a strong ethical outlook and a heightened sensitivity to attitudes and morals."[3]

In his work, Celaya employs autobiography, allusions, and references to religious thinkers and poets, including Nietzsche, Kierkegaard, Leo Tolstoy, and Paul Celan to construct a complex personal aesthetic steeped in literature and philosophy, and he has long made a case for artists to be prophets again: "The prophet, unlike the mystic, returns to the world."[4] He writes, "Joseph Beuys, Herman Melville, Marcel Broodthaers, Ayn Rand, and Albert Pinkham Ryder were prophets, not because they sat around theorizing but because they showed us something of the future and of ourselves.... The prophet becomes a prophet through his or her work."[5]

In 2017, *The First Kierkegaard* was installed alongside several paintings by Ryder, their caliginous mood and spirituality, as well as Ryder's preference for using bitumen instead of black paint, finding echoes in Celaya's painting.

---

1 Søren Kierkegaard, *Fear and Trembling/Repetition*, ed. and trans. H. V. Hong and E. H. Hong (Princeton, NJ: Princeton University Press, 1983), 70.

2 Kierkegaard, *Fear and Trembling/Repetition*, 156.

3 "The Prophet," in *Enrique Martínez Celaya, Collected Writings and Interviews, 2010–2017* (Lincoln: University of Nebraska Press, 2010), 236.

4 Celaya, "The Prophet," 234.

5 Celaya, "The Prophet," 237.

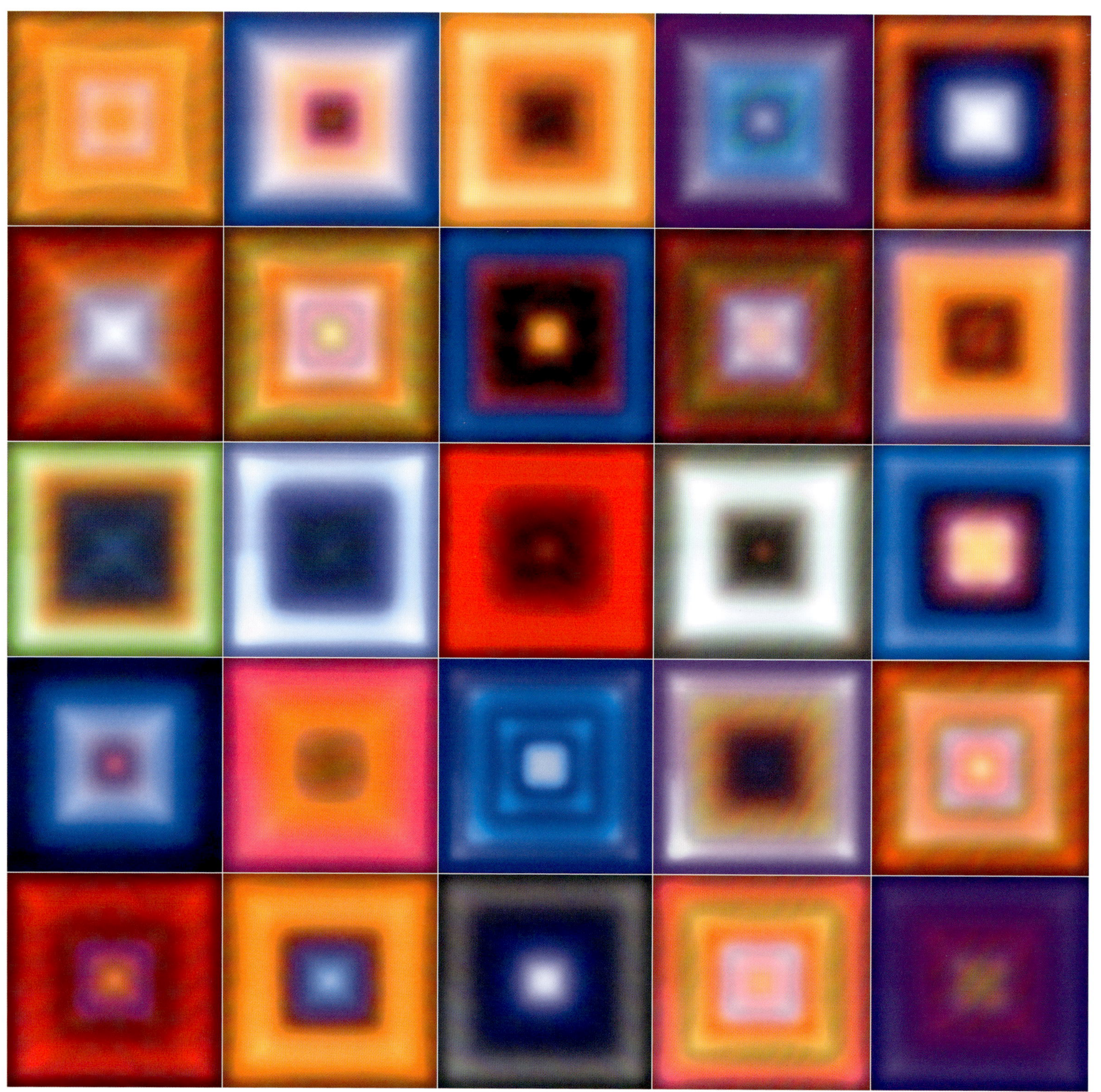

199
Leo Villareal
Scramble, 2011
Light-emitting diodes, custom software, circuitry, wood, and Plexiglas,
60 × 60 in.
The Phillips Collection, Washington, DC, The Dreier Fund for Acquisitions, 2012.

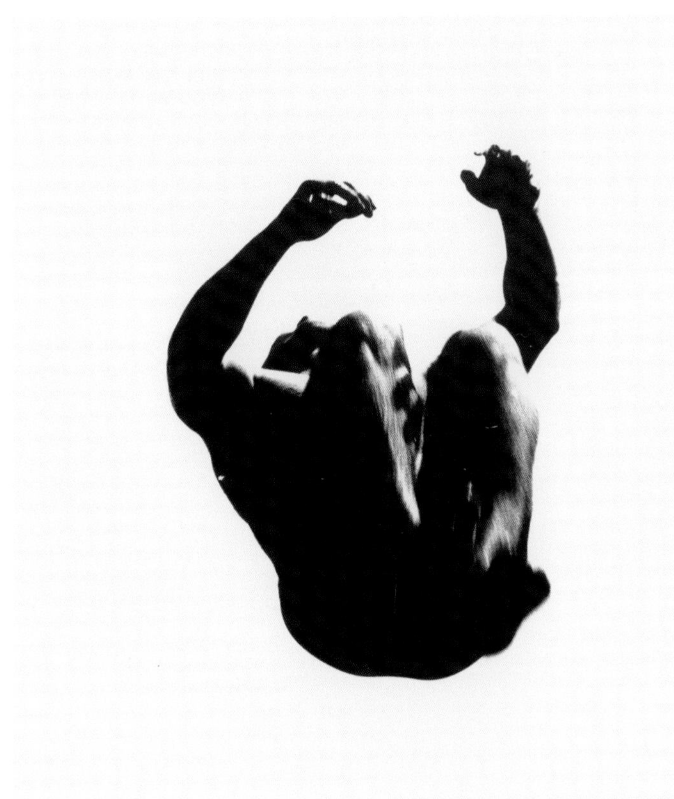

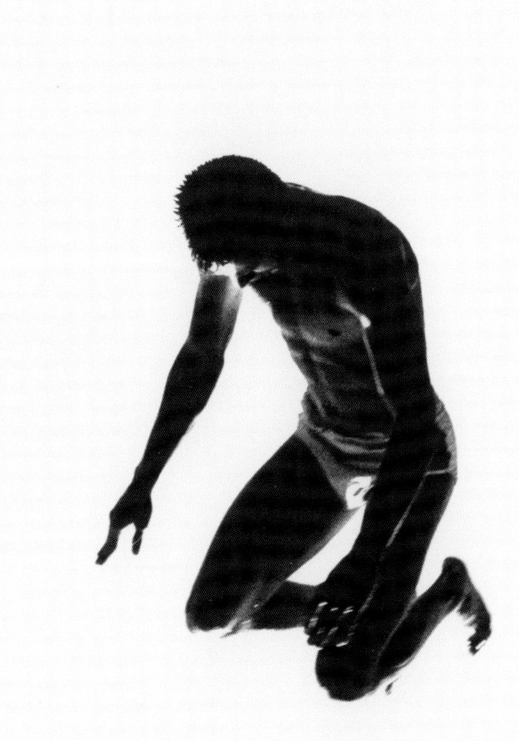

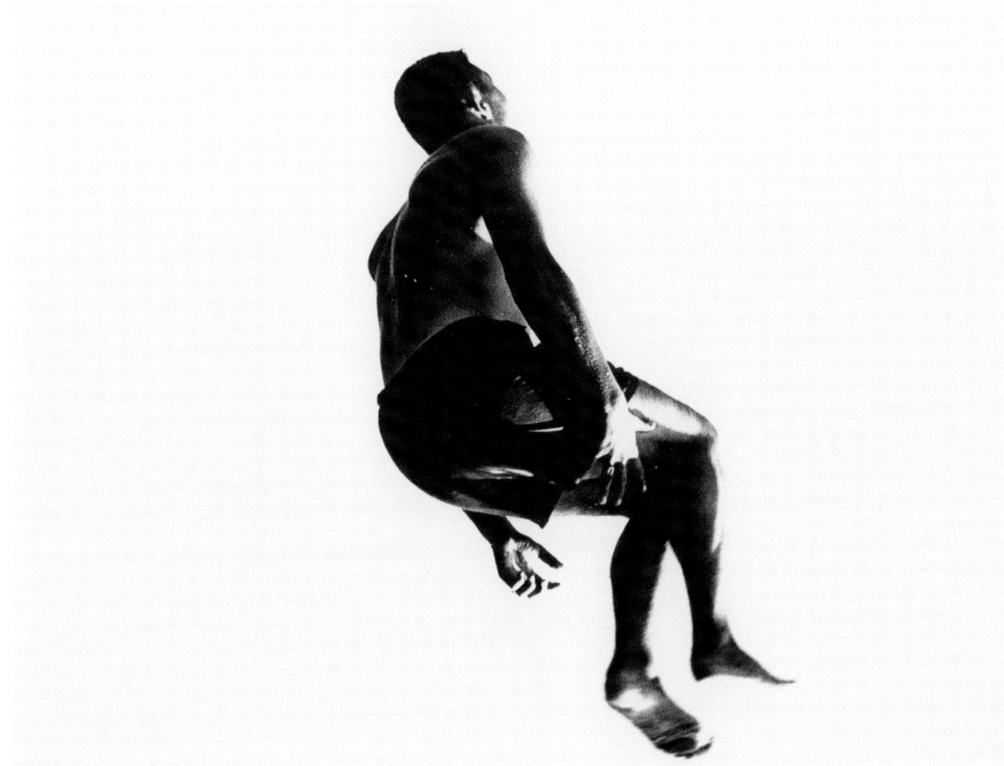

200 (top left)
Aaron Siskind
***Pleasures and Terrors of Levitation #200*, 1956**
Gelatin silver print,
14 × 11 in.
The Phillips Collection, Washington, DC,
Gift of Fern M. Schad, 2005.

201 (top right)
Aaron Siskind
***Pleasures and Terrors of Levitation #32*, 1965**
Gelatin silver print,
14 × 11 in.
The Phillips Collection, Washington, DC,
Gift of Fern M. Schad, 2005.

202 (bottom)
Aaron Siskind
***Pleasures and Terrors of Levitation #169*, 1954**
Gelatin silver print,
11 × 14 in.
The Phillips Collection, Washington, DC,
Gift of Fern M. Schad, 2005.

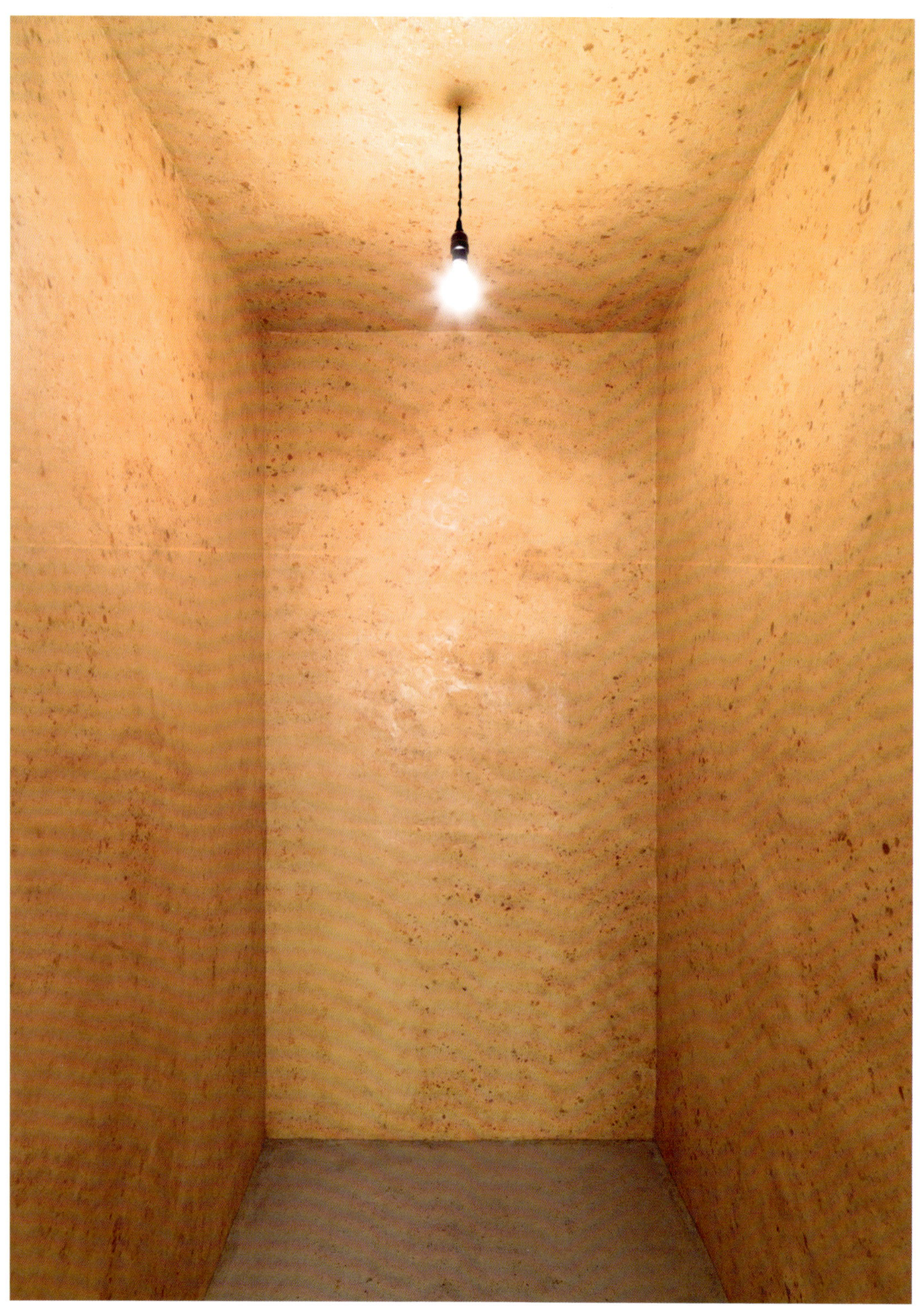

203
Wolfgang Laib
Wax Room: Wohin bist Du gegangen – wohin gehst Du? (Where have you gone – where are you going?), 2013
Beeswax and light bulb.
The Phillips Collection, Washington, DC,
The Dreier Fund for Acquisitions; gifts in memory of trustee Caroline Macomber; Brian Dailey and Paula Ballo Dailey; a community of online contributors; and a partial gift of the artist. Wax donated by Sperone Westwater.

WOLFGANG LAIB
WAX ROOM: WOHIN BIST DU GEGANGEN – WOHIN GEHST DU? (WHERE HAVE YOU GONE – WHERE ARE YOU GOING?), 2013

Klaus Ottmann

Born in Metzingen, Germany, in 1950, the son of a physician, Wolfgang Laib initially followed his father's path. In 1972, upon returning to Germany after a three-month stay in India, where he had been studying the quality of the local drinking water for his medical dissertation, Laib discovered a large black rock, about three feet long, in a field near his house. Inspired by his memories of the simple shapes of quotidian and ceremonial objects in India, he brought the rock home and, although he had never formally studied art, set to work carving it into a perfect ovoid object called a *brahmanda* (in India, a stone *brahmanda* symbolizes the unity of male and female principles and the wholeness of the universe). As he worked, Laib realized that he had become dissatisfied with medical science, which he felt addressed human needs imperfectly. He decided to become an artist instead of a physician.

Since then, Laib has created objects of great simplicity and purity: "milkstones"—rectangular slabs of polished white marble with barely perceptible depressions on their upper surfaces that he fills with milk; fields of yellow or orange pollen that he sifts onto the floors of galleries or museums; and rooms lined with beeswax. Identifying with no artistic school or movement, Laib has distanced himself from Western European aesthetic traditions. Specifically, he rejects the notion of the autonomous creative ego that emerged in the Renaissance, which has led, he believes, to the prevalent, uniquely Western concept of the artistic self. He has little interest in contemporary art apart from his own practice, and has forged few friendships with other artists, remaining true for more than thirty years to his solitary pursuit. He is inspired equally by the natural environment of his native southern Germany, where he lives in a small village outside Biberach, and by non-Western art and religion, especially those of his second home near Madurai, in Tamil Nadu, India.

In 2013, Laib installed *Where have you gone - where are you going?*, the first permanent site-specific installation initiated at The Phillips Collection since the Rothko Room in 1960. Laib's life-sized wax rooms, built out of beeswax blocks or shaped from melted beeswax and "activated" by the dim light of a bare bulb suspended from the ceiling, are considered among his signature works. These small, echoing, and cocoon-like chambers offer a personal, meditative experience that is immediate and intense, with the comforting scent of beeswax.

For Laib, The Phillips Collection was a logical choice for his first permanent wax room in a museum because of the Phillips's intimate and experiential character. While at the Phillips to participate in the Conversations with Artists series in October 2012, Laib visited the Rothko Room for the first time; it left a profound impression. "A wax chamber has a very deep and open relationship to Rothko's paintings," he explains, because to enter a wax room is to be "in another world, maybe on another planet and in another body."[1] Laib's wax rooms are directed inward, forcing the viewer into a mental suspension of everyday reality. The intense smell and color of these rooms seem to induce a loss of awareness of self or place. For Laib, art is an act of participation and of sharing—participating in nature and sharing that experience with others. His works are not merely visual experiences, but serve as contributions to social and spiritual change.

---

1 https://www.phillipscollection.org/collection/laib-wax-room. Accessed April 2020.

ART DONORS TO THE PHILLIPS COLLECTION, 2000–2020

The following is a list of donors who have given or promised works of art to The Phillips Collection between January, 2000 and August, 2020.

Anonymous
Jonathan and Roseann Aaronsohn
Natalie R. Abrams
Christopher Addison
Rebecca B. and Julius W. Allen
Carolyn S. Alper
American Abstract Artists
American Academy of Arts and Letters
Joe Amrhein and Susan Swenson
Madeline and Stephen Anbinder
Karel Appel Foundation
Lila Oliver Asher
Liane Atlas
Michael and Joyce Axelrod
Helena and Ramis Barquet
The Barrett Collection
Mr. and Mrs. William Beadleston
Gifford Beal Family
C. Richard Belger and Evelyn Craft Belger
Sandra and David Berler
Diane and Norman Bernstein
Max Berry
The Estate of Jake Berthot
Geoffrey B. Biddle
Beatriz and Graham Bolton
Tanya Bonakdar Gallery
Marcia T. Boogaard
David Boul and Tom O'Briant
Jack Boul
Luther W. Brady
Marcella Louis Brenner
Tom and Judy Brody
The Honorable Ann and Donald A. Brown
Robert Brown
Renee Butler
Susan and Dixon Butler
Calvin Cafritz
Dennis Cannaday
Iris & B. Gerald Cantor Foundation
Constance Caplan
Norman and Carolyn K. Carr
Enrique Martínez Celaya
Marion Oates Charles
Ching Ho Cheng Estate
William and Sandra Christenberry
Sandra Cinto
Earl and Susan Cohen
Armida B. Colt
Susan Conway
The Hereward Lester Cooke Memorial Fund
Trustees of the Corcoran Gallery of Art
Lisa and Matthew Cowan
B. J. and Carol Cutler
Renato d'Agostin
Brian Dailey and Paula Ballo Dailey
Barbara Dash
Estate of Rudolf de Crignis
Mr. and Mrs. Willem de Looper
Joseph Del Valle
Zöe and Joel Dictrow
Joseph P. DiGangi
Editions Fawbush
Robert and Mercedes Eichholz
John Elderfield
Marjorie Phillips Elliott
Betsey Ely
Joan Fabry and Michael Klein
The Feitelson/Lundeberg Art Foundation
Adam and Susan Finn
Jordan and Devinah Finn
Lisa Finn
Dorothy Fisher
Jim and Sandy Fitzpatrick
John and Birgit Ford
Helen C. Frederick
Elizabeth French
William Freyvogel and Carla White Freyvogel
Lee and Maria Friedlander
Alfred and Pie Friendly
Vittorio Gallo
Lucinda and Carlos Garcia
Cam and Wanda Garner
Sandra Gering
Archive Luigi Ghirri
Léonard Gianadda
Sam Gilliam
Arthur and Carol Goldberg
Henry H. and Carol Brown Goldberg
Roy Goldberg and Keith Sherman
Marion F. and Norman W. Goldin
Barbara K. Gordon and Herbert Gordon
Antony Gormley
Milton Gottesman
Paula Gottesman
Graham Holdings Company
Dawn Greene
Miriam Schapiro Grosof
Michael Gross and Shelley Singer
Wendy A. Grossman
Dr. and Dr. J. Kurt Grovenburg
Harry Grubert
Agnes Gund
Donna and Arthur Hartman
Hemphill Gallery
The Hepworth Estate
Tayo Heuser
Bernhard Hildebrandt
Bonnie and Harold Himmelman
Anne S. Hobler
Joseph and Sharon Holston
Erin Hoover
Lynne and Joseph Horning
Chris Hughes
Margaret Stuart Hunter
Clay J. Ide
The Rosalind Gersten Jacobs and Melvin Jacobs Collection
David Jay
Beau and Linda Lichtenberg Kaplan
Paul Kasmin Gallery
Laine R. and Norton N. Katz
Louis and Annette Kaufman Trust
Joe and Nancy Keithley
Dean Kessmann
Elizabeth Klee
Jae Ko
Randy Kohls
Ann Kohs
Richard M. Krause
Oleg Kudryashov
Sara M. Kuniyoshi
Michelle and Stan Kurtz
Wolfgang Laib
Steve LaMantia
Mark Lane and Marcia Gregory
Mariagrazia Oliva Lapadula
Elysa Lazar
Archivio Bice Lazzari
Mr. and Mrs. Marc E. Leland

Galerie Lelong & Co.
Saul E. Levi
Mirella and Dani Levinas
Aaron and Barbara Levine
The Lichtenberg Family Foundation
The Joseph and Charlotte Lichtenberg Collection
Barbara Liotta
Alan Lipton
Scott Little
Lilliane Litton
Gene Locks
Shaun Lucas
Raymond Machesney
Mel and Gail Mackler
Caroline M. Macomber
Patricia B. Madlener
Wendy Makins
Robert Mann Gallery
B. Thomas Mansbach
Marie M. Martin
Marsha Mateyka
Jerri Mattare
Alfred H. McAdams
Jean Meisel
Morley and Jean Melden
linn meyers
Nathan and Jeanette Miller
Susan P. Millies
A. Fenner Milton
Betty Milton
Ina Milton
Kent and Marcia Minichiello
Claudia Minicozzi
Renato Miracco
Victoria Munroe
Henry Myers
Minna Newman Nathanson and Jim Nathanson
Francis Naumann
George M. Neall III and Lisa Forman Neall
Manuel Neri Trust
Lowell Nesbitt
Bea Nettles
Benjamin Nicolette
Francesco Nonino
Julia J. Norrell
Jean Nowak
Ny Carlsbergfondet
Peter Ocko and Kate Axelrod
Frederick P. Ognibene
Patrick Oliphant
Kristina Olitski
The Ossorio Foundation
Marco Paoli
Christine Anne Parker
Dr. and Mrs. Ronald A. Paul
Vesna Pavlović
Sandra Payson
Elizabeth J. Peake
Alan Pensler
Seymour Perlin, M.D. and Ruth Rudolph Perlin
Phillips Contemporaries
Gifford and Joann K. Phillips
James L. Phillips
Leo and Nina Pircher
Anna Paola Pizzocaro
Heather Podesta
Tony Podesta
Kenneth Polin
Andrea Pollan
Estate of Richard Pousette-Dart
Nicholas and Sheila Pye
Jack Rachlin
John Raimondi and Ralph T. Cantin
Lyn Rales
Lynn and Marcus Raskin
John and Diane Rehm
Anne S. Reich
Family of Anita Reiner
Toni A. Ritzenberg
Jean Reed Roberts
Bernardí Roig
Maria Roque-Lopes
Suzanne Rose
Fondation Georges Rouault
Michael A. Rubenstein and Juliet Rubenstein
Seymour and Janet Rubin
John and Joy Safer
Mrs. Walter S. Salant
Roger and Victoria Sant
Savas Private Collection
Fern M. Schad
Joan S. and Richard H. Schmidt
Penelope Schmidt and Robert Yarber
Dennis and Debra Scholl
Victoria Schonfeld
Sean Scully
Francine Seders Gallery
Daniel Shapiro
Kate Shepherd
Ranjani Shettar and Talwar Gallery
Robert Shimshak and Marion Brenner
John and Sara Shlesinger
Sharon Simpson
Aaron Siskind Foundation
Philip M. Smith
Bosco Sodi
Federico Solmi
Souls Grown Deep Foundation
Patti and Jerry Sowalsky
Sperone Westwater
Jonathan Spingarn
Susan and Louis Stamberg
Bob Stana and Tom Judy
A. Stancioff and R. Chanler
David W. Steadman
Robert and Kathi Steinke
Jill and Jeffrey Stern
Samuel A. Stern
Sidney Stolz and David Hatfield
Frances and Bayard Storey
Renée Stout
Kerry H. Stowell
Alice Phillips Swistel
Estate of Agnes Gordon Tack
Stephen Talasnik
The Thiebaud Family
Patrick A. Thomas
Gail and John Thomason
Larry and Brenda Thompson
Richard E. Thompson
Leslie Tonkonow and Klaus Ottmann
Elizabeth Hutton Turner
Rolf and Nancy Valtin
Xavier Veilhan
Michal Venera
Paolo Ventura
Mr. and Mrs. Duane Vieth
Dorothy and Herbert Vogel
Trish and George Vradenburg
Tanja Wagner Gallery
The Andy Warhol Foundation for the Visual Arts
Weber & Weber Gallery
Mary E. Weinmann
Brian Weinstein
Linda and Steve Weitz
Robert S. Wennett and Mario Cader-Frech Foundation
Michael Werner
Henry and Betsy Werronen
Brett Weston Archive
Auldlyn Higgins Williams and E.T. Williams Jr.
Wade Wilson
Shelly Wischhusen
Gabriel Wisdom
Beverly and Christopher With
Bernhard and Marlene Witkop
Alan and Irene Wurtzel
Charles M. Young
Lucia Young
Margot and Paul Zimmerman
Stephen R. Zwirn

DONORS TO THE PHILLIPS COLLECTION CENTENNIAL CAMPAIGN

We sincerely thank all donors who made gifts in honor of the 100th anniversary of our founding for the Centennial Campaign. These generous gifts of all sizes from trustees, friends, members, foundations, and other organizations have enabled us to flourish and will help sustain our beloved museum for generations to come. Below we are pleased to recognize those who made leadership gifts as of August 2020.

* Indicates planned gift

$10,000,000 AND ABOVE

Sherman Fairchild Foundation

$5,000,000-$9,999,999

Anonymous

Victoria and Roger Sant*

$1,000,000-$4,999,999

Anonymous

Carolyn S. Alper

C. Richard Belger and Evelyn Craft Belger

The Morris & Gwendolyn Cafritz Foundation

Estate of Frauke de Looper

John and Gina Despres*

The Marion F. Goldin Charitable Fund*

Lynne and Joseph Horning*

Robert and Arlene Kogod

The Andrew W. Mellon Foundation

Estate of Gifford Phillips

Estate of Jack Rachlin

Mr. and Mrs. Thomas D. Rutherfoord, Jr.*

Jodie H. and David A. Slaughter*

George Vradenburg and The Vradenburg Foundation*

Alan and Irene Wurtzel*

$500,000-$999,999

Robert and Mercedes Eichholz Foundation

Henry Luce Foundation

Mr. John D. Macomber*

Dr. and Mrs. Ronald A. Paul

$250,000-$499,999

Anonymous (2)

Esthy and James Adler*

Susan and Dixon Butler*

Estate of Helen and Charles Crowder

Henry H. and Carol Brown Goldberg

A. Fenner Milton*

James D. Parker*

Judy and Leo E. Zickler*

$100,000-$249,999

Mr. John P. Cahill*

DC Commission on the Arts and Humanities

Bill DeGraff*

Lindsay and Henry Ellenbogen

Barbara and Bob Hall*

Institute of Museum and Library Services

Sachiko Kuno Foundation

Estate of R. Robert and Ada H. Linowes

Sandra L. Mabry*

B. Thomas Mansbach

Bradford Maupin*

Carol Melton and Joseph M. Hassett

Robert E. Meyerhoff and Rheda Becker

Estate of Sheila A. Morgenstern

Prince Charitable Trusts

Robert C. Rea*

Sharon Percy Rockefeller

George Swygert and Lori Jenkins*

Richard E. Thompson*

Linda and Steve Weitz

Elizabeth H. Williams and Thomas Moore

$50,000-$99,999

Anonymous

Estate of Dorothy Bunevich

Mr. and Mrs. Bernard J. Cutler

Robert and Debra Drumheller

Philip L. Graham Fund

Institute for Contemporary Expression

Mirella and Dani Levinas

Estate of Raymond Machesney

Leslie Sawin*

Sally Wells*

Leslie Whipkey and Lee Hoffman

THE PHILLIPS COLLECTION EXHIBITION HISTORY, 1999–2021

The Phillips Collection presented the following exhibitions for which it served as either an organizer or a presenting venue.

* Indicates a corresponding catalogue

1999

TPC.1999.1
Photographs from the Collection of Dr. and Mrs. Joseph D. Lichtenberg. January 12–April 25, 1999. Organizing institution: The Phillips Collection.

TPC.1999.2
An Adventurous Spirit: Calder at The Phillips Collection. January 23–June 8, 1999. Organizing institutions: The Phillips Collection and The Calder Foundation.

TPC.1999.3
An American Century of Photography from Dry-Plate to Digital: Selections from the Hallmark Photographic Collection. January 23–March 28, 1999. Organizing institution: The Phillips Collection.

TPC.1999.4
Spirits of the South: The Julia J. Norrell Collection. February 18–June 15, 1999. Organizing institution: The Phillips Collection.

TPC.1999.5*
Georgia O'Keeffe: The Poetry of Things. April 17–July 18, 1999. Organizing institution: The Phillips Collection. Traveled to 3 additional venues.

TPC.1999.6
Judith Rothschild: An Artist's Search. May 15–August 1, 1999. Organizing institution: The Phillips Collection.

TPC.1999.7*
Renoir to Rothko: The Eye of Duncan Phillips. September 25, 1999–January 23, 2000. Organizing institution: The Phillips Collection.

2000

TPC.2000.1*
Honoré Daumier. February 19–May 14, 2000. Organizing institutions: The Phillips Collection, The National Gallery of Canada, and Réunion des Musées Nationaux, Paris. Traveled to 2 additional venues.

TPC.2000.2*
An Irish Vision: Works by Tony O'Malley. April 8–July 9, 2000. Organizing institutions: The Phillips Collection and Crawford Municipal Art Gallery, Cork, Ireland.

TPC.2000.3
A Collector's Cabinet: Whistler's Lithographs and 20th Century American Prints from the Collection of Steven Block. June 7–August 20, 2000. Organizing institution: The Phillips Collection.

TPC.2000.4*
Ben Shahn's New York: The Photography of Modern Times. June 10–August 27, 2000. Organizing institutions: Harvard University Art Museums, Cambridge, MA. Traveled to 3 additional venues.

TPC.2000.5*
Degas to Matisse: Impressionist Masterworks from the Detroit Institute of Arts. September 23, 2000–January 21, 2001. Organizing institutions: The Phillips Collection and The Detroit Institute of Arts, MI.

TPC.2000.6*
William Scharf: Paintings, 1984–2000. November 18, 2000–July 2, 2001. Organizing institution: The Phillips Collection. Traveled to The Frederick R. Weisman Museum of Art, Malibu, CA, October 20–December 15, 2001.

2001

TPC.2001.1*
Wayne Thiebaud: A Paintings Retrospective. February 10–April 29, 2001. Organizing institution: Fine Arts Museums of San Francisco, CA. Traveled to 3 additional venues.

TPC.2001.2*
Over the Line: The Art and Life of Jacob Lawrence. May 27–August 19, 2001. Organizing institution: The Phillips Collection. Traveled to 5 additional venues.

TPC.2001.3
Morris Graves. July 14–November 14, 2001. Organizing institution: The Phillips Collection.

TPC.2001.4*
Impressionist Still Life. September 22, 2001–January 13, 2002. Organizing institutions: The Phillips Collection and the Museum of Fine Arts, Boston, MA. Traveled to 1 additional venue.

2002

TPC.2002.1
Corot to Picasso: European Masterworks from the Smith College Museum of Art. February 16–May 12, 2002. Organizing institution: Smith College Museum of Art, Northampton, MA.

TPC.2002.2
John Walker. February 16–August 4, 2002. Organizing institution: The Phillips Collection.

TPC.2002.3
Howard Hodgkin. May 18–July 18, 2002. Organizing institution: The Phillips Collection.

TPC.2002.4*
Edward Weston: Photography and Modernism. June 1–August 18, 2002. Organizing institution: Museum of Fine Arts, Boston, MA.

TPC.2002.5
Willem de Looper: A Birthday Celebration. September 20, 2002–January 19, 2003. Organizing institution: The Phillips Collection.

TPC.2002.6*
Pierre Bonnard: Early and Late. September 22, 2002–January 19, 2003. Organizing institutions: The Phillips Collection and the Denver Art Museum, CO. Traveled to 1 additional venue.

2003

TPC.2003.1*
Margaret Bourke-White: The Photography of Design, 1927–1936. February 15–May 11, 2003. Organizing institution: The Phillips Collection. Traveled to 8 additional venues.

TPC.2003.2*
Marsden Hartley. June 7–September 7, 2003. Organizing institution: Wadsworth Atheneum Museum of Art, Hartford, CT.

TPC.2003.3
Surrealism and Modernism from the Collection of the Wadsworth Atheneum Museum of Art. October 4, 2003–January 18, 2004. Organizing institution: Wadsworth Atheneum Museum of Art, Hartford, CT.

2004

TPC.2004.1*
Discovering Milton Avery: Two Devoted Collectors, Louis Kaufman and Duncan Phillips. February 14–May 16, 2004. Organizing institution: The Phillips Collection.

TPC.2004.2
Revelation: Georges Rouault at Work. June 12–September 25, 2004. Organizing institution: The Phillips Collection.

TPC.2004.3*
August Sander: Photographs of the German Landscape. June 12–September 25, 2004. Organizing institution: The Phillips Collection.

TPC.2004.4
Aaron Siskind: New Relationships in Photography. June 12–September 25, 2004. Organizing institution: The Phillips Collection.

TPC.2004.5*
Calder/Miró. October 9, 2004–January 23, 2005. Organizing institutions: Fondation Beyeler, Basel, Switzerland, and The Phillips Collection.

2005

TPC.2005.1*
Modigliani: Beyond the Myth. February 26–May 29, 2005. Organizing institution: The Jewish Museum, New York, NY.

TPC.2005.2
East Meets West: Hiroshige at The Phillips Collection. June 25–September 4, 2005. Organizing institution: The Phillips Collection.

TPC.2005.3*
Sean Scully: Wall of Light. October 22, 2005–January 8, 2006. Organizing institution: The Phillips Collection. Traveled to the Modern Art Museum of Fort Worth, TX, and two other museums from February 11, 2006 to January 14, 2007.

2006

TPC.2006.1*
Degas, Sickert and Toulouse-Lautrec: London and Paris, 1870–1910. February 18–May 14, 2006. Organizing institution: Tate Britain, London, UK.

TPC.2006.2
The Renoir Returns: A Celebration of Masterworks at The Phillips Collection. April 15–July 30, 2006. Organizing institution: The Phillips Collection.

TPC.2006.3*
Klee and America. June 17–September 10, 2006. Organizing institution: The Menil Collection, Houston, TX.

TPC.2006.4*
When We Were Young: New Perspectives on the Art of the Child. June 17–September 10, 2006. Organizing institutions: The Phillips Collection and the Krannert Art Museum, University of Illinois. Traveled to 1 additional venue.

TPC.2006.5*
The Société Anonyme: Modernism for America. October 14, 2006–January 21, 2007. Organizing institution: Yale University Art Gallery, New Haven, CT.

TPC.2006.6
El Lissitzky: Futurist Portfolios. October 14, 2006–January 21, 2007. Organizing institution: The Phillips Collection. Traveled to 3 additional venues.

2007

TPC.2007.1*
Moving Pictures: American Art and Early Film, 1880–1910. February 17–May 20, 2007. Organizing institution: Williams College Museum of Art, Williamstown, MA.

TPC.2007.2
Lyrical Color: Morris Louis, Gene Davis, Kenneth Noland and the Washington Color School. April 14–July 29, 2007. Organizing institution: The Phillips Collection.

TPC.2007.3*
American Impressionism: Paintings from The Phillips Collection. June 16–September 16, 2007. Organizing institution: The Phillips Collection.

TPC.2007.4*
Impressionists by the Sea. October 20, 2007–January 13, 2008. Organizing institutions: The Phillips Collection, the Royal Academy of Arts, London, UK, and the Wadsworth Atheneum Museum of Art, Hartford, CT. Traveled to 2 additional venues.

2008

TPC.2008.1*
Degas to Diebenkorn: The Phillips Collects. February 9–May 25, 2008. Organizing institution: The Phillips Collection.

TPC.2008.2
The Great American Epic: Jacob Lawrence's Migration Series. May 3–October 26, 2008. Organizing institution: The Phillips Collection.

TPC.2008.3*
Diebenkorn in New Mexico. June 21–September 7, 2008. Organizing institution: The Harwood Museum of Art, University of New Mexico.

TPC.2008.4*
Brett Weston: Out of the Shadow. June 21–September 7, 2008. Organizing institutions: The Phillips Collection and the Oklahoma City Museum of Art, OK. Traveled to 1 additional venue.

TPC.2008.5*
Christo and Jeanne-Claude: Over the River, A Work in Progress. October 11, 2008–January 25, 2009. Organizing institution: The Phillips Collection.

TPC.2008.6
Scale Matters: Photographs from the Joseph and Charlotte Lichtenberg Collection. November 1, 2008–February 1, 2009. Organizing institution: The Phillips Collection.

2009

TPC.2009.1*
Morandi: Master of Modern Still Life. February 21–May 24, 2009. Organizing institutions: The Phillips Collection and the Museo di Arte Moderna e Contemporanea di Trento e Rovereto (MART), Rovereto, Italy.

TPC.2009.2
Intersections. *dBfoundation: This is not that CAFÉ*. May 7–December 31, 2009. Organizing institution: The Phillips Collection.

TPC.2009.3*
Paint Made Flesh. June 20–September 13, 2009. Organizing institution: Frist Center for the Visual Arts, Nashville, TN.

TPC.2009.4*
Man Ray, African Art, and the Modernist Lens. October 10, 2009–January 10, 2010. Organizing institution: International Arts & Artists, Washington, DC.

TPC.2009.5
Object as Subject: Photographs of the Czech Avant-Garde. October 14, 2009–February 7, 2010. Organizing institution: The Phillips Collection.

TPC.2009.6
Intersections. *Jennifer Wen Ma: Brain Storm*. October 15, 2009–January 3, 2010. Organizing institutions: Transformer, Shigeko Bork Mu Projects, and The Phillips Collection.

TPC.2009.7
Intersections. *Barbara Liotta: Icarus*. October 22, 2009–January 21, 2010. Organizing institution: The Phillips Collection.

TPC.2009.8
Intersections. *Tayo Heuser: Pulse*. November 19, 2009–October 31, 2010. Organizing institution: The Phillips Collection.

2010

TPC.2010.1*
Georgia O'Keeffe: Abstraction. February 6–May 9, 2010. Organizing institutions: The Phillips Collection, the Whitney Museum of American Art, New York,

NY, and the Georgia O'Keeffe Museum, Santa Fe, NM. Traveled to 2 additional venues.

TPC.2010.2
Intersections. *linn meyers: at the time being*. February 11–August 22, 2010. Organizing institution: The Phillips Collection.

TPC.2010.3
Intersections. *Regi Müller: Flurries.* April 1, 2010–May 15, 2011. Organizing institution: The Phillips Collection.

TPC.2010.4*
Pousette-Dart: Predominantly White Paintings. June 5–September 12, 2010. Organizing institution: The Phillips Collection.

TPC.2010.5*
Robert Ryman: Variations and Improvisations. June 5–September 12, 2010. Organizing institution: The Phillips Collection.

TPC.2010.6
Intersections. *Kate Shepherd: Relation to and yet not (homage to Mondrian).* June 10–September 5, 2010. Organizing institution: The Phillips Collection.

TPC.2010.7
Side by Side: Oberlin's Masterworks at the Phillips. September 11, 2010–January 16, 2011. Organizing institutions: The Phillips Collection and the Allen Memorial Art Museum, Oberlin College, Oberlin, OH.

TPC.2010.8
Intersections. *Jae Ko: Force of Nature.* September 30, 2010–February 20, 2011. Organizing institution: The Phillips Collection.

TPC.2010.9*
Truth Beauty: Pictorialism and the Photograph as Art 1845–1945. October 9, 2010–January 9, 2011. Organizing institutions: George Eastman House International Museum of Photography and Film, Rochester, NY, and Vancouver Art Gallery, BC, Canada.

TPC.2010.10
Coburn and the Photographic Portfolio. October 9, 2010–January 9, 2011. Organizing institution: The Phillips Collection.

2011

TPC.2011.1*
David Smith Invents. February 12–May 15, 2011. Organizing institution: The Phillips Collection.

TPC.2011.2*
Philip Guston: Roma. February 12–May 15, 2011. Organizing institutions: The City of Rome and the Museo Carlo Bilotti – Aranciera di Villa Borghese, in partnership with the American Academy in Rome.

TPC.2011.3
Intersections. *Nicholas and Sheila Pye: The Coronation*. February 17–May 22, 2011. Organizing institution: The Phillips Collection.

TPC.2011.4
One-on-One: Peter Doig / Georges Braque. March 17–May 11, 2011. Organizing institution: The Phillips Collection.

TPC.2011.5
Intersections. *A. Balasubramaniam: Sk(in).* May 26–October 30, 2011. Organizing institution: The Phillips Collection.

TPC.2011.6
Intersections. *Lee Boroson: Lunar Bower*. May 26, 2011–May 6, 2012. Organizing institution: The Phillips Collection.

TPC.2011.7*
Kandinsky and the Harmony of Silence: Painting with White Border. June 11–September 4, 2011. Organizing institutions: The Phillips Collection and The Solomon R. Guggenheim Foundation. Traveled to 1 additional venue.

TPC.2011.8
Stella Sounds: The Scarlatti K Series. June 11–September 4, 2011. Organizing institution: The Phillips Collection.

TPC.2011.9
Intersections. *Allan deSouza: The World Series*. June 23–October 30, 2011. Organizing institution: The Phillips Collection.

TPC.2011.10*
Degas's Dancers at the Barre: Point and Counterpoint. October 1, 2011–January 8, 2012. Organizing institution: The Phillips Collection.

2012

TPC.2012.1
French Drawings from the Aaronsohn Collection. February 2–April 29, 2012. Organizing institution: The Phillips Collection.

TPC.2012.2*
Snapshot: Painters and Photography, Bonnard to Vuillard. February 4–May 6, 2012. Organizing institutions: The Phillips Collection, the Van Gogh Museum, Amsterdam, and the Indianapolis Museum of Art, IN. Traveled to 2 additional venues.

TPC.2012.3
Intersections. *Alyson Shotz: Ecliptic.* February 16–May 27, 2012. Organizing institution: The Phillips Collection.

TPC.2012.4
Intersections. *Sandra Cinto: One Day, After the Rain*. May 19, 2012–August 18, 2013. Organizing institution: The Phillips Collection.

TPC.2012.5
Antony Gormley: Drawing Space. June 2–September 9, 2012. Organizing institution: The Phillips Collection.

TPC.2012.6
Jasper Johns: Variations on a Theme. June 2–September 9, 2012. Organizing institutions: The Phillips Collection in collaboration with the John and Maxine Belger Foundation.

TPC.2012.7
John Cage at the Phillips. June 2–September 9, 2012. Organizing institution: The Phillips Collection.

TPC.2012.8
Political Wits, 100 Years Apart: Daumier and Oliphant at the Phillips. September 6, 2012–January 31, 2013. Organizing institution: The Phillips Collection.

TPC.2012.9*
Per Kirkeby: Paintings and Sculpture. October 6, 2012–January 6, 2013. Organizing institution: The Phillips Collection.

TPC.2012.10
Picturing the Sublime: Photographs from the Joseph and Charlotte Lichtenberg Collection. October 11, 2012–February 17, 2013. Organizing institution: The Phillips Collection.

TPC.2012.11
Intersections. *Xavier Veilhan: IN(balance)*. November 3, 2012–February 10, 2013. Organizing institution: The Phillips Collection.

2013

TPC.2013.1*
Angels, Demons, and Savages: Pollock, Ossorio, Dubuffet. February 9–May 12, 2013. Organizing institutions: The Phillips Collection and the Parrish Art Museum, Water Mill, NY. Traveled to 1 additional venue.

TPC.2013.2
Intersections. *Jeanne Silverthorne: Vanitas!* February 28–June 2, 2013. Organizing institution: The Phillips Collection.

TPC.2013.3
Next Stop Italy: A Journey into Italian Contemporary Photography. March 9–May 5, 2013. Organizing institution: The Phillips Collection.

TPC.2013.4*
Georges Braque and the Cubist Still Life, 1928–1945. June 8–September 1, 2013. Organizing institutions: The Phillips Collection and the Mildred Lane Kemper Art Museum, Washington University, St. Louis, MO. Traveled to 1 additional venue.

TPC.2013.5*
Ellsworth Kelly: Panel Paintings 2004–2009. June 22–September 22, 2013. Organizing institution: The Phillips Collection.

TPC.2013.6
Intersections. *Bernhard Hildebrandt: A Conjugation of Verb*. June 27–September 22, 2013. Organizing institution: The Phillips Collection.

TPC.2013.7
History in the Making: 100 Years After the Armory Show. August 1, 2013–January 5, 2014. Organizing institution: The Phillips Collection.

TPC.2013.8*
Van Gogh Repetitions. October 12, 2013–February 2, 2014. Organizing institutions: The Phillips Collection and The Cleveland Museum of Art, OH. Traveled to 1 additional venue.

TPC.2013.9
Intersections. *John F. Simon Jr.: Points, Lines and Colors in Succession.* October 17, 2013–February 9, 2014. Organizing institution: The Phillips Collection.

TPC.2013.10
Shaping a Modern Identity: Portraits from the Joseph and Charlotte Lichtenberg Collection. October 24, 2013–January 12, 2014. Organizing institution: The Phillips Collection.

2014

TPC.2014.1
Intersections. *Jean Meisel: 50–65 Horizon Line.* January 23–May 4, 2014. Organizing institution: The Phillips Collection.

TPC.2014.2*
Made in the USA: American Masters from The Phillips Collection, 1850–1970. March 1–August 21, 2014. Organizing institution: The Phillips Collection.

TPC.2014.3
Intersections. *Vesna Pavlović: Illuminated Archive.* May 22–September 28, 2014. Organizing institution: The Phillips Collection.

TPC.2014.4
O'Keeffe and Friends: Dialogues with Nature. September 11, 2014–May 3, 2015. Organizing institution: The Phillips Collection.

TPC.2014.5*
Neo-Impressionism and the Dream of Realities: Painting, Poetry, Music. September 27, 2014–January 11, 2015. Organizing institution: The Phillips Collection.

TPC.2014.6
A Tribute to Anita Reiner. October 14, 2014–January 4, 2015. Organizing institution: The Phillips Collection.

TPC.2014.7
Intersections. *Bernardí Roig: NO/ Escape.* October 25, 2014–April 5, 2015. Organizing institution: The Phillips Collection.

2015

TPC.2015.1
Jacob Lawrence: Struggle … From the History of the American People. January 10–August 9, 2015. Organizing institution: The Phillips Collection.

TPC.2015.2*
Hiroshi Sugimoto: Conceptual Forms and Mathematical Models. February 7–May 10, 2015. Organizing institution: The Phillips Collection.

TPC.2015.3*
Man Ray–Human Equations: A Journey from Mathematics to Shakespeare. February 7–May 10, 2015. Organizing institutions: The Phillips Collection and The Israel Museum, Jerusalem.

TPC.2015.4
Modern Vision: American Sculptors' Drawings from the Linda Lichtenberg Kaplan Collection. May 21–September 6, 2015. Organizing institution: The Phillips Collection.

TPC.2015.5*
Intersections @ 5: Contemporary Art Projects at the Phillips. May 28–October 25, 2015. Organizing institution: The Phillips Collection.

TPC.2015.6
American Moments: Photographs from The Phillips Collection. June 6–September 13, 2015. Organizing institution: The Phillips Collection.

TPC.2015.7
One-on-One: Carol Brown Goldberg / Henri Matisse. June 9–September 6, 2015. Organizing institution: The Phillips Collection.

TPC.2015.8
Jill O'Bryan: one billion breaths in a lifetime. June 9–December 7, 2015. Organizing institution: The Phillips Collection.

TPC.2015.9
Postwar Germanic Expressions: Gifts from Michael Werner. September 12, 2015–April 17, 2016. Organizing institution: The Phillips Collection.

TPC.2015.10
Question Bridge: Black Males. October 8, 2015–February 28, 2016. Organizing institution: The Phillips Collection.

TPC.2015.11*
Gauguin to Picasso: Masterworks from Switzerland. October 10, 2015–January 10, 2016. Organizing institutions: The Phillips Collection and the Museo Nacional Centro de Arte Reina Sofia in collaboration with the Im Obersteg Foundation and the Rudolf Staechelin Family Trust.

2016

TPC.2016.1
Intersections. *Helen Frederick: Acts of Silence.* February 4–May 1, 2016. Organizing institution: The Phillips Collection.

TPC.2016.2*
Seeing Nature: Landscape Masterworks from the Paul G. Allen Family Collection. February 6–May 8, 2016. Organizing institutions: The Portland Art Museum, OR, Seattle Art Museum, WA, and the Paul G. Allen Family Collection.

TPC.2016.3*
William Merritt Chase: A Modern Master. June 4–September 11, 2016. Organizing institutions: The Phillips Collection, the Museum of Fine Arts, Boston, MA, the Fondazione Musei Civici di Venezia, Venice, and the Terra Foundation for American Art. Traveled to 2 additional venues.

TPC.2016.4
Intersections. *Bettina Pousttchi: Double Monuments.* June 9–October 2, 2016. Organizing institution: The Phillips Collection.

TPC.2016.5*
Karel Appel: A Gesture of Color – Paintings and Sculptures, 1947–2004. June 18–September 18, 2016. Organizing institutions: The Phillips Collection in close collaboration with the Karel Appel Foundation, Amsterdam.

TPC.2016.6*
People on the Move: Beauty and Struggle in Jacob Lawrence's Migration Series. October 8, 2016–January 8, 2017. Organizing institutions: The Phillips Collection, The Museum of Modern Art, New York, NY, in collaboration with the Schomburg Center for Research in Black Culture, Harlem, NY.

TPC.2016.7*
Whitfield Lovell: The Kin Series and Related Works. October 8, 2016–January 8, 2017. Organizing institution: The Phillips Collection.

TPC.2016.8
One-on-One: Enrique Martínez Celaya / Albert Pinkham Ryder. October 13, 2016–April 2, 2017. Organizing institution: The Phillips Collection.

TPC.2016.9*
Intersections. *Arlene Shechet: From Here on Now.* October 20, 2016–May 7, 2017. Organizing institution: The Phillips Collection.

TPC.2016.10*
Jake Berthot: From the Collection and Promised Gifts. November 19, 2016–April 2, 2017. Organizing institution: The Phillips Collection.

2017

TPC.2017.1
Jacob Lawrence's The Life of Toussaint L'Ouverture. January 7–April 30, 2017. Organizing institution: The Phillips Collection.

TPC.2017.2*
Toulouse-Lautrec Illustrates the Belle Époque. February 4–April 30, 2017. Organizing institutions: The Phillips Collection and the Montreal Museum of Fine Arts, QC, Canada. Traveled to 1 additional venue.

TPC.2017.3
George Condo: The Way I Think. March 11–June 25, 2017. Organizing institution: The Phillips Collection.

TPC.2017.4*
Markus Lüpertz. May 27–September 3, 2017. Organizing institution: The Phillips Collection.

TPC.2017.5
Moving Forward, Looking Back: A Collection Still in the Making – Selections from The Phillips Collection Archives. June 26, 2017–December

31, 2020. Organizing institution: The Phillips Collection.

TPC.2017.6*
Renoir and Friends: Luncheon of the Boating Party. October 7, 2017–January 7, 2018. Organizing institution: The Phillips Collection.

2018

TPC.2018.1
To Future Women. January 21–February 18, 2018. Organizing institutions: The Phillips Collection, supported by local DC-based institutions and organizations including Halcyon Arts Lab, IA&A at Hillyer, Stable and ArtTable.

TPC.2018.2*
Ten Americans: After Paul Klee. February 3–May 6, 2018. Organizing institutions: The Phillips Collection and the Zentrum Paul Klee, Bern, Switzerland.

TPC.2018.3*
Marking the Infinite: Contemporary Women Artists from Aboriginal Australia. June 2–September 9, 2018. Organizing institutions: The Nevada Museum of Art, Reno, NV, and the Kluge-Ruhe Aboriginal Art Collection of the University of Virginia.

TPC.2018.4*
Intersections. *Richard Tuttle: It Seems Like It's Going to Be.* September 13–December 30, 2018. Organizing institution: The Phillips Collection.

TPC.2018.5*
Nordic Impressions: Art from Åland, Denmark, the Faroe Islands, Finland, Greenland, Iceland, Norway, and Sweden, 1821–2018. October 13, 2018–January 13, 2019. Organizing institution: The Phillips Collection.

TPC.2018.6*
Bice Lazzari: The Poetry of Mark-Making. October 23, 2018–February 24, 2019. Organizing institutions: The Phillips Collection, the Embassy of Italy, Washington, DC, and the Archivio Bice Lazzari, Rome.

2019

TPC.2019.1*
Zilia Sánchez: Soy Isla (I Am an Island). February 16–May 19, 2019. Organizing institution: The Phillips Collection. Traveled to 2 additional venues.

TPC.2019.2
One-on-One: Maggie Michael / Arthur Dove. February 21–May 5, 2019. Organizing institution: The Phillips Collection.

TPC.2019.3*
Jeanine Michna-Bales: Photographs of the Underground Railroad. March 2–May 12, 2019. Organizing institution: The Phillips Collection.

TPC.2019.4
Intersections. *Ranjani Shettar: Earth Songs for a Night Sky.* May 16–August 25, 2019. Organizing institution: The Phillips Collection.

TPC.2019.5
The Warmth of Other Suns: Stories of Global Displacement. June 22–September 22, 2019. Organizing institutions: The Phillips Collection in partnership with the New Museum, New York, NY.

TPC.2019.6
Dear Dove, Dear Phillips, Dear Stieglitz Reading Room Exhibition. July 23, 2019–July 19, 2020. Organizing institution: The Phillips Collection.

TPC.2019.7
Intersections. *Los Carpinteros: Cuba Va!* October 10, 2019–January 12, 2020. Organizing institution: The Phillips Collection.

TPC.2019.8*
Bonnard to Vuillard: The Intimate Poetry of Everyday Life. The Nabi Collection of Vicki and Roger Sant. October 26, 2019–January 26, 2020. Organizing institution: The Phillips Collection.

2020

TPC.2020.1*
Moira Dryer: Back in Business. February 8–December 13, 2020. Organizing institution: The Phillips Collection.

TPC.2020.2*
Riffs and Relations: African American Artists and the European Modernist Tradition. February 29, 2020–January 3, 2021. Organizing institution: The Phillips Collection.

TPC.2020.3
Digital Intersections. *Luca Buvoli: Picture: Present (An episode from "Astrodoubt and The Quarantine Chronicles" in 12 scenes).* July 20–August 7, 2020. Organizing institution: The Phillips Collection.

TPC.2020.4
Hopper in Paris. October 10, 2020–January 10, 2021. Organizing institution: The Whitney Museum of American Art, New York, NY.

2021

TPC.2021.1
Intersections. *Marley Dawson. ghosts.* May 20–September 5, 2021. Organizing institution: The Phillips Collection.

TPC.2021.2
Seeing Differently: The Phillips Collects for a New Century. February 20–September 12, 2021. Organizing institution: The Phillips Collection.

TPC.2021.3
Jacob Lawrence: American Struggle. June 26–September 19, 2021. Organizing institution: Peabody Essex Museum, Salem, MA.

TPC.2021.4
Intersections. *Sanford Biggers. Mosaic.* October 16, 2021–January 2, 2022. Organizing institution: The Phillips Collection.

TPC.2021.5
David Driskell: Icons of Nature and History. October 16, 2021–January 9, 2022. Organizing institutions: High Museum of Art, Atlanta, GA, and Portland Museum of Art, ME.

TPC.2021.6
Alma Thomas: A Creative Life. October 30, 2021–January 23, 2022. Organizing institutions: The Columbus Museum, GA, and the Chrysler Museum of Art, Norfolk, VA.

THE COLLECTION ON TOUR 2000–2020

Since 1922 the Phillips has been collaborating with institutions, foundations, and sponsors to share its artwork. When the museum underwent renovations in the 1980s and early 2000s, the Phillips toured its cherished masterpieces at home and abroad in Asia, Australia, and Europe. In 2006, the Phillips's *European Masterworks* exhibition returned home after a world tour that was seen by over two million people. In addition, *To See as Artists See: American Art from The Phillips Collection* featured nearly 100 works that traveled to Europe and Asia before visiting US venues, and made its grand homecoming in spring 2014. Major European and American artwork tours have traveled throughout the US and abroad since 2000.

2000–2009

Masterworks from The Phillips Collection at the Bellagio. Las Vegas, NV. September 1, 2000–March 4, 2001.

Art Beyond Isms: Masterworks from El Greco to Picasso in The Phillips Collection. Also toured under the title *European Masterworks.* Museum of Fine Arts, Houston, TX. September 22, 2002–January 5, 2003. Phoenix Art Museum, AZ. January 23–May 4, 2003. Albright-Knox Art Gallery, Buffalo, NY. May 23–September 1, 2003. Denver Art Museum, CO. October 4, 2003–January 4, 2004. Frist Center for Visual Arts, Nashville, TN. February 6–May 16, 2004. Fondation Pierre Gianadda, Martigny, Switzerland. May 27–September 27, 2004. Los Angeles County Museum of Art, CA. October 17, 2004–January 2, 2005. The Cleveland Museum of Art, OH. February 20–May 30, 2005. Mori Arts Center, Tokyo, Japan. June 17–September 4, 2005. Museum of Modern and Contemporary Art, Rovereto, Italy. September 17–November 13, 2005. Musée de Luxembourg, Paris, France. November 28, 2005–March 26, 2006.

Jacob Lawrence: The Migration Series from The Phillips Collection. Frist Center for the Visual Arts, Nashville, TN. February 6–May 16, 2004. Columbus Museum of Art, OH. June 11–August 31, 2004.

In the American Grain. Dove, Hartley, Martin, O'Keeffe and Stieglitz. The Stieglitz Circle at The Phillips Collection. Santa Barbara Museum of Art, CA. February 14–May 9, 2004. The Philbrook Museum of Art, Tulsa, OK. June 6–August 22, 2004. Georgia O'Keeffe Museum, Santa Fe, NM. October 1, 2004–January 2, 2005. Norton Museum of Art, West Palm Beach, FL. February 19–May 8, 2005. The Newark Museum, NJ. June 8–September 4, 2005. The Currier Gallery of Art, Manchester, NH. October 1, 2005–January 2, 2006.

American Impressionism: Paintings from The Phillips Collection, organized by The Phillips Collection, supported by a grant from the National Endowment for the Humanities as part of the American Masterpieces program. The Dixon Gallery and Gardens, Memphis, TN. October 28, 2007–January 6, 2008. Memorial Art Gallery, University of Rochester, NY. April 12–June 15, 2008. Montgomery Museum of Fine Arts, AL. July 4–October 19, 2008. Oklahoma City Museum of Art, OK. November 6, 2008–January 18, 2009. Society of the Four Arts, Palm Beach, FL. March 13–April 15, 2009. Museum of Fine Arts, Santa Fe, NM. June 5–September 13, 2009. Grand Rapids Art Museum, MI. October 2, 2009–January 3, 2010.

Jacob Lawrence: The Migration Series. McNay Art Museum, San Antonio, TX. January 10–March 25, 2007. Columbia Museum of Art, SC. April 14–June 24, 2007. Figge Art Museum, Davenport, IA. September 29–October 28, 2007. Whitney Museum of American Art, New York, NY. November 14, 2007–January 6, 2008. Mississippi Museum of Art, Jackson, MS. January 26–April 6, 2008.

Da Corot a Picasso: la Phillips Collection di Washington/From Corot to Picasso: The Phillips Collection in Washington. Palazzo Baldeschi al Corso, Perugia, Italy. September 15, 2008–January 18, 2009.

2010–2020

To See as Artists See: American Art from The Phillips Collection, 1850–1960. Museo di Arte Moderna e Contemporanea di Trento e Rovereto (MART), Rovereto, Italy. June 5–September 12, 2010. Fundación MAPFRE, Madrid, Spain. October 5, 2010–January 16, 2011. National Art Center, Tokyo, Japan. September 28–December 12, 2011. Frist Center for the Visual Arts, Nashville, TN. February 2–May 6, 2012. Amon Carter Museum of American Art, Fort Worth, TX. October 6, 2012–January 6, 2013. Tampa Museum of Art, FL. February 2–April 28, 2013.

Conversations: Impressionist and Modern Masterworks from The Phillips Collection. Daejeon Museum of Art, South Korea. July 2–October 22, 2014. Hangaram Art Museum, Seoul Arts Center, South Korea. November 25, 2014–March 12, 2015. Palazzo delle Esposizioni, Rome, Italy. October 15, 2015–February 15, 2016. CaixaForum Barcelona, Spain. March 11–June 19, 2016. Fundación "la Caixa," Madrid, Spain. July 16–October 22, 2016.

American Mosaic: Picturing Modern Art through the Eye of Duncan Phillips. Orange County Museum of Art, Newport Beach, CA. August 6–December 4, 2016.

From Homer to Hopper: Experiment and Ingenuity in American Art. Brandywine River Museum of Art, Chadds Ford, PA. February 25–May 21, 2017.

From Hopper to Rothko: America's Road to Modern Art. Museum Barberini, Potsdam, Germany. June 17–October 3, 2017.

A Modern Vision: European Masterworks from The Phillips Collection. Kimbell Art Museum, Fort Worth, TX. May 14–August 13, 2017. Mitsubishi Ichigokan Museum, Tokyo, Japan. October 17, 2018–February 3, 2019. High Museum of Art, Atlanta, GA. April 6–July 14, 2019. Milwaukee Art Museum, WI. November 15, 2019–March 22, 2020.

The Artist Sees Differently: Modern Still Lifes from The Phillips Collection. Princeton University Art Museum, Princeton, NJ. January 23–April 29, 2018.

From Winslow Homer to Georgia O'Keeffe: American Paintings from The Phillips Collection. Taft Museum of Art, Cincinnati, OH. February 9–May 19, 2019.

From Homer to Hopper: American Art from The Phillips Collection, Washington, DC. Vero Beach Museum of Art, FL. February 1–May 31, 2020.

THE PHILLIPS COLLECTION PUBLICATION HISTORY, 1999–2020

The following list comprises books or exhibition catalogues published, co-published, or edited by The Phillips Collection or members of its staff since 1999.

1999

Daumier: 1808–1879. Texts by Henri Loyrette, Michael Pantazzi, Ségolène Le Men, Édouard Papet, and Michel Melot. Ottawa: National Gallery of Canada 1999; Paris: Galeries nationales du Grand Palais, 1999; Washington, DC: The Phillips Collection, 2000.

Passantino, Erika D., ed., David W. Scott, consulting ed. *The Eye of Duncan Phillips: A Collection in the Making*. Washington, DC: The Phillips Collection in association with Yale University Press, 1999.

The Phillips Collection. *Duncan Phillips 1886–1966: Centennial Exhibition*. Introduction by Eliza E. Rathbone. 3rd ed. Washington, DC: The Phillips Collection, [1986] 1999.

Turner, Elizabeth H. *Georgia O'Keeffe: The Poetry of Things*. Washington, DC: The Phillips Collection and Yale University Press, in association with Dallas Museum of Art, 1999.

2000

Kramer, Hilton, et al. *William Scharf: Paintings, 1984–2000*. Preface by Eliza Rathbone. Washington, DC: The Phillips Collection, 2000.

Nesbett, Peter T., and Michelle DuBois, eds. *Over the Line: The Art and Life of Jacob Lawrence*. Seattle: University of Washington Press in association with Jacob and Gwendolyn Lawrence Foundation, 2000.

Phillips, Stephen Bennett, Karen Wilkin, and Charles H. Sawyer. *Degas to Matisse: Impressionist and Modern Masterworks*. The Phillips Collection in cooperation with The Detroit Institute of Arts. London: Merrell in association with The Phillips Collection, 2000.

The Phillips Collection. *An Irish Vision: Works by Tony O'Malley*. Text by Peter Murray. Washington, DC: The Kennedy Center and The Phillips Collection with Gandon Editions, 2000.

2001

Rathbone, Eliza E., and George M. Shackelford, et al. *Impressionist Still Life*. Washington, DC: The Phillips Collection in association with Harry N. Abrams, 2001.

Thompson, Jeffrey E. *At Home with the Impressionists: Masterpieces of French Still-life Painting*. Washington, DC: The Phillips Collection; New York: Universe, 2001.

2002

Leach, Deba Foxley. *I See You, I See Myself: The Young Life of Jacob Lawrence*. Washington, DC: The Phillips Collection, 2002.

Phillips, Stephen B. *Margaret Bourke-White: The Photography of Design, 1927–1936*. New York: Rizzoli International in association with The Phillips Collection, 2002.

Rathbone, Eliza E., and Johanna Halford-MacLeod. *Art Beyond Isms: Masterworks from El Greco to Picasso in The Phillips Collection*. Washington, DC: The Phillips Collection in association with Third Millennium, 2002.

Turner, Elizabeth H. *Pierre Bonnard: Early and Late*. London: Philip Wilson in collaboration with The Phillips Collection, 2002.

2003

Halford-MacLeod, Johanna. *Renoir: Luncheon of the Boating Party*. London: Scala in association with The Phillips Collection, 2003.

Wright, Suzanne. *The Choice Is Yours: An Art Activity Handbook for Young Artists Highlighting the Art and Life of Jacob Lawrence*. Washington, DC: The Phillips Collection, 2003.

2004

Fondation Pierre Gianadda. With an essay by Eliza E. Rathbone [and texts by Johanna Halford-MacLeod]. *Chefs-d'oeuvre de la Phillips Collection Washington*. Martigny, Switzerland: Fondation Pierre Gianadda in collaboration with The Phillips Collection, 2004.

Phillips, Stephen Bennett, et al. *August Sander: Photographs of the German Landscape*. Washington, DC: The Phillips Collection, 2004.

Rathbone, Eliza E. *Discovering Milton Avery: Two Devoted Collectors, Louis Kaufman and Duncan Phillips*. Washington, DC: The Phillips Collection, 2004.

Turner, Elizabeth H., and Oliver Wick, eds. *Calder/Miró*. London: Philip Wilson in collaboration with The Phillips Collection and Fondation Beyeler, 2004.

2005

Phillips, Stephen B., ed. *Sean Scully: Wall of Light*. New York: Rizzoli International in association with The Phillips Collection, 2005.

Prat, Jean-Louis, and Eliza E. Rathbone. *La Collection Phillips à Paris*. Paris and Milan: Musée du Luxembourg and Skira in collaboration with The Phillips Collection, 2005.

Rathbone, Eliza E., and Johanna Halford-MacLeod. *Da Goya a Manet, da Van Gogh a Picasso: The Phillips Collection*. Rovereto and Milan: Museo di Arte Moderna e Contemporanea di Trento e Rovereto (MART) and Mazzotta in collaboration with The Phillips Collection, 2005.

2006

Helfenstein, Josef, and Elizabeth Hutton Turner, eds. *Klee and America*. Houston: The Menil Foundation and Hatje Cantz Verlag, 2006.

2007

Frank, Susan Behrends. *American Impressionists: Painters of Light and the Modern Landscape*. New York: Rizzoli International in association with The Phillips Collection, 2007.

2008

Christo, et al. *Christo and Jeanne-Claude: Over the River: Project for Arkansas River, State of Colorado: A Work in Progress.* Foreword by Jay Gates. Introduction by Jonathan David Fineberg. Hong Kong: Taschen, 2008.

Gates, Jay, and Vittorio Sgarbi. *Da Corot a Picasso, da Fattori a De Pisis: la Phillips collection di Washington e la collezione Ricci Oddi di Piacenza.* Perugia and Milan: Arte Moderna e Contemporanea in association with Silvana Editoriale, 2008.

Phillips, Stephen B., ed. *Brett Weston: Out of the Shadow.* Oklahoma City, OK: Oklahoma City Museum of Art in association with The Phillips Collection, 2008.

The Phillips Collection. *Degas to Diebenkorn: The Phillips Collects.* Essay by Jay Gates. [Reprinted from Winter 2008 issue of *The Phillips Collection Magazine*] Washington, DC: The Phillips Collection, 2008.

2009

Fergonzi, Flavio, and Elisabetta Barisoni. *Morandi: Master of Modern Still Life.* Washington, DC: The Phillips Collection, 2009.

Haskell, Barbara, et al. *Georgia O'Keeffe: Abstraction.* New York: Whitney Museum of American Art, The Phillips Collection, and Georgia O'Keeffe Museum in association with Yale University Press, 2009.

2010

Anfam, David, and Carter Ratcliff. *Pousette-Dart: Predominantly White Paintings.* Washington, DC: The Phillips Collection, 2010.

Frank, Susan Behrends, ed. With an essay by Elisabetta Barisoni. *American Art 1850–1960: Capolavori dalla Phillips Collection di Museo di Washington.* Rovereto and Milan: Museo di Arte Moderna e Contemporanea di Trento e Rovereto (MART) and Silvana Editoriale in association with The Phillips Collection, 2010.

———. With essays by Dore Ashton and María Dolores Jiménez Blanco. *Made in USA: Arte Americano de la Phillips Collection.* Madrid: Fundación Mapfre in association with The Phillips Collection and TF. Editores. 2010.

Sretenović, Vesela. *Robert Ryman: Variations + Improvisations.* Washington, DC: The Phillips Collection, 2010.

2011

Frank, Susan Behrends. With essays by Sarah Hamill and Peter Stevens. *David Smith Invents.* Washington, DC: The Phillips Collection in association with Yale University Press, 2011.

———, ed. With essays by Dore Ashton and Hanako Nishino. *To See as Artists See: American Art from The Phillips Collection.* Tokyo: The National Art Center and The Yomiuri Shimbun in association with The Phillips Collection, 2011.

Rathbone, Eliza E., and Elizabeth Steele. *Degas's Dancers at the Barre: Point and Counterpoint.* Washington, DC: The Phillips Collection in association with Yale University Press, 2011.

———, and Susan Behrends Frank. With an essay by Robert Hughes. *Master Paintings from The Phillips Collection.* Washington, DC: The Phillips Collection in association with D Giles Limited, 2011.

Smithgall, Elsa, et al. *Kandinsky and the Harmony of Silence: Painting with White Border.* Washington, DC: The Phillips Collection in association with Yale University Press, 2011.

2012

Kosinski, Dorothy M., and Klaus Ottmann. *Per Kirkeby: Paintings and Sculpture.* New Haven, CT: Yale University Press in association with The Phillips Collection, 2012.

2013

Butler, Karen K., Renée Maurer, et al. *Georges Braque and the Cubist Still Life, 1928–1945.* St. Louis, MO: Mildred Lane Kemper Art Museum and The Phillips Collection in association with DelMonico, Prestel, 2013.

Frank, Susan Behrends, ed. With an essay by Eliza E. Rathbone. *Made in the U.S.A.: American Art from The Phillips Collection, 1850–1970.* New Haven, CT: Yale University Press in association with The Phillips Collection, 2013.

Ottmann, Klaus, and Dorothy M. Kosinski. *Angels, Demons, and Savages: Pollock, Ossorio, Dubuffet.* New Haven, CT: Yale University Press in association with The Phillips Collection and The Parrish Art Museum, 2013.

Rathbone, Eliza E., William H. Robinson, Elizabeth Steele, and Marcia Steele. *Van Gogh Repetitions.* New Haven, CT: Yale University Press in association with The Phillips Collection and The Cleveland Museum of Art, 2013.

Sretenović, Vesela. *Ellsworth Kelly: Panel Paintings 2004–2009.* Washington, DC: The Phillips Collection, 2013.

2014

Frank, Susan Behrends, et al. *Ingres to Kandinsky: From The Phillips Collection.* Seoul, South Korea: Hangaram Art Museum, Seoul Arts Center (SAC), 2014.

Homburg, Cornelia. *Neo-Impressionism and the Dream of Realities: Painting, Poetry, Music.* New Haven, CT: Yale University Press in association with The Phillips Collection, Washington, DC, 2014.

2015

Dickerman, Leah, and Elsa Smithgall, eds. *Jacob Lawrence: The Migration Series.* New York: The Museum of Modern Art and The Phillips Collection, 2015.

Frank, Susan Behrends, ed. With an essay by Claudio Zambianchi. *Impressionisti e Moderni. capolavori dalla Phillips Collection di Washington.* Rome and Milan: Palazzo delle Esposizioni and Silvana Editoriale in association with The Phillips Collection, 2015.

Grossman, Wendy A., and Edouard Sebline, eds. *Man Ray. Human Equations: A Journey from Mathematics to Shakespeare.* Ostfildern: Hatje Cantz in association with The Phillips Collection, 2015.

Kosinski, Dorothy, Renée Maurer, et al. *Gauguin to Picasso, Masterworks from Switzerland: The Staechelin and Im Obersteg Collections.* Washington, DC: The Phillips Collection in association with D Giles Limited, 2015.

Ottmann, Klaus. *Hiroshi Sugimoto: Conceptual Forms and Mathematical Models.* Ostfildern: Hatje Cantz in association with The Phillips Collection, 2015.

Sretenović, Vesela. *Intersections @ 5: Contemporary Art Projects at the Phillips.* Washington, DC: The Phillips Collection, 2015.

2016

Frank, Susan Behrends, ed. With an essay by Alex Mitrani. *Impresionistas y Modernos: Obras maestras de la Phillips Collection.* Washington, DC: Barcelona and Madrid: The Phillips Collection in association with Obra Social "la Caixa," 2016.

Goldfarb, Hilliard T., Giles Genty, and Renée Maurer. *Toulouse-Lautrec Illustrates the Belle Époque.* Paris: Editions Hazen in association with The Phillips Collection, 2016.

Lewis, Sarah E., et al. *Whitfield Lovell: KIN.* Introduction by Irving Sandler. New York: Skira Rizzoli in association with The Phillips Collection, 2016.

Ottmann, Klaus. *A Gesture of Color: Karel Appel. Paintings and Sculptures, 1947–2004.* Munich/Berlin and Washington, DC: Sieveking Verlag and The Phillips Collection, 2016.

———. *Arlene Shechet: From Here On Now.* Washington, DC: The Phillips Collection, 2016.

———, and Eliza E. Rathbone, *Jake Berthot: From the Collection and Promised Gifts.* Washington, DC: The Phillips Collection, 2016.

Smithgall, Elsa, et al. *William Merritt Chase: A Modern Master.* Foreword by D. Frederick Baker. Washington, DC: The Phillips Collection in association with Yale University Press, 2016.

2017

Kosinski, Dorothy M., and Evelyn Hankins. *Markus Lüpertz: Hirshhorn Museum and Sculpture Garden and The Phillips Collection.* Washington, DC: The Phillips Collection and Hirshhorn Museum and Sculpture Garden in association with Sieveking Verlag, 2017.

Rathbone, Eliza E. *Renoir and Friends: Luncheon of the Boating Party.* Washington, DC: The Phillips Collection in association with D Giles Limited, 2017.

Westheider, Ortrud, and Michael Philipp, eds. *From Hopper to Rothko: America's Road to Modern Art.* Washington, DC: Potsdam: The Phillips Collection in association with the Museum Barberini, 2017. English edition, trans. Donald Goodwin, Amy Klement, Miranda Robbins, Jennifer Taylor. Munich: Prestel Verlag, 2017.

Zentrum Paul Klee and The Phillips Collection. *Ten Americans: After Paul Klee.* New York: Zentrum Paul Klee and The Phillips Collection in association with Prestel, 2017.

2018

Miracco, Renato. *Bice Lazzari: The Poetry of Mark-Making.* Washington, DC: The Phillips Collection, 2018.

Ottmann, Klaus. *Nordic Impressions: Art from Åland, Denmark, the Faroe Islands, Finland, Greenland, Iceland, Norway, and Sweden, 1821–2018.* Washington, DC: The Phillips Collection, 2018.

Sretenović, Vesela. *Richard Tuttle: It Seems Like It's Going To Be.* Washington, DC: The Phillips Collection, 2018.

Yasui, Hiroo, and Renée Maurer. *The Phillips Collection: A Modern Vision.* Tokyo: Mitsubishi Ichigokan Museum in association with The Phillips Collection, 2018.

2019

Smithgall, Elsa, ed. *Bonnard to Vuillard: The Intimate Poetry of Everyday Life.* New York: Rizzoli Electa in association with The Phillips Collection, 2019.

Sretenović, Vesela. *Zilia Sánchez: Soy Isla.* New Haven, CT: Yale University Press in association with The Phillips Collection, 2019.

2020

Childs, Adrienne L., Renée Maurer, and Valerie C. Oliver. *Riffs and Relations: African American Artists and the European Modernist Tradition.* New York: Rizzoli Electa in association with The Phillips Collection, 2020.

Ottmann, Klaus. *Jennifer Bartlett & Pierre Bonnard: In and Out of the Garden.* Washington, DC: The Phillips Collection in association with D Giles Limited, 2020.

Siegel, Lily, and Valerie Smith. *Moira Dryer: Back in Business.* Introduction by Klaus Ottmann. Washington, DC: The Phillips Collection, 2020.

INDEX

Page numbers in *italics* indicate illustrations

CONTRIBUTORS

heather ahtone

heather ahtone is senior curator at First Americans Museum (FAM) in Oklahoma City, Oklahoma. A citizen of the Chickasaw Nation and descended from the Choctaw Nation, she examines the intersection of indigenous cultural knowledge and contemporary art. Since 1993, she has curated numerous exhibitions. She publishes regularly and seeks opportunities to broaden discourse on contemporary indigenous arts around the world. She and her team are preparing a celebration of the histories and culture of Oklahoma's tribal communities, for the planned launch of FAM in May 2021.

Taylor Renee Aldridge

Taylor Renee Aldridge is a writer and independent curator based in Detroit, Michigan. She has organized exhibitions at the Detroit Institute of Arts; Detroit Artist Market; Cranbrook Art Museum in Bloomfield Hills, Michigan; and The Luminary in St. Louis, Missouri. In 2015, along with art critic Jessica Lynne, she co-founded *ARTS.BLACK*, a journal of art criticism for Black perspectives. Her writing has appeared in *Artforum*, *Art Newspaper*, *Art21*, *ARTnews*, *Canadian Art*, *Contemporary And (C&)*, *Detroit Metro Times*, *Hyperallergic*, and SFMOMA's *Open Space*. She earned her MLA from Harvard University and her BA from Howard University.

Dominique Baqué

An *Art Press* columnist for twenty years, Dominique Baqué has published extensively on photography, the image, and contemporary art. Her many books include *Pour un nouvel art politique* (2004) and *L'Effroi du présent. Figurer la violence* (2009), as well as monographs on Georges Tony Stoll (2005), Thierry Dreyfus (2013), Dorothée Smith (2013), Pierre-François Grimaldi (2016), and Claude de Soria (2016), among others. She is the author of recent books on Anselm Kiefer (*Anselm Kiefer, entre mythe et concept*, 2015) and Cy Twombly (*Cy Twombly, sous le signe d'Apollon et de Dionysos*, 2016). Her most recent book is *Helmut Newton. Magnifier le désastre* (2019).

Tina Baum

Tina Baum is from Garramilla (Darwin), in Australia's Northern Territory. A proud member of the Gulumirrgin (Larrakia)/Wardaman/Karajarri peoples of the Northern Territory and Western Australia, she has over thirty years' experience working with First Nation artists and communities in museums and galleries throughout Australia. She has been the Curator of Aboriginal and Torres Strait Islander Art at the National Gallery of Australia, Canberra, since 2005. She has published widely in exhibition catalogues, magazines, and journals. *Defying Empire: 3rd National Indigenous Art Triennial* (2017) and *Emerging Elders* (2009) are among the exhibitions she has curated recently.

Enrique Martínez Celaya

Enrique Martínez Celaya is an internationally renowned artist, author, and former scientist, whose work has been exhibited and collected by major institutions around the world. He is the author of books and papers on art, poetry, philosophy, and physics. The first provost professor of humanities and arts at the University of Southern California, Celaya is also a Montgomery Fellow at Dartmouth College. His work is held in over fifty public collections internationally, among them the Metropolitan Museum of Art, New York; the Whitney Museum of American Art, New York; the Los Angeles County Museum of Art; The Phillips Collection, Washington, DC; the State Hermitage Museum, St. Petersburg; and the Moderna Museet, Stockholm.

Adrienne L. Childs

Adrienne L. Childs is an art historian, independent curator, and associate of the W.E.B. Du Bois Research Institute at the Hutchins Center for African and African American Research at Harvard University. She is curator of the exhibition *Riffs and Relations: African American Artists and the European Modernist Tradition* (2020) at The Phillips Collection. She is co-curator of the recent exhibition *The Black Figure in the European Imaginary* at the Cornell Fine Arts Museum at Rollins College. She contributed to *The Image of the Black in Western Art*, Volume V, and is co-editor of the book *Blacks and Blackness in European Art of the Long Nineteenth Century*.

Makeba Clay

Makeba Clay is a nationally recognized diversity and inclusion expert and leadership strategist, with more than twenty years' experience in the field. She is also a certified mediator. The Phillips Collection's first chief diversity officer, she is responsible for implementing an institution-wide inclusion plan to develop cultural competency and build an equity mindset among museum staff and trustees. Professional accolades she has garnered include the 2015 Higher Education Excellence in Diversity Award from *INSIGHT Into Diversity* magazine. Clay has made transformational contributions toward organizational equity, diversity, and inclusion goals in institutions of higher education and cultural organizations, including American University, College of Southern Maryland, Princeton University, and Smithsonian National Museum of African Art.

Kate Cowcher

Kate Cowcher is lecturer in art history at the University of St Andrews. She completed her PhD at Stanford University in 2017 and is currently working on a book about art during the Ethiopian Revolution. Her research interests include modern and contemporary art in Africa, African cinema, and the Cold War. She was the postdoctoral fellow in Modern and Contemporary Art at the University of Maryland Center for Art and Knowledge at The Phillips Collection in 2017–18.

Jessica Stafford Davis

Jessica Stafford Davis is the founder of The Agora Culture, a national online multicultural arts platform, and *Art on the Vine*, Martha's Vineyard's annual exhibition. Her priority is making the arts accessible. She serves on the National Board of ArtTable and the Advisory Council for George Mason University School of Art.

David C. Driskell

An internationally acclaimed artist, curator, professor, and scholar, the late David C. Driskell contributed significantly to scholarship in the history of art on the role of Black artists in America. He received ten honorary doctoral degrees, authored seven books on the subject of African American art, co-authored four others, and published more than forty catalogues from exhibitions he curated. His articles and essays on African American art have appeared in major publications throughout the world. His work, represented in numerous public and private collections, has been featured in exhibitions in the United States, Europe, and Africa. In 2020–21, an artist retrospective, *David Driskell: Icons of Nature and History*, organized by the High Museum of Art and Portland Museum of Art, will tour to four venues, including The Phillips Collection.

John Edmonds

John Edmonds is an American artist and photographer, who was first publicly recognized for his intimate portraits of lovers, close friends, and strangers. He received his MFA from Yale University and his BFA from the Corcoran School of the Arts and Design. His practice expands upon art historical portraiture and figuration to include individuals from his own creative community in New York and beyond. In 2019, he was included in the 79th Whitney Biennial.

Susan Behrends Frank

Susan Behrends Frank, PhD, is a curator at The Phillips Collection specializing in European and American modernism. Since joining the Phillips, she has curated many exhibitions, a significant number of them permanent collection-related shows that have presented the museum's European and American collections to audiences in Germany, Italy, Japan, South Korea, and Spain, as well as in the US. Currently, she is co-organizing with the Art Gallery of Ontario an international loan show, *Picasso: Painting the Blue Period* for 2021–22, and is co-editor of the exhibition catalogue. Her publications include *American Impressionists: Painters of Light and the Modern Landscape* (2007), *David Smith Invents* (2011), and *Made in the U.S.A.: American Art from The Phillips Collection, 1850–1970* (2013).

Antony Gormley

Born in London, Antony Gormley makes sculptures, installations, and public artworks that investigate the relationship of the human body to space. His work has developed the potential opened up by sculpture since the 1960s through a critical engagement with both his own body and those of others. Gormley continually tries to identify the space of art as a place of becoming in which new behaviors, thoughts, and feelings can arise.

Wendy A. Grossman

Independent scholar Wendy A. Grossman, PhD, is an art historian and curator affiliated with The Phillips Collection, the University of Maryland, College Park, and NYU Washington, DC. She has lectured internationally and published widely on topics in the history of photography, twentieth-century European and American modernisms, the intersections of non-Western and Western art, dada, surrealism, contemporary art, and the artist Man Ray.

Jeffreen M. Hayes

Jeffreen M. Hayes, PhD, merges her curatorial practice with her role as a cultural leader in supporting artists. As an advocate for racial inclusion, equity and access, she creates approaches for community participation, particularly for those in under-represented groups. Her curatorial projects include *Silos* (2016); *Augusta Savage: Renaissance Woman* (2019); *AfriCOBRA: Messages to the People* (2019); *AfriCOBRA: Nation Time* (2019); and *Embracing the Lens: The BlackFlorida Project* (2020). As the executive director of Threewalls, Hayes provides strategic vision for the artistic direction and impact of the organization in Chicago. Under her leadership, Threewalls works with artists to help manifest the organization's vision of art connecting segregated communities, people, and experiences.

Liesbeth Heenk

Liesbeth Heenk studied in London at the Courtauld Institute of Art, where she wrote her dissertation on Vincent van Gogh's drawings. After working as a print expert in the international auction business, she set up her own publishing house, Amsterdam Publishers. She is the author of *Howard Hodgkin Prints: A Catalogue Raisonné*, published by Thames & Hudson in 2003.

Mary Jane Jacob

Mary Jane Jacob is a curator and writer who has championed public, site-specific, and socially engaged art. She is a professor at the School of the Art Institute of Chicago and the author of *Dewey for Artists*, published by the University of Chicago Press in 2018. She is currently organizing an exhibition of pioneering Polish artist Magdalena Abakanowicz for Tate Modern, London.

Fred L. Joiner

Fred L. Joiner is a poet and curator based in Chapel Hill, North Carolina. Poet Laureate of Carrboro, North Carolina, he was a fellow of the Academy of American Poets Laureate in 2019. His work has appeared or is forthcoming in *Furious Flower: Seeding the Future of African American Poetry*, *Callaloo*, *Gargoyle*, and *Fledgling Rag*, among other publications. Joiner has read his work, curated exhibitions, and organized public programs in the United States and abroad. He is a co-founder of the Center for Poetic Thought and is on the board of directors of the American Poetry Museum and the ARCH Development Corporation. He is also board chair of the Orange County (NC) Arts Commission.

Franz W. Kaiser

German-born Franz W. Kaiser is a curator and art historian. Working in France, Germany, and the Netherlands, he has realized numerous art exhibitions and written on a wide range of subjects. He has curated several exhibitions of the work of Karel Appel, whom he knew personally.

Dorothy Kosinski

Dorothy Kosinski, PhD, Vradenburg Director and CEO of The Phillips Collection, joined the Phillips in 2008, after serving as senior curator of painting and sculpture at the Dallas Museum of Art. At the Phillips, she launched a major partnership with the University of Maryland and established a satellite campus in Southeast DC at the Town Hall Education Arts Recreation Campus (THEARC). Kosinski has diversified and expanded the museum's collection and programming, notably hiring the museum's first chief diversity officer. In August 2013, President Barack Obama appointed her to the National Council on the Humanities. She received a BA from Yale University and an MA and PhD from the Institute of Fine Arts at New York University.

Lauren Kroiz

Lauren Kroiz, associate professor in the History of Art Department and faculty director of the Phoebe A. Hearst Museum of Anthropology at University of California, Berkeley, is the author of *Cultivating Citizens: The Regional Work of Art in the New Deal Era* (2018) and *Creative Composites: Modernism, Race, and the Stieglitz Circle* (2012), for which she won The Phillips Collection Book Prize. Kroiz is also a former postdoctoral fellow at The Phillips Collection's Center for the Study of Modern Art.

Raina Lampkins-Fielder

Paris-based Raina Lampkins-Fielder is the curator and program officer for Souls Grown Deep Foundation and Community Partnership, dedicated to promoting the work and legacy of African American artists from the South. Previously, she was the artistic director and curator of the American Center for Art and Culture (formerly Mona Bismarck American Center) in Paris. She served as Associate Director, Helena Rubinstein Chair of Education at the Whitney Museum of American Art, New York, and has held posts at the Brooklyn Museum of Art, the New Museum of Contemporary Art, New York, and the Andy Warhol Museum in Pittsburgh.

Jacqueline E. Lawton

Playwright and producer Jacqueline E. Lawton is an advocate for access, diversity, equity, and inclusion in the American theater. She received her MFA in playwriting from the University of Texas at Austin. She is a 2012 TCG Young Leaders of Color award recipient and an alumna of National New Play Network, Arena Stage's Playwrights' Arena in Washington, DC, and Center Stage's Playwrights Collective. She is an assistant professor in the Department of Dramatic Art at the University of North Carolina at Chapel Hill, where she is also a dramaturge for PlayMakers Repertory Company. She is the Dramatist Guild's North Carolina Regional Representative.

Whitfield Lovell

Whitfield Lovell received a BFA from the Cooper Union School of Art and also studied art throughout Europe. He has received international acclaim for his work, which links drawings with found objects. Using vintage photographs of African Americans as his source material, he evokes charged and mysterious narratives of a collective past. Lovell has received many accolades, including a MacArthur Foundation Fellowship and an honorary doctorate from Lehman College, Bronx, New York, and his work is in the permanent collections of numerous museums throughout the United States. The Phillips Collection hosted a solo show of his work, *The Kin Series and Related Works*, in 2016.

Jennifer Wen Ma

Jennifer Wen Ma's artistic practice bridges disciplines as varied as installation, painting, drawing, video, performance, theater, and public art. She often brings together unlikely elements in a single piece, creating sensitive, poetic and poignant works. Ma has exhibited internationally, in the United States (Metropolitan Museum of Art, Lincoln Center Festival, and Solomon R. Guggenheim Museum—all New York; The Phillips Collection, Washington, DC), China (Ullens Center for Contemporary

Art, National Art Museum of China, both Beijing), and Spain (Guggenheim Bilbao). Ma's work has been shown at the Sydney Biennale, Echigo-Tsumari Triennial, and Singapore Biennale. She was a core creative-team-member of the 2008 Beijing Olympics opening ceremony, receiving an Emmy Award for its US broadcast.

Renée Maurer

Renée Maurer is associate curator at The Phillips Collection, where she has developed special installations featuring artists including Sam Gilliam, William Christenberry, and Morris Louis. Exhibitions she has coordinated and managed include *Riffs and Relations: African American Artists and the European Modernist Tradition*, guest curated by Adrienne L. Childs in 2020; *A Modern Vision: European Masterworks from The Phillips Collection* and its tour (2017–20); *Toulouse-Lautrec Illustrates the Belle Époque* (2017); *American Moments: Photographs from The Phillips Collection* (2015); *Gauguin to Picasso: Masterworks from Switzerland, the Staechelin and Im Obersteg Collections* (2015); *Georges Braque and the Cubist Still Life: 1928–1945* (2013); and *Jasper Johns: Variations on a Theme* (2012).

Kent Mitchell Minturn

Kent Mitchell Minturn is an art historian and critic based in New York City. He has published widely on American and European twentieth-century art. His essay on Alfonso Ossorio and Jean Dubuffet appeared in the exhibition catalogue *Art Brut in America: The Incursion of Jean Dubuffet*, published by the American Folk Art Museum, New York, in 2015.

Jed Morse

Jed Morse is chief curator at the Nasher Sculpture Center in Dallas. He has organized and contributed to numerous exhibitions and publications on modern and contemporary sculpture, including *David Smith: Drawing and Sculpting* (2006); *Matisse: Painter as Sculptor* (2007); and *Return to Earth: Ceramic Sculpture of Fontana, Melotti, Miró, Noguchi, and Picasso, 1943–1963* (2013); as well as commissions and exhibitions of work by Diana Al-Hadid, Barry X Ball, Phyllida Barlow, Tony Cragg, Martin Creed, Michael Dean, Luke Fowler, Alex Israel, Nathan Mabry, Ernesto Neto, Anna-Bella Papp, Giuseppe Penone, Jaume Plensa, Bettina Pousttchi, Eva Rothschild, Sterling Ruby, Joel Shapiro, Alyson Shotz, and Erick Swenson. He is currently working on a retrospective of modernist sculptor and designer Harry Bertoia.

Charmaine A. Nelson

Charmaine A. Nelson is a professor of art history at McGill University. She has made ground-breaking contributions to the fields of the visual culture of slavery, race and representation, and Black Canadian studies. Nelson has published seven books, including *Slavery, Geography, and Empire in Nineteenth-Century Marine Landscapes of Montreal and Jamaica* (2016) and *Towards an African Canadian Art History: Art, Memory, and Resistance* (2018). She has been featured in broadcast and news media, including by CBC, BBC One, PBS, *Huffington Post Canada*, and *The Walrus*. Most recently, she was the William Lyon Mackenzie King Visiting Professor of Canadian Studies at Harvard University (2017–18).

Alexander Nemerov

Alexander Nemerov is the author of various essays on photographers, including William Eggleston, Rachel Harrison, Todd Hido, Clay Jordan, Deana Lawson, Danny Lyon, Clifford Ross, and Bill Yates. He has published books on Ralph Eugene Meatyard (*American Mystic*, 2017) and Diane Arbus (*Silent Dialogues*, 2015). His book *Soulmaker*, on the photographer Lewis Hine, was short-listed for the 2016 Marfield Prize for Arts Writing. Writing in the *Guardian*, novelist Ali Smith named his book *Summoning Pearl Harbor* one of the best books of 2018. He teaches at Stanford University.

Jeremy Ney

Jeremy Ney has been director of music at The Phillips Collection since October 2018. Prior to working at the Phillips, he worked for the Philharmonia Orchestra in London, and the S&R Foundation in Washington, DC, where he managed an artist residency, award scheme, and concert series. Ney earned his MMus in Musicology from King's College London. His dissertation focused on the connections between music and the visual arts, exploring a contemporary piece of music composed in response to a painting by Cy Twombly.

Bruce Nixon

Bruce Nixon is an independent scholar who has written extensively about contemporary art on the West Coast. He is the author of *Ginnever: Perspectives* (2020) and *Manuel Neri and the Assertion of Modern Figurative Sculpture* (2017), among many other publications.

Nontobeko Ntombela

Nontobeko Ntombela is a lecturer at the Wits School of Arts, University of the Witwatersrand, Johannesburg, South Africa. From time to time, as part of her creative research practice, she produces and participates in curatorial projects.

Klaus Ottmann

Klaus Ottmann is chief curator and deputy director for academic affairs at The Phillips Collection. The exhibitions he has curated there include *Nordic Impressions: Art from Åland, Denmark, the Faroe Islands, Finland, Greenland, Iceland, Norway, and Sweden, 1821–2018* (2018); *George Condo: The Way I Think* (2017); *Karel Appel: A Gesture of Color* (2016); *Hiroshi Sugimoto: Conceptual Forms and Mathematical Models* (2015); and *Angels, Demons, and Savages: Pollock, Ossorio, Dubuffet* (2013, co-curated with Dorothy Kosinski). He oversaw the permanent installation of the Phillips's *Wax Room* created by Wolfgang Laib. Ottmann, who is publisher and editor of Spring Publications, is the translator and editor of Yves Klein's complete writings, *Overcoming the Problematics of Art:*

The Writings of Yves Klein (2006), and is the translator of works by F. W. J. Schelling. In 2016, Ottmann was made a Chevalier of the Order of Arts and Letters by the French Ministry of Culture.

Eliza E. Rathbone

Educated in art history at Smith College, New York University, and the Courtauld Institute of Art, Eliza E. Rathbone spent nearly thirty-eight years as a curator at the National Gallery of Art and The Phillips Collection in Washington, DC, before becoming chief curator emerita of The Phillips Collection in 2014. In these capacities, she worked on the growth and care of collections, researched and organized numerous special exhibitions, and authored accompanying catalogues on nineteenth- and twentieth-century American and European art, collaborating with major institutions in the United States and abroad.

Bridget Riley

About her training as an artist, Bridget Riley says: "I found that I had to learn to draw before I could even attempt to paint, and in learning to draw I learned to see. As Boudin said to young Monet, 'Learn to draw, learn to see.' And in learning to see I found my way into working as a painter. I looked to the past for friends and relatives, so to speak, in the painter's world of organized sight, which I hoped to enter. In the impressionists and post-impressionists, I saw a common interest in perception and I found evidence of 'the golden chain,' to which Renoir and the other impressionists consciously added their links, a golden chain that stretches back through Delacroix, Courbet, Corot, Constable and Claude, to Veronese, Titian, and Bernini." Riley lives, works, and writes in London, Cornwall, and France.

Ellington Robinson

Based in Washington, DC, and the Virgin Islands, Ellington Robinson earned a BA in English from Morehouse College, in Atlanta, Georgia, and his MFA in painting and mixed media from the University of Maryland, College Park, where he received the Anne Truitt Fellowship, David C. Driskell Graduate Assistant Fellowship, and David C. Driskell Award of Excellence Teaching Fellowship. His work has been acquired by the Studio Museum in Harlem; The Phillips Collection, Washington, DC; the Grand Crossing Library in Chicago; and the Art in Embassies Program (for the American Embassy in Oslo, Norway), among other institutions.

Bernardí Roig

The multidisciplinary work of Bernardí Roig—sculpture, video, drawing, painting, and text—uses a distilled, minimalist, conceptual language to reflect obsessively on isolation, the erotic impulse, and desire, and to place representation of the human figure at the epicenter of its concerns. His obsessive, unsettling works can be understood as mechanisms of loneliness rife with the urgency to "speak from the impossibility of speech," seeking out figures and images for an unhinged time. He had a solo exhibition at The Phillips Collection in 2014, curated by Vesela Sretenović, as part of the Intersections program.

Susan Rothenberg

Susan Rothenberg was born in Buffalo, New York, in 1945 and died in May 2020 in New Mexico, where she lived and worked. Her work is in numerous collections, including the National Gallery of Art, Washington, DC; the Metropolitan Museum of Art, New York; the Museum of Modern Art, New York; the Whitney Museum of American Art, New York; the Walker Art Center, Minneapolis; Tate, London; and the Stedelijk Museum, Amsterdam. Retrospective exhibitions of her work have been held at the Hirshhorn Museum and Sculpture Garden, Washington, DC; the Albright-Knox Art Gallery, Buffalo; Dallas Museum of Art; and Los Angeles County Museum of Art, among others.

Sean Scully

Sean Scully was born in Dublin, Ireland in 1945 and today lives and works between New York, Bavaria, and London. His work is in the collection of virtually every major museum around the world. In 2014, he became the only Western artist to have a career retrospective exhibition in China. Recent solo exhibitions include *Landline* at the Hirshhorn Museum and Sculpture Garden, Washington, DC; a retrospective—*Vita Duplex*—at the Staatliche Kunsthalle Karlsruhe, Germany; *Sea Star* at the National Gallery, London; and the first major exhibition of his sculptures at the Yorkshire Sculpture Park, UK. A major fifty-year career retrospective, *The Shape of Ideas*, will open at the Philadelphia Museum of Art in 2021, before traveling to the Modern Art Museum of Fort Worth, Texas.

Alyson Shotz

Alyson Shotz lives and works in Brooklyn, New York. Her work is in public collections, including the Solomon R. Guggenheim Museum, New York; the Guggenheim Bilbao, Spain; the Hirshhorn Museum and Sculpture Garden, Washington, DC; the Whitney Museum of American Art, New York; and the San Francisco Museum of Modern Art. It has been widely exhibited in group and solo shows in the United States and abroad. Shotz was an Arts Institute research fellow at Stanford University in 2014–15 and a Sterling Visiting Scholar at Stanford University in 2012. She received a Pollock Krasner Award in 1999 and 2010, and the Saint Gaudens Memorial Fellowship in 2007, and she was the Happy and Bob Doran Artist in Residence at Yale University Art Gallery in 2005–6.

Elsa Smithgall

Elsa Smithgall is senior curator at The Phillips Collection. She has directed more than a dozen critically acclaimed exhibitions and has authored and/or edited numerous publications, including *Bonnard to Vuillard: The Intimate Poetry of Everyday Life—The Nabi Collection of Vicki and Roger Sant* (2019); *Ten Americans: After Paul Klee* (2017); *People on the Move: Beauty and Struggle in Jacob Lawrence's Migration Series* (2016); *Whitfield Lovell: The Kin Series and Related Works* (2016); and *William Merritt Chase:*

A Modern Master (2016). Smithgall holds an MA in art history from the University of Texas, Austin, and received a Certificate in Museum Executive Leadership from the Getty Leadership Institute.

Bosco Sodi

Mexican-born Bosco Sodi is known for his richly textured, vividly colored large-scale paintings. He finds emotive power in the essential crudeness of the materials that he uses to execute his paintings. Focusing on material exploration, the creative gesture, and the spiritual connection between the artist and his work, Sodi seeks to transcend conceptual barriers. To distance his works from associations beyond their immediate existence, he leaves many of his paintings untitled. The work itself becomes a memory, a relic symbolic of the artist's conversation with the raw material that brought the painting into creation. Sodi's influences range from art informel—artists such as Antoni Tàpies and Jean Dubuffet—to master colorists such as Willem de Kooning and Mark Rothko, and to the bright hues of his native heritage.

Vesela Sretenović

Since 2009, Vesela Sretenović, PhD, has been senior curator of modern and contemporary art at The Phillips Collection, where one of her initiatives is Intersections, a series in which contemporary artists—national and international, emerging and established—create new work to engage with the museum's permanent collection and architecture. She has organized numerous solo exhibitions of prominent artists, including Antony Gormley, Ellsworth Kelly, Robert Ryman, Richard Tuttle and, most recently, a first museum retrospective of Cuban artist Zilia Sánchez. Prior to joining the Phillips, Sretenović spent ten years as curator at the David Winton Bell Gallery, Brown University, while teaching contemporary art and art theory at the Rhode Island School of Design, Providence.

Renée Stout

Raised in Pittsburgh, Pennsylvania, Renée Stout received her BFA from Carnegie-Mellon University in 1980. She lives and works in Washington, DC, and now creates in a variety of media, including painting, mixed-media sculpture, and installation. Among the awards she has won is a Joan Mitchell Foundation grant. Her work is in many national and international collections.

Lou Stovall

Born in Athens, Georgia, Lou Stovall studied at the Rhode Island School of Design and at Howard University (BFA). Since 1962, he has lived and worked in Washington, DC. Stovall's prints and drawings are part of numerous public and private collections throughout the world. Though his craft is that of a printmaker, Stovall's passion for art extends beyond a single medium. His drawings and silkscreen prints have earned him grants from the National Endowment for the Arts and the Stern Family Fund. Through his direction of Workshop, Inc., the professional printmaking facility he founded in 1968, Stovall has nurtured a strong artistic community in Washington, DC.

Elizabeth Hutton Turner

Elizabeth Hutton Turner, PhD, served as senior curator at The Phillips Collection, where she helped establish an interdisciplinary Center for the Study of Modern Art, and organized more than twenty-five exhibitions on such artists as Alexander Calder, Paul Klee, Jacob Lawrence, and Georgia O'Keeffe. In 2007, she was appointed professor at the University of Virginia, and served from 2008 to 2013 as its first vice-provost for the arts. Since 2015, Turner has taught, emphasizing object-based research and engaging her students in developing her new exhibitions at the Montreal Museum of Fine Arts, the Fralin Museum of Art at the University of Virginia, The Phillips Collection, and the Peabody Essex Museum in Salem, Massachusetts. Current writing projects include "Unexpected O'Keeffe" and "Alexander Calder: A Biography of Objects."

Jenna Wortham

Jenna Wortham is a staff writer for the *New York Times Magazine* and co-host of the arts and culture podcast *Still Processing*. She is the co-editor of the forthcoming visual anthology *Black Futures*, due out from One World in 2020.

CREDITS

PLATES

2, © Ralph Gibson

10, © 2020 The Jacob and Gwendolyn Knight Lawrence Foundation, Seattle / Artists Rights Society (ARS), New York

11, © William Christenberry

12, 13, © Joel Meyerowitz

17, © The Estate of Jörg Immendorff, Courtesy Galerie Michael Werner, Märkisch Wilmersdorf, Köln & New York

18, © 2020 Estate of Ching Ho Cheng / Artists Rights Society (ARS), New York

20, © Smoking Dogs Films; Courtesy Smoking Dogs Films and Lisson Gallery

21–23, © 2014 Jeanine Michna-Bales

24, © 2013 Jeanine Michna-Bales

25, © Benny Andrews Estate; Courtesy of Michael Rosenfeld Gallery LLC, New York, NY

27, © 2020 Karel Appel Foundation / Artists Rights Society (ARS), New York / c/o Pictoright Amsterdam

28, © Kara Walker

29, © Los Carpinteros; Courtesy Sean Kelly, New York

36, © 2020 Artists Rights Society (ARS), New York / VG Bild-Kunst, Bonn

38, © 2020 Banco de México Diego Rivera Frida Kahlo Museums Trust, Mexico, D.F. / Artists Rights Society (ARS), New York

39, © David Bates

40, © 2020 T.H. and R.P. Benton Testamentary Trusts / UMB Bank Trustee / Licensed by VAGA at Artists Rights Society (ARS), New York

41, © 2020 The Milton Avery Trust / Artists Rights Society (ARS), New York

49, © 2020 Artists Rights Society (ARS), New York

50–52, © Die Photographische Sammlung / SK Stiftung Kultur – August Sander Archiv, Cologne / Artists Rights Society (ARS), New York 2020

56, © Cardinal Point Press

61, © 2020 Center for Creative Photography, Arizona Board of Regents / Artists Rights Society (ARS), New York

62, © linn meyers

65, 66, © 2020 Artists Rights Society (ARS), New York / VG Bild-Kunst, Bonn

68, 70, 71, © 2020 Artists Rights Society (ARS), New York

69, © 2020 Artists Rights Society (ARS), New York / VEGAP, Madrid

72 © 2012 Artists Rights Society (ARS), New York

73, © 2020 Estate of Gene Davis / Artists Rights Society (ARS), New York

74, © 2020 The Estate of David Smith / Licensed by VAGA at Artists Rights Society (ARS), NY

75, © Estate of Poul Gernes

76, © 2020 Estate of Lucy T. Pettway / Artists Rights Society (ARS), New York

78, © 2020 Mary Lee Bendolph / Artists Rights Society (ARS), New York

79, © 2020 Estate of Aolar Mosely / Artists Rights Society (ARS), New York

81, © Modern Ancient Brown, Inc.

86, © the artist, c/o Buku-Larrŋgay Mulka Centre

87, © the artist, licensed by Aboriginal Artists Agency Ltd, courtesy Milingimbi Artists

88, © Joe Guymala, c/o Injalak Arts & Crafts Aboriginal Corporation

89–91, © the artist, c/o Buku-Larrŋgay Mulka Centre

92, © William Christenberry

93, © 1979 Amon Carter Museum of Art

95, 96, © 2020 Al Held Foundation, Inc. / Licensed by Artists Rights Society (ARS), New York

102–104, © 2020 Alex Katz / Licensed by VAGA at Artists Rights Society (ARS), New York

106–109, © Estate of Rudolf de Crignis

110, © 2020 Calder Foundation, New York / Artists Rights Society (ARS), New York

115, © 1993 Marcella Louis Brenner; © 2020 Maryland Institute College of Art (MICA), Rights Administered by Artists Rights Society (ARS), New York, All Rights Reserved

117, © Estate of the artist

119, © The Feitelson/Lundeberg Art Foundation

120, © William Christenberry

122, © Arlene Shechet

123, © Amy Cutler

126, © Kate Shepherd, Courtesy of Galerie Lelong & Co.

127, © Hiroshi Sugimoto; Courtesy of the artist and Marian Goodman Gallery

128, © 2020 Artists Rights Society (ARS), New York / ADAGP, Paris

137, © 2020 Artists Rights Society (ARS), New York / VG Bild-Kunst, Bonn

141, © The Richard Diebenkorn Foundation

143, © 2017 Janet Taylor Pickett

146, © John Walker, courtesy of Alexandre Gallery, New York

147, © 2020 Wayne Thiebaud / Licensed by VAGA at Artists Rights Society (ARS), New York

148–150, © 2020 Estate of Hale Woodruff / Licensed by VAGA at Artists Rights Society (ARS), New York

151, 152, © Jean Bubley and the Esther Bubley Estate

156–159, © Allan deSouza | Courtesy Talwar Gallery, New York | New Delhi

164, © Eggleston Artistic Trust

165, © Ralph Gibson

166, © Bridgeman Images

172, © 2020 Helen Frankenthaler Foundation, Inc. / Artists Rights Society (ARS), New York / Tyler Graphics Ltd., Mt. Kisco, New York

173, © Joseph Marioni

174, © Gift of Mariagrazia Oliva Lapadula and the Archivio Bice Lazzari, Rome 2018

175, © Harold Edgerton, MIT, Courtesy of Palm Press, Inc.

176, © 2020 The Jacob and Gwendolyn Knight Lawrence Foundation, Seattle / Artists Rights Society (ARS), New York

177, © 2020 Artists Rights Society (ARS), New York

181, © 2020 Richard Serra / Artists Rights Society (ARS), New York

182, © 2020 Susan Rothenberg / Artists Rights Society (ARS), New York

183, © 2020 Artists Rights Society (ARS), New York / ADAGP, Paris

184, © 2020 Susan Rothenberg / Artists Rights Society (ARS), New York

185, © Man Ray 2015 Trust / Artists Rights Society (ARS), New York / ADAGP, Paris 2021

186, © 2020 Artists Rights Society (ARS), New York / VG Bild-Kunst, Bonn

188, © 2020 Artists Rights Society (ARS), New York / VG Bild-Kunst, Bonn

189, © 2020 Estate of Richard Pousette-Dart / Artists Rights Society (ARS), New York

190, © 2020 The Murray-Holman Family Trust / Artists Rights Society (ARS), New York

193, © 2020 Dedalus Foundation, Inc. / Artists Rights Society (ARS), New York

196, © 1998 Kate Rothko Prizel & Christopher Rothko / Artists Rights Society (ARS), New York

197, © Collection Van Abbemuseum, Eindhoven, The Netherlands; Photo: Peter Cox, Eindhoven, The Netherlands

198, © Enrique Martínez Celaya

203, Photo: Lee Stalsworth

FIGURES

Page 10, Photo: Lee Stalsworth

Figs. 2–9, Photo: Lee Stalsworth

Fig. 10, Image courtesy the Fine Arts Museums of San Francisco

Fig. 11, © RMN-Grand Palais / Art Resource, NY; Photo: Stéphane Maréchalle

Fig. 14, © 2020 Karel Appel Foundation / Artists Rights Society (ARS), New York / c/o Pictoright Amsterdam

Fig. 15, Photo: Robert Lautman, 2006

Fig. 16, © 1998 Kate Rothko Prizel & Christopher Rothko / Artists Rights Society (ARS), New York

Page 32 (left), Photo: Clara E. Sipprel

Page 32 (right), Photo: Sylvia Salmi Solow; Image courtesy of Morris Library, Southern Illinois University

Page 42, Photo: Allan Northern

Fig. 25, Photo: Lee Stalsworth

Fig. 27, © 2020 Artists Rights Society (ARS), New York / ADAGP, Paris

Figs. 28–30, Photos: Allan Northern

Figs. 33–35, © 2020 Artists Rights Society (ARS), New York

Fig. 39, Photo: Fred Joiner

Fig. 42, © 2020 The Jacob and Gwendolyn Knight Lawrence Foundation, Seattle / Artists Rights Society (ARS), New York

Fig. 45, © 2020 Mike Kelley Foundation for the Arts. All Rights Reserved / Licensed by VAGA at Artists Rights Society (ARS), NY

Fig. 46, © Estate of Seymour Lipton; Courtesy of Michael Rosenfeld Gallery LLC, New York, NY

Fig. 50, Art © Estate of David Smith / Licensed by VAGA, New York

Fig. 51, © Antony Gormley

Fig. 52, © Antony Gormley; Photo: David Parry / © Royal Academy of Arts

Fig. 54, Image courtesy the Fine Arts Museums of San Francisco

Fig. 57, © Die Photographische Sammlung / SK Stiftung Kultur – August Sander Archiv, Cologne / Artists Rights Society (ARS), New York 2020

Fig. 58, Courtesy the artist and neugerriemschneider, Berlin; Photo: Jens Ziehe, Berlin

Fig. 60, © Kerry James Marshall. Photography courtesy Denver Art Museum

Fig. 61, © Joseph Holston 2002

Figs. 63, 64, © McCord Museum

Figs. 65, 66, Bruce Davidson/ Magnum Photos

Page 90, Photo: Allan Northern

Figs. 67, 68, Photo: Allan Northern

Figs. 69–70, Photo: Lee Stalsworth

Fig. 71, © The Phillips Collection

Fig. 73, Photo © Estate of Henri Cartier-Bresson / SAIF, Paris / VAGA, New York; Henri Cartier-Bresson/ Magnum Photos

Page 102, Photo: Allan Northern

Figs. 76–78, Photo: Allan Northern

Figs. 79–83, Photo: Lee Stalsworth

Page 112, Photo: Allan Northern

Fig. 85, Photo: Lee Stalsworth

Figs. 86–89, Photo: Allan Northern

Fig. 90, © 2020 The Jacob and Gwendolyn Knight Lawrence Foundation, Seattle / Artists Rights Society (ARS), New York

Fig. 91, © 2020 Karel Appel Foundation / Artists Rights Society (ARS), New York / c/o Pictoright Amsterdam

Fig. 92, Courtesy Galerie Michael Werner, Märkisch Wilmersdorf, Cologne & New York; © 2020 Markus Lüpertz / Artists Rights Society (ARS), New York / VG Bild-Kunst, Germany

Fig. 94, © 2020 Calder Foundation, New York / Artists Rights Society (ARS), New York

Fig. 95, © RMN-Grand Palais / Art Resource, NY; Photo: Stéphane Maréchalle

Fig. 96, © Frédéric Jaulmes

Fig. 97, © Man Ray 2015 Trust / Artists Rights Society (ARS), New York / ADAGP, Paris

Fig. 98, Collection Van Abbemuseum, Eindhoven, The Netherlands; Photo: Peter Cox, Eindhoven, The Netherlands

Seeing Differently: The Phillips Collects for a New Century
is organized by The Phillips Collection, Washington, DC.

The presentation of the exhibition and its publication are generously supported by the Henry Luce Foundation.

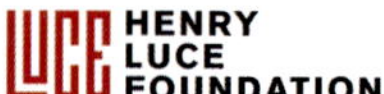

Additional support is provided by the National Endowment for the Humanities.

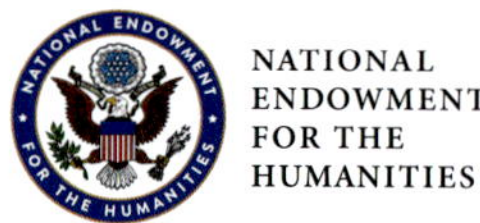

With support from The Phillips Collection's Exhibitions Endowment Fund, which is generously supported by the Sherman Fairchild Foundation, Robert and Debra Drumheller, and The Marion F. Goldin Charitable Fund; and from the Frauke and Willem de Looper Charitable Fund.

Special thanks to our key academic partner, University of Maryland, a global leader in research, entrepreneurship, and innovation.

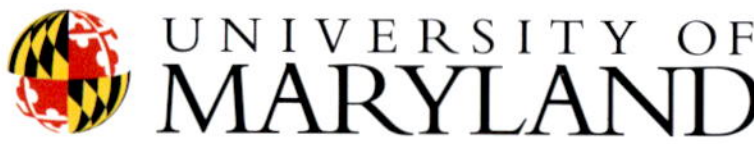

First published in the United States of America in 2021 by
The Phillips Collection
1600 21st Street, NW
Washington, DC 20009
www.phillipscollection.org

In association with GILES
An imprint of D Giles Limited
66 High Street
Lewes, BN7 1XG, UK
gilesltd.com

Library of Congress Control Number: 2020918520
ISBN: 978-1-911282-76-1 (Hardcover edition)

For The Phillips Collection:
Dorothy Kosinski, Vradenburg Director and CEO
Klaus Ottmann, Chief Curator, Deputy Director for Curatorial and Academic Affairs
Elsa Smithgall, Senior Curator
Kathryn S. Rogge, Exhibitions Coordinator and Manager of Academic Initiatives
Johanna Halford-MacLeod and Alexander Karelis, Editors

For D Giles Limited:
Copy-edited and proofread by Jenny Wilson
Designed by Ocky Murray
Produced by D Giles Limited
Printed and bound in China

Front cover illustration:
Janet Taylor Pickett, *And She Was Born*, 2017
Acrylic on canvas with printed paper collage, 30 x 30 in.
The Phillips Collection, Washington, DC,
The Dreier Fund for Acquisitions, 2020.

Back cover illustrations:
Jennifer Wen Ma, *Brain Storm*, 2009, Single-channel video, The Phillips Collection, Washington, DC, The Dreier Fund for Acquisitions, 2014; Mary Lee Bendolph, *"Housetop" variation*, detail, 1998, Printed and multi-colored cotton and wool fabrics, 72 × 76 in., The Phillips Collection, Washington, DC, Museum purchase, and gift of the Souls Grown Deep Foundation from the William S. Arnett Collection, 2019; Simone Leigh, *No Face (Crown Heights)*, detail, 2018, Terracotta, graphite ink, salt-fired porcelain, epoxy, 20 × 8 × 8 in., The Phillips Collection, Washington, DC, Director's Discretionary Fund, 2019; Aimé Mpane, *Mapasa*, detail, 2012, Acrylic and mixed media on two wood panels, each: 12 1/2 x 12 in., The Dorothy and Herbert Vogel Award, 2012; Poul Gernes, *Untitled (stripe series with ochre as recurring color)*, 1965, Sixteen enamel on hardboards, each: 48 × 48 in., The Phillips Collection, Washington, DC, Acquired in 2019 with support from the Ny Carlsbergfondet.

Frontispiece:
Aimé Mpane, *Maman Calcule*, detail, 2013
Acrylic and mixed media on pieces of wood with monofilament, 83 × 73 in.
The Phillips Collection, Washington, DC,
The Dreier Fund for Acquisitions, 2019.

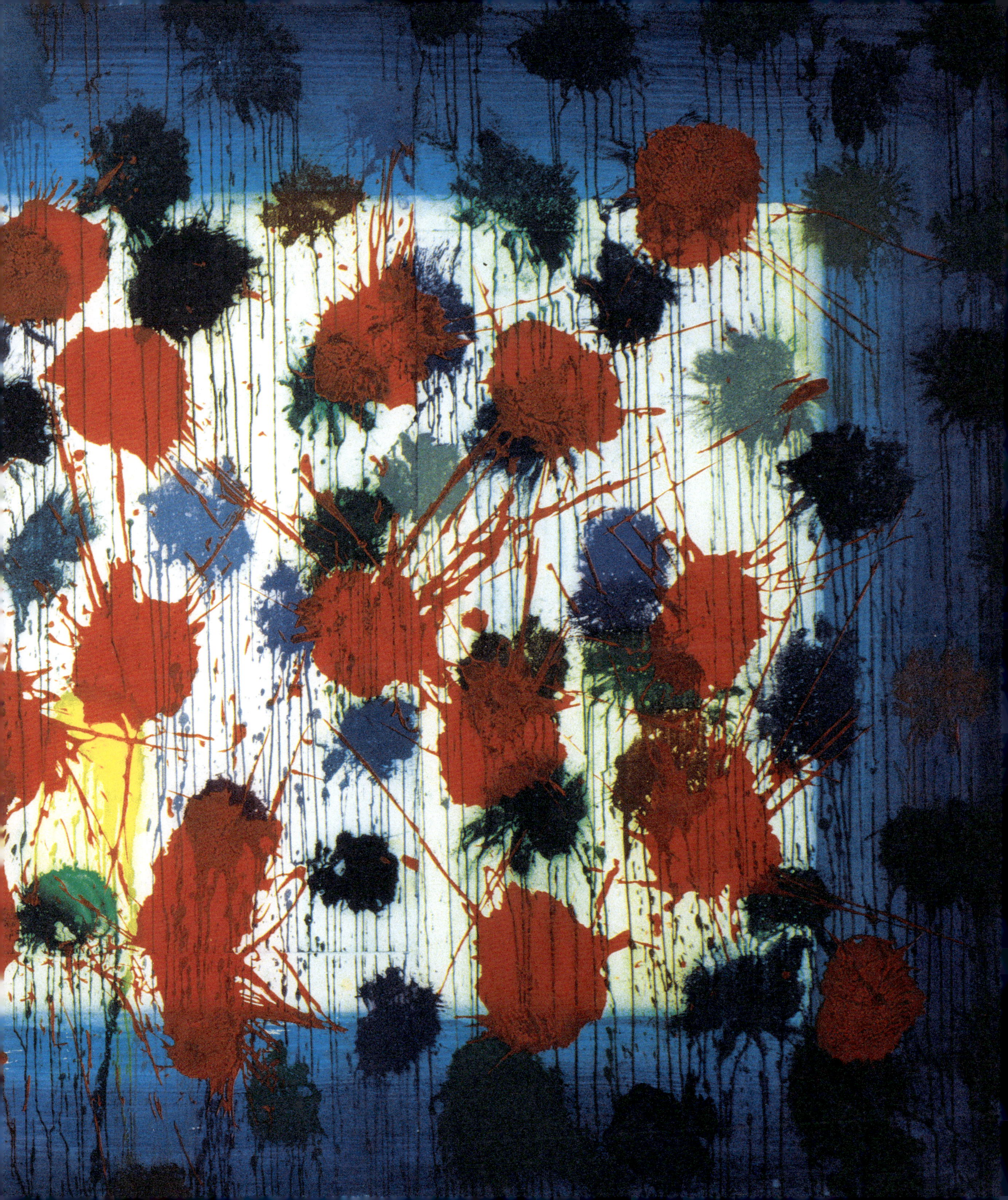

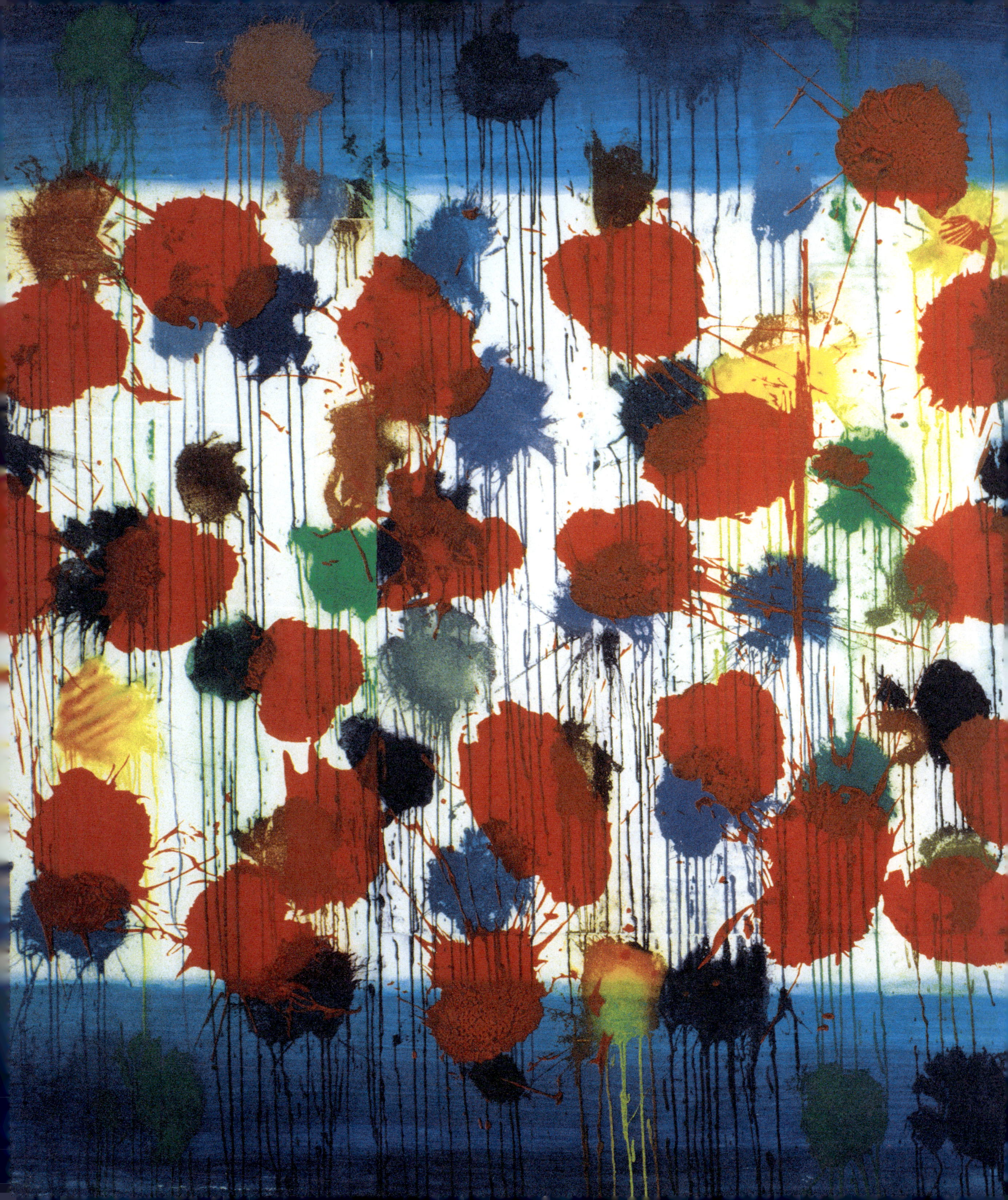